DELUXE EDITION

D1178344

 **MapArt**

Calgary &
Southern Alberta Atlas

CONTENTS

See the inside back cover for **Edmonton & Northern Alberta Atlas** coverage.

Cities & Towns

Airdrie 68-69	Canmore 58-59	Lake Louise 56
Banff 57	Chestermere 70	Lethbridge 82-89
Beiseker 69	Coaldale 85	Medicine Hat 92-95
Bellevue 81	Cochrane 60-61	Olds 62
Black Diamond 75	Coleman 79	Okotoks 75-76
Blairmore 80	Crossfield 62	Red Deer 64-67
Bragg Creek 78	Drumheller 72-73	Redwood Meadows . . .61
Brooks 90	High River 77	Strathmore 71
Calgary Key Map 2-3	Innisfail 63	Taber 91
Calgary 6-55	Irricana 69	Turner Valley 74

Information Panels

Cinemas 10	Hospitals 11	Points of Interest 46
Calgary Districts 46	Hotels & Motels 14	Shopping Centres 8
Golf Courses 15	Parks & Recreation 40	

Street Index 96

Thank you for purchasing this product! We work hard to ensure all of our products are accurate, up-to-date, and clear. For the many customers who have offered suggestions since the previous edition, we appreciate your interest in helping us to improve the maps. You can reach us by e-mail at inquiries@mapart.com, or by telephone at 905-436-2525, or by fax at 905-723-6677. Please include the product name and date, page number, and co-ordinates to help us identify your concern.

come see us @ www.mapart.com

MapArt. DIRECTION + DESIGN

CARTOGRAPHIC TEAM

Malcolm Buchan   Brent Carey   Michael Foell   Karen Gillingham   Werner Mantei   Carl Nanders
Dave Scott   Samiha Sleiman   Matthew Wadley   Craig White   Marlene Ziobrowski

© **MapMedia Corp.** 2005 Edition
Published by Peter Heiler Ltd.
Distributed by **MapArt Publishing Ltd.**
70 Bloor St. E., Oshawa, Ontario L1H 3M2
☎ 905-436-2525   FAX 905-723-6677

Printed in Canada  Imprimé au Canada

Scale 1:147 000 — 0 1 2 Kilometres / kilomètres

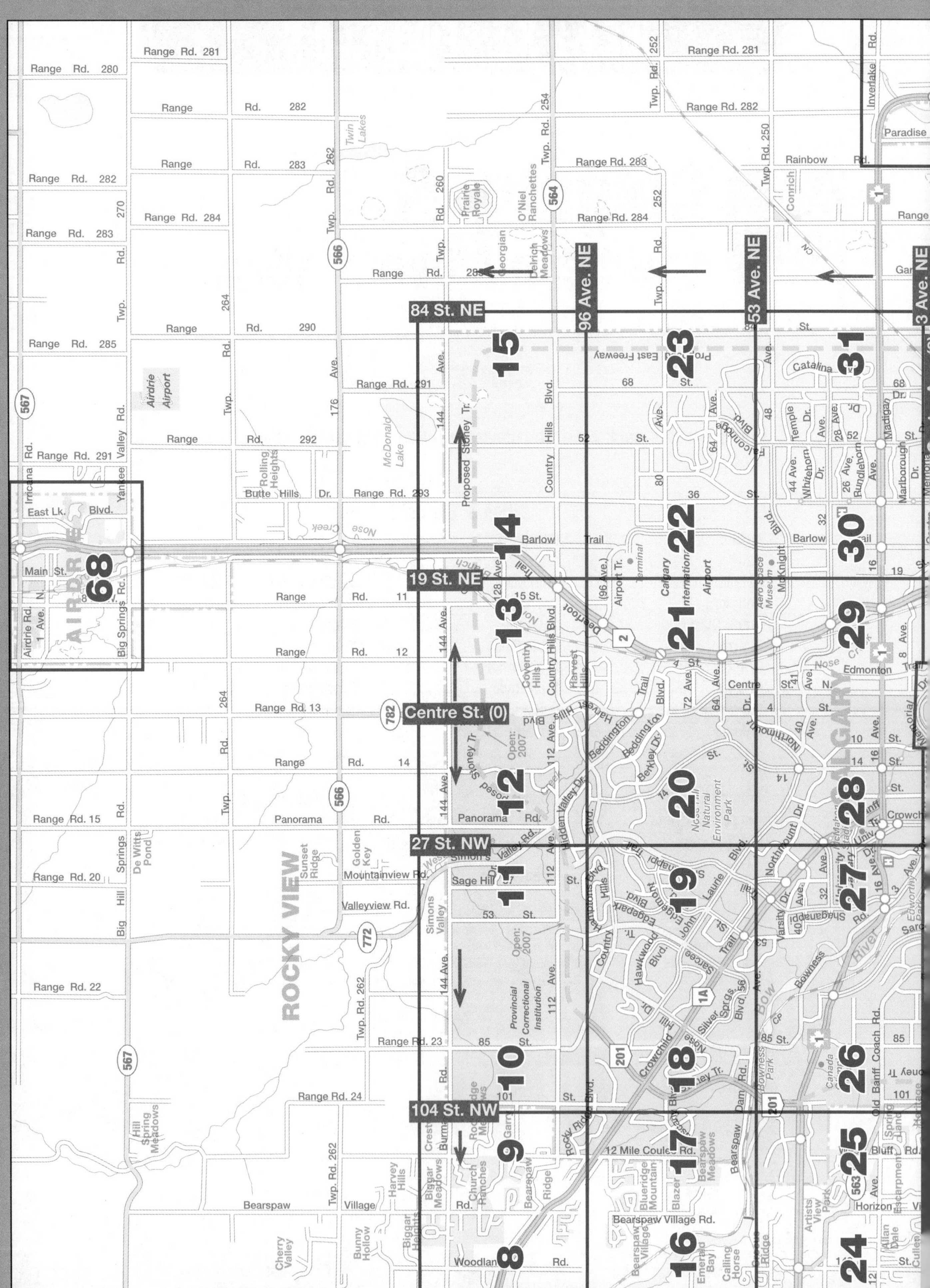

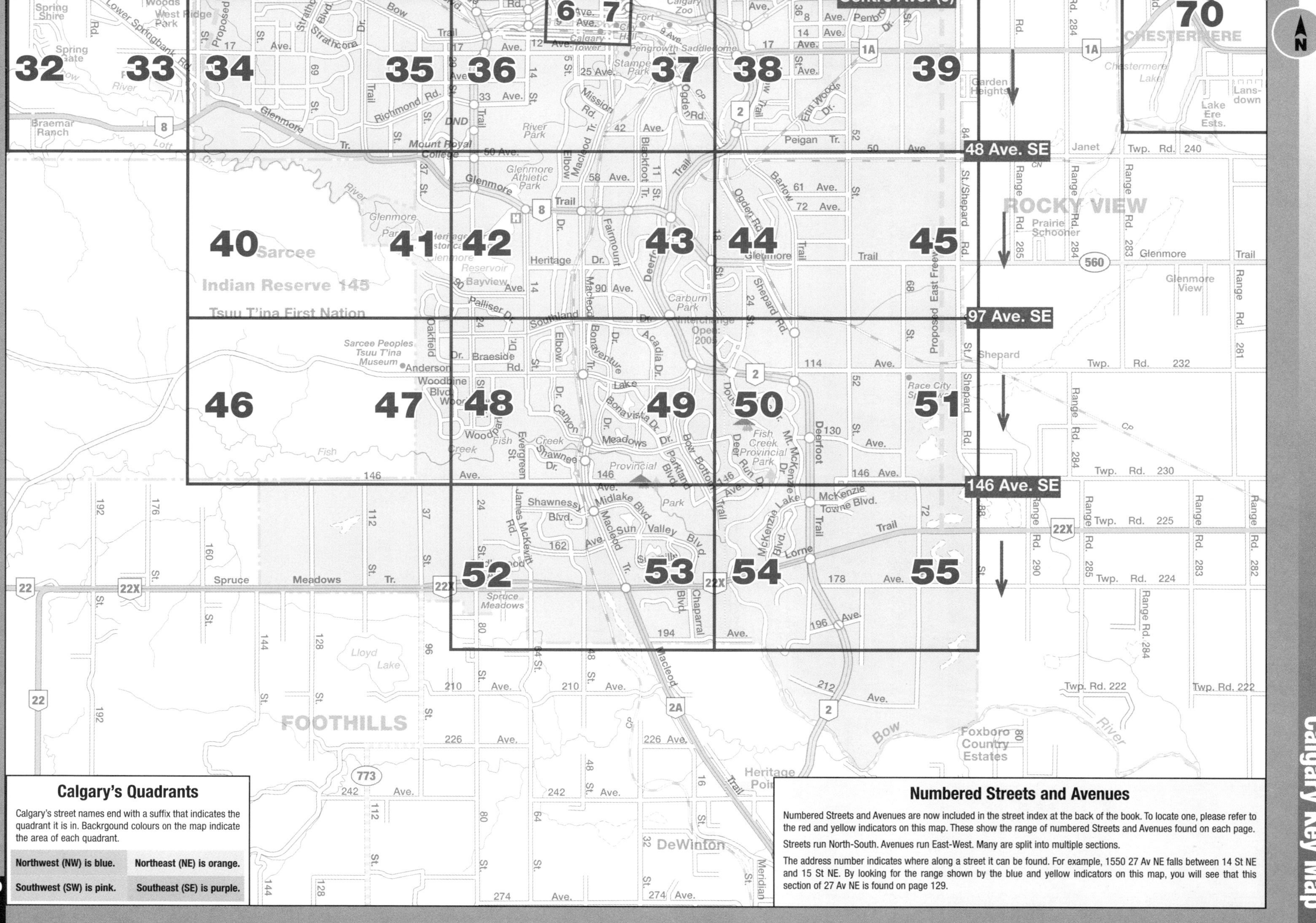

Numbered Streets and Avenues

Numbered Streets and Avenues are now included in the street index at the back of the book. To locate one, please refer to the red and yellow indicators on this map. These show the range of numbered Streets and Avenues found on each page. Streets run North-South. Avenues run East-West. Many are split into multiple sections.

The address number indicates where along a street it can be found. For example, 1550 27 Av NE falls between 14 St NE and 15 St NE. By looking for the range shown by the blue and yellow indicators on this map, you will see that this section of 27 Av NE is found on page 129.

Calgary's Quadrants

Calgary's street names end with a suffix that indicates the quadrant it is in. Background colours on the map indicate the area of each quadrant.

Northwest (NW) is blue.   Northeast (NE) is orange.

Southwest (SW) is pink.   Southeast (SE) is purple.

Calgary Area Map

Scale 1:147 000
0 1 2 Kilometres kilomètres
To Kathyrn
To Delacour
To Red Deer & Edmonton
To Cochrane
To Canmore & Banff
AIRDRIE
ROCKY VIEW
Airdrie Airport
Calgary International Airport
Aero Space Museum
Nose Hill Natural Environment Park
University of Calgary
McMahon Stadium
Canada Olympic Park
Provincial Correctional Institution
McDonald Lake
Twin Lakes
De Witts Pond
Prairie Royale
O'Niel Ranchettes
Delrich Meadows
Georgian
Rolling Heights
Sunset Ridge
Golden Key
Simons Valley
Hill Spring Meadows
Crestview
Burma
Rock Ridge Meadows
GlenGarry
Church Ranches
Bearspaw
Ridge
Harvey Hills
Biggar Meadows
Biggar Heights
Bunny Hollow
Cherry Valley
Bearspaw Village
Blueridge Mountain
Blazer
Bearspaw Meadows
Emerald Bay
Calling Horse
Crocus Ridge
Artists View Park
Bowness Park
Allan Dale
Cullen Creek
Escarpment
Spring Land
Heritage
Edworthy Park
Coventry Hills
Harvest Hills
Conrich
Barlow Trail
Deerfoot Trail
Country Hills Blvd.
Stoney Tr.
Proposed Stoney Tr.
Proposed East Freeway
Open: 2007
Crowchild Tr.
Sarcee Trail
Shaganappi Trail
Edmonton Trail
Memorial Dr.
Bearspaw Village Rd.
12 Mile Coulee Rd.
Old Banff Coach Rd.
Nose Creek
West Nose Creek
Bow River
CN
CP
Range Rd. 280
Range Rd. 281
Range Rd. 282
Range Rd. 283
Range Rd. 284
Range Rd. 285
Range Rd. 290
Range Rd. 291
Range Rd. 292
Range Rd. 293
Range Rd. 11
Range Rd. 12
Range Rd. 13
Range Rd. 14
Range Rd. 15
Range Rd. 20
Range Rd. 22
Range Rd. 23
Range Rd. 24
Twp. Rd. 250
Twp. Rd. 252
Twp. Rd. 254
Twp. Rd. 260
Twp. Rd. 262
Twp. Rd. 264
Twp. Rd. 270
Panorama Rd.
Mountainview Rd.
Valleyview Rd.
Simon's Valley Rd.
Sage Hill Dr.
Big Hill Springs Rd.
Yankee Valley Rd.
Irricana Rd.
East Lk. Blvd.
Butte Hills Dr.
Main St.
8 St. W.
Airdrie Rd.
Woodland Rd.
Bearspaw Village
567
566
564
782
772
563
201
1A
2
1

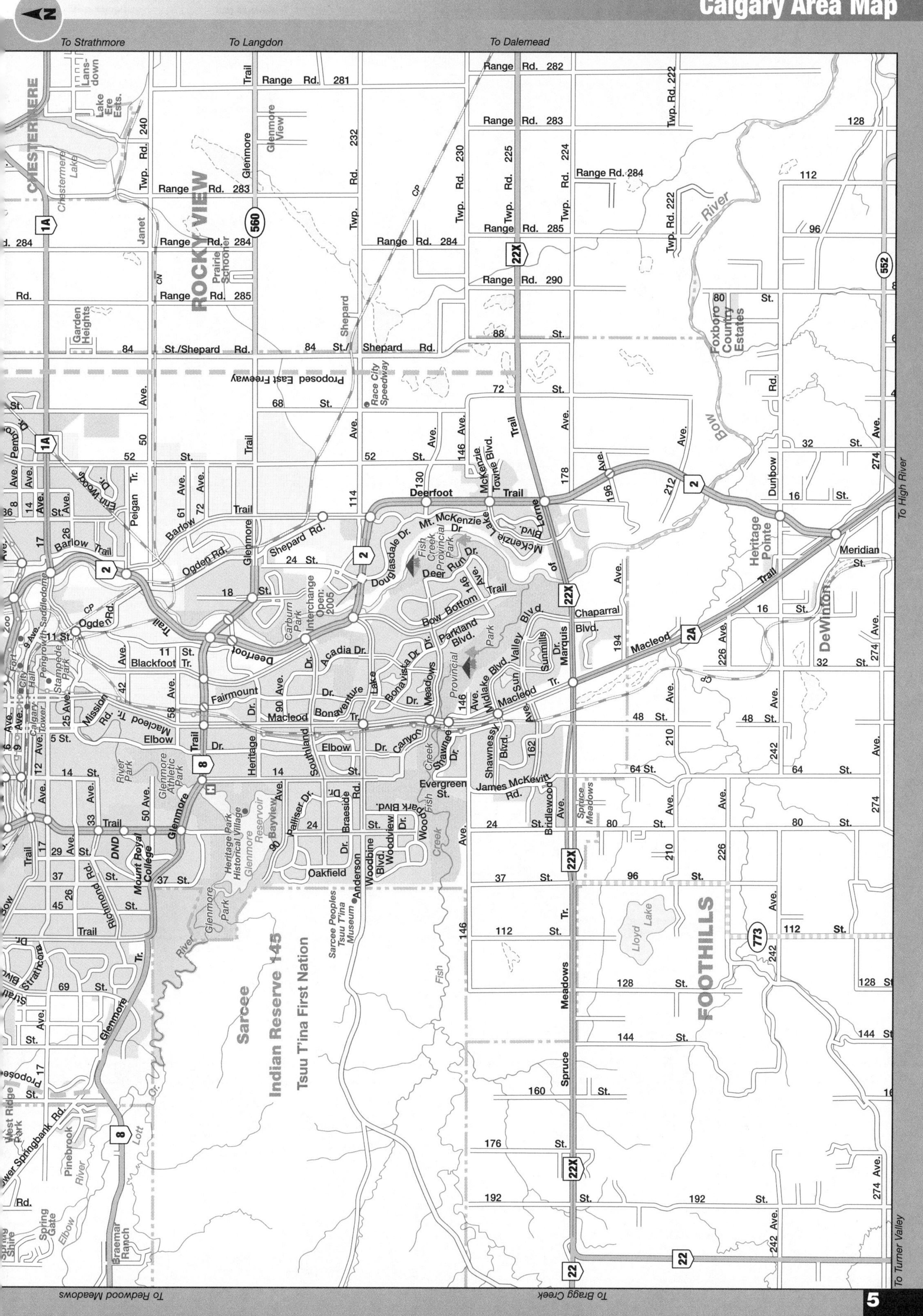
To Strathmore
To Langdon
To Dalemead
To Redwood Meadows
To Bragg Creek
To High River
To Turner Valley
CHESTERMERE
ROCKY VIEW
FOOTHILLS
Sarcee Indian Reserve 145
Tsuu T'ina First Nation
Proposed East Freeway
Fish Creek Provincial Park
Heritage Pointe
DeWinton
Foxboro Country Estates
Lloyd Lake
Bow River
Race City Speedway
Heritage Park Historical Village
Glenmore Reservoir
Sarcee Peoples Tsuu T'ina Museum

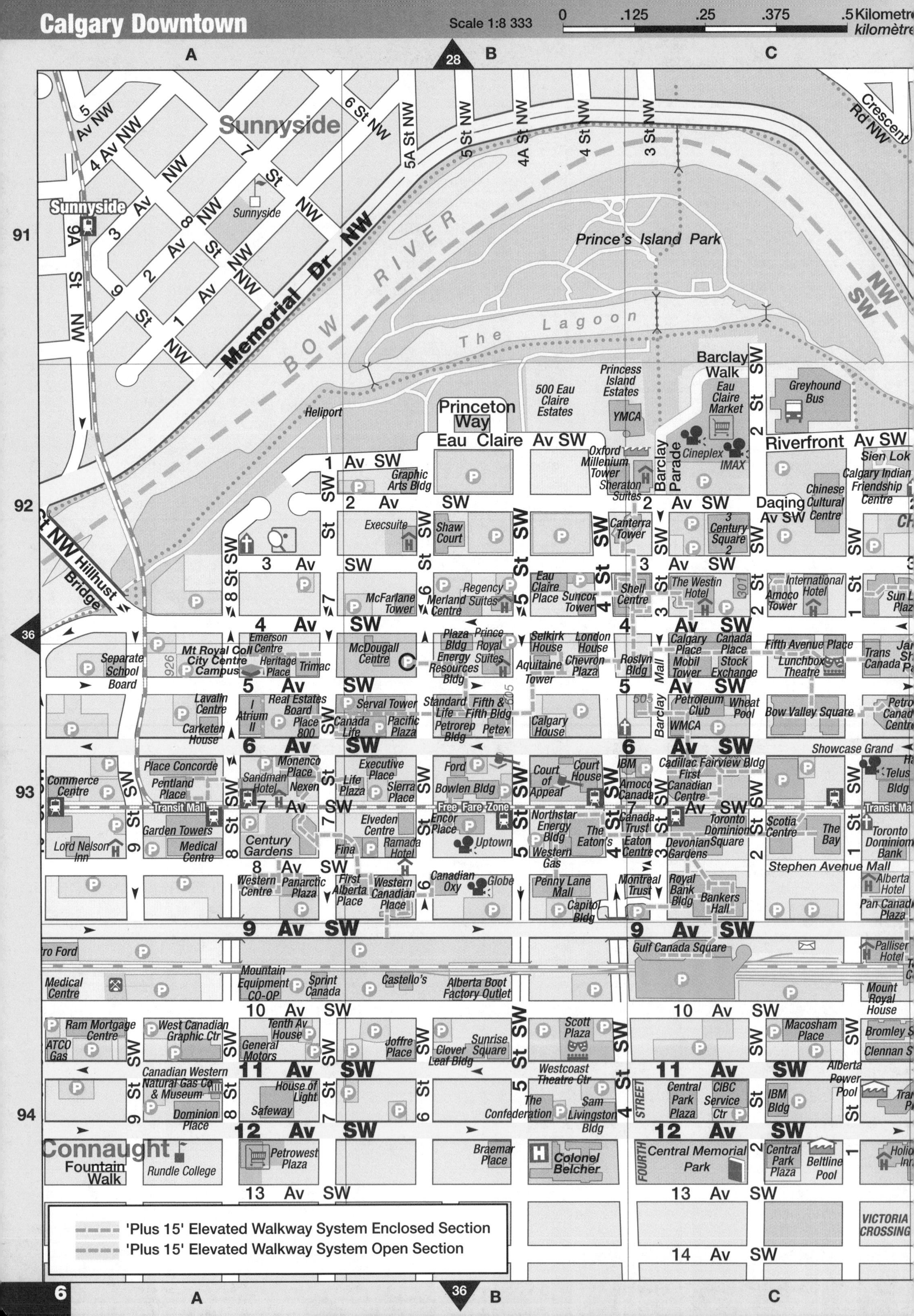

Calgary Downtown

Scale 1:8 333

0 .125 .25 .375 .5 Kilometre
kilomètre

A   28   **B**   **C**

Sunnyside

91

Sunnyside

92

36

93

94

Prince's Island Park

The Lagoon

BOW RIVER

Memorial Dr NW

Heliport

Princeton Way
Eau Claire Av SW

500 Eau Claire Estates

Princess Island Estates

YMCA

Barclay Walk
Eau Claire Market

Greyhound Bus

Cineplex IMAX

Riverfront Av SW

Sien Lok

Calgary Indian Friendship Centre

Oxford Millenium Tower
Sheraton Suites

Chinese Cultural Centre

Daqing Av SW

1 Av SW
Graphic Arts Bldg

2 Av SW

Execsuite
Shaw Court

Canterra Tower

Century Square 2

3 Av SW
McFarlane Tower

Regency Merland Suites Centre

Eau Claire Place
Suncor Tower

Shell Centre

The Westin Hotel

Amoco Tower

International Hotel

Sun L Plaza

4 Av SW

Emerson Centre
McDougall Centre

Plaza Bldg / Prince Royal Suites
Energy Resources Bldg

Selkirk House / London House
Aquitaine Tower / Chevron Plaza

Calgary Place
Mobil Tower

Canada Place
Stock Exchange

Fifth Avenue Place

Lunchbox Theatre

Trans Canada

Jai

Mt Royal Coll City Centre Campus
Heritage Place / Trimac

Roslyn Bldg

5 Av SW

Lavalin Centre
I Atrium II

Real Estates Board Place 800

Serval Tower
Canada Life / Pacific Plaza

Standard Fifth & Life Fifth Bldg
Petrorep Petex

Calgary House

Petroleum Club
WMCA

Wheat Pool

Bow Valley Square

Petro Canad Centre

Separate School Board

Carketen House

6 Av SW

Showcase Grand

Commerce Centre

Place Concorde
Pentland Place

Sandman Hotel
Monenco Place / Nexen

Executive Place
Life Plaza / Sierra Place

Ford
Bowlen Bldg

Court of Appeal

Court House

IBM
Amoco Canada

Cadillac Fairview Bldg
First Canadian Centre

Telus Bldg

Transit Mall

7 Av SW

Transit Mall

Garden Towers

Century Gardens

Elveden Centre
Ramada Hotel / Fina

Free Fare Zone

Encor Place
Uptown

Northstar Energy Bldg
Western Gas

The Eaton's

Eaton Centre

Canada Trust

Toronto Dominion Square
Devonian Gardens

Scotia Centre

The Bay

Toronto Dominion Bank

Lord Nelson Inn

Medical Centre

8 Av SW

Western Centre
Panarctic Plaza

First Alberta Place
Western Canadian Place

Canadian Oxy / Globe

Penny Lane Mall
Capitol Bldg

Montreal Trust

Royal Bank Bldg
Bankers Hall

Stephen Avenue Mall

Alberta Hotel
Pan Canad Plaza

9 Av SW   **9 Av SW**

Ford

Medical Centre

Mountain Equipment CO-OP
Sprint Canada

Castello's

Alberta Boot Factory Outlet

Gulf Canada Square

Palliser Hotel

Mount Royal House

Ram Mortgage Centre
ATCO Gas

West Canadian Graphic Ctr

Tenth Av House
General Motors

Joffre Place
Clover Leaf Bldg

Sunrise Square

Scott Plaza

10 Av SW

Macosham Place

Bromley Ct
Clennan A

11 Av SW

Canadian Western Natural Gas Co & Museum

House of Light
Safeway

Westcoast Theatre Ctr

The Confederation

Sam Livingston Bldg

Central Park Plaza

CIBC Service Ctr

IBM Bldg

Alberta Power Pool

Tra Pa

Dominion Place

12 Av SW

Petrowest Plaza

Braemar Place

Colonel Belcher

Central Memorial Park

Central Park Plaza

Beltline Pool

Holid Int

Connaught
Fountain Walk

Rundle College

13 Av SW   13 Av SW

VICTORIA CROSSING

14 Av SW

'Plus 15' Elevated Walkway System Enclosed Section
'Plus 15' Elevated Walkway System Open Section

6   **A**   36   **B**   **C**

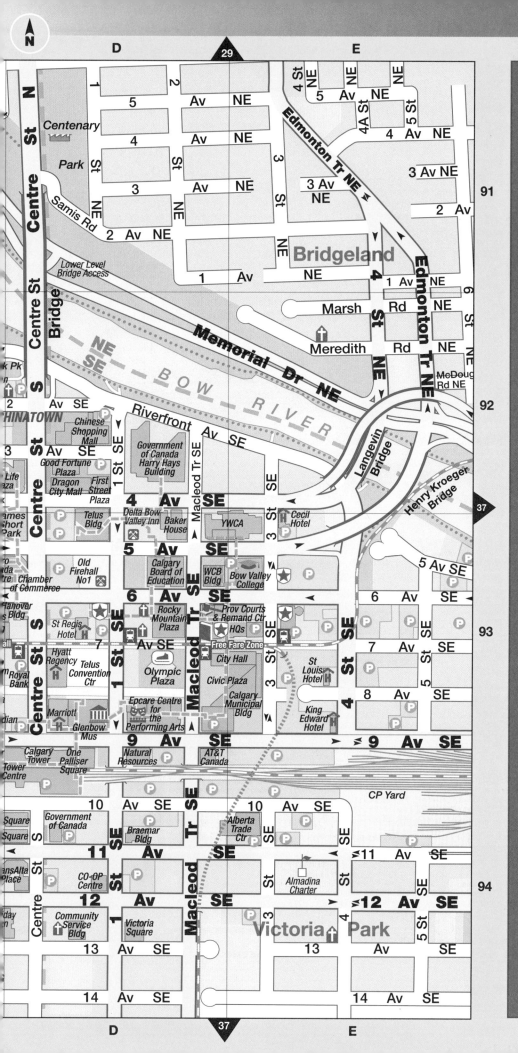

Downtown Calgary Major Buildings

AGT Tower .D92-93
Amoco Tower .C92
Aquitaine Tower B93
Atrium A93
Baker House .D93
Bankers Hall .C93
Bowlen Bldg. B93
Bromley Square C-D94
Cadillac Fairview Bldg. C93
Calgary Board of Education D93
Calgary House B93
Calgary Place C92-93
Calgary Real Estate Board A93
Calgary Tower D94
Canada Life A-B93
Canada Place C92-93
Canada Trust B-C93
Canadian Oxy B93
Canterra Tower B-C92
Century Square C92
Chevron Plaza B93
Chamber of Commerce D93
City Hall E93
Civic Plaza D-E93
Commerce Centre A93
Court House B93
Court of Appeal B93
Devonian Gardens C93
Dominion Place A94
Dragon City D92
Eau Claire Estates B92
Eau Claire Place B92
Elvedon Centre B93
Emerson Centre A92-93
Encor Place B93
Energy Resources Bldg. B93
Epcare Centre for the Perfoming Arts .D93
Fifth Avenue Place C92-93
Fina A-B93
First Alberta Place A-B93
First Canadian Centre C93
Ford B93
Government of Canada Harry Hays
   Building .D92
Gulf Canada Square C94
Hanover Bldg. D93
Heliport A92
Lavalin Centre A93
Life Plaza A-B93
McDougall Centre B93
McFarlane Tower B92
Mobil Tower C93
Monenco Place A93
Montreal Trust B-C93
Municipal Bldg. D-E93
Northstar Energy Bldg. B93
Nova A93
One Palliser Square D94
Pacific Plaza B93
Pan Canadian Plaza C-D93
Panarctic Plaza A93
Pentland Place A93
Petex B93
Petro Canada Centre C-D93
Petroleum Club C93
Place 800 . . . . .A93
Place Concorde A93
Provincial Court & Remand Centre
   Headquarters D-E93
Rocky Mountain Plaza D93
Roslyn Bldg. B-C93
Royal Bank Bldg. C93
Selkirk House B92-93
Shaw Court B92
Shell Centre B-C92
Sierra Place B93
Standard Life B93
Stock Exchange A93
Sun Life Plaza C-D92
Suncor Tower B92
Telus Convention Centre D93
Toronto Dominion Square C93
Tower Centre D94
TransAlta Place C-D94
Trimac A93
Western Canadian Place B93
Western Centre A93
Western Gas B93
Wheat Pool C93

0   .25   .5   .75   **1 Kilometre**
kilomètre

V   W   X   Y

1

Woodland   Way

**Woodland
Estates**

**Westledge
Estates**

32   165 St

Township Rd 260   Woodland   Cl   144 Av /
Township Rd 260 (Burma Rd)

Woodland Gn

Range Rd   Lochend   Dr
**Lochend
Estates**
Lochend   Dr

149 St   Woodland   La   Woodland Pl

2

Lochend Rd

**New Woods
Estates**

To Cochrane - Page 61

Bow   Valley   Tr

31 Rd

Sparrow   Pl

1A

Range Rd

3

MUNICIPAL   DISTRICT   OF   ROCKY   VIEW

Coyote   Valley   Rd

149 St

CP

B O W

R I V E R

Shopping Centres & DISTRICTS

Avenida Place *Calgary* **49** P28	Eau Claire Market *Calgary* **6** C92	Park Place S.C. *Lethbridge* **83** E7
BARCLAY MALL *Calgary* **6** C93	ELECTRIC AVENUE *Calgary* . . .**6** A94	Parkland Mall *Red Deer* **64** E5
Bay, The *Calgary* **6** C93	Fairway Shopping Plaza *Lethbridge* . .	Penny Lane Mall *Calgary* **6** B93
Beddington Shop. Ctr. *Calgary*	. . . .**88** J10-11	Richmond Square *Calgary* .**35** I19-20
. . . .**20-21** O7-8 P7-8	Forest Lawn S.C. *Calgary* .**38** W17-18	Riverbend S.C. *Calgary* **44** S-T24
Beddington Square *Calgary* .**20** O7-8	FOURTH STREET *Calgary* . .**36** O17-18	Samson Mall *Lake Louise* **56** C4
Bow Valley Square *Calgary* **6** C93	Franklin Mall *Calgary* **28** V15	Scotia Centre *Calgary* **6** C93
Brentwood Village *Calgary* . . .**27** K12	Gaetz Av Crossing Shop Ctr *Red Deer*	Scott Plaza *Calgary* **6** B94
Bower Place S.C. *Red Deer* . .**66** J-K5	. . . .**66** J-K5	Shawnessy Centre *Calgary* . .**53** P32
Canyon Meadows S.C. *Calgary***48** N27	Glenmore Landing *Calgary* .**42** M-N25	Shawnessy Village *Calgary* . .**53** P32
Cassils Centre Mall *Brooks* . . .**90** B2	Greentree Mall *Drumheller* . .**73** D7-8	Signal Hill Centre *Calgary* .**35** H19-20
Castleridge Mall *Calgary* **30** W11	Heritage Plaza *Calgary* .**42-43** O-P24	Southcentre *Calgary* **49** P27
Centre Village Mall *Lethbridge* .**83** E8	Hunterhorn Plaza *Calgary* . . .**21** P-O9	Southland Crossing *Calgary* .**42** O25
CHINATOWN *Calgary* **6** C-D92	KENSINGTON CROSSING *Calgary* . .	Southpointe Common S.C. *Red Deer* .
Chinook Centre *Calgary* **42** O22	. . . .**36** N16	. . . .**66** K5
Co-Op Shop. Centre *Calgary* . .**48** L26	Lake Bonavista Promenade *Calgary* .	Southwood Centre *Calgary* . .**48** N26
College Value Mall *Lethbridge*	. . . .**49** Q28	Southview Mall *Medicine Hat* **95** J5-6
. . . .**88** H-J10	Macleod Mall *Calgary* . .**42-43** O-P25	Stadium Shopping Ctr. *Calgary***27** K14
Country Fair Plaza *Calgary***20-21** O-P9	Macleod Plaza *Calgary* .**42-43** O-P25	STEPHEN AVENUE MALL *Calgary***6** C93
Country Hills Towne Centre *Calgary* . .	Macleod Trail Ctr. *Calgary*	Strathcona Town Sq. *Calgary* .**34** G16
. . . .**13** P-Q4	. . . .**42-43** O-P25	Sunridge Mall *Calgary* **30** U-V13
Crossroads Market *Calgary* . .**30** T14	Magrath Market Place *Lethbridge* . . .	Toronto Dominion Sq. *Calgary* .**6** C93
Crowchild Square *Calgary* **19** I10	. . . .**88** H10	Tower Lane Mall *Airdrie* **68** C3
Crowfoot Plaza *Calgary* **18** F8	Market Mall *Calgary* **27** I12	Trans Canada Mall *Calgary* **31** X14-15
Crowsnest Mall *Crowsnest Pass*	Marlborough Mall *Calgary* .**30** V15-16	UPTOWN 17: THE AVENUE *Calgary* . .
. . . .**80** E6-7	Medicine Hat Mall *Medicine Hat* **95** J7	. . . .**36** N17
Dalhousie Station *Calgary* **19** I10	Midnapore Mall *Calgary* **53** P31	Village Square *Calgary* **31** X13
Deer Park Mall *Red Deer* **67** H8	Mountain View Plaza *Olds* **62** B3	Westbrook Shop. Ctr. *Calgary* . . . . .
Deer Valley Centre *Calgary* .**49** R-S29	North Hill Shop. Ctr. *Calgary***28** M-N14	. . . .**35** J-K17
Deerfoot Mall *Calgary* **21** Q-R10	Northgate Vlg. Mall *Calgary***38** V15-16	Westhills Towne Centre *Calgary* . . . .
Eastgate Mall *Innisfail* **63** B4	Northland Vlg. Shoppes *Calgary*	. . . .**35** H20
Eastview S.C. *Red Deer* **67** H7	. . . .**27** J11	Willow Park Shopping Centre *Calgary*
Eaton Centre *Calgary* **6** B-C93	Park Meadows S.C. *Lethbridge* .**84** C9	. . . .**49** P26

Springbank

Heights

Rd

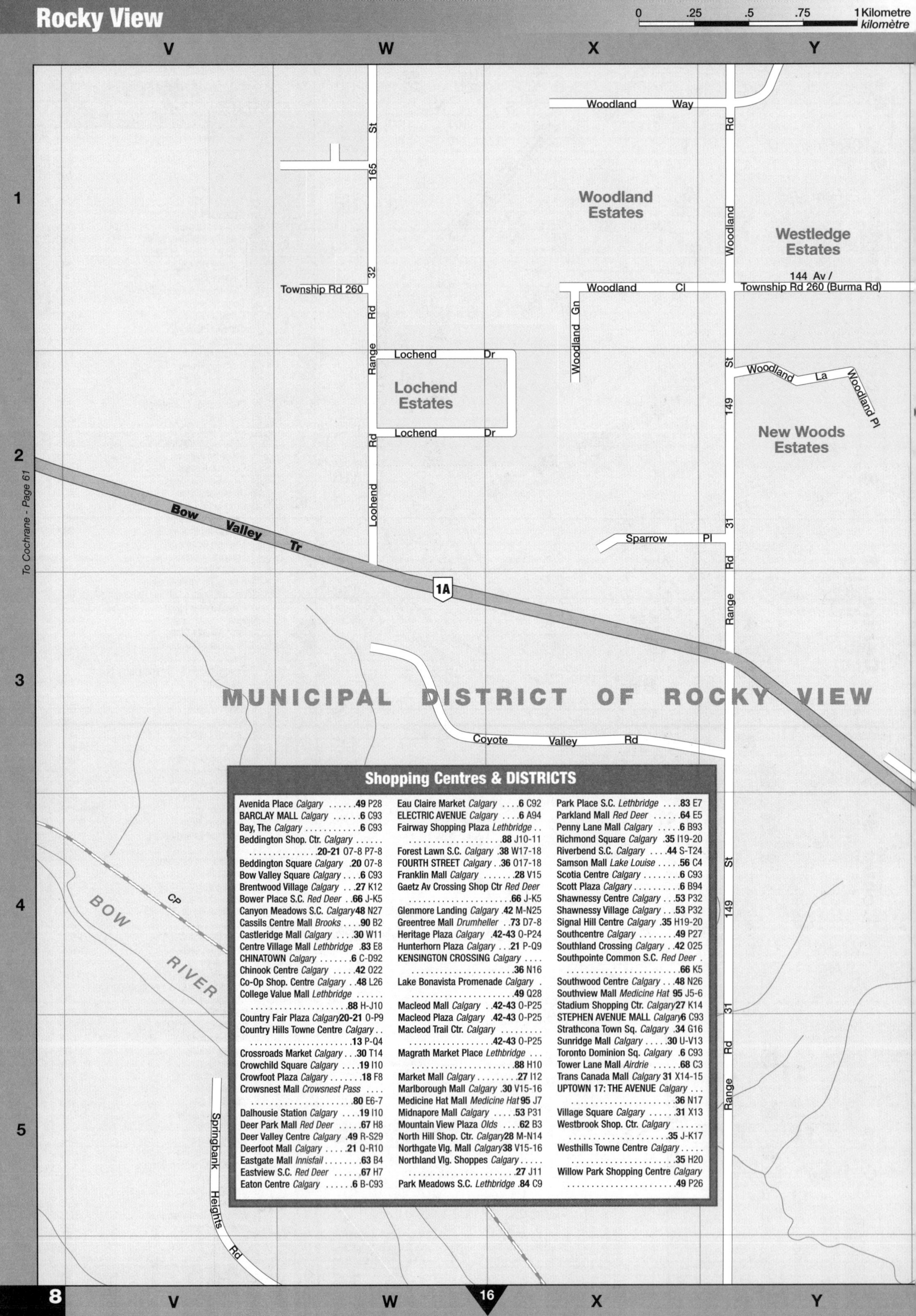

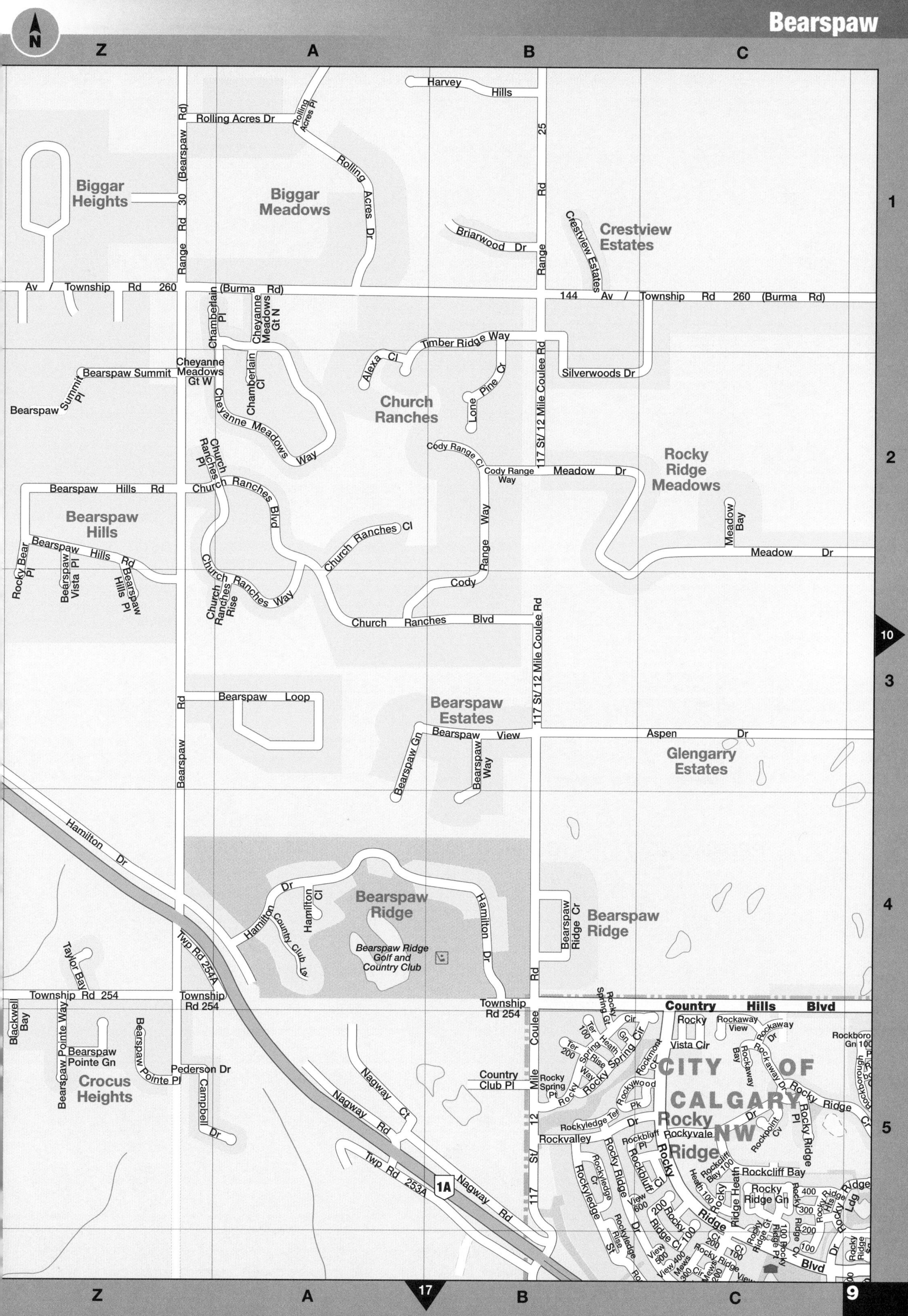

N

Z A B C

Biggar
Heights

Biggar
Meadows

Harvey   Hills

Rolling Acres Dr

Rolling Acres Pl

Rolling Acres Dr

Range   Rd   30   (Bearspaw   Rd)

25

Range   Rd

Briarwood   Dr

Crestview Estates

Crestview
Estates

1

Av / Township   Rd   260

144   Av / Township   Rd   260   (Burma   Rd)

(Burma   Rd)

Chamberlain Pl

Cheyanne
Meadows
Gt N

Cheyanne
Meadows
Gt W

Bearspaw Summit Pl

Bearspaw Summit

Bearspaw   Summit   Pl

Chamberlain   Ct

Cheyanne   Meadows   Way

Chamberlain Ct

Alexa   Cl

Timber Ridge Way

Lone   Pine   Ct

Church
Ranches

Silverwoods Dr

117 St / 12 Mile Coulee Rd

Rocky
Ridge
Meadows

2

Bearspaw   Hills   Rd

Church Ranches Pl

Church   Ranches   Blvd

Cody Range Cl

Cody Range
Way

Meadow   Dr

Meadow
Bay

Bearspaw
Hills

Rocky Bear Pl

Bearspaw   Hills   Rd

Bearspaw Vista Pl

Bearspaw Hills Pl

Church Ranches   Cl

Range   Way

Church   Ranches

Church   Ranches   Way

Church Ranches Rise

Cody

Meadow   Dr

Church   Ranches   Blvd

117 St / 12 Mile Coulee Rd

10

3

Rd

Bearspaw   Loop

Bearspaw
Estates

Bearspaw   View

Aspen   Dr

Glengarry
Estates

Bearspaw   Gn

Bearspaw Way

Bearspaw   Rd

Hamilton   Dr

Hamilton

Hamilton Dr

Country Club Ln

Hamilton Ct

Bearspaw
Ridge

Bearspaw Ridge
Golf and
Country Club

Hamilton   Dr

Bearspaw   Ridge Cr

Bearspaw
Ridge

Rd

4

Taylor Bay

Township   Rd   254

Blackwell Bay

Township
Rd 254A

Township
Rd 254

Township
Rd 254

Country
Club Pl

Country   Hills   Blvd

CITY   OF
CALGARY
NW

Rocky
Ridge

Crocus
Heights

Bearspaw Pointe Way

Bearspaw
Pointe Gn

Bearspaw Pointe Pl

Pederson Dr

Campbell   Dr

Nagway   Ct

Nagway   Rd

Twp   Rd   253A

1A

Nagway   Rd

12   Mile   Coulee

117   St

Rocky
Spring Gn

Rocky Spring Gt

Rocky
Spring Heath

Rocky
Spring Pt

Rocky
Spring Way

Rockvalley

Rockyledge Ter

Rockyledge

Rockyledge
Dr

Rockyledge
View 600

Rockyledge
View 200

Rockyledge
View 500

Rocky   Cir

Rockaway
View

Rocky
Vista Cir

Rockmont
Gn

Rockwood
Pk

Rockbluff Pl

Rockbluff
Cr

Rockyvale
View

Rockaway
Bay

Rockaway   Dr

Rockpoint Cv

Rocky
Ridge
Pl

Rockboro
Gn 100

Rocky   Ridge

Rockcliff Bay

Rocky
Ridge Gn

Rocky Ridge Gt 200

Rocky Ridge
Rise

Rocky Ridge
View 400

Rocky Ridge
View 500

Rocky Ridge
View 300 Cir

Mavis Ridge Cl

Rocky   Ridge

Rocky Ridge
Ldg

Rocky Ridge
Blvd

5

Z   A   17   B   C   9

1 Kilometre
kilomètre

0   .25   .5   .75   1

MUNICIPAL DISTRICT

144 Av / Township Rd 260 (Burma Rd)

CITY OF

West View Secondary

PROVINCIAL   **CORRECTIONAL**   **INSTITUTION**

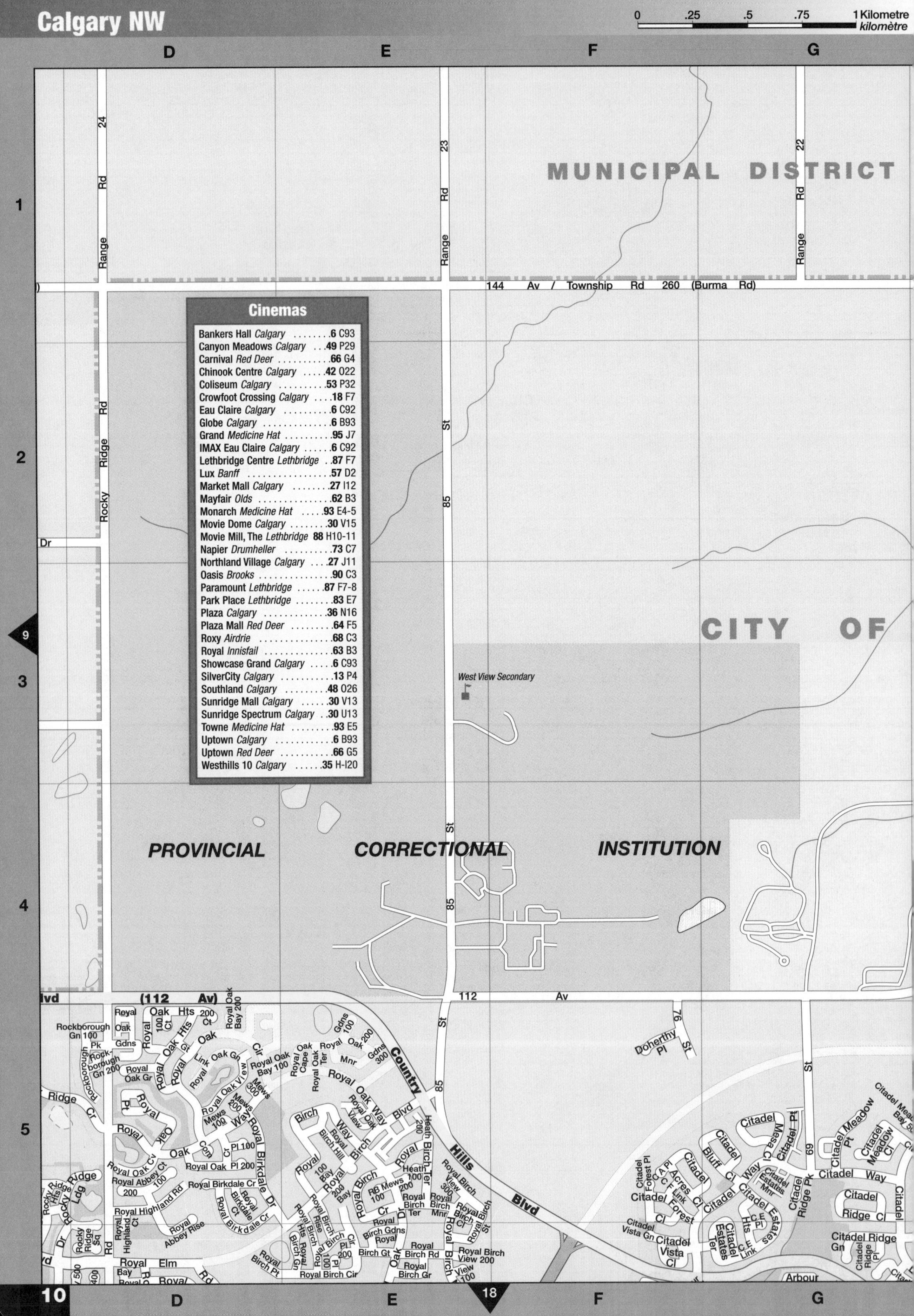

Cinemas

Bankers Hall *Calgary*	.6 C93
Canyon Meadows *Calgary*	.49 P29
Carnival *Red Deer*	.66 G4
Chinook Centre *Calgary*	.42 O22
Coliseum *Calgary*	.53 P32
Crowfoot Crossing *Calgary*	.18 F7
Eau Claire *Calgary*	.6 C92
Globe *Calgary*	.6 B93
Grand *Medicine Hat*	.95 J7
IMAX Eau Claire *Calgary*	.6 C92
Lethbridge Centre *Lethbridge*	.87 F7
Lux *Banff*	.57 D2
Market Mall *Calgary*	.27 I12
Mayfair *Olds*	.62 B3
Monarch *Medicine Hat*	.93 E4-5
Movie Dome *Calgary*	.30 V15
Movie Mill, The *Lethbridge*	88 H10-11
Napier *Drumheller*	.73 C7
Northland Village *Calgary*	.27 J11
Oasis *Brooks*	.90 C3
Paramount *Lethbridge*	.87 F7-8
Park Place *Lethbridge*	.83 E7
Plaza *Calgary*	.36 N16
Plaza Mall *Red Deer*	.64 F5
Roxy *Airdrie*	.68 C3
Royal *Innisfail*	.63 B3
Showcase Grand *Calgary*	.6 C93
SilverCity *Calgary*	.13 P4
Southland *Calgary*	.48 O26
Sunridge Mall *Calgary*	.30 V13
Sunridge Spectrum *Calgary*	.30 U13
Towne *Medicine Hat*	.93 E5
Uptown *Calgary*	.6 B93
Uptown *Red Deer*	.66 G5
Westhills 10 *Calgary*	.35 H-I20

(112 Av)   112 Av

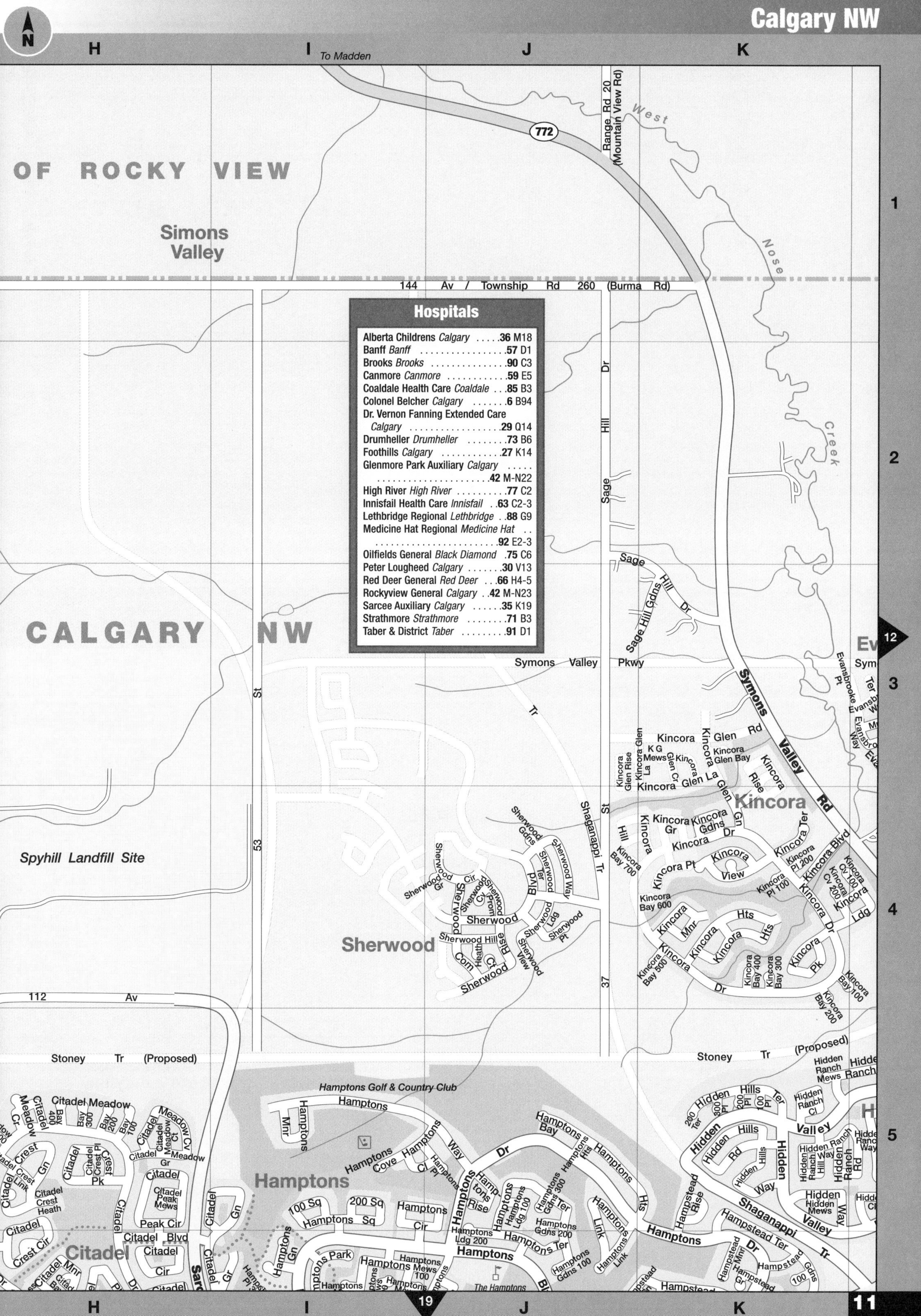

N

H I J K

To Madden

772

Range Rd 20 (Mountain View Rd)

West

OF ROCKY VIEW

Simons Valley

Nose Creek

1

144 Av / Township Rd 260 (Burma Rd)

Hospitals

Alberta Childrens *Calgary*	**36** M18
Banff *Banff*	**57** D1
Brooks *Brooks*	**90** C3
Canmore *Canmore*	**59** E5
Coaldale Health Care *Coaldale*	**85** B3
Colonel Belcher *Calgary*	**6** B94
Dr. Vernon Fanning Extended Care *Calgary*	**29** Q14
Drumheller *Drumheller*	**73** B6
Foothills *Calgary*	**27** K14
Glenmore Park Auxiliary *Calgary*	**42** M-N22
High River *High River*	**77** C2
Innisfail Health Care *Innisfail*	**63** C2-3
Lethbridge Regional *Lethbridge*	**88** G9
Medicine Hat Regional *Medicine Hat*	**92** E2-3
Oilfields General *Black Diamond*	**75** C6
Peter Lougheed *Calgary*	**30** V13
Red Deer General *Red Deer*	**66** H4-5
Rockyview General *Calgary*	**42** M-N23
Sarcee Auxiliary *Calgary*	**35** K19
Strathmore *Strathmore*	**71** B3
Taber & District *Taber*	**91** D1

CALGARY NW

Sage Hill Dr

Sage Hill Dr

Sage Hill Gdns

2

Symons Valley Pkwy

Ev
Sym
12
3

Kincora Glen Rd

Kincora Glen
K G Mews
Kincora Glen La
Kincora Glen Cr
Kincora Glen Bay
Kincora Glen La
Kincora Glen Gn
Kincora Glen Rise
Rise

Kincora

Kincora Gr
Kincora Gdns
Kincora Dr
Kincora
Kincora Pt
Kincora View
Kincora Pl 200
Kincora Pl 100
Kincora Blvd
Kincora CV 100
Kincora CV 200
Kincora Dr
Kincora Ldg

Spyhill Landfill Site

53 St

Shaganappi Tr

Sherwood Gdns
Sherwood Gr
Sherwood Cir
Sherwood Prom
Sherwood Dr B
Sherwood Ter
Sherwood Way
Sherwood Ldg
Sherwood Pt

Kincora Bay 700
Kincora Bay 600
Kincora Bay 500
Kincora Bay 400
Kincora Bay 300
Kincora Bay 200
Kincora Bay 100
Kincora Mnr
Kincora Hts
Kincora Hts
Kincora Pk

Sherwood
Sherwood Hill Com
Keath
Sherwood Rise
Sherwood View
Sherwood Pt
Sherwood

37 St

4

112 Av

Stoney Tr (Proposed)

Stoney Tr (Proposed)

Hidden Ranch Mews
Hidden Ranch

Hamptons Golf & Country Club

Hamptons

Citadel Meadow
Citadel Meadow Cr
Meadow Cv
Meadow Gr
Citadel Meadow Bay 400/300/200/100
Citadel Crest Gn
Citadel Crest Link
Citadel Crest Pk
Citadel Crest Heath
Citadel Crest Cir
Citadel Mnr

Hamptons Mnr
Hamptons
Hamptons Cove
Hamptons Way
Hamptons
Hamptons Rise
Hamptons Dr
Hamptons Bay
Hamptons Hts
Hamptons Ter

Hidden Hills Ter
Hidden Ranch Pl 100/200
Hidden Ranch Cl
Hidden Valley
Hidden Hills
Hidden Hills Rd
Hidden Ranch Rd
Hidden Ranch Way
Hidden Ranch Hill
Hidden Way
Hidden Mews
Hidden Cl

Hamptons

Citadel
Citadel Peak Pk
Citadel Peak Cir
Citadel Gn
Citadel Blvd
Citadel Cir
Citadel Cir

100 Sq
200 Sq
Hamptons Sq
Hamptons Cir
Hamptons Gn
Hamptons Park
Hamptons Mews 100
Hamptons Ldg 200
Hamptons Ldg 100
Hamptons Gdns 200
Hamptons Gdns 100
Hamptons Ter

Hamptons

Hampstead Ter
Hampstead Rise
Hampstead Gdns
Hampstead Mnr
Hidden Valley
Shaganappi Tr

Citadel
Citadel Crest Cir

The Hamptons

Hamptons Blvd

Hamptons Link
Hampstead Dr
Hampstead Link

5

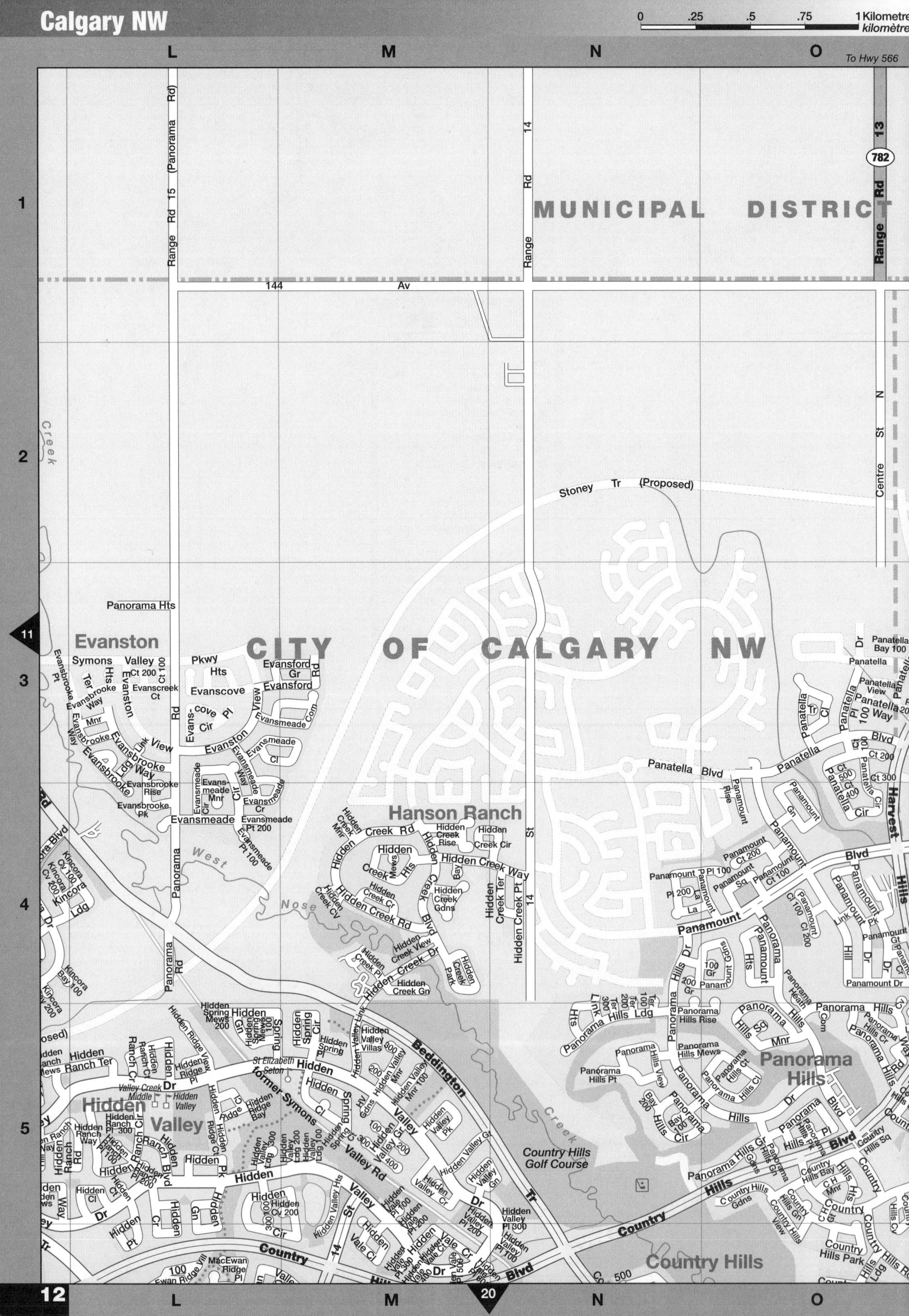

0   .25   .5   .75   1 Kilometre
kilomètre

L   M   N   O

To Hwy 566

1

Range Rd 15 (Panorama Rd)

Range Rd 14

Range Rd 13

782

MUNICIPAL   DISTRICT

Centre St N

144   Av

2

Stoney   Tr   (Proposed)

Creek

Panorama Hts

11

Evanston

CITY   OF   CALGARY   NW

Panatella Bay 100
Panatella

Panatella View
Panatella 20

3

Symons   Valley
Hts

Pkwy
Hts

Evansford
Gr
Evansford

Evanston Ct 100
Ct 200

Panatella 100 Way

Evansbrooke Pt

Ter
Way

Evanston

Evanscreek
Ct

View Rd

Panatella Tr

Panatella
Blvd

Panatella Cir

Evansbrooke Way

Mnr

Evanscove Pl

Evanscove
Cir

Evansmeade Com

Ct 100
Panatella Ct 200

Evanston Link View

Evanston

Evansmeade
Cl

Ct 300

Evansbrooke Ldg

Evansmeade Way

Panatella Blvd

Panamount Rise

Evansbrooke Way

Evansbrooke Rise

Evansmeade Cr

Evansmeade
Mnr

Harvest Hills

Panamount Gn

Evansbrooke Pk

Evansmeade
Ct

Panamount
Ct 200

Panamount
Pk

Evansmeade

Evansmeade
Pt 200

Hanson Ranch

Hidden Creek Rise

Hidden Creek Cir

St

Panamount Pl 100

Panamount
Sq

Panamount
Ct 100

Panamount Blvd

Kincora Blvd

Panorama Rd

Evansmeade Pt 100

Hidden Creek Mnr

Creek Rd

Hidden Creek Mews

Hidden
Creek
Hts

Hidden Creek Bay

Hidden Creek Way

Panamount Pl 200

Panamount
La

Panamount
Ct 100 Ct 200

Panamount Dr

4

Kincora Dr

Kincora
Ct 100
Kincora
Ct 200

Kincora Ldg

Panorama Rd

West

Nose

Hidden
Creek Gr

Hidden Creek Cv

Hidden Creek Rd

Hidden Creek Gdns

Hidden Creek Blvd

14 St

Hidden Creek Pt

Panorama Hills Dr

100
Gr

Panam
Gr

Panorama Hills

Panamount Heath

Panamount Dr

Kincora Bay 100

Kincora Ct 200

Hidden Creek Pl

Hidden Creek View

Hidden Creek Dr

Hidden Creek Park

Hidden Creek Gn

Panorama Hills Ldg

Panorama Hills

Panorama Com

Panorama Hills Way

(Proposed)

Hidden Ranch Mews

Hidden
Ranch Ter

Hidden Spring Mews 200

Hidden Spring Gn

Hidden Spring Cir

Hidden Valley Villas

Beddington Tr

Panorama Hills Hts

Panorama Hills View

Panorama Hills Rise

Panorama Hills Mews

Panorama Hills Sq

Panorama Hills Mnr

Panorama Hills Cl

Panorama Hills

5

Hidden Ranch Cr

Hidden Ranch
Ct

Hidden Ridge View

Hidden Ridge

St Elizabeth Seton

Hidden Spring

Hidden Valley Gr

Hidden Valley Mnr 100

Panorama Hills Pt

Panorama Hills Bay 200

Panorama Hills Gr

Panorama Hills Pl

Panorama Hills Blvd

Hidden Ranch Way

Valley Creek Dr

Former Symons

Hidden Valley

Hidden Ridge Bay

Hidden Ridge Pk

Hidden

Hidden Valley Ct

Hidden Valley Pk

Country Hills Golf Course

Panorama Hills Cir

Country Hills Sq

Hidden Valley

Hidden Ranch Pl 300

Hidden Valley Rd

Hidden Valley Gn

Panorama Hills Gr

Country Hills Bay

C H Mnr

Hidden Ranch Rd

Hidden Ranch Blvd

Hidden Valley

Hidden Valley Cr

Panorama Hills Gdns

C Hills Gn

Country Hills View

Hidden Ranch Pt 200

Hidden

Hidden Valley Cv 200

Country Hills Blvd

Country Hills Gdns

Country Hills Park

Country Hills Dr

Hidden Ranch Way

Hidden
Cl

Hidden Gn

Hidden Ranch Dr

Hidden Valley Hts

14 St

Hidden Vale Cl

Hidden Valley Dr

Hidden Valley Pt 200

Hidden Valley Pt 300

Creek

Country Hills

Country Hills Park

Hidden Dr

Hidden Pt

Country Pl

Hidden Cir

MacEwan Ridge Vill

MacEwan Ridge Pl

Valley

Hidden Vale Ct

Hidden Dr

Hidden Valley Pt 100

Ewan Ridge

100

12

L   M   20   N   O

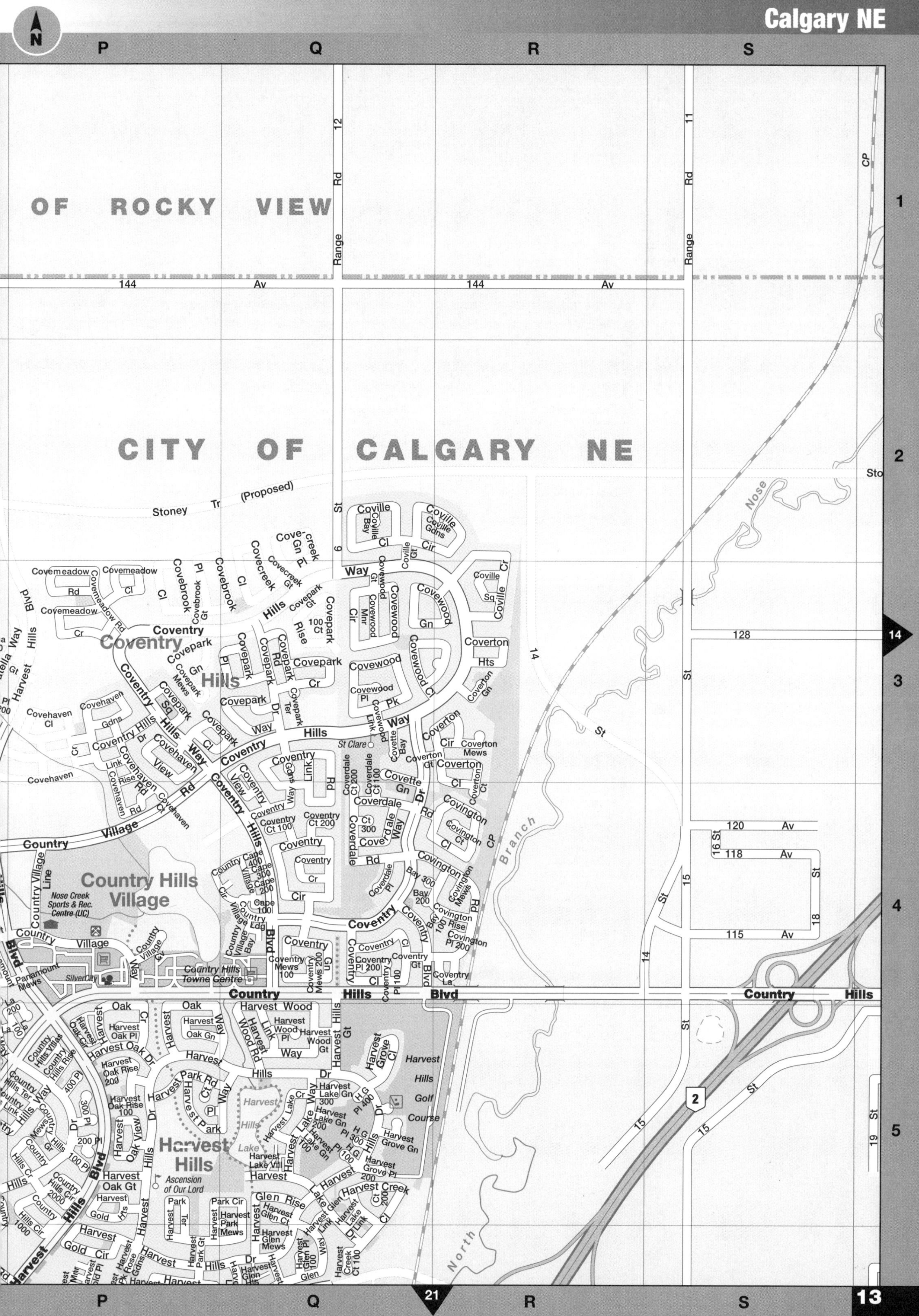

OF ROCKY VIEW

CITY OF CALGARY NE

Coventry

Coventry Hills

Country Hills Village

Nose Creek Sports & Rec. Centre (UC)

SilverCity

Country Hills Towne Centre

Harvest Hills

Ascension of Our Lord

Harvest Lake

Harvest Hills Golf Course

0 .25 .5 .75 1 Kilometre
kilomètre

To Airdrie - Page 68

T U V W

MUNICIPAL DISTRICT OF

CP
Creek
Deerfoot Tr
Barlow Tr
St
Range Rd 293
Range Rd 292
144 Av
52 St

Stoney Tr (Proposed)
24 St

13
Av

Deerfoot Tr
Barlow Tr
Stonehill Dr
Stonehill Gt

Hills Blvd
Country Hills Blvd

Ldg
Freeport Dr
Freeport Pl
Freeport Blvd
Freeport St
Freeport Business Park
Freeport Way
19 St
Barlow Tr

36 St
52 St

100 Av

T U 22 V W

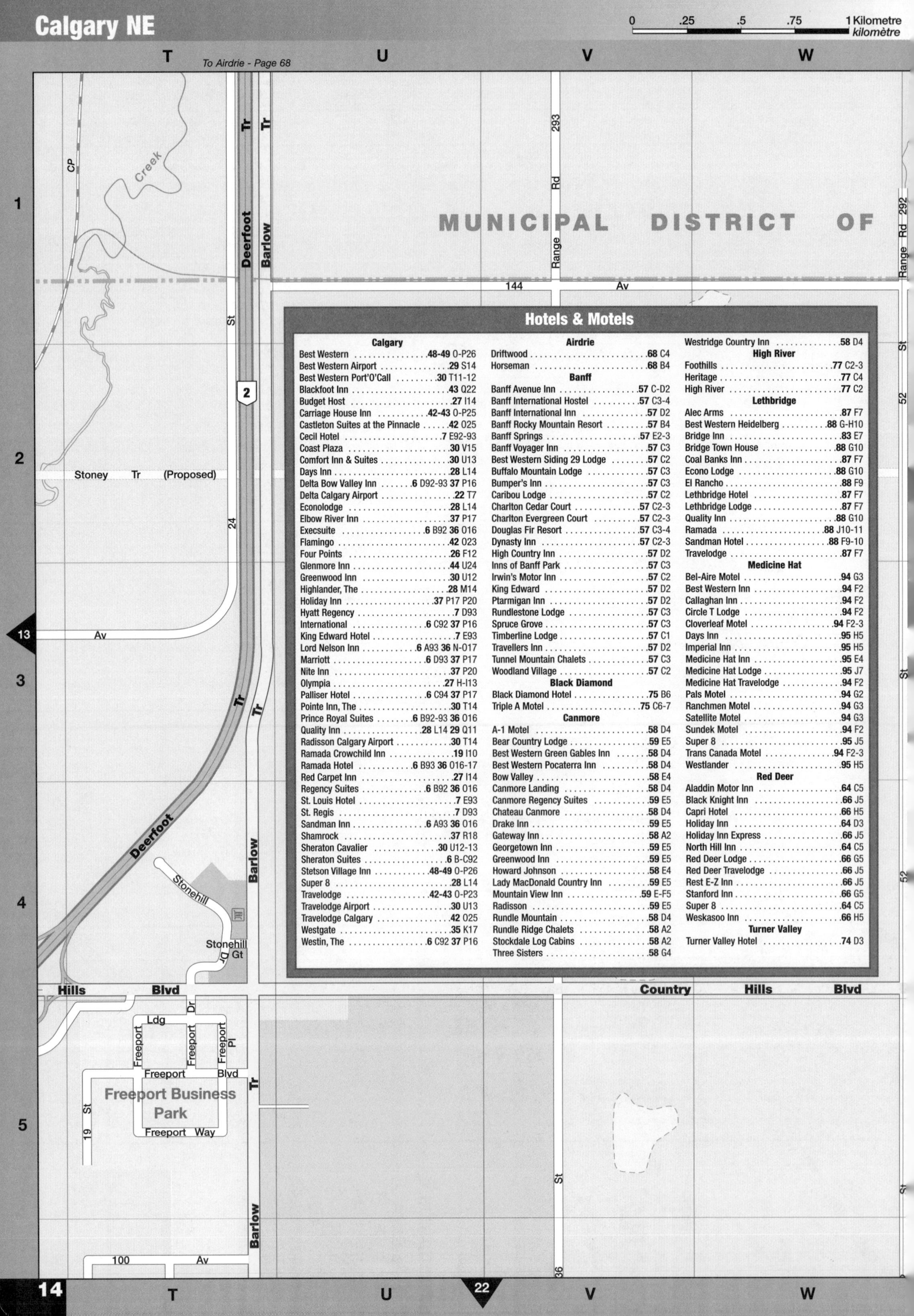

Hotels & Motels

Calgary

Best Western	.48-49 O-P26
Best Western Airport	.29 S14
Best Western Port'O'Call	.30 T11-12
Blackfoot Inn	.43 Q22
Budget Host	.27 I14
Carriage House Inn	.42-43 O-P25
Castleton Suites at the Pinnacle	.42 O25
Cecil Hotel	.7 E92-93
Coast Plaza	.30 V15
Comfort Inn & Suites	.30 U13
Days Inn	.28 L14
Delta Bow Valley Inn	.6 D92-93 37 P16
Delta Calgary Airport	.22 T7
Econolodge	.28 L14
Elbow River Inn	.37 P17
Execsuite	.6 B92 36 O16
Flamingo	.42 O23
Four Points	.26 F12
Glenmore Inn	.44 U24
Greenwood Inn	.30 U12
Highlander, The	.28 M14
Holiday Inn	.37 P17 P20
Hyatt Regency	.7 D93
International	.6 C92 37 P16
King Edward Hotel	.7 E93
Lord Nelson Inn	.6 A93 36 N-O17
Marriott	.6 D93 37 P17
Nite Inn	.37 P20
Olympia	.27 H-I13
Palliser Hotel	.6 C94 37 P17
Pointe Inn, The	.30 T14
Prince Royal Suites	.6 B92-93 36 O16
Quality Inn	.28 L14 29 Q11
Radisson Calgary Airport	.30 T14
Ramada Crowchild Inn	.19 I10
Ramada Hotel	.6 B93 36 O16-17
Red Carpet Inn	.27 I14
Regency Suites	.6 B92 36 O16
St. Louis Hotel	.7 E93
St. Regis	.7 D93
Sandman Inn	.6 A93 36 O16
Shamrock	.37 R18
Sheraton Cavalier	.30 U12-13
Sheraton Suites	.6 B-C92
Stetson Village Inn	.48-49 O-P26
Super 8	.28 L14
Travelodge	.42-43 O-P23
Travelodge Airport	.30 U13
Travelodge Calgary	.42 O25
Westgate	.35 K17
Westin, The	.6 C92 37 P16

Airdrie

Driftwood	.68 C4
Horseman	.68 B4

Banff

Banff Avenue Inn	.57 C-D2
Banff International Hostel	.57 C3-4
Banff International Inn	.57 D2
Banff Rocky Mountain Resort	.57 B4
Banff Springs	.57 E2-3
Banff Voyager Inn	.57 C3
Best Western Siding 29 Lodge	.57 C2
Buffalo Mountain Lodge	.57 C3
Bumper's Inn	.57 C3
Caribou Lodge	.57 C3
Charlton Cedar Court	.57 C2-3
Charlton Evergreen Court	.57 C2-3
Douglas Fir Resort	.57 C3-4
Dynasty Inn	.57 C2-3
High Country Inn	.57 D2
Inns of Banff Park	.57 C3
Irwin's Motor Inn	.57 C2
King Edward	.57 D2
Ptarmigan Inn	.57 D2
Rundlestone Lodge	.57 C3
Spruce Grove	.57 C3
Timberline Lodge	.57 C1
Travellers Inn	.57 D2
Tunnel Mountain Chalets	.57 C3
Woodland Village	.57 C2

Black Diamond

Black Diamond Hotel	.75 B6
Triple A Motel	.75 C6-7

Canmore

A-1 Motel	.58 D4
Bear Country Lodge	.59 E5
Best Western Green Gables Inn	.58 D4
Best Western Pocaterra Inn	.58 D4
Bow Valley	.58 E4
Canmore Landing	.58 D4
Canmore Regency Suites	.59 E5
Chateau Canmore	.58 D4
Drake Inn	.59 E5
Gateway Inn	.58 A2
Georgetown Inn	.59 E5
Greenwood Inn	.59 E5
Howard Johnson	.58 E4
Lady MacDonald Country Inn	.59 E5
Mountain View Inn	.59 E-F5
Radisson	.59 E5
Rundle Mountain	.58 D4
Rundle Ridge Chalets	.58 A2
Stockdale Log Cabins	.58 A2
Three Sisters	.58 G4

High River

Westridge Country Inn	.58 D4
Foothills	.77 C2-3
Heritage	.77 C4
High River	.77 C2

Lethbridge

Alec Arms	.87 F7
Best Western Heidelberg	.88 G-H10
Bridge Inn	.83 E7
Bridge Town House	.88 G10
Coal Banks Inn	.87 F7
Econo Lodge	.88 G10
El Rancho	.88 F9
Lethbridge Hotel	.87 F7
Lethbridge Lodge	.87 F7
Quality Inn	.88 G10
Ramada	.88 J10-11
Sandman Hotel	.88 F9-10
Travelodge	.87 F7

Medicine Hat

Bel-Aire Motel	.94 G3
Best Western Inn	.94 F2
Callaghan Inn	.94 F2
Circle T Lodge	.94 F2
Cloverleaf Motel	.94 F2-3
Days Inn	.95 H5
Imperial Inn	.95 H5
Medicine Hat Inn	.95 E4
Medicine Hat Lodge	.95 J7
Medicine Hat Travelodge	.94 F2
Pals Motel	.94 G2
Ranchmen Motel	.94 G3
Satellite Motel	.94 G3
Sundek Motel	.94 F2
Super 8	.95 J5
Trans Canada Motel	.94 F2-3
Westlander	.95 H5

Red Deer

Aladdin Motor Inn	.64 C5
Black Knight Inn	.66 J5
Capri Hotel	.66 H5
Holiday Inn	.64 D3
Holiday Inn Express	.66 J5
North Hill Inn	.64 C5
Red Deer Lodge	.66 G5
Red Deer Travelodge	.66 J5
Rest E-Z Inn	.66 J5
Stanford Inn	.66 G5
Super 8	.64 C5
Weskasoo Inn	.66 H5

Turner Valley

Turner Valley Hotel	.74 D3

N

X   Y   291 Rd   Range Rd   Z   290 Rd   Range Rd

McDonald Lake

ROCKY VIEW

Range Rd 292

1

144   Av   144   Av   Township   Rd   260

52 St

CITY OF CALGARY NE

2

Stoney   Tr   (Proposed)

Golf Courses

Banff Springs Hotel G C *Banff* **57** D-E4	Innisfail G C *Innisfail* **63** A1
Bearspaw Ridge G & C C *Rocky View* . . .**9** A-B4	Lakeside Greens G & C C *Chestermere* . .**70** E2
Bridge Valley G C *Lethbridge* **83** E5	Lakeview G C *Calgary* **42** M22
Brooks G C *Brooks* **90** D4	Land-O-Lakes G & C C *Coaldale* **85** C1
Buffalo Run G C *Rocky View* **47** J28-29	Lethbridge C C *Lethbridge* **87** H7
Calgary Elks Lodge & G C *Calgary* . .**29** Q-R13	Links (The) of Gleneagles *Cochrane* **61** B7
Calgary G & C C *Calgary* **42** N21	Lynx Ridge G C *Rocky View* **17** A-B9
Canmore G C & Curling C *Canmore* . .**58** C-D3	Maple Ridge G C *Calgary* **49** R26-27
Canyon Meadows G & C C *Calgary* . .**48** M-N28	McCall Lake G C *Calgary* **29** S12
Cochrane G C *Cochrane* **60** D4	McKenzie Meadows G C *Calgary* **54** T33
Confederation Park G C *Calgary* **28** M13	Medicine Hat G C *Medicine Hat* **93** D6
Connaught G C *Medicine Hat* **95** H5	Paradise Canyon G C *Lethbridge* **87** K8
Cottonwood Coulee G C *Medicine Hat*	Paradise Valley Par 3 G C *Medicine Hat* . .**94** H3
. . . .**94** H2-3 J2-3	Pinebrook G & C C *Rocky View* **33** B-C18
Country Hills G C *Calgary* **12** N5 **20** O6	Red Deer G & C C *Red Deer* **66** G2-3
Crowsnest Pass G & C C *Crowsnest Pass*	Redwood Meadows G C *Redwood Meadows* . . .
. . . .**80** D-E7	. . . .**61** C1
D'Arcy Ranch G C *Okotoks* **76** B2	Richmond Green G C *Calgary* **36** L19
Douglasdale Estates G C *Calgary* . . .**50** U28	River Bend G C *Red Deer* **65** A7
Earl Grey G C *Calgary* **42** M22	Shaganappi Point G C *Calgary* . . .**35-36** K16-17
Elbow Springs G C *Rocky View* **33** B-C20	Shawnee Slopes G C *Calgary* **48** N30
Fox Hollow G C *Calgary* **29** R13	Silver Springs G & C C *Calgary* **19** H10
Glencoe G & C C *Rocky View* **32** X-Y19	Silvertip G & C C *Canmore* **59** D6
Hamptons G & C C *Calgary* **11** I-J5	Strathmore G C *Strathmore* **71** C2
Harvest Hills G C *Calgary* **13** Q-R5	Taber G C *Taber* **91** D2
Henderson Lake G C *Lethbridge* **88** G11	Turner Valley G C *Turner Valley* **74** D4-5
Highland G & C C *Calgary* **28-29** P11-12	Valley Ridge G C *Calgary* **25** B10 C11
Highwood G & C C *Highwood* **77** B1-2	Willow Park G & C C *Calgary* **49** Q26-27
Inglewood G & Curling C *Calgary* . . .**38** T18-19	Woodside G C *Airdrie* **68** B1-2

3

120   Av

84

52 St

4

To Delacour

Country   Hills   Blvd   **Twp Rd 254**   564

Proposed East Freeway

68 St

5

52 St

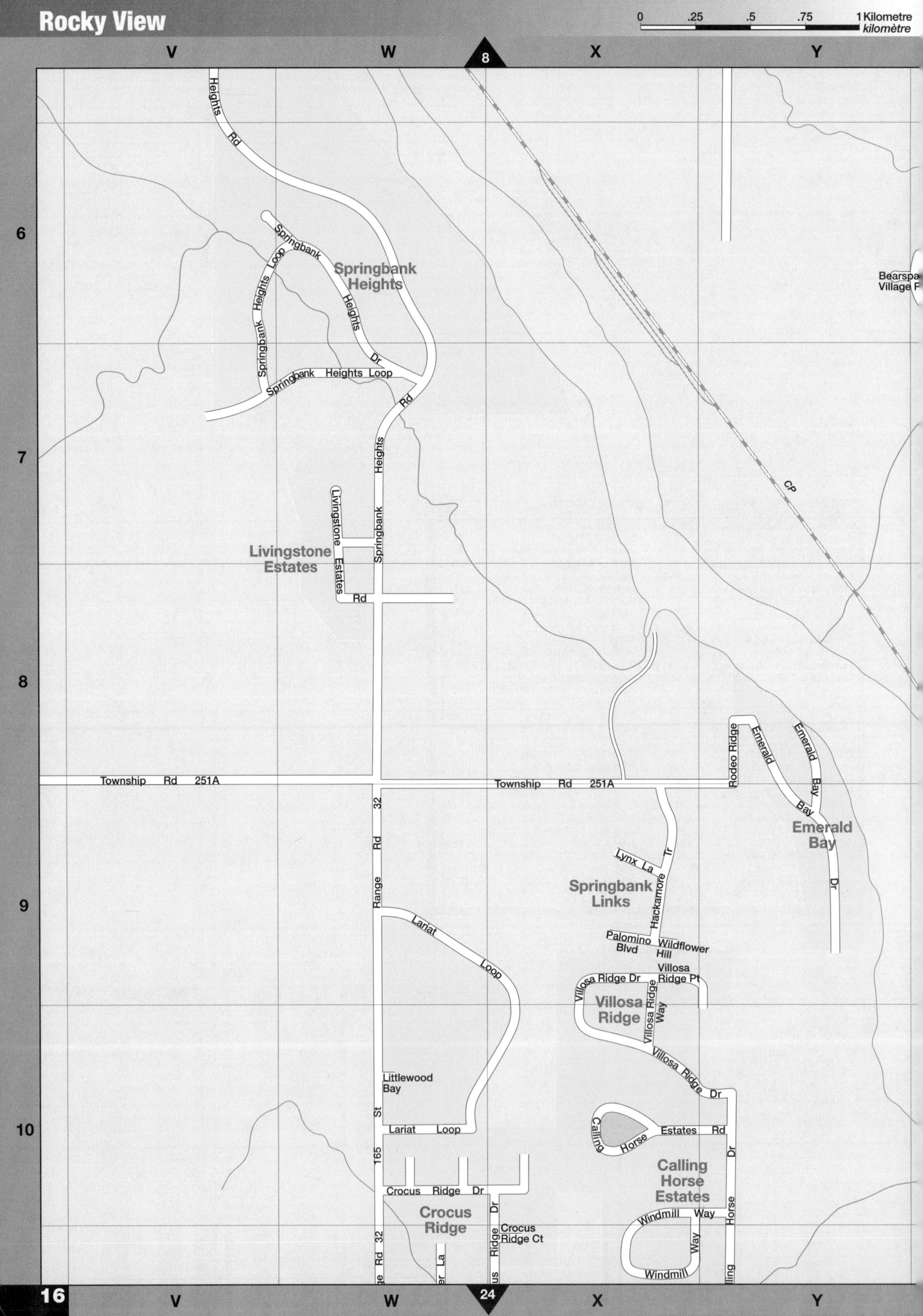

0   .25   .5   .75   1 Kilometre
kilomètre

V   W   8   X   Y

6

Heights Rd

Springbank
Heights Loop

**Springbank
Heights**

Springbank Heights Dr

Springbank Heights Loop

Rd

7

Springbank Heights Rd

Livingstone Estates

**Livingstone
Estates**

Livingstone Estates Rd

CP

Bearspa
Village P

8

Rodeo Ridge

Emerald
Bay

Emerald Bay

**Emerald
Bay**

Dr

Township Rd 251A   Township Rd 251A

Range Rd 32

Lynx La

Hackamore Tr

**Springbank
Links**

Palomino Blvd   Wildflower Hill

9

Lariat Loop

Villosa Ridge Dr   Villosa Ridge Pt

Villosa Ridge Way

**Villosa
Ridge**

Villosa Ridge Dr

Range Rd 32

St 165

Littlewood
Bay

Lariat Loop

Calling Horse

Estates Rd

Dr

**Calling
Horse
Estates**

10

Crocus Ridge Dr

Crocus Ridge Dr

**Crocus
Ridge**

Crocus Ridge Ct

Windmill Way

Windmill Way

Horse Dr

lling

Range Rd 32   er La   us Ridge Dr

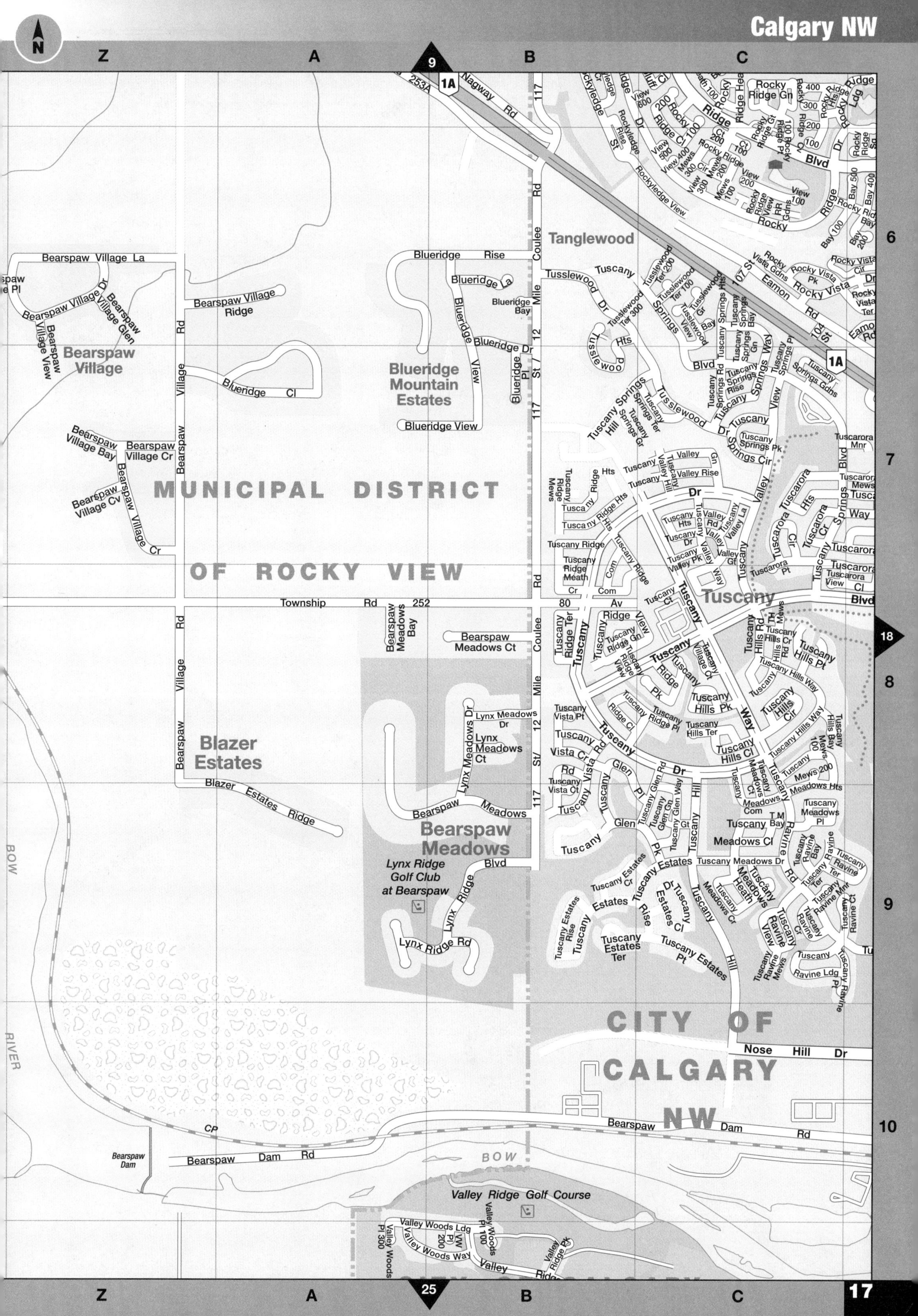
Z
A
B
C
9
25
18
6
7
8
9
10
Tanglewood
Bearspaw Village
Blueridge Mountain Estates
MUNICIPAL DISTRICT OF ROCKY VIEW
Blazer Estates
Bearspaw Meadows
Lynx Ridge Golf Club at Bearspaw
Tuscany
CITY OF CALGARY NW
Valley Ridge Golf Course
Bearspaw Dam
BOW RIVER
Township Rd 252
12 Mile Coulee Rd
117 St
Bearspaw Village Rd
Nose Hill Dr
Bearspaw Dam Rd
Tuscany Blvd
Rocky Ridge Blvd
Nagway Rd
1A
CP

0 .25 .5 .75 1 Kilometre kilomètre
D
E
10
F
G
6
7
8
9
10
17
Royal Oak
Arbour Lake
Crowfoot Park
Crowfoot Plaza
Crowfoot Centre
Crowfoot Arena
Crowfoot Crossing
St Ambrose
Watergrove Mobile Home Park
Scenic Acres
Monsignor E L Doyle
Crowchild Twin Arenas
St Sylvester
Silver Springs
WO Mitchell
Bearspaw Water Treatment Plant
Bow Centre Place
Baker Park
Bowmont Park
Bow River
Bowness Park
Stoney Tr
Crowchild Tr
Nose Hill Dr
John Laurie Blvd
Country Hills Blvd
Citadel Way
Arbour Lake Rd
Crowfoot Way
Ranchlands Blvd
Scenic Acres Blvd
Silver Springs Blvd
Silver Springs Rd
Bearspaw Dam Rd
Scenic Bow Rd
Hawkwood Blvd
Tuscany Blvd
Schubert
Scurfield Dr
Silver Ridge Dr
Silver Mead Rd
Silverview Way
Silverdale Rd
201
1A

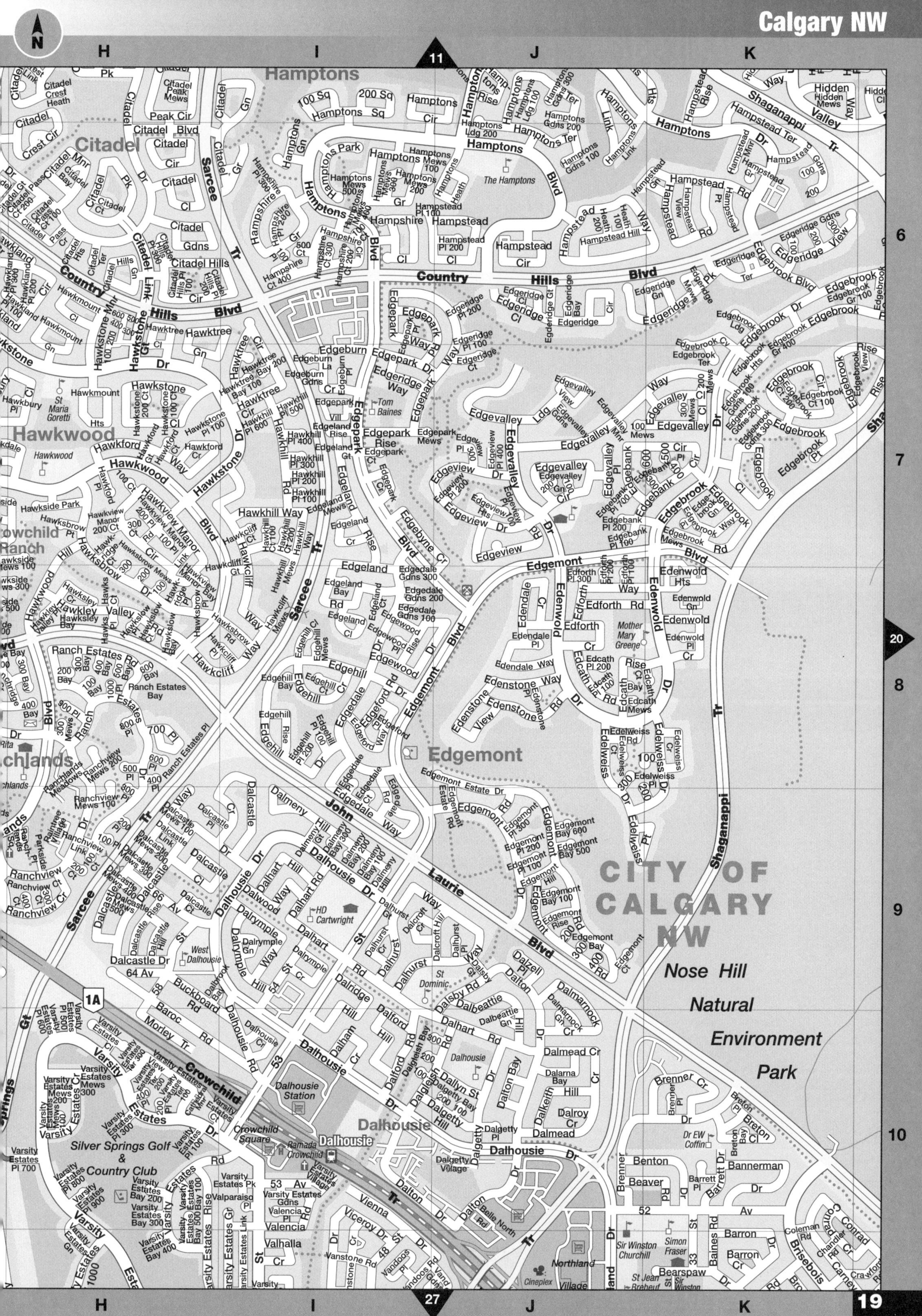

CITY OF
CALGARY
NW

Nose Hill

Natural

Environment

Park

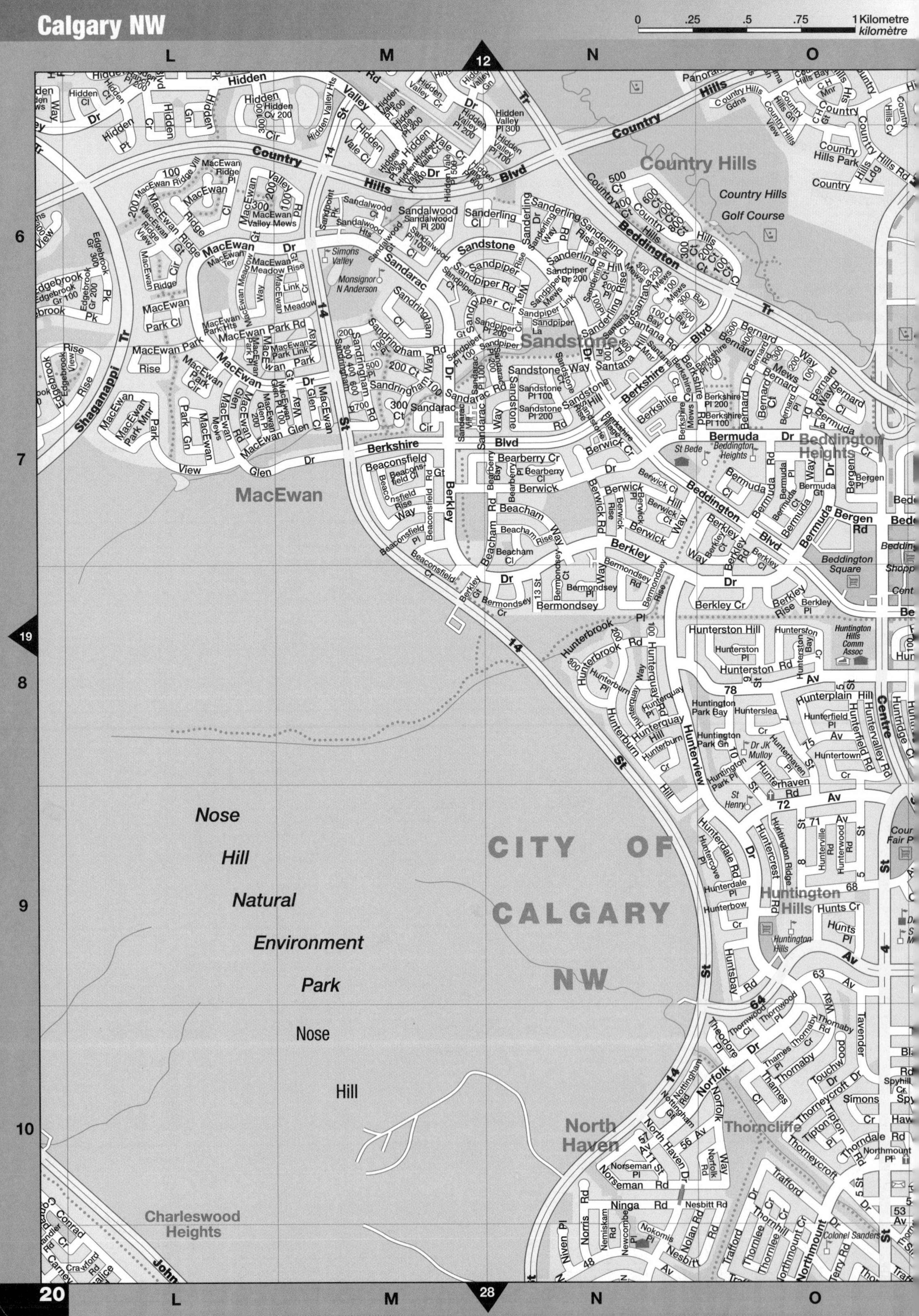

1 Kilometre
kilomètre

0   .25   .5   .75

Country Hills

Country Hills
Golf Course

Sandstone

Beddington
Heights

Bermuda

Beddington
Square

Beddington
Shopp
Cent

MacEwan

Shaganappi Tr

Berkshire

Berkley

Berkley Cr

Huntington Hill
Hills
Comm
Assoc

Huntington Hills

Hunterplain Hill

Centre

Nose

Hill

Natural

Environment

Park

Nose

Hill

CITY   OF

CALGARY

NW

Huntington
Hills

North
Haven

Thorncliffe

Charleswood
Heights

John

P
Q
R
S
13
29
22
6
7
8
9
10
Harvest Hills Business Park
Confluence Park
CITY OF CALGARY NE
CALGARY INTERNATIONAL AIRPORT
Deerfoot Business Centre
Deerfoot Mall
Skyline East
Skyline West
Thorncliffe Heights
Laycock Park
Hunterhorn Plaza
Deerfoot Tr
Airport Tr
(96 Av)
Beddington Tr
Beddington Blvd
64 Av
Aviation Park Blvd
Aviation Way
Nose Creek
North

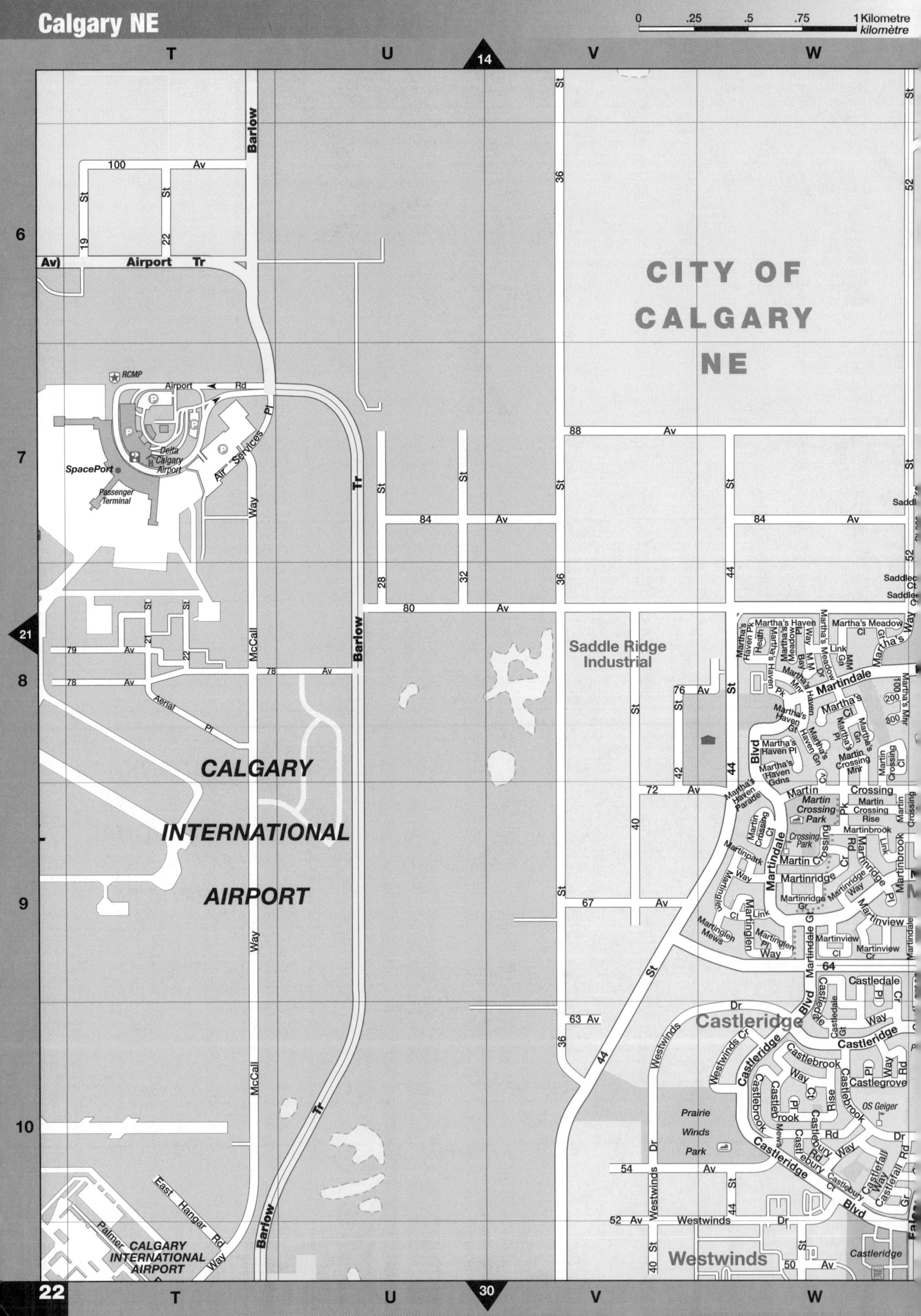

CITY OF
CALGARY
NE

CALGARY
INTERNATIONAL
AIRPORT

Saddle Ridge
Industrial

Castleridge

Westwinds

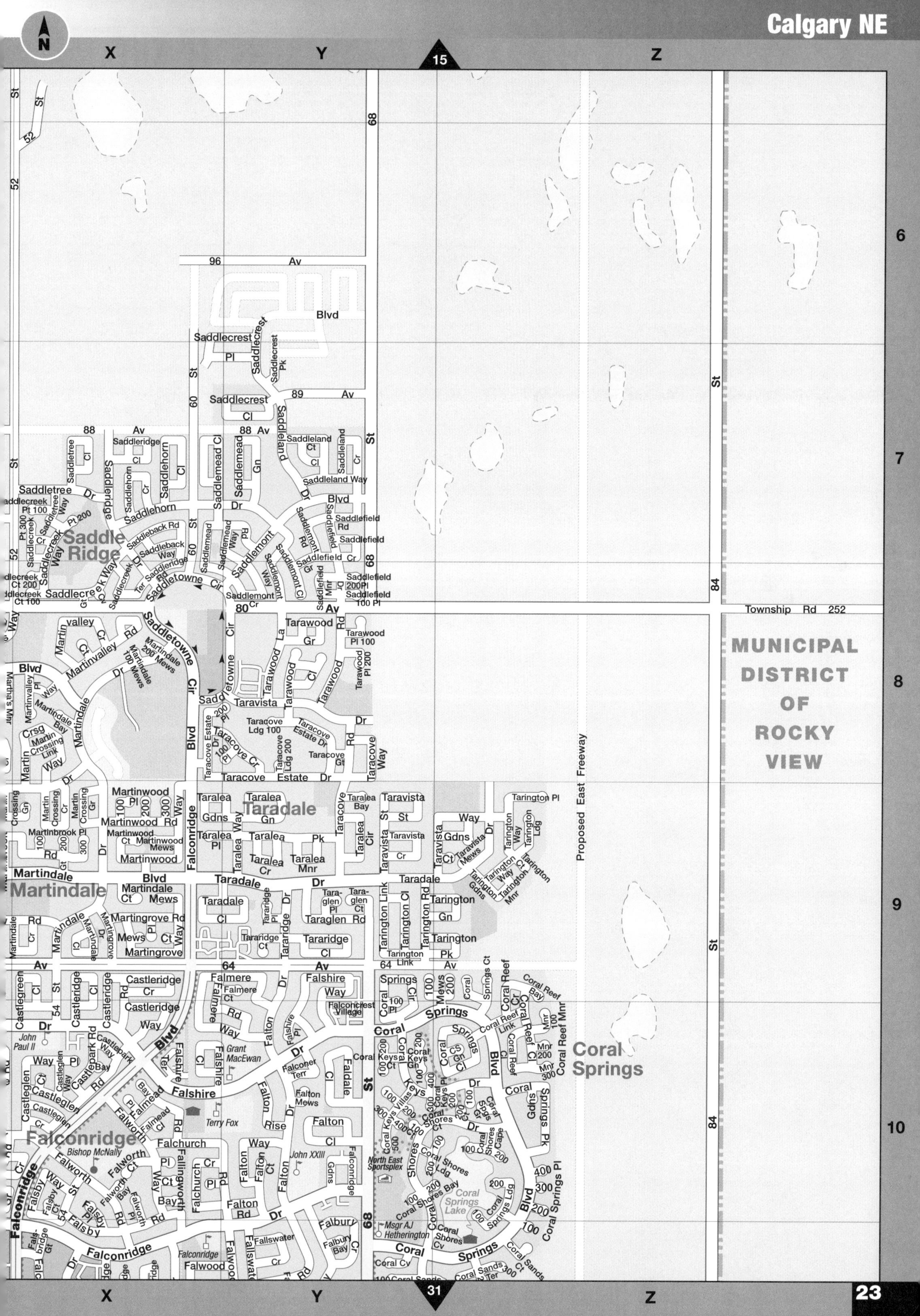
X
Y
15
Z
6
7
8
9
10
96 Av
Blvd
Saddlecrest Pl
Saddlecrest Cl
89 Av
88 Av
60 St
68 St
84 St
Saddle Ridge
Saddletowne Cir
80 Av
Township Rd 252
MUNICIPAL
DISTRICT
OF
ROCKY
VIEW
Taradale
Martindale
Martindale Blvd
Taradale Dr
Proposed East Freeway
64 Av
Coral Springs
Coral Springs Blvd
Falconridge
Falconridge Blvd
Falshire Dr
Coral Springs Lake
North East Sportsplex
X
Y
31
Z

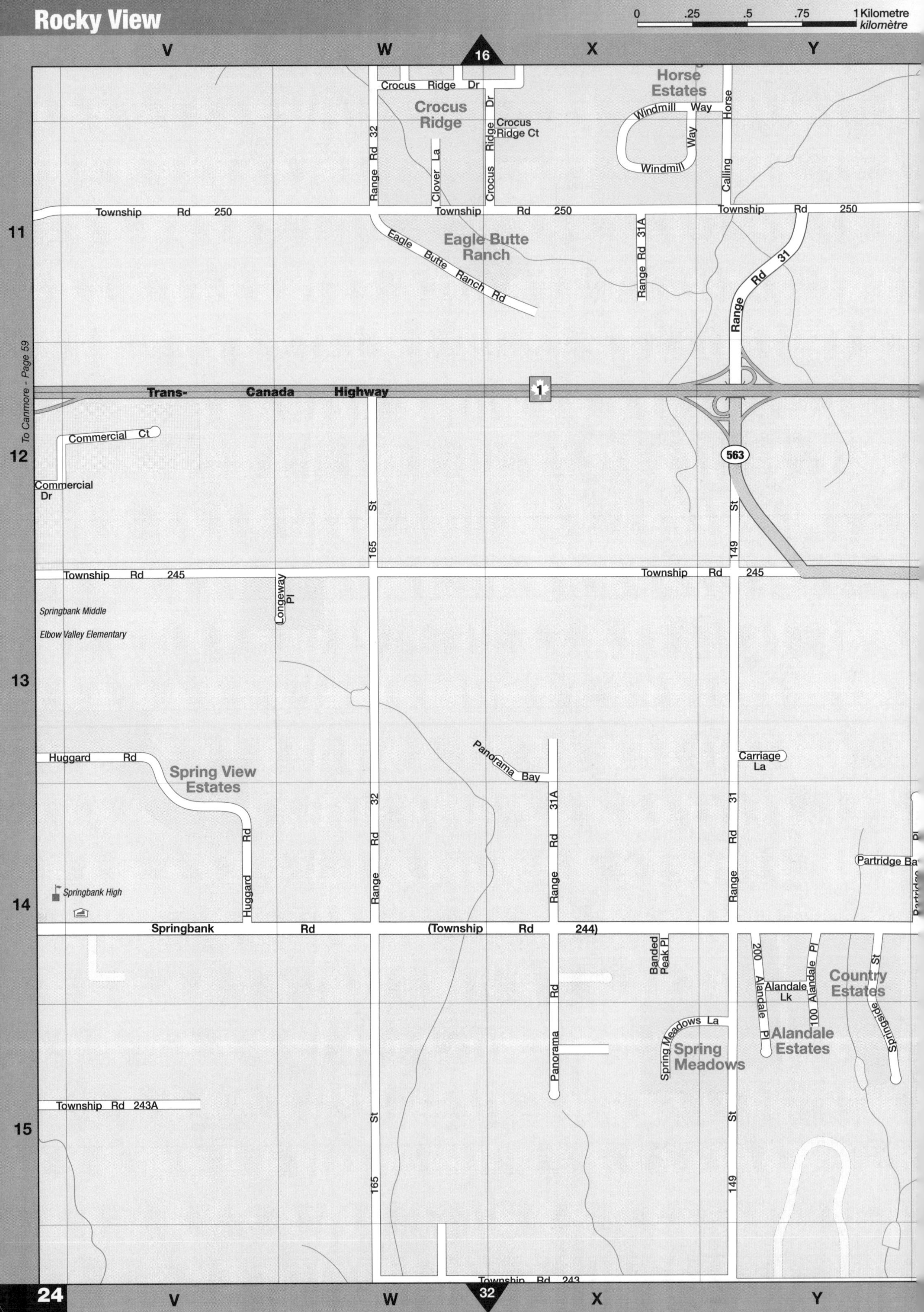

Crocus Ridge Dr

Crocus Ridge

Crocus Ridge Ct

Horse Estates

Windmill Way

Windmill

Range Rd 32

Clover La

Crocus Ridge Dr

Calling

Horse

Township Rd 250

Township Rd 250

Township Rd 250

11

Eagle Butte Ranch Rd

Eagle Butte Ranch

Range Rd 31A

Range Rd 31

Trans- Canada Highway **1**

To Canmore - Page 59

Commercial Ct

563

12

Commercial Dr

165 St

149 St

Township Rd 245

Township Rd 245

Longeway Pl

Springbank Middle

Elbow Valley Elementary

13

Panorama Bay

Carriage La

Huggard Rd

Spring View Estates

Huggard Rd

Range Rd 32

Range Rd 31A

Range Rd 31

Partridge Ba

Springbank High

14

Springbank Rd (Township Rd 244)

Panorama Rd

Banded Peak Pl

200 Alandale Pl

Alandale Pl 100

Springside St

Country Estates

Alandale Lk

Spring Meadows La

Panorama

Spring Meadows

Alandale Estates

Partridge

Township Rd 243A

165 St

149 St

15

Township Rd 243

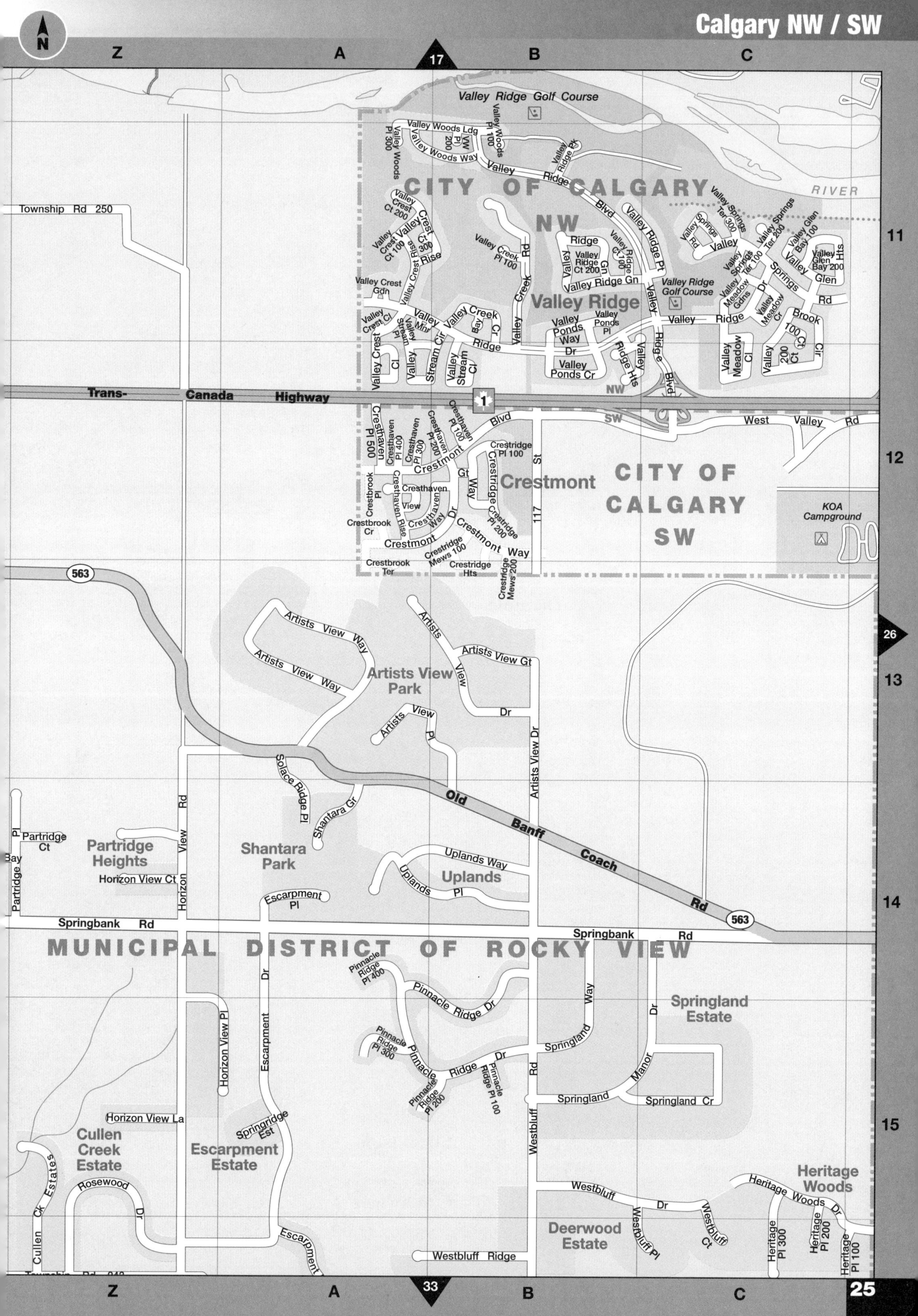
Z
A
17
B
C
Valley Ridge Golf Course
City of Calgary NW
Valley Ridge
Valley Ridge Golf Course
River
Township Rd 250
Trans-Canada Highway
1
City of Calgary SW
Crestmont
KOA Campground
563
Artists View Park
Shantara Park
Partridge Heights
Uplands
Old Banff Coach Rd
Springbank Rd
Municipal District of Rocky View
Springland Estate
Cullen Creek Estate
Escarpment Estate
Heritage Woods
Deerwood Estate
11
12
13
14
15
26
33

0 .25 .5 .75 1 Kilometre kilomètre
D E F G
18
Bowmont Park
Scenic Bow Rd
Bow Centre Place
Baker Park
Bowness Park
Bowness Lagoon
Greenwood
Greenwood Village Mobile Home Park
Greenbriar
Bowness
Belvedere-Parkway
Bowness Rd
Stoney Tr
201
Trans-Canada Highway
Olympic Hall of Fame
Canada Olympic Park
Bobsled & Luge Tracks
70m & 90m Ski Jumping Towers
Four Points
Bowcroft
Thomas B Riley
Our lady of the Assumption
KOA Campground
Chinook Winds Adventist Academy
CITY OF CALGARY SW
Winter Hts
Stoney Tr (Proposed)
Old Banff Coach Rd
Sarcee
Patterson
West Spring Farms
West Springs
Springside
Coach Hill
Heritage Woods
11
12
13
14
15
25
D E F G
34

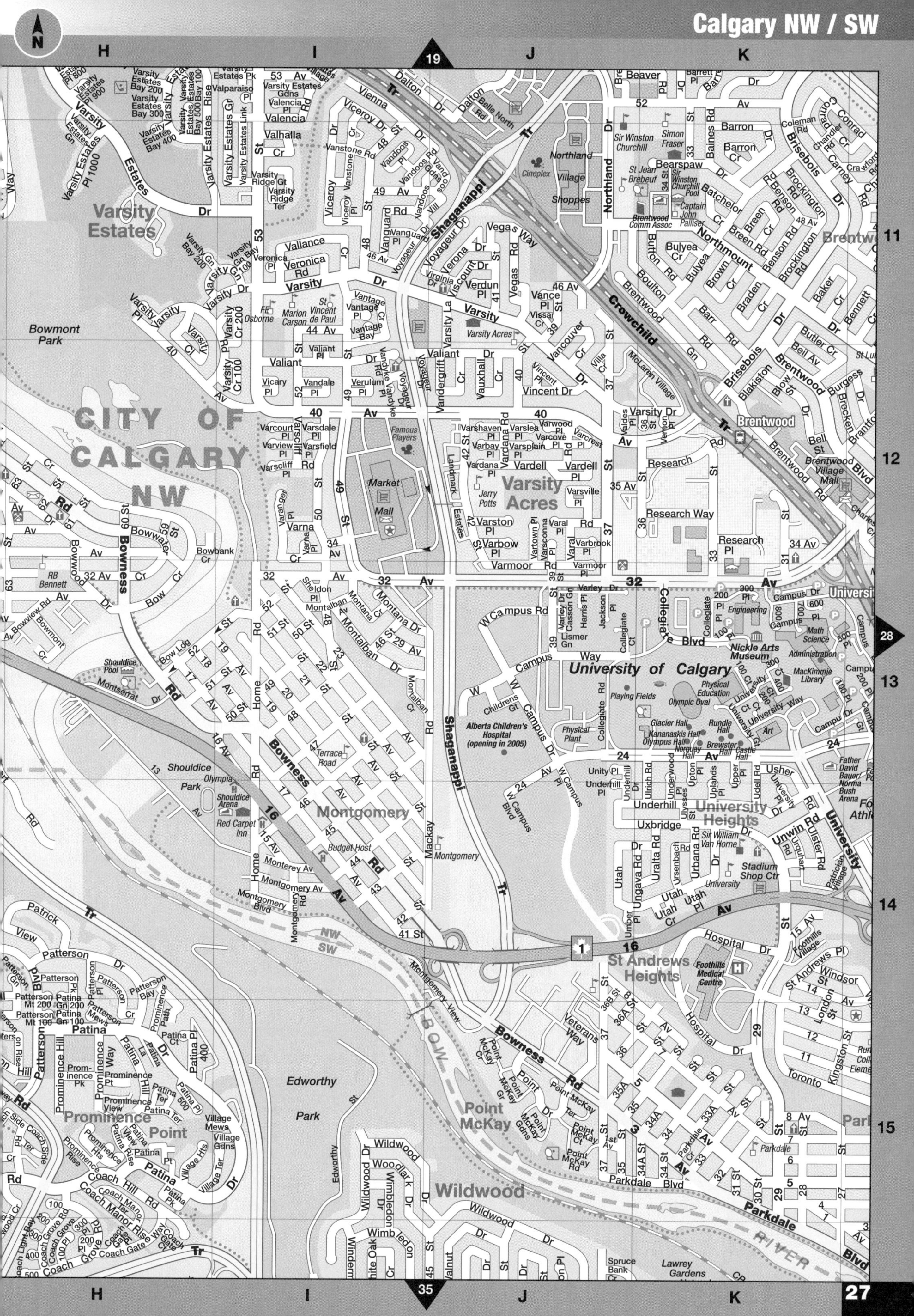
H
I
19
J
K
11
12
13
14
15
28
35
CITY OF CALGARY NW
Varsity Estates
Bowmont Park
Varsity Acres
University of Calgary
University Heights
Montgomery
St Andrews Heights
Point McKay
Wildwood
Prominence Point
Edworthy Park
Brentwood
Shouldice Park
Crowchild Tr
Shaganappi Tr
Bowness Rd
16 Av
32 Av
40 Av
Varsity Dr
Varsity Estates Dr
Northland Dr
Northland Village Shoppes
Market Mall
Famous Players
Sir Winston Churchill
Simon Fraser
Brentwood Village Mall
Alberta Children's Hospital (opening in 2005)
Foothills Medical Centre
Stadium Shop Ctr
Olympic Oval
Nickle Arts Museum
MacKimmie Library
Research Way
Research Pl
Campus Dr
Collegiate Blvd
University Dr
Shouldice Arena
Red Carpet Inn
Budget Host
Montgomery View
Parkdale Blvd
Patterson
Patina
Coach Hill Rd
Bow River
NW
SW
Lawrey Gardens
Spruce Bank Cr

Calgary NW
0 .25 .5 .75 1 Kilometre kilomètre
L M N O
20
36
27
28
11
12
13
14
15
Charleswood Heights
Nose Hill Natural Environment Park
Foothills Estate
Brentwood
Laurie Blvd
John Laurie Blvd
McKnight Blvd
North Haven
Highwood
Cambrian Heights
CITY OF CALGARY NW
Queen's Park Cemetery
Charleswood
North Capitol Hill Park
Collingwood
Confederation Park Golf Course
Banff Trail
Rosemont
North Mount Pleasant
Capitol Hill
Confederation Park
Mount Pleasant
Pleasant Heights
University
Foothills Athletic Park
McMahon Stadium
Foothills Baseball Stadium
North Hill Shopping Centre
Lions Park
Southern Alberta Institute of Technology
SAIT/ACA/Jubilee
Alberta College of Art
Rosedale
Briar Hill
Upper Hillhurst
Riley Park
Sunnyside
Parkdale
West Hillhurst
Hillhurst
Kensington Crossing
Prince's Island
Eau Claire
Memorial
Crowchild
16 Av
14 St
10 St
Northmount
Charleswood Dr
Crescent Rd
SEE DOWNTOWN
28

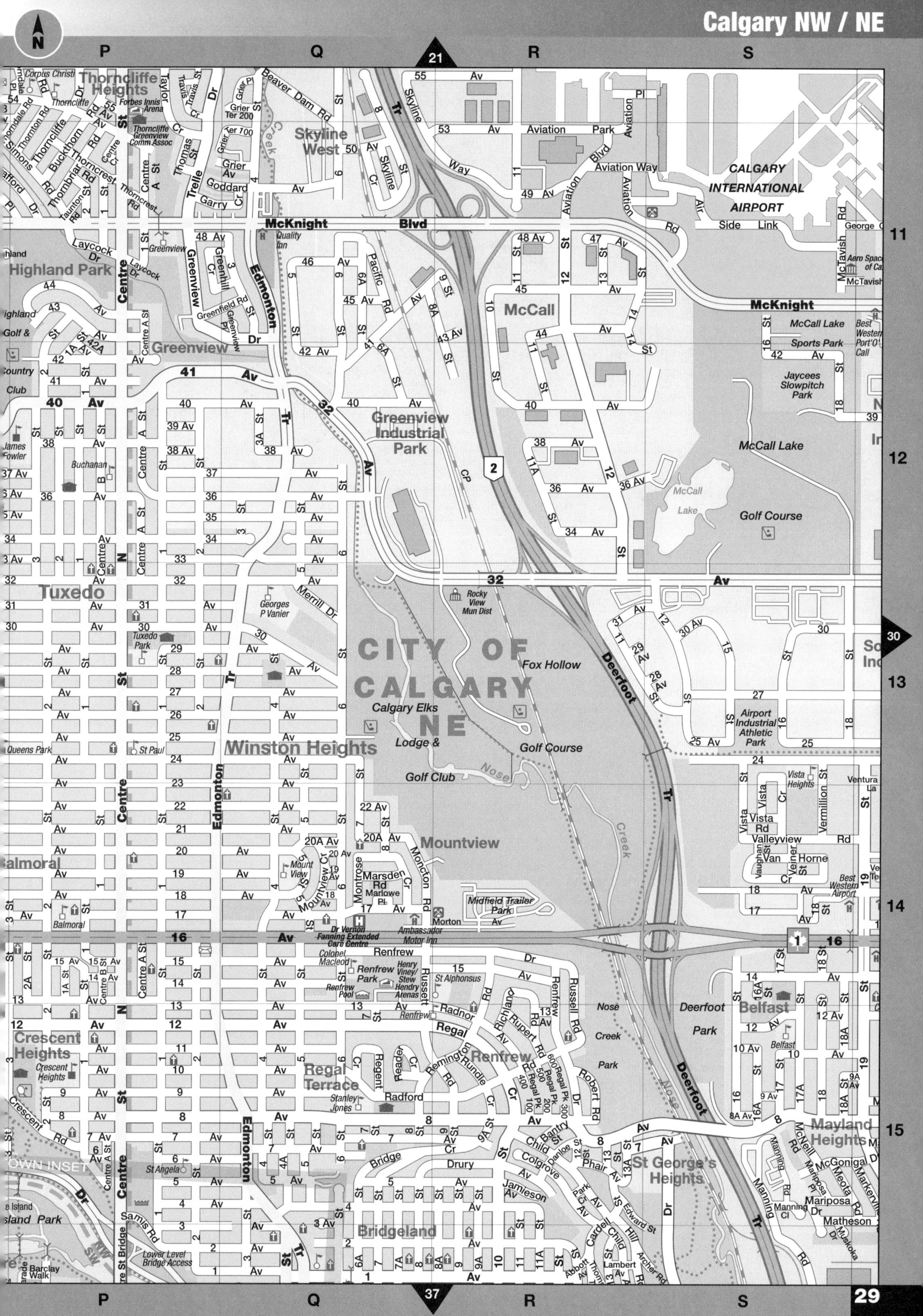
P
Q
R
S
21
11
12
13
14
15
30
37
Thorncliffe Heights
Forbes Innis Arena
Thorncliffe Greenview Comm Assoc
Skyline West
CALGARY INTERNATIONAL AIRPORT
Aviation Park
Aviation Way
Aviation Blvd
McKnight Blvd
Quality Inn
Highland Park
Greenview
McCall
McCall Lake
Sports Park
Jaycees Slowpitch Park
Greenview Industrial Park
McCall Lake
Golf Course
Tuxedo
Georges P Vanier
CITY OF CALGARY NE
Rocky View Mun Dist
Fox Hollow
Calgary Elks Lodge & Golf Club
Golf Course
Airport Industrial Athletic Park
Winston Heights
Mountview
Vista Heights
Balmoral
Midfield Trailer Park
Dr Vernon Fanning Extended Care Centre
Ambassador Motor Inn
Renfrew Park
Henry Viney/Stew Hendry Arenas
St Alphonsus
Deerfoot Tr
Deerfoot Park
Belfast
Nose Creek Park
Crescent Heights
Regal Terrace
Renfrew
Mayland Heights
St George's Heights
Bridgeland
Centre St
Edmonton Tr
16 Av
32 Av
Calgary Elks

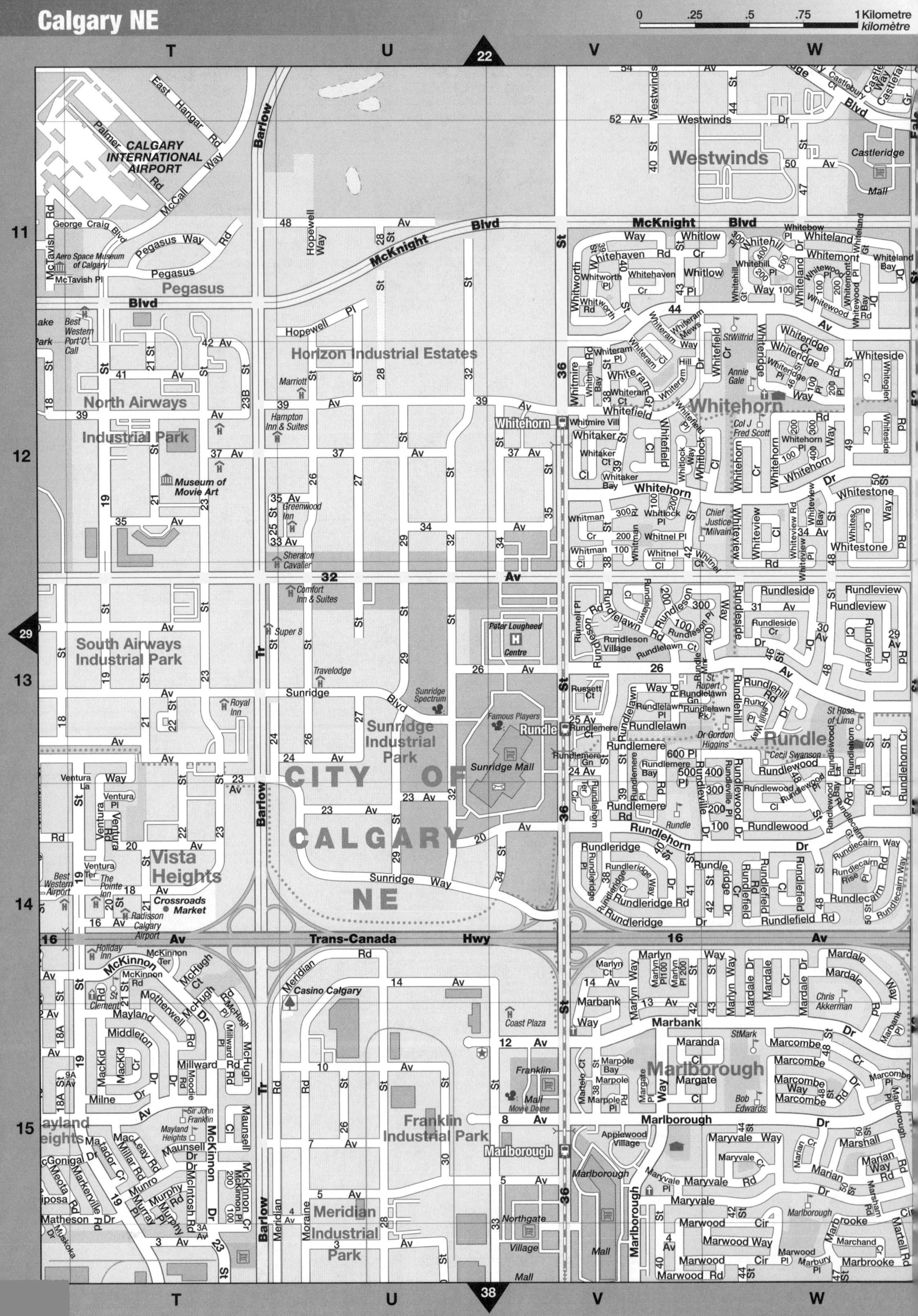
0 .25 .5 .75 1 Kilometre kilomètre
CALGARY INTERNATIONAL AIRPORT
Westwinds
Castleridge Mall
Pegasus
Horizon Industrial Estates
North Airways Industrial Park
Whitehorn
South Airways Industrial Park
Peter Lougheed Centre
Sunridge Industrial Park
Sunridge Mall
Rundle
CITY OF CALGARY NE
Vista Heights
Crossroads Market
Trans-Canada Hwy
Casino Calgary
Marlborough
Franklin Mall
Franklin Industrial Park
Meridian Industrial Park
Mayland Heights
Marlborough Mall
Northgate Village Mall
McKnight Blvd
Barlow Tr
36 St
32 Av
16 Av
Museum of Movie Art
Aero Space Museum of Calgary

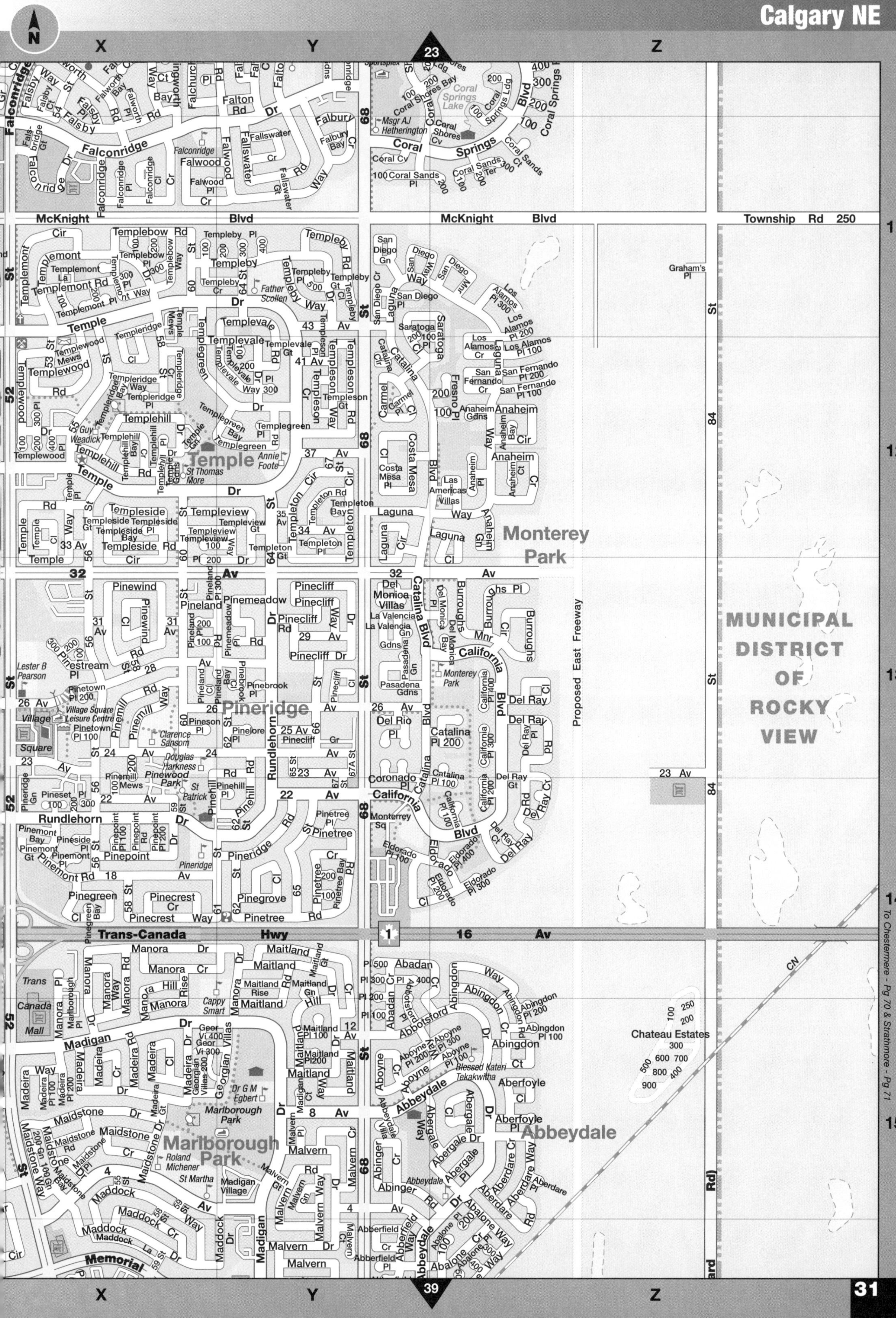

N

X   Y   23   Z

Falconridge

Falsby Way · Falsby · Falworth · Falton Rd · Falbury · Falbury Bay
Falsbridge · Falconridge Dr · Falwood Cr · Falwood Pl · Falwood Cr · Fallswater Cr · Falbury Bay · Fallswater Way

SportsPlex · Coral Shores · Coral Springs Blvd · 400 300 200 100
Coral Springs Lake · Msgr AJ Hetherington · Coral Shores Cv · Coral Sands
Coral Cv · 100 Coral Sands Pl · Coral Sands Ter · Coral Sands Pl 100
Coral Springs

McKnight Blvd   **McKnight Blvd**   **Township Rd 250**   **11**

Templebow Rd · Templeby Pl · Templeby Rd · Templemont
Templemont La · Templemont Pl · Templeby · Templeby Way · Templeby Gt · Templeby Way 500
Templemont Rd · Templemont Pl · Father Scollen · San Diego Gn · San Diego Cir · Diego Way · Diego Mnr · Los Alamos Pl 300 · Graham's Pl

Temple · Templevale · Temple Mews · Templewood · 43 Av · Templeson Way · Templeson Rd · San Diego · Saratoga · Los Alamos Cr · Los Alamos Pl 200 · Los Alamos Pl 100
Templeridge · Templegreen · Templevale Gt · 41 Av · Templeson Way 300 · Catalina Ct · Catalina · San Fernando Cr · San Fernando Pl 200 · San Fernando Pl 100
Templewood · Guy Weadick · Templehill · Templegreen Bay · Templegreen · Annie Foote · Carmel Pl · Carmel · 200 · Fresno Pl · Anaheim Gdns · Anaheim · Anaheim Bay · Anaheim Cir
Temple Dr · St Thomas More · 37 Av · Costa Mesa · Costa Mesa Pl · Las Americas Villas · Anaheim Gn · Anaheim

Temple Rd · Templeside · Templeview · Templeton Rd · Templeton Bay · Laguna · Laguna Way · **Monterey Park**
33 Av · Templeside Pl · Templeview Gt · 35 Av · 34 Av · Templeton Gt · Templeton · Laguna Cir · Laguna Cl
Temple Cir · Templeside Rd · Templeview 100 · 60 · Templeton Cir · 64 St · Laguna

32 · **32 Av** · Monterey Park · **MUNICIPAL DISTRICT OF ROCKY VIEW**

Pinewind · Pinecliff · Pineland · Pinemeadow · Pinecliff · Del Monica Villas · Burroughs Pl
31 Av · Pinewind Cl · Pineland 200 · Pinemeadow Way · 29 Av · Pinecliff Rd · La Valencia · La Valencia Gn · Burroughs Mnr · Burroughs
Pinestream Pl · Pinewind Cl · Pineland Cl · Pinebrook · Pinecliff Dr · La Valencia Gdns · Pasadena Gn · **California Blvd** · Del Ray
Lester B Pearson · Pinetown Pl 200 · Pineland · Pasadena Gdns · Monterey Park · California · Del Ray
Village Square Leisure Centre · Pinetown Pl 100 · **Pineridge** · Pinelore · 26 Av · Del Rio · Catalina · Del Ray Gt · **Proposed East Freeway**
Clarence Sansom · Pinelore Pl · 25 Av · Pinecliff Gr · Del Rio · Catalina Pl 200 · **23 Av**
Douglas Harkness · Pinewood Park · St Patrick · Pinehill · Coronado · Catalina Pl 100 · California Pl 100

Rundlehorn · Pinemill Mews · 22 Av · Pinetree · Monterey Sq · **California Blvd** · Del Ray
Pinemont Bay · Pineside · Pinepoint · Pineridge Cr · Pinetree Cr · Eldorado Pl 100 · Eldorado Bay · Eldorado 400
Pinemont Gt · Pinemont Rd · 18 Av · Pineridge · 65 St · Eldorado · Eldorado 300
Pinegreen · Pinecrest Cr · Pinegrove · Pinetree · Eldorado Pl 200

14

Trans-Canada Hwy · **1** · **16 Av** · To Chestermere · Pg 70 & Strathmore · Pg 71

Manora Dr · Maitland · Abadan · Way · Abingdon · CN
Trans Pl · Manora Way · Manora · Maitland Rise · Maitland Gn · Abadan Pl 500 · Abingdon Cr · Abingdon
Trans Canada Mall · Manora Hill · Maitland · Abadan · Abbotsford · Abingdon Ct · **Chateau Estates**
Madigan · Cappy Smart · Geo Geo Vi 300 · 12 Av · Maitland Pl · Aboyne · Aboyne Pl · Abingdon
Madeira · Georgian Villas · Maitland Way · Aboyne · Blessed Kateri Tekakwitha · Aberfoyle
Madeira Pl · Dr G M Egbert · Marlborough Park · Malvern · Aboyne · Aberfoyle Pl · **Abbeydale**
Maidstone · **Marlborough Park** · 8 Av · Malvern Rd · **Abbeydale Way** · Abergale · Aberdare Way
Maidstone · Roland Michener · St Martha · Madigan Village · Malvern Way · Abergale Pl · Aberdare
Maddock · 4 · Madigan · Malvern Dr · Abinger Cr · Abergale · Abalone Way 200 · Aberdare
Maddock La · Maddock Rd · Malvern Way · Abberfield · Abalone Way 400
Memorial · Malvern Dr · Abberfield Pl · Abbeydale Dr · Abalone

X   Y   39   Z

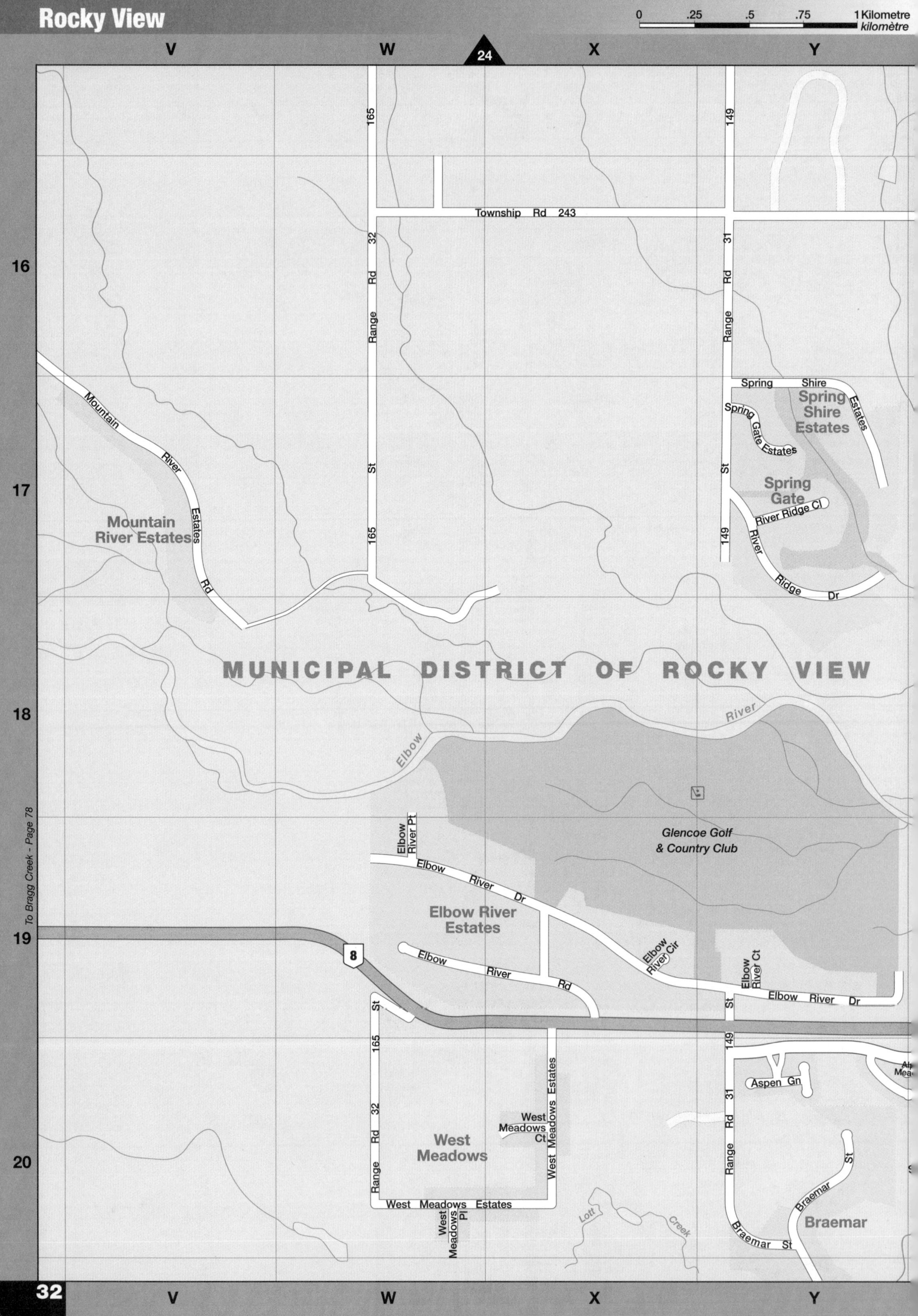

0 .25 .5 .75 1 Kilometre
kilomètre

V W 24 X Y

165

Range Rd 32

Township Rd 243

149

16

Range Rd 31

Spring Shire

Spring Shire Estates

Spring Gate Estates

St

165

17

Mountain River Estates

Mountain River Estates Rd

St

149

Spring Gate

River Ridge Cl

River Ridge Dr

MUNICIPAL DISTRICT OF ROCKY VIEW

18

Elbow

River

Glencoe Golf & Country Club

Elbow River Pt

Elbow River Dr

19

Elbow River Estates

8

Elbow River Rd

Elbow River Cir

St

Elbow River Ct

Elbow River Dr

To Bragg Creek - Page 78

St

165

Range Rd 32

West Meadows Estates

West Meadows Ct

West Meadows Estates

149

Range Rd 31

Aspen Gn

Alp Mea

20

West Meadows

Braemar St

Braemar St

Braemar

West Meadows Pl

West Meadows Estates

Lott

Creek

N

Cullen Creek Estate

Escarpment Estate

Springbank Est

Cullen Ck Estates

Rosewood Dr

Escarpment Pk

Township Rd 243

Conrad Pl

Westbluff

Westbluff Dr

Westbluff Pl

Westbluff Ct

Deerwood Estate

Heritage Woods

Heritage Woods Dr

Heritage Pl 300

Heritage Pl 200

Heritage Pl 100

Westbluff Ridge

Westbluff Bay

Westwood Rd

Wild Rose Dr

Westridge Park

16

Clear Mountain Rise

Robinson Rd

Westridge Park Dr

Westmeadows Rd

Horizon View Rd

Range Rd 25

Lower Springbank Rd

17

Township Rd 242

34

Pinetree Dr

Lower Springbank Rd

18

Pinebrook Golf & Country Club

Pinebrook Way

Pineridge Way

Pinetree Dr

Pinecone La

Pinebrook Estate

19

Granite Ridge

Stonepine Ct

Stonepine Dr

Stonepine Cv

Range Rd 30

ELBOW

RIVER

Clearwater Park

Tr

Lott Creek Dr

pine eadows

Sweetwater Pl

Snowberry Gt

Whispering Woods Ter

Misty Morning Dr

Bent Tree Ct

Bent Tree Pl

Majestic Gt

Majestic Pl

8

Reflection Cv

Majestic View

Snowberry View

Snowberry Pl

Snowberry

Snowberry Cir

Diamond Pl

Willow

Range Rd 25

Lott Creek Blvd

Glenmore

Elbow Springs Golf Courses

20

Elbow Valley

Lott Creek Dr

Lott Creek Hollow

Fisher

Fishermans Pt

Fishermans Bend

Fishermans Ldg

Crooked Pond Gn

Wolfwillow Ridge

Wolfwillow Pt

Coulee Ridge

Crooked Pond Way

Owl Haven

Wolfwillow La

Wolfwillow Way

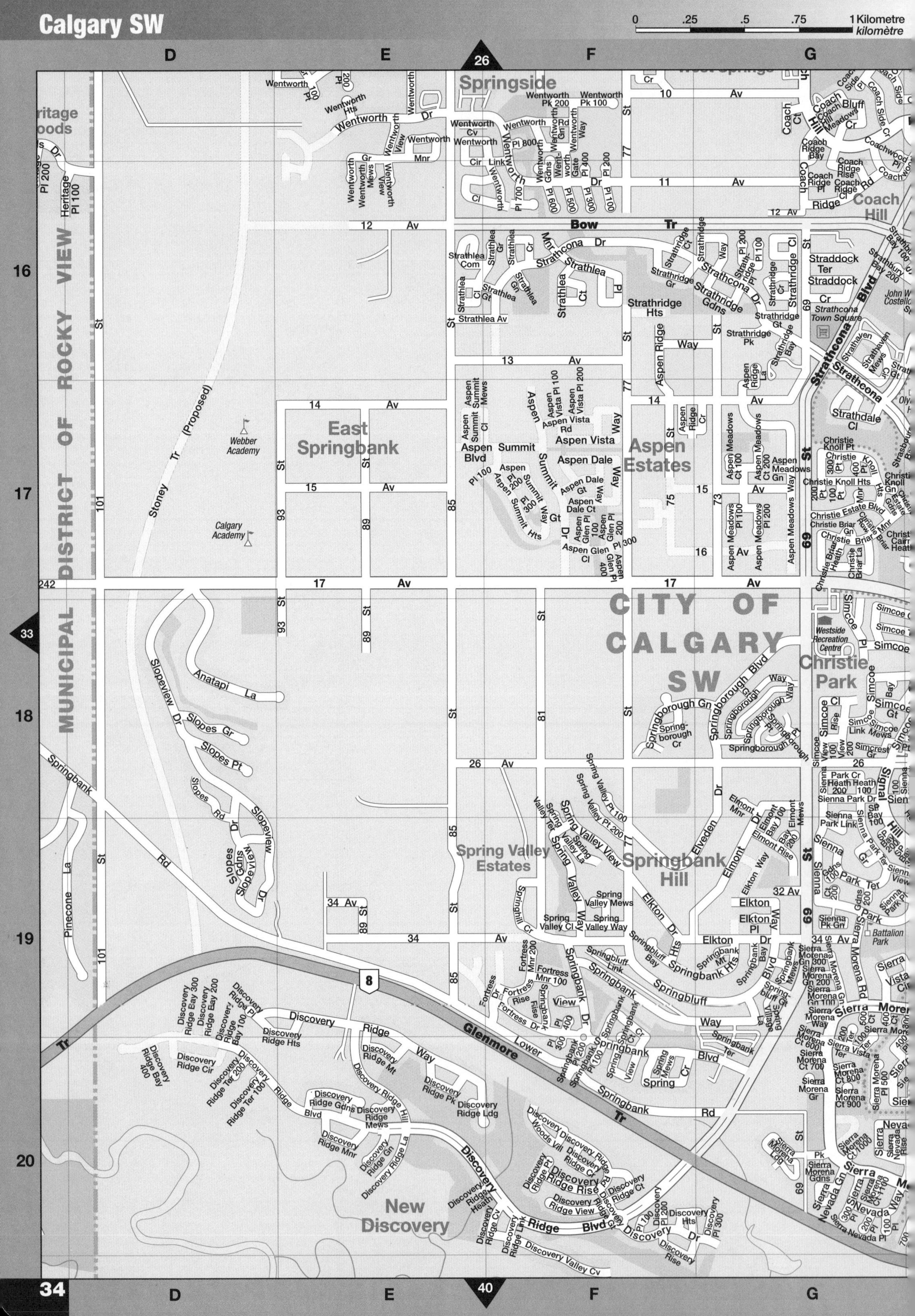

0 .25 .5 .75 1 Kilometre
kilomètre

Springside

West Springs

Coach Hill

Heritage Woods

MUNICIPAL DISTRICT OF ROCKY VIEW

Wentworth

Stoney Tr (Proposed)

Webber Academy

East Springbank

Calgary Academy

Strathlea

Strathcona

Strathridge Hts

Aspen Ridge

Strathridge Pk

Strathdale Cl

Christie Knoll Pt

Strathcona Town Square

John E Costello

Aspen Summit

Aspen Estates

Aspen Vista

Aspen Dale

Aspen Meadows

Christie Estate Blvd

Christie Briar

Christie Cairn Heath

CITY OF CALGARY SW

Westside Recreation Centre

Simcoe

Christie Park

Springborough Blvd

Springborough Gn

Springborough Cr

Anatapi La

Slopeview Dr

Slopes Gr

Slopes Pt

Slopes Rd

Springbank Rd

Pinecone La

Spring Valley Estates

Spring Valley View

Spring Valley Mews

Spring Valley Cl

Spring Valley Way

Springbank Hill

Elmont Dr

Elkton Dr

Elkton

Elkton Pl

Springbluff

Springbank Hts

Springbank Blvd

Sienna Park Dr

Sienna Hill

Sienna Park Gn

Battalion Park

Sierra Morena

Sierra Vista

Sierra Morena Rd

8

Glenmore

Discovery Ridge Bay

Discovery Ridge Cir

Discovery Ridge Mnr

Discovery Ridge

Discovery Ridge Hts

Discovery Ridge Mt

Discovery Ridge Pk

Discovery Ridge Ldg

Discovery Ridge Gdns

Discovery Ridge Mews

Springbank Tr

Fortress Mnr

Fortress Dr

Fortress Rise

Springbank Lower

Spring Mews

Sierra Nevada

Sierra Morena Gr

New Discovery

Discovery Woods Vill

Discovery Ridge Rise

Discovery Ridge View

Discovery Ridge Ct

Discovery Ridge Blvd

Discovery Ridge Heath

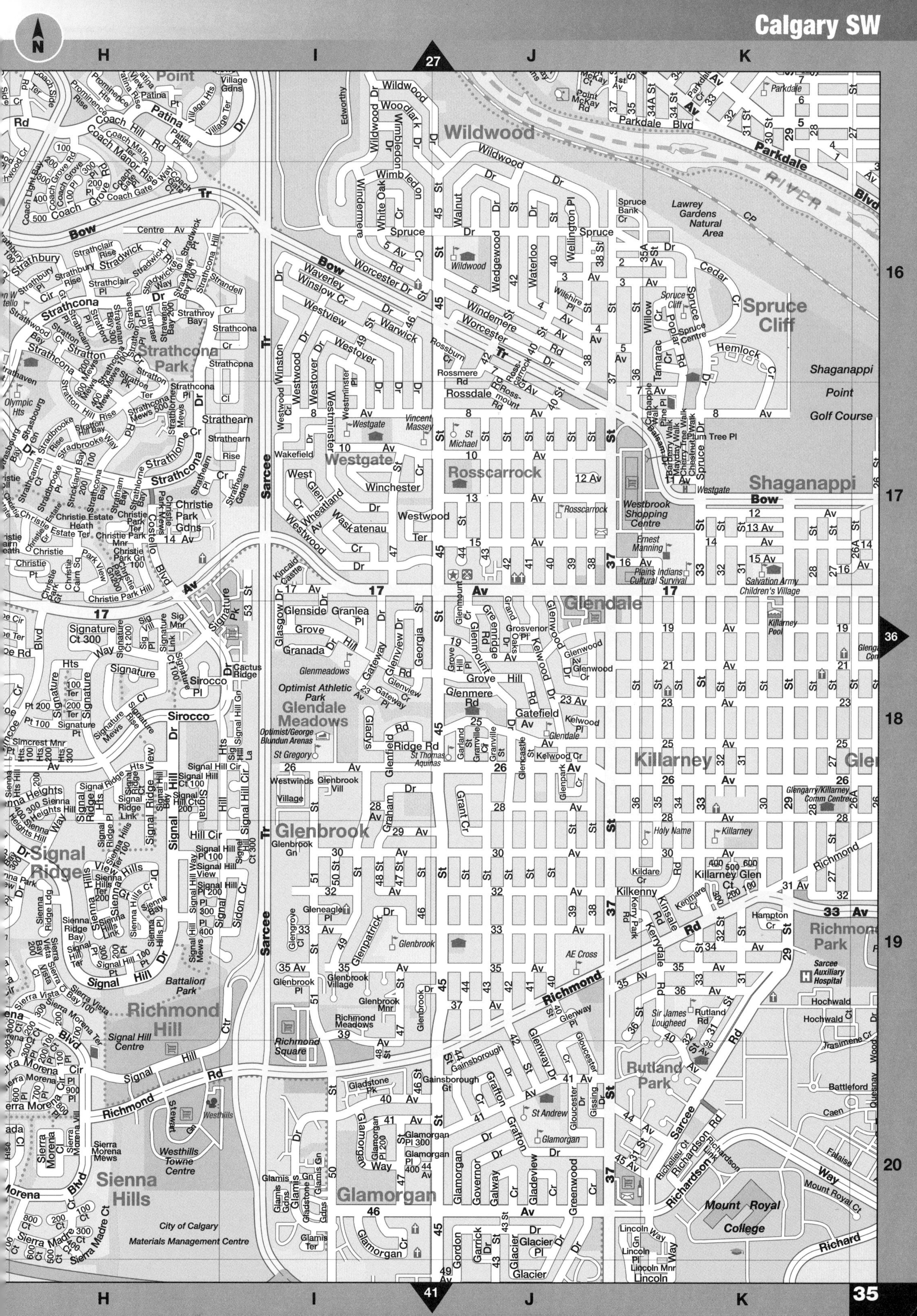
N
H
I
J
K
27
41
36
16
17
18
19
20
Wildwood
Spruce Cliff
Shaganappi Point Golf Course
Shaganappi
Lawrey Gardens Natural Area
River
Parkdale Blvd
Bow Tr
Strathcona Park
Westgate
Rosscarrock
Westbrook Shopping Centre
Ernest Manning
Plains Indians Cultural Survival
Salvation Army Children's Village
Glendale
Killarney Pool
Killarney
Glengarry/Killarney Comm Centre
Optimist Athletic Park
Glendale Meadows
Optimist/George Blundun Arenas
Glenbrook
Signal Ridge
Battalion Park
Richmond Hill
Signal Hill Centre
Richmond Square
Richmond Rd
Sarcee Tr
Richmond Park
Sarcee Auxiliary Hospital
Rutland Park
Westhills Towne Centre
Sienna Hills
Glamorgan
City of Calgary Materials Management Centre
Mount Royal College
17 Av
Signal Hill Ctr
Crowchild Tr
37 St
45 St

0 .25 .5 .75 1 Kilometre kilomètre
L
M
N
O
28
42
35
16
17
18
19
20
SEE DOWNTOWN
Riley Park
Hillhurst
West Hillhurst
Sunnyside
Prince's Island
Eau Claire
The Lagoon
BOW
Memorial
Kensington
Westmount
Bowness
Broadview
Brownsea Dr
Memorial Dr
NW
SW
Louise Bridge
Kensington Crossing
Gladstone Rd
Queen Elizabeth Sr
Queen Elizabeth Elem
Louise Dean Centre
Madeleine d'Houet
St John Fine Arts
Calgary Science Centre & Centennial Planetarium
Athabasca University
Pumphouse Theatres
Pumphouse Rd
Greyhound Bus Terminal
Greyhound Way
Mewata Stadium
Lord Nelson Inn
Sandman Inn
Ramada Hotel
Eaton Centre
Court House
Heliport
Princeton Way
Eau Claire Av
YMCA
Sheraton Suites
Execsuite
Regency House
Prince Royal Inn
Energy Resources
Barclay Mall
Shaganappi Point
Golf Course
Sunalta
10 Av
CP
Scarboro
Sovereign
Jacques Lodges
Sandhurst Av
Surrey St
Sunalta
Scotland St
Short Rd
Sharon Av
Sudbury Av
Scarboro Av
Shelbourne
Superior Av
Sunset Av
State Rd
Sonora Av
Sunderland
Salem
Senlac St
Summer St
Summit St
Suffolk St
Alex Ferguson
Sacred Heart
Connaught
Canadian Western Natural Gas Museum
Fountain Walk
Rundle College
Best Western Downtown
Scott Plaza
Colonel Belcher Hospital
Central Memorial Park
Fourth Street
Uptown 17: The Avenue
17 Av
Naval Museum of Alberta
HMCS Tecumseh
Tecumseh Rd
Alberta Childrens Hospital
Knob Hill
Bankview
Dr Gordon Townsend
Glengarry Seniors' Comm Centre
Glengarry
Knob Hill
St Charles
Osborne Cr
Richmond Rd
Crowchild Tr
Bagot
Cameron
Mount Royal
Royal
Colborne
Sydenham Rd
Durham
Amherst St
Prospect
Carleton St
Morrison St
Montreal Av
Wolfe
Frontenac
Dorchester Av
Hillcrest
Earl Grey
Earl Grey Cr
Garden Cr
Garden La
Hope St
Cliff St
College La
Western Canada
Mount Royal College Holy Cross Campus
Mission
Killarney Aquatic Centre
Richmond
Chinook College
CITY OF CALGARY
King Edward
South Calgary
SW
Marda Loop
Quebec Av
Montcalm
Talon St
Laval Av
Frontenac Av
Maquette St
Cartier St
Champlain St
Cabot St
Valois Av
Glencoe
Glencoe Rd
Elbow Dr
Park
Premier Way
Joliet Av
Alfege St
Verchere St
Levis Av
Ridge Rd
Pitt Av
Council
Rideau Park
Rideau Rd
Richmond Park
Richmond Green Golf Course
Sarcee Auxiliary Hospital
Keller Hall
Dieppe
Trasimene Cr
Calais
Battleford
Caen
Falaise
Quesnay Wood Dr
Lamone Av
Breskens
Normandy Dr
Garrison Gt
Sorrel Mews
Garrison
Somme Mews
Somme Av
Somme Blvd
Marda Link
Scarpe Dr
Cambrai
Ypres Gn
Ypres Mews
Ypres Way
Julien
Flanders Av
Flanders Park
Woods
Amiens
Mons Av
Moreuil Ct
Passchendale
Quentin
Currie
Museum of the Regiments
Calgary Centennial Arenas
Bishop Carroll
Ste-Marguerite-Bourgeoys
Richard Rd
Mount Royal Ct
Dr Oakley
Learning Centre
Altadore
Altadore Av
Acton Av
William Reid
Elbow Park
Elbow Park La
Sifton Blvd
Crestview Rd
River Park
ELBOW RIVER
Riverdale
Riverdale Av
Lansdowne Av
Britannia
Britannia Dr
Coronation
Madison
Edinburgh
Anne
Elizabeth
Crown
Charles Av
Imperial Way
Crescent
Brunswick Av
Cliffe
Elboya
St Anthony
Stanley
Edison
Stanley Park

N
P
Q
R
S
29
43
38
16
17
18
19
20
TOWN INSET
Bridgeland
St George's Heights
Riverside
Calgary Zoo Extension
Zoo
Calgary Zoo, Botanical Garden & Prehistoric Park
St George's Island
St Patrick Island
Bridgeland/Memorial
Memorial Dr
Fort Calgary Historic Park
Deane House Historic Site
Victoria Park
City Centre
7 Avenue Transit Mall
Stephen Avenue Mall
Chinatown
Glenbow Museum
Calgary Tower
Olympic Plaza
Municipal Bldg
Conv Ctr
Bow Valley College
James Short Park
Eau Claire Market
Prince's Island Park
Barclay Walk
IMAX
Riverfront Av
Langevin Bridge
Centre St Bridge
Lower Level Bridge Access
St Angela
Langevin
Victoria Crossing
Holiday Inn
Victoria Park Comm Ctr
Almadina Charter
Rouleauville Square
St Mary's
Lindsay Park
Lindsay Park Sports Centre
Victoria Pk./Stampede
Stampede Park
Stampede Casino
Stampede Corral
Pengrowth Saddledome
Roundup Centre
The Grain Academy
Elbow River Inn & Casino
Big Four Building
Stampede Horse Track
Erlton/Stampede
Erlton
Ramsay
Ramsay Comm Assoc
Ste Anne
Shamrock
Burns Avenue
Grandview
Mills Estate
Inglewood Pool
Inglewood
Sam Livingston Fish Hatchery
Pearce Estate
Colonel Walker
Wildlands Park
Blackfoot Trail
17 Av
26 Av
Union Cemetery
Burnsland Cemetery
Burnsland
Chinese Cemetery
St Mary's Cemetery
Roxboro
Mission
College Campus
CITY OF CALGARY SE
Highfield
Cash Casino
Frank Sisson's Silver Dollar Casino
Stage West
DND
Bonnybrook
Ogden
Ogden Rd
Waste Treatment Plant
Quality Hotel & Conference Centre
39 Avenue
Holiday Inn
Nite Inn
Stanley Park
Macleod Tr
Blackfoot Tr
Bow River
Elbow River
CP

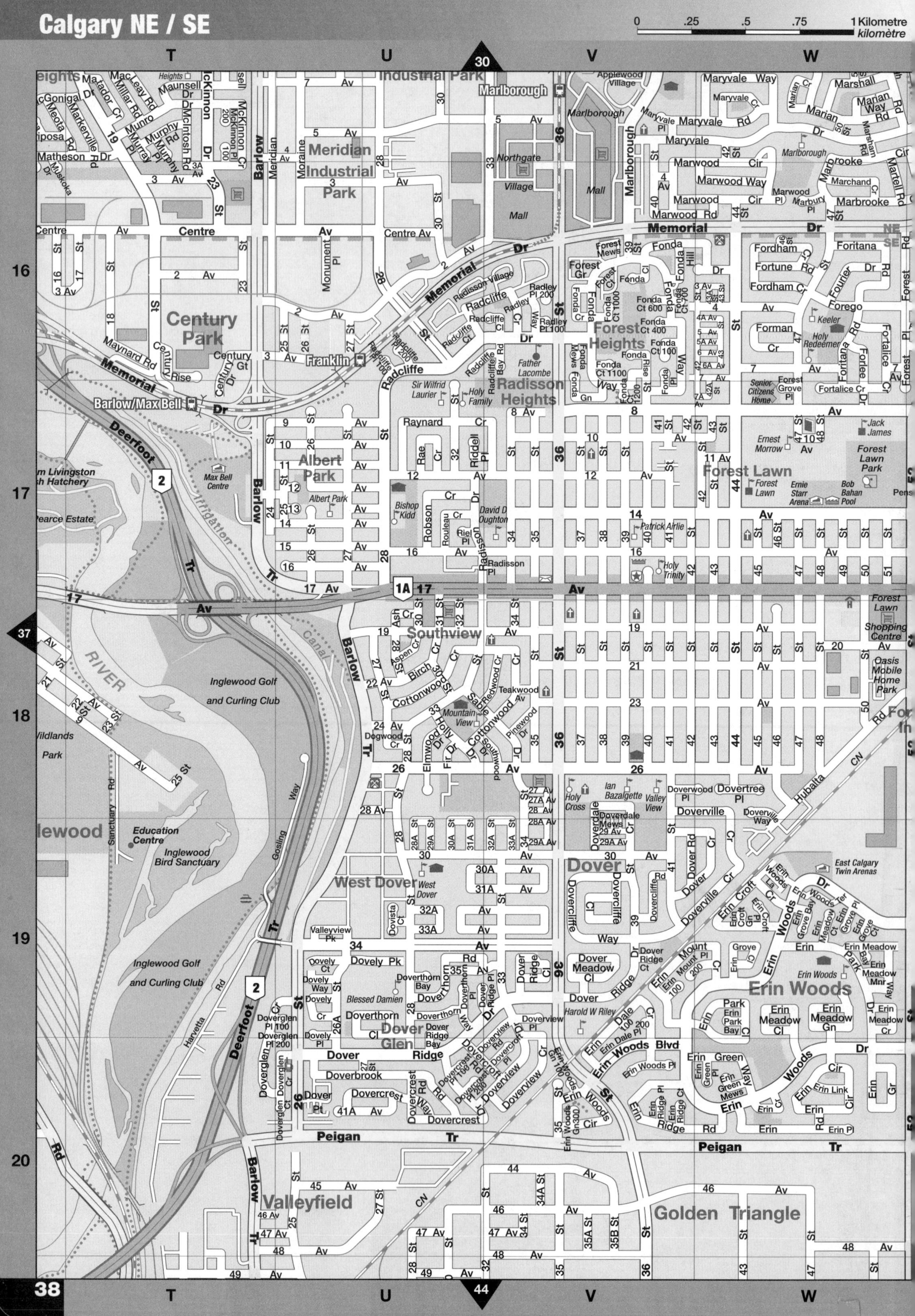
0
.25
.5
.75
1 Kilometre
kilomètre
T
U
V
W
30
44
37
16
17
18
19
20
Meridian Industrial Park
Marlborough
Marlborough Mall
Northgate Village Mall
Memorial Dr
Centre Av
Century Park
Franklin
Barlow/Max Bell
Radisson Heights
Forest Heights
Forest Lawn
Albert Park
Max Bell Centre
Deerfoot Tr
Barlow Tr
17 Av
Southview
Inglewood Golf and Curling Club
RIVER
Irrigation Canal
Inglewood Bird Sanctuary
Education Centre
Wildlands Park
Pearce Estate
West Dover
Dover
Dover Glen
Erin Woods
East Calgary Twin Arenas
Valleyfield
Golden Triangle
Peigan Tr
Forest Lawn Shopping Centre
Oasis Mobile Home Park
Ernie Starr Arena
Bob Bahan Pool
Hubalta Rd
CN
36 St
52 St

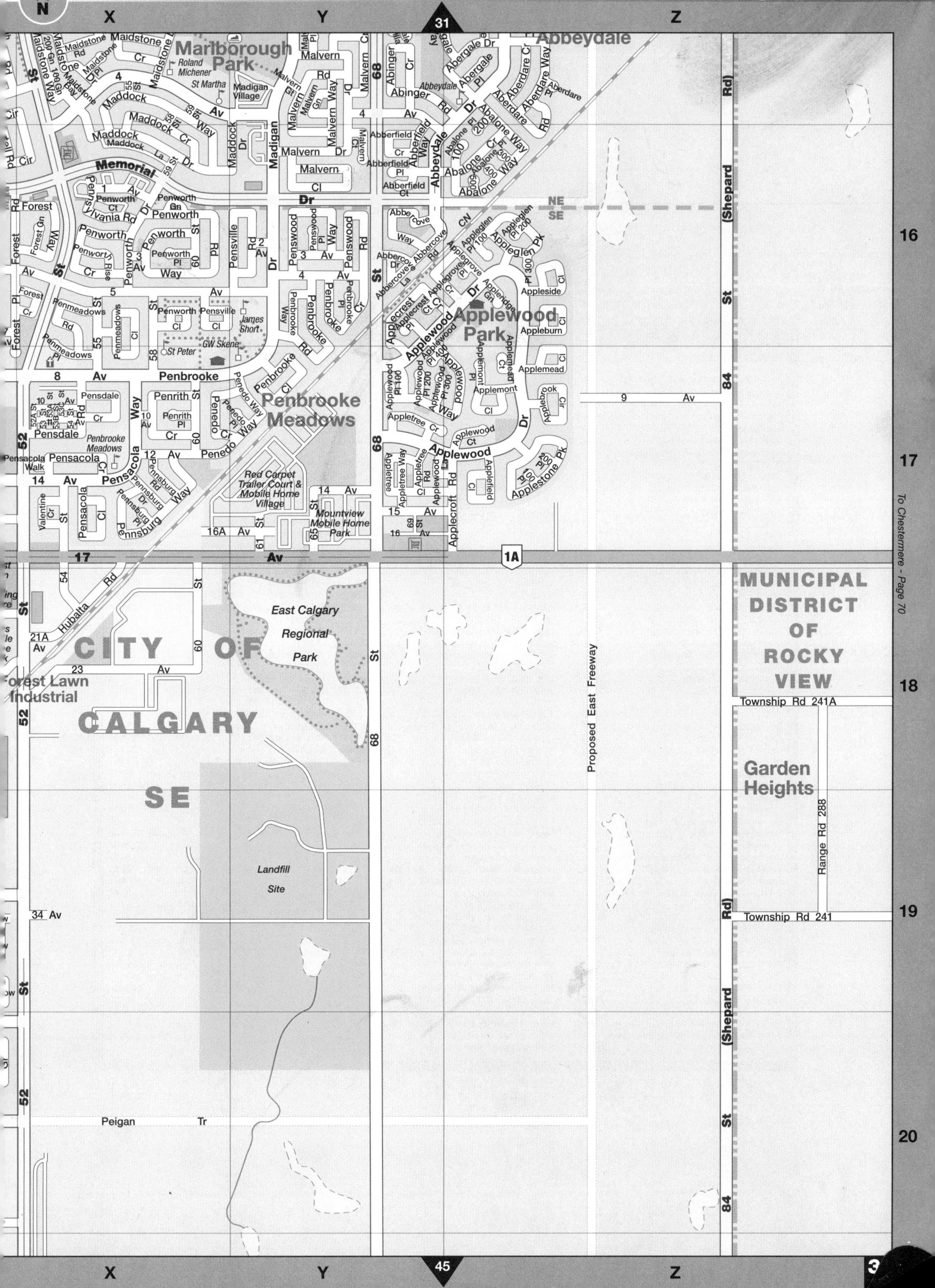

N

X   Y   31   Z

Marlborough Park

Abbeydale

Maidstone Maidstone Rd
Maidstone Cr
Maidstone Way
200 Gn 100 Gn
Roland Michener
St Martha
Madigan Village
Malvern Cr
Malvern St
Malvern Way
Malvern Rd
Malvern Dr
Malvern Cl
Abinger Cr
Abinger Rd
Abergale Dr
Abergale Pl
Aberdare Way
Aberdare Ct
Aberdare Rd
Aberdare Dr
Abberfield Way
Abberfield Cr
Abberfield Pl
Abberfield Ct
Abbeydale Dr
Abalone Pl
Abalone Way
Abalone Cl
Abalone Rd
Abbercove Way
Abbercove La
CN
NE / SE

4 Av
Maddock Way
Maddock Cr
Maddock La
Maddock Dr
Maddock Av
Memorial
Penworth Ct
Penworth Gn
Penworth Dr
Penworth Rise
Penworth Cr
Penworth Rd
Penworth Pl
Penworth Way
Forest Gn
Forest Dr
Forest Way
Forest Cr
Forest Pl
Sylvania Rd
Pensville Rd
Penswood Rd
Penswood Pl
Penbrooke Rd
Penbrooke Way
Penbrooke Cl
Penbrooke St
James Short
GW Skene
St Peter
Penmeadows Rd
Penmeadows Cl

Applewood Park
Appleglen
Appleglen Pk
Applegrove Pl
Applegrove Way
Appledge Dr
Applecrest
Applecrest Ct
Applebrook
Appleburn
Appleside
Applemead
Applemont Pl
Applemont Ct
Applewood Dr
Appletree Ct
Appletree Way
Appletree
Applefield Ct
Applecroft Rd
Applestone Pk

8 Av
Penbrooke
Penbrooke Meadows
Pensdale Cr
Penrith Cr
Penrith Pl
Penedo Way
Penedo Cr
Penedo Pl
Pensdale
Penbrooke Meadows
Pensacola Walk
Pensacola Cl
Pensacola Way
Pennsburg Way
Pennsburg
14 Av
Valentine Cr
Red Carpet Trailer Court & Mobile Home Village
Mountview Mobile Home Park
15 Av
16 Av
16A Av
14 Av

1A

17 Av

CITY OF CALGARY SE

Hubalta Rd
54 St
60 St
68 St
52 St
21A Av
23 Av
Forest Lawn Industrial

East Calgary Regional Park

Landfill Site

34 Av

Peigan Tr

MUNICIPAL DISTRICT OF ROCKY VIEW

84 St
9 Av
Shepard Rd

Township Rd 241A

Garden Heights

Range Rd 288

Township Rd 241

16

17

18

19

20

X   Y   45   Z

Proposed East Freeway

To Chestermere - Page 70

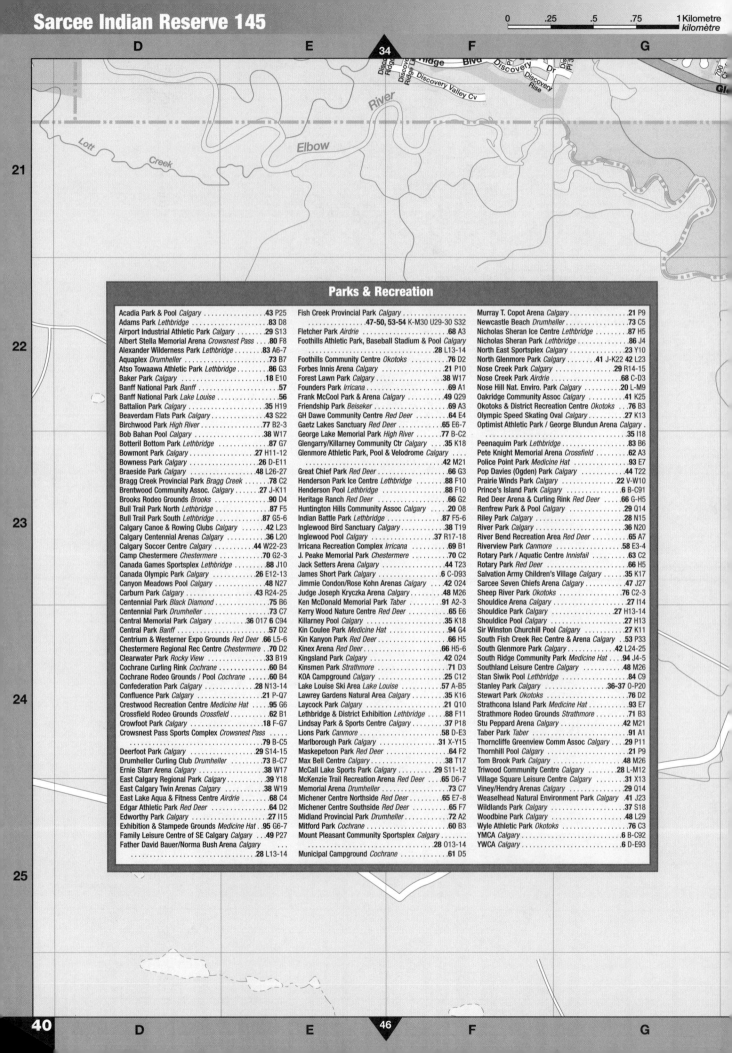

0   .25   .5   .75   1 Kilometre
kilomètre

Parks & Recreation

Acadia Park & Pool *Calgary* 43 P25
Adams Park *Lethbridge* 83 D8
Airport Industrial Athletic Park *Calgary* 29 S13
Albert Stella Memorial Arena *Crowsnest Pass* . . .80 F8
Alexander Wilderness Park *Lethbridge* 83 A6-7
Aquaplex *Drumheller* 73 B7
Atso Towaawa Athletic Park *Lethbridge* 86 G3
Baker Park *Calgary* 18 E10
Banff National Park *Banff* 57
Banff National Park *Lake Louise* 56
Battalion Park *Calgary* 35 H19
Beaverdam Flats Park *Calgary* 43 S22
Birchwood Park *High River* 77 B2-3
Bob Bahan Pool *Calgary* 38 W17
Botteril Bottom Park *Lethbridge* 87 G7
Bowmont Park *Calgary* 27 H11-12
Bowness Park *Calgary* 26 D-E11
Braeside Park *Calgary* 48 L26-27
Bragg Creek Provincial Park *Bragg Creek* 78 C2
Brentwood Community Assoc. *Calgary* 27 J-K11
Brooks Rodeo Grounds *Brooks* 90 D4
Bull Trail Park North *Lethbridge* 87 F5
Bull Trail Park South *Lethbridge* 87 G5-6
Calgary Canoe & Rowing Clubs *Calgary* 42 L23
Calgary Centennial Arenas *Calgary* 36 L20
Calgary Soccer Centre *Calgary* 44 W22-23
Camp Chestermere *Chestermere* 70 G2-3
Canada Games Sportsplex *Lethbridge* 88 J10
Canada Olympic Park *Calgary* 26 E12-13
Canyon Meadows Pool *Calgary* 48 N27
Carburn Park *Calgary* 43 R24-25
Centennial Park *Black Diamond* 75 B6
Centennial Park *Drumheller* 73 C7
Central Memorial Park *Calgary* 36 O17 6 C94
Central Park *Banff* 57 D2
Centrium & Westerner Expo Grounds *Red Deer* .66 L5-6
Chestermere Regional Rec Centre *Chestermere* . .70 D2
Clearwater Park *Rocky View* 33 B19
Cochrane Curling Rink *Cochrane* 60 B4
Cochrane Rodeo Grounds / Pool *Cochrane* 60 B4
Confederation Park *Calgary* 28 N13-14
Confluence Park *Calgary* 21 P-Q7
Crestwood Recreation Centre *Medicine Hat* 95 G6
Crossfield Rodeo Grounds *Crossfield* 62 B1
Crowfoot Park *Calgary* 18 F-G7
Crowsnest Pass Sports Complex *Crowsnest Pass* .
. . . . .79 B-C5
Deerfoot Park *Calgary* 29 S14-15
Drumheller Curling Club *Drumheller* 73 B-C7
Ernie Starr Arena *Calgary* 38 W17
East Calgary Regional Park *Calgary* 39 Y18
East Calgary Twin Arenas *Calgary* 38 W19
East Lake Aqua & Fitness Centre *Airdrie* 68 C4
Edgar Athletic Park *Red Deer* 64 D2
Edworthy Park *Calgary* 27 I15
Exhibition & Stampede Grounds *Medicine Hat* . .95 G6-7
Family Leisure Centre of SE Calgary *Calgary* . . .49 P27
Father David Bauer/Norma Bush Arena *Calgary* . . .
. . . . .28 L13-14

Fish Creek Provincial Park *Calgary* . . . .
. . . . .47-50, 53-54 K-M30 U29-30 S32
Fletcher Park *Airdrie* 68 A3
Foothills Athletic Park, Baseball Stadium & Pool *Calgary*
. . . . .28 L13-14
Foothills Community Centre *Okotoks* 76 D2
Forbes Innis Arena *Calgary* 21 P10
Forest Lawn Park *Calgary* 38 W17
Founders Park *Irricana* 69 A1
Frank McCool Park & Arena *Calgary* 49 Q29
Friendship Park *Beiseker* 69 A3
GH Dawe Community Centre *Red Deer* 64 E4
Gaetz Lakes Sanctuary *Red Deer* 65 E6-7
George Lake Memorial Park *High River* 77 B-C2
Glengarry/Killarney Community Ctr *Calgary* . . .35 K18
Glenmore Athletic Park, Pool & Velodrome *Calgary* . . .
. . . . .42 M21
Great Chief Park *Red Deer* 66 G3
Henderson Park Ice Centre *Lethbridge* 88 F10
Henderson Pool *Lethbridge* 88 F10
Heritage Ranch *Red Deer* 66 G2
Huntington Hills Community Assoc *Calgary* 20 O8
Indian Battle Park *Lethbridge* 87 F5-6
Inglewood Bird Sanctuary *Calgary* 38 T19
Inglewood Pool *Calgary* 37 R17-18
Irricana Recreation Complex *Irricana* 69 B1
J. Peake Memorial Park *Chestermere* 70 C2
Jack Setters Arena *Calgary* 44 T23
James Short Park *Calgary* 6 C-D93
Jimmie Condon/Rose Kohn Arenas *Calgary* . . .42 O24
Judge Joseph Kryczka Arena *Calgary* 48 M26
Ken McDonald Memorial Park *Taber* 91 A2-3
Kerry Wood Nature Centre *Red Deer* 65 E6
Killarney Pool *Calgary* 35 K18
Kin Coulee Park *Medicine Hat* 94 G4
Kin Kanyon Park *Red Deer* 66 H5
Kinex Arena *Red Deer* 66 H5-6
Kingsland Park *Calgary* 42 O24
Kinsmen Park *Strathmore* 71 D3
KOA Campground *Calgary* 25 C12
Lake Louise Ski Area *Lake Louise* 57 A-B5
Lawrey Gardens Natural Area *Calgary* 35 K16
Laycock Park *Calgary* 21 Q10
Lethbridge & District Exhibition *Lethbridge* 88 F11
Lindsay Park & Sports Centre *Calgary* 37 P18
Lions Park *Canmore* 58 D-E3
Marlborough Park *Calgary* 31 X-Y15
Maskepetoon Park *Red Deer* 64 F2
Max Bell Centre *Calgary* 38 T17
McCall Lake Sports Park *Calgary* 29 S11-12
McKenzie Trail Recreation Arena *Red Deer* 65 D6-7
Memorial Arena *Drumheller* 73 C7
Michener Centre Northside *Red Deer* 65 E7-8
Michener Centre Southside *Red Deer* 65 F7
Midland Provincial Park *Drumheller* 72 A2
Mitford Park *Cochrane* 60 B3
Mount Pleasant Community Sportsplex *Calgary* . . . . . .
. . . . .28 O13-14
Municipal Campground *Cochrane* 61 D5

Murray T. Copot Arena *Calgary* 21 P9
Newcastle Beach *Drumheller* 73 C5
Nicholas Sheran Ice Centre *Lethbridge* 87 H5
Nicholas Sheran Park *Lethbridge* 86 J4
North East Sportsplex *Calgary* 23 Y10
North Glenmore Park *Calgary* 41 J-K22 42 L23
Nose Creek Park *Calgary* 29 R14-15
Nose Creek Park *Airdrie* 68 C-D3
Nose Hill Nat. Enviro. Park *Calgary* 20 L-M9
Oakridge Community Assoc *Calgary* 41 K25
Okotoks & District Recreation Centre *Okotoks* . . .76 B3
Olympic Speed Skating Oval *Calgary* 27 K13
Optimist Athletic Park / George Blundun Arena *Calgary* .
. . . . .35 I18
Peenaquim Park *Lethbridge* 83 B6
Pete Knight Memorial Arena *Crossfield* 62 A3
Police Point Park *Medicine Hat* 93 E7
Pop Davies (Ogden) Park *Calgary* 44 T22
Prairie Winds Park *Calgary* 22 V-W10
Prince's Island Park *Calgary* 6 B-C91
Red Deer Arena & Curling Rink *Red Deer* . . .66 G-H5
Renfrew Park & Pool *Calgary* 29 O14
Riley Park *Calgary* 28 N15
River Park *Calgary* 36 N20
River Bend Recreation Area *Red Deer* 65 A7
Riverview Park *Canmore* 58 E3-4
Rotary Park / Aquatic Centre *Innisfail* 63 C2
Rotary Park *Red Deer* 66 H5
Salvation Army Children's Village *Calgary* 35 K17
Sarcee Seven Chiefs Arena *Calgary* 47 J27
Sheep River Park *Okotoks* 76 C2-3
Shouldice Arena *Calgary* 27 I14
Shouldice Park *Calgary* 27 H13-14
Shouldice Pool *Calgary* 27 H13
Sir Winston Churchill Pool *Calgary* 27 K11
South Fish Creek Rec Centre & Arena *Calgary* . .53 P33
South Glenmore Park *Calgary* 42 L24-25
South Ridge Community Park *Medicine Hat* 94 J4-5
Southland Leisure Centre *Calgary* 48 M26
Stan Siwik Pool *Lethbridge* 84 C9
Stanley Park *Calgary* 36-37 O-P20
Stewart Park *Okotoks* 76 D2
Strathcona Island Park *Medicine Hat* 93 E7
Strathmore Rodeo Grounds *Strathmore* 71 B3
Stu Peppard Arena *Calgary* 42 M21
Taber Park *Taber* .91 A1
Thorncliffe Greenview Comm Assoc *Calgary* . . .29 P11
Thornhill Pool *Calgary* 21 P9
Tom Brook Park *Calgary* 48 M26
Triwood Community Centre *Calgary* 28 L-M12
Village Square Leisure Centre *Calgary* 31 X13
Viney/Hendry Arenas *Calgary* 29 O14
Weaselhead Natural Environment Park *Calgary* . .41 J23
Wildlands Park *Calgary* 37 S18
Woodbine Park *Calgary* 48 L29
Wyle Athletic Park *Okotoks* 76 C3
YMCA *Calgary* .6 B-C92
YWCA *Calgary* .6 D-E93

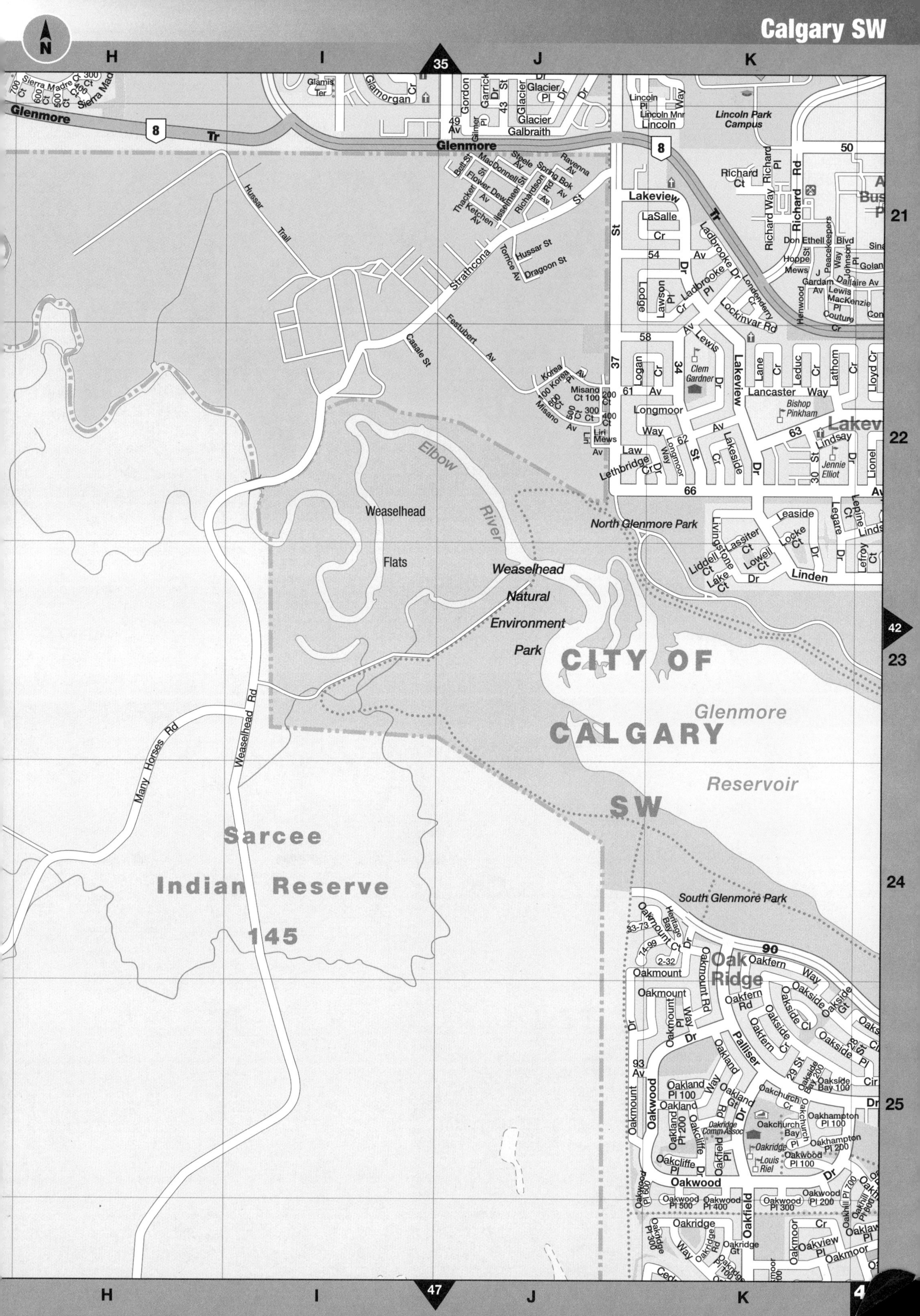

N

Glamis
Ter
Glamorgan

Glenmore

8

Tr

Glenmore

Glenmore

8

Tr

Gordon
Garrick Dr
43 St
Glacier Pl
Glacier
Galbraith

Lincoln
Pl
Lincoln Mnr
Lincoln

Lincoln Park
Campus

50

21

49 Av

Richard
Ct

Richard Way
Richard
Richard Rd

Don Ethell Bv
Peacekeepers Blvd
J Johnson
Dallaire Av
Gardam
Av
Lewis
MacKenzie
Pl
Couture
Cr
Sina

Golan

Bell St
MacDonnell St
Flower Dewinet
St
Steele
Av
Spring Bok
Richardson
Rd
Ravenna
Av

Thacker
Ketchen Av
Torrice Av
Hussar St
Dragoon St

Strathcona

Hussar
Trail

Festubert
Av

Casale St

LaSalle
Cr
54
Av
Lakeview

Loppa Rd
Ladbrooke Dr
Ladbrooke Pl
Londonderry

Henwood

Hoppe
Mews

Lawson
58
Av
Lewis
Lockinvar Rd

61
Av
Logan
Ct
Clem
Gardner
34
Dr

Lakeview

Lane
Cr
Leduc
Cr
Lathom
Cr
Lloyd Cr

Lancaster Way
Bishop
Pinkham
63
Lindsay
Jennie
Elliot
Lionel

Lakev

22

Korea
100 Korea
90 Ct
Misano
Ct 100
200
Ct
300
Ct
400
Ct

Misano
Av
Liri
Mews

Law
Av
Lethbridge
66

37 St

Longmoor
Way
62
St
Longmoor
Way
Lakeside
Dr
Lakeside
Cr

Elbow

River

Weaselhead

Flats

Weaselhead

Natural

Environment

Park

North Glenmore Park

Leaside

Livingstone
Liddell
Lassiter
Ct
Locke
Ct
Lowell
Ct
Lake
Ct
Lake
Dr

Linden

Legare
Ct
Lepine
Ct
Jeffroy

Linds

Av

CITY OF

CALGARY

SW

Glenmore

Reservoir

42

23

Weaselhead Rd

Many Horses Rd

Sarcee

Indian Reserve

145

24

South Glenmore Park

Oakmount
Bay
33-73
74-99
(2-32)
Oakmount
Heritage
Cr

90

Oakfern
Way

Oak
Ridge

Oakfern
Rd
Oakside Cl
Oakside
Oakside
Oakside
Oakside Bay 100
Oakside
Cir

Oakmount
Dr
Oakcommunity Way
Oakmount

Palliser
Dr
93
Av

Oakland
Way
Oakland
Gt
Oakland
Dr
Oakchurch
Bay
Oakchurch Pl
Oakhampton
Bay
Oakhampton
Pl 100

Oakland
Pl 100
Oakland
Pl 200
Oakridge
Comm Assoc
Louis
Riel
Oakwood
Pl 100
Oakwood
Pl 200

25

Oakwood
Dr

Oakcliffe
Pl

Oakridge
Dr

Oakwood

Oakwood
Pl 500
Oakwood
Pl 400
Oakwood
Pl 300
Oakwood
Pl 200

Oakfield

Oakmoor

Oakl

Oakridge
Way
Oakridge
Rd
Oakridge
Gt

Oakridge

Oakview
Pl
Oakmoor
Pl

Cr

Sierra Madre Ct
700 Ct
600 Ct
500 Ct
400 Ct
Sierra Mad

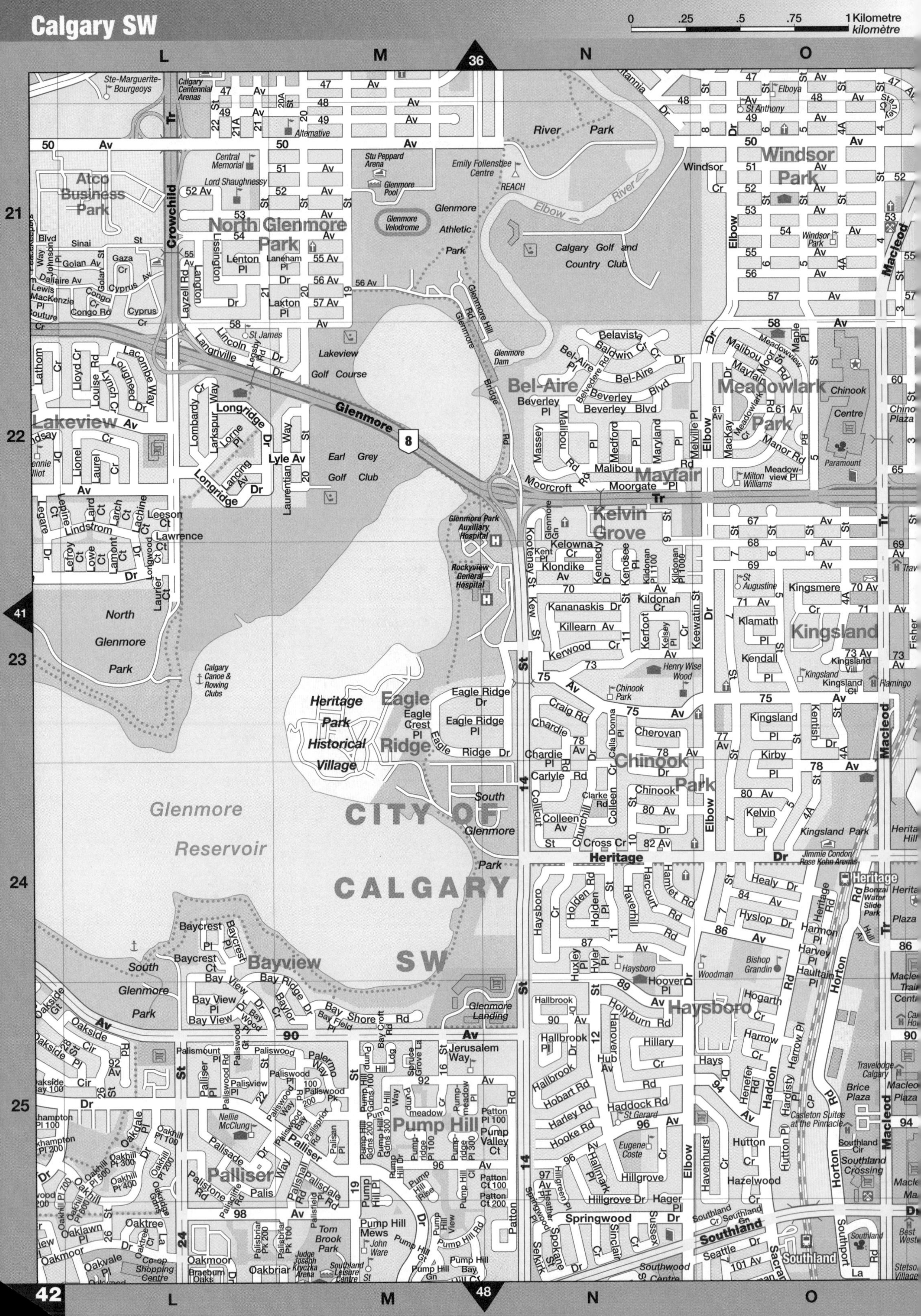
0 .25 .5 .75 1 Kilometre kilomètre
L M N O
36
41
48
21
22
23
24
25
Crowchild Tr
Glenmore Tr
Macleod Tr
North Glenmore Park
Atco Business Park
Lakeview
Windsor Park
Bel-Aire
Meadowlark Park
Mayfair
Kelvin Grove
Kingsland
Chinook Park
Eagle Ridge
Haysboro
Bayview
Palliser
Pump Hill
Glenmore Reservoir
CITY OF CALGARY SW
River Park
Elbow River
Glenmore Athletic Park
Calgary Golf and Country Club
Lakeview Golf Course
Earl Grey Golf Club
Heritage Park Historical Village
North Glenmore Park
South Glenmore Park
Glenmore Velodrome
Glenmore Pool
Stu Peppard Arena
Emily Follensbee Centre
Glenmore Dam
Glenmore Park Auxiliary Hospital
Rockyview General Hospital
Calgary Canoe & Rowing Clubs
Chinook Centre
Heritage Dr
Southland Dr
Elbow Dr
14 St
90 Av
Glenmore Landing
Southland Crossing
Jimmie Condon/Rose Kohn Arenas

N
P
Q
R
S
37
44
49
21
22
23
24
25
Manchester
Burns Industrial Park
Blackfoot Inn
Chinook
Chinook Plaza
Glenmore
Blackfoot Tr
Deerfoot Tr
Fairview Industrial Park
Fairview
Travelodge
Glendeer Business Park
East Fairview Industrial Park
CITY OF CALGARY SE
Heritage Dr
Heritage Meadows Way
Heritage Hill
Heritage Plaza
Macleod Trail Centre
Macleod Plaza
Macleod Mall
Best Western
Stetson Village
Carriage House Inn
Acadia
Acadia Park
Acadia Pool
Lord Beaverbrook
Dr Norman Bethune
Andrew Davison
Le Roi Daniels
St Matthew
Fred Parker
David Thompson
Alice M Curtis
St Cecilia
Willow Park
Blackfoot Mobile Home Park
Carburn Park
Beaverdam Flats Park
BOW RIVER
Waste Treatment Plant
Millican Estates
Lynnwood Ridge
Ogden
Riverbend
Riverbend Shopping Centre
Banting And Best
Jack Setters Arena
Southland Dr
Glenmore Tr
Riverview Mews
Highfield Cr
Manitou Rd
Fairmount Dr
Centre St
Macleod Tr
Ogden Rd
Riverview Cir
Lysander Dr
Lynnview Rd
Riverbend Dr
Rivervalley Dr
Riverbirch Rd
Riverside Rd
Riverbrook Way
CP
CN

0
.25
.5
.75
1 Kilometre
kilomètre
T
U
V
W
38
50
43
21
22
23
24
25
Ogden Shops
Foothills
Industrial
Park
South Foothills
Industrial Park
Cepeear
Ogden
Lynnwood
Ridge
Riverbend
Pop Davies (Ogden) Park
Banting And Best
Sherwood Community
Jack Setters Arena
St Bernadette
Calgary Soccer Centre
Glenmore Inn & Conference Centre
Riverbend Shopping Centre
Holy Angels
Caravan Trailer Court
South Hill Mobile Home Park
Irrigation
Canal
Glenmore
Tr
Barlow
Tr
Ogden
Rd
Ogden Dale Rd
Ogden Dale Pl
Shepard
Rd
Shepard Pl
Millican Rd
Crestwood Rd
Lynnwood Dr
Lynndale Cr
Lynnover Cr
Lytton Cr
Ogmoor Pl
Acres Rd
Rivercrest Dr
Riverglen Dr
Rivercroft Cl
Riverstone Rd
Riverstone Cl
Riverwood Cl
River Rock Way
River Rock Rd
Olympia Bay
Olympia Dr
Olympia Cr
50 Av
54 Av
61 Av
64 Av
72 Av
76 Av
80 Av
90 Av
98 Av
CN
CP

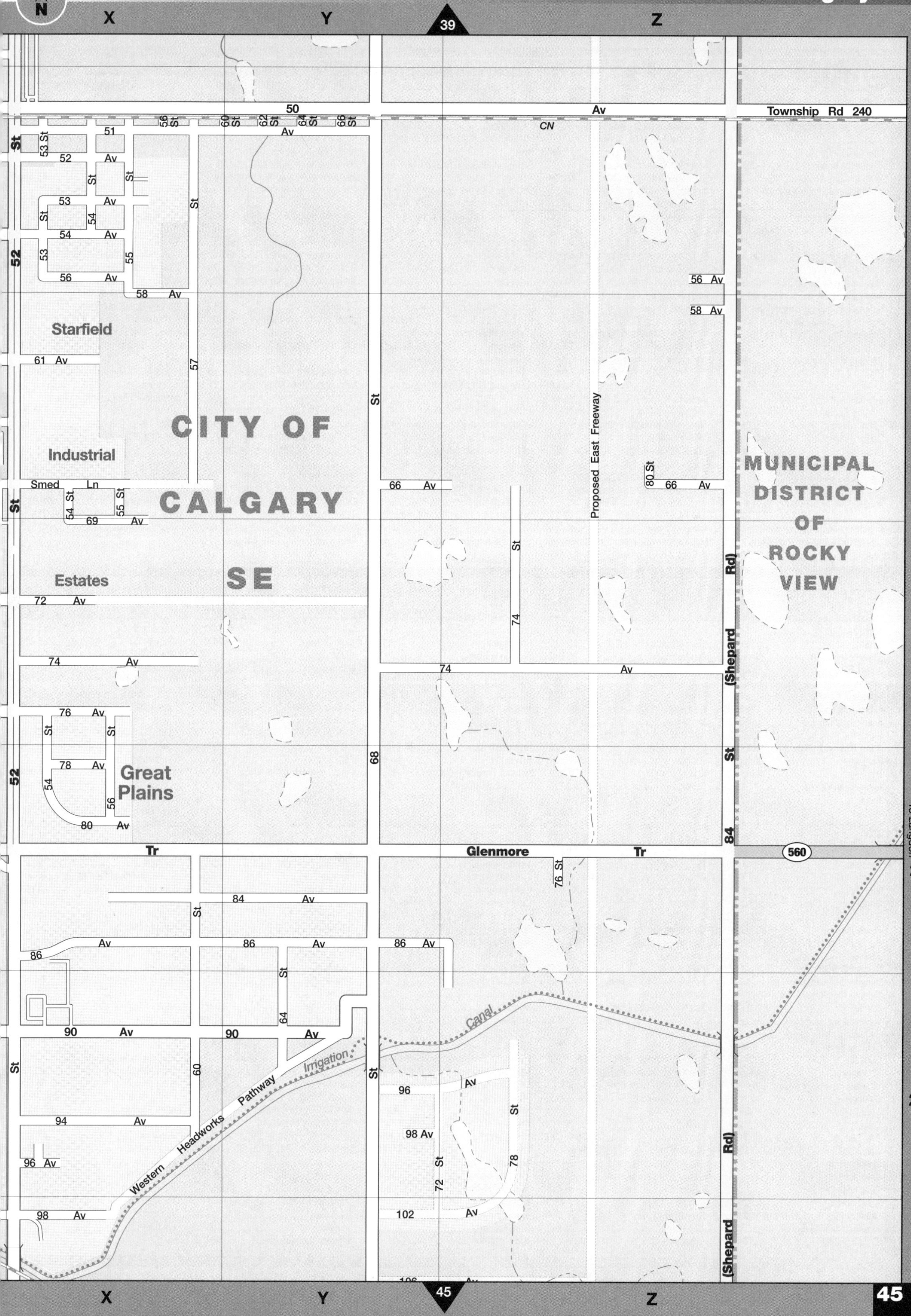

N

X   Y   **39**   Z

50   Av   Township Rd 240

CN

21

St

53 St

51

52

53 St

52   Av

St

St

53   Av

54

54   Av

St

53

55

56   Av

58 Av

56 Av

58 Av

Starfield

57

61 Av

22

CITY OF

St

Proposed East Freeway

Industrial

Smed Ln

CALGARY

66 Av

80 St 66 Av

MUNICIPAL

54 St 55 St

69   Av

DISTRICT

St

SE

St

OF

Estates

ROCKY

72 Av

74

VIEW

23

74   Av

74   Av

(Shepard

76 Av

St

St

78 Av

68

Great
Plains

54

St

52

56

80 Av

84

Tr   Glenmore   Tr   **560**

24

76 St

To Langdon

84   Av

St

86 Av   Av   86 Av

86

St

64

90   Av   **90**   **Av**

Canal

60

St

96 Av

St

Irrigation

Western Headworks Pathway

94   Av

98 Av

St

78

St

25

96 Av

St

72

98 Av

102   Av

Rd)

(Shepard

106   Av

X   Y   **45**   Z

0 .25 .5 .75 1 Kilometre kilomètre

D E 40 F G

Points of Interest

Aero Space Museum of Alberta *Calgary* .30 T11
Airdrie Town Hall *Airdrie* .68 B3
Alberta Birds of Prey Centre *Coaldale* .85 A1
Alberta College of Art *Calgary* .28 N15
Athabasca University *Calgary* .36 N16
Banff Airfield *Banff* .57 A4
Banff Park Museum National Historic Site *Banff* .57 D2
Beiseker Town Hall *Beiseker* .69 A1
Black Diamond Town Hall *Black Diamond* .75 B6
Bonzai Water Slide Park *Calgary* .42 O24
Bow Centre Place *Calgary* .18 D-E10
Bow Falls *Banff* .57 E2-3
Bow Valley College *Calgary* .37 P-Q16
Bow Valley Ranch *Calgary* .53 S32
Bowman Arts Centre *Lethbridge* .87 F8
Brewery Gardens *Lethbridge* .87 F7
Brooks & District Museum *Brooks* .90 B-C4
Brooks Town Hall *Brooks* .90 C2
Calgary Centre for the Performing Arts *Calgary* .6 D93
Calgary Chinese Cultural Centre *Calgary* .6 C92
Calgary City Hall *Calgary* .6 D-E93
Calgary Int'l Airport *Calgary* .21-22 S-T8
Calgary Main Post Office *Calgary* .6 C94
Calgary Science Centre and Centennial Planetarium *Calgary* .36 N16
Calgary Tower (Tourist Info) *Calgary* .6 D94
Calgary Zoo, Botanical Garden & Prehistoric Park *Calgary* .37 R17
Canadian Badlands Passion Play *Drumheller* .72 C4
Canadian Western Natural Gas Company Museum *Calgary* .6 A94
Canmore Nordic Ctr. *Canmore* .58 E2
Canmore Town Hall *Canmore* .58 E4
Cascade Rock Garden *Banff* .57 E2
Cash Casino *Calgary* .37 Q20
Casino Lethbridge *Lethbridge* .87 F8
Centennial Museum *Canmore* .58 E4
Coaldale Town Hall *Coaldale* .85 B3
Cochrane Art Gallery *Cochrane* .61 C5
Cochrane Town Hall *Cochrane* .60 B4
Cochrane Ranch Historic Site *Cochrane* .60 A3-4
County of Wheatland Office *Strathmore* .71 E2
Crossfield Town Hall *Crossfield* .62 A3
Crowsnest Museum *Crowsnest Pass* .79 C3
Crowsnest Pass Arts & Crafts Gallery *Crowsnest Pass* .80 E7-8
Crowsnest Pass Municipal Hall *Crowsnest Pass* .79 C4
Deane House Historic Site *Calgary* .37 R17
Devonian Gardens *Calgary* .6 C93
Drumheller City Hall *Drumheller* 73 C6
Drumheller Dinosaur & Fossil Museum *Drumheller* .73 C7
Energy Resources Bldg *Calgary* 6 B93
Fish Creek Interpretive Ctr. *Calgary* .53 S32
Fort Calgary Historic Park *Calgary* .37 Q17
Frank Sisson's Silver Dollar Casino *Calgary* .37 Q-R20
Funland Amusement Park *Drumheller* .73 B5
Gas Plant National Historic Site *Turner Valley* .74 D4
Glenbow Museum *Calgary* .6 D93
Grain Academy, The *Calgary* 37 P-Q17
Greyhound Bus Terminal *Calgary* .36 M16-17
Henderson Rose Garden *Lethbridge* .88 F-G10
Heritage Park Historical Village *Calgary* .42 M23-24
High River Town Hall *High River* 77 C2
Hillcrest Bible Institute *Medicine Hat* .95 H5-6
Historic RCMP Barracks & Pk. *Canmore* .58 E4
Homestead Antique Museum *Drumheller* .73 B5-6
Illingworth Kerr Gallery *Calgary* .28 N15
Innisfail Town Hall *Innisfail* .63 B3
Irricana Village Hall *Irricana* .69 B1
Lethbridge City Hall *Lethbridge* .87 F8
Lethbridge Community College *Lethbridge* .88 J9-10
Lunchbox Theatre *Calgary* .6 C93
Luxton Museum *Banff* .57 E1
McMahon Stadium *Calgary* .28 L14
Medicine Hat College *Medicine Hat* .94 G4
Medicine Hat Mun. Airport *Medicine Hat* .94 G1
Medicine Hat Convention Centre *Medicine Hat* .93 D5
Medicine Hat Museum & Art Gallery *Medicine Hat* .94 F3
Mewata Stadium *Calgary* .36 N16-17
Mount Royal College *Calgary* .35 K20
Mountain View Mus. *Olds* .62 BB-C34
Museum of Movie Art *Calgary* .30 T12
Museum of the Highwood *High River* .77 C2-3
Museum of the Regiments *Calgary* .36 L20
Naval Museum of Alberta / HMCS Tecumseh *Calgary* .36 L17-18
Newell County Office *Brooks* .90 C4
Nickle Arts Museum *Calgary* .27 K13
Nikka Yuko Japanese Garden *Lethbridge* .88 G10
Nose Creek Valley Museum *Airdrie* .68 D3
Okotoks Station Cultural Centre *Okotoks* .76 C3
Okotoks Town Hall *Okotoks* .76 C2
Olds Agriculture College *Olds* .62 C4
Olds Town Hall *Olds* .62 B4
Olympic Hall of Fame *Calgary* .26 D-E12
Olympic Plaza *Calgary* .6 D93
Pengrowth Saddledome *Calgary* .37 Q18
Pioneer Acres Site *Irricana* .69 A1
Pumphouse Theatres *Calgary* .36 M16
Race City Speedway *Calgary* 51 Y-Z27
Red Deer City Hall *Red Deer* .66 G5
Red Deer College *Red Deer* .66 J4
Rocky View Mun. Dist. Offices *Calgary* .29 R13
Royal Tyrell Museum of Palaeontolgy *Drumheller* .72 A1
St. George's Island *Calgary* 37 R-S17
St. Patrick Island *Calgary* .37 Q-R16
Sam Livingston Fish Hatchery *Calgary* .37 S17
Sarcee Peoples Tsuu T'ina Museum *Calgary* .47 J27
Sir Alexander Galt Museum *Lethbridge* .87 F6-7
South Alberta Art Gallery *Lethbridge* .87 E-F7
Southern Alberta Institute of Technology (SAIT) *Calgary* .28 N14
Southern Alberta Jubliee Auditorium *Calgary* .28 N15
Snell Gardens *Red Deer* .64 F5
Spruce Meadows Equestrian Centre *Calgary* .52 M-N34
Stage West Theatre *Calgary* .37 Q20
Stampede Casino *Calgary* .37 P-Q18
Stampede Park *Calgary* .37 P-Q18
Stockmen's Memorial Museum and Library *Cochrane* .61 B-C5
Strathmore Town Hall *Strathmore* .71 D2
Taber Town Hall *Taber* .91 D2
Turner Valley Town Hall *Turner Valley* .74 C-D3
University of Calgary *Calgary* 27 J-K13
University of Lethbridge *Lethbridge* .87 H5-6
White Museum *Banff* .57 D1-2
Whoop-Up Park *Lethbridge* 88 G11-12
World's Largest Dinosaur *Drumheller* .73 B7

Calgary Districts

Abbeydale .31 Z15
Acadia .43 P25
Airways Industrial Park .30 T12-13
Albert Park .38 U17
Altadore .36 M20
Applewood Park .39 Z16
Arbour Lake .18 F-G6
Aspen Estates .34 F17
Balmoral .28-29 O-P14
Banff Trail .28 L-M13
Bankview .36 M-N18
Bayview .42 L-M24
Beddington Heights .20 O7
Bel-Aire .42 N22
Belfast .29 S14-15
Bonavista Downs .49 R-S28
Bonnybrook .37 S19-20
Bowness .26 F11
Braeside .48 M27
Brentwood .28 K-L11
Briar Hill .28 M15
Bridgeland .37 Q-R16
Bridlewood .52 L-M33
Burns Avenue .37 R18
Burns Industrial Park .43 Q-R22
Burnsland .37 Q19
Cambrian Heights .28 N12
Canyon Creek Estates .48 N29
Canyon Meadows .48 N-O27 N-O28
Capitol Hill .28 M13
Castleridge .22 W10
Cedarbrae .47-48 K-L27
Century Park .38 T16
Cepeear .44 U23
Charleswood .28 L-M13
Charleswood Heights .28 L10-11
Chinook Park .42 N-O24
Christie Park .34 G18
Citadel .19 H6
City Centre .37 P16
Coach Hill .34 G16
Collingwood .28 M-N13
Connaught .36 N-O17
Copperfield .55 Y32
Coral Springs .23 Z10
Country Hills .20 N-O6
Country Hills Village .13 P4
Coventry Hills .13 P-Q3
Cranston .54 U-V34
Crescent Heights .29 P15
Crestmont .25 B12
Crowchild Ranch .18-19 G-H7
Dalhousie .19 I10
Deer Ridge .50 T30
Deer River Estates .50 T29
Deer Run .54 T31
Deerfoot Business Centre .21 Q-R9
Diamond Cove .49 S27-28
Douglas Glen .50 T26-27
Douglasdale .50 T-U28
Dover .38 V19
Dover Glen .38 U19-20
Eagle Ridge .42 M23
East Springbank .34 E17
Eau Claire .36-37 O-P16
Edgemont .19 I-J8
Elbow Park .36 N-O19
Elboya .36-37 O-P20
Erin Woods .38 W19
Erlton .37 P18
Evanston .12 L3
Evergreen .52 L-M31
Evergreen Estate .48 M30
Falconridge .23 X10
Fairview .43 P23
Fairview Industrial Park .43 P23
Foothills Estate .28 M11
Foothills Industrial Park .44 V-W22 V-W23
Forest Heights .38 V16
Forest Lawn .38 W17
Forest Lawn Industrial .38-39 W-X18
Franklin Industrial Park .30 U15
Freeport Business Park .14 T5
Garrison Woods .36 L19-20
Glamorgan .35 I20
Glenbrook .35 I19
Glencoe .36 N-O19
Glendale .35 J17-18
Glendale Meadows .35 I18
Glendeer Business Park .43 R23
Glengarry .36 L18
Golden Triangle .38 V-W20
Grandview .37 Q18
Greenbriar .26 E12
Greenview .29 P-Q12
Greenwood .26 D11
Hamptons .11 I5
Hanson Ranch .12 M-N4
Harvest Hills .13 P-Q5
Hawkwood .19 H7
Haysboro .42 N-O25
Hidden Valley .12 L5
Highfield .37 Q-R20
Highland Park .29 P11
Highwood .28 O11-12
Hillhurst .36 N16
Horizon Industrial Estates .30 U12
Huntington Hills .20 O9
Inglewood .37-38 S-T19
Kelvin Grove .42 N22
Killarney .35 J-K18
Kincora .11 K4
Kingsland .42 O23
Knob Hill .36 L-M18
Lake Bonavista .49 Q28
Lake Chaparral .53 R34
Lakeview .41-42 K-L22
Lynnwood Ridge .43-44 S-T21 S22
MacEwan .20 L-M7
Manchester .43 P-Q21
Maple Ridge .49 R26
Marlborough .30 V-W15
Marlborough Park .31 X-Y15
Martindale .23 X9
Mayfair .42 N-O22
Mayland Heights .29-30 S-T15
McKenzie .54 U-V32
McKenzie Lake .54 V31-32
McKenzie Towne .54 V-W31
Meadowlark Park .42 O22
Meridian Industrial Park .38 U15-16
Midnapore .53 Q32
Millican Estates .43 S22
Millrise .52 N-O31
Mills Estate .37 R-S18
Mission .36-37 O-P18
Monterey Park .31 Z12-13
Montgomery .27 I14
Mount Pleasant .28 O14
Mount Royal .36 N18
Mountain Park .54 T-U32
Mountview .29 Q-R14
New Brighton .51 X30
North Glenmore Park .42 L-M21
North Haven .20 N10
North Mount Pleasant .28 O13
Oak Ridge .41 K24-25
Ogden .43-44 S-T24
Palliser .42 L25
Panorama Hills .12 O5
Parkdale .28 L15
Parkland .49 R30
Patterson .26 G14
Pegasus .30 T11
Penbrooke Meadows .39 Y17
Pineridge .31 Y13
Pleasant Heights .28 N14
Point McKay .27 J15
Prominence Point .27 H15
Pump Hill .42 M25
Queensland Downs .49 R-S29
Radisson Heights .38 V17
Ramsay .37 Q17
Ranchlands .18-19 G-H8
Regal Terrace .29 Q15
Renfrew .29 R15
Richmond Hill .35 H19
Richmond Park .35-36 K-L19
Rideau Park .36 O19
Riverbend .43-44 S-T25
Riverdale .36 N20
Riverside .37 R-S16
Rocky Ridge .9 C5
Rosedale .28 O14
Rosemont .28 N13
Rosscarrock .35 J17
Roxboro .36-37 O-P19
Royal Oak .18 D-E6
Rundle .30 W13
Saddle Ridge .23 X8
Saddle Ridge Industrial .22 V8
St. Andrews Heights .27 J-K14
St. George's Heights .29 R-S15
Sandstone .20 N6
Scenic Acres .18 E8
Scarboro .36 M17
Shaganappi .35 K17
Shawnee Slopes .48 N30
Shawnessy .52 N-O32
Shawville .53 P33
Shepard Industrial Park .50 U26
Sherwood .11 I-J4
Sienna Hills .35 H20
Signal Ridge .35 H19
Silver Springs .18 G10
Skyline East .21 Q-R10
Skyline West .29 Q11
Somerset .52 N33
South Calgary .36 M19
South Foothills Industrial Park 44 W25
Southview .38 U18
Southwood .48 N-O26
Springside .26 E-F15
Spruce Cliff .35 K16
Stanley Park .37 P20
Starfield Industrial Estates 45 X22-23
Strathcona Park .35 H16
Sunalta .36 L17
Sundance .53 R33
Sunnyside .28 O15
Sunridge Industrial Park .30 U13
Tanglewood .17 B6
Taradale .23 Y9
Temple .31 X-Y12
Thorncliffe .20 O10
Thorncliffe Heights .21 P10
Tuscany .17 C8
Tuxedo .29 P13
University Heights .27 K14
Upper Hillhurst .28 M15
Valley Ridge .25 B11
Valleyfield .38 T-U20
Varsity Acres .27 J12
Varsity Estates .27 H11
Victoria Park .37 Q17
Vista Heights .30 T14
West Dover .38 U19
West Hillhurst .28 L-M15
West Springs .26 F-G15
Westgate .35 I17
Westmount .36 M16
Whitehorn .30 V-W12
Wildwood .27 J15
Willow Park .49 P26
Windsor Park .42 O21
Winston Heights .29 Q13
Woodbine .47 K28
Woodlands .48 M28

D E F G

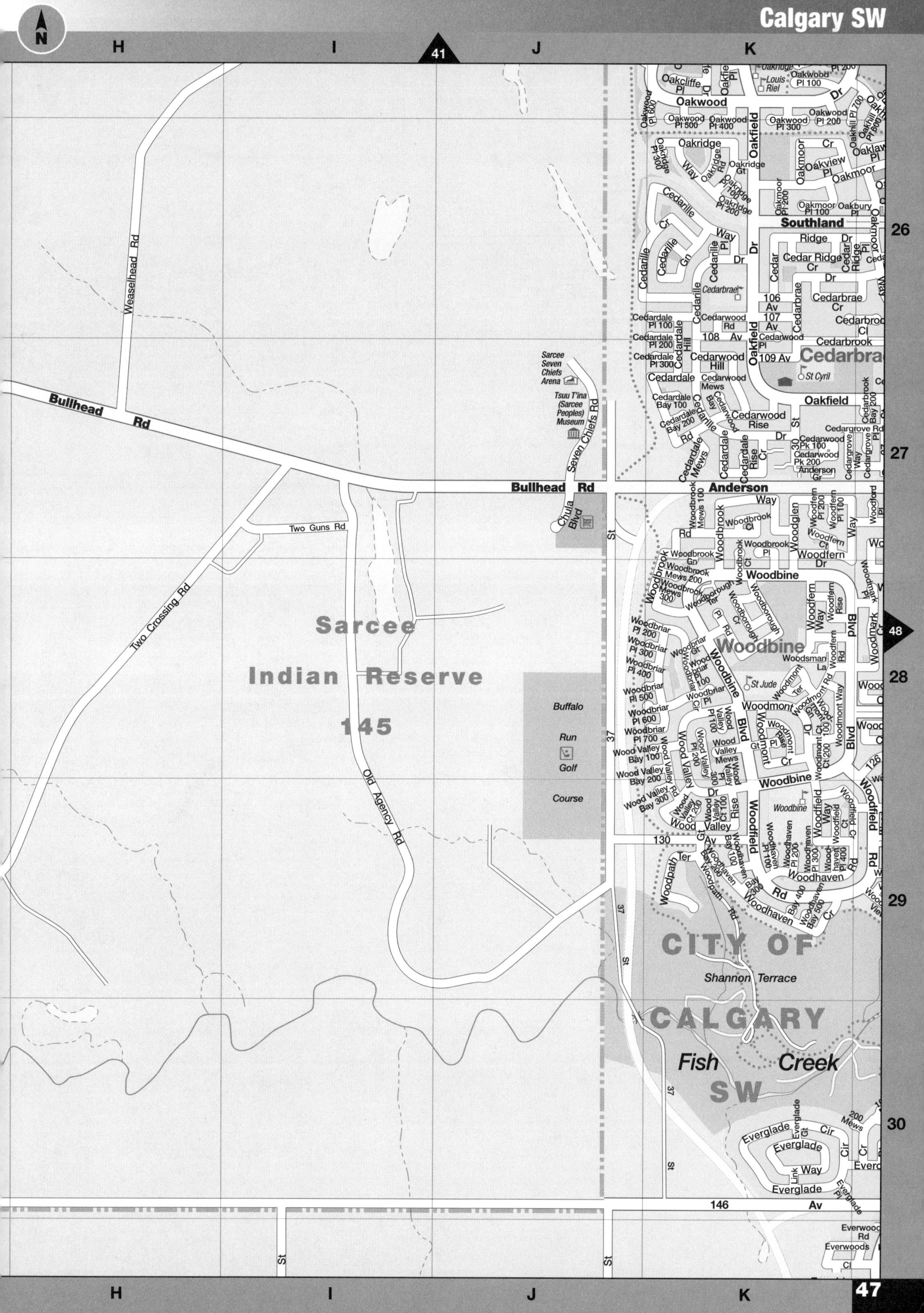

N

Oakcliffe Pl
Oakwood Pl 200
Louis Riel
Oakwood Pl 100
Oakcliffe Pl
Oakfield
Oakwood
Oakwood Pl 500
Oakwood Pl 400
Oakwood Pl 300
Oakwood Pl 200
Oakhill Dr
Oaklaw

Oakridge Pl 300
Cr
Oakmoor
Oakview
Oakmoor
Way
Oakridge Way
Oakridge Gt
Oakmoor Pl 200
Oakbury Pl

Cedarille Cr
Cedarille Gn
Way
Cedarille Dr
Oakridge Dr
Southland
Oakmoor Pl 100

Cedar Ridge Dr
Cedar Ridge Cr
Cedar Ridge Dr
Cedarbrae Cr

Cr
Cedarille Gn
Cedarille Dr
Cedarbrae
106 Av
107 Av
108 Av
Cedarbrook Cl

Cedardale Pl 100
Cedardale Pl 200
Cedardale Pl 300
Cedardale Hill
Cedarwood Rd
Cedarwood Hill
Cedarbra
Cedarbrook

Cedardale Mews
Cedarwood Mews
109 Av
St Cyril
Cedarbrook Bay 200
Cedarbrook Bay 100

Sarcee Seven Chiefs Arena
Tsuu T'ina (Sarcee Peoples) Museum
Seven Chiefs Rd
Cedardale Bay 100
Cedardale Mews
Cedarwood Rise
Oakfield
27

Cedardale Mews
Cedardale Bay 200
Cedarille
Cedarwood Rise Dr
Cedargrove Rd
Cedargrove Way
Cedargrove Gr
Pk 100
Pk 200

Cedarwood Rise Cr
Cedarwood Anderson Gr

Bullhead   Rd

Bullhead   Rd
Anderson

Chula Blvd
Woodbrook Mews 100
Woodbrook Rd
Woodbrook Cl
Woodglen
Way
Woodfern Pl 200
Woodfern Pl 100
Way

Two Guns Rd
Woodbrook Gn
Woodbrook Mews 200
Woodbrook Pl
Woodfern Ct
Woodfern Dr

Woodbrook Mews 300
Woodborough Ter
Woodbine
Woodbine
Woodfern Way
Woodfern Rise

Two Crossing Rd
Woodbriar Pl 200
Woodbriar Pl 300
Woodbriar Pl 400
Woodbriar Cr
Woodborough Pl
Woodbine Blvd
Woodbine
Woodsman La
Woodfern Rd
Woodmark Blvd
◆48
28

Sarcee

Woodbriar Pl 500
Woodbriar Pl 600
Woodbriar Pl 700
Woodbriar Cr
Woodbine Blvd
St Jude
Woodmont Dr
Woodmont Way

Indian   Reserve
Wood Valley Bay 100
Wood Valley Bay 200
Wood Valley Mews
Wood Valley Cr
Wood Valley Pl 100
Wood Valley Pl 200
Wood Valley Pl 300
Woodmont
Woodmont Ct
Woodmont Cr
Blvd
126

145
Buffalo
Wood Valley Bay 300
Wood Valley Dr
Wood Valley Rise
Woodbine
Woodfield Ct
Woodfield Rd

Run
Old Agency Rd
Wood Valley
Woodfield Rise
Woodbine
Woodfield
Woodfield Way

Golf
130
Woodpath Ter
Woodhaven Pl 100
Woodhaven Pl 200
Woodhaven Pl 300
Woodhaven Pl 400

Course
37 St
Woodpath Ter
Woodpath Bay
Woodhaven Bay 100
Woodhaven Rd
Woodhaven
Woodhaven Bay 400
Woodhaven Bay 500
29

CITY OF

Shannon Terrace

37 St
CALGARY

37 St
Fish   Creek
SW
200 Mews

Everglade Gt
Everglade Cir
Everglade Cir

Everglade Link
Everglade Way
Everglade
30

146   Av

Everwood Rd
Everwoods

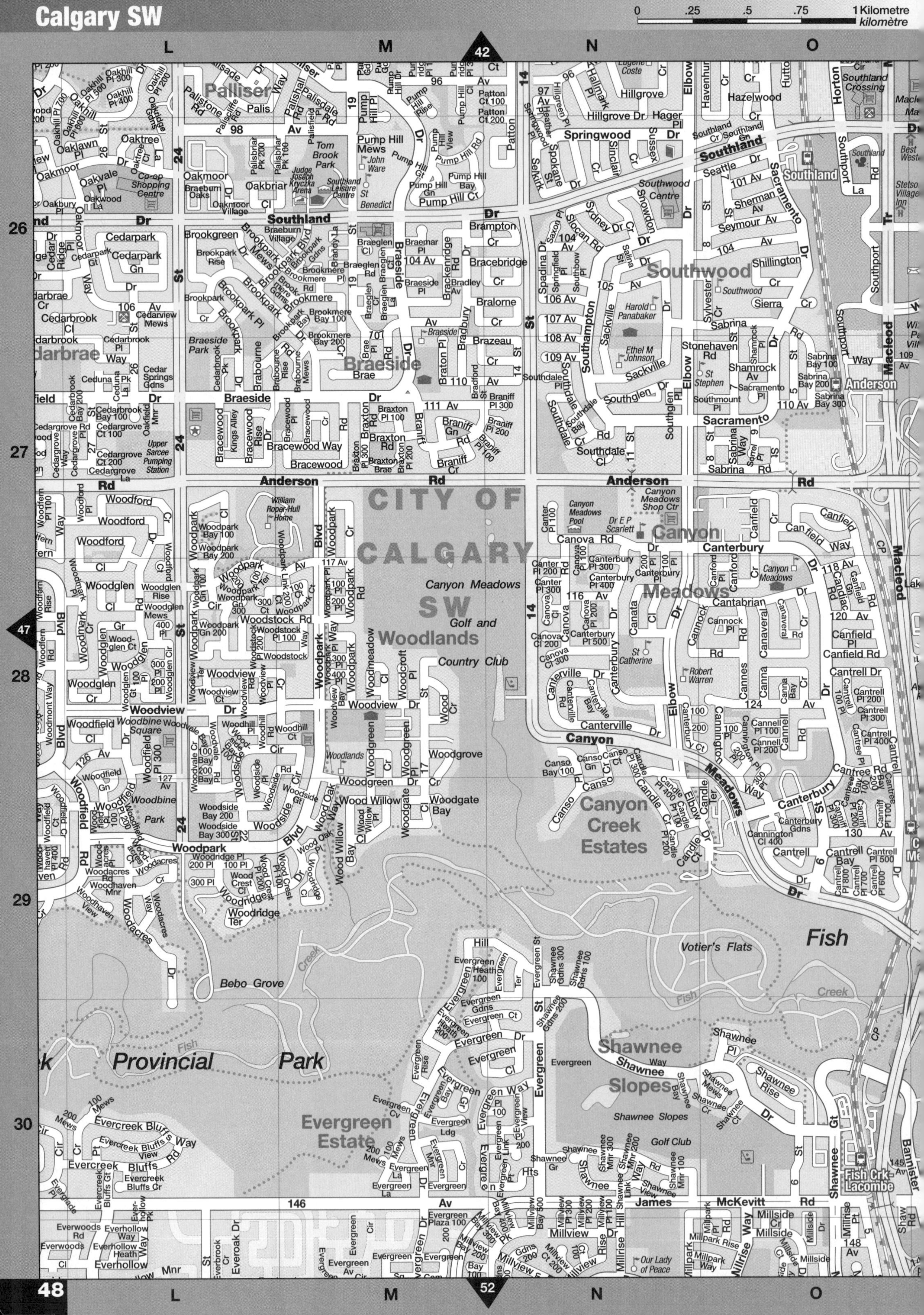
0 .25 .5 .75 1 Kilometre kilomètre
L
M
N
O
42
47
52
26
27
28
29
30
CITY OF CALGARY SW
Palliser
Braeside
Southwood
Canyon Meadows
Canyon Creek Estates
Shawnee Slopes
Evergreen Estate
Fish Creek Provincial Park
Canyon Meadows Golf and Woodlands Country Club
Shawnee Slopes Golf Club
Southland Drive
Anderson Rd
Macleod Tr
Canyon Meadows Dr
Woodpark Blvd
Woodview Dr
Elbow Dr
14 St
24 St
146 Av
James McKevitt Rd
Southland Leisure Centre
Southwood Centre
Canyon Meadows Shop Ctr
Co-op Shopping Centre
Woodbine Square
Upper Sarcee Pumping Station
William Roper-Hull Home
Tom Brook Park
Braeside Park
Woodbine Park
Votier's Flats
Bebo Grove
Southland
Anderson
Fish Crk Lacombe
Southland Crossing

CITY OF CALGARY

Provincial SE

Canyon Meadows

Willow Park

Willow Park Golf and Country Club

Maple Ridge

Maple Ridge Golf Course

Bonavista Downs

Diamond Cove

Bonavista

Lake Bonavista

Lake Bonaventure

Queensland Downs

Parkland

Deer Ridge

Southcentre

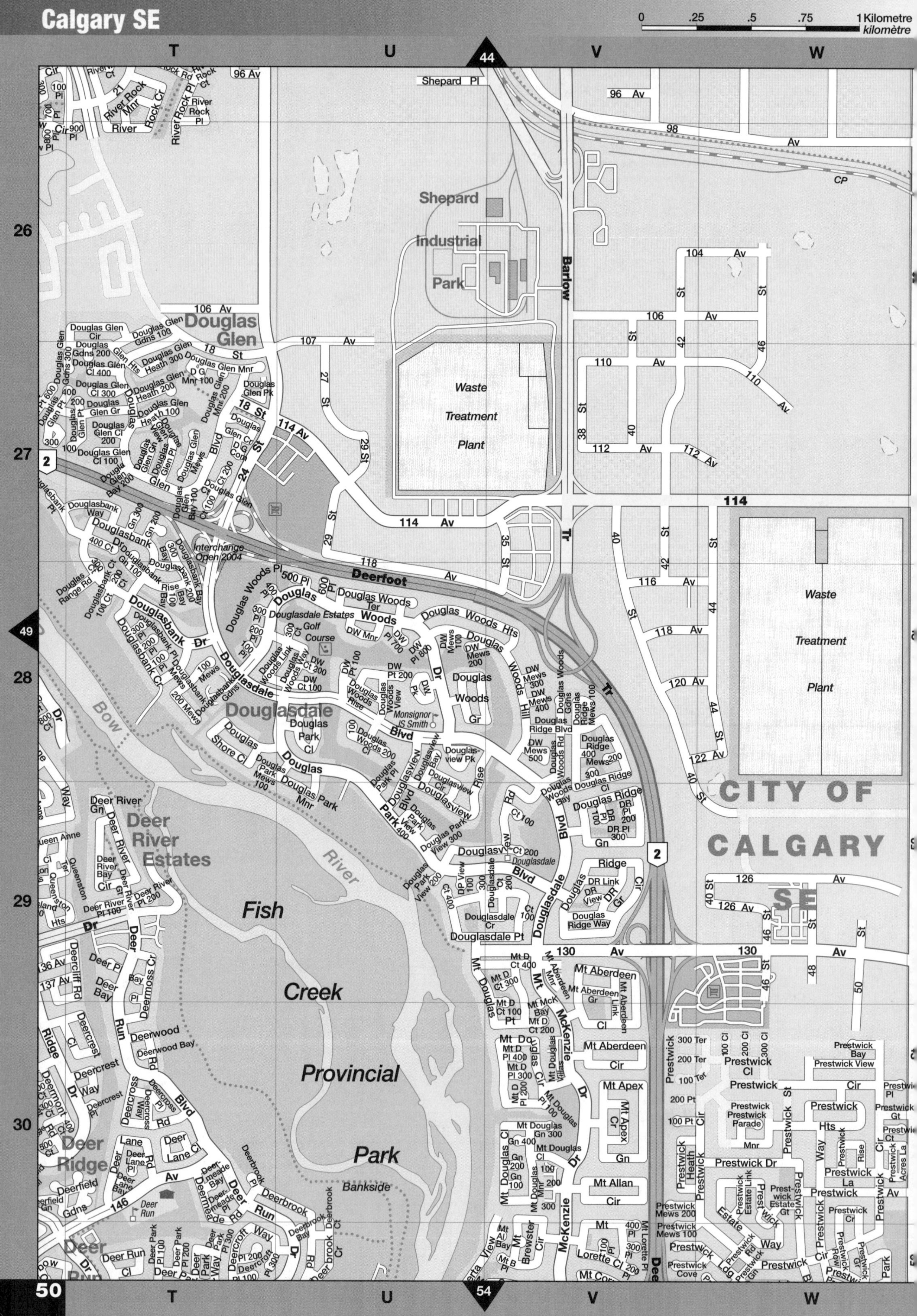

0   .25   .5   .75   1 Kilometre
kilomètre

T   U   **44**   V   W

Shepard Pl

96 Av

Shepard

Industrial

Park

Barlow

98
Av

CP

104   Av

St   St

106   Av

42   St   46   St

110   Av   110
Av

38 St   40 St

112   Av   112 Av

26

106 Av

Douglas Glen   Douglas Glen Gdns 100
Douglas Glen Cir   Douglas Glen
Douglas Gdns 200   18 St
Douglas Glen Cl 400   Douglas Glen Heath 300   Douglas Glen Mnr
Douglas Glen Pt 500   Douglas Glen Cl 300   D G Mnr 100
Douglas Glen 400   Douglas Glen Heath 200   Douglas Glen Pk
Douglas Glen 200   18 St
Douglas Glen Cl 200   Douglas Glen
Douglas Glen Ct 300   Douglas Glen Cres
Douglas Glen Cl 100   Douglas Glen Pl   Douglas Glen Blvd   24 St
Douglasbank Pt   Douglas Glen Mews   Douglas Glen Bay 100   Douglas Glen

107 Av

114 Av

29 St   27 St

Waste

Treatment

Plant

114

27

2

Douglasbank Way   Douglasbank
Douglasbank Dr   Douglasbank Gr 100
Douglasbank 400 Ct   Douglasbank Rise 100   Douglasbank Crt 100
Douglas Range Rd   300 Mews 200   Douglasdale
Douglasbank Ct 100   200 Mews
Douglasbank Cr

29 St   35 St

114   Av

118   Av

Deerfoot   Av

40 St   42 St

116   Av

44 St

118   Av

Waste

Treatment

Plant

49

Douglas Woods Pl   500 Pl   600
Douglas   Douglas Woods Ter
Douglasbank Dr   Pl 300   Douglas   **Woods**
Douglasdale Estates   DW Mnr   Douglas Woods Hts
Douglas   Golf   DW   Pt 700
Dr   200   Course   DW Mnr 100
Douglas Link   DW   Pt 600   Douglas Woods
Douglas Woods Way   DW   Pt 100   Mews 100
100   DW Ct 200   DW Pk   DW Mews
Douglasdale   DW Ct 100   Douglas   Douglas Woods Gdns

28

Dr   Douglas   Woods Rise   Douglas   Woods Hill
Douglasdale Blvd   Douglas Woods 200   Woods   DW Mews 400
Douglasdale   W Ct 100   **Blvd**   Gr   Douglas Ridge Blvd   Douglas Ridge Mews 100
Douglasdale   Monsignor IS Smith   DW Mews 500   Douglas Ridge
Douglas   Douglas Park Cl   Douglasview Pk   Mews 200   300
Douglas   Shore Cl   Douglas Park Mews 100   Douglas Park Mnr   Douglasview Bay   Douglas Ridge
Douglas Park   Douglasview   Douglas Ridge Blvd
Douglasview   Blvd   Gn   Douglas Ridge

CITY OF

40 St

126   Av

CALGARY

Deer River Gn   Deer River
Deer River Bay   Deer River   Douglasview   Rd   DR Pl 100
Queen Anne   Deer River   Douglas Park View 300   Ct 100   DR Pl 200
Queenston   Deer River Cir   Douglas Park View 400   Blvd   DR Pl 300
Queenston   Deer River Pl 100   Park View 200   Douglasdale   Ridge
Queenston   Deer River Pl 200   Douglasv   Blvd   DR Link
Hts   Douglas Park View 200   Douglasdale   DR View Gt   Cir
Fish   Douglas Park View 100   Douglasdale Cr   Douglas Ridge Way

S E

126   Av

46 St   48 St   50 St

29

Dr   Deer   Douglasdale Pt   **130**   Av   **130**   Av
36 Av   Deer Pl   Mt D Ct 400
137 Av   Deer Bay   Mt Douglas   Mt D Ct 300   Mt Aberdeen
Deercliff Rd   Deer Bay   Mt McK Bay   Mt Aberdeen Gr   Mt Aberdeen Link
Deercrest Rd   Deerwood   Mt Do Ct 100   Mt Douglas Villas   Mt Aberdeen Cl

Creek

Deerwood Bay   Mt D Ct 200   Mt Aberdeen   Cir   Prestwick 300 Ter   Prestwick Bay
Deercrest Way   Mt Do Pl 400   Mt Douglas Cl   Prestwick View
100 Cl   200 Cl   300 Cl

Ridge   Deermont   Deercross Rd   Mt D Pl 100   Mt Aberdeen   Prestwick 300 Ter   Prestwick Cl
Deercross   Mt D Pl 200   Mt Douglas Cres   200 Ter
Blvd   Deercross Pl   Mt Apex   100 Ter   Prestwick St   Prestwick Cir
200 Pt   Prestwick   Prestwick Hts

Provincial

Mt Apex Cr   Prestwick Parade   Prestwick Way   Prestwick Rise

30

Deer   Deer Cres   Deer Lane   Mt Douglas Gn 300   100 Pt   200 Pt   Prestwick
Ridge   Deerfield   Deer Lane Pl   Mt Douglas Cl   Prestwick Heath   Prestwick Dr
Deerbrook   Mt Douglas Gn 400   Prestwick Estate

Park

146   Av   Deer Run   Bankside   Mt Douglas Gn 200   Prestwick Mews 200   Prestwick
Deermeade Pl   Mt Douglas Gn 100   Prestwick Estate Link   Prestwick Mews 100   La
Deer   Deermeade Bay   Prestwick Estate Gt   Prestwick Acres La
Deer Park Run   Deerbrook   Mt Al Bay   Mt Brewster Cir   Prestwick Cove

50

Deer   Deer Park Pl 100   Deercroft Way   Mt Al   Mt B   Mt B Bay
Deer Dr   Deer Park Pl 200   Deerbrook Cr   Mt Al Pl   Lorette Ct   Prestwick
Run   Deer Park Pl 300   Mt Co

McKenzie

Dr

T   U   **54**   V   W

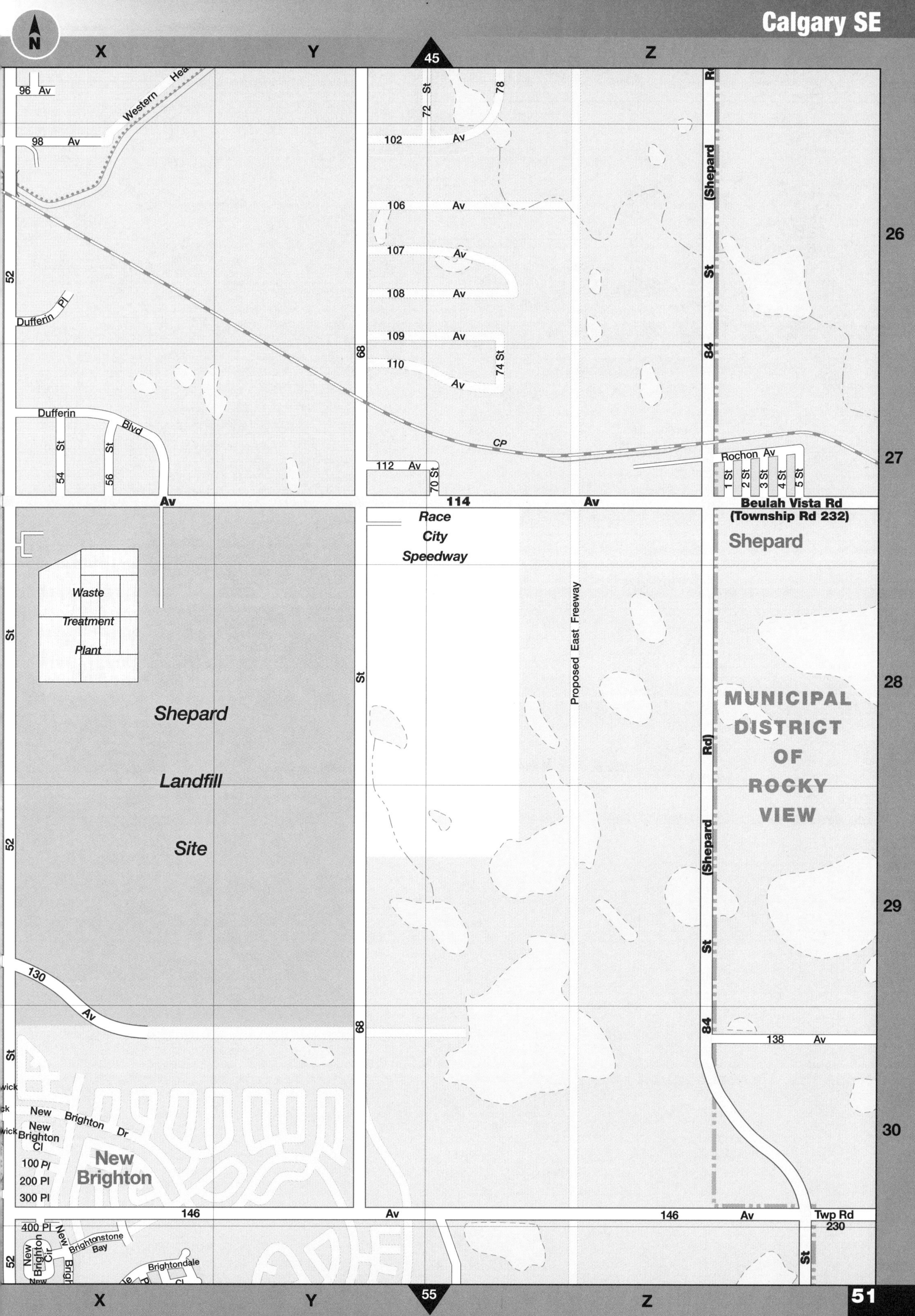

N

X   Y   45   Z

96 Av

Western Hea

98 Av

72 St

78

102   Av

106   Av   **26**

52

Dufferin Pl

107   Av

108   Av

74 St

68

109   Av

110

Av

Dufferin   Blvd

54 St

56 St

CP

Rochon Av   **27**

112 Av

70 St

1 St
2 St
3 St
4 St
5 St

Av   114   Av

Beulah Vista Rd
(Township Rd 232)

Race
City
Speedway

Shepard

St

St

Waste

Treatment

Plant

Proposed East Freeway

MUNICIPAL   **28**

DISTRICT

Shepard

OF

Landfill

Rd)

ROCKY

52

Site

(Shepard

VIEW

130

St

29

Av

68

St

84

138   Av

New Brighton Dr

wick
New
k   New
wick Brighton Cl

30

100 Pl
St
200 Pl

New
Brighton

300 Pl

146   Av   146   Av

Twp Rd
230

400 Pl

New Brighton Cir

Brightonstone
Bay

Brightondale

52

St

X   Y   55   Z

48

CITY OF
CALGARY
SW

MUNICIPAL
DISTRICT
OF
FOOTHILLS

Evergreen

Millrise

Shawnessy

Bridlewood

Somerset

Spruce
Meadows
Equestrian
Centre

L   M   N   O

Park
Fish
Creek
Provincial
Park
Midnapore
Sundance
Shawville
Heron Flats
Lake Midnapore
Lake Sundance
Lake Chaparral
Lake Sikome
CITY OF CALGARY SE
Macleod Tr
Sun Valley Blvd
Marquis of
Sheriff King Rd
Midlake Blvd
Midpark Blvd
Bow Bottom Tr
Chaparral Blvd
194 Av
190 Av
Shawnessy Centre
Midnapore Mall
South Fish Creek Recreation Centre
Fish Creek Interpretive Centre
Bow Valley Ranch
To Okotoks - Page 76 & High River - Page 77

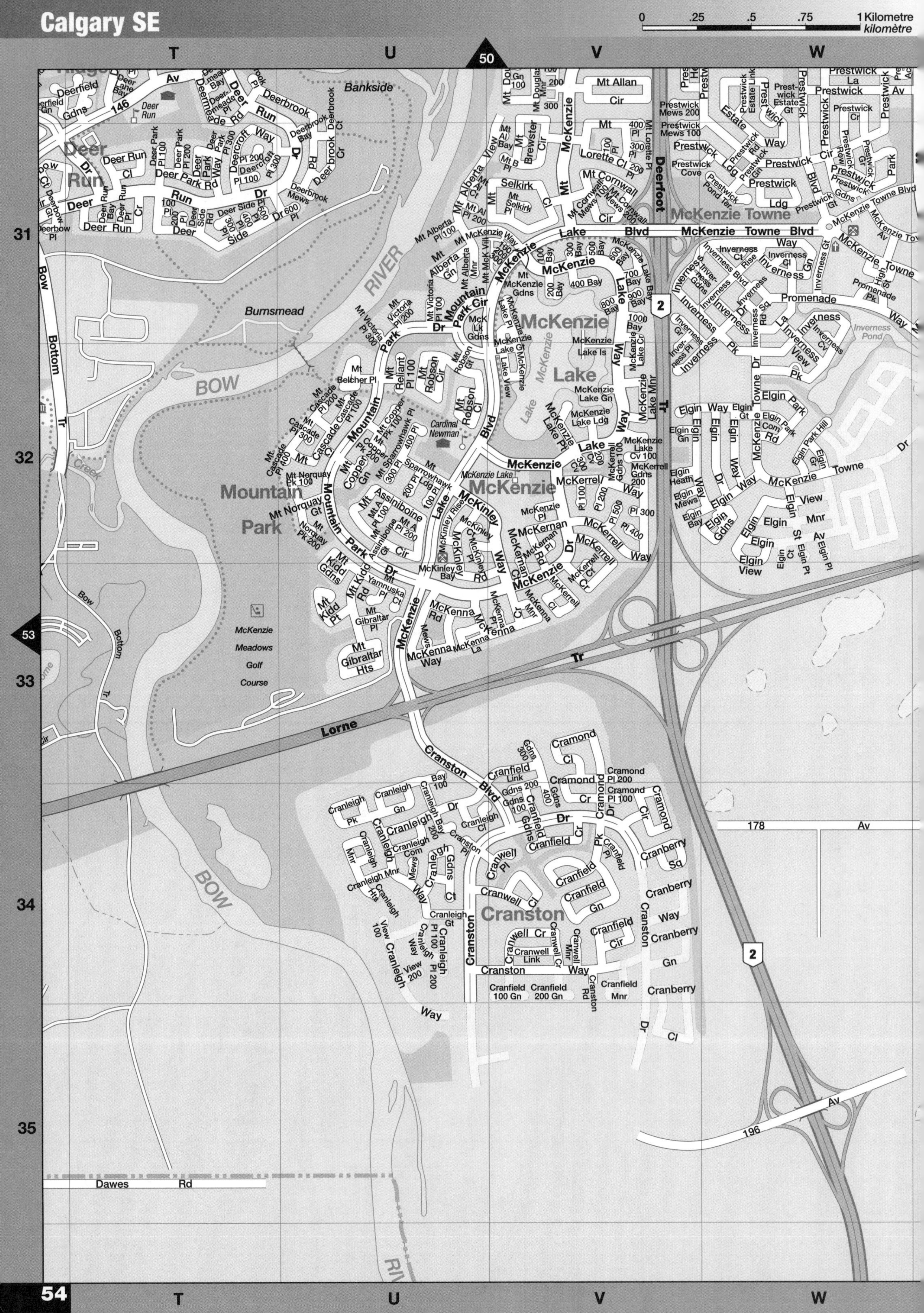
0 .25 .5 .75 1 Kilometre
kilomètre
T U V W
50
53
31
32
33
34
35
Deer Run
Bankside
Burnsmead
BOW RIVER
Mountain Park
McKenzie Lake
McKenzie Towne
McKenzie Meadows Golf Course
Cardinal Newman
Cranston
Lorne Tr
Deerfoot Tr
Bow Bottom Tr
McKenzie Lake Blvd
McKenzie Towne Blvd
Inverness Pond
178 Av
196 Av
Dawes Rd
Prestwick
Elgin
Cranfield
Cranleigh
Cranberry
Cramond
Cranwell

T U V W

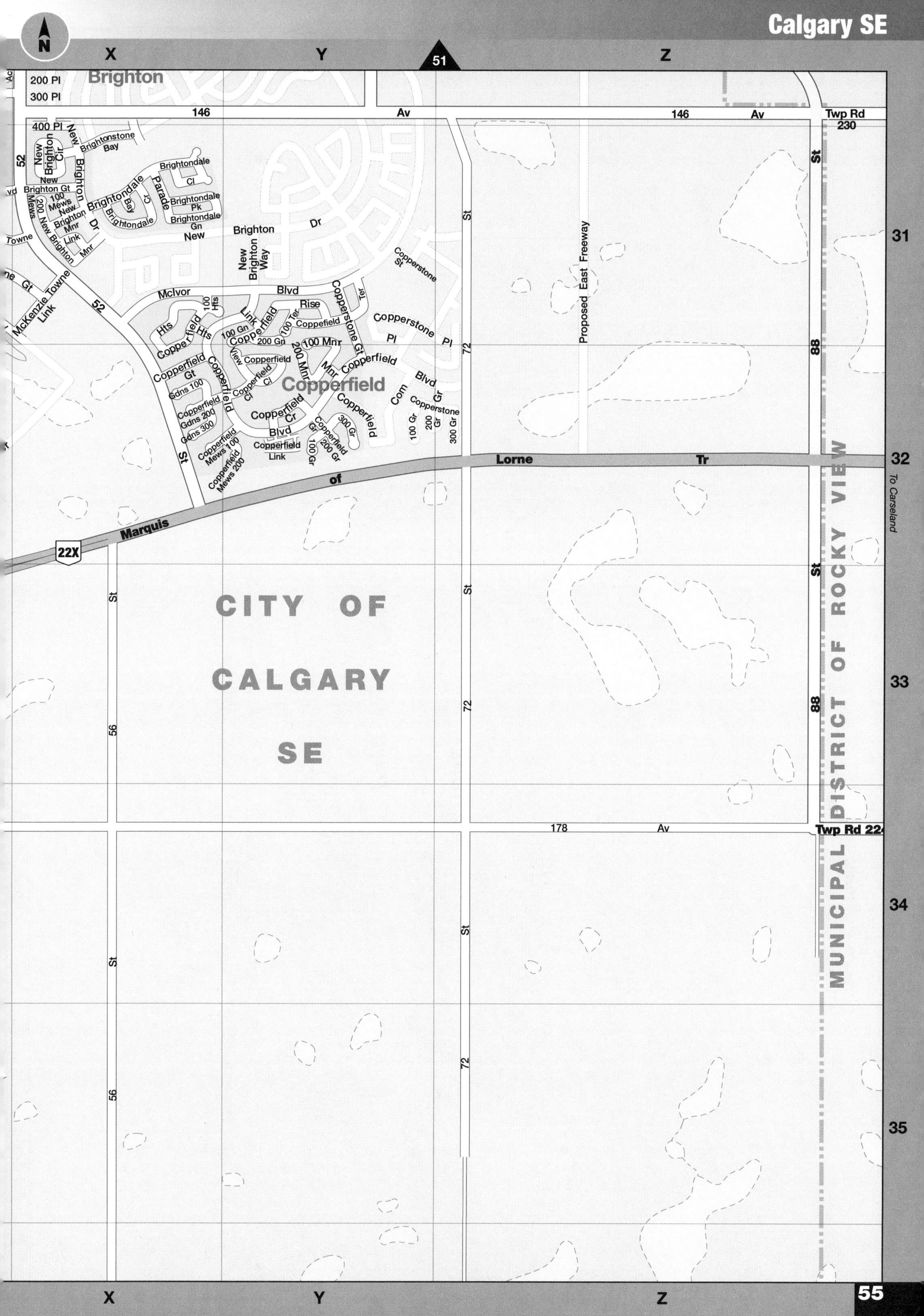
N
X
Y
51
Z
Brighton
200 Pl
300 Pl
146
Av
146
Av
Twp Rd
230
400 Pl
New Brighton Cir
New Brighton
Brightonstone Bay
52
Brightondale Cl
Brightondale Parade
Brightondale Pk
Brightondale Gn
New
Brighton Gt
100 Mews
New Brighton Mnr
200 New Brighton Mews
Link
Mnr
Brightondale Bay
Cr
Dr
New
Brighton
Dr
Towne
New Brighton Way
Copperstone St
Copperstone
McKenzie Towne Link
Gt
52
McIvor
Blvd
100 Hts
Rise
Copperstone Gt
Ter
Link
Copperfield
100 Ter
Coppefield
Copperstone
Pl
Pl
Hts
Hts
100 Gn
Copperfield
200 Gn
100 Mnr
200 Mnr
Copperfield
Copperfield View
Copperfield Cl
Copperfield Gt
Gdns 100
Copperfield Gdns 200
Gdns 300
Copperfield
Copperfield Cl
Copperfield
Mnr
Blvd
Gr
Com
Copperstone
100 Gr
200 Gr
300 Gr
Copperfield Cr
Copperfield
300 Gr
Blvd
Copperfield Link
100 Gr
200 Gr
Copperfield
Copperfield Mews 100
Copperfield Mews 200
St
72
St
Proposed East Freeway
St
88
Lorne
Tr
of
Marquis
22X
To Carseland
CITY OF
CALGARY
SE
St
56
St
72
St
88
MUNICIPAL DISTRICT OF ROCKY VIEW
178
Av
Twp Rd 224
St
St
72
56
31
32
33
34
35
X
Y
Z

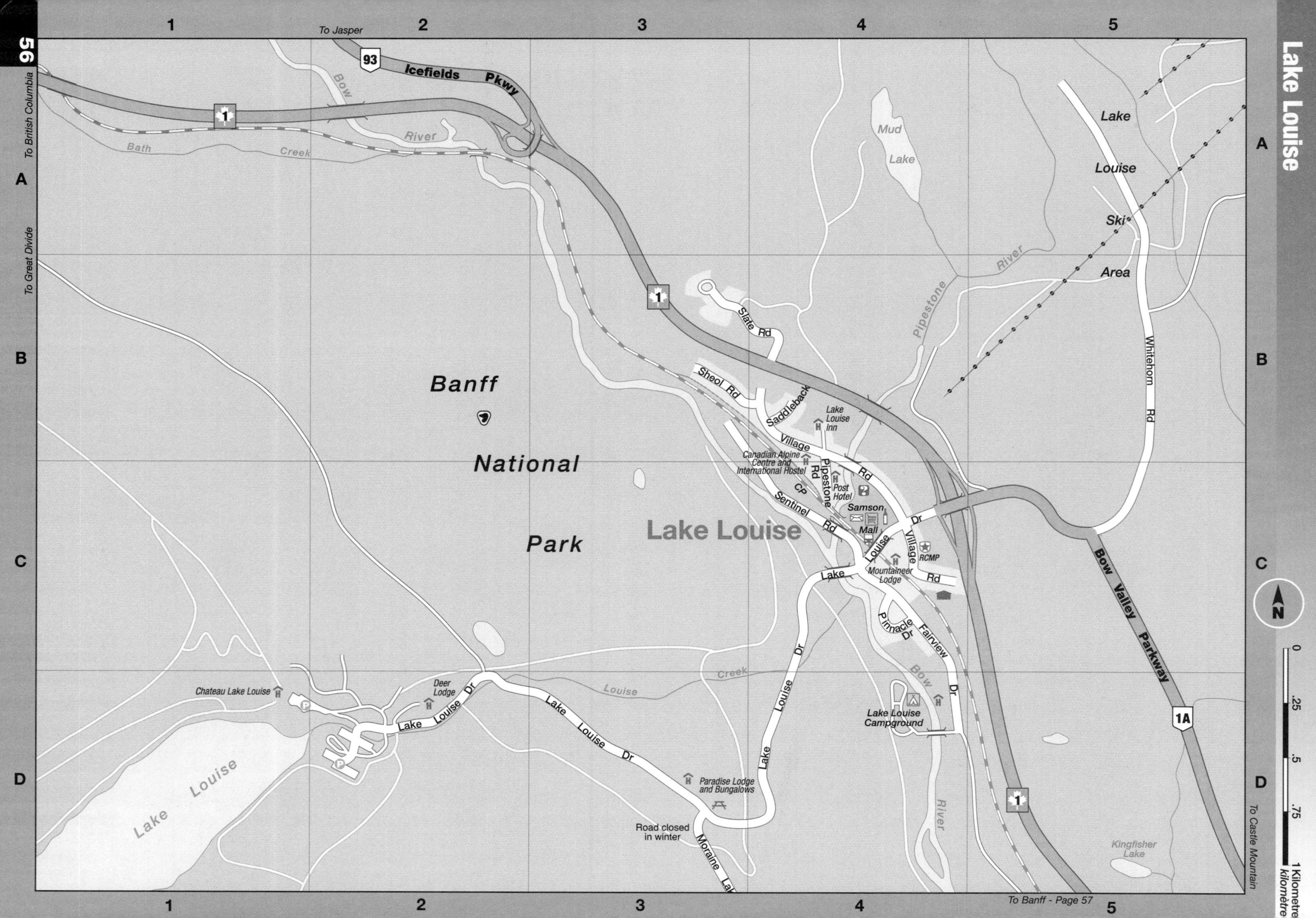

0   .25   .5   .75   1 Kilometre
kilomètre

To Castle Mountain

Whitehorn   Rd

Lake Louise Ski Area

Bow Valley Parkway

1A

Kingfisher Lake

River

To Banff – Page 57

Pipestone River

Mud Lake

RCMP

Village   Dr

Fairview   Dr

Bow

Pinnacle Dr

Mountaineer Lodge

River

Lake Louise Campground

Louise   Rd

Samson Mall

Lake Louise Inn

Pipestone   Rd

Post Hotel

Sentinel   Rd

Village   Rd

CP

Canadian Alpine Centre and International Hostel

Saddleback   Rd

Slate   Rd

Sheol   Rd

Lake   Louise   Dr

Lake

Lake Louise

Creek

Louise

Paradise Lodge and Bungalows

Moraine   Lak

Road closed in winter

Banff

National

Park

Icefields   Pkwy

Bow

River

Lake   Louise   Dr

Deer Lodge

93

To Jasper

Bath

Creek

Chateau Lake Louise

Lake   Louise

To Great Divide

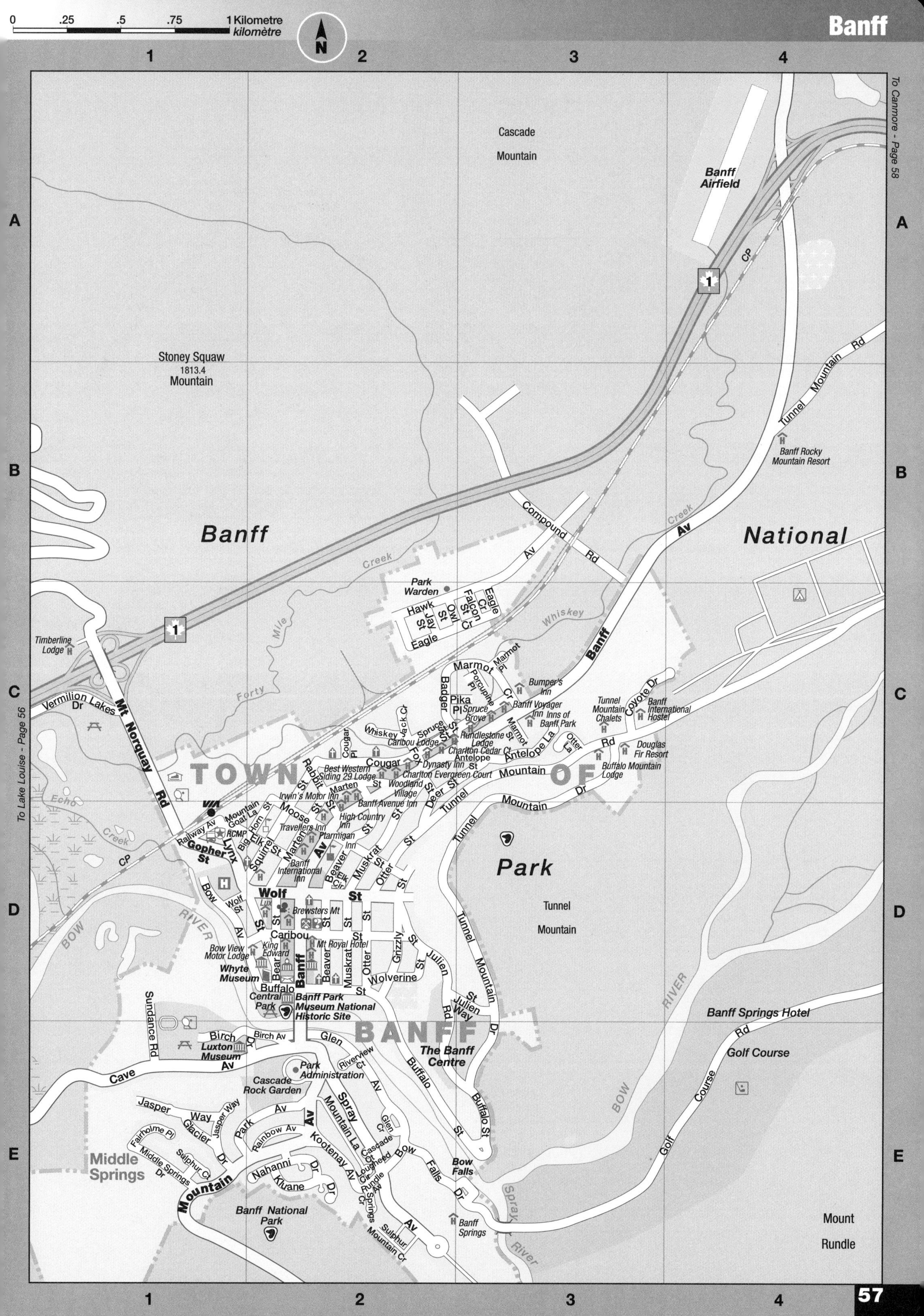

0 .25 .5 .75 1 Kilometre
kilomètre

N

1   2   3   4

A

Cascade
Mountain

Banff
Airfield

CP

B

Stoney Squaw
1813.4
Mountain

Banff

Creek

Compound Rd

Av

Banff Rocky
Mountain Resort

Tunnel Mountain Rd

National

B

Timberline
Lodge

Vermilion Lakes
Dr

Mt Norquay Rd

Forty Mile

Creek

Whiskey

Creek

Av

Banff Av

Park
Warden

Eagle Cr
Falcon Cr
Owl St
Jay St
Hawk St
Eagle St

Marmot Pl
Marmot Cr

Porcupine

Badger St

Pika Pl

Spruce
Grove

Bumper's Inn

Banff Voyager
Inn Inns of
Banff Park

Marmot St

Coyote Dr

Tunnel
Mountain
Chalets

Banff
International
Hostel

C

C

Echo

Creek

CP

Whiskey Jack Ck

Caribou Lodge

Spruce St

Rundlestone
Lodge

Charlton Cedar Ct

Antelope La

Antelope St

Otter La

Rd

Douglas
Fir Resort

Buffalo Mountain
Lodge

TOWN

Cougar

Cougar Pt

Fox St

Deer St

Dynasty Inn

Charlton Evergreen Court

Woodland
Village

Mountain Av

Mountain Dr

OF

Rabbit St

Best Western
Siding 29 Lodge

Marten St

Tunnel St

Mountain

PARK

VIA

Railway Av

Mountain Goat La

Irwin's Motor Inn

Moose St

Banff Avenue Inn

Deer St

D

Gopher St

Lynx St

RCMP

Big Horn St

Squirrel St

Marten St

Travellers Inn

High Country
Inn

Ptarmigan
Inn

Beaver St

Muskrat St

Otter St

Tunnel Mountain Dr

Tunnel
Mountain

Park

Tunnel

Mountain

D

H

Banff
International
Inn

Elk St

Beaver Cir

Grizzly St

Jullen St

RIVER

BOW

Wolf St

Lux

Caribou St

Brewsters Mt

King Edward

Mt Royal Hotel

Beaver St

Muskrat St

Otter St

Wolverine St

Jullen Rd

Jullen Way

RIVER

BOW

Banff Springs Hotel

Bow View
Motor Lodge

Whyte
Museum

Bear St

Banff

Av

Banff Park
Museum National
Historic Site

Buffalo
Central
Park

Buffalo St

Golf Course

Golf Course Rd

Golf Course

E

Sundance Rd

Birch
Luxton
Museum

Birch Av

Av

Park
Administration

Cascade
Rock Garden

Glen

Riverview Ct

Spray Av

Buffalo Av

BANFF

The Banff
Centre

E

Cave

Jasper Way

Glacier Dr

Jasper Way

Park Dr

Rainbow Av

Mountain La

Kootenay Av

Spray Av

Glen Av

Cascade Ct

Lougheed Ct

Bow Falls

Bow
Falls Dr

Banff
Springs

Mount

Rundle

Fairholme Pl

Middle Springs Dr

Sulphur Ct

Nahanni Dr

Kluane Dr

Rundle Av

Sulphur Mountain Cr

Spray River

Middle
Springs

Mountain Av

Banff National
Park

To Canmore - Page 58

To Lake Louise - Page 56

0 .25 .5 .75 1 Kilometre
kilomètre

To Banff - Page 57

Harvie Heights

Grotto Rd
Rundle Dr
Spray Dr
Bow River Rd
Rundle Ridge Chalets
Birch Av
Cascade Dr
Stockade Log Cabins
Banff Boundary Lodge
Gateway Inn
Bow Cr
River Rd
Cedar Av
Access Rd
Dogwood Av

A

DISTRICT OF BIGHORN EAST

Bow
River

Harvie Heights Rd

B

KANANASKIS COUNTRY

Banff Trail

Canmore Golf Course & Curling Club

Seasonal Campground
2801
Ray McBride St
Best Western Pocaterra Inn
Rundle Mountain
Chateau Canmore
Westridge Country Inn
Palliser Tr
Bow Valley Av
Akai Motel
A-1 Motel
Canmore Ldg
Rocky Mtn
Best Western Green Gables Inn
Teepee Town
Industrial St
1A

Larch
Riverside
900 Pl
800 Larch Pl
700 Larch
600 Larch
500 Larch
400 Larch Pl
300 Larch Pl
200 Larch Pl
100 Larch Pl
Larch Pl
Larch Ct
Larch Pl
1000 Larch
1100 Larch
Canmore Comm Ctr
Woodside La
11 Av
1737
Loop
17 St
Canmore Coll 1808
17
16 St
12 Av
11 Av
Lions Park
Fairholm
16 St
Pinewood
Aspen Ind Park
Canmore Station
Howard Johnson
15
14
13 St
Birchwood Cr
14 Av
1 Av
Spring Cr
Spring Creek Ct
13 St
12A St
12 St
11 St
Car Regen
Bear Ct
Bow River Seniors Lodge
13 St
Mt Rundle
Railway Av
Paint Box Ldg
Mallard Alley
Policeman's
Engine Bridge
Riverview Park
11
Mt Peechee Pl
10 Av
9 Av
10
St
9 St
Centennial Mus
Canmore Mus
9 St
Bow Valley
Riverview Pl
Main St (8 St)
Bridge Rd
Rundle Dr
River Rd
Historic RC Barracks &
(7 St) Veteran's Way
Our Lady of Snows
Centennial Park
Lawrence Grassi
6
5
4
2A St
8 St
7 St

C

D

E

Stadium
Canmore Nordic Centre
Rundle Forebay

MUNICIPAL DISTRICT OF BIGHORN WEST

Spray Trail
Dorien
742
Smith

Evergreen Cir
Squirrel Ct
Ashley Ct
MacDonald Pl
Three St
100 Grassi
200 Grassi
300 Grassi
St Barbara's
Mineside
Rundle Plant La
Sisters Dr
Rundle Ct
Rundle Dr
Three Sisters Dr
Riverside
Bridge
River
Millennium

F

Rundleview Estates
Deer Dr
Wilson
Rundleview Dr
Olympic Dr
China Ct
Patrician St
Prendergast Pl
Spray Lakes Rd
Loop
Prospect Tr
Prospect Rise
Prospect Ct
Prospect His
Prospect
Prospect Ct

Creek
Canmore

Quarry Lake

Carey Dr
Padmore
Carey
McNeill
Morris
Van Horne
Walker
Walker

G

Grassi Lake

Peaks of Grassi
Lawrence
Wilson
Kamenka Gn
Three Sisters
The Village
Grassi Peaks Dr
Ridge
Sheilan
Way
91

H

1   2   3   4

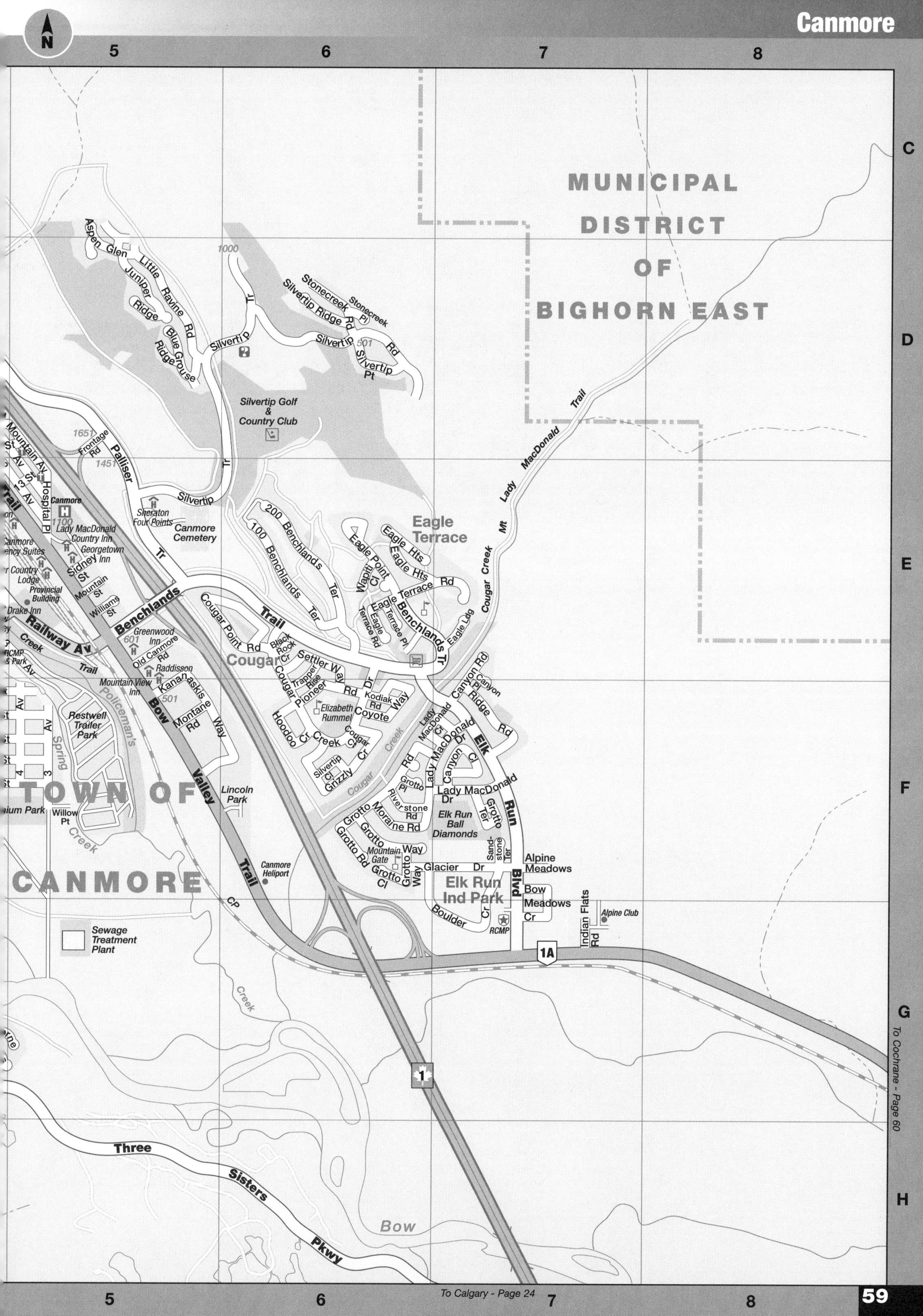
5
6
7
8
C
D
E
F
G
H
MUNICIPAL DISTRICT OF BIGHORN EAST
TOWN OF CANMORE
Silvertip Golf & Country Club
Eagle Terrace
Canmore Cemetery
Sheraton Four Points
Lady MacDonald Country Inn
Georgetown Inn
Provincial Building
Drake Inn
Greenwood Inn
Old Canmore Rd
Raddisson
Mountain View Inn
Restwell Trailer Park
Lincoln Park
Willow Pt
Canmore Heliport
Sewage Treatment Plant
Elizabeth Rummel
Elk Run Ball Diamonds
Elk Run Ind Park
RCMP
Alpine Club
Alpine Meadows
Bow Meadows Cr
Indian Flats Rd
Mt Lady MacDonald Trail
Cougar Creek
Benchlands Trail
Bow Valley Trail
Palliser Tr
Silvertip Tr
Three Sisters Pkwy
Railway Av
Elk Run Blvd
Lady MacDonald Dr
Glacier Dr
Boulder Cr
Bow
1A
1
To Cochrane - Page 60

To Calgary - Page 24

0   .25   .5   .75   **1 Kilometre**
kilomètre

To Canmore - Page 59

1   **2**   **3**   **4**

To Rocky Mountain House

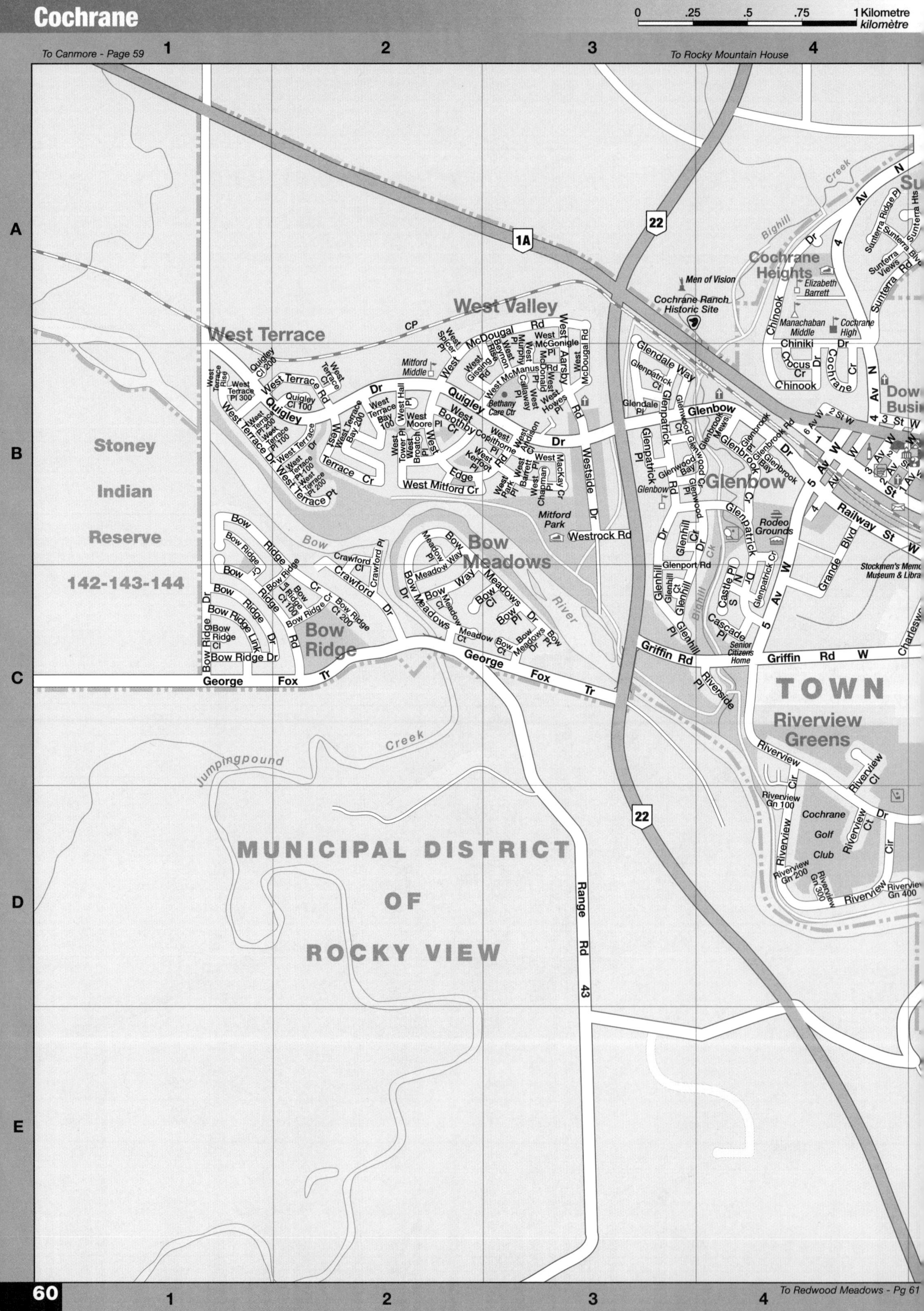

A

1A

Men of Vision

Cochrane Ranch
Historic Site

Cochrane
Heights

Elizabeth
Barrett

Sunterra Ridge Pl
Sunterra Hts
Sunterra
Views
Sunterra Blvd
Sunterra Rd

Chinook

Manachaban
Middle

Cochrane
High

Chiniki

Crocus
Cr

Cochrane

Av N

Dr

Chinook

Down
Busi

22

West Valley

West
Spur

CP

McDougal
Pl

West
McGonigle
Pl

West McManus
Pl

West
Callaway

West Aarsby
Rd
Rd
West
Murphy
Pl
Rd
West
Howes
Pl

McDougal Rd
West

West Terrace

West
Gissing Rise

West
Benyon

Bethany
Care Ctr

Quigley Cl 200

Quigley

West Terrace Rd

Quigley Cl 100

Quigley
Bay 100

West Terrace
Rise

West
Terrace

Dr

West Hall
Pl

West
Boothby

West
Moore
Pl

West
Copithorne

Johnston
Pl

West AC

Dr

Glendale Way

Glenpatrick
Ct

Glendale
Pl

Glenbow

Glenpatrick

Glenbrook Rd

Glenwood Mews
Glenwood Mews

Glenwood Glenwood

Glenbrook
Bay

Glenbrook

2 St W

3 St W

1
Av
W

Glenbow

B

Stoney

Indian

Reserve

142-143-144

West
Terrace
Pl 300

West
Terrace
Pl 200

West Terrace Dr

West
Terrace
T 100

West
Terrace Cr

West
Terrace
Pt

West
Terrace
Pl 200

West
Tower Pl

Dr

West Terrace
Bay 200

West
Broach

West
Kerfoot

West
Barrett

West
Park

MacKay Cr

Westside

West Mitford Cr

Dr

Glenpatrick
Pl

Glenwood
Rd

Glenbow Rd

Glenbow

Glenpatrick

Railway
St W

Av
W

Mitford
Park

Westrock Rd

Mitford
Middle

Bow

Bow Ridge

Bow Ridge Cl

Bow
Ridge

Crawford
Cl

Bow
Ridge Dr

Crawford Pl

Crawford
Dr

Bow
Meadows

Meadow Way

Bow
Meadows

Meadows Cr

Meadows
Pl

Bow
Meadows Dr

River

Rodeo
Grounds

Glenhill

Glenport Rd

Glenhill
Ct

Glenpatrick Cr

Glenhill
Ct

Castle Pl
S

Stockmen's Memo
Museum & Libra

Bow Ridge

Bow Ridge Cr

Bow Ridge Rd

Bow Ridge Ct 100

Bow Ridge Ct 200

Bow Ridge Link

Bow
Ridge
Cl

Bow Ridge Dr

Bow
Ridge

Meadows
Ct

Meadow
Ct

Bow
Meadow
Dr

Bow
Meadows
Pl

Bow
Meadows

Glenhill
Ct

Glenhill
Cr

Glenhill

Cascade
Pl

Senior
Citizens
Home

Griffin Rd

Bighill

C

George

Fox

Tr

George

Fox

Tr

Griffin   Rd   W

Riverview

Riverside

Charleswo

TOWN

Riverview
Greens

Creek

Jumpingpound

Riverview

Riverview
Gn 100

Cochrane
Golf
Club

Riverview Cir

Riverview
Gn 200

Riverview
Dr

Riverview
Ct

Riverview
Cir

Riverview
Gn 300

Riverview
Gn 400

MUNICIPAL DISTRICT

D

OF

ROCKY VIEW

Range Rd 43

22

E

1   **2**   **3**   **4**

To Redwood Meadows - Pg 61

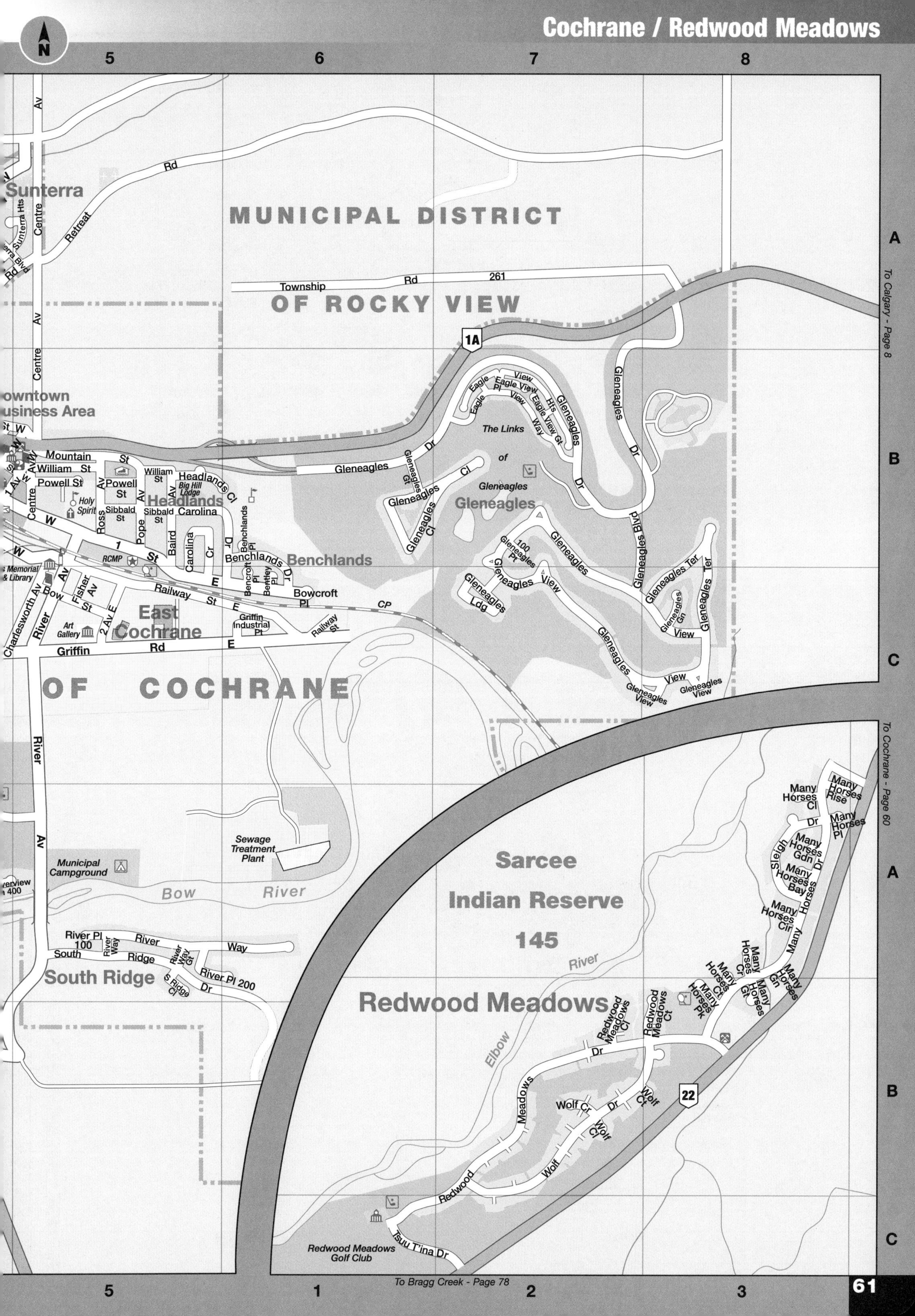

N

5   6   7   8

Sunterra

Rd

Sunterra Hts
Sunterra Blvd
Centre
Retreat

MUNICIPAL DISTRICT

Township Rd 261

OF ROCKY VIEW

1A

Downtown
Business Area

Eagle View
Eagle View Pl
Eagle View Gt
Eagle View Way
Eagle View Dr

Gleneagles Hts
Gleneagles Dr

The Links
of
Gleneagles

Gleneagles

Gleneagles Gt
Gleneagles Cl
Gleneagles Ct
Gleneagles Pt

Mountain
William St
Powell St
Holy Spirit
Big Hill Lodge
William St
Sibbald St
Headlands
Carolina
Headlands Cl
Headlands Pl
Benchlands Dr
Benchlands Pl

Centre Av W
1 Av W
Ross Av
Powell Av
Pope
Baird
Carolina
Cr
Carolina Dr

Gleneagles Dr

Gleneagles Blvd

Gleneagles Ter
Gleneagles Ter

100
Gleneagles Pt
Gleneagles View
Gleneagles Cir

RCMP
Benchlands
Bencroft Pl
Bentley Pl

Benchlands

Bowcroft Pl

Gleneagles Ldg

Gleneagles View

Memorial
& Library
Bow Av
Fisher St
River Av
2 Av E

Railway St
E

Griffin Industrial Pt
Railway St
CP

Art Gallery
East Cochrane

Charlesworth Av

Gleneagles View
Gleneagles View

OF COCHRANE

Griffin Rd
E

River Av

River

Sarcee
Indian Reserve
145

Many Horses Rise
Many Horses Cl
Many Horses Pl
Many Horses Dr
Many Horses Gdn
Many Horses Bay
Many Horses Cir

Sewage
Treatment
Plant

Municipal
Campground
Riverview 400

River
Bow

Many Horses Ct
Many Horses Cir
Many Horses Gt
Many Horses Cir

River Pl 100
River Way
South
River Way Gt
River Ridge
South Ridge
S Ridge Ct
River Pl 200
River Way Dr

River
Way

River

Redwood Meadows

Elbow

Redwood Meadows Ct
Redwood Meadows Ct
Meadows Pk

Meadows

Redwood Meadows Dr

Wolf Cr
Wolf Dr
Wolf Ct
Wolf Ct

22

Wolf

Redwood

Tsuu T'ina Dr

Redwood Meadows
Golf Club

5   1   2   3

A

B

C

A

B

C

To Calgary - Page 8

To Cochrane - Page 60

To Bragg Creek - Page 78

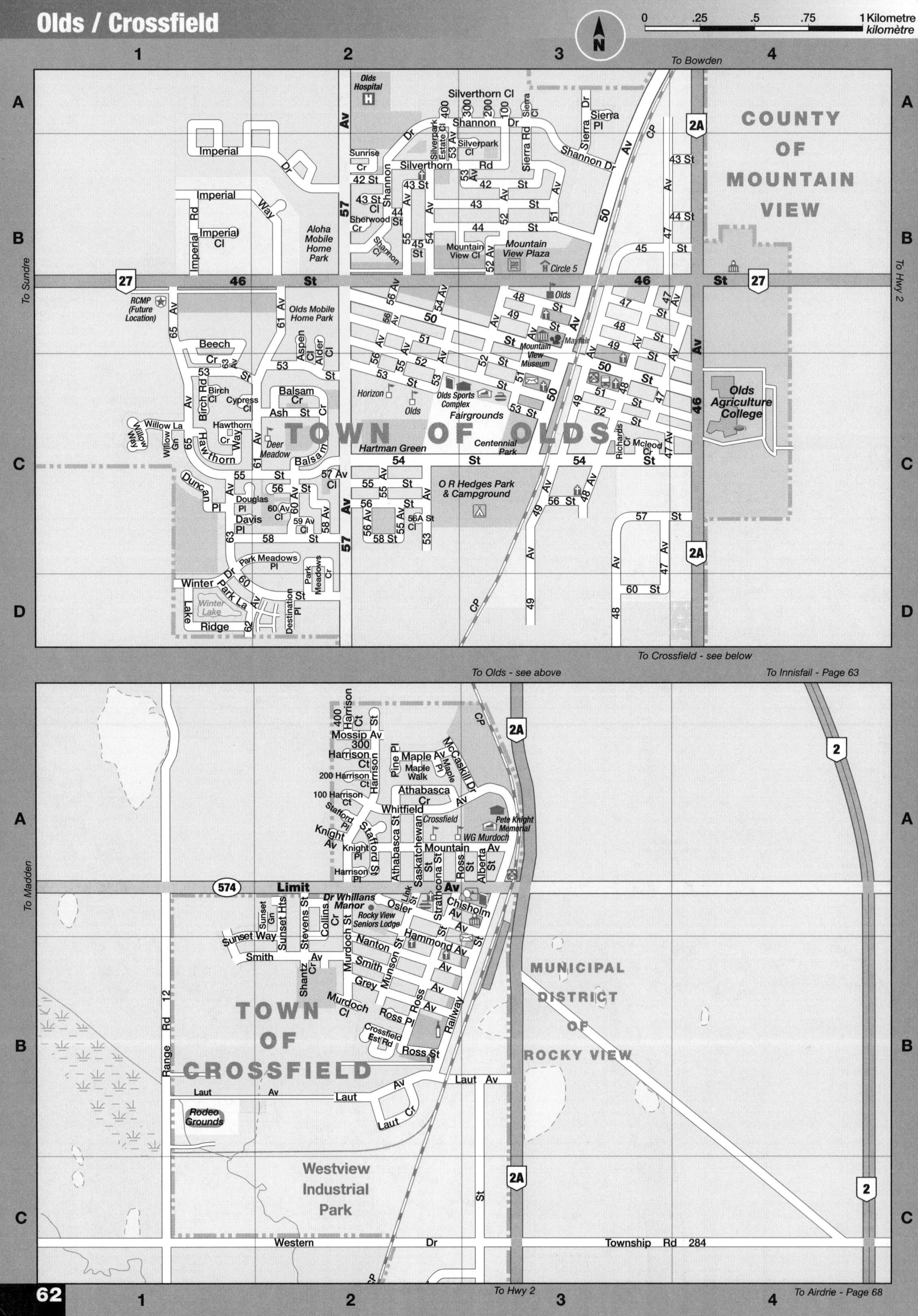

TOWN OF OLDS

COUNTY OF MOUNTAIN VIEW

Olds Hospital

Silverthorn Cl

RCMP (Future Location)

Aloha Mobile Home Park

Olds Mobile Home Park

Mountain View Plaza

Circle 5

Mountain View Museum

Olds Sports Complex

Fairgrounds

Centennial Park

Hartman Green

O R Hedges Park & Campground

Olds Agriculture College

Winter Lake

Park Meadows Pl

Deer Meadow

To Bowden

To Sundre

To Hwy 2

To Crossfield - see below

To Olds - see above

To Innisfail - Page 63

TOWN OF CROSSFIELD

MUNICIPAL DISTRICT OF ROCKY VIEW

Pete Knight Memorial

WG Murdoch

Dr Whillans Manor

Rocky View Seniors Lodge

Rodeo Grounds

Westview Industrial Park

Limit

Township Rd 284

Western Dr

To Madden

To Hwy 2

To Airdrie - Page 68

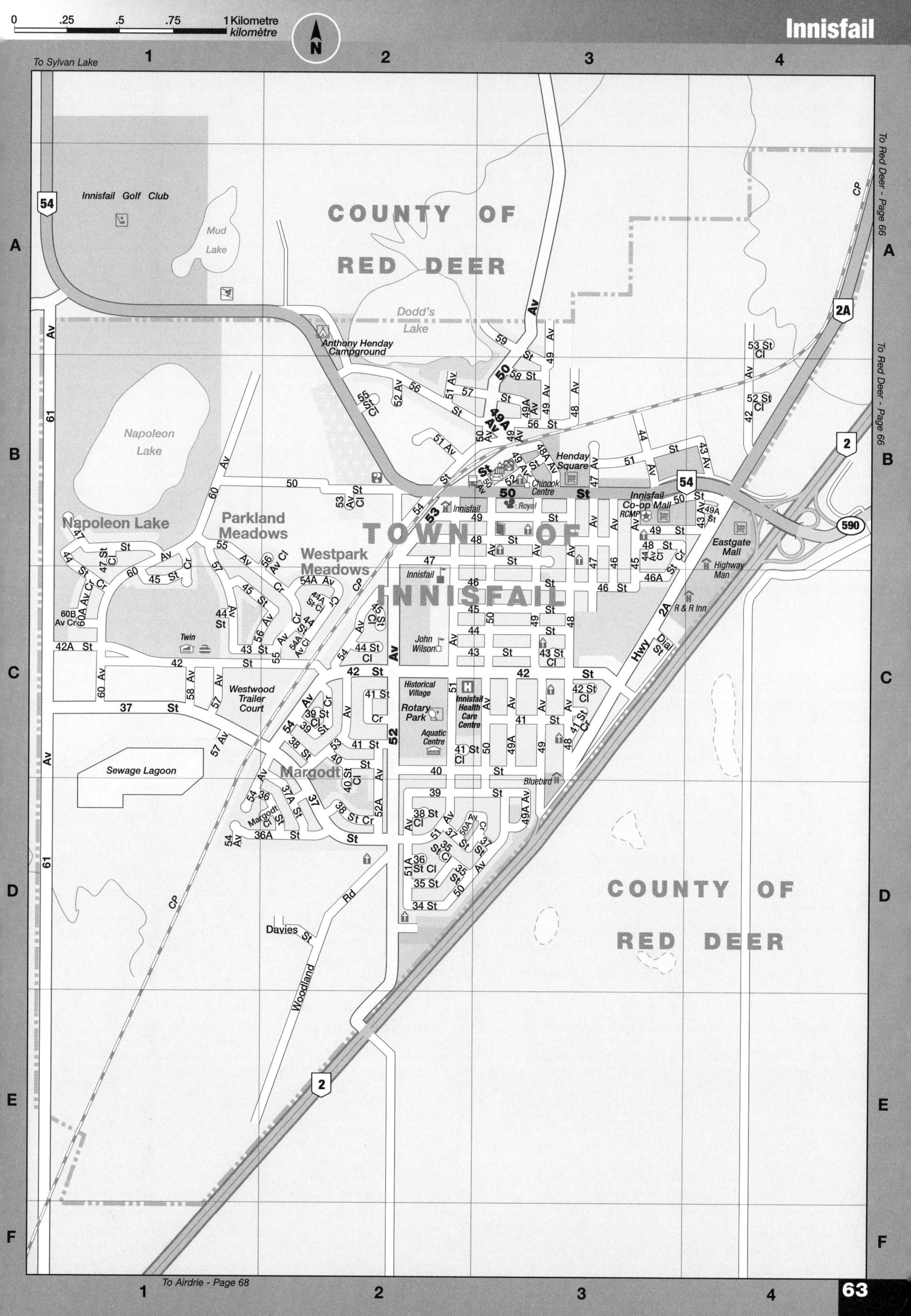

0 .25 .5 .75 1 Kilometre
kilomètre

N

1   2   3   4

To Sylvan Lake

54

Innisfail Golf Club

Mud Lake

COUNTY OF

RED DEER

Dodd's Lake

Anthony Henday Campground

2A

2

Napoleon Lake

Napoleon Lake

Parkland Meadows

Westpark Meadows

TOWN OF

INNISFAIL

Henday Square

Chinook Centre

Innisfail Co-op Mall

RCMP

Eastgate Mall

Highway Man

R & R Inn

54

590

Innisfail

Royal

Innisfail

John Wilson

Twin

Westwood Trailer Court

Historical Village

Rotary Park

Aquatic Centre

Innisfail Health Care Centre

H

Bluebird

Sewage Lagoon

Margodt

Davies St

Woodland Rd

CP

COUNTY OF

RED DEER

2

To Airdrie - Page 68

To Red Deer - Page 66

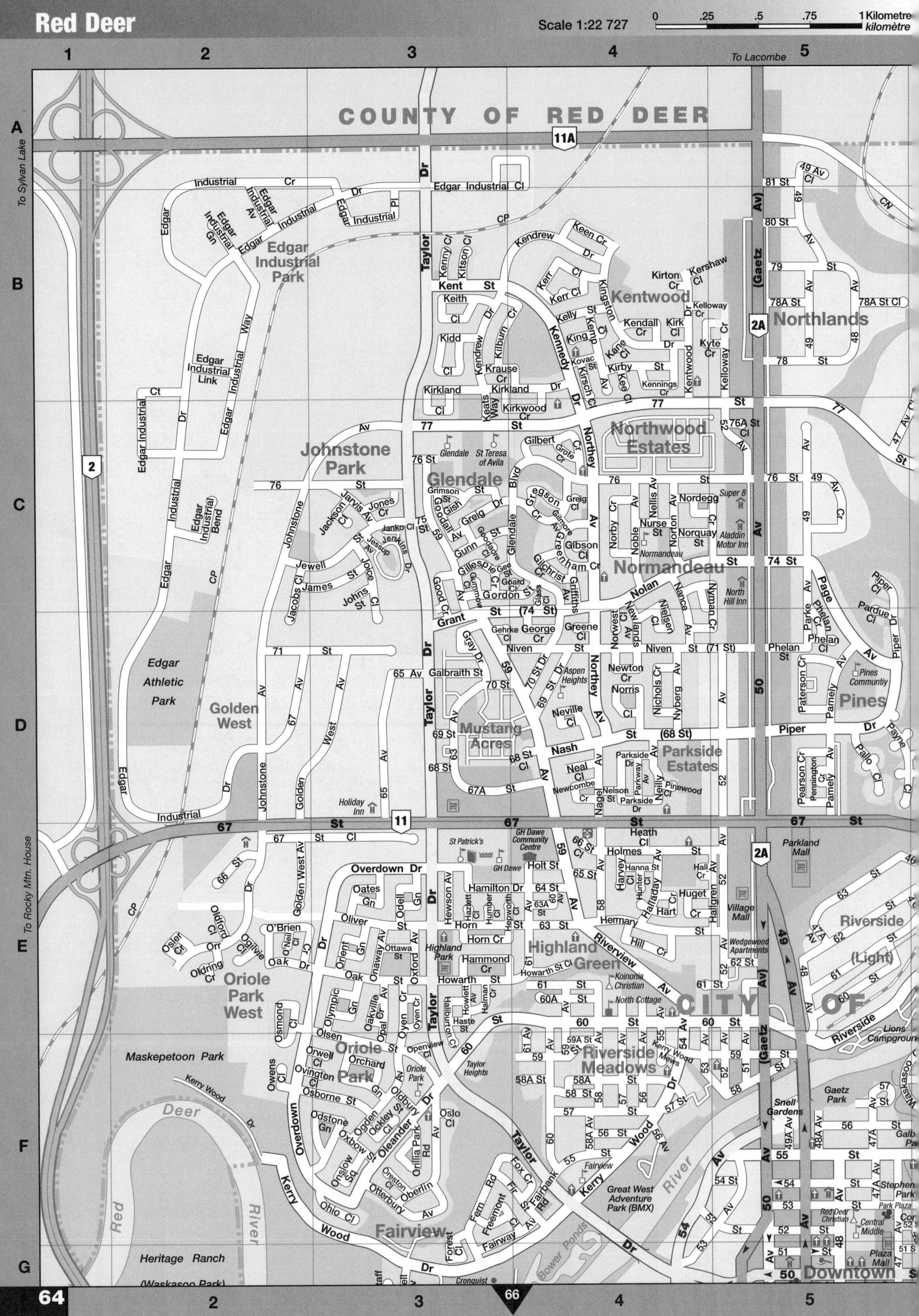

Red Deer

Scale 1:22 727

0 .25 .5 .75 1 Kilometre
kilomètre

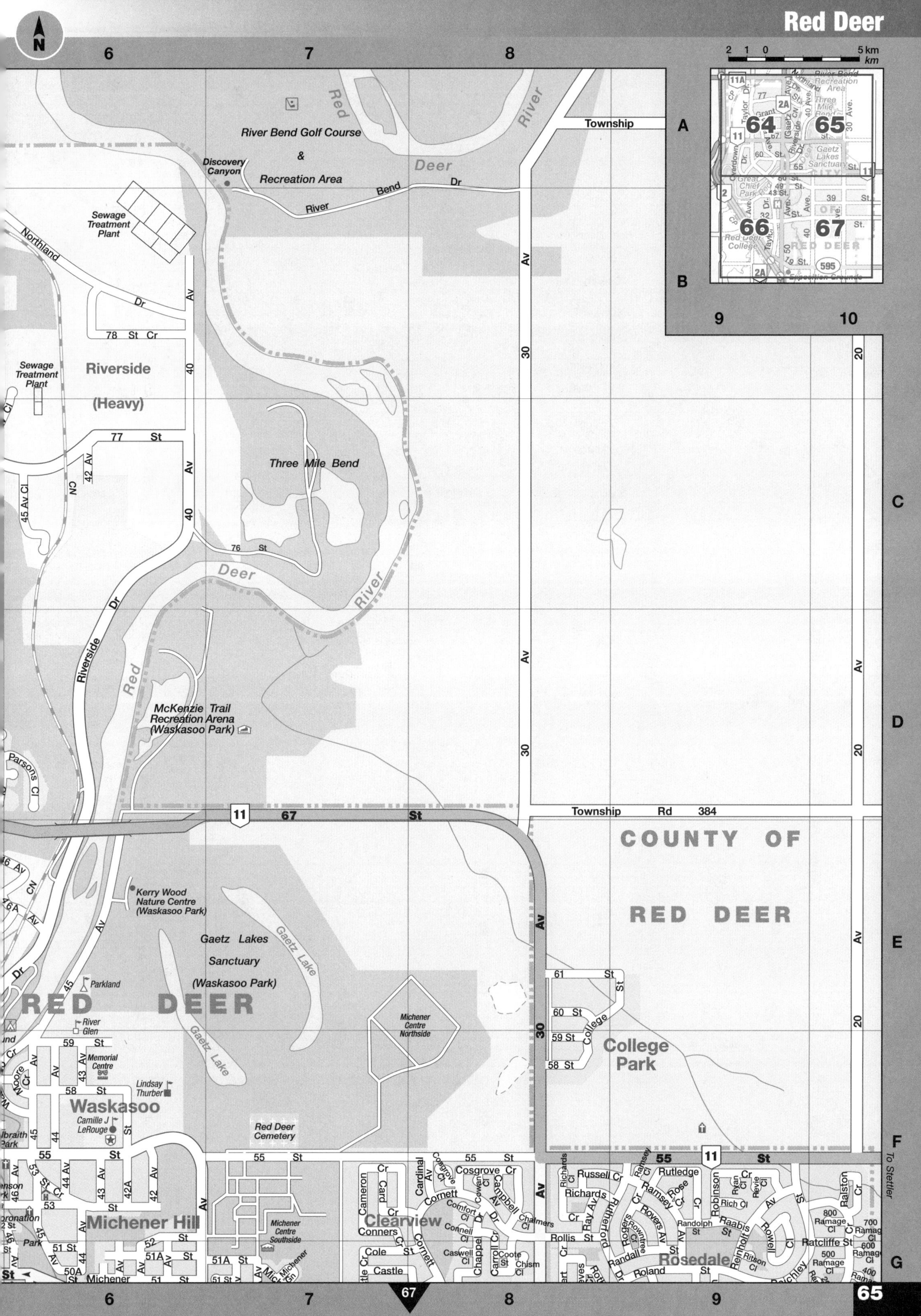

River Bend Golf Course
&
Recreation Area
Discovery Canyon
Sewage Treatment Plant
Northland Dr
78 St Cr
Riverside (Heavy)
77 St
Three Mile Bend
76 St
Riverside Dr
Red Deer River
McKenzie Trail Recreation Arena (Waskasoo Park)
Township Rd 384
COUNTY OF RED DEER
Kerry Wood Nature Centre (Waskasoo Park)
Gaetz Lakes Sanctuary (Waskasoo Park)
Gaetz Lake
Michener Centre Northside
RED DEER
College Park
Waskasoo
Red Deer Cemetery
Michener Hill
Michener Centre Southside
Clearview
Rosedale
55 St
67 St
30 Av
40 Av
20 Av
Township
To Stettler

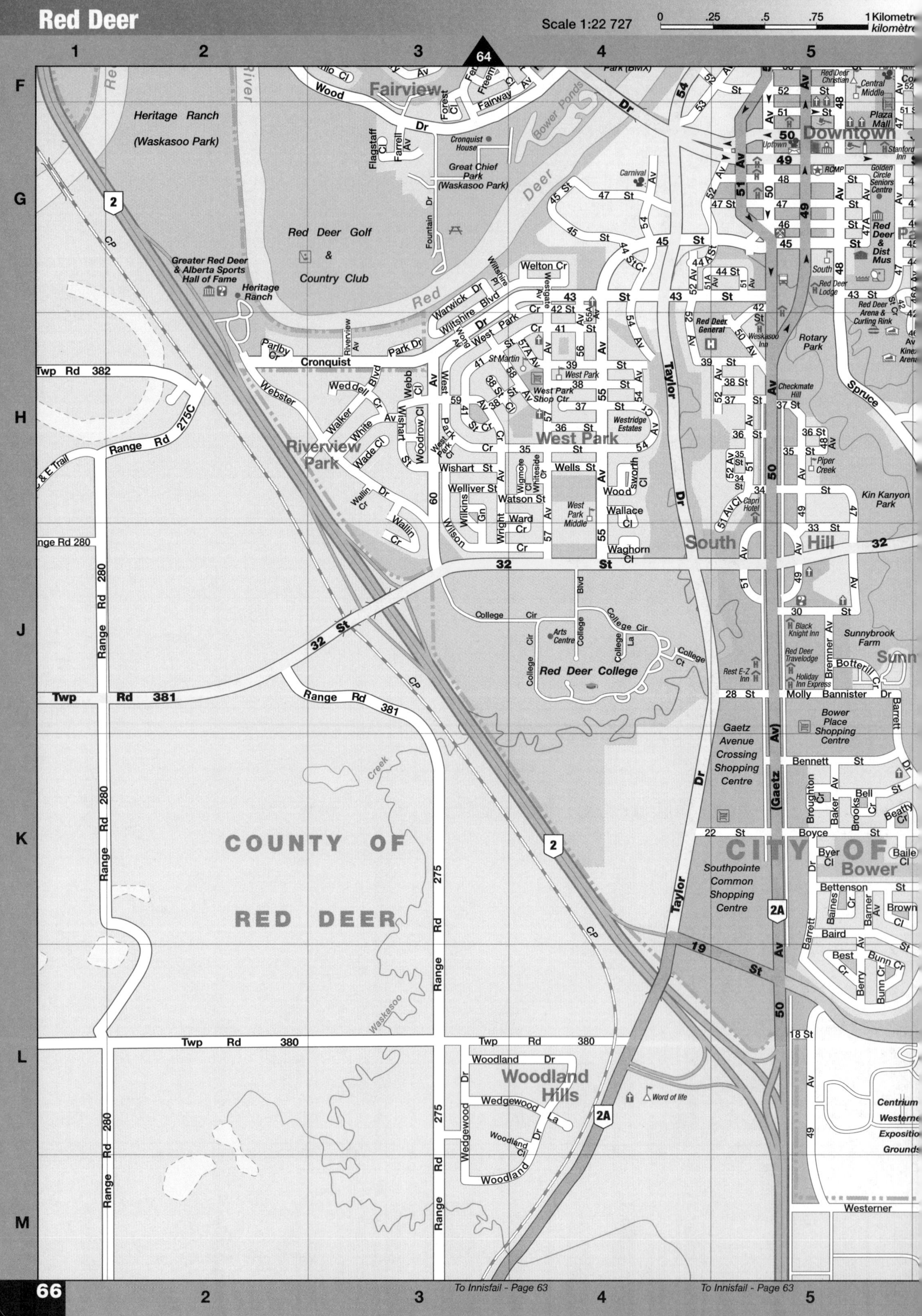
Scale 1:22 727
0 .25 .5 .75 1 Kilometre kilomètre
64
Heritage Ranch
(Waskasoo Park)
Red Deer Golf
&
Country Club
Greater Red Deer
& Alberta Sports
Hall of Fame
Heritage
Ranch
Fairview
Cronquist
House
Great Chief
Park
(Waskasoo Park)
Bower Ponds
Red Deer River
Carnival
Downtown
Red Deer
Christian
Central
Middle
Plaza
Mall
Uptown
RCMP
Stanford
Inn
Golden
Circle
Seniors
Centre
Red
Deer
&
Dist
Mus
South
Red Deer
Lodge
Red Deer
Arena &
Curling Rink
Rotary
Park
Red Deer
General
Weskasoo
Inn
Checkmate
Hill
Spruce
Riverview
Park
West Park
West Park
Shop Ctr
St Martin
Westridge
Estates
West
Park
Middle
Piper
Creek
Kin Kanyon
Park
Capri
Hotel
South
Hill
College Cir
Arts
Centre
Red Deer College
Black
Knight Inn
Red Deer
Travelodge
Holiday
Inn Express
Rest E-Z
Inn
Sunnybrook
Farm
Molly Bannister Dr
Gaetz
Avenue
Crossing
Shopping
Centre
Bower
Place
Shopping
Centre
Bennett St
Boyce St
(Gaetz Av)
Southpointe
Common
Shopping
Centre
CITY OF
Bower
Taylor Dr
19 St
COUNTY OF
RED DEER
Twp Rd 382
Twp Rd 381
Twp Rd 380
Range Rd 280
Range Rd 275
Range Rd 381
32 St
Creek
Waskasoo
CP
Woodland
Hills
Woodland Dr
Wedgewood La
Word of life
Centrium
Westerner
Exposition
Grounds
Westerner
18 St
To Innisfail - Page 63
To Innisfail - Page 63

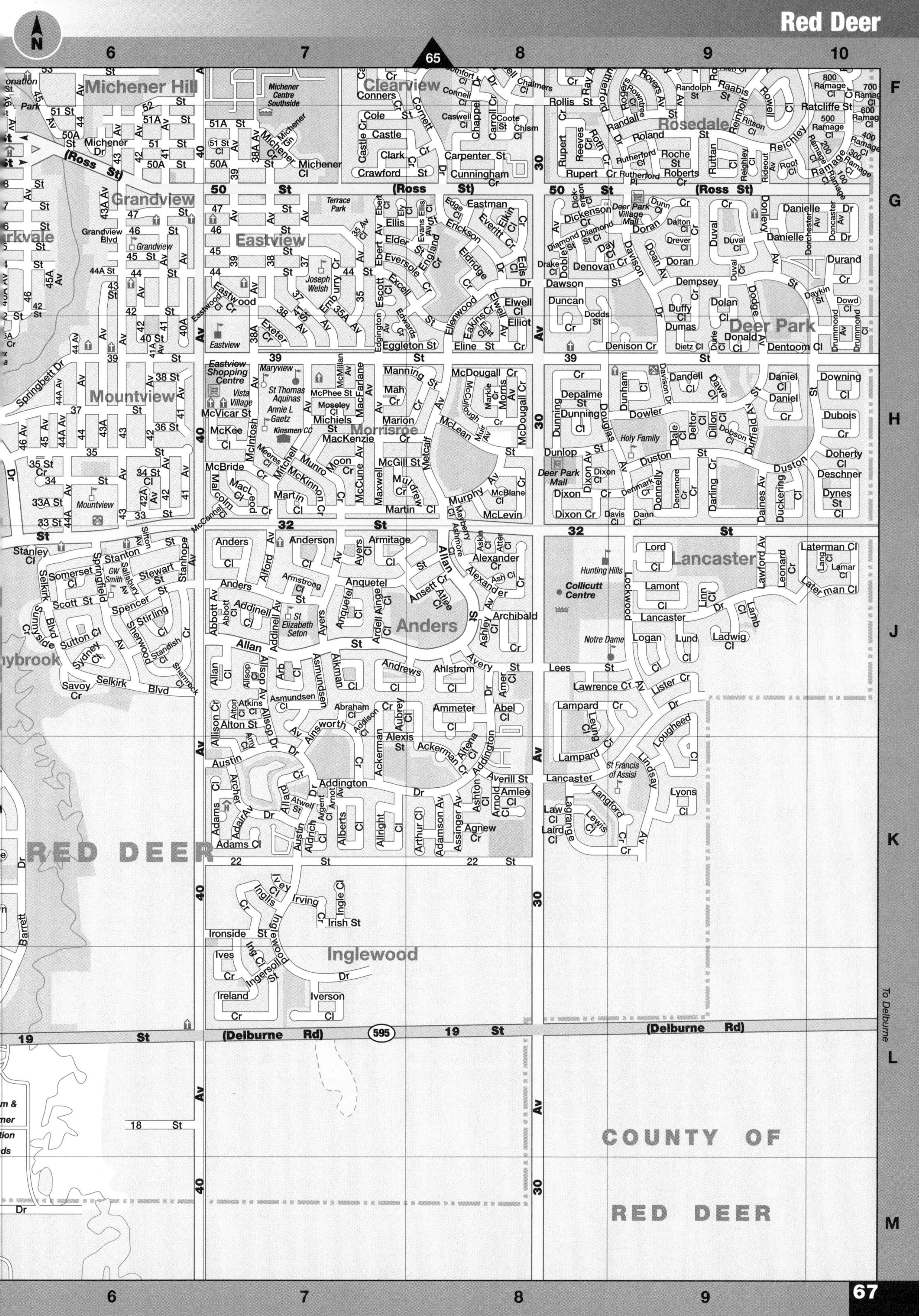

Michener Hill
Michener Centre Southside
Clearview
Rosedale
Grandview
Eastview
Terrace Park
Joseph Welsh
Deer Park
Deer Park Village Mall
Mountview
Eastview Shopping Centre
Vista Village
Maryview
St Thomas Aquinas
Annie L Gaetz
Kinsmen CC
Morrisroe
Holy Family
Deer Park Mall
Lancaster
Hunting Hills
Collicutt Centre
Notre Dame
Anders
St Elizabeth Seton
St Francis of Assisi
Inglewood
RED DEER
COUNTY OF RED DEER
(Ross St)
50 St
39 St
32 St
22 St
19 St
(Delburne Rd)
595
40 Av
30 Av
To Delburne
65

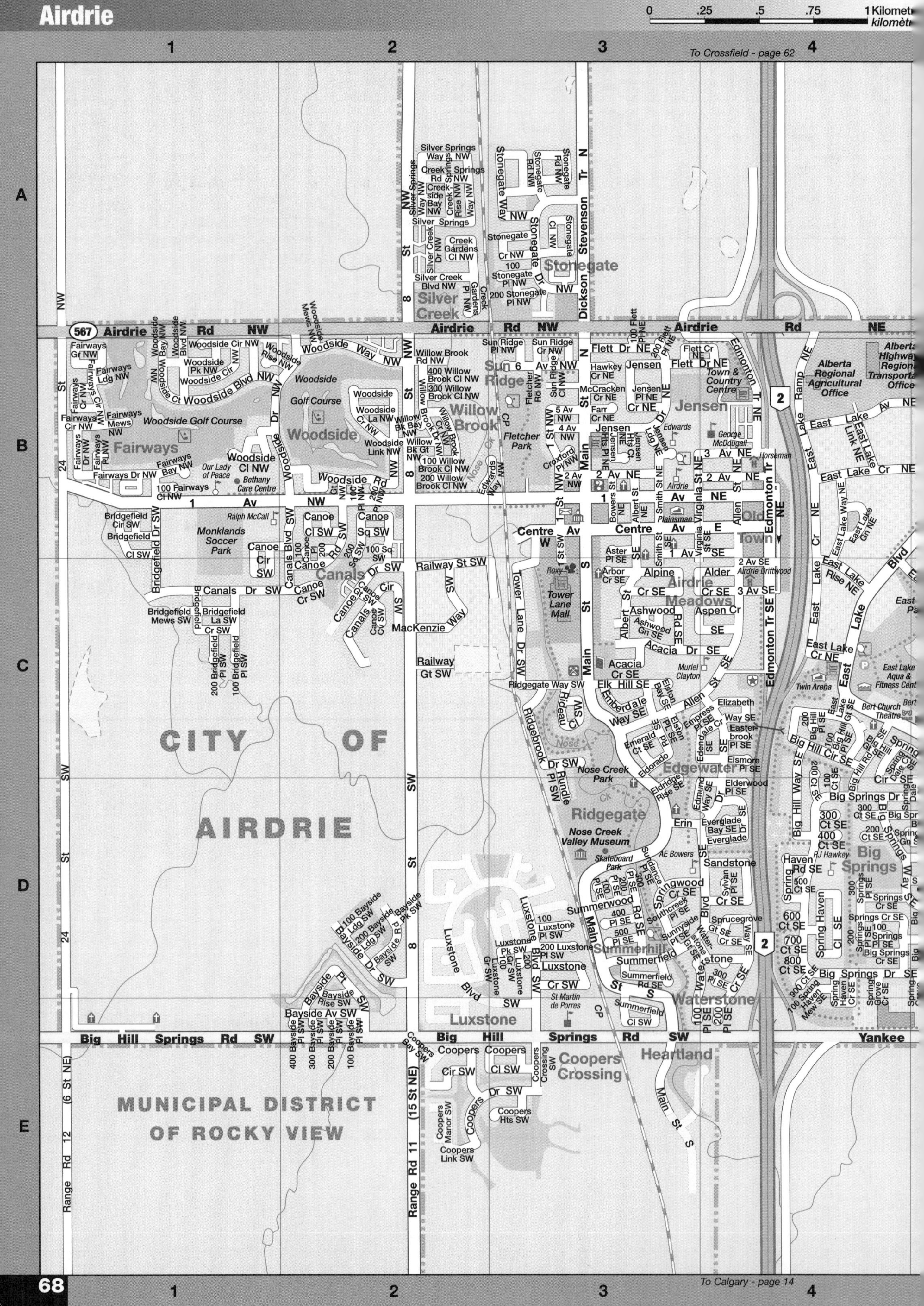
0 .25 .5 .75 1 Kilometre kilomètre
1 2 3 4
A B C D E
To Crossfield - page 62
To Calgary - page 14
567 Airdrie Rd NW
Airdrie Rd NE
CITY OF AIRDRIE
MUNICIPAL DISTRICT OF ROCKY VIEW
Silver Creek
Stonegate
Sun Ridge
Willow Brook
Fairways
Woodside
Woodside Golf Course
Jensen
Old Town
Canals
Airdrie Meadows
Edgewater
Ridgegate
Big Springs
Summerhill
Waterstone
Luxstone
Coopers Crossing
Heartland
Monklands Soccer Park
Fletcher Park
Nose Creek Park
Nose Creek Valley Museum
Tower Lane Mall
Town & Country Centre
Alberta Regional Agricultural Office
East Lake Aqua & Fitness Centre
Twin Arena
Bert Church Theatre
Big Hill Springs Rd SW
Yankee
1 Av NW
Centre Av
Main St S
Edmonton Tr NE
Edmonton Tr SE
East Lake Blvd
8 St NW
8 St SW
Range Rd 11 (15 St NE)
Range Rd 12 (6 St NE)
24 St NW
Dickson Stevenson Tr N
Railway St SW
Tower Lane Dr SW
Ridgegate Way SW
Allen St SE
Big Hill Way SE
Sierra Springs Dr SE
Luxstone Blvd SW
Bayside Dr SW
Coopers Dr SW
CP
Nose Ck
2

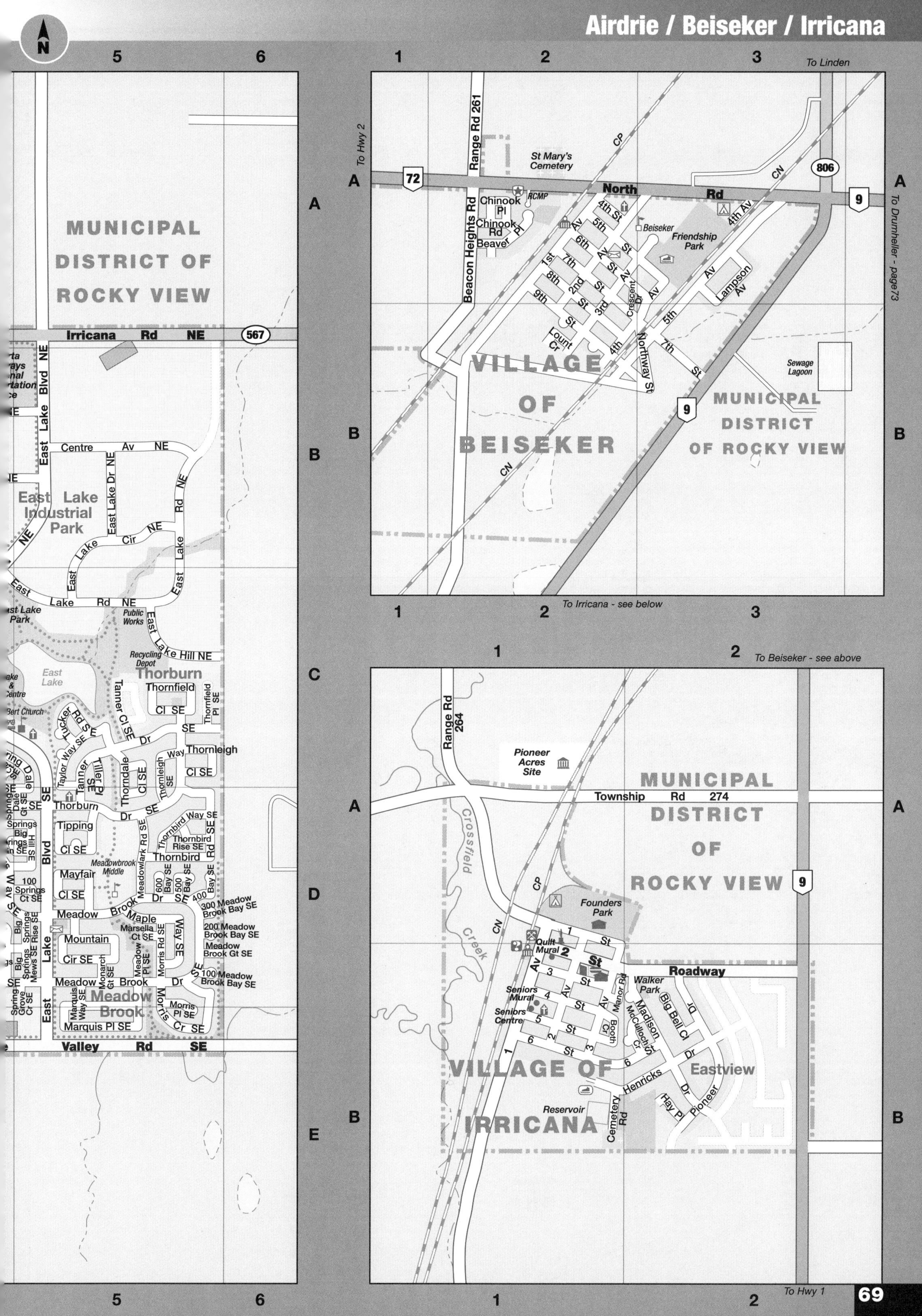
MUNICIPAL DISTRICT OF ROCKY VIEW
Irricana Rd NE
567
East Lake Blvd NE
Centre Av NE
East Lake Industrial Park
East Lake Dr NE
East Lake Cir NE
East Lake Rd NE
Public Works
East Lake Hill NE
Recycling Depot
East Lake
Thorburn
Thornfield Cl SE
Thornfield Pl SE
Tanner Cl SE
Tucker Rd SE
Taylor Way SE
Tiller Pl
Thorndale Cl SE
Thornleigh Way
Thornleigh Cl SE
Thorburn Dr SE
Tipping Cl SE
Thornbird Way SE
Thornbird Rise SE
Thornbird Rd SE
Meadowbrook Middle
Mayfair Cl SE
Meadowlark Rd SE
600 Bay SE
500 Bay SE
400 Bay SE
300 Meadow Brook Bay SE
200 Meadow Brook Bay SE
Meadow Brook Gt SE
100 Meadow Brook Bay SE
Meadow Brook Dr
Maple Way SE
Marsella Ct SE
Mountain Cir SE
Monarch Gt SE
Meadow Pl SE
Morris Rd SE
Morris Pl SE
Morris Cr SE
Marquis Way SE
Marquis Pl SE
Meadow Brook
Valley Rd SE
100 Springs Ct SE
Big Springs Rise SE
Big Springs Mews SE
Spring Grove Cr SE
To Hwy 2
To Linden
Range Rd 261
St Mary's Cemetery
72
North Rd
806
9
RCMP
Chinook Pl
Chinook Rd
Beaver Pl
Beacon Heights Rd
4th St
5th Av
6th Av
7th St
8th Av
9th
1st St
2nd St
3rd St
4th Av
5th
7th St
Crescent Dr
Beiseker
Friendship Park
4th Av
Lampson Av
Lount Cr
Northway St
CP
CN
VILLAGE OF BEISEKER
Sewage Lagoon
MUNICIPAL DISTRICT OF ROCKY VIEW
To Drumheller - page73
To Irricana - see below
To Beiseker - see above
Range Rd 264
Pioneer Acres Site
Township Rd 274
MUNICIPAL DISTRICT OF ROCKY VIEW
Crossfield Creek
Founders Park
Quilt Mural
1 St
2 St
Roadway
3 Av
4 Av
5 St
6 St
Seniors Mural
Seniors Centre
Manor Rd
Walker Park
Booth Cr
McCulloch Cr
Madison St
Big Bell Cl
Dr
Eastview
Henricks Dr
Hay Pl
Pioneer Dr
Reservoir
Cemetery Rd
VILLAGE OF IRRICANA
To Hwy 1

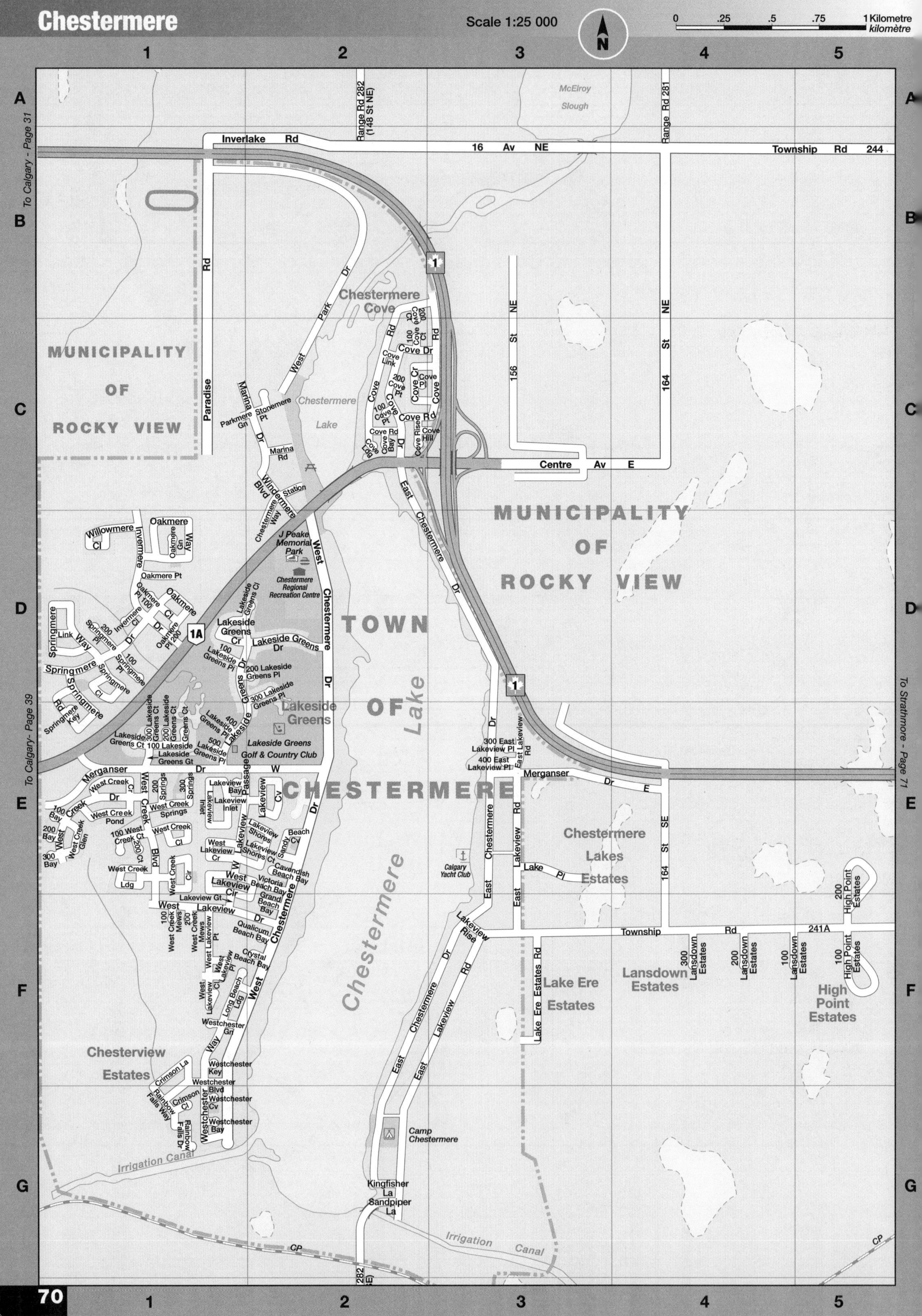

Scale 1:25 000

N

0   .25   .5   .75   1 Kilometre
kilomètre

A

To Calgary - Page 31

Inverlake   Rd

16   Av   NE

Township   Rd   244

Range Rd 282 (148 St NE)

Range Rd 281

McElroy Slough

B

1

Chestermere Cove

200 Cove Ct
100 Cove Ct
Cove Dr
Cove Link
200 Cove Pt
100 Cove Pt
Cove Pl
Cove Rd
Cove Rd
Cove Rise
Cove Hill
Cove Rd
Cove Bay
Cove

156 St NE

164 St NE

Centre   Av   E

C

MUNICIPALITY
OF
ROCKY VIEW

Paradise   Rd

West   Park   Dr

Marina Gr
Parkmere
Stonemere Pt
Marina Rd

Chestermere Lake

Windermere   Way

Chestermere   Blvd

Station

D

Willowmere Cl
Oakmere Gn
Oakmere Way

Invermere
Oakmere Pt

Oakmere Dr
200 Invermere Cl
100
Oakmere
Oakmere Pt 200

Springmere Way
Link
200 Springmere Dr
100
Springmere Ct
Springmere
Springmere Dr
Springmere Key
Rd
Springmere Cl

1A

J Peake Memorial Park

Chestermere Regional Recreation Centre

Lakeside Greens Cl
Lakeside Greens Cr
Lakeside Greens Dr
100 Lakeside Greens Pl
200 Lakeside Greens Pl
300 Lakeside Greens Pl

Lakeside   Greens   Dr

MUNICIPALITY
OF
ROCKY VIEW

TOWN

1   Chestermere   Dr

E

Springmere
300 Lakeside Greens Ct
200 Lakeside Greens Ct
100 Lakeside Greens Ct
400 Lakeside Greens Pl
500 Lakeside Greens Pl

Lakeside Greens Gt

Lakeside Greens Golf & Country Club

Lakeside Greens

OF   Lake

Merganser Springs
West Creek Cr
West Creek Dr
200 West Creek Springs
300 West Creek Springs
West Creek Pond
100 West Creek Ct
100 Bay
West Creek Glen
200 Bay
West Creek Cl
West Creek Cir
300 Bay
West Creek Ldg

Passage   Dr   W

Lakeview Bay
Lakeview Inlet
Lakeview Shores
Lakeview Shores Ct

Beach
Sandy Cv
Cavendish Beach Way

Merganser   Dr   E

300 East Lakeview Pl
400 East Lakeview Pl

East   Lakeview   Rd

Chestermere   Dr

CHESTERMERE

CHESTERMERE

Chestermere Lakes Estates

164 St SE

High Point Estates
200

F

West Creek Mews
100 West Creek Mews
200 West Creek Mews

West Lakeview Cir
West Lakeview Gt
West Lakeview Mews

West Lakeview Dr
West Lakeview Way

Victoria Beach Bay
Grand Beach Bay
Qualicum Beach Bay
Crystal Beach Bay
Long Beach

Chestermere   Lake

Calgary Yacht Club

East   Chestermere   Rd

East   Lakeview   Rd

Lake   Pl

Lakeview   Rise

Chestermere Lakes Estates

Township   Rd   241A

300 Lansdown Estates
200 Lansdown Estates
100 Lansdown Estates

High Point Estates
100

Lansdown Estates

High Point Estates

To Strathmore - Page 71

Chesterview Estates

Westchester Key
Westchester Blvd
Westchester Cv
Westchester Bay

Crimson La
Crimson Cl
Rainbow Falls Way
Rainbow Falls Dr

Lake Ere Estates Rd

Lake Ere Estates

Lansdown Estates

High Point Estates

G

Irrigation Canal

East   Chestermere   Dr

East   Lakeview   Rd

Camp Chestermere

Kingfisher La
Sandpiper La

Irrigation   Canal

282 (E)(E) NE

CP

CP

To Calgary - Page 39

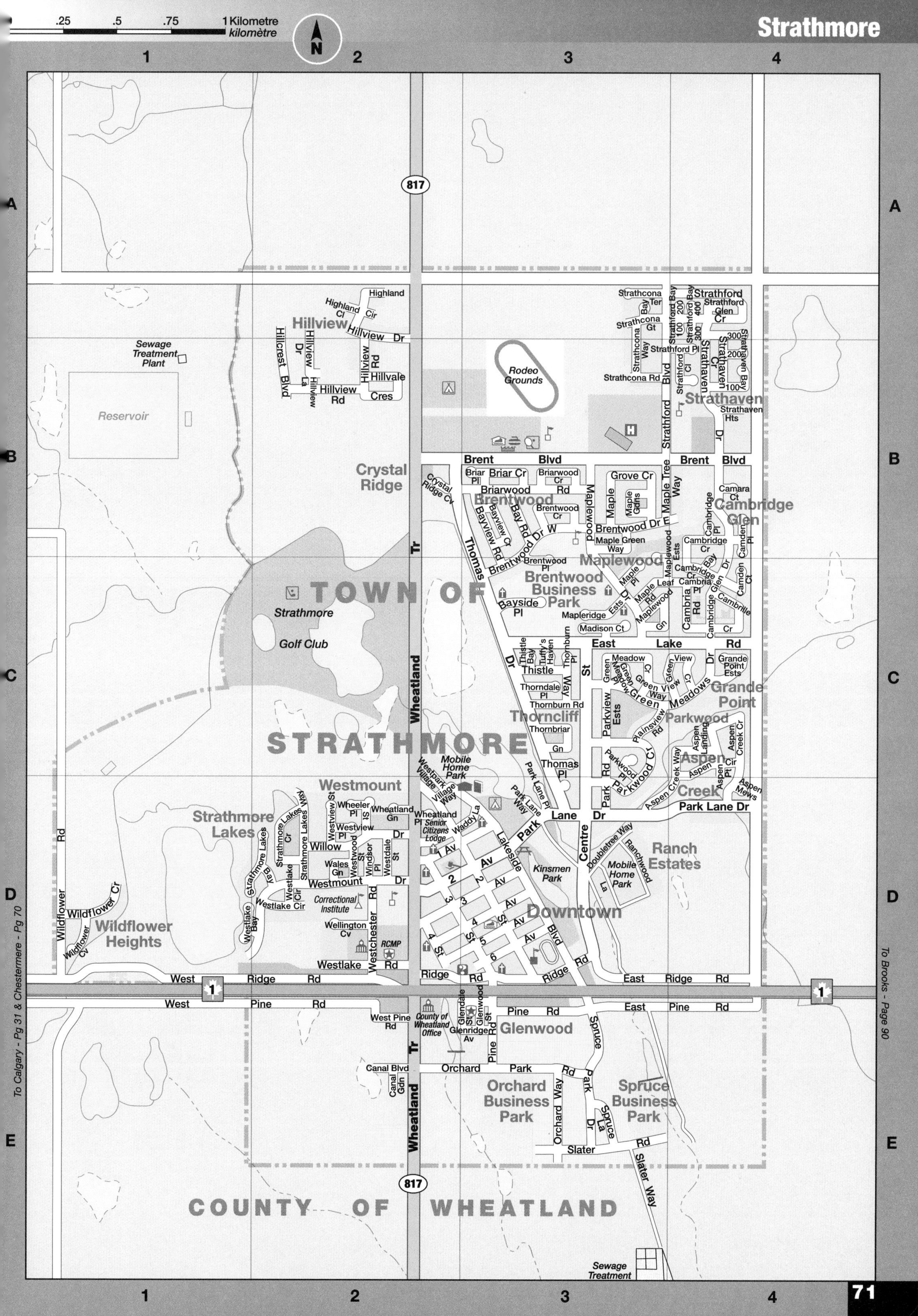
Strathmore
.25
.5
.75
1 Kilometre
kilomètre
N
1
2
3
4
A
B
C
D
E
817
Highland
Highland Cl
Cir
Hillview
Hillview Dr
Hillcrest Blvd
Hillview Dr
Hillview La
Hillview Rd
Hillvale
Hillview Rd
Cres
Sewage Treatment Plant
Reservoir
Rodeo Grounds
Strathcona Ter
Strathcona Bay
Strathcona Gt
Strathcona Way
Strathcona Rd
Strathford Bay 100
Strathford Bay 200
Strathford Bay 300
Strathford Bay 400
Strathford Glen
Strathford Cr
Strathford Pl
Strathford Ct
Strathford Blvd
Strathaven Cr
Strathaven Bay
300
200
100
Strathaven
Strathaven Hts
Strathaven Dr
H
Brent Blvd
Crystal Ridge
Crystal Ridge Cv
Briar Pl
Briar Cr
Briarwood Cr
Briarwood Rd
Brentwood
Bayview Rd
Bayview Cr
Bay Rd
Brentwood Cr
Brentwood Dr W
Brentwood Pl
Brentwood Dr
Maplewood
Maple
Maple Gdns
Grove Cr
Maple Tree Way
Maple Green Way
Maplewood
Maplewood Ests
Maple Pl
Maple Rd
Leaf
Maplewood Gn
Maple Ests
Mapleridge
Madison Ct
Cambridge Pl
Camara Ct
Cambridge Glen
Cambridge Cr
Cambridge Bay
Camden Pl
Camden Ct
Cambridge Cr
Cambria Pl
Cambria Rd
Cambridge Glen
Cambridge Dr
Cambrille
Cr
Thomas Dr
Brentwood Business Park
Bayside Pl
TOWN OF
STRATHMORE
Strathmore Golf Club
Wheatland Tr
East Lake Rd
Thistle Bay
Tuffy's Haven
Thornburn Pl
Thistle
Thorndale Pl
Thornburn Rd
Thornburn Way
St
Meadow Cr
Green Meadow
Green View Way
Green View Cr
Meadows
Grande Point Ests
Grande Point
Parkview Ests
Plainsview Rd
Parkwood
Thorncliff
Thornbriar Gn
Thomas Pl
Park Lane Pl
Park Lane Way
Parkwood Pl
Parkwood Ct
Park Rd
Aspen Landing
Aspen Creek Way
Aspen Creek Cr
Aspen Cir
Aspen Pt
Aspen
Aspen Creek
Aspen Mews
Park Lane Dr
Lane Dr
Mobile Home Park
Westpark Village
Village Way
Wheatland Senior Citizens Lodge
Waddy La
Westmount
Strathmore Lakes
Strathmore Lakes Cr
Strathmore Lakes Way
Westview St
Wheeler Pl
Wheatland Gn
Westview Pl
Willow Dr
Westwood St
Windsor Pl
Westdale St
Wales Gn
Westmount Dr
Strathmore Lakes Bay
Westlake Cir
Correctional Institute
Westchester Rd
Wellington Cv
RCMP
Westlake Rd
Wildflower Rd
Wildflower Cr
Wildflower Heights
Wildflower Cv
Westlake Bay
1 Av
2 Av
3 Av
4 St
5
6
Lakeside Blvd
Park
Kinsmen Park
Centre St
Doubletree Way
Ranchwood
Mobile Home Park
La
Ranch Estates
Downtown
Ridge Rd
West Ridge Rd
East Ridge Rd
1
West Pine Rd
East Pine Rd
West Pine Rd
County of Wheatland Office
Glendale St
Glenwood St
Glenridge Av
Pine Rd
Glenwood
Spruce
Canal Blvd
Canal Gdn
Orchard Park Rd
Orchard Business Park
Orchard Way
Park Dr
Spruce La
Spruce Business Park
Slater Rd
Slater Way
COUNTY OF WHEATLAND
Sewage Treatment
To Calgary - Pg 31 & Chestermere - Pg 70
To Brooks - Page 90
71

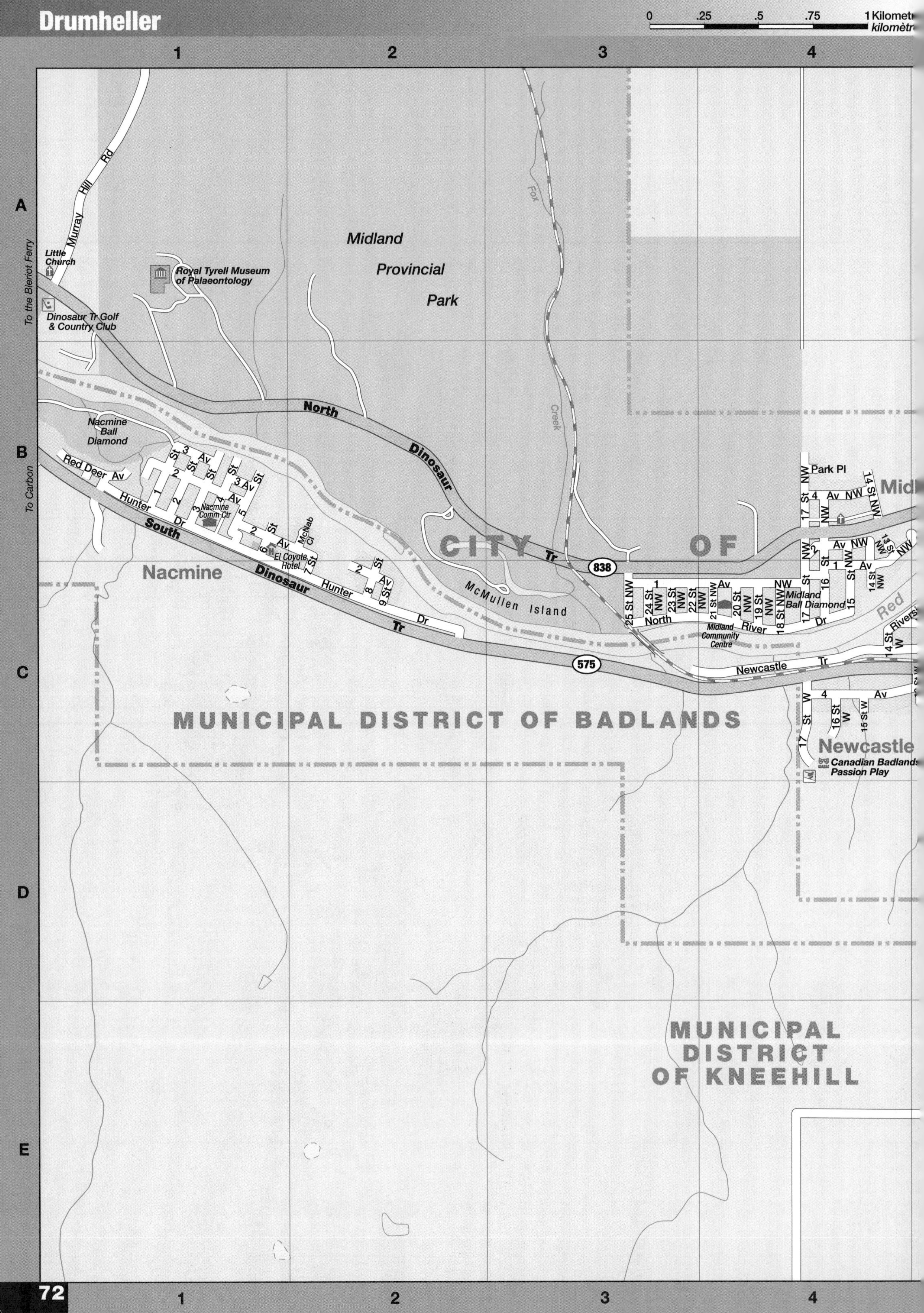

0 .25 .5 .75 1 Kilometr
kilomètre

1 2 3 4

A

Midland

Provincial

Park

Little
Church

Royal Tyrell Museum
of Palaeontology

To the Bleriot Ferry

Murray Hill Rd

Dinosaur Tr Golf
& Country Club

Fox

Creek

B

Nacmine
Ball
Diamond

Red Deer Av

To Carbon

Hunter

North

Dinosaur

Nacmine
Comm Ctr

McNab
Ct

El Coyote
Hotel

South

Nacmine

Dinosaur

Hunter

Tr

Dr

C I T Y

Tr

838

McMullen Island

O F

Park Pl

14 St NW

17 St NW

4 Av NW

Midl

13 St NW

Av NW

25 St NW

24 St NW

North

23 St NW

22 St NW

21 St NW

20 St NW

Av

19 St NW

Midland
Community
Centre

River

18 St NW

17 St NW

Dr

16

15

14 St NW

Midland
Ball Diamond

Red

Riversi

C

MUNICIPAL DISTRICT OF BADLANDS

575

Newcastle

Tr

4 Av

16 St W

15 St W

17 St W

Newcastle

Canadian Badlands
Passion Play

D

**MUNICIPAL
DISTRICT
OF KNEEHILL**

E

1 2 3 4

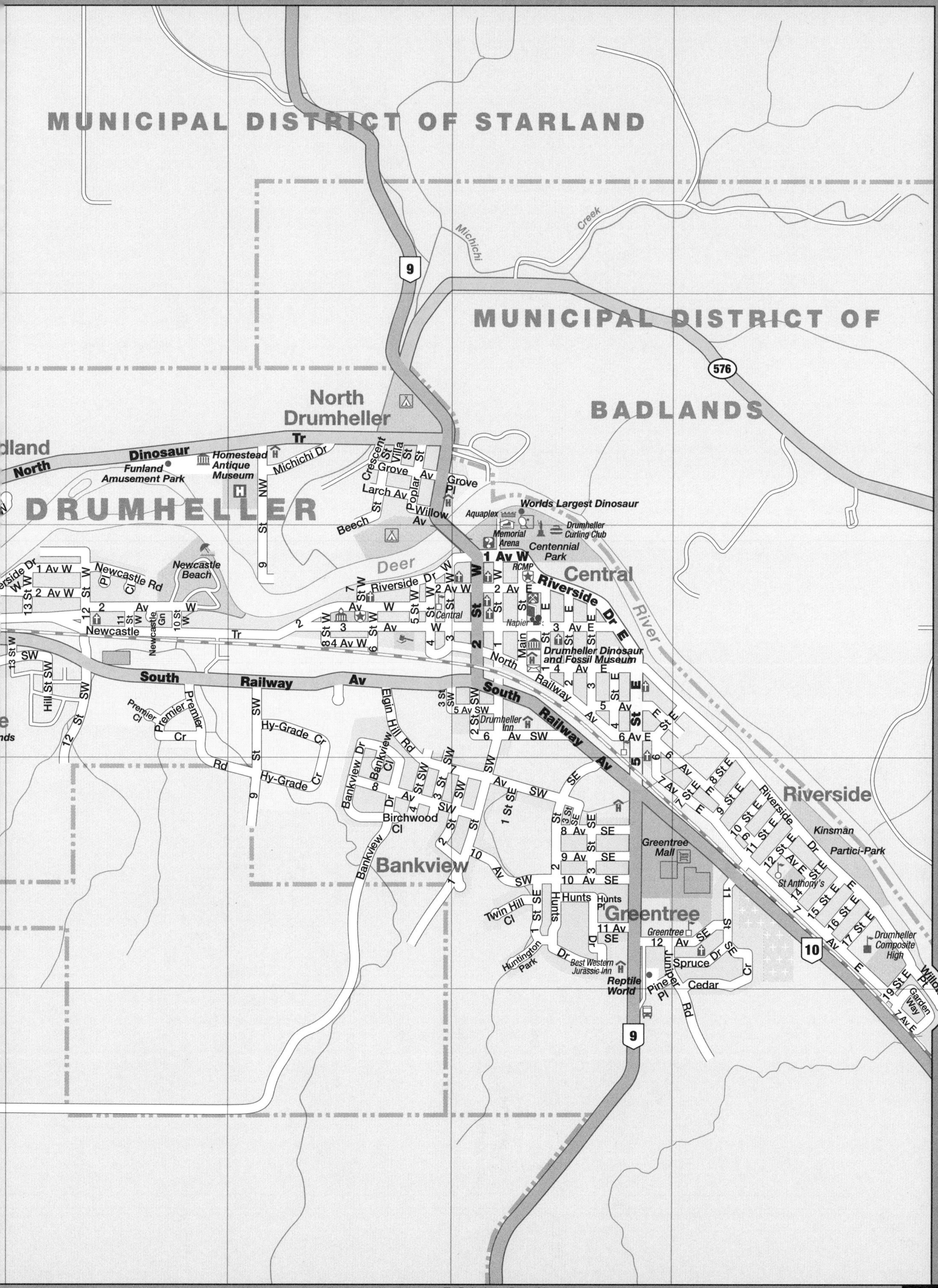

N

5 6 7 8

To Stettler

A

MUNICIPAL DISTRICT OF STARLAND

Creek

Michichi

9

MUNICIPAL DISTRICT OF

576

B

North
Drumheller

Tr

To Michichi

Dinosaur
North

Homestead
Antique
Museum

Michichi Dr

Crescent St
Grove St
Villa Av
Poplar
Grove Pl

Worlds Largest Dinosaur

DRUMHELLER

Funland
Amusement Park

NW St

Larch Av

Beech St

P. Willow Av

Aquaplex

Drumheller
Curling Club

Newcastle Rd

Newcastle
Beach

Deer

Memorial
Arena

Centennial
Park

Riverside Dr W
1 Av W
2 Av W

13 St W

12 Av

11 Av W

Newcastle Gn
10 St W

Newcastle

Tr

1 Av W
Riverside Dr
2 St W
3 Av W
8 St
4 Av W

Central Av

Riverside Dr W
2 St W
Central

RCMP

1 Av W
2 Av

Napier

3 Av

Riverside Dr

Central

Riverside Dr

5 St E

Main St
North
Railway

Drumheller Dinosaur
and Fossil Museum

C

13 St SW
Hill St SW
12 St

South Railway Av

Premier Cl
Premier Cr
Premier Rd

Hy-Grade Cr

Hy-Grade Cr

9 St

Elgin Hill Rd

Bankview Dr

3 St SW

South Railway Av

Drumheller Inn

2 St SW
5 St W
6 St W

3 St SW

6 Av

5 Av

6 Av E

7 Av E
8 St E

Riverside
Dr

Kinsman
Partici-Park

Bankview Dr

Birchwood Cl

Bankview

3 St SW
AV St
AV St SW

1 St SE

3 St SE
8 Av SE

9 Av SE

10 Av SE

10 St E
11 St E
12 Av E
14 St E
15 St E
16 St E

Riverside

St Anthony's

D

Twin Hill Cl

Huntington
Park

10 Av SW

Hunts Dr

Hunts Pl

11 Av SE

Greentree
Mall

Greentree

12 Av

Spruce
Dr

St SE
Cr

11 St E

17 St E

10

Drumheller
Composite
High

Willow

Best Western
Jurassic Inn

Reptile
World

Juniper Pl
Pine St

Cedar

Garden
Way

9

19 St E
7 Av E

To Rosedale

E

5 6 7 8

Turner Valley

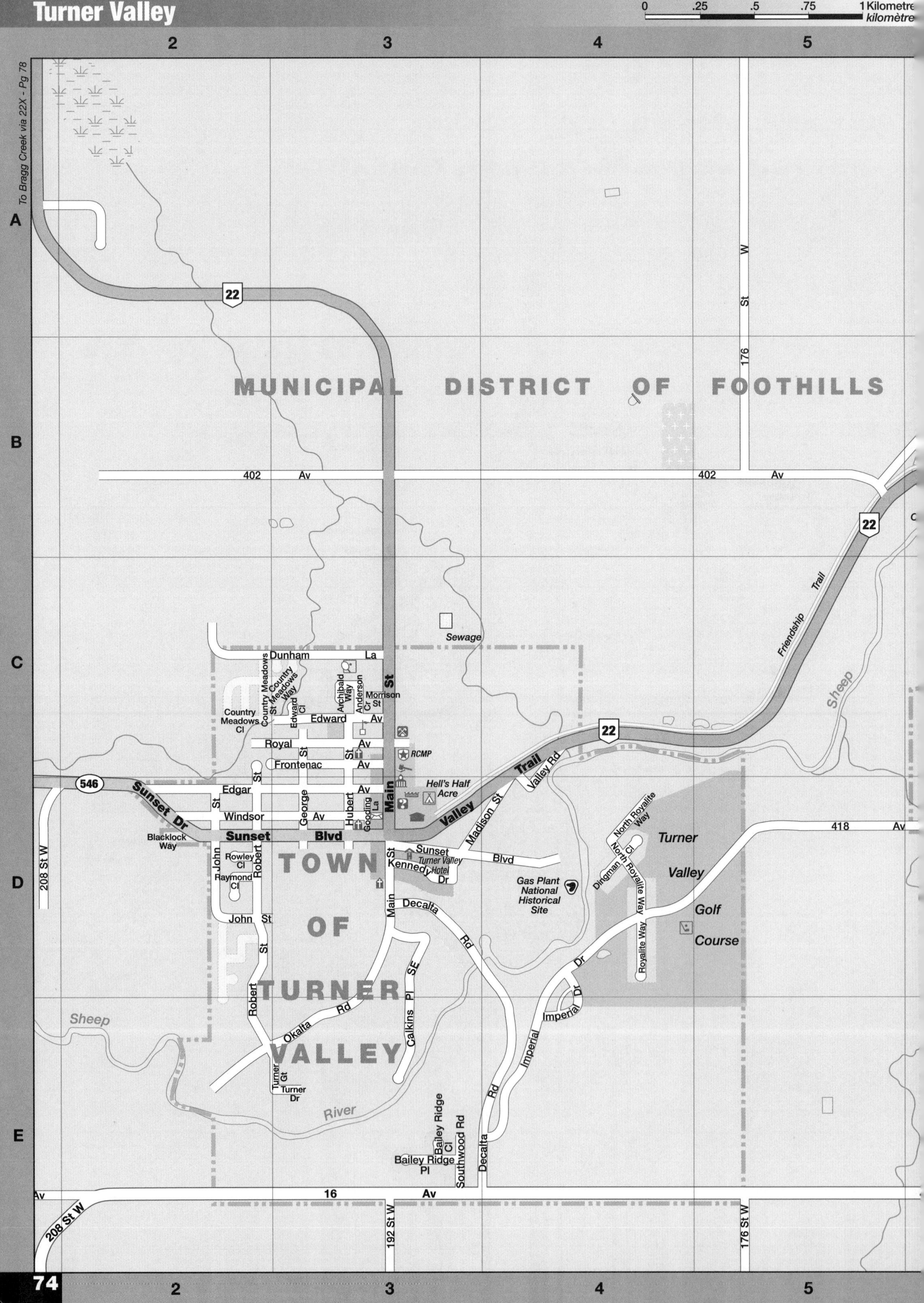

0   .25   .5   .75   1 Kilometre
kilomètre

2   3   4   5

To Bragg Creek via 22X - Pg 78

A

22

MUNICIPAL   DISTRICT   OF   FOOTHILLS

B

402   Av   402   Av

176 St W

22

Sewage

Friendship Trail

C

Dunham   La

Country Meadows Way
Country Country Meadows St
Archibald Way
Morrison St
Anderson Cr
Edward Cl
Country Meadows Cl
Edward Av
St
St
Royal Av
St
Frontenac Av
Main St
22
Sheep
Valley Rd
Edgar Av
Hell's Half Acre
Valley Trail
Windsor Av
George Av
Hubert La
Gooding La
RCMP

546   Sunset Dr

Madison St

North Royalite Way

418   Av

Sunset   Blvd
Blacklock Way
Robert St
Rowley Cl
John St
Raymond Cl
Sunset Blvd
Kennedy Dr
Turner Valley Hotel
Gas Plant National Historical Site
Dingman Cl
North Royalite Way
Royalite Way

Turner Valley Golf Course

D

208 St W

TOWN OF TURNER VALLEY

John St
Main St
Decalta
Robert St
Okalta Rd
Calkins Pl SE
Imperial Dr
Imperial Rd
Decalta Rd

Sheep

Turner Gt
Turner Dr

River

Bailey Ridge Cl
Bailey Ridge Pl
Southwood Rd

E

Av   16   Av

208 St W   192 St W   176 St W

74

2   3   4   5

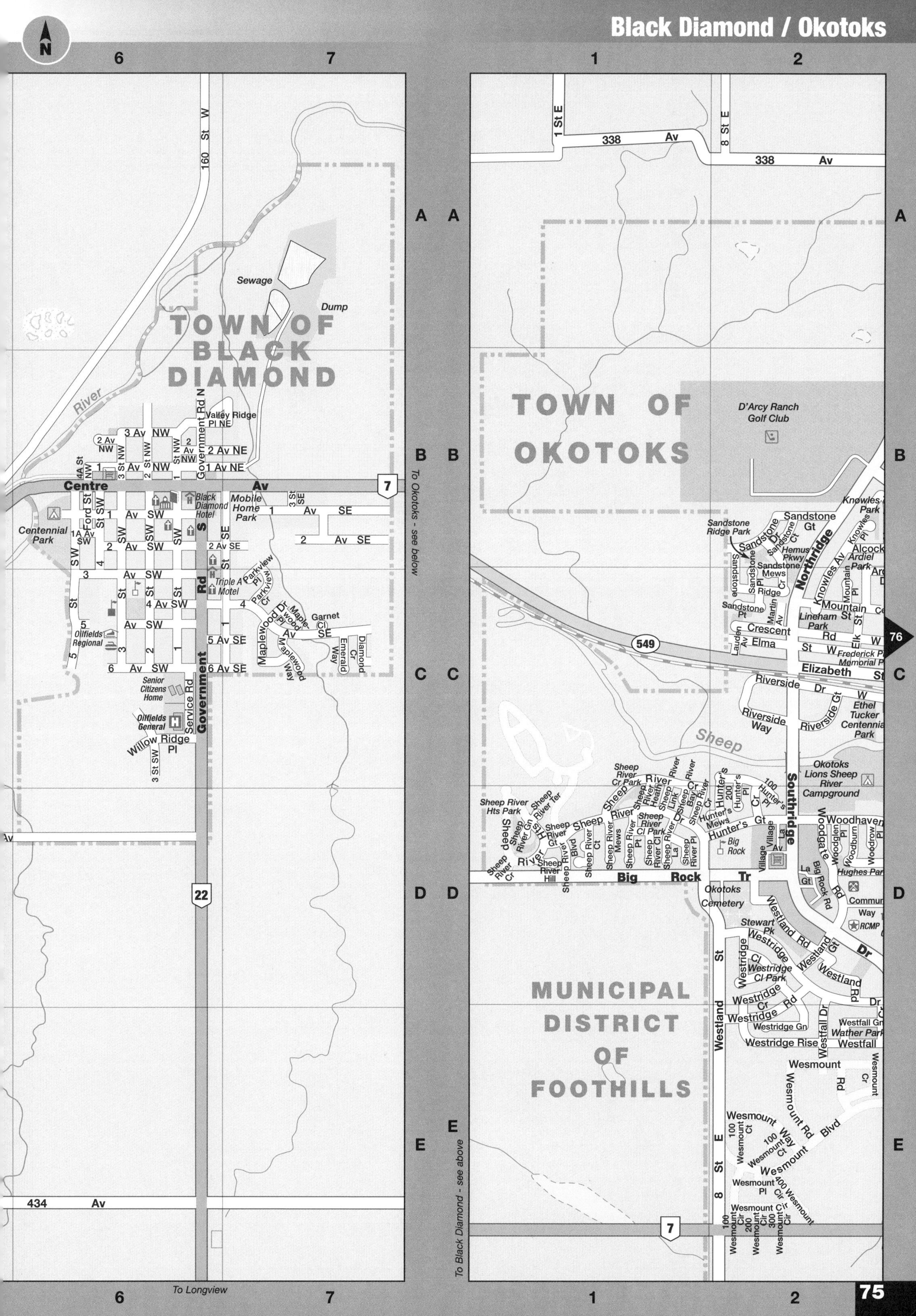
TOWN OF BLACK DIAMOND
TOWN OF OKOTOKS
MUNICIPAL DISTRICT OF FOOTHILLS
Sewage
Dump
Centennial Park
Oilfields Regional
Senior Citizens Home
Oilfields General
Black Diamond Hotel
Mobile Home Park
Triple A Motel
Centre Av
Government Rd S
Government Rd N
Valley Ridge Pl NE
Willow Ridge Pl
Service Rd
Maplewood Dr
Garnet Cl
Emerald Way
Diamond Cr
Parkview Pl
Parkview Cr
160 St W
434 Av
338 Av
1 St E
8 St E
To Okotoks - see below
To Black Diamond - see above
To Longview
D'Arcy Ranch Golf Club
Sandstone Ridge Park
Sandstone Gt
Northridge Dr
Knowles Park
Alcock Ardiel Park
Lineham Park
Crescent Rd
Elma St W
Elizabeth St
Frederick Pl
Memorial P
Riverside Dr W
Riverside Way
Riverside Gt
Ethel Tucker Centennial Park
Sheep River
Okotoks Lions Sheep River Campground
Sheep River Hts Park
Sheep River Cr Park
Hunter's Gt
Southridge Dr
Big Rock Tr
Big Rock
Okotoks Cemetery
Stewart Pk
Westridge Cl Park
Westridge Rd
Westridge Gn
Westridge Rise
Westland Rd
Westland St
Westfall Dr
Westfall Gn
Wather Park
Wesmount Rd
Wesmount Blvd
Wesmount Way
Wesmount Cr
Wesmount Pl
Wesmount Cir
Woodhaven
Woodgate
Hughes Park
Community Way
RCMP
549
7
22
76
A
B
C
D
E
1
2
6
7

0   .25   .5   .75   **1 Kilometre**
kilomètre

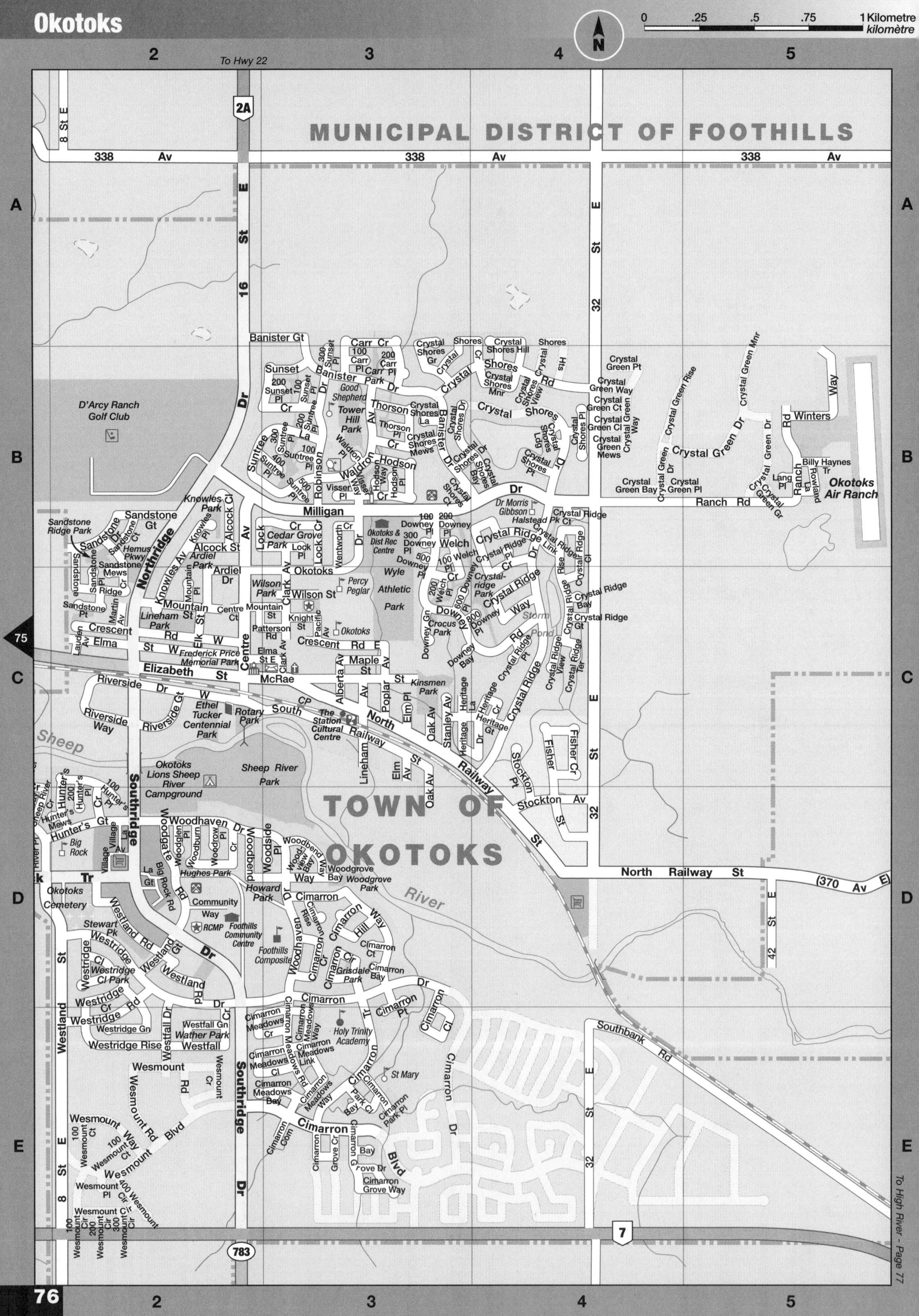

MUNICIPAL DISTRICT OF FOOTHILLS

338   Av   338   Av   338   Av

A   **A**

D'Arcy Ranch
Golf Club

B   **B**

Banister Gt   Carr Cr   Crystal   Shores   Crystal Shores Hill
100   Crystal Shores Gr   Shores
Sunset   Carr   Carr Pl   Shores   Crystal Shores Mnr   Crystal Green Pt   Crystal Green Mnr   Winters
200   Banister Dr   Park Dr   Crystal Shores View   Crystal Green Way   Crystal Green Rise   Way
Sunset Pl   Good Shepherd   Crystal   Crystal Green Dr   Crystal Green Dr
Cr   Thorson   Shores La   Crystal Shores Mnr   Crystal Green Way   Crystal Green Ct   Winters
Tower Hill Park   Thorson   Crystal   Crystal Green Cl   Crystal Green Way   Ranch Rd
Suntree   Cr   Crystal Shores Mews   Crystal   Crystal Green Mews   Billy Haynes Tr
300   Waldron   Hodson   Shores   Shores   Crystal Green   Okotoks
400   Robinson   Cr   Bay   Crystal Green Bay   Crystal Green Pl   Lang Pl   Ranch Rd   Air Ranch
100   Visser   Hodson   Crystal Shores Pt   Crystal Green   Ranch Rd   Okotoks
500   Suntree   Cr   Crystal Shores Bay   Ranch Rd   Air Ranch
Milligan   Hodson Cr   Crystal Shores Dr   Dr Morris Gibbson   Crystal Ridge

Knowles Park   Dr   100 Downey   200   Halstead Pk   Crystal Ridge
Sandstone Gt   Alcock Ct   Cedar Grove   Pl   Downey   Welch   Crystal Ridge Link
Sandstone Ridge Park   Alcock St   Park   Lock Pl   300 Downey Pl   Crystal Ridge   Crystal Ridge Bay
Knowles Av   Ardiel Park   Lock   500 Downey Pl   Welch Cr   Crystalridge Park   Crystal Ridge
Sandstone Mews   Ardiel Dr   Okotoks   Wyle   100   Crystal Ridge Bay
Sandstone Mountain St   Wentworth   Okotoks & Dist Rec Centre   200 Welch   Downey Gn   Crystal Ridge Gt
Ridge   Centre Ct   Wilson Park   Clark Av   600   Crystal Ridge   Crystal Ridge
Sandstone Pt   Lineham Park Rd   Mountain St   Knight St   Welch   Downey Pl   Way   Crystal Ridge View
Martin   Mountain Ct   Patterson Rd   Pacific St   Percy Peglar   800 Downey   Storm   Crystal Ridge Ter
Crescent   Elma   Elk   W   Elma St E   Okotoks   Crocus Park   Downey Bay   Pond   Crystal Ridge
Lauden   Elma   St   W   Crescent   Rd E   Fisher Cr

75

C   Elizabeth St   Frederick Price Memorial Park   McRae   Maple St   Kinsmen Park   Fisher   **C**
Riverside Dr   Alberta Av   Poplar St   Heritage
Riverside Gt   Ethel Tucker Centennial Park   W   South   North   Oak Av   Stanley Av   Heritage Cr   Stockton
Riverside Way   Rotary Park   The Station Cultural Centre   Railway   Heritage Gt   Pt   Fisher
Sheep   Ethel   Elm Pl   Stockton Av

Okotoks Lions Sheep River Campground   Sheep River Park   Lineham   Elm Av   Oak Av   Railway   St   Stockton

Hunter's   **TOWN OF**   Stockton Av
Hunter's Pl   200   Woodhaven Dr   **OKOTOKS**   North Railway St   (370 Av E)
Hunter's Cr   100   Woodburn   Woodrow   Woodbend   Woodbend Way
D   Hunter's Mews   Gt   Pl   Woodside   Way   Woodgrove Bay   River   **D**
Village   Big Rock   Hughes Park   Woodbend   Woodgrove Park
Okotoks Cemetery   Big Rock Rd   Howard Park   Community Way   Cimarron Way   42 St E   Southbank Rd
Stewart Pk   RCMP   Foothills Community Centre   Cimarron Rise   Cimarron Hill
Westridge   Westland Rd   Foothills Composite   Cimarron Cr   Cimarron Ct   Cimarron Ct
Westland Gt   Cimarron Cr   Grisdale Park   Cimarron Bay
Westridge Cl   Westland Rd   Cimarron Dr
Westridge Cl Park   Westland   Dr   Cimarron   Cimarron Pt
Westridge Cr   Dr   Cimarron Meadows Cr   Cimarron Tr
Westridge Rd   Westfall Gn   Wather Park   Cimarron Meadows Cr   Holy Trinity Academy
Westridge Rise   Westfall   Cimarron Meadows Link   St Mary
Wesmount   Cimarron Meadows Rd   Cimarron Meadows Way   Southbank Rd
Wesmount Cr   Cimarron Meadows Cl   Cimarron Park Cl
E   Wesmount Rd   Cimarron Meadows Bay   Cimarron Park Pl   **E**
Wesmount Way   Southridge Dr   Cimarron Meadows Way   Cimarron Park Way
100 Wesmount Way   Cimarron Com   Blvd   Cimarron Grove Cr
200 Wesmount Ct   Cimarron Bay   Cimarron Grove Dr
Wesmount Pl   Cimarron   Grove Way
100 Wesmount Cir   400 Wesmount Cir
200 Wesmount Cir   300 Wesmount Cir

Page 77
To High River - Page 77
To Hwy 22
To High River

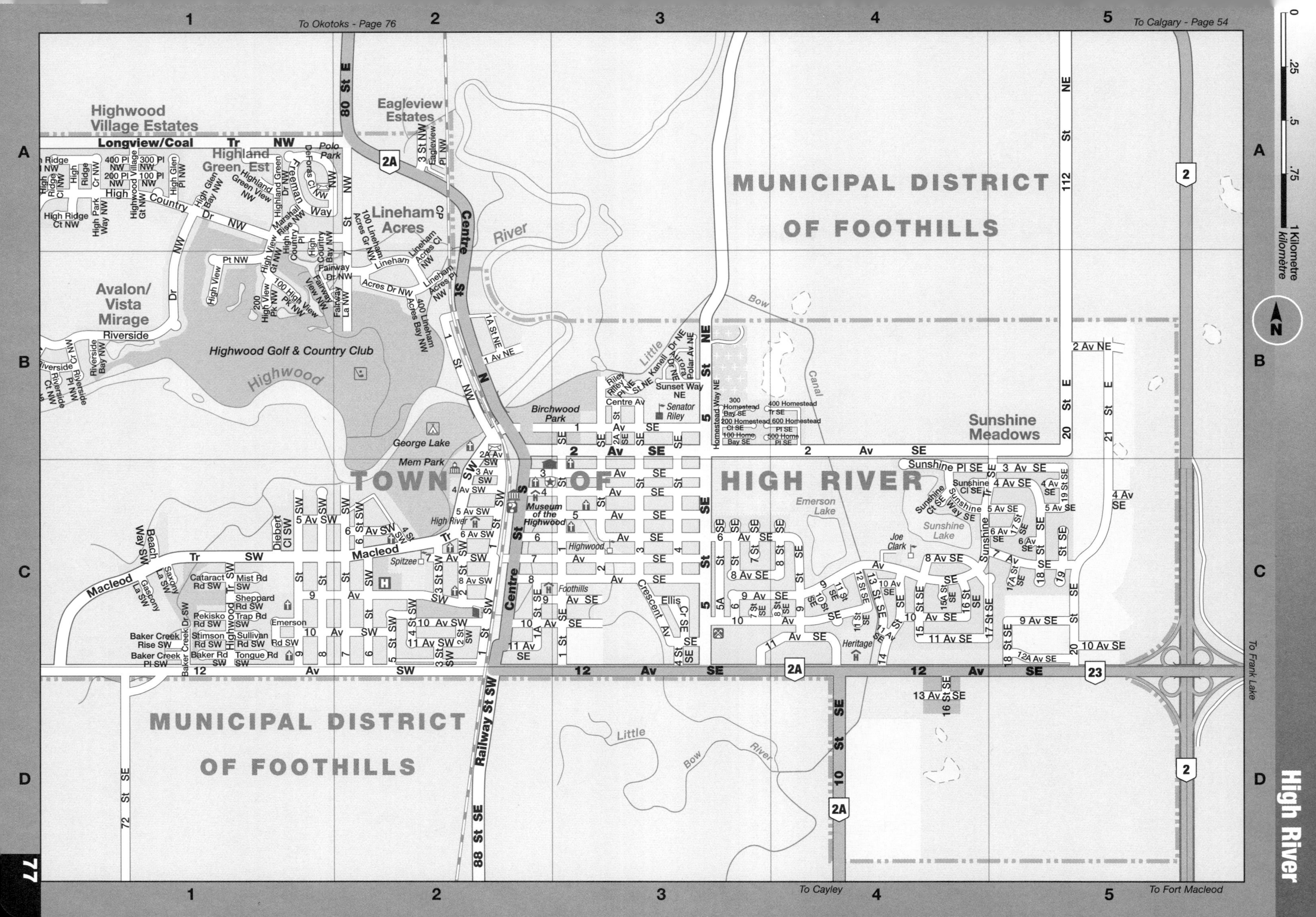

0
.25
.5
.75
1 Kilometre
kilomètre
N
A
B
C
D
1
2
3
4
5
To Okotoks - Page 76
To Calgary - Page 54
To Frank Lake
To Cayley
To Fort Macleod
MUNICIPAL DISTRICT
OF FOOTHILLS
TOWN OF HIGH RIVER
Highwood Village Estates
Eagleview Estates
Highland Green Est
Polo Park
Lineham Acres
Avalon/ Vista Mirage
Highwood Golf & Country Club
Highwood
River
Little Bow
Canal
Birchwood Park
George Lake
Mem Park
Senator Riley
Museum of the Highwood
High River
Spitzee
Foothills
Sunshine Meadows
Emerson Lake
Sunshine Lake
Joe Clark
Heritage
Longview/Coal Tr NW
High Country Dr NW
Centre St
Railway St SW
88 St SE
80 St E
112 St NE
20 St E
21 St E
10 St SE
72 St SE
2 Av SE
12 Av SE
12 Av SW
Macleod Tr
Beach Way SW
Crescent Av
Sunshine Pl SE
Homestead Way NE
2A
2
23

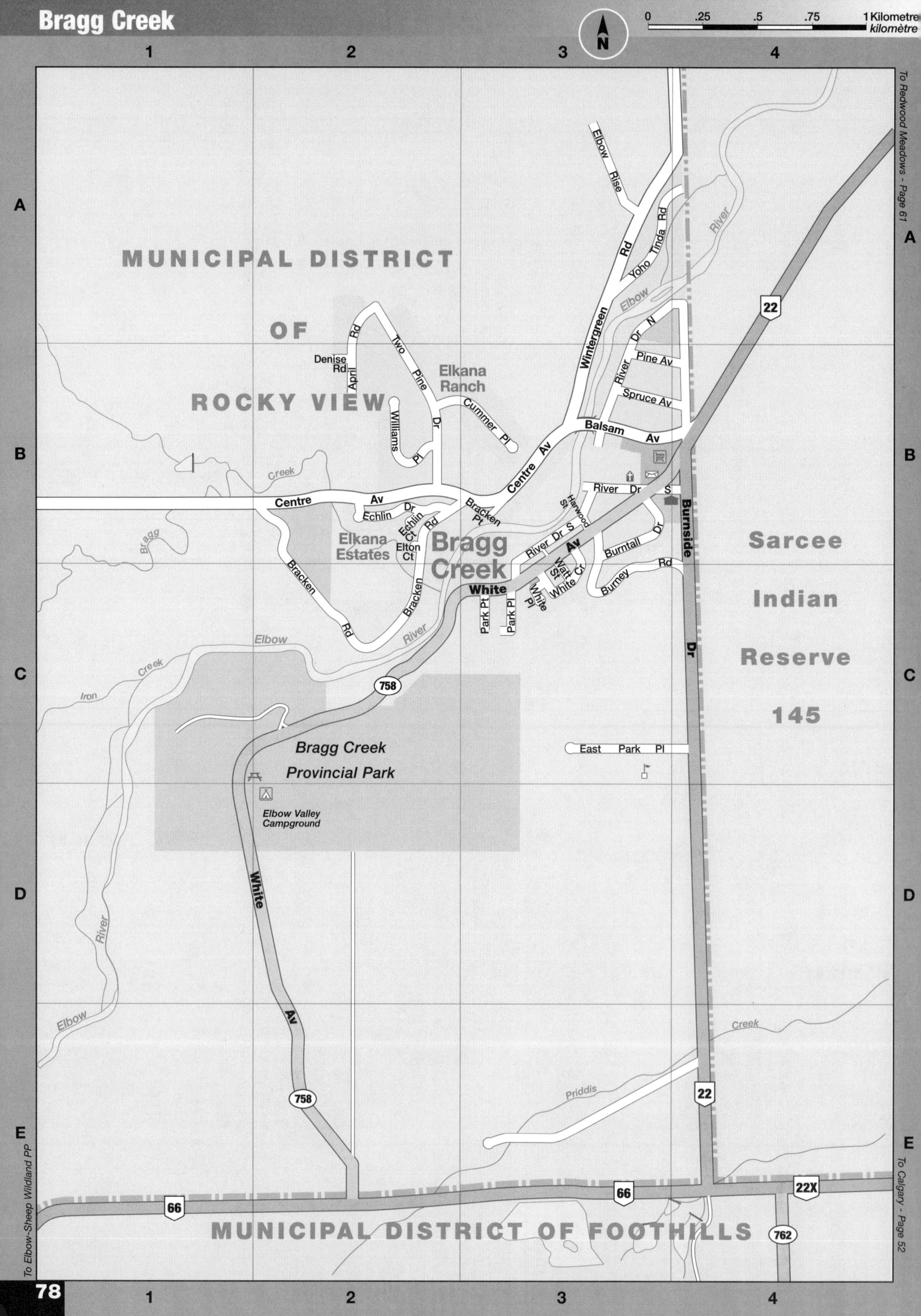

0   .25   .5   .75   **1 Kilometre**
kilomètre

N

1   2   3   4

A

MUNICIPAL DISTRICT

OF

ROCKY VIEW

Denise
Rd
April
Rd
Two Pine
Williams Pl
Dr
Elkana
Ranch
Cummer Pl

Elbow Rise

Yoho Tinda Rd

Wintergreen Rd

River Dr N
Elbow

22

Pine Av

Spruce Av

B

Centre   Av

Echlin Dr
Echlin Ct
Elton Ct
Bracken Rd

Bracken Pt
Centre   Av

Elkana
Estates

**Bragg
Creek**

White

Park Pt
Park Pl

Balsam   Av

River   Dr   S

Harwood St
Watt St
White Cr
White Pl
River Dr S   Av

Burntall Dr
Burney Rd

Burnside   Dr

Sarcee

Indian

Reserve

145

C

Bragg   Creek

Elbow   Creek

Iron   Creek

758

Bragg Creek
Provincial Park

Elbow Valley
Campground

East   Park   Pl

D

White   Av

Elbow   River

758

Priddis   Creek

22

E

66

66

762

22X

To Redwood Meadows - Page 61
To Calgary - Page 52
To Elbow-Sheep Wildland PP

MUNICIPAL DISTRICT OF FOOTHILLS

1   2   3   4

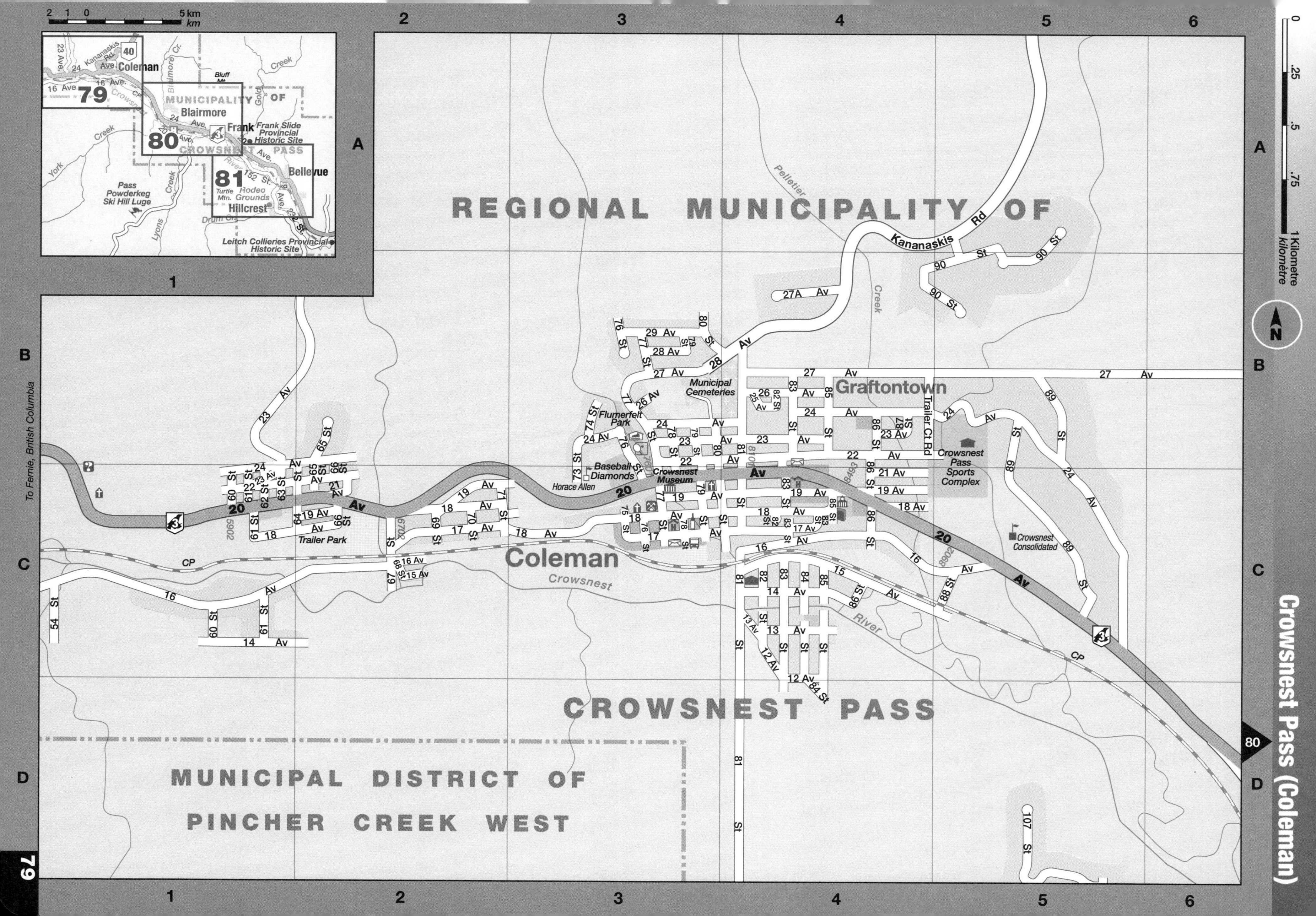
0 .25 .5 .75 1 Kilometre kilomètre
N
80
REGIONAL MUNICIPALITY OF
CROWSNEST PASS
MUNICIPAL DISTRICT OF
PINCHER CREEK WEST
Coleman
Graftontown
Kananaskis Rd
Crowsnest Pass Sports Complex
Crowsnest Consolidated
Trailer Ct Rd
Municipal Cemeteries
Flumerfelt Park
Baseball Diamonds
Horace Allen
Crowsnest Museum
Trailer Park
Pelletier Creek
Crowsnest River
CP
20 Av
To Fernie, British Columbia
Coleman
Blairmore
Frank
Frank Slide Provincial Historic Site
Bellevue
Hillcrest
Leitch Collieries Provincial Historic Site
Pass Powderkeg Ski Hill Luge
Turtle Mtn.
Rodeo Grounds
Bluff Mtn.
2 1 0 5 km km
79
80
81

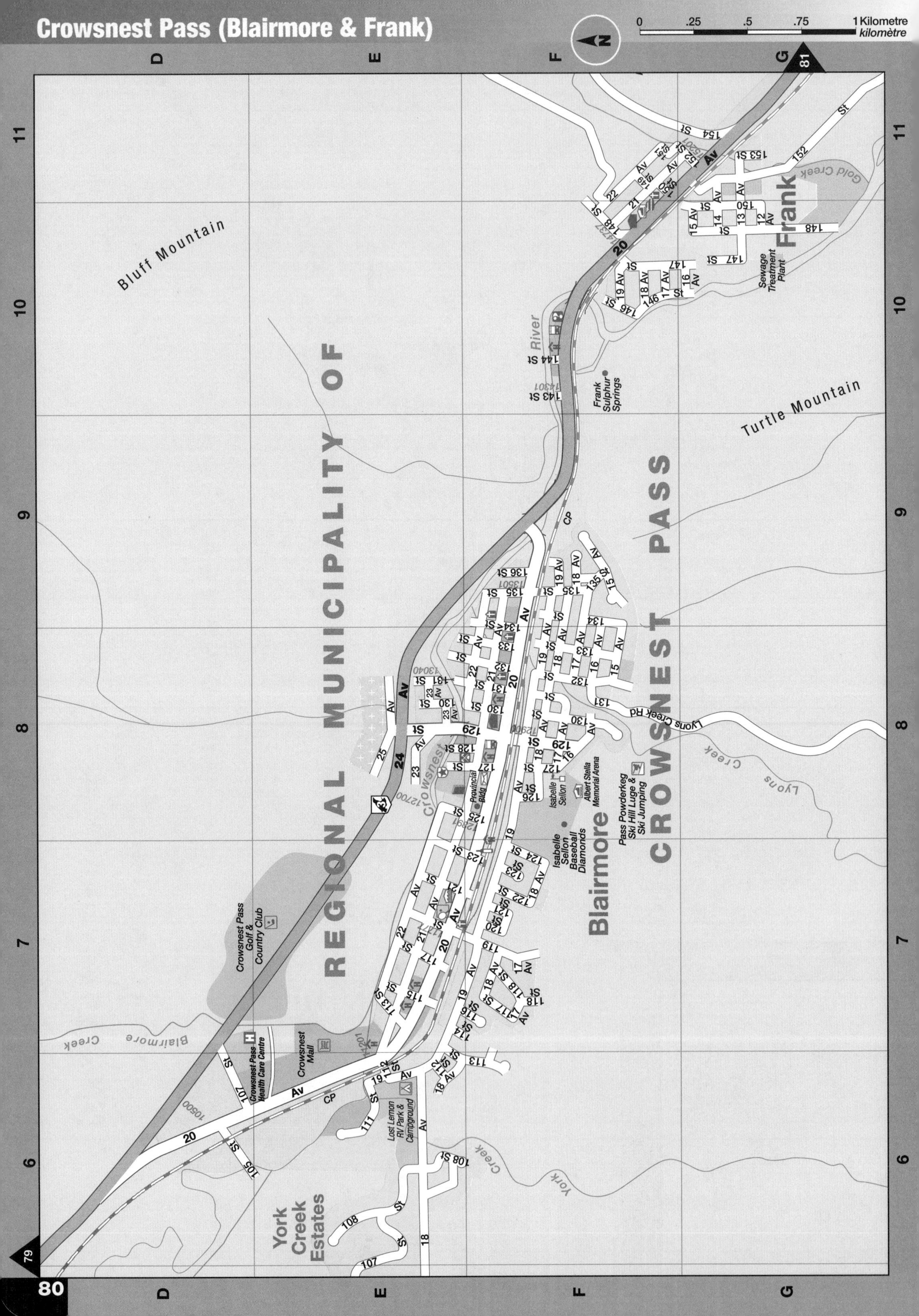
0
.25
.5
.75
1 Kilometre
kilomètre
Bluff Mountain
Turtle Mountain
REGIONAL MUNICIPALITY OF CROWSNEST PASS
Frank
Blairmore
York Creek Estates
Crowsnest Pass Golf & Country Club
Crowsnest Pass Health Care Centre
Crowsnest Mall
Lost Lemon RV Park & Campground
Provincial Bldg
Isabelle Sellon
Albert Stella Memorial Arena
Isabelle Sellon Baseball Diamonds
Pass Powderkeg Ski Hill Luge & Ski Jumping
Frank Sulphur Springs
Sewage Treatment Plant
Lyons Creek Rd
Crowsnest River
Blairmore Creek
York Creek
Lyons Creek
Gold Creek
CP
20 Av
24 Av
Bldg
79
81

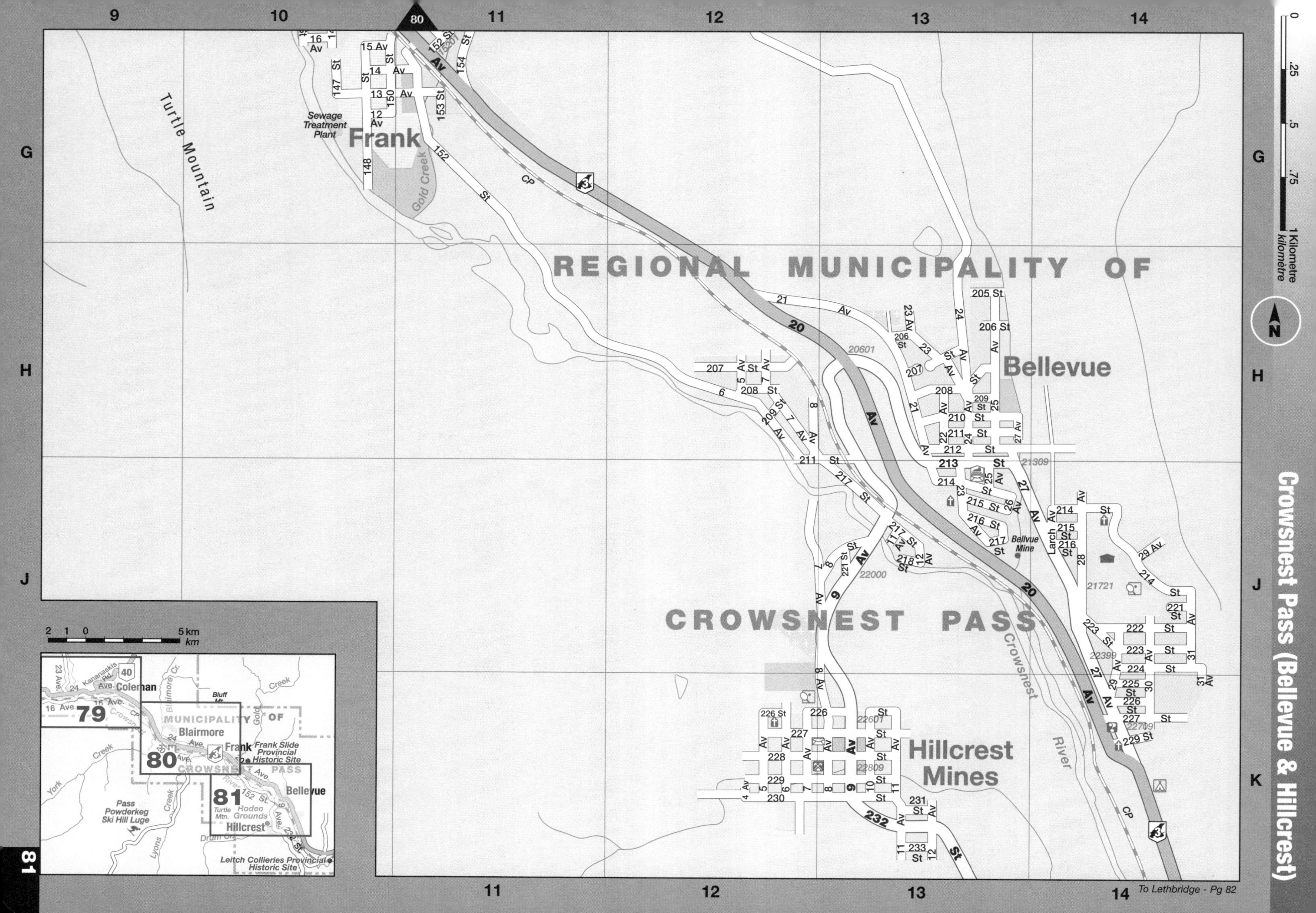
0 .25 .5 .75 1 Kilometre kilomètre
N
REGIONAL MUNICIPALITY OF CROWSNEST PASS
Bellevue
Hillcrest Mines
Frank
Turtle Mountain
Sewage Treatment Plant
Gold Creek
Crowsnest River
Bellvue Mine
CP
To Lethbridge - Pg 82
Coleman
Blairmore
Frank Slide Provincial Historic Site
Rodeo Grounds
Hillcrest
Pass Powderkeg Ski Hill Luge
Leitch Collieries Provincial Historic Site
79
80
81

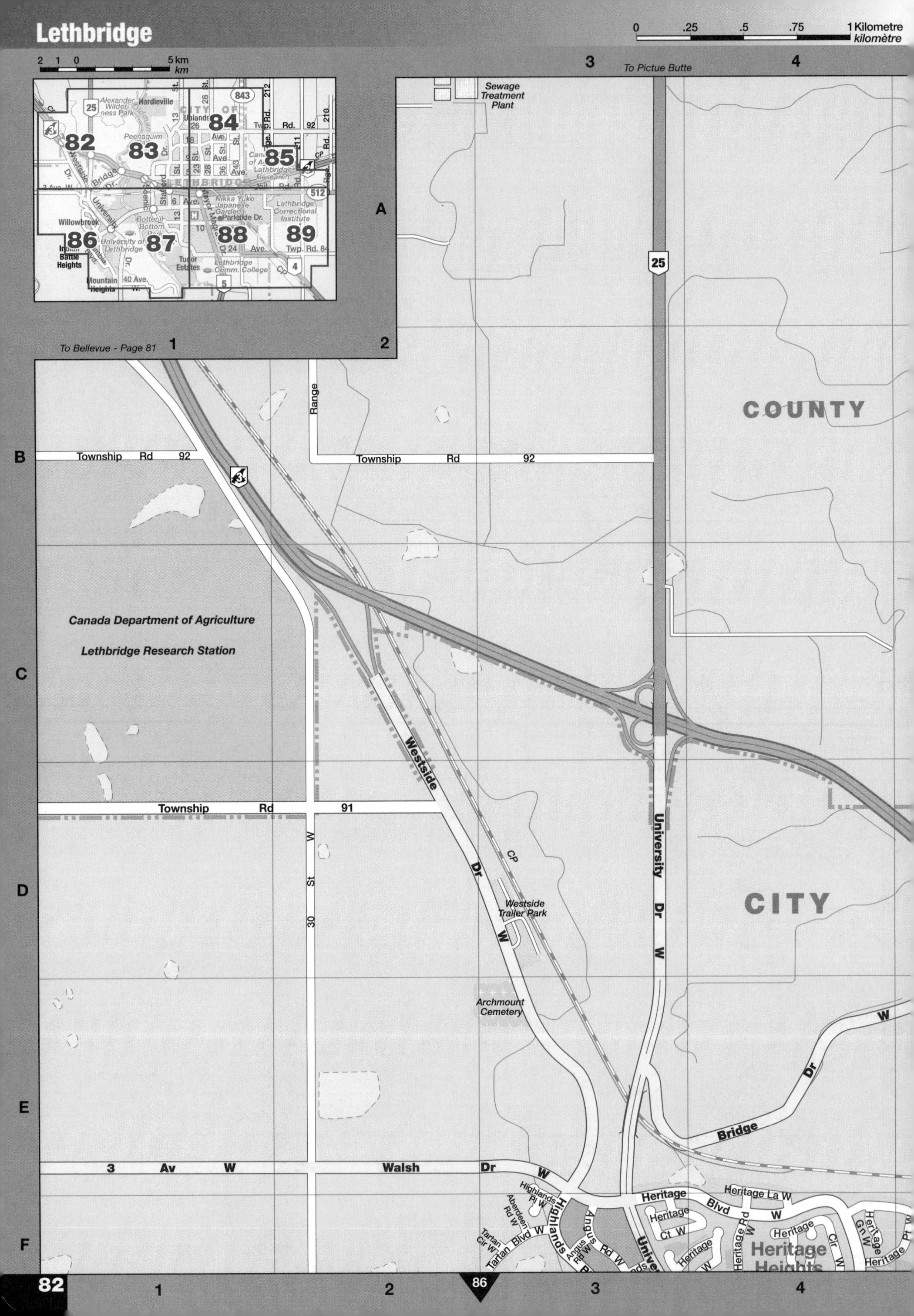

Lethbridge

2 1 0   5 km
km

82   83   84   85
86   87   88   89

Alexander Wilderness Park
Hardieville
Peenaquim

3   To Pictue Butte   4

A

COUNTY

Sewage Treatment Plant

25

B   Township   Rd   92

Township   Rd   92

Range

C

Canada Department of Agriculture

Lethbridge Research Station

Westside   Dr   W

CP

University   Dr   W

CITY

D   Township   Rd   91

St   W

30

Westside Trailer Park

E   *Archmount Cemetery*

Bridge   Dr   W

3   Av   W   Walsh   Dr   W

Highlands Pl W
Aberdeen Rd W
Tartan Cir W
Tartan Blvd W
Angus Rd W

Heritage
Heritage   Blvd   W
Heritage La W
Heritage Ct W
Heritage Rd W
Heritage Cir W
Heritage Gn W

F   *Heritage Heights*

To Bellevue - Page 81   1   2

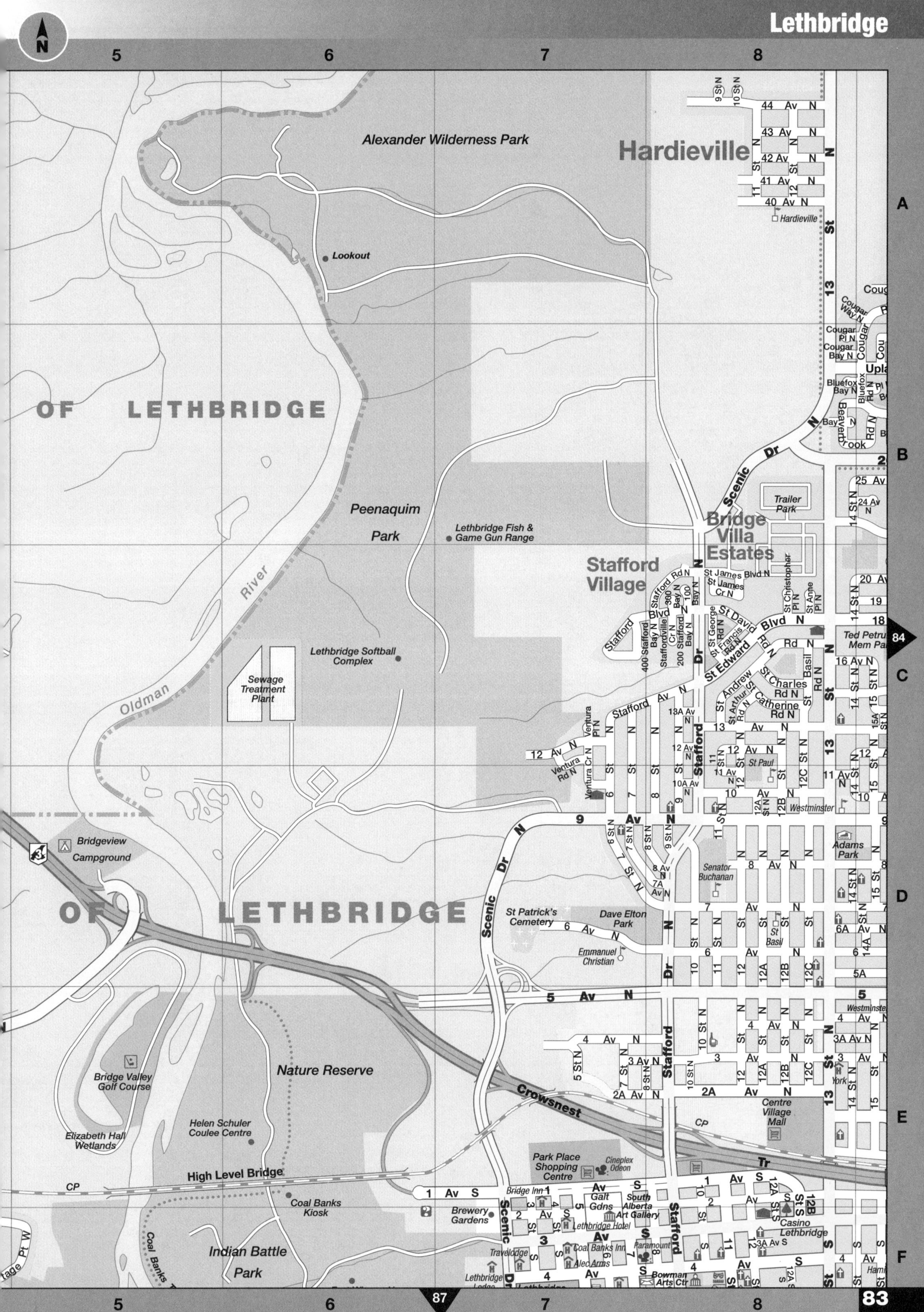
Alexander Wilderness Park
Hardieville
Lookout
OF LETHBRIDGE
Peenaquim Park
Lethbridge Fish & Game Gun Range
Oldman River
Sewage Treatment Plant
Lethbridge Softball Complex
Stafford Village
Bridge Villa Estates
Trailer Park
Bridgeview Campground
St Patrick's Cemetery
Dave Elton Park
Emmanuel Christian
Senator Buchanan
Adams Park
Ted Petrunia Mem Park
Nature Reserve
Bridge Valley Golf Course
Elizabeth Hall Wetlands
Helen Schuler Coulee Centre
High Level Bridge
Coal Banks Kiosk
Indian Battle Park
Park Place Shopping Centre
Cineplex Odeon
Centre Village Mall
Brewery Gardens
Galt Gdns
South Alberta Art Gallery
Lethbridge Hotel
Casino Lethbridge
Crowsnest Tr
Scenic Dr
Stafford Dr
13 St
5 Av N
9 Av N
1 Av S
2A Av N
3 Av S
4 Av S
Bowman Arts Ctr
Travelodge
Coal Banks Inn
Alec Arms
Paramount
Bridge Inn
Westminster
York
St Basil
St Paul

0 .25 .5 .75 1 Kilometr
kilomètre

9   10   11   12

A

Cougar Way N
Marmot Rd N
Cougar Way N
Cougar Rd
Lynx Pl
Lynx Rd N
Cougar Pl N
Cougar Cr N
Kodiak
Blvd
Grizzly Ter N
Cougar Bay N
Uplands
Blvd
Ermineglen Rd N
Ermineview Rd N
Bluefox Bay N
Beaverun Pl N
Ermine Run N
Ermine Pl N
Ermineglen Pl N
Erminebend Pl N
Grizzly Ter N
Bluefox Pl N
Ermine Pl N
Beaverbrook Rd N
Foxbend Cr N
Bluefox Blvd
Kodiak Blvd N
Uplands
Beaverpond Ct N
Bay N
Ermineview Way N
Kodiak Cr N

B

26   Av   N   26   Av   N

25 Av N   25 Av N   Eagle Rd
14 St N
16 St N
17 St N
19 St N
22 St N
24 Av N
Oriole Rd N
Pheasant Rd N
Robin Rd N
Quail Pl N
Churchill
24 Av N
24 Av N
24 Av N
23   Av   Meadowlark   Blvd N
31 St N
39 St N
41 St N
Industrial Park
Park Meadows
Hawthorne Pl N
16 St N
20 Av N   20 Av N
Heather Rd N
Hawthorne Rd N
Meadowlark
18   Av   19 Av N   Park Meadows Blvd N
18   Av   N
16 Av N   Larkspur Cl N
Heather
Greenview Cl N
Honeysuckle Cl N
16 St N
18 St N
29 St N
31
33 St N
36 St N
39 St N
41 St N
43   St   N

83

C

Ted Petrunia Mem Park
Park Meadows
Primrose Cl N
14 Av N   14 Av N
16 Av N
Stan Siwik Pool
Winston Churchill
Park Meadows Shopping Centre
15 Av N
14 Av N
13 Av N
25 St
27 St
28   St   N
29 St N
30 St N
31
33
36
39
41
43   St   N
14 St N
16 St N
17 St
19 St N
13
14 Av N
12
11A Av N
22 St N
12 Av N
11A Av N
11A Av N
10A Av N
12
C I T Y   O F
13
12 Av N
18 St N
18A St N
10A Av N
27A
10 Av N
10
Wilson

D

9   Av   N   9   Av   N
Galbraith
8A Av N   8A Av N   8A
Adams Park
14 St N
15 St
8 Av N   8 Av N
29 St N
8   Av   N
Shackleford
Industrial Park
7A Av N   7A
7A Av N
18A St N
24 St N
7A Av N
7
32
6A Av N
6A
6A Av N
30
6   Av   N
6   Av
6A Av N
14A
5A   Av   N
McKillop Pl N
L E T H B R I D G E
41 St N
43   St   N

E

5   Av   N   5   Av   Av   N
Westminster Pool
21A Av N
4 Av N   4 Av N
26 St N
29 St N
Anderson
Industrial Park
Westminster
DND
4 Av N
17 St N
3A Av N
3 Av N
2B Av
Magrath Dr N
31 St
33
36
39 St N
43   St
York
2A Av N
2A   N
20A St N
2   2A
26 St N
28 St N
30 St N
35 St N
36 St
CP
Canada
of Agr
Lethbridg
17 St N
1A Av N
Mayor
22
2   26   Av   N
Tr

F

Crowsnest
3 St S
9 Av S
2 Av S
32 St S
34 St S
WT Hill Blvd S
2 Av S
4
Fairview
St Francis
Lethbridge Collegiate
Catholic Central
Sandman Hotel
Leaside Av
Cassino St S
Falaise St S
Dieppe Blvd S
Normandy
Corvette
Astra
Ortona St S
3 Av S
3A Av S
44
4 Av S
Hamilton
St Mary's
4 Av S

88

9   10   11   12

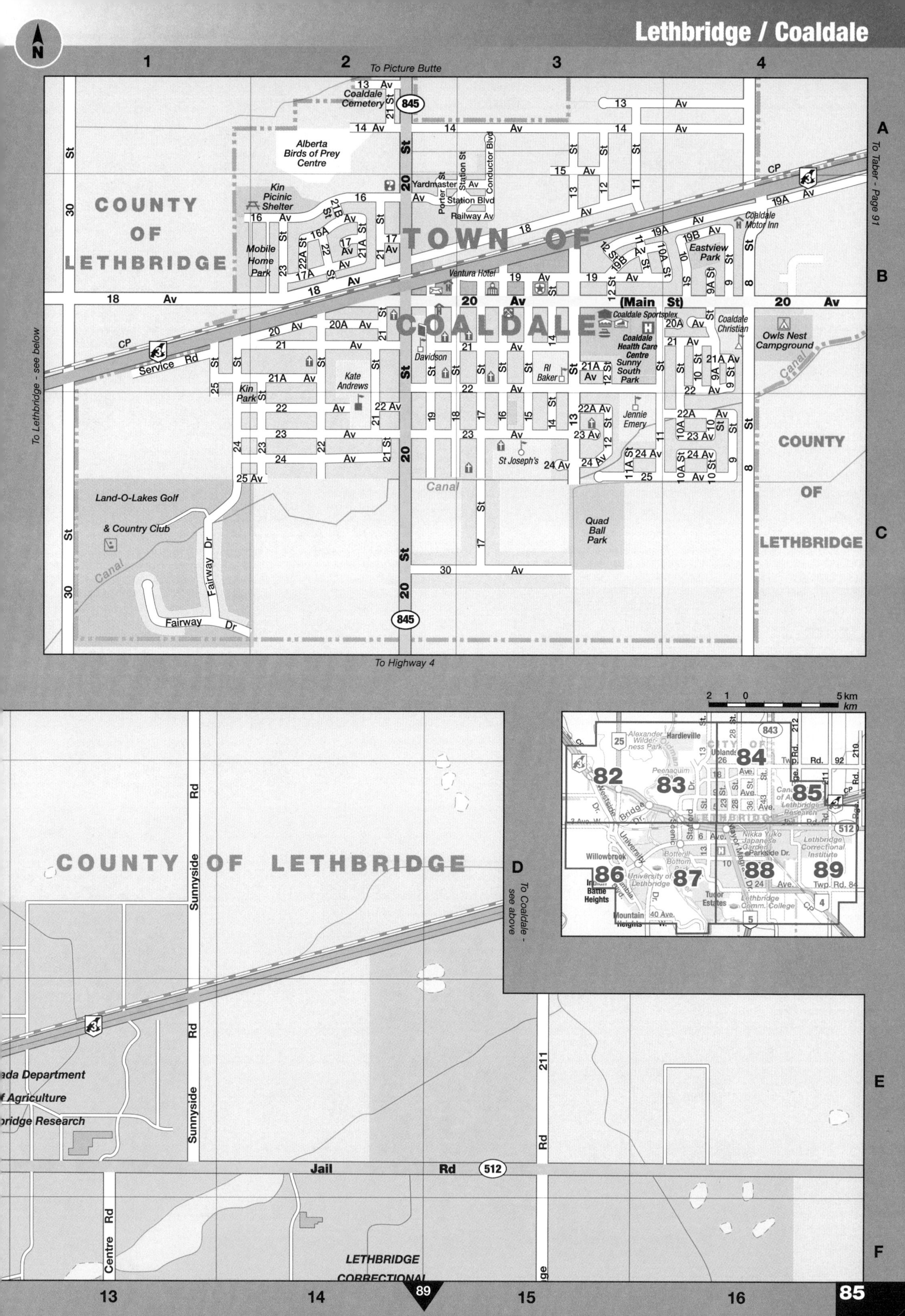
Lethbridge / Coaldale
To Picture Butte
Coaldale Cemetery
845
Alberta Birds of Prey Centre
Kin Picinic Shelter
Mobile Home Park
COUNTY OF LETHBRIDGE
TOWN OF COALDALE
Yardmaster Av
Station St
Conductor Blvd
Station Blvd
Porter St
Railway Av
Ventura Hotel
20 Av (Main St)
Coaldale Sportsplex
Coaldale Health Care Centre
Sunny South Park
Coaldale Christian
Owls Nest Campground
Coaldale Motor Inn
Eastview Park
Davidson
Kate Andrews
Kin Park
RI Baker
Jennie Emery
St Joseph's
Service Rd
CP
Canal
Land-O-Lakes Golf & Country Club
Fairway Dr
Quad Ball Park
30 Av
To Highway 4
To Taber - Page 91
To Lethbridge - see below
COUNTY OF LETHBRIDGE
To Coaldale - see above
Sunnyside Rd
Jail Rd
512
211 Rd
Centre Rd
Canada Department of Agriculture Lethbridge Research
LETHBRIDGE CORRECTIONAL
CITY OF LETHBRIDGE
82
83
84
85
86
87
88
89
Alexander Wilderness Park
Hardieville
Uplands
Peenaquim
Westside Dr.
Bridge Dr.
University Dr.
Scenic Dr.
Stafford Dr.
Mayor Magrath Dr.
Willowbrook
Indian Battle Heights
University of Lethbridge
Botterill Bottom Park
Nikka Yuko Japanese Garden
Parkside Dr.
Lethbridge Correctional Institute
Lethbridge Research
Tudor Estates
Lethbridge Comm. College
Mountain Heights
Twp. Rd. 84
843
25
4
5
2 1 0 5 km
13
14
15
16
89
85

0
.25
.5
.75
1 Kilometre
kilomètre
82
3 Av W
Walsh Dr W
30 St W
24 Av W
25 St W
Heritage Heights
Willowbrook
Atso Towaawa Athletic Park
Mike Mountain Horse School
Indian Battle Heights
Fr Leonard Van Tighem
Children of St Martha
Rutgers Park
Nicholas Sheran Lake
Nicholas Sheran Park
Sheridan Park
Columbia Park
University Dr
Whoop-Up Dr
Benton Dr W
McMaster Blvd
Columbia Blvd
Temple Blvd
Simon Fraser Blvd W
Red Crow Blvd W
Jerry Potts Blvd
Heritage Blvd W
Garry Dr W
Highlands Blvd W
Squamish Blvd W
Blackfoot Blvd W
Chilcotin Blvd W
Mohawk Blvd W
Castle Mountain W
Cascade Blvd
2 1 0 5 km
82
83
84
85
86
87
88
89
CITY OF LETHBRIDGE
Hardieville
Alexander Wilderness Park
Uplands
Peenaquim
Willowbrook
Indian Battle Heights
Mountain Heights
Tudor Estates
University of Lethbridge
Nikka Yuko Japanese Garden
Lethbridge Research
Lethbridge Correctional Institute
Lethbridge Comm. College
a
Riverview Pkwy W
Canyon Ct W
Canyoncrest Pl
Canyon Blvd W
100 Canyon Terr W
200 Canyon Terr W
Canyon Cl W
Canyon Gardens W
Canyon Ct W
Canyon Gn W
Paradise Canyon Golf Course
LETHBRIDGE
Paradise Canyon
1 2 3 4 6 7 8
E F G H J K L

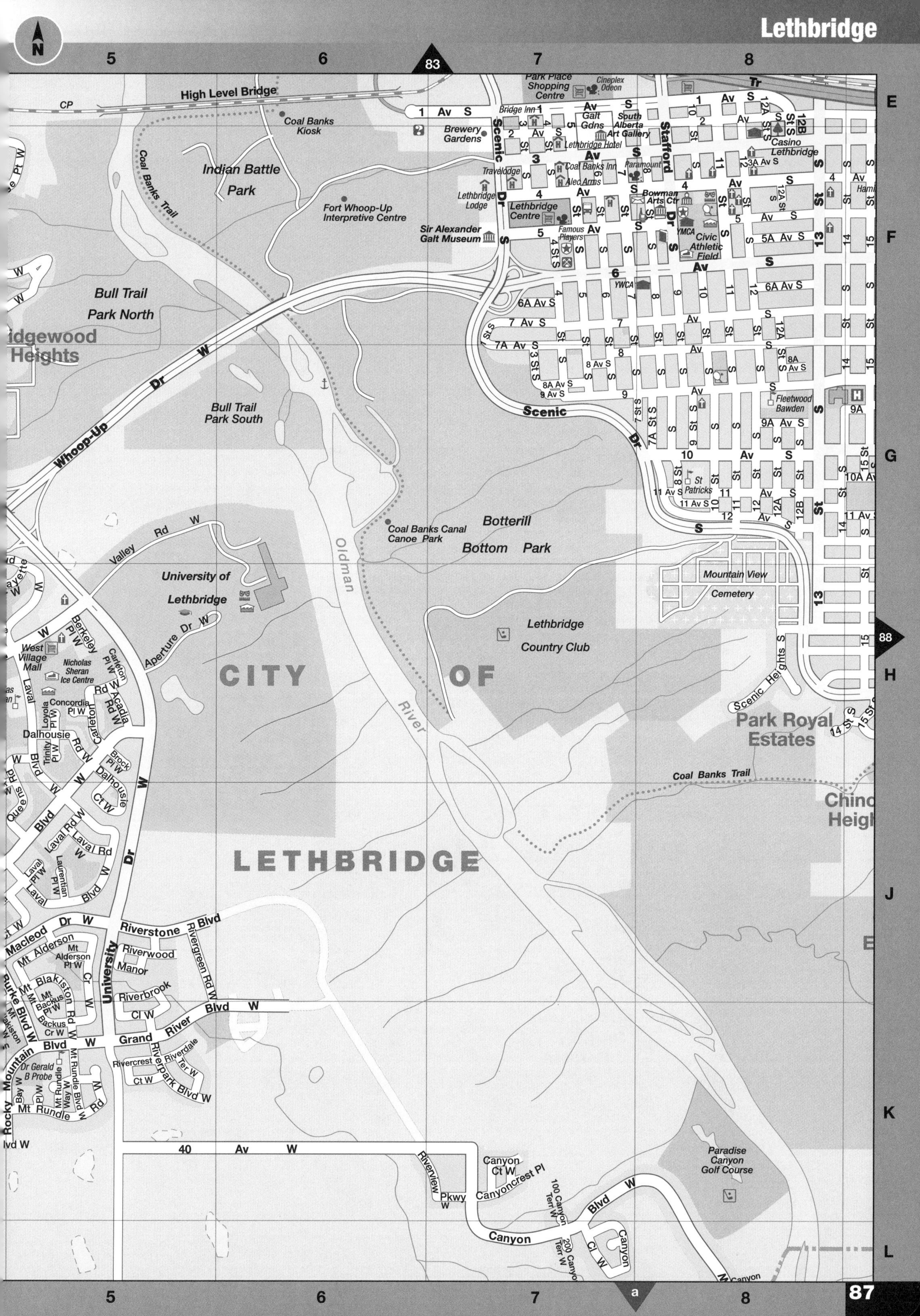

N

CP

High Level Bridge

Coal Banks Kiosk

Indian Battle Park

Coal Banks Trail

Brewery Gardens

Fort Whoop-Up Interpretive Centre

Sir Alexander Galt Museum

Bridge Inn
Park Place Shopping Centre
Cineplex Odeon
Galt Gdns
South Alberta Art Gallery
Lethbridge Hotel
Coal Banks Inn
Alec Arms
Travelodge
Lethbridge Lodge
Lethbridge Centre
Casino Lethbridge
Paramount
Bowman Arts Ctr
YMCA
Famous Players
Civic Athletic Field
YWCA
Fleetwood Bawden

idgewood Heights

Bull Trail Park North

Whoop-Up Dr W

Valley Rd W

Bull Trail Park South

Oldman

Scenic Dr S

Scenic Dr

St Patricks

Coal Banks Canal Canoe Park

Botterill

Bottom Park

Mountain View Cemetery

University of Lethbridge

Aperture Dr W

West Village Mall

Barkeley Pl W
Carleton Rd W
Acadia Rd W
Nicholas Sheran Ice Centre
Concordia Pl W
Loyola Pl W

Dalhousie

Laval

Trinity Pl W
Brock Pl W
Dalhousie Ct W

River

CITY

Lethbridge Country Club

OF

Scenic Heights S

Park Royal Estates

Chino Heigh

Queens
Blvd
Laval Rd W
Laval Rd
Laval Pl W
Laurentian Pl W
Laval

LETHBRIDGE

Coal Banks Trail

Macleod Dr W

Riverstone Blvd

University Dr

Rivergreen Rd W

Riverwood Manor

Riverbrook

Mt Alderson
Mt Alderson Pl W
Blakiston Rd
Mt Backus Pl W
Mt Backus Cr W
Cl W
Blvd W

Burke Blvd W

Grand River Blvd W

Rocky Mountain Blvd

Dr Gerald B Probe
Mt Rundle Blvd W
Mt Rundle Pl W
Bay W
Mt Rundle Rd
Rivercrest Ct W
Riverpark Blvd W
Riverdale Tier W
Riverdale Ter W

Blvd W

40 Av W

Riverview Pkwy

Canyon Ct W
Canyoncrest Pl

Paradise Canyon Golf Course

100 Canyon Terr W
200 Canyon Terr W

Canyon Blvd W

Canyon

Canyon Cl W

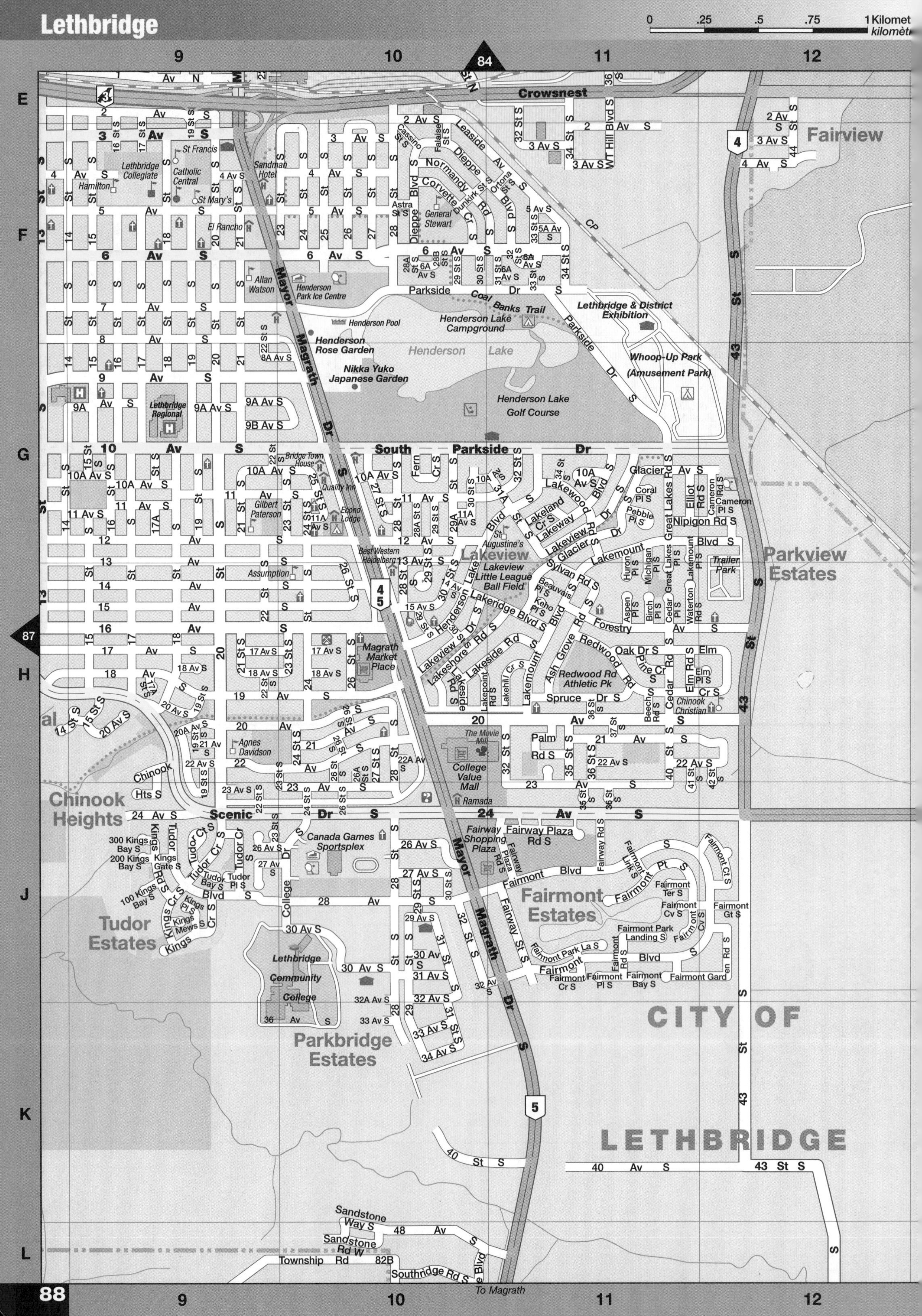
0 .25 .5 .75 1 Kilomet
kilomèt
84
87
9
10
11
12
E
F
G
H
J
K
L
Crowsnest
Fairview
Lethbridge Collegiate
St Francis
Catholic Central
St Mary's
Hamilton
Sandman Hotel
El Rancho
General Stewart
Allan Watson
Henderson Park Ice Centre
Henderson Pool
Henderson Rose Garden
Nikka Yuko Japanese Garden
Henderson Lake Campground
Coal Banks Trail
Henderson Lake
Henderson Lake Golf Course
Lethbridge & District Exhibition
Whoop-Up Park (Amusement Park)
Lethbridge Regional
Mayor Magrath Dr
South Parkside Dr
Parkside Dr
Bridge Town House
Quality Inn
Gilbert Paterson
Econo Lodge
Best Western Heidelberg
Assumption
St Augustine's
Lakeview
Lakeview Little League Ball Field
Parkview Estates
Trailer Park
Magrath Market Place
Redwood Rd Athletic Pk
Chinook Christian
Agnes Davidson
The Movie Mill
College Value Mall
Ramada
Chinook Heights
Scenic Dr S
Canada Games Sportsplex
Fairway Shopping Plaza
Fairway Plaza Rd S
Fairmont Estates
Tudor Estates
Lethbridge Community College
Parkbridge Estates
CITY OF LETHBRIDGE
Sandstone Way S
Sandstone Rd W
Township Rd 82B
Southridge Rd S
To Magrath
43 St S
40 Av S
24 Av S
4
5

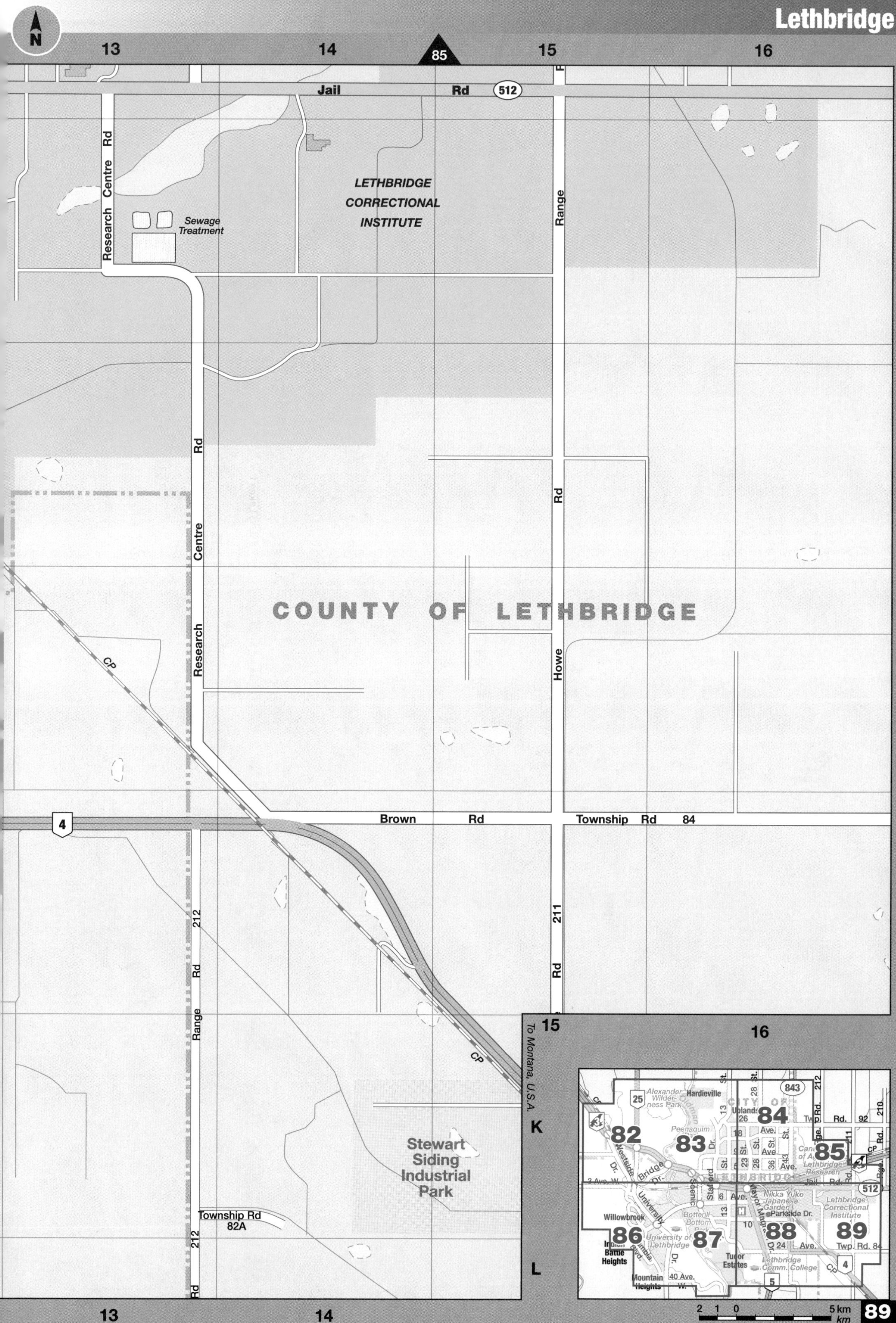

N

13   14   ▲85   15   16

E

Jail   Rd   512

Research Centre Rd

Sewage
Treatment

LETHBRIDGE
CORRECTIONAL
INSTITUTE

Range

F

G

Research   Centre   Rd

Rd

CP

COUNTY   OF   LETHBRIDGE

Howe

H

4

Brown   Rd   Township Rd 84

212

211

J

Range   Rd

Rd

CP

15   16

To Montana, U.S.A.

K

Stewart
Siding
Industrial
Park

212

Township Rd
82A

L

13   14

CITY OF LETHBRIDGE inset:

Alexander Wilder-ness Park   Hardieville   843   212

25   Uplands

82   Peenaquim   83   84   85   Canada Lethbridge Research Jail   512

Nikka Yuko Japanese Garden   Parkside Dr.   Lethbridge Correctional Institute

Willowbrook   Botterill Bottom   University of Lethbridge   Tudor Estates   Lethbridge Comm. College   Twp. Rd. 84

86   87   88   89

Indian Battle Heights

Mountain Heights   40 Ave. W.   5   4

2 1 0   5 km
km

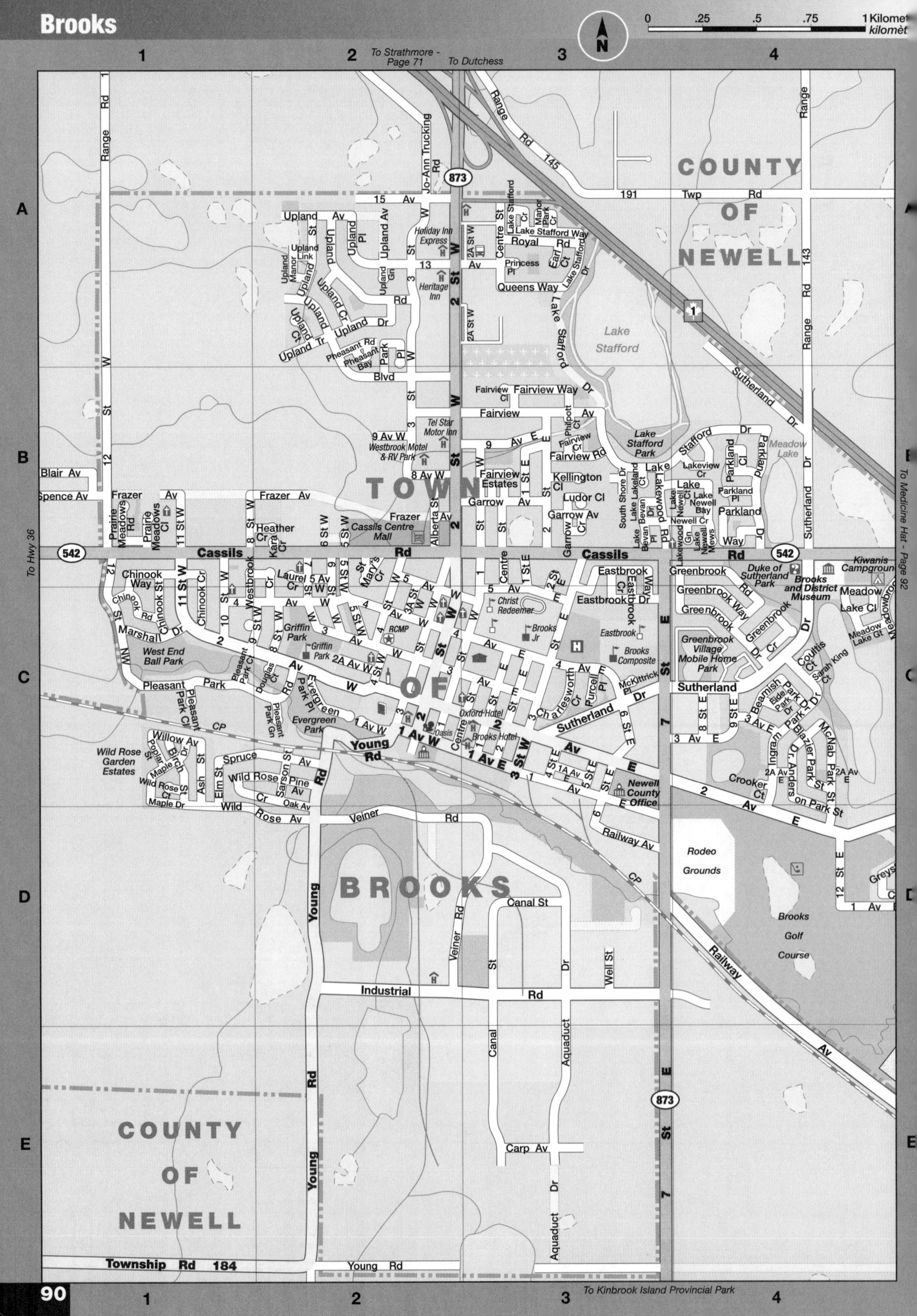

To Strathmore - Page 71
To Dutchess
To Hwy 36
To Medicine Hat - Page 92
To Kinbrook Island Provincial Park
COUNTY OF NEWELL
TOWN OF BROOKS
Lake Stafford
Lake Stafford Park
Meadow Lake
Cassils Rd
Holiday Inn Express
Heritage Inn
Tel Star Motor Inn
Westbrook Motel & RV Park
Cassils Centre Mall
West End Ball Park
Griffin Park
Christ Redeemer
Brooks Jr
Brooks Composite
Greenbrook Village Mobile Home Park
Duke of Sutherland Park
Brooks and District Museum
Kiwanis Campground
Oxford Hotel
Brooks Hotel
Newell County Office
Evergreen Park
Wild Rose Garden Estates
Rodeo Grounds
Brooks Golf Course
Industrial Rd
Township Rd 184

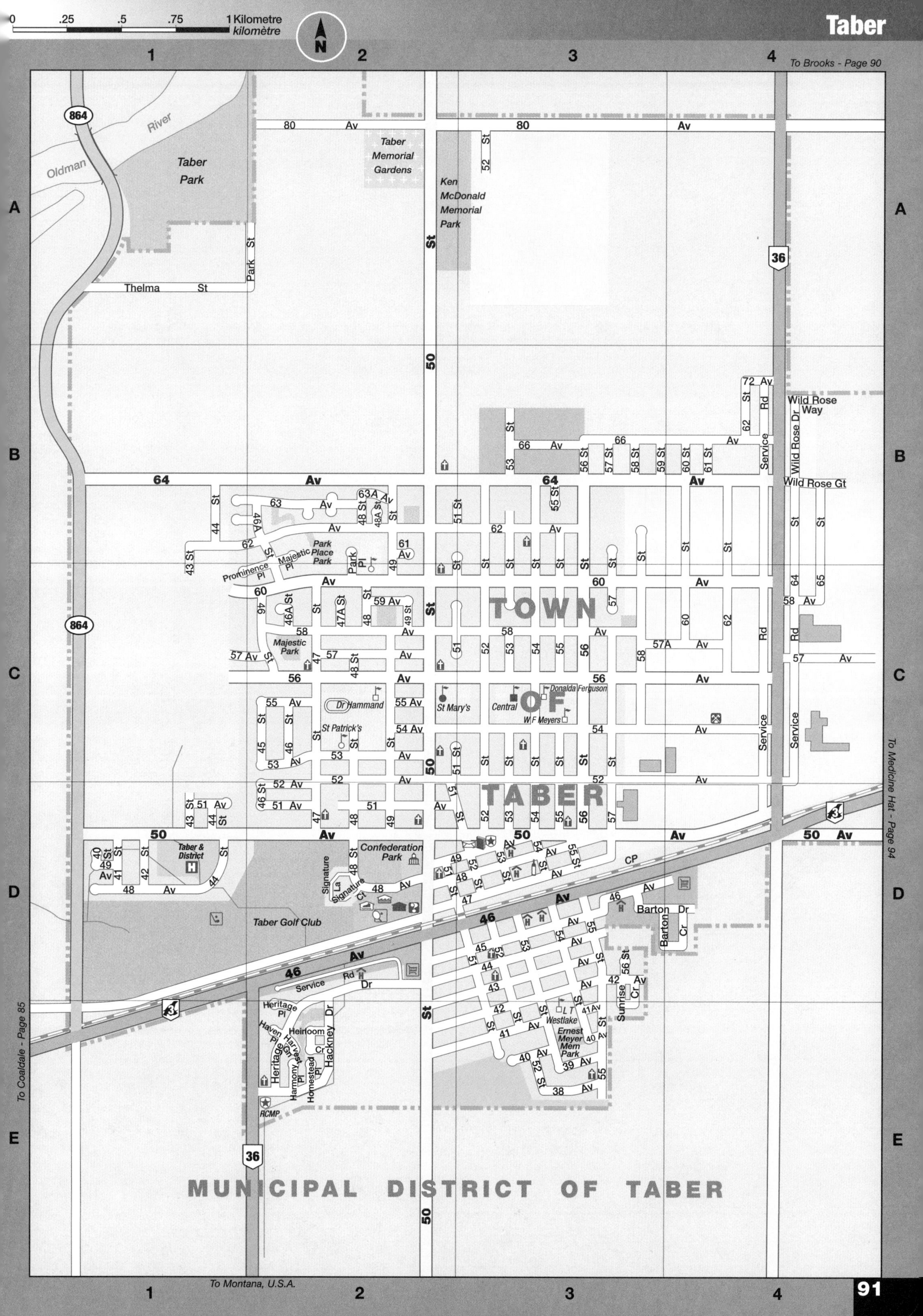

0 .25 .5 .75 1 Kilometre kilomètre
N
To Brooks - Page 90
To Medicine Hat - Page 94
To Coaldale - Page 85
To Montana, U.S.A.
Oldman River
Taber Park
Taber Memorial Gardens
Ken McDonald Memorial Park
Park Place Park
Majestic Park
Confederation Park
Taber & District
Taber Golf Club
Ernest Meyer Mem Park
RCMP
St Mary's
Central
Donalda Ferguson
W F Meyers
Dr Hammand
St Patrick's
L T Westlake
TOWN OF TABER
MUNICIPAL DISTRICT OF TABER
80 Av
64 Av
60 Av
56 Av
50 Av
46 Av
50 St
Thelma St
Park St
Wild Rose Way
Wild Rose Gt
Wild Rose Dr
Service Rd
Barton Dr
Barton Cr
Sunrise Cr
Heritage Pl
Haven Pl
Harvest Gn
Heirloom Cr
Hackney Dr
Harmony Pl
Homestead Pl
Heritage Gn
Signature La
Signature Ct
Prominence Pl
Majestic Pl
Service Rd Dr
CP

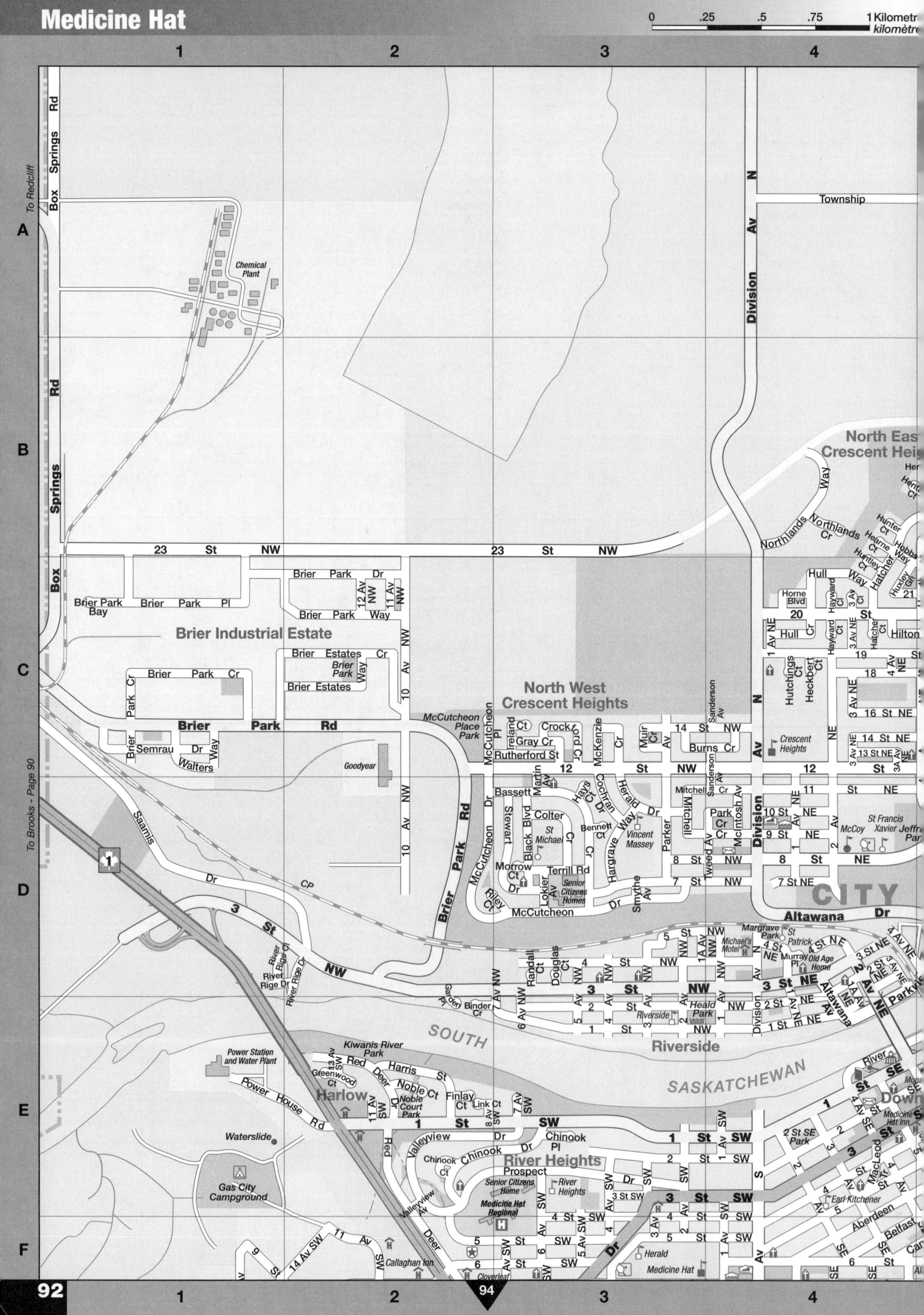

1 2 3 4

A

Township

To Redcliff

Box Springs Rd

Chemical Plant

Division Av

N

North East Crescent Heights

B

Box Springs Rd

Her

Way

Northlands Cr

Northlands

Heritage Ct

Hunter Ct

Hearne Way

Huntley Ct

Hatchet

Huxley Way

21

23 St NW

23 St NW

Hull

Hayward Way

Horne Blvd

3 Av NE

20

1 Av NE

Hull Cr

Hayward Ct

Hatchet St

Hilton

Brier Park Dr

12 Av NW

11 Av NW

Brier Park Pl

Brier Park Bay

Brier Park Way

Brier Industrial Estate

10 Av NW

19 St

4 Av NE

18 St

3 Av NE

16 St NE

C

Brier Estates Cr

Brier Park Way

North West Crescent Heights

Sanderson Av

Hutchings Ct

Heckbert Ct

Brier Park Cr

Park Cr

Brier Estates

Crescent Heights

3 Av NE

14 St NE

3A St NE

13 St NE

Brier Park Rd

McCutcheon Place Park

McCutcheon

Ireland Ct

Crock

Gray Cr

McKenzie

Muir Av

14 St NW

Burns Cr

Sanderson Av

Division Av

N

12 St NE

Brier Semrau Dr Way

Walters

Goodyear

10 Av NW

Rutherford St

12 St NW

Bassett

Martin

Hays Ct

Cochran

Herald

Mitchell

Mitchell

11 St NE

10 St NE

St Francis Xavier Jeffr Par

D

10 Av NW

Brier Park Rd

McCutcheon Dr

Stewart

Black Blvd

Colter

St Michael

Bennett

Hargrave Way

Vincent Massey

Parker

Park Cr

McCoy

9 St NE

Saamis Dr

CP

Morrow Ct

Terrill Rd

Senior Citizens Homes

Smythe Av

Tweed Av

McIntosh Av

8 St NW

7 St NE

CITY

1

3 St NW

River Rige Dr

River Rige Dr

Riley Dr

Lokier Dr

McCutcheon Dr

Margrave Park

Michael's Motel

St Patrick

Murray

Old Age Home

Altawana Dr

To Brooks - Page 90

Randall St

Douglas St

1 Av NW

4 St

3 St NE

3 St NE

4 Av NE

2 Av NE

Parkvi

Garden Pl

Binder Cr

6 Av NW

5 Av NW

3 St NW

Heald Park

Division Av

3 St NE

Altawana Av

E

Power Station and Water Plant

Kiwanis River Park

13 Av SW

Red

Harris

Deer

Noble Ct

Finlay Ct

Link Ct

7 Av SW

1 Av NW

Riverside NW

1 Av NW

Riverside

SASKATCHEWAN

River

SE St

Power House Rd

Greenwood Ct

Harlow

11 Av SW

Valleyview Dr

Noble Court Park

1 St SW

8 Av SW

Chinook Pl

1 St SW

2

1 St SW

Medicine Hat Inn

Down

Waterslide

Chinook Ct

Chinook

Chinook

River Heights

Prospect

River Heights

2

Dr

1 St SW

2 St SE Park

S

Gas City Campground

Valleyview Av

Deer

Senior Citizens Home

Medicine Hat Regional

H

3 St SW

4 Av SW

3 St SW

3 St SW

3 Av SW

MacLeod

3

Earl Kitchener

Aberdeen

F

14 Av SW

11 Av SW

Callaghan Inn

Cloverleaf

5

6

4 Av SW

5 Av SW

5 St SW

Dr

Herald

Medicine Hat

Belfast

Parkview
Medicine Hat Golf Course
Sewage Lagoon
OF MEDICINE HAT
RIVER
Police Point Park
Police Point Park Interpretive Centre
Strathcona Island Park
Heritage Pavilion
North Flats
Veinerville
Athletic Ball Park
Arena & Convention Centre
Senior Citizens Home
Lions Park
Strathcona Centre
Webster Niblock
Train Station
Ranchlands Blvd
Robinson Rd
Bridge St
41A
92
93
94
95
A
B
C
D
E
F
5
6
7
8

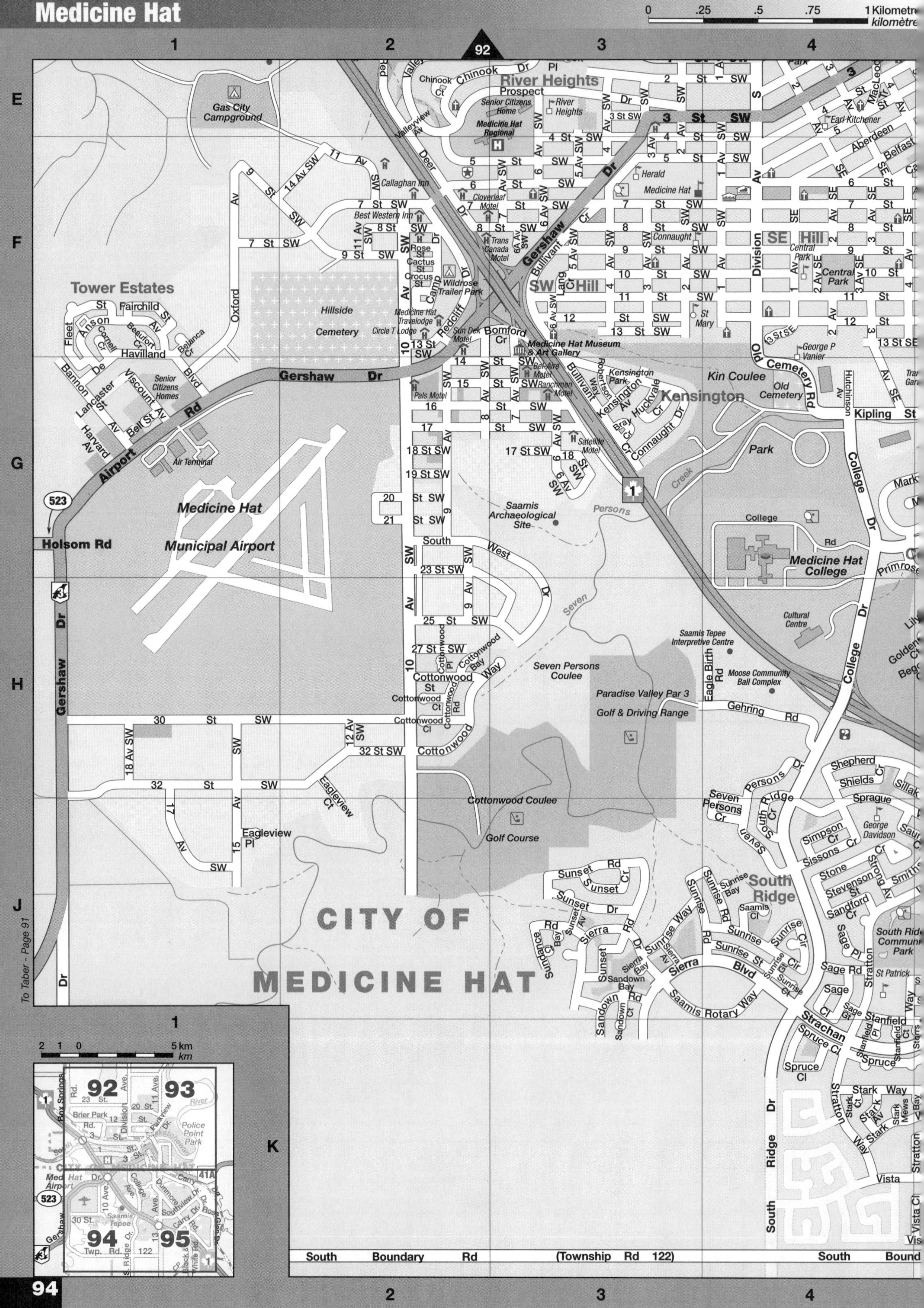
0 .25 .5 .75 1 Kilometre
kilomètre
92
River Heights
Gas City Campground
Senior Citizens Home
Medicine Hat Regional
Callaghan Inn
Best Western Inn
Cloverleaf Motel
Trans Canada Motel
Herald
Medicine Hat
Connaught
SE Hill
Central Park
Earl Kitchener
Aberdeen
Belfast
Tower Estates
Fairchild
Anson
Cornell
Beaufort
Belanca
Havilland
Fleet
Bannon
Lancaster
Viscount
Senior Citizens Homes
Harvard
Bell
Hillside Cemetery
Oxford
Rose
Cactus
Crocus
Camp
Wildrose Trailer Park
Medicine Hat Travelodge
Circle T Lodge
Redcliff
Sun Dek Motel
Bomford
Medicine Hat Museum & Art Gallery
SW Hill
Lang
Bullivant
Gershaw Dr
St Mary
George P Vanier
Old Cemetery Rd
Kin Coulee
Old Cemetery
Hutchinson
Kipling
Kensington
Robertson Way
Kensington Park
Huckvale
Bray
Connaught Dr
Bel-Aire Motel
Ranchmen Motel
Pals Motel
Satellite Motel
Park
Creek
Airport Rd
Air Terminal
523
Holsom Rd
Medicine Hat Municipal Airport
Saamis Archaeological Site
Persons
Seven
South West Dr
College Dr
College Rd
Medicine Hat College
Primrose
Cultural Centre
Saamis Tepee Interpretive Centre
Eagle Birth Rd
Moose Community Ball Complex
Seven Persons Coulee
Paradise Valley Par 3 Golf & Driving Range
Gehring Rd
Cottonwood
Cottonwood Pl
Cottonwood Bay
Cottonwood Way
Cottonwood Ct
Cottonwood Cl
Cottonwood Rd
30 St SW
32 St SW
18 Av SW
Eagleview Ct
Eagleview Pl
Cottonwood Coulee Golf Course
Gershaw Dr
Persons Dr
Seven Persons Cr
South Ridge Cr
Shepherd
Shields
Sprague
George Davidson
Simpson Cr
Sissons Cr
Stone
Stevenson St
Strong
Sandford Cr
Smith
Sunset Rd
Sunset Cr
Sunset Dr
Sunset Bay
Sundance
Sierra Rd
Sierra Dr
Sierra Bay
Sandown Bay
Sandown Rd
Sandown Ct
Sunrise Way
Sunrise Rd
Sunrise Bay
Saamis Cl
Sunrise Cir
Sunrise St
Sunrise Ct
Sierra Blvd
Saamis Rotary Way
South Ridge
South Ridge Community Park
Sage Pl
Sage Rd
Sage Ct
Sage Cl
St Patrick
Stratton Way
Stanfield
Strachan
Spruce Cl
Spruce Ct
Stark Way
Stark Ct
Stark Av
Stark Mews
Vista
Vista Cl
South Ridge Dr
CITY OF MEDICINE HAT
South Boundary Rd (Township Rd 122)
To Taber - Page 91
2 1 0 5 km
92
93
94
95
Box Springs
Brier Park Rd.
Division Ave.
Parkview Dr.
River
Police Point Park
Med Hat Airport
College Ave.
Dunmore Rd.
Carry Dr.
10 Ave.
30 St.
Saamis Tepee
Gershaw
Twp. Rd. 122
S. Ridge Dr.
Black & White Rd.
41A
523
1
2
3
4
E
F
G
H
J
K

N

5 6 93 7 8

E
F
G
H
J
K

To Highway 41

Veinerville

Shirley Av
Cartwright Av
Christman Av
Natalie Av

Robinson Rd

Porters Hill

41A

Day

Creek

St

CP

Rotary Park
Prince
Queen
Allowance
Woodr
Yuill
Washing
Minto

Dominion
North Flats
Queen
Coburg

Elm
Elm Street

Bridge St
Clay Av
Steel
Steel Street Park
Wood
Poffen
London
St

Bridge
Porcelain Av
Brick Av
Shale Av
Iron St
Rose St

Medalta Clay Products Interpretive Centre
Medalta Av

Strathcona Island Park

Heritage Pavilion

Industrial Av

Creek

Olive
S
Foundry
Railway St
St
Factory
CP

Mill St
Smelter
Factory

Elevator St
Persons
Carry Dr

Seven

Spencer
Marshall
Marshall Av

Craven Dr
Ravine Dr
Crestwood Dr
16 SE
St SE
Crestwood Dr

Crestwood Cr
Collins Cr
Corbitt Way
Carr
Castelan
Church St
Cook Ct
Cousins
Cowan
Cobb Rd
Cockrill Ct

Armories

Leinweber Park
Armories

Cuyler

Carry Dr

Cook Ct

Carter Ct
Chow Av
Clark
Currie
Clendel Cr
Cooney Rd

East Glen

East Glen
East Glen
East Glen
East Glen Cr
East Glen Cr

Ross Heights
Ross Heights Cr
Ross Heights Pl
Ross Heights Ct

Marlborough
Kwick
Morris Ct
Milne Pl
McNeely Ct

Upland Dr

17
16 Av SE
13 St SE
15 Av SE
16 Av SE
17 Av SE
19
18 Av SE
20 Av SE
19 Av SE
20 Av SE

St Thomas Aquinas

Exhibition & Stampede Grounds

Kinplex

Ewart Av
Elliott St
Eden Av
Elder Av
East Glen
East Glen
Glen
East Glen

College Dr
Connaught
Bluebell
Sunflower
Buttercup
Violet Ct
Camas Ct
Begonia Ct
Clematis
Lupine Ct
Clover Ct
Iris
Larkspur
Primrose

Dr
Upland
22 St SE
23 St SE
24
25
26
27 St
28

Norwood Tot Lot
Jackson St
Burton Pl
Lamb
17 Av SE
17 Av SE

21 St SE
23 St SE
24
20
26 St SE
28 St SE

22 Av
Higdon Av
Thompson

McCaig Ct

Amos St
Rohan Pl
Cavan Av
Gardner Pl
Porter Pl
Woolley Pl

Crescent View

Crestwood Recreation Centre
Crestwood

Southview
Southview
Collier
Rd
Cameron
Campbell
Cairney
Clelland
Cairns Way
Cane Rd

Crockett Way
Cook Rd
Craig Rd
Collie

Cypress

Clark
Currie Ct
Carswell Way

Dr
Ross
Glen

Rossdale
Rossdale
Rossdale Way

Ross Heights Pl
Ross Heights Ct

Connaught Golf Club

13

Hillcrest Bible Institute
30
15 Av SE
Norwood
31 St SE

Southview
Southview Ct
Southdale Ct
15 Av SE
17 Av SE

Dr

Calder Cir
Calder Gn
Calder
Calder
Calder Pl
Calder Bay
Calder Rd

Calder
Cook Rd
Cooper Rd
Cunliffe

Southview
Carry
Carry

Mother Teresa

Ross
Glen
Ross
Glen
Ross Glen Cr

Rossdale
Rossdale
Rossdale
Rossdale

Southview
Southview Mall

Days Inn
Westlander
Imperial Inn
Super 8 Motel

Park
Park Meadows Ct
Vintage Meadows Pl
Vintage Meadows

Dunmore Rd

Red Oak
Red Oak Blvd
Rideau
Rideau Ct
Rideau Gn

Cameron Way
Cameron

Rossland
Rossland
Rossland Blvd

Rossland
Rossland Pl
Rossmere
Rossmere Pl

Ross View Pl
Ross View
Ross View Cl
Ross View Bay

Ross View

Shannon
Silcher
Stapeford
Smeaton
Stock St
Sharpe Cr
Slack
Sprague
Smith
Schneider

Meadows La
Meadows Park
Sandstone
Comfort Inn & Suites

Meadowland

Grand

Red Oak Blvd
Radigson Av
Radisson
Rideau Gn

Ross Haven
Ross Haven
Ross Haven Pl
Ross Haven Av
Ross Haven Pl

Ross Glen
Ross Glen

Rossland
Rossland

Robinson Dr
Robinson Av
Robinson Rd

Trans
Canada

Medicine Hat Mall
Medicine Hat Lodge

Carry
Trans Canada Way

Rossmere Rd
Rae
Rossmere
Rae
Rae St
Rae Av

Rice Pl
Rice
Rice Bay

Stafford St
Schuler
Simmons
Swan
Scott Cr
Stein Cl
Spruce
Scott Gn
Scott
Way
Stanfield
Storrs
Sonegate Cr

SE Av

Strachan
Strachan Ct

Rd

Ross
Glen
Ross
Redwood
Redwood Bay
Redwood Way
Redwood Dr
Redwood St

Rae St
Rae Av
Haven
Rundle Wall
Rundle Pl
Rundle Cr

Rossmere
Glen
Ross View

Robinson Dr

Rice
Rice Cr
Rice Gn
Rice
Turner
Turner Gn
Turner Cr

Rice Pl
Rice Bay
Taylor Ct

Spruce Meadows
Scott Ct
Scott Bay
Way

South Ridge Estates Mobile Home Park

Stratton Dr
Vista Cl
Vista

Black & White Tr

1

Turner
Turner Gn
Turner Cr
Turner Cr
Ross
Glen Dr
Turner Cr
Turner Ct
Turner Rd

Taylor
Taylor
Taylor Pl
Taylor Ct

Taylor
Taylor Cr
Taylor Bay
Taylor Cir
Taylor Rd
Taylor Blvd
Taylor Mews

CP

South Boundary Rd
Boundary Rd
54 St

Street Index

Street Generics and Abbreviations

Av ....Avenue	Com ....Common	Frwy .....Freeway	Hill ....Hill	Mews .....Mews	Pl ....Place	Ter ....Terrace
Bay ....Bay	Cr ......Crescent	Gdns ....Gardens	Hts ......Heights	Mnr ......Manor	Pt ....Point	Tr ....Trail
Blvd ...Boulevard	Ct ....Court	Gn ....Green	Hwy ......Highway	Path ......Path	Rd ....Road	View ......View
Cape ....Cape	Cv ....Cove	Gr ....Grove	La ....Lane	Pk ....Park	Rise ......Rise	Vill ....Villas
Cir ....Circle	Dr ....Drive	Gt ....Gate	Ldg ......Landing	Pkwy ....Parkway	Sq ....Square	Walk ....Walk
Cl ....Close	Expwy .Expressway	Heath .....Heath	Link ....Link	Ptwy ....Pathway	St ....Street	Way ....Way

How to use the index

To find a street, search through the alphabetically arranged columns. A three letter code beside the street name indicates which municipality the street is located in. Note the page number and the reference square to the right of the street name. For example, to find the location of Abbercove Way:

Abbercove Way NE *CAL* 39 Y16

Turn to page 39 and locate the square Y16. Scan the square to find the street.

Comment utiliser l'index

Les noms de rues sont arrangés par ordre alphabétique. Un code de trois lettres à côté du nom indique la municipalité dans laquelle se trouve la rue. Prenez note du numéro de page et des coordonnées à la droite du nom. Par exemple, pour trouver la rue Huntington:

Huntington St NE *CAL* 21 Q8

Tourner à la page 21 et trouver le carré Q8. Vous y trouverez la rue Huntington.

Community Codes / Codes des communautés

AIRDRIE, CITY OF ....AIR	COALDALE, TOWN OF ....COD	OKOTOKS, TOWN OF ....OKO
BANFF, TOWN OF ....BAN	COCHRANE, TOWN OF ....COC	OLDS, TOWN OF ....OLD
BEISEKER, VILLAGE OF ....BEI	CROSSFIELD, TOWN OF ....CRS	Redwood Meadows (SARCEE IR 145) ..RDW
Bellevue (CROWSNEST PASS) ....CRO	Coleman (CROWSNEST PASS) ....CRO	RED DEER, CITY OF ....RED
BLACK DIAMOND, TOWN OF ....BLD	DRUMHELLER, CITY OF ....DRU	ROCKY VIEW, MUNICIPAL DISTRICT OF
Blairmore (CROWSNEST PASS) ....CRO	HIGH RIVER, TOWN OF ....HIG	(CALGARY OUTSKIRTS) ....RCY
Bragg Creek (ROCKY VIEW) ....BRG	INNISFAIL, TOWN OF ....INN	STRATHMORE, TOWN OF ....STM
BROOKS, TOWN OF ....BRO	IRRICANA, VILLAGE OF ....IRR	TABER, TOWN OF ....TAB
CALGARY, CITY OF ....CAL	Lake Louise (BANFF NAT. PARK) ....LKL	TURNER VALLEY, TOWN OF ....TVY
CANMORE, TOWN OF ....CAN	LETHBRIDGE, CITY OF ....LET	
CHESTERMERE, TOWN OF ....CHE	MEDICINE HAT, CITY OF ....MED	

Calgary's Numbered Roads

Calgary's numbered roads are now included in this index. In Calgary numbered streets run north-south, numbered avenues run east-west. Centre St and Centre Av run through the middle of the city, and numbers increase as you move farther from the centre. Use the key map on pages 2-3 to determine which page a numbered street will fall on.

Street Addresses

It's easy to determine the location of a building by its address on a numbered road. As an example, 3556 15 Av NW is found between 34 St NW and 35 St NW.

Highways | 2 | Routes provinciales

1 BAN 57 A4 C1	2 S CAL ...49 S27 50 V29 53 Q35 54 V31 W34	5 LET 88 H10 K11	23 HIG 77 C-D5
1 BRO 90 A4	2 AIR 68 B4 D4	7 BLD 75 B7	25 LET 82 A3
1 CAL 25 B12 26 F12-13 27 J14	2 CRS 62 A4 C4	7 OKO 75 E1 76 E4	27 OLD 62 B1 B4
...........28 O14 29 S14 31 Y14	2 HIG 77 A5 D5	8 CAL 34 E19 41 H21 K21 42 M22 43 Q22	36 TAB 91 A4 E1
1 CAN 58 A2 D4 59 G6	2 INN 63 B4 E2	8 RCY 32 W20 33 A20	41A MED 95 F5 F8
1 CHE 70 B3 D3	2 RED 64 C1 66 G2 K4	8 BEI 69 A4 B3	54 INN 63 A1 B3-4
1 LKL 56 A1 D5	2A CRS 62 A3 C3	9 DRU 73 A6 E7	66 BRG 78 E1 E3
1 MED 92 D1 94 G3 95 K7-8	2A HIG 77 A2 D4	9 IRR 69 A2	72 BEI 69 A1
1 RCY 24 X12	2A INN 63 A4	10 CHE 73 D-E8	93 LKL 56 A2
1 STM 71 D-E1 D-E4	2A OKO 76 A2	11 RED 64 D-E3 65 D-E7 F9	201 CAL 18 E6 D9 26 D11
1A CAL 9 B5 17 C7 19 H9 28 L13 38 U17 39 Z17	2A OLD 62 A-B4 C4	11A RED 64 A4	549 OKO 75 C1
1A CAN 58 C3 59 G7	2A RED 64 B5 E5 66 K5 L4	22 BLD 75 D6	560 RCY 45 Z24
1A CHE 70 D1	3 COD 85 A-B4 B1	22 BRG 78 A4 E4	563 RCY 24 Y12 25 C14
1A COC 60 A3 61 A-B7	3 CRO ...79 C1 C5 80 E8 81 G11 K14	22 COC 60 A3 D3	783 OKO 168 E2
1A LKL 56 D5	3 LET 82 B1 83 D5 84 E9 85 E13	22 RDW 69 B3	
1A RCY 8 W3	3 MED 94 H1	22 TVY 74 A1 C4	
2 N CAL 13 S5 14 T2	3 TAB 91 D4 E1	22X CAL ...52 M33-34 53 S34 55 X32	
.....21 Q7 29 R12 38 T17 T19 43 R22 R24	4 LET 88 F12 89 J13	22X BRG 78 E4	

1 Av BEI 69 A2	1 Av NW MED 92 D-E4	1 St RCY 51 Z27	1 St SE CAL
1 Av CAN 58 D4 59 E5	1 Av S LET 83 E6-7 E7 E8	1 St E BRO 90 B3 B-C3 C3	.....7 D92-94 37 P16-17 P20 43 P21 53 P31
1 Av IRR 69 B1	1 Av SE AIR 68 B3-4	1 St E COC 61 B-C5	1 St SE DRU 73 D7
1 Av STM 71 D2-3	1 Av SE BLD 75 B7	1 St E DRU 73 C7	1 St SE HIG 77 B-C3 C3
1 Av E BRO 90 C2-3 C-D3 D4	1 Av SE HIG 77 B3	1 St E OKO 75 A1	1 St SE MED 92 E4 93 E5
1 Av N LET 84 E9	1 Av SE MED 94 F4	1 St NE CAL	1 St SW AIR 68 B-C3
1 Av NE AIR 68 B3-4	1 Av SW BLD 75 B6	.......7 D91 29 P11 P12-13 P13-15 P15	1 St SW BLD 75 B-C6
1 Av NE BLD 75 B6-7	1 Av SW CAL ..6 A-B92 26 D12 36 O16	1 St NE MED 92 E43 D5	1 St SW CAL
1 Av NE CAL .7 D-E91 37 P-Q16 Q-R16 39 X16	1 Av SW MED 92 E4 E4 94 F4 F4	1 St NW AIR 68 B3	.......6 C92-94 37 P16-17 P18 P19 P20 43 P21
1 Av NE HIG 77 B2	1 Av W BRO 90 B2	1 St NW BLD 75 B6	1 St SW DRU 73 D7
1 Av NW AIR 68 B1-2	1 Av W COC 60 B4 61 B5	1 St NW CAL 29 P11 P12 P13 P14 P14-15	1 St SW HIG 77 C2
1 Av NW BLD 75 B6	1 Av W DRU 73 C5 C7	1 St NW HIG 77 B2	1 St SW MED 92 E2-4
1 Av NW CAL ...6 A91 27 K15 28 O15	1 St CAN 58 F4 59 F5	1 St NW MED 92 E3-4	1 St W BRO 90 B3 C2-3
.......36 L16 L-M16 M16 N16 O16	1 St DRU 72 B1	1 St S LET 87 F-G7	1 St W DRU 73 C7
1 Av NW DRU 72 B-C4 C3-4	1 St IRR 69 A-B1	1 St SE BLD 75 B-C7	1A Av E BRO 90 C3

1A Av N LET 84 E9
1A Av NE MED 92 D-E4
1A Av NW MED 92 D3-4
1A Av SW BLD 75 B6
1A St NE HIG 77 B2
1A St NW CAL 29 P11-12 P14
1A St SE CAL 43 P21
1A St SE HIG 77 C2
1A St SW CAL . . .37 P19-20 43 P21 P22
2 Av BEI 69 A2
2 Av CAN 58 E4 59 E5
2 Av DRU 72 B1 B1-2 C2
2 Av IRR 69 B1
2 Av STM 71 D2-3
2 Av E BRO 90 C3 C-D4
2 Av E COC 61 C5
2 Av E DRU 73 C7
2 Av N LET 84 E9
2 Av NE AIR 68 B3 B4
2 Av NE BLD 75 B6-7
2 Av NE CAL 7 D91 E91 37 P-Q16 37 P16
2 Av NE HIG 77 B5
2 Av NW AIR 68 B3
2 Av NW BLD 75 B6
2 Av NW CAL
. . . . . .6 A91 28 015 36 L16 L-M16 M16 N16
2 Av NW DRU 72 B4
2 Av S LET
. . .83 E8 84 E10 E12 E9 87 F7 88 F11 F12
2 Av SE AIR 68 C4
2 Av SE BLD 75 B6-7
2 Av SE CAL
. . . . . .7 D92 37 P16 38 T16 U-V16 39 Y16
2 Av SE HIG 77 C3
2 Av SE MED 92 E4 94 F4 F4
2 Av SW BLD 75 B6
2 Av SW CAL
. . . . . .6 A-B92 C92 26 D13 35 J-K16 36 016
2 Av SW MED 92 E3 94 F3
2 Av W BRO 90 C1-2
2 Av W COC 60 B4 61 B5
2 Av W DRU 73 C5 C6 C6-7
2 St CAN 58 F4 59 F5
2 St DRU 72 B1
2 St IRR 69 B1
2 St RCY 51 Z27
2 St STM 71 D3
2 St E BRO 90 B3 B-C3 C3
2 St E DRU 73 C7
2 St NE CAL
. . . . .7 D91 21 P6 29 P12-13 P14-15 37 P16
2 St NE MED 92 D4 E4
2 St NW BLD 75 B6
2 St NW CAL .29 P11 P11-12 P12 P13-15 P15
2 St NW MED 92 E3-4
2 St SE CAL . . .43 P21-22 P25 49 P26
2 St SE DRU 73 D7
2 St SE HIG 77 B-C3
2 St SE MED 92 E4 93 D5-6 E5 E5
2 St SW BLD 75 B-C6
2 St SW CAL
. . . . . .6 C92-94 37 P16-17 P17-18 P19 43 P21
2 St SW DRU 73 C7 D6-7
2 St SW HIG 77 C2
2 St SW MED 92 E3-4
2 St W BRO 90 B2-3 C2
2 St W COC 60 B4 61 B5
2 St W DRU 73 C7
2A Av E BRO 90 C4
2A Av N LET . .83 E7-E8 E8 84 E10 E9
2A Av NE MED 92 D-E4
2A Av NW MED 92 D-E3
2A Av SW HIG 77 C2
2A Av W BRO 90 C2
2A St CAN 58 F4
2A St NW CAL 29 P14
2A St SE CAL 37 P18
2A St SE HIG 77 B3
2A St W BRO 90 A3
2B Av N LET 84 E9
3 Av BEI 69 A-B2
3 Av CAN 59 F5
3 Av DRU 72 B1
3 Av IRR 69 B1
3 Av STM 71 D2-3
3 Av CI MED 92 C4
3 Av E BRO 90 C2-3 C4
3 Av E DRU 73 C7
3 Av N LET 83 E8 84 E9
3 Av NE AIR 68 B4
3 Av NE CAL
. . . . .7 D-E91 37 P-Q16 Q16 38 T16 U16
3 Av NE MED 92 C4 D4
3 Av NW BLD 75 B6
3 Av NW CAL
. . .6 A91 27 J-K15 28 015 36 L16 L-M16 M16
3 Av NW MED 92 D-E3
3 Av S LET 87 F7-8 88 F10 F11 F12 F9
3 Av SE AIR 68 C4

3 Av SE CAL
. .7 D92 37 P16 S16 38 T16 T-U16 W16 39 Y16
3 Av SE HIG 77 C2-3 C5
3 Av SE MED 92 E4 94 F4 F4 F-G4
3 Av SW BLD 75 C6
3 Av SW CAL
. . .6 A-B92 C92 35 J16 J-K16 36 016 37 P16
3 Av SW HIG 77 C2
3 Av SW MED 92 E4 94 F3 F3
3 Av W BRO 90 C2
3 Av W COC 60 B4
3 Av W DRU 73 C6
3 Av W LET 82 E1
3 St CAN 58 F4 59 F5
3 St DRU 72 B1
3 St IRR 69 B1
3 St RCY 51 Z27
3 St STM 71 D2-3
3 St E BRO 90 C3
3 St E DRU 73 C7
3 St NE CAL
. . . .7 E91 21 P6 P-Q9 29 Q11 Q12 Q15 37 Q16
3 St NE MED 92 D4
3 St NW BLD 75 B6
3 St NW CAL
. . . . . .6 C91 28 014 015 29 P12 P14 P15
3 St NW HIG 77 A2
3 St NW MED 92 D1-2 D3-4
3 St S LET 83 E7 87 F7 G7
3 St SE BLD 75 B7
3 St SE CAL . . .7 E92-94 37 Q16-17 Q17 Q18
. . . . .43 P21-22 P25 49 P26
3 St SE DRU 73 D7
3 St SE HIG 77 C2
3 St SE MED 92 E4 93 E5 E5-6
3 St SW BLD 75 B-C6
3 St SW CAL
. . . . .6 C92-93 36 016-17 019 42 021 43 P22
3 St SW DRU 73 C6-7 D6
3 St SW HIG 77 C2
3 St SW MED 92 E3-4
3 St W BRO 90 C2 C3
3 St W COC 60 B4 61 B5
3 St W DRU 73 C7
3A Av N LET 83 E8 84 E9
3A Av NE CAL 30 T15 38 T16
3A Av NE MED 92 C4
3A Av S LET 87 F8
3A St NE CAL 29 Q12
3A St W BRO 90 C2
4 Av BEI 69 A3 B2
4 Av CAN 59 F5
4 Av CRO 81 K12
4 Av STM 71 D3
4 Av E BRO 90 C2-3 C3
4 Av E DRU 73 C7
4 Av N COC 60 A-B4
4 Av N LET 83 E7 E8 84 E10 E9
4 Av NE CAL 7 D-E91 29 P-Q15 Q-R15
. . . . .30 U15 31 X15 Y15 38 V16
4 Av NE MED 92 C4 D4 93 C-D5 D5
4 Av NW AIR 68 B3
4 Av NW CAL
. . . . . .6 A91 27 K15 28 L15 L-M15 N-015
4 Av NW DRU 72 B4
4 Av NW MED 92 D-E3
4 Av S LET 87 F7-8 88 F10 F12 F9 F9
4 Av SE BLD 75 C6-7
4 Av SE CAL .7 D-E92 37 P16 38 W16 39 Y16
4 Av SE HIG 77 C2-3 C5
4 Av SE MED 92 E4 94 F4 F4 F5
4 Av SW BLD 75 C6
4 Av SW CAL .6 A-C92 35 J16 36 016 37 P16
4 Av SW DRU 72 C4 73 C5
4 Av SW HIG 77 C2
4 Av SW MED 92 E3 94 F3 F3
4 Av W BRO 90 C1-2 C2
4 Av W COC 60 B4
4 Av W DRU 73 C7
4 St BEI 69 A2
4 St CAN 58 F4 59 F5
4 St DRU 72 B1
4 St IRR 69 B1
4 St RCY 51 Z27
4 St STM 71 D2
4 St E BRO 90 C4
4 St E DRU 73 C7
4 St NE CAL 7 E91-92 21 P9-10 Q10 Q8
. . . . .29 Q11 Q13-15 Q15 37 Q16
4 St NE MED 92 D4 93 D5
4 St NW CAL
. . . . . .6 B91 20 09-10 28 011-15 36 016
4 St NW HIG 77 B2
4 St S LET 83 E7 87 F7 F7-G7
4 St SE CAL
. . . . . .7 E93-94 37 Q16-17 Q19-20 43 Q21-22
4 St SE HIG 77 B-C3 C3
4 St SE MED 92 E4 93 E5 E5-6
4 St SW BLD 75 B-C6

4 St SW CAL 6 C92-94
. . .36 016-18 019 019-20 020 42 021 52 033-34
4 St SW DRU 73 D6
4 St SW HIG 77 C2
4 St SW MED 92 E3-4 94 F3-4
4 St W BRO 90 B-C2 C2
4 St W DRU 73 C6
4A Av NE CAL . . .7 E91 21 Q9-10 29 Q15
4A St NW BLD 75 B6
4A St NW CAL . .6 B91 28 013 014-15 015
4A St SW CAL
. . . .36 019-20 020 42 021 022-23 023 024
5 Av BRO 90 C3
5 Av CAN 58 E4 F4
5 Av CRO 81 H12 K12
5 Av CRO 73 C7
5 Av STM 71 D3
5 Av E DRU 73 C7
5 Av N LET 83 E7-8 84 E10-11 E9
5 Av NE CAL .7 D-E91 29 P-Q15 015 30 U-V15
5 Av NE MED 93 C5 D5
5 Av NW AIR 68 B3
5 Av NW CAL .6 A91 27 K15 28 L-M15 M-15
5 Av NW MED 92 D-E3
5 Av S LET 87 F7-8 F8 88 F10 F11 F9
5 Av SE BLD 75 C6-7
5 Av SE CAL
. . . . . .7 D-E93 37 P16 Q16 38 W16 39 X16
5 Av SE HIG 77 C3 C5
5 Av SE MED 92 E4 93 E5 95 F5
5 Av SW BLD 75 C6
5 Av SW CAL .6 A-C93 35 I16 36 016 37 P16
5 Av SW DRU 73 C7
5 Av SW HIG 77 C1-2 C2
5 Av SW MED 94 F3
5 Av W BRO 90 B-C2
5 Av W COC 60 B-C4
5 St BEI 69 A2
5 St CAN 58 F4 59 F5
5 St DRU 72 B1
5 St IRR 69 B1
5 St RCY 51 Z27
5 St E BRO 90 C3
5 St E DRU 73 C-D7
5 St N LET 83 E7
5 St NE CAL
. .7 E91 29 Q11 Q12-13 Q13-14 Q14-15 Q15
5 St NE HIG 77 B3
5 St NE MED 93 D5
5 St NW CAL
. . .6 B91 20 010 09 28 013 013-14 014-15
5 St S LET 83 E7 87 F7 F-G7
5 St SE CAL 7 E93-94 37 Q16-17 Q17
. . . . .43 Q21 Q22 Q23 Q25 49 Q26
5 St SE HIG 77 C3
5 St SE MED 92 E4 93 E5 75 B-C6
5 St SW BLD 75 B-C6
5 St SW CAL 6 B92-94
. . . .36 016-17 018 019 019-20 020
. . . . .42 021-22 023-24 48 027
5 St SW HIG 77 C2
5 St SW MED 94 F2-3 F3-4
5 St W BRO 90 B2 C2
5 St W DRU 73 C6
5A Av N LET . . .83 D8 84 D9 D9-10 D10
5A Av S LET 87 F8 88 F11
5A Av SE CAL 38 W16
5A St NW CAL 6 B91 28 015
5A St SE HIG 58 D-E4 E4 F4
5A St SW CAL . . .36 018 019 020
6 Av CAN 58 E4 F4
6 Av CRO 81 H12 K12
6 Av STM 71 D3
6 Av E DRU 73 C7 D8
6 Av N LET 83 D7-8 84 D10 D11 D9
6 Av NE CAL 29 P-Q15
6 Av NE MED 93 C5
6 Av NW AIR 68 B3
6 Av NW CAL . .27 K15 28 L15 L-M15 M-N15
6 Av NW MED 92 D-E3
6 Av S LET 87 F7-8 88 F10-11 F9
6 Av SE BLD 75 C6-7
6 Av SE CAL 7 D-E93 37 P16 38 W16
6 Av SE HIG 77 C2-3 C3-4 C5
6 Av SE MED 93 E5
6 Av SW BLD 75 C6
6 Av SW CAL . . .6 A-C93 36 016 37 P16
6 Av SW DRU 73 C7
6 Av SW HIG 77 C2
6 Av SW MED 92 E3 94 F3 G3
6 Av W COC 60 B4
6 St BEI 69 A2
6 St BRO 90 B-C2
6 St CAN 58 E4
6 St DRU 72 B1-2
6 St IRR 69 B1
6 St E BRO 90 C3 C-D3
6 St E DRU 73 C7-8 D7

6 St N LET 83 C-D7 D7
6 St NE CAL 7 E91-92 13 Q2 21 Q10 Q6
. . . . .29 Q11 Q11-12 Q12-15 Q15 37 Q16
6 St NE MED 93 D5
6 St NW CAL .6 B91 28 013 014 014-15 015
6 St S LET 87 F7 F-G7
6 St SE CAL 37 Q16-17 Q17 Q18
. . . . .43 Q21 Q22 Q23 Q24-25 53 Q31
6 St SE HIG 77 C3
6 St SE MED 94 F4 95 F5 F5
6 St SW CAL 6 B92-94
. . . . .36 016-17 017 019 020
. . . .42 021-23 48 027 029 030 52 033
6 St SW HIG 77 C2
6 St SW MED 94 F2-3
6 St W BRO 90 B2
6 St W DRU 73 C6
6A Av N LET . . .83 D8 84 D10 D9
6A Av S LET . . .87 F7 F8 88 F10 F11
6A Av SE CAL 38 W16
6A Av SW MED 94 F3
6A St NE CAL . .29 Q11 Q12 Q15 37 Q16
6A St NW CAL 28 014-15
6A St SW CAL 36 020
7 Av CAN 58 E4 E-F4
7 Av CRO 81 H12 J12-13 K12
7 Av E DRU 73 D7-8 D8
7 Av N LET 83 D8 84 D10 D9
7 Av NE CAL .29 P-Q15 Q-R15 R-S15 30 U15
7 Av NE MED 93 B-C5 C5
7 Av NW CAL
. . .27 K15 28 L15 L-M15 M15 N15 015
7 Av NW MED 92 D-E3
7 Av S LET 87 F7 F7-8 88 F9
7 Av SE CAL 7 D-E93 37 Q17 R17 S18 38 W16
7 Av SE HIG 77 C2-3 C5
7 Av SW CAL . . .6 A-C93 35 J16-17 J-K17
7 Av SW DRU 73 D7
7 Av SW HIG 77 C2
7 Av SW MED 92 E3 94 F3 G3
7 St BEI 69 A2
7 St BRO 90 B-C2
7 St CAN 58 E4
7 St E BRO 90 C3 E3
7 St E DRU 73 D8
7 St N LET 83 C-D7 D7 E7
7 St NE CAL . .21 Q10 29 Q13-14 Q15 37 Q16
7 St NE MED 92 D4 93 D5
7 St NW CAL
. . . . . .6 A91 20 08 28 013 014 014-15 015
7 St NW HIG 77 A-B2
7 St NW MED 92 D3-4
7 St S LET 87 F7 F-G7 G7-8
7 St SE CAL . . .37 Q19-20 020 43 Q25 49 Q26
7 St SE HIG 77 C3-4
7 St SE MED 94 F4 95 F5 F5
7 St SW CAL 6 A92-94
. . . . .36 016-17 017-18 019 020
. . . . . . .42 022-24 48 026 026-27
7 St SW HIG 77 C2
7 St SW MED . . .94 F1-2 F2 F2-3 F3-4
7 St W DRU 73 C6
7A Av N LET . . .83 D8 84 D10 D9
7A Av S LET 87 F-G7 G8
7A St NE CAL 29 Q15 37 Q16
7A St NW CAL 28 014-15
7A St SW CAL 36 019
8 Av BRO 90 B2
8 Av CAN 58 D-E4 E4
8 Av CRO 81 J12-13 K12-13
8 Av N LET 83 D8 84 D10 D11 D9
8 Av NE CAL 29 P-R15 S15 30 T15 V15 31 Y15
8 Av NE MED 93 C5
8 Av NW CAL
. . .27 J14 K15 28 M15 M-N15 29 P15
8 Av S LET 87 G7 G7-8 88 F-G9
8 Av SE CAL 7 E93 37 Q17 R17 R-S17 S18
. . . . . . .38 T18 V17 V-W17 39 X17
8 Av SE DRU 73 D7
8 Av SE HIG 77 C2-3 C3-4 C4
8 Av SE MED 95 F5
8 Av SW CAL . . .6 A-B93 35 I-K17 36 017
8 Av SW DRU 73 D6-7
8 Av SW HIG 77 C2
8 Av SW MED 92 E3 94 G2
8 St BEI 69 A2
8 St CAN 58 E4
8 St COD 85 B-C4
8 St DRU 72 B-C2
8 St E BRO 90 C4
8 St E DRU 73 D8
8 St E OKO 76 A2 E2
8 St N LET 83 C-D8 D7-8 E7-8
8 St NE CAL
. . . . .21 Q10 Q9 29 Q11 Q14 Q15 37 Q16
8 St NE MED 92 D4 93 D5
8 St NW AIR 68 A-B2
8 St NW CAL . . .6 A91 20 09 28 014 015

8 St NW *MED* . . . **92** D3-4
8 St S *LET* . . . **87** F8 F-G8
8 St SE *CAL* . . . **37** Q19-20 R17 R17-18
8 St SE *HIG* . . . **77** C4
8 St SE *MED* . . . **94** F4 **95** F5 F5
8 St SW *AIR* . . . **68** C-D2
8 St SW *CAL* . . **6** A92-94 **36** O16-18 O19 O20 . . . **42** O21 **48** O26 O27
8 St SW *HIG* . . . **77** C1
8 St SW *MED* . . . **94** F2 F2-3 F3-4
8 St W *BRO* . . . **90** B1-2 C2
8 St W *DRU* . . . **73** C6
8A Av N *LET* . . . **84** D10 D9
8A Av NE *CAL* . . . **29** S15
8A Av S *LET* . . . **87** G7 G8 **88** G9-10
8A St NE *CAL* . . . **29** Q11 R12 R15 **37** R16
8A St SW *CAL* . . . **36** N19
9 Av *BRO* . . . **90** B3
9 Av *CAN* . . . **58** E4
9 Av *CRO* . . . **81** J13 K13
9 Av N *LET* . . . **83** D7-8 **84** D10-11 D9
9 Av NE *CAL* . . . **29** P-Q15 S15
9 Av NE *MED* . . . **93** C5 C-D5
9 Av NW *CAL* . . . **28** L15 M15 O15 **29** P15
9 Av S *LET* . . . **87** G7 G7-8 **88** G9
9 Av SE *CAL* . **7** D-E94 **37** P17 R17 **38** T18 U17
9 Av SE *DRU* . . . **73** D7
9 Av SE *HIG* . . . **77** C2-3 C3-4 C4 C5
9 Av SW *CAL* **6** A-C94 **26** E-F15 **36** O17 **37** P17
9 Av SW *HIG* . . . **77** C1-2
9 Av SW *MED* . . . **94** G2
9 Av W *BRO* . . . **90** B2
9 St *BEI* . . . **69** A-B2
9 St *CAN* . . . **58** E4
9 St *COD* . . . **85** B4 C4
9 St *DRU* . . . **72** C2
9 St E *BRO* . . . **90** C4
9 St E *DRU* . . . **73** D8
9 St N *LET* . . . **83** A8 C-D8 D8
9 St NE *CAL* . . **21** R10 R9 **29** R11 R15 **37** R16
9 St NE *MED* . . . **92** D4
9 St NW *CAL* . . . **6** A91 **20** O8 . . . **28** O12 O13 O14 O14-15 O15 **36** O16
9 St NW *DRU* . . . **73** B-C6
9 St S *LET* . . . **87** F-G8 G8
9 St SE *CAL* . . **37** R17 R17-18 R19-20 **43** R21
9 St SE *HIG* . . . **77** C4
9 St SE *MED* . . . **94** F4 **95** F5 F5
9 St SW *CAL* . . . **6** A93-94 **36** N17 N18 N19 N20 N-O16 **42** N22
9 St SW *DRU* . . . **73** C-D6
9 St SW *HIG* . . . **77** C1
9 St SW *MED* . . . **94** F1-2 F3-4
9 St W *BRO* . . . **90** C2
9A Av S *LET* . . . **87** G8 **88** G9 G9-10
9A St *COD* . . . **85** B4
9A St NE *CAL* . . . **29** R15 R15 **37** R16
9A St NW *CAL* . . . **6** A91 **28** N15 **36** N16
9B Av S *LET* . . . **88** G9-10
10 Av *CAN* . . . **58** E3
10 Av *CRO* . . . **81** K13
10 Av N *LET* . . . **83** D8 **84** D10 D11-12 D9
10 Av NE *CAL* . . . **29** P-Q15 S15 **30** U15
10 Av NE *MED* . . . **93** C5
10 Av NW *CAL* . . . **28** L15 M15 O15 **29** P15
10 Av NW *MED* . . . **92** C2 C-D2
10 Av S *LET* . . . **87** G8 **88** G9
10 Av SE *CAL* . . . **7** D94 **37** P17 R17 **38** U17 V17 W17 **39** X17
10 Av SE *DRU* . . . **73** D7
10 Av SE *HIG* . . . **77** C2-3 C3-4 C4 C5
10 Av SW *CAL* . . . **6** A-C94 **26** F-G15 **35** I-J17 **36** M-O17 **37** P17
10 Av SW *DRU* . . . **73** D7
10 Av SW *HIG* . . . **77** C1-2 C2
10 Av SW *MED* . . . **94** F-J2
10 St *CAN* . . . **58** E4
10 St *COD* . . . **85** B4 C4
10 St E *DRU* . . . **73** D8
10 St N *LET* . . . **83** A8 D8 E8
10 St NE *CAL* . . . **21** R10 R8-9 **29** R11-12 R15 **37** R16
10 St NE *MED* . . . **92** D4
10 St NW *CAL* . . . **6** A92 **20** O8-9 **28** N12-15 **36** N16
10 St S *LET* . . . **83** E8 **87** F8 F-G8 G8
10 St SE *CAL* . . . **37** R17 R19 **43** R22 **49** R28
10 St SE *HIG* . . . **77** C4 D4
10 St SE *MED* . . . **94** F4 **95** F5 F5
10 St SW *CAL* . . . **6** A93-94 **36** N16 N17 N18-19 N20 **52** O32
10 St SW *MED* . . . **94** F3-4
10 St W *BRO* . . . **90** B-C1
10 St W *DRU* . . . **73** C5
10A Av N *LET* . . . **83** D8 **84** D10
10A Av S *LET* . . **88** G9 G9-10 G10 G10-11 G11
10A St *COD* . . . **85** B3-4 B-C4 C4
10A St NW *CAL* . . . **28** N15 **36** N16
11, Range Rd *RCY* . . . **13** S1
11 Av *CAN* . . . **58** D3 D-E3
11 Av *CAN* . . . **58** E3
11 Av *CRO* . . . **81** J13 K13
11 Av N *LET* . . . **83** C-D8 D8 **84** C-D10 D9
11 Av NE *CAL* . . . **29** P-Q15
11 Av NE *MED* . . . **93** A-C5 C-D5
11 Av NW *CAL* . . . **27** K15 **28** L15 M15 N15 O15 **29** P15
11 Av NW *MED* . . . **92** C2
11 Av S *LET* . . . **87** G8 **88** G10 G9-10
11 Av SE *CAL* . . . **7** D-E94 **37** P-Q17 R17 **38** U17 W17
11 Av SE *DRU* . . . **73** D7
11 Av SE *HIG* . . . **77** C2 C4 C4-5
11 Av SW *CAL* . . . **6** A-C94 **34** F-G16 **36** M-O17 **37** P17
11 Av SW *HIG* . . . **77** C2
11 Av SW *MED* . . . **92** E2 **94** F2
11 Range Rd (15 St. NE) *AIR* . . . **68** E2
11 St *CAN* . . . **58** E4
11 St *COD* . . . **85** A-B3 B3 B-C3
11 St E *DRU* . . . **73** D8
11 St N *LET* . . . **83** A8 C-D8 D8
11 St NE *CAL* . . . **21** R9-10 **29** R11 R12 R15 R-S13 **37** R16
11 St NE *MED* . . . **92** D4 **93** D5
11 St NW *CAL* . . **20** N10 **28** N14 N15 **36** N16
11 St S *LET* . . . **87** F8 G8
11 St SE *CAL* . . . **37** R17 R18 R19 R19-20 R20 **43** R21-23
11 St SE *DRU* . . . **73** D8
11 St SE *HIG* . . . **77** C4
11 St SE *MED* . . . **94** F4 **95** F5 F5
11 St SW *CAL* . . . **36** N16-17 N18 N19 **42** N23 N24 **48** N27
11 St SW *MED* . . . **94** F3-4
11 St W *BRO* . . . **90** B1 B-C1
11 St W *DRU* . . . **73** C5
11A Av N *LET* . . . **84** C10 C9-10 D9-10
11A Av S *LET* . . . **88** G10
11A St *COD* . . . **85** C3
11A St NE *CAL* . . . **29** R12 R15 **37** R16 R16
11A St NW *CAL* . . . **28** N15 **36** N16
11A St SE *CAL* . . . **37** R19-20
12, Range Rd *CRS* . . . **62** B1
12, Range Rd *RCY* . . . **13** Q1
12 Av *CAN* . . . **58** D-E3
12 Av (Bellevue) *CRO* . . . **81** J13 K13
12 Av (Blairmore) *CRO* . . . **80** G10
12 Av (Coleman) *CRO* . . . **79** C-D4
12 Av N *LET* . . . **83** C7 C8 **84** C10 C10-11 C9
12 Av NE *CAL* . . **29** P-Q15 S15 **30** V15 **31** Y15
12 Av NW *CAL* . . **27** K15 **28** L15 L-N15 **29** P15
12 Av NW *MED* . . . **92** C2
12 Av S *LET* . . . **87** G8 **88** G10 G9-10
12 Av SE *CAL* . . . **7** D-E94 **37** P-Q17 **38** U17 U-V17 **39** X17
12 Av SE *DRU* . . . **73** D7-8
12 Av SE *HIG* . . . **77** C3 C4-5
12 Av SE *MED* . . . **95** H5
12 Av SW *CAL* . . . **6** A-C94 **34** E16 G16 . . . **35** K17 **36** L17 M-O17 **37** P17
12 Av SW *HIG* . . . **77** C1-2
12 Av SW *MED* . . . **94** H2
12 Range Rd *AIR* . . . **68** E1
12 Range Rd (6 St. NE) *AIR* . . . **68** E1
12 St *CAN* . . . **58** E4
12 St *COD* . . . **85** A-B3 B3 C3
12 St E *BRO* . . . **90** D4
12 St E *DRU* . . . **73** D8
12 St N *LET* . . . **83** A8 C-D8 D8 E8
12 St NE *CAL* . . . **29** R11-12 S13 **37** R16
12 St NE *MED* . . . **92** C4 **93** C5
12 St NW *BRO* . . . **90** B-C1
12 St NW *CAL* . . . **28** N14 N15 **36** N16
12 St NW *MED* . . . **92** C3
12 St S *LET* . . . **87** F8 G8
12 St SE *CAL* . . . **37** R17 R20 **43** R22 R23
12 St SE *HIG* . . . **77** C4
12 St SE *MED* . . . **94** F4 **95** F5 F5
12 St SW *CAL* . . . **36** N17-18 N19 **42** N25
12 St SW *DRU* . . . **73** C5
12 St SW *MED* . . . **94** F3
12 St W *BRO* . . . **90** A-B1
12 St W *DRU* . . . **73** C5
12 Mile Coulee Rd NW *CAL* **9** B4-5 **17** B6-9
12A Av SE *HIG* . . . **77** C5
12A St *CAN* . . . **58** E4
12A St N *LET* . . . **83** D8 E8
12A St NE *CAL* . . . **29** R15 **37** R16
12A St S *LET* . . . **83** E8 **87** F8 F8 F-G8 G8
12A St SE *CAL* . . . **43** R21
12B St N *LET* . . . **83** C-D8 D8 E8
12B St S *LET* . . . **83** E8 **87** F8 G8
12C St N *LET* . . . **83** C-D8 D8 E8
13, Range Rd *RCY* . . . **12** O1
13 Av *BRO* . . . **90** A2-3
13 Av *COD* . . . **85** A2 A3-4
13 Av (Blairmore) *CRO* . . . **80** G10-11
13 Av (Coleman) *CRO* . . . **79** C4
13 Av N *LET* . . . **83** C8 **84** C10 C9
13 Av NE *CAL* . . . **29** P-Q15 S14-15
13 Av NW *CAL* . . . **27** K15 **28** L15 M15 O15 **29** P14
13 Av S *LET* . . . **88** G9-10 H9-10
13 Av SE *CAL* . . . **7** D-E94 **37** P-Q17 **38** U17
13 Av SE *HIG* . . . **77** D4
13 Av SE *MED* . . . **95** G5 H-K6
13 Av SW *CAL* . . . **6** A-C94 **34** E-F16 . . . **35** J17 K17 **36** M-O17 **37** P17
13 Av SW *MED* . . . **92** E2
13 St *CAN* . . . **58** E3 E4 **59** E5
13 St *COD* . . . **85** A-B3 B-C3
13 St N *LET* . . . **83** A8 C8 E8
13 St NE *CAL* . . . **29** R11 R15 **37** R16
13 St NE *MED* . . . **92** C4 **93** C-D5
13 St NW *CAL* . . . **28** N14 N15 **36** N16 N16
13 St NW *DRU* . . . **72** B4
13 St S *LET* . . . **87** F8 G-H8
13 St SE *CAL* . . . **37** R17 **43** R21
13 St SE *HIG* . . . **77** C4
13 St SE *MED* . . . **94** F4 F4 **95** F5
13 St SW *CAL* . . . **36** N17 N18 N19
13 St SW *MED* . . . **94** F3 F-G2
13 St W *DRU* . . . **73** C5
13A Av N *LET* . . . **83** C8
13A St NE *CAL* . . . **29** R15
13A St SE *CAL* . . . **37** R-S20
13A St SW *CAL* . . . **36** N19
14, Range Rd *RCY* . . . **12** N1
14 Av *COD* . . . **85** A2-4
14 Av (Blairmore) *CRO* . . . **80** G10-11
14 Av (Coleman) *CRO* . . . **79** C1-2 C4
14 Av N *LET* . . . **84** C10 C11 C11-12 C9
14 Av NE *CAL* . . . **29** P-Q14 S14 **30** U14 V14
14 Av NW *CAL* . . . **27** K14 **28** L14 L-N14 O14 **29** P14
14 Av S *LET* . . . **88** H10 H9-10
14 Av SE *CAL* . . . **7** D-E94 **37** P-Q17 S17 . . . **38** U17 V-W17 **39** X17 Y17
14 Av SE *MED* . . . **95** G5-6
14 Av SW *CAL* . . . **6** C94 **34** E17 F-G17 . . . **35** H17 K17 **36** L17 M-O17 **37** P17
14 Av SW *MED* . . . **94** F2
14 St *CAN* . . . **58** E3-4 E4
14 St *COD* . . . **85** B3 C3
14 St E *DRU* . . . **73** D8
14 St N *LET* . **83** B8 C8 D8 E8 **84** B9 C9 D9 E9
14 St NE *CAL* . . . **13** R3 S4 **29** R11 S12
14 St NE *MED* . . . **92** C4 **93** C5
14 St NW *CAL* . . . **12** M5 **20** M6-7 N8-10 **28** N11-15 **36** N16
14 St NW *DRU* . . . **72** B4 C4
14 St NW *MED* . . . **92** C3-4
14 St S *LET* . . . **87** F8 G8 H8 **88** F9 G9 H9
14 St SE *CAL* . . . **37** R17 S17 S19-20
14 St SE *HIG* . . . **77** C4
14 St SW *CAL* . . . **36** N17-19 **42** N23-25 **48** N26-28
14 St SW *MED* . . . **94** G2-3
14 St W *DRU* . . . **72** C4 **73** C5
14A St N *LET* . . . **84** D9
14A St SE *CAL* . . . **37** S17 S19 S20
14A St SW *CAL* . . . **36** N18 N19 N20 **42** N21
15, Range Rd (Panorama Rd) *RCY* . . **12** L1
15 Av *BRO* . . . **90** A2
15 Av *COD* . . . **85** A-B3
15 Av (Blairmore) *CRO* . . . **80** F8 F9 G10-11
15 Av (Coleman) *CRO* . . . **79** C2 C4
15 Av N *LET* . . . **84** C10 C9
15 Av NE *CAL* . . . **29** P-Q14 R14
15 Av NW *CAL* . . . **27** K14 **29** P14
15 Av S *LET* . . . **88** H10 H9-10
15 Av SE *CAL* . . . **37** S17 **38** U17 **39** Y17
15 Av SE *MED* . . . **95** G6 G-H6
15 Av SW *CAL* . . . **34** E17 G17 **35** J17 K17 **36** L17 M-O17 **37** P17
15 Av SW *MED* . . . **94** H-J1
15 St *CAN* . . . **58** D4 E3-4 **59** D5
15 St *COD* . . . **85** B-C3
15 St E *DRU* . . . **73** D8
15 St N *LET* . . . **84** C9 C-D9 D9 E9
15 St NE *CAL* . . . **13** S3-5 S5 **21** S6 **29** S13
15 St NE *MED* . . . **93** C5
15 St NW *CAL* . . . **28** M13 M14 M15 **36** M16
15 St NW *DRU* . . . **72** C4
15 St S *LET* . . . **88** F9 F-G9 G-H9 H9
15 St SE *CAL* . . . **37** S17 S18 S19-20 **43** S21 S25 **53** S34-35
15 St SE *HIG* . . . **77** C4
15 St SW *CAL* . . . **36** N16-17 N17 N18 N19 N20 **42** N21
15 St SW *MED* . . . **94** G2-3
15 St W *DRU* . . . **72** C4
15A St N *LET* . . . **84** C9
15A St SE *CAL* . . . **37** S18 S19-20
15A St SE *HIG* . . . **77** C4
15A St SW *CAL* . . . **36** M18 M19-20
16 Av *COD* . . . **85** B2
16 Av (Blairmore) *CRO* . . . **80** F8 G10
16 Av (Coleman) *CRO* . . . **79** C1 C2 C4
16 Av N *LET* . . . **83** C8 **84** C10-11 C9
16 Av NE *CAL* . . **29** P-S14 **30** T-W14 **31** X-Z14
16 Av NE *CHE* . . . **70** B3
16 Av NW *CAL* . . . **26** G13 **27** H-I13 I-K14 **28** L-O14
16 Av S *LET* . . . **88** H9-10
16 Av SE *CAL* . . . **38** U17 U-W17 **39** Y17
16 Av SE *MED* . . . **95** G6 H6
16 Av SW *CAL* . . . **34** G17 **35** J-K17 K17 **36** L17 M-O17
16 St *CAN* . . . **58** D-E3 D-E4
16 St *COD* . . . **85** B-C3
16 St E *DRU* . . . **73** D8
16 St E *OKO* . . . **76** A2
16 St N *LET* . . . **84** B9 B-C9 C9 C-D9 D9 E9
16 St NE *CAL* . . **13** S4 **29** S11-12 S13 S14-15
16 St NE *MED* . . . **92** C4 **93** C5
16 St NW *CAL* . . . **28** M13 M14 M15 **36** M16
16 St NW *DRU* . . . **72** B-C4
16 St S *LET* . . . **84** E9 **88** F9 F-G9 G9
16 St SE *CAL* **.37** S16 S17 S18 S19-20 **43** S23
16 St SE *HIG* . . . **77** C4-5 C-D4
16 St SE *MED* . . . **95** G6
16 St SW *CAL* . . . **36** M16-17 M17 M18 M18-19 M20 **42** M21 M25
16 St SW *MED* . . . **94** G2-3
16 St W *DRU* . . . **72** C4
16A Av *COD* . . . **85** B2
16A Av SE *CAL* . . . **39** X-Y17
16A St NE *CAL* . . . **29** S14 S15
16A St NE *MED* . . . **93** C5
16A St NW *CAL* . . . **28** M13 M15 **36** M16
16A St SE *CAL* . . . **37** S17 S18 S19-20
16A St SW *CAL* . . . **36** M18 M20
16B St SW *CAL* . . . **36** M18
17 Av *COD* . . . **85** B2
17 Av (Blairmore) *CRO* . . **80** F10 F7 F8 F8-9
17 Av (Coleman) *CRO* . . . **79** C2 C3-4 C4
17 Av NE *CAL* . . . **29** P14 Q14 S14 **30** T14
17 Av NW *CAL* . . . **27** H13 I14 **28** M14 N-O14 **29** P14
17 Av S *LET* . . . **88** H10 H9 H9-10
17 Av SE *CAL* . . . **37** Q-R17 R17 S17 **38** T-W17 **39** X-Y17
17 Av SE *MED* . . . **95** G6 H6
17 Av SW *CAL* . . . **34** E-G17 **35** H-K17 **36** L-O17 **37** P17
17 Av SW *MED* . . . **94** J1
17 St *CAN* . . . **58** D3 D4
17 St *COD* . . . **85** B-C3
17 St E *DRU* . . . **73** D8
17 St N *LET* . . . **84** B9 B-C9 C9 C-D9 D9 E9
17 St NE *CAL* . . . **29** S14 S15
17 St NE *MED* . . . **93** C5
17 St NW *CAL* . . . **28** M13 M14 M15 **36** M16
17 St NW *DRU* . . . **72** B4 B-C4
17 St S *LET* . . . **84** E9 **88** F9 F-G9 G-H9
17 St SE *CAL* . . **37** S17 S18-19 S20 **38** T16
17 St SE *HIG* . . . **77** C5
17 St SE *MED* . . . **95** G6
17 St SW *CAL* . . . **36** M17 M18 M18-19 M20 **42** M21 **48** M28
17 St SW *MED* . . . **94** G2-3
17 St W *DRU* . . . **72** C4
17A Av *COD* . . . **85** B2
17A St NE *CAL* . . . **29** S14-15
17A St NW *CAL* . . . **28** M13 M15
17A St S *LET* . . . **88** G9 H9
17A St SE *CAL* . . . **37** S17 S20 **43** S22
17A St SE *HIG* . . . **77** C5
17A St SW *CAL* . . . **36** M18
17B St SW *CAL* . . . **36** M18
18 Av *COD* . . . **85** B1-3
18 Av (Blairmore) *CRO* **.80** E6 F10 F7 F8 F8-9
18 Av (Coleman) *CRO* . . . **79** C1-2 C3-4 C4
18 Av N *LET* . . . **84** C10-11 C9
18 Av NE *CAL* . . **29** P-Q14 S14 **30** T14 **31** X14
18 Av NW *CAL* . . . **27** H13 I13 **28** M14 N-O14 **29** P14
18 Av S *LET* . . . **88** H10 H9 H9-10
18 Av SE *CAL* . . . **37** P18 R18
18 Av SE *MED* . . . **95** G6
18 Av SW *CAL* . . . **36** O18 O18 **37** P18
18 Av SW *MED* . . . **94** H1
18 St *COD* . . . **85** B-C3
18 St *RED* . . . **66** L5 **67** L6
18 St N *LET* . . . **84** B-C9 C-D9 D9 E9
18 St NE *CAL* . . . **13** S4 **29** S12 S13 S14 S15
18 St NE *MED* . . . **92** C4 **93** C5
18 St NW *CAL* . . . **28** M13 M14 M15 **36** M16
18 St NW *DRU* . . . **72** C4
18 St S *LET* . . . **88** F9 F-G9 G-H9
18 St SE *CAL* . . **38** T16 **43** S22 S23-25 **49** S27
18 St SE *HIG* . . . **77** C5
18 St SW *CAL* . **36** M17 M18 M18-19 M19-20
18 St SW *MED* . . . **94** G2 G3

18A St N *LET* 84 C-D9 D9
18A St NW *CAL* 28 M15 36 M16
18A St SE *CAL* 43 S22
18A St SW *CAL* 36 M18
19 Av *COD* .85 B3
19 Av (Blairmore) *CRO* .80 E6 E-F7 F10 F8-9
19 Av (Coleman) *CRO* 79 C2 C3-4 C4
19 Av N *LET* 84 C9
19 Av NE *CAL* 29 P-Q14
19 Av NW *CAL*
. . . . .27 H13 I14 28 M14 N-O14 29 P14
19 Av S *LET* 88 H9-10
19 Av SE *CAL* 37 R18 R-S18 38 U-W18
19 Av SE *MED* 95 H6
19 Av SW *CAL*
. . . . . .35 J-K18 K18 36 L18 L-M18 O18 37 P18
19 St *COD* 85 B-C2
19 St *RED* 66 K-L4 L5 67 L6 L8
19 St E *DRU* 73 D-E8
19 St N *LET* 84 B9 C9 C-D9 D9 E9
19 St NE *CAL* 14 T5 30 T12-13 T14-15 38 T16
19 St NE *MED* 92 C4 93 C5
19 St NW *CAL* 28 M11-15 36 M16
19 St NW *DRU* 72 C4
19 St S *LET* 84 E9 88 F9 F-G9 G9 H9 H-J9
19 St SE *CAL* 37 S18 38 T16 44 T22
19 St SE *HIG* 77 C5
19 St SE *MED* 95 G6
19 St SW *CAL* 36 M17 M18 M18 M20
. . . . .42 M21 M25 48 M26
19 St SW *MED* 94 G2
19A Av *COD* 85 B3-4
19A St NE *MED* 93 C5
19A St SW *CAL* 36 M17-18 M18
19B Av *COD* 85 B3
20, Range Rd (Mountain View Rd) *RCY* .
. . . . .11 J1
20 Av *RED* 65 B-E10
20 Av (Bellevue) *CRO* .81 H12-13 J13-14 K14
20 Av (Blairmore) *CRO*
. . . . .80 D-E6 E7 F10 F8-9 G11
20 Av (Coleman) *CRO* 79 C1-5
20 Av (Main St) *COD* 85 B3-4
20 Av N *LET* 84 C9
20 Av NE *CAL* 29 P-Q14 30 T14 U-V14
20 Av NW *CAL* . .27 I13-14 28 L-O14 29 P14
20 Av S *LET* 88 H10-11 H9 H9-10
20 Av SE *CAL* 37 R18 S18 38 W18
20 Av SE *MED* 95 G6 H6
20 Av SW *CAL* 36 M18 O18 37 P18
20 St *COD* 85 A-C2
20 St E *HIG* 77 B5
20 St N *LET* 84 B9 C9 C-D9 D9 E9
20 St NE *CAL* 30 T14
20 St NE *MED* 92 C4 93 C5 C5-6
20 St NW *CAL* . .28 M14 M14-15 M15 36 M16
20 St NW *DRU* 72 C4
20 St S *LET* 88 F9 F-G9 G9 H9
20 St SE *CAL* 37 S18 44 T22 T23
20 St SE *HIG* 77 C5
20 St SE *MED* 95 G6
20 St SW *CAL* . . .36 M18-20 42 M21 M22
20 St SW *MED* 94 G2
20A Av *COD* 85 B2 B4
20A Av S *LET* 88 H9
20A St N *LET* 84 E9
20A St NW *CAL* 28 M14-15
20A St SE *CAL* 44 T23-24
20A St SW *CAL* 36 M20 42 M21
21 Av *COD* 85 B2 B3 B4
21 Av (Bellevue) *CRO* .81 H12-13 H-J13
21 Av (Blairmore) *CRO* .80 E7 F10-11 F8 G11
21 Av (Coleman) *CRO* 79 C2 C4
21 Av N *LET* 84 C9
21 Av NE *CAL* 29 P-Q14
21 Av NW *CAL* .27 I13 28 M-N14 O14 29 P14
21 Av S *LET* 88 H10 H11 H9
21 Av SE *CAL* 37 R18 38 V-W18
21 Av SE *MED* 95 G6
21 Av SW *CAL*
. . . .35 K18 36 L18 L-M18 M-N18 O18 37 P18
21 St *COD* 85 A2 B2 B-C2
21 St E *HIG* 77 B5
21 St N *LET* 84 D9
21 St NE *CAL* . . .22 T8 30 T12 T13 T14 T14-15
21 St NE *MED* 92 C4 93 C5 C5-6
21 St NW *CAL*
. . . . .28 M13-14 M14-15 M15 36 M16
21 St NW *DRU* 72 C4
21 St S *LET* 88 F9 F-G9 G9 H9
21 St SE *CAL* 37 S18 44 T23 T25
21 St SE *MED* 95 G6
21 St SW *CAL* . . .36 L20 M18-19 42 L21 L21
21 St SW *MED* 94 G2
21A Av *COD* 85 B2 B3 B4
21A Av SE *CAL* 39 X18
21A St *COD* 85 B2
21A St N *LET* 84 E9
21A St NW *CAL* 28 L14-15

21A St SE *CAL* 44 T23
21A St SW *CAL* 36 L20 42 L21 L21
21B St *COD* 85 B2
22, Range Rd *RCY* 10 G1
22 Av *COD* 85 B3 B-C4 C2
22 Av (Blairmore) *CRO* 80 E8
22 Av (Coleman) *CRO* 79 B3-4 B4 C1-2
22 Av NE *CAL* 29 P-Q14 31 X14 Y14
22 Av NW *CAL* 27 I13 28 M14 N14 O14 29 P14
22 Av S *LET* 88 H11 H11-12 H9 H9-10
22 Av SE *CAL* 37 Q-R18 38 S18 U18
22 Av SE *MED* 95 H6-7
22 Av SW *CAL*
. . . . . .36 L-M18 M18 M-N18 O18 37 P18
22 St *COD* 85 B2 B-C2
22 St *RED* 66 K4-5 67 K7 K8
22 St N *LET* 84 B9 C9 D9 E9
22 St NE *CAL* 22 T8 30 T13 T13-14
22 St NE *MED* 93 B-C5
22 St NW *CAL* .28 L13-14 L14-15 L15 36 L16
22 St NW *DRU* 72 C3-4
22 St S *LET* 88 F-G9 G9-10 H9
22 St SE *CAL* 38 T18 T20 44 T21 T23
22 St SE *MED* 95 G5-6
22 St SW *CAL*
. . .36 L17 L18 L18-19 L20 42 L21 L25 48 L29
22A Av *COD* 85 C3 C4
22A Av S *LET* 88 H10
22A St *COD* 85 B2
22A St NW *CAL* 28 L13-14 L14-15
22A St SE *CAL* 44 T23
22A St SW *CAL* 36 L18
23, Range Rd *RCY* 10 E1
23 Av *COD* 85 C2-3 C4
23 Av (Bellevue) *CRO* 81 H13 J13
23 Av (Blairmore) *CRO* 80 E8
23 Av (Coleman) *CRO* .79 B1-2 B3-4 B4 C1
23 Av N *LET* 84 B9
23 Av NE *CAL*
. . . . .29 P-Q13 30 T13-14 U14 31 X13 Y13 Z13
23 Av NW *CAL* . .27 I13 28 N-O14 O14 29 P14
23 Av S *LET* 88 H-J11 J10 J9
23 Av SE *CAL* 37 Q-R18 38 V-W18 39 X18
23 Av SW *CAL*
. . . . .35 J-K18 36 L18 M18 O18 37 P18
23 St *COD* 85 B2 C2
23 St N *LET* 84 B-C9 D10
23 St NE *CAL* 30 T12-14
23 St NW *CAL*
. . . . . . .28 L12 L13 L13-14 L14-15 L15 36 L16
23 St NW *DRU* 72 C3
23 St NW *MED* 92 B-C1
23 St S *LET* .88 F10 G10 H10 H9-10 J10 J9-10
23 St SE *CAL* 38 T16 T18 44 T21 T23 T25
23 St SE *MED* 95 G5-6 G6
23 St SW *CAL* 36 L17 L18
23 St SW *MED* 94 G2
23A St NW *CAL* 28 L13
24, Range Rd *RCY* 10 D1
24 Av *COD* 85 C2 C3 C4
24 Av (Bellevue) *CRO* 81 H13
24 Av (Blairmore) *CRO* 80 E8
24 Av (Coleman) *CRO*
. . . . .79 B3 B3-4 B4 B5 B-C1 B-C2 C5
24 Av N *LET* 84 B11 B11-12 B9
24 Av NE *CAL*
. . . . .29 P-Q13 S13 30 T13 U13 V13 31 X-Y13
24 Av NW *CAL* 27 J-K13 28 L-M13 O13 29 P13
24 Av S *LET* 88 J10-11 J9
24 Av SE *CAL* 37 Q-R18 38 S18 U18
24 Av W *LET* 86 J1 J2-3
24 St *COD* 85 B-C1
24 St N *LET* 84 C10 C-D10 D10 E10
24 St NE *CAL* 30 T13
24 St NE *AIR* 68 A-B1
24 St NW *CAL* 28 L12-13 L14 L14-15
24 St NW *DRU* 72 C3
24 St S *LET* 88 F10 G10 H10 J10
24 St SE *CAL* 38 T17 44 T21 T23-25 50 T26-27
24 St SE *MED* 95 G-H5 H6
24 St SW *AIR* 68 C-D1
24 St SW *CAL*
. . . . . . .36 L17 42 L25 48 L26-28 52 L31-33
24A St NW *CAL* 28 L15
24A St SE *CAL* 44 T23-24
24A St SW *CAL* 36 L17-18 L19
25, Range Rd *RCY* 9 B1 33 B17 B20
25 Av *COD* 85 C2 C3-4
25 Av (Bellevue) *CRO* 81 H13 J13
25 Av (Blairmore) *CRO* 80 E8
25 Av (Coleman) *CRO* 79 B4
25 Av N *LET* 83 B8 84 B9 B9
25 Av NE *CAL*
. . . . .29 P-Q13 S13 30 T13 V13 31 X13 Y13
25 Av NW *CAL* .28 L-M13 M13 O13 29 P13
25 Av SE *CAL* 37 Q18

25 Av SW *CAL*
. . . . . .35 J-K18 36 L18 M18 O18 37 P18
25 St *COD* 85 B1
25 St N *LET* 84 C10 C-D10 D10
25 St NE *CAL* 30 T12
25 St NW *CAL* 28 L15 36 L16
25 St NW *DRU* 72 C3
25 St S *LET* 88 F10 G10
25 St SE *CAL* . . .38 T16 T17 U20 44 T21
25 St SE *MED* 95 H5 H5-6
25 St SW *CAL* 36 L18
25 St SW *MED* 94 H2
25 St W *LET* 86 J3
25A St SW *CAL* 36 L17-18
26 Av (Bellevue) *CRO* 81 J13
26 Av (Coleman) *CRO* 79 B3 B4
26 Av N *LET* 84 B10-11 B9-10
26 Av NE *CAL*
. . . . .29 P-Q13 30 U-W13 31 X13 X-Y13
26 Av NW *CAL* 28 L13 O13 29 P13
26 Av S *LET* 88 J10 J9-10
26 Av SE *CAL* 37 R18 S18 38 U-W18
26 Av SW *CAL*
. . .34 E-G18 35 H18 I-K18 36 L-M18 O18 37 P18
26 St N *LET* 84 D10 D10
26 St NE *CAL* 30 U12-13 U15
26 St NW *CAL* 28 L11 L15 36 L16
26 St S *LET* 88 F10 G-H10 H10 H-J10
26 St SE *CAL*
. . . . .38 U16 U17 U19-20 44 U21 U24
26 St SE *MED* 95 H6
26 St SW *CAL*
. . . . . . .36 L17-18 42 L25 48 L26 L26-27
26A St N *LET* 84 D10
26A St NE *CAL* 38 U19 44 U23
26A St SW *CAL* 36 L17 L18
27 Av (Bellevue) *CRO* 81 H13 J13-14
27 Av (Coleman) *CRO* 79 B3 B4 B5
27 Av NE *CAL* 29 P-Q13 S13 30 T13
27 Av NW *CAL* 28 L13 M13 O13 29 P13
27 Av S *LET* 88 J10 J9-10
27 Av SW *CAL* 36 M18 37 P18
27 St N *LET* 84 C10 D10
27 St NE *CAL* 30 U12 U13
27 St NW *CAL* 27 K15 28 L15
27 St S *LET* 88 F10 G10 H10
27 St SE *CAL*
. . . . .38 U16 U17 U18 U20
. . . . .44 U21 U23-24 U24 50 U27
27 St SE *MED* 95 H5 H5-6
27 St SW *CAL* 35 K17-18 K19 48 L27
27 St SW *MED* 94 H2
27A Av *CRO* 79 B4
27A St N *LET* 84 C-D10
28 Av (Bellevue) *CRO* 81 J14 K14
28 Av (Coleman) *CRO* 79 B3 B3-4
28 Av NE *CAL* 29 P-Q13 S13 31 X13
28 Av NW *CAL* 28 L13 O13 29 P13
28 Av S *LET* 88 J10
28 Av SE *CAL* 37 S18 38 U18
28 Av SW *CAL* 35 J18 K18 36 L18 M18 37 P18
28 St *RED* 66 J5
28 St N *LET* 84 A10 C10 E10
28 St NE *CAL* 30 U11-12 U15 38 U16
28 St NW *CAL* 27 K15
28 St S *LET* 88 F-K10
28 St SE *CAL*
. . . . . .38 U16 U17 U18 U18-19 U19 U20 44 U21 U24
28 St SE *MED* 95 H6
28 St SW *CAL* 35 K17-18 41 K25 42 L25
28A St S *LET* 88 F10 G10
28A St SE *CAL* 38 U19
28B St S *LET* 88 H10
29 Av *COD* 85 C3
29 Av (Bellevue) *CRO* 81 J14 J-K14
29 Av (Coleman) *CRO* 79 B3
29 Av NE *CAL* 29 P-Q13 R-S13 30 W13 31 Y13
29 Av NW *CAL* .26 G13 27 I13 28 O13 29 P13
29 Av SW *CAL* 35 I19 36 M19 O19 37 P19
29 St N *LET* 84 C10 D10 E10
29 St NE *CAL* 30 U13 U14
29 St NW *CAL* 27 K14-15
29 St S *LET* 88 F10 G10 G-H10 H10 J10
29 St SE *CAL* 44 U22 U25 U-V25 50 U27
29 St SE *MED* 95 H6
29 St SW *CAL* 35 K18-19 41 K25
29A St S *LET* 88 G10
29A St SE *CAL* 38 U19 44 U23
30, Range Rd *RCY* 9 Z1 33 Z19
30 Av *COD* 85 C2-3
30 Av *CRO* 79 B4
30 Av *RED* 65 B-F8 67 G-M8
30 Av NE *CAL* 29 P-Q13 S13 30 T13 W13
30 Av NW *CAL*
. . . . .26 G13 27 H13 28 N-O13 29 P13
30 Av S *LET* 88 J10 J9-10
30 Av SE *CAL* 37 S19 38 U-V19
30 Av SW *CAL*
. . . . .35 I-K19 36 L19 M19 O19 O19 37 P19 P19

30 St *COD* 85 A-C1
30 St *RED* 66 J5
30 St N *LET* 84 C10 D10 E10
30 St NW *CAL* 27 K15
30 St S *LET* 88 F10 G10 G-H10 H10 J10
30 St SE *CAL*
. . . . . .38 U18 U20 44 U21 U24 U-V22 V23
30 St SE *MED* 95 H6
30 St SW *CAL* 35 K18 47 K27
30 St SW *MED* 94 H1
30 St W *LET* 82 D2 86 G2 J2
30A Av SE *CAL* 38 U-V19
30A St SE *CAL* 38 U19
31 Av *CRO* 81 J14 J-K14
31 Av NE *CAL* 29 P13 R13 30 W13 31 X13
31 Av NW *CAL*
. . .26 G13 27 H13 28 M-N13 N-O13 O13 29 P13
31 Av SW *CAL* 35 K19 36 M19 O19 37 P19
31 St N *LET* 84 C11 E10-11
31 St NW *CAL* 27 K12 K15
31 St S *LET* 88 F11
31 St SE *CAL* 38 U18 44 U24
31 St SE *MED* 95 H6
31 St SW *CAL* 35 J-K20 K17-18 K19
31A, Range Rd *RCY* 24 X11 X14
31A Av SE *CAL* 38 U-V19
31A St S *LET* 88 G11
31A St SE *CAL* 38 U19
32, Range Rd *RCY*
. . . . .8 W1-2 16 W9 24 W11 W14 32 W16 W20
32 Av NE *CAL* . .29 P-Q13 Q12 R-S13 30 T-W13 31 X-Z13
32 Av NW *CAL* 26 G13 27 H13 I-K13
. . . . .28 M-N13 N-O13 O13 29 P13
32 Av S *LET* 88 J10-11
32 Av SE *CAL* 37 P19 R19 S19
32 Av SW *CAL*
. . .34 G19 35 I19 J19 K19 36 L19 M19 N19 O19
32 St SE *CAL* 66 J3-4 J5 67 H-J7 J8-9
32 St E *OKO* 76 A-D4 E4
32 St N *LET* 84 D11
32 St NE *CAL* 22 U7-8 30 U11-14
32 St NW *CAL* 27 K15
32 St S *LET* 84 E11 88 F11 G11 H11 J11
32 St SE *CAL* 38 U17 U18 V20 44 V21
32 St SW *CAL* 35 K17-18 K19 K19-20
32 St SW *MED* 94 H1 H2
32A Av S *LET* 88 J-K10
32A St SE *CAL* 38 V19
33, Range Rd *RCY* 16 V9 24 V14 32 V16
33 Av NE *CAL* 29 P-Q12 30 T-U12 31 X12
33 Av NW *CAL*
. . . . . .26 E11 F12 G12 27 H12 28 O12 29 P12
33 Av S *LET* 88 K10
33 Av SW *CAL*
. . . . . .35 I19 J19 K19 36 L-M19 O19 37 P19
33 St *RED* 66 J5 67 H6
33 St N *LET* 84 C11 E11
33 St NE *CAL* 30 V15 38 V16
33 St NW *CAL* 19 K10 27 K11 K12 K15
33 St S *LET* 88 F11
33 St SE *CAL* 38 U18 V19 44 V24
33 St SW *CAL* 35 K17-18 K19
33A Av SE *CAL* 38 V19
33A St *RED* 67 V19
33A St NW *CAL* 27 K15
33A St SE *CAL* 38 V19
34 Av NE *CAL*
. . . . . .29 P-Q12 R12 30 U-V12 W12 31 Y12
34 Av NW *CAL* 26 E11 F-G12 G12
. . . . .27 H12 I12 K12 28 L12 O12 29 P12
34 Av SE *CAL*
. . . . . .37 P-Q19 Q-R19 R-S19 38 U-V19 39 X19
34 Av SW *CAL* 34 E-F19 G19
. . . . .35 K19 36 M-O19 O19 37 P19
34 St *INN* .63 D2
34 St *RED* 66 H5 67 H6
34 St Cl *RED* 67 H6
34 St NE *CAL* 30 V12 V15
34 St NW *CAL* 27 K15
34 St S *LET* 84 E11 88 F11 G11
34 St SE *CAL* 38 V17-18 V18-19 V20
34 St SW *CAL* 35 K18 41 K22
34A St NW *CAL* 27 K15
34A St SE *CAL* 38 V20
35 Av *RED* 67 G7
35 Av Cl *RED* 67 G7
35 Av NE *CAL* 29 P-Q12 30 T12 T-U12
35 Av NW *CAL*
. . .26 F-G12 G12 27 J-K12 28 O12 29 P12
35 Av SW *CAL* 35 I19 I-J19 J-K19 36 M19
35 St *INN* .63 D2
35 St *RED* 66 H4 H5 67 H6
35 St Cl *INN* 63 D2
35 St Cr *RED* 67 H6
35 St NE *CAL* 30 V12
35 St NW *CAL* 27 J-K15
35 St S *LET* 88 H11 J11

35 St SE CAL
  .38 V17 V18 V20 44 V21 V22 V23-24 50 V27-28
35 St SW CAL .35 K18
35A Av RED .67 G-H7
35A St NW CAL 27 J-K15
35A St SE CAL 38 V20
35A St SW CAL 35 K16
35B St SE CAL 38 V20
36 St NE CAL 29 P-Q12 R12
36 Av NW CAL
  . . . . . . .26 E11 F12 F-G12 G12 28 O12 29 P12
36 Av S LET 88 K9-10
36 Av SE CAL 37 P-Q19 S19
36 Av SW CAL
  . . . . .35 K19 36 M19 N-O19 O19 37 P19
36 St INN 63 D1-2
36 St RED 66 H4 H5 67 H6
36 St Cl INN 63 D2
36 St N LET 84 C11 E11
36 St NE CAL . .14 V3-5 22 V6-10 30 V11-15
36 St NW CAL 27 J-K15 K12
36 St S LET 84 E11 88 H11 J11
36 St SE CAL . .38 V16-20 44 V21 V21-22 V24
36 St SW CAL 35 J16 J18 J19
36A St INN .63 D1-2
36A St NW CAL 27 J15
36B St NW CAL 27 J14-15
37 Av RED 67 G7
37 Av NE CAL .29 P-Q12 30 T-U12 V12 31 Y12
37 Av NW CAL 26 F-G12 28 O12 29 P12
37 Av SW CAL . . .35 J19 36 M19 O19 37 P19
37 St INN 63 C1 D2 D3
37 St RED 66 H4 H5 67 H6
37 St NW CAL 27 J11-12 J14-15
37 St S LET .88 H11
37 St SE CAL 38 V17 V18 V20 44 V21
37 St SW CAL
  . . . . .35 J16-20 41 J21-22 47 J27-29 K30
37A St INN 63 D2
38 Av RED 67 G-H7
38 Av TAB 91 E3
38 Av NE CAL 29 P12 Q12 R12
38 Av NW CAL 29 P12
38 Av SE CAL 37 R-S19
38 Av SW CAL 36 M19 M-O19 37 P19
38 St INN 63 C2
38 St RED 66 H3-4 H4 H5 67 H6
38 St Cl INN .63 D2
38 St Cl RED 66 H3-4
38 St Cr INN .63 D2
38 St NE CAL . .30 V12 V12-13 V13-14 V15
38 St SE CAL 38 V17-18
38 St SW CAL 35 J16 J17 J19
38A Av RED 67 G7 G-H7
38A Av SE CAL 37 P-Q19
38A Av SW CAL 37 P19
39 Av RED 67 G7
39 Av LET 91 E3
39 Av NE CAL . . .29 P12 30 T12 U12 U-V12
39 Av NW CAL 26 F-G12 28 N-O12
39 Av SE CAL 37 P20
39 Av SW CAL 35 I19-20 K20 36 M20 N20 O20
39 St INN .63 C2 D2-3
39 St RED 66 H4 H4-5 67 H6-9
39 St Cl INN .63 C2
39 St N LET 84 C11 E11
39 St NE CAL 30 V12 V13-14
39 St NW CAL 27 J11 J13
39 St SE CAL 38 V16 V17-18 V19
39 St SW CAL 35 J17 J19
40 Av RED 65 B-C6 F6 67 G-M6
40 Av TAB 91 E3
40 Av N LET .83 A8
40 Av NE CAL 29 P-Q12 Q12 R12
40 Av NW CAL
  . . . . . . .26 F12 27 H-J12 28 N12 O12 29 P12
40 Av S LET 88 K10-11
40 Av SW CAL
  . . . . . .35 I20 K19-20 36 M20 O20 37 P20
40 Av W LET 87 K5-6
40 St INN .63 C2 C2-3
40 St RED 67 H6
40 St TAB 91 D1
40 St Cl INN .63 C2
40 St NE CAL 22 V9 30 V14 V15 38 V16
40 St NW CAL 27 J12
40 St S LET .88 H11
40 St SE CAL . .38 V17 V18 44 V21-24 V24-25
  . . . . .50 V27-28 54 V33-35
40 St SW CAL 35 J16 J17 J19
40A Av RED .67 G-H6
41 Av RED 67 G6 G-H6 H6
41 Av TAB 91 E3
41 Av N LET .83 A8
41 Av NE CAL 29 P-Q12 30 T12 31 Y12
41 Av NW CAL 26 D12 F12 29 P12
41 Av SE CAL 37 Q20 S20
41 Av SW CAL . . .35 I-J20 36 M20 37 P20
41 St INN .63 C2 C3

41 St RED 66 H3-4 H4 67 G-H7
41 St TAB 91 D1
41 St Cl INN .63 C2-3
41 St Cr INN 63 C2 C3
41 St Cr RED .66 H3
41 St N LET .84 C12
41 St NE CAL 30 V14
41 St NW CAL 27 I14 J11
41 St S LET .84 C12
41 St SE CAL 38 V17 V18-19
41 St SW CAL 35 J17 J19
41A MED .95 F5 F8
41A Av RED 67 H6
41A Av SE CAL 38 U20
42 Av INN 63 B4
42 Av RED 65 C6 F6 67 G6-H6 H6
42 Av TAB 91 D3 D-E3
42 Av N LET .83 A8
42 Av NE CAL 29 Q12 S12 30 T12
42 Av NW CAL 28 O12 29 P12
42 Av SE CAL 37 P-R20 R20 S20
42 Av SW CAL 36 M20 O20 37 P20
42 St INN 63 C1 C2-3
42 St OLD 62 B2 B3
42 St RED 66 G4 G-H5 67 G6 G-H6
42 St TAB 91 D1
42 St Cl INN .63 C3
42 St Cr RED 66 G-H5
42 St E OKO .76 D5
42 St NE CAL . .22 U8 30 V12 V14-15 W14 W15
42 St NW CAL 27 I14 J12
42 St S LET 88 H-J12
42 St SE CAL . .38 V17-18 V-W17 W16-17 W17
  . . . . .44 V22 V24 50 V27
42 St SW CAL 35 J16 J17 J19-20
42A Av RED 67 H6
42A St INN 63 C1
42A St RED 65 F6
42A St SE CAL 38 W17
43, Range Rd COC 60 D3
43 Av INN 63 B4
43 Av RED 65 F6 67 G6 H6 H6
43 Av TAB 91 D3
43 Av N LET .83 A8
43 Av NE CAL 29 R11 31 Y11
43 Av NW CAL .26 F11-12 G11-12 29 P11
43 Av SE CAL 37 R20
43 Av SW CAL 36 M20 37 P20
43 St INN 63 C1-2 C2-3
43 St OLD 62 B2 B3 B3-4
43 St RED 66 G4 G4-5 G5 67 G6
43 St TAB 91 B-C1 D1
43 St Cl INN .63 C3
43 St Cl OLD .62 B2
43 St N LET 84 C12 D-E12
43 St NE CAL 30 V11 W14-15
43 St NW CAL 27 I14
43 St S LET 88 F-G12 H12 J-K12 L12
43 St SE CAL 38 W16 W17 W17-18
43 St SW CAL 35 J17 J19 J20
43A Av RED 67 G6 H6
43A St SE CAL 38 W16
44 Av INN 63 B3
44 Av RED 65 F6 F6 67 G6 H6
44 Av TAB 91 D3
44 Av Cl INN .63 B3
44 Av N LET .83 A8
44 Av NE CAL 29 R11 30 V-W11
44 Av NW CAL
  . . .26 D11 F11 F12 G11 27 I11 28 O11 29 P11
44 Av SE CAL 37 R20 38 V20
44 Av SW CAL 35 J-K20 36 M20
44 St INN 63 C1 C2-3
44 St OLD 62 B2 B3 B3-4
44 St RED 66 G5 G5 67 G6 G6 G7
44 St TAB 91 B1 D1
44 St Cl INN .63 C2
44 St Cr INN 63 B-C1
44 St NE CAL . . .22 V9-10 W10 W8 38 W16
44 St NW CAL 27 I14
44 St S LET .84 E12
44 St SE CAL
  . . . . . .38 W16-18 44 W21-24 W24-25 50 W28
44 St SW CAL 35 J17 J19 J20
44A Av RED 67 H6 H-J6
44A St RED 66 G4-5 67 G6
44A St Cl INN .63 C2
45 Av INN 63 B3
45 Av RED 65 E6 F6 67 H6
45 Av TAB 91 D3
45 Av Cl RED .65 C6
45 Av NE CAL 29 Q11 R11
45 Av SE CAL 38 U20
45 Av SW CAL
  . . . . .35 J-K20 36 M20 M-N20 37 P20
45 St INN 63 C1-2 C2-3
45 St OLD 62 B2 B3-4
45 St RED 66 G4 G5 67 G6 G7

45 St TAB 91 C2
45 St Cl INN .63 C2
45 St Cr INN 63 B-C1
45 St NW CAL 27 I13-14
45 St SE CAL 38 W17-18
45 St SW CAL 35 J16-20
45A Av RED 67 G6
46 Av INN 63 B3
46 Av OLD 62 C4
46 Av RED 64 E5 65 E6 F6 67 G6
46 Av TAB 91 D2 D3
46 Av NE CAL 29 Q11
46 Av NW CAL . . .26 D11 E-F11 27 J11
46 Av SE CAL . . .37 Q-R20 38 V-W20 43 S21
46 Av SW CAL
  . . . . .35 I-J20 36 M20 O20 37 P20
46 St INN 63 C2-3
46 St OLD 62 B2 B3-4
46 St RED 66 G5 G5 67 G6 G6
46 St TAB 91 C2 D2
46 St NE CAL 30 W12 W13
46 St NW CAL 27 I13 I13-14
46 St SE CAL
  . . . . . . .38 W17 W18 44 W21-22 W23-24 W24
46 St SE CAL 50 W29
46 St SW CAL 35 I19 I20
46A Av RED 64 E5 65 E6 66 G5 67 G6
46A Av Cr RED 66 H5 67 H6
46A St TAB 91 B2 C2
46A St Cr INN 63 B-C3
47 Av INN 63 B3
47 Av OLD 62 B3 B4 C3-4 D3
47 Av RED 64 F5 66 G5 G5 H-J5
47 Av TAB 91 D3
47 Av Cl RED 64 C5 65 B6 C6
47 Av NE CAL 29 R11
47 Av NW CAL 26 D11 E-F11
47 Av SE CAL 38 U-V20
47 Av SW CAL . . .36 L20 M20 O20 37 P20
47 St INN 63 B3 B2-3
47 St OLD .62 B-C3
47 St RED 66 G4 G4-5 G5 67 G6
47 St TAB 91 C2 C-D2
47 St Cl INN 63 B-C1
47 St NE CAL 30 W11 38 W16
47 St NW CAL 27 I13
47 St SE CAL 38 W16-17 W17-18 W20 44 W21
47 St SW CAL 35 I17 I19 I20
47A Av RED 64 E5 F5 66 G5
47A St TAB 91 C2
48 Av INN 63 B3 B-C3
48 Av OLD 62 C3 D3
48 Av RED 64 B5 E5 F5 66 G-H5
48 Av TAB 91 D1 D2 D2-3
48 Av NE CAL 29 P-Q11 R11 30 U11
48 Av NW CAL 26 E-F11 28 L11 N11
48 Av S LET 88 K-L10 L11
48 Av SE CAL 37 Q-R20 38 U20 V20 W20
48 Av SW CAL 36 M20 N-O20 O20
48 St INN 63 B2-3 B3
48 St OLD 62 B-C3 C3
48 St RED 66 G5 G5 67 G6
48 St TAB 91 B2 C2 C-D2 D2
48 St E OKO .76 E5
48 St NE CAL . .30 W12-13 W13-14 W14 W15
48 St NW CAL 27 I11 I13
48 St SE CAL
  . . . . . . .38 W17-18 44 W21-24 W24-25 50 W29
48 St SW CAL 35 I19 I20
48A Av INN 63 B3
48A Av RED 64 F5
48A St TAB 91 B2
49 Av INN 63 A-B3 B3 B-C3
49 Av OLD 62 B-D3
49 Av RED 64 B5 C5 E5 F5 66 G5 H5 J5 L5
49 Av TAB 91 D1 D2-3
49 Av Cl RED 64 A-B5
49 Av NE CAL 29 R11
49 Av NW CAL 27 I11
49 Av SE CAL 38 T-U20 U20
49 Av SW CAL . .41 J21 42 L-M21 M21 O21
49 St INN 63 B2-3 B3
49 St OLD 62 C3
49 St RED 66 G5 67 G6 G6
49 St TAB 91 B-C2 C2 C-D2
49 St NE CAL 30 W12
49 St NW CAL 27 I12 I13
49 St SE CAL 38 W17
49 St SW CAL 35 I19
49A Av INN 63 B3 C3 D3
49A Av RED 64 F5
49A St INN 63 B4
50 Av INN 63 A-B3 B-C3 D2-3
50 Av OLD 62 C4
50 Av RED 64 B-F5 66 G-M5
50 Av TAB 91 D1-4
50 Av NE CAL 29 Q11 30 W11
50 Av SE CAL . . .43 P20 44 T-W21 45 X-Z21
50 Av SW CAL .41 K21 42 L-M21 O21 43 P21

50 St INN 63 B2-3 B4
50 St OLD 62 C2-3 C3
50 St RED 66 G5 67 G6 G7 G8-9
50 St TAB 91 A-E2
50 St NE CAL 14 W5 30 W13-14 W14
50 St NW CAL 27 I12 I13
50 St SE CAL 38 W17-18 44 W21
50 St SE CAL 50 W29
50 St SW CAL 35 I19 I20
50A Av INN .63 D2-3
50A St RED 67 G6 G7
51 Av INN 63 B2 C-D2
51 Av OLD 62 B3 C3
51 Av RED 64 E-F5 66 G5 H5 J5
51 Av TAB 91 D1-2
51 Av Cl RED .66 H-J5
51 Av SE CAL .43 P-Q21 Q21 44 T21 45 X-Y21
51 Av SW CAL 42 M21 O21
51 St INN 63 B3
51 St OLD 62 C2-3 C3
51 St RED 66 G5 67 G6
51 St TAB 91 B2-3 C2-3 D2 D-E3
51 St Cl RED .67 G7
51 St NE CAL 30 W13-14
51 St NW CAL 27 H-I13 I13
51 St SE CAL
  . . . . . . .38 W17 W20 44 W21 W22 W23 W24
51 St SW CAL 35 I18-19
51A Av INN 63 D2
51A Av RED 66 G4-5
51A St RED 67 G6 G7
52 Av INN 63 C2
52 Av OLD 62 B3 C3
52 Av RED . .64 B5 C5 D5 E5 F5 66 G4-5 H4 H5
52 Av TAB 91 C3-4 C-D2
52 Av NE CAL 30 V11
52 Av NW CAL 19 J-K10
52 Av SE CAL 43 P21 44 T21 45 X21
52 Av SW CAL . . .42 L21 M21 O21 43 P21
52 St INN 63 B3
52 St OLD 62 C2-3 C3
52 St RED 64 F5 65 F6 67 G6
52 St TAB 91 A3 B-D3 D3 D-E3 E3
52 St Cl INN .63 B4
52 St NE CAL
  . . . . . . .14 W2-5 15 X5 22 W6-8 23 X6 30 W11-15
52 St NW CAL 27 H-I13 I12 I13
52 St SE CAL
  . . . . . . .39 X16-20 45 X21-25 51 X26-30 55 X32
52A Av INN .63 C-D2
52A St SE CAL 39 X17
53 Av INN 63 C2
53 Av OLD 62 B2 B2-3 C2 C-D2
53 Av RED 64 F4-5 66 G4-5
53 Av TAB 91 C2
53 Av Cl INN .63 B2
53 Av NE CAL 29 I10 20 O10
53 Av NW CAL 19 I10 20 O10
53 Av SE CAL .43 P21 P-Q21 44 T21 45 X21
53 Av SW CAL . . .42 L-M21 O21 43 P21
53 St OLD 62 C1 C2 C3
53 St RED 64 F5
53 St TAB 91 B3 B-C3 C-D3 D3 D-E3
53 St Cl INN 63 A-B4
53 St Cr RED .65 F6
53 St NE CAL 31 X12
53 St NW CAL . .11 I3-4 19 I9-10 27 I11
53 St SE CAL 39 X17 45 X21 X23-24
53 St SW CAL 35 I17-18
53A St SE CAL 39 X17
53B St SE CAL 39 X17
53C St SE CAL 39 X17
54 Av INN 63 C2 D1
54 Av OLD 62 B2 B-C2
54 Av RED 64 E-F4 F4 66 G4 G4 H4
54 Av TAB .91 C2 C3-4
54 Av Cr RED .66 H4
54 Av NE CAL 22 V-W10
54 Av NW CAL 18 G10 20 O10 29 P11
54 Av SE CAL 44 U-V21 V-W21 45 X21
54 Av SW CAL 41 K21 42 L-M21 O21
54 St CRO 79 C1
54 St INN 63 B2
54 St MED 95 K8
54 St OLD 62 C2-3 C3
54 St RED 64 F5
54 St TAB 91 B-C3 C-D3 D3 D-E3
54 St NW CAL 31 I9
54 St SE CAL 39 X17 X17-18 45 X21
54A Av Cl INN .63 C2
54A Av Cr INN .63 C2
55 Av OLD 62 B2 C2 C-D2
55 Av RED 64 E-F4 66 H4 H-J4
55 Av TAB 91 C2
55 Av Cr INN 63 B1 C1-2 C2
55 Av NE CAL 21 Q-R10
55 Av SW CAL . . .42 M21 O21 43 P21
55 St OLD 62 C1-2 C2
55 St RED 64 F4 F5 65 F6 F7 F8-9

55 St / 133 St

55 St TAB ... 91 B3 B-C3 C-D3 D3 E3
55 St Cl INN ... 63 B2
55 St NE CAL ... 31 X12 X15
55 St SE CAL ... 31 X15 39 X16-17 45 X21
55A Av RED ... 66 G-H4
56 Av INN ... 63 C1-2
56 Av OLD ... 62 B-C2 C2 C-D2
56 Av RED ... 64 F4 66 G-H4
56 Av TAB ... 91 C2-4
56 Av Cl INN ... 63 B-C2
56 Av NE CAL ... 21 P10
56 Av NW CAL ... 20 N-O10
56 Av SE CAL ... 44 U-V21 W21 45 X21
56 Av SW CAL ... 42 M21 O21
56 St INN ... 63 B2-3
56 St OLD ... 62 C2 C3
56 St RED ... 64 F4 F5
56 St TAB ... 91 B3 B-D3 D3
56 St NE CAL ... 31 X12-14
56 St SE CAL ... 45 X21 X24
56A St Cl OLD ... 62 C-D2
57 Av INN ... 63 B-C1 C1
57 Av OLD ... 62 B2 C-D2
57 Av RED ... 64 F4 66 H4 H-J4
57 Av TAB ... 91 C1-2 C2 C4
57 Av Cl OLD ... 62 C2
57 Av NE CAL ... 21 Q-R10
57 Av NW CAL ... 20 N10
57 Av SE CAL ... 44 U21
57 Av SW CAL ... 42 M21 O21 43 P21
57 St INN ... 63 B2-3
57 St OLD ... 62 C-D3
57 St RED ... 64 F4 F5
57 St TAB ... 91 B3 B-D3
57 St SE CAL ... 45 X21-22
57A Av RED ... 66 H4
57A Av TAB ... 91 C3-4
58 Av INN ... 63 C1
58 Av OLD ... 62 C-D2
58 Av RED ... 64 E4 F4 66 H3-4
58 Av TAB ... 91 C2 C3
58 Av NW CAL ... 18 E-F10
58 Av SE CAL ... 44 U21-22 V-W22 45 X22
58 Av SW CAL ... 41 J-K22 42 L-M22 O22
58 St INN ... 63 B3
58 St OLD ... 62 D2
58 St RED ... 64 F4 F5 65 F6 F8
58 St TAB ... 91 B3 B-C3
58 St NE CAL ... 31 X12 X14 X15
58 St NW CAL ... 19 H9
58 St S LET ... 89 J13 L13
58 St SE CAL ... 39 X16-17
58A Av RED ... 64 F4
58A St RED ... 64 F4
59 Av RED ... 64 C3 D3-4 E4 E-F4
59 Av TAB ... 91 C2
59 Av Cl OLD ... 62 C-D2
59 Av NW CAL ... 21 P10
59 Av SE CAL ... 43 Q22 R22
59 Av SW CAL ... 43 P22
59 St INN ... 63 A-B3
59 St RED ... 64 F4 F5 65 F6 F8
59 St TAB ... 91 B3
59 St NE CAL ... 31 X14 X15 39 X16
59 St NW CAL ... 27 H12
59A Av SE CAL ... 43 S22
59A St RED ... 64 F4
60 Av INN ... 63 B-C1
60 Av OLD ... 62 C2
60 Av RED ... 64 E4 F4 66 H-J3
60 Av TAB ... 91 C2-4
60 Av Cl OLD ... 62 C-D2
60 Av NE CAL ... 21 P10
60 Av NW CAL ... 18 E10
60 Av SE CAL ... 43 P-Q22 R22 44 V22
60 Av SW CAL ... 42 O22 43 P22
60 St CRO ... 79 C1
60 St OLD ... 62 D1-2 D3
60 St RED ... 64 E4 E4-5 E5 65 E8
60 St TAB ... 91 B4 B-C4
60 St NE CAL ... 31 X11 X12-13
60 St NW CAL ... 27 H12
60 St SE CAL ... 39 X16 X17 X18 45 X24-25 X-Y21
60A Av Cr INN ... 63 C1
60A St RED ... 64 E4
60B Av Cr INN ... 63 C1
61 Av INN ... 63 A-D1
61 Av OLD ... 62 B-C2 C1
61 Av RED ... 64 E4 F4
61 Av TAB ... 91 B2
61 Av NW CAL ... 18 E-F10 G10
61 Av SE CAL ... 43 P22 44 U-W22 45 X22
61 Av SW CAL ... 41 J-K22 42 O22 43 P22
61 St CRO ... 79 C1
61 St RED ... 64 E4 E4-5 E5 65 E8-9
61 St TAB ... 91 B4
61 St NE CAL ... 31 X-Y14
61 St NW CAL ... 27 H12
61 St SE CAL ... 39 Y17
62 Av OLD ... 62 D1
62 Av TAB ... 91 B1-3
62 Av NW CAL ... 18 E-F10 G10
62 Av SE CAL ... 43 P-Q22 S22 44 V22
62 Av SW CAL ... 41 K22
62 St CRO ... 79 C1
62 St RED ... 64 E5
62 St TAB ... 91 B-C4
62 St NE CAL ... 31 Y13 Y14
62 St NW CAL ... 27 H12
62 St SE CAL ... 45 Y21
63 Av OLD ... 62 C1 C-D1
63 Av RED ... 64 D3 E5
63 Av TAB ... 91 B2
63 Av NE CAL ... 22 V9
63 Av NW CAL ... 20 O9
63 Av SW CAL ... 41 K22 42 L22
63 St CRO ... 79 C1
63 St RED ... 64 E4
63 St NW CAL ... 26 G12-13 27 H12
63A Av TAB ... 91 B2
63A St RED ... 64 E4
64 Av TAB ... 91 B1-4
64 Av NE CAL ... 21 Q9 22 W9 23 X-Y9
64 Av NW CAL ... 18 F9 19 H9 20 O9
64 Av SE CAL ... 43 Q22 R22 S22 44 T22 V22 V-W22 W22
64 St CRO ... 79 C1-2
64 St RED ... 64 E4
64 St TAB ... 91 B-C4
64 St NE CAL ... 31 Y11 Y12-13
64 St NW CAL ... 26 G12
64 St SE CAL ... 45 Y21 Y25
65 Av OLD ... 62 C1
65 Av RED ... 64 D3
65 Av NE CAL ... 21 Q-R9
65 Av NW CAL ... 18 G9
65 Av SE CAL ... 43 P22
65 Av SW CAL ... 42 O22 43 P22
65 St CRO ... 79 B2 B-C2
65 St RED ... 64 E4
65 St TAB ... 91 B-C4 C4
65 St NE CAL ... 31 Y13 Y14
65 St NW CAL ... 26 G12
65 St SE CAL ... 39 Y17
66 Av TAB ... 91 B3 B3-4
66 Av NW CAL ... 18 G9 19 H9
66 Av SE CAL ... 43 S22 44 T22 V22 W22 45 X22 Y22
66 Av SW CAL ... 41 K22 42 L22 O22 43 P22
66 St CRO ... 79 B-C2 C2
66 St RED ... 64 E2
66 St Cl RED ... 64 E4
66 St NE CAL ... 31 Y13
66 St NW CAL ... 26 G11 G12
66 St SE CAL ... 45 Y21
67 Av RED ... 64 D2
67 Av NE CAL ... 22 V9
67 Av NW CAL ... 18 F9
67 Av SW CAL ... 42 O22
67 St CRO ... 79 C2
67 St RED ... 64 E3-5 65 D7-8
67 St Cl RED ... 64 E2-3
67 St NE CAL ... 31 Y12 Y14
67 St NW CAL ... 26 G11 G12 G12-13
67A St RED ... 64 D3-4
67A St NE CAL ... 31 Y13
68 Av RED ... 64 D2
68 Av NE CAL ... 21 Q-R9
68 Av NW CAL ... 18 F9 20 O9 21 P9
68 Av SE CAL ... 44 W22
68 Av SW CAL ... 42 O23
68 St CRO ... 79 C2
68 St RED ... 64 D3
68 St Cl RED ... 64 D3-4
68 St NE CAL ... 15 Y5 23 Y10 Y6-7 31 Y11-15
68 St NW CAL ... 26 G11 G13
68 St SE CAL 39 Y16-20 45 Y21-25 51 Y26-30
69 Av SE CAL ... 44 T23 45 X23
69 Av SW CAL ... 42 O23
69 St CRO ... 79 C2
69 St RED ... 64 D3
69 St Dr RED ... 64 D4
69 St NW CAL ... 10 G5 26 F-G11 G12 G13
69 St SE CAL ... 39 Y17
69 St SW CAL ... 26 G14 34 G16 G17-20
70 Av SE CAL ... 44 V23
70 Av SW CAL ... 42 N23 O23
70 St CRO ... 79 C2
70 St RED ... 64 D3-4
70 St Dr RED ... 64 D4
70 St NW CAL ... 26 F-G11 G12
70 St SE CAL ... 51 Z27
71 Av NW CAL ... 18 F9 20 O9
71 Av SE CAL ... 43 P23 Q23 44 T23
71 Av SW CAL ... 42 O23
71 St CRO ... 79 C2
71 St RED ... 64 D2-3
71 St NW CAL ... 18 G9 26 G12
72 Av TAB ... 91 B4
72 Av NE CAL ... 21 P8-9 Q-R9 22 V-W9
72 Av NW CAL ... 20 O9
72 Av SE CAL ... 44 T23 V-W23
72 St NW CAL ... 18 G10 26 F11 G12
72 St SE CAL ... 45 Y-Z25 55 Z31-35
72 St SE HIG ... 77 D1
73 Av SE CAL ... 42 O23 43 P23 R23 44 V23
73 Av SW CAL ... 42 N23 O23
73 St CRO ... 79 B-C3
73 St NW CAL ... 26 F11 G12
73 St SW CAL ... 26 G14-15 34 G16-17
74 Av SE CAL ... 44 T23 V23 W23 45 X23 Z23
74 St CRO ... 79 B3
74 St RED ... 64 C5
74 St NW CAL ... 26 F-G12
74 St SE CAL ... 45 Z23 51 Z27
75 Av NW CAL ... 20 O8
75 Av SE CAL ... 44 V-W23
75 Av SW CAL ... 42 N-O23
75 St CRO ... 79 C3
75 St RED ... 64 C3
75 St NW CAL ... 18 F9 26 F11-12
75 St SW CAL ... 34 F17
76 Av SE CAL ... 43 S23 44 T23 V-W23 45 X23
76 St CRO ... 79 B3 C3
76 St RED ... 64 C2-3 C3 C4-5 C5
76 St NW CAL ... 10 F5 26 F12
76A St Cl RED ... 64 C5
77 Av SE CAL ... 43 Q23 44 T-U23 W24
77 Av SW CAL ... 42 O23
77 St CRO ... 79 B3 C3
77 St RED ... 64 B-C4 C3 C5 65 C6
77 St NW CAL ... 26 F11-12
77 St SW CAL ... 26 F14-15 34 F16-19
78 Av NE CAL ... 21 P8 22 T-U8
78 Av NW CAL ... 20 O8
78 Av SE CAL ... 44 T24 V24 V-W24 45 X24
78 Av SW CAL ... 42 N23 O24
78 St CRO ... 79 B3 C3
78 St RED ... 64 B5
78 St Cr RED ... 65 B6
78 St NW CAL ... 18 F8-9 26 F12
78 St SE CAL ... 45 Z25
78A St RED ... 64 B5
78A St Cl RED ... 64 B5
79 Av NE CAL ... 22 T8
79 Av SE CAL ... 43 Q24
79 St CRO ... 79 B3 C3
79 St RED ... 64 B5
79 St NW CAL ... 26 F11 F12
80 Av TAB ... 91 A2-4
80 Av NE CAL ... 22 U-W8 23 X-Y8
80 Av NW CAL ... 17 B8
80 Av SE CAL ... 44 T24 T-U24 U-V24 V-W24 45 X24
80 Av SW CAL ... 42 N24 O24
80 St CRO ... 79 B3 B-C3
80 St RED ... 64 B5
80 St E HIG ... 77 A2
80 St NW CAL ... 26 F11 F12
80 St SE CAL ... 45 Z22
81 St CRO ... 79 B-C4 C-D4
81 St RED ... 64 A-B5
81 St NW CAL ... 26 F11 F11-12 F12
81 St SW CAL ... 26 F14-15 34 F18
82 Av SW CAL ... 42 N24
82 St CRO ... 79 B4 C4 D4
82 St NW CAL ... 26 F11
82B, Township Rd LET ... 88 L10
83 Av SE CAL ... 43 P24 44 T-U24
83 St CRO ... 79 B4 C4
83 St NW CAL ... 26 E12 F11
84 Av NE CAL ... 22 W7
84 Av SE CAL ... 43 P24 44 U24 45 Y24
84 Av SW CAL ... 42 O24
84 St CRO ... 79 C4 D4
84 St NE CAL ... 15 Z3-5 23 Z6-10 31 Z11-14
84 St NW CAL ... 18 E10 26 E11
84 St SE CAL 39 Z16-20 45 Z21-25 51 Z26-30
85 Av SE CAL ... 44 U24
85 St CRO ... 79 B4 C4
85 St NW CAL ... 10 E2-5 26 E11-12
85 St SW CAL ... 26 E14-15 34 E16-18
86 Av SE CAL ... 42 O24 43 P24 44 U24 45 X-Y24
86 Av SW CAL ... 42 O24
86 St CRO ... 79 B4 B-C4 C4
86 St NW CAL ... 26 E11
87 Av SW CAL ... 42 N24
87 St CRO ... 79 B4
87 St NW CAL ... 18 E10 26 E11
88 Av NE CAL ... 23 Y7
88 Av SE CAL ... 43 P-Q25
88 St CRO ... 79 C5
88 St NW CAL ... 26 E11
88 St SE CAL ... 55 Z31-33
88 St SE HIG ... 77 D2
89 Av NE CAL ... 23 X7 Y7
89 Av SW CAL ... 42 N24-25
89 St CRO ... 79 B5 B-C5 C5
89 St NW CAL ... 26 E11
89 St SW CAL ... 26 E15 34 E18 E19
90 Av SE CAL ... 42 O25 43 P25 44 U-W25 45 X25 Y25
90 Av SW CAL ... 41 K24-25 42 N25
90 St CRO ... 79 A-B5 B4-5
91 Av SE CAL ... 44 T25 V25
92 Av SE CAL ... 43 P25 Q25 44 V25 45 X25
92 Av SW CAL ... 42 L25 M-N25
93 Av SW CAL ... 41 J-K25
93 St SW CAL ... 34 E18
94 Av SE CAL ... 42 O25 43 P25 Q25 45 X25
94 Av SW CAL ... 42 O25
95 St NW CAL ... 26 D11-12
96 Av NE CAL ... 21 P6 R-S6 S6 22 T6 23 X-Y6
96 Av NW CAL ... 18 D6
96 Av SE CAL 43 P25 44 T25 V25 45 X25 Y-Z25
96 Av SW CAL ... 42 M-N25 N25
97 Av SE CAL ... 43 Q25
97 Av SW CAL ... 42 N25
97 St SW CAL ... 26 D12
98 Av SE CAL ... 45 Y25 50 V-W26 51 X26
98 Av SW CAL ... 48 L-M26
99 Av SE CAL ... 49 P-Q26
100 Av NE CAL ... 22 T6
101 Av SW CAL ... 48 O26
101 St SW CAL ... 26 D12 D14-15 34 D16-19
102 Av SE CAL ... 51 Y-Z26
104 Av SW CAL ... 48 M26 N26 O26
104 St NW CAL ... 17 C6
105 Av SW CAL ... 48 N26
105 St CRO ... 80 D-E6
106 Av SE CAL ... 50 T26 51 Y-Z26
106 Av SW CAL ... 47 K26 48 L26 N26
107 Av SE CAL ... 45 Y-Z25 50 U26-27
107 Av SW CAL ... 47 K26 48 M26 N26
107 St CRO ... 80 D6 E6
107 St NW CAL ... 17 C6
108 Av SE CAL ... 51 Y-Z26
108 Av SW CAL ... 47 K26 48 N26
108 St CRO ... 80 E6 E-F6
109 Av SE CAL ... 51 Y-Z26
109 Av SW CAL ... 47 K27 48 N27
110 Av SE CAL ... 51 Y-Z27
110 Av SW CAL ... 48 M-N27 O27
111 Av SW CAL ... 48 M27
111 St CRO ... 80 E6
112 Av NW CAL ... 10 D-G4 11 H4 12 O4
112 Av SE CAL ... 51 Y27
112 St CRO ... 80 E6 E6-7
112 St NE HIG ... 77 A5
113 St CRO ... 80 E7 E-F6
114 Av SE CAL ... 50 U-W27 51 X-Z27
114 St CRO ... 80 E-F7
115 Av NE CAL ... 13 S4
115 St CRO ... 80 E7
116 Av SE CAL ... 50 V28
116 Av SW CAL ... 48 N28
116 St CRO ... 80 F7
117 Av SW CAL ... 48 M27
117 St CRO ... 80 E7 F7
117 St (12 Mile Coulee Rd) RCY . 9 B1-2 B3
117 St NW CAL ... 9 B5 17 B6-9
117 St SW CAL ... 25 B12
118 Av NE CAL ... 13 S4
118 Av SE CAL ... 50 U27-28 V28
118 Av SW CAL ... 48 O28
118 St CRO ... 80 F7
119 St CRO ... 80 E-F7
120 Av NE CAL ... 13 S4 15 Z4
120 Av SE CAL ... 49 Q-R28 50 V28
120 Av SW CAL ... 48 O28
120 St CRO ... 80 F7
121 St CRO ... 80 E7 F7
122 Av SE CAL ... 50 V-W28
122 St CRO ... 80 F7
123 St CRO ... 80 E-F7 F7
124 Av SW CAL ... 48 O28
124 St CRO ... 80 F7
125 St CRO ... 80 E-F8
126 Av SE CAL ... 50 W29
126 Av SW CAL ... 48 L28
126 St CRO ... 80 F8
127 Av SW CAL ... 48 L28-29
127 St CRO ... 80 E-F8 F8
128 Av NE CAL ... 13 S3 14 T3
128 St CRO ... 80 E-F8
129 Av SE CAL ... 49 P29
129 St CRO ... 80 F8
130 Av SE CAL ... 50 V29
130 Av SW CAL ... 47 K29 48 O29
130 St CRO ... 80 E8 F8
131 St CRO ... 80 E8 F8
132 St CRO ... 80 E-F8 F8
132 St SE CHE ... 70 E1
133 St CRO ... 80 E-F8 F8

134 St CRO 80 F8-9 F9
135 Av SE CAL 49 P29
135 St CRO 80 F9
136 Av SE CAL 49 S29 50 T29
136 St CRO 80 F9
137 Av SE CAL 49 R-S30 S29 50 T29
138 Av RCY 51 Z30
138 Av SE CAL 49 S30
143, Range Rd BRO 90 A4
143 St CRO 80 F10
143A, Range Rd BRO 90 A3
144 Av (Burma Rd) RCY 8 Y1 9 Z1 B-C1
144 Av NE CAL 14 V1
144 Av NW CAL 10 F-G1 11 H-K1 12 L-M1
144 St CRO 80 F10
145, Range Rd BRO 90 A1
145 Av SE CAL 48 O30
146 Av SE CAL 49 P30 50 T30 51 X-Z30 53 S31
146 Av SW CAL 47 K30 48 L-M30
146 St CRO 80 F10 F-G10
147 St CRO 80 F-G10 G10
148 Av SW CAL 52 O31
148 St CRO 80 F10 G10
148 St NE CHE 70 A-B2
148 St SE CHE 70 G2
149 Av SE CAL 53 P31
149 St CRO 80 F11
149 St RCY 8 Y2 Y4 24 Y12 Y15 32 Y19-20
150, Range Rd BRO 90 C1
150 St CRO 80 F-G11 G10-11
151 Av SE CAL 53 P31
151 St CRO 80 F11
152 St CRO 80 G11
153 Av SE CAL 53 P31
153 St CRO 80 G11
154 Av SW CAL 52 N31
154 St CRO 80 G11
156 St NE CHE 70 C3
157 Av SW CAL 52 O31
159 Av SW CAL 52 O32
162 Av SE CAL 53 P32
162 Av SW CAL 52 M-N32
164 St NE CHE 70 C4
164 St SE CHE 70 E4
165 St RCY 8 W1 16 W10 24 W12 W15 32 W17-20
170 Av SW CAL 52 L-M33
171 Av SW CAL 52 N33
178 Av SE CAL 54 W34 55 X-Z34
180 St NE CHE 70 C-D5
181 St RCY 16 V10 24 V12 V15
184, Township Rd BRO 90 E1
186 Av SW CAL 52 L34
190 Av SE CAL 53 P35
194 Av SE CAL 52 O35 53 P-S35
196 Av SE CAL 54 W35
201 NW CAL 18 D9 E6 26 D11
205 St CRO 81 H13
206 St CRO 81 H13
207 St CRO 81 H12 H13
208 St CRO 81 H12 H13
209 St CRO 81 H12 H13
210 St CRO 81 H13
211 St CRO 81 H13 H-J12
212 St CRO 81 H13
213 St CRO 81 H-J13
214, Range Rd LET 88 L10
214 St CRO 81 J13 J14
215 St CRO 81 J13 J14
216 St CRO 81 J13 J14
217 St CRO 81 J13
218 St CRO 81 J13
221 St CRO 81 J13 J14
222 St CRO 81 J14
223 St CRO 81 J14
224, Township Rd RCY 55 Z34
224 St CRO 81 J-K14
225 St CRO 81 K14
226 St CRO 81 K12 K12-13 K14
227 St CRO 81 K12-13 K14
228 St CRO 81 K12-13
229 St CRO 81 K12-13 K14
230, Township Rd RCY 51 Z30 55 Z31
230 St CRO 81 K12-13
231 St CRO 81 K13
232, Township Rd RCY 51 Z27
232 St CRO 81 K13
233 St CRO 81 K13
240, Township Rd RCY 45 Z21
241, Township Rd RCY 33 A19
241A, Township Rd RCY 33 A18
242, Township Rd RCY 33 C17
243, Township Rd RCY 32 W-X16 Y16 33 Z16
243A, Township Rd RCY 24 V15
244, Township Rd CHE 70 B5
245, Township Rd RCY 24 V13 X-Y13
250, Township Rd RCY 24 V11 W-X11 Y11 25 Z11
250, Township Rd RCY 25 A11
251A, Township Rd RCY 16 V8-9 X8-9
252, Township Rd RCY 17 A8 A-B8
253A, Township Rd RCY 9 A5
254, Township Rd RCY 9 A4 B4-5
254, Township Rd RCY 9 Z4 Z4-5
254A, Township Rd RCY 9 Z4
260, Township Rd CAL 10 F-G1 11 I-K1
260, Township Rd RCY 8 W1
260, Township Rd RCY 9 A1
260, Township Rd (Burma Rd) RCY 8 Y1 9 Z1 B-C1
261, Range Rd BEI 69 A2
261, Township Rd COC 61 A6-7
264, Range Rd IRR 69 A1
274, Township Rd IRR 69 A1-2
275, Range Rd CHE 70 D5
275, Range Rd RED 66 K-M3
275C, Range Rd RED 66 H2
280, Range Rd CHE 70 A-B4
280, Range Rd RED 66 J-M1
282, Range Rd CHE 70 A-B2 E1 G2
284, Township Rd CRS 62 C3-4
285, Range Rd RCY 9 A1
288, Range Rd RCY 33 A19
290, Range Rd CAL 15 Z1
290, Range Rd RCY 15 Y1
291, Range Rd CAL 15 Y1
291, Range Rd RCY 14 W1 15 X1
291 Range Rd AIR 69 B6
291 Range Rd AIR 69 D6
292, Range Rd CAL 14 W1 15 X1
292, Range Rd RCY 14 V1
293, Range Rd CAL 14 V1
338 Av OKO 75 A1 76 A2-4
370 Av E OKO 76 D4
380, Township Rd RED 66 L2-4
381, Range Rd RED 66 J2-3
381, Township Rd RED 66 J1-2
382, Township Rd RED 66 H1-2
384, Township Rd RED 65 D8-9
390, Township Rd RED 65 A8-9
434 Av BLD 75 E6
434 Av TVY 74 E1

A

Abadan Cr NE CAL 31 Y14-15 Y-Z14
Abadan Pl 100 to 500 NE CAL 31 Y14-15
Abalone Cr NE CAL 39 Z16
Abalone Pl 100 to 500 NE CAL 31 Z15 39 Z16
Abalone Way NE CAL 31 Z15 39 Z16
Abbercove Dr NE CAL 39 Y16
Abbercove La NE CAL 39 Y16
Abbercove Rd NE CAL 39 Y-Z16
Abbercove Way NE CAL 39 Y16
Abberfield Cr NE CAL 39 Y16
Abberfield Ct NE CAL 39 Y16
Abberfield Pl NE CAL 39 Y16
Abberfield Way NE CAL 39 Y16
Abbeydale Dr NE CAL 31 Y-Z15 39 Y-Z16
Abbeydale Villa NE CAL 31 Y15
Abbotsford Dr NE CAL 31 Y-Z15
Abbotsford Pl NE CAL 31 Y14-15
Abbott Av RED 67 J7
Abbott Av NE CAL 37 R16
Abbott Cl RED 67 J7
Abbott Pl SE CAL 43 Q25
Abel Cl RED 67 J8
Aberdare Cr NE CAL 31 Z15
Aberdare Pl NE CAL 31 Z15
Aberdare Rd NE CAL 31 Z15 39 Z16
Aberdare Way NE CAL 31 Z15
Aberdeen Rd SE CAL 43 P-Q24
Aberdeen Rd W LET 86 F3
Aberdeen St MED 92 E4 93 E5 94 F4
Aberfoyle Cl NE CAL 31 Z15
Aberfoyle Pl NE CAL 31 Z15
Abergale Cl NE CAL 31 Z15
Abergale Dr NE CAL 31 Y-Z15
Abergale Pl NE CAL 31 Z15
Abergale Way NE CAL 31 Z15
Abingdon Cr NE CAL 31 Z14-15
Abingdon Ct NE CAL 31 Z15
Abingdon Pl 100 200 NE CAL 31 Z15
Abingdon Rd NE CAL 31 Z14-15
Abingdon Way NE CAL 31 Z14-15
Abinger Cr NE CAL 31 Y15
Abinger Rd NE CAL 31 Y-Z15
Aboyne Cr NE CAL 31 Y15
Aboyne Pl 100 to 300 NE CAL 31 Y-Z15
Aboyne Way NE CAL 31 Y-Z15
Abraham Cl RED 67 J7
Acacia Cr SE AIR 68 C3
Acacia Dr SE AIR 68 C3-4
Academy Dr SE CAL 43 Q25
Acadia Dr SE CAL 43 P-Q25 49 Q26-29 R27
Acadia Rd W LET 87 H5
Access Rd CAN 58 A2
Ackerman Cr RED 67 J-K7 K8
Acres Dr NW HIG 77 B2
Acres Rd SE CAL 44 T22
Acton Av SW CAL 36 M20 42 M21-22
Adair Av RED 67 K7
Adams Cl RED 67 K7
Adams Cr SE CAL 43 P25
Adamson Av RED 67 K8
Addinell Av RED 67 J7
Addinell Cl RED 67 J7
Addington Dr RED 67 J-K8 K7
Addison Cl RED 67 J7
Addison Dr SE CAL 43 Q24
Addison Pl SE CAL 43 Q24
Adelaide St SE CAL 37 Q-R17
Adrian Pl SE CAL 43 Q25 49 Q26
Aerial Pl NE CAL 22 T8
Aero Dr NE CAL 21 R8
Aero Gt NE CAL 21 R8
Aero Rd NE CAL 21 R-S8 S9
Agate Cr SE CAL 43 Q25 49 Q26
Agnew Cr RED 67 K8
Ahlstrom Cl RED 67 J8
Aikman Cl RED 67 J7
Ainge Cl RED 67 J7
Ainsworth Cr RED 67 J-K7
Air Services Pl NE CAL 22 T7
Air Side Link NE CAL 29 S11
Airdrie Rd NE AIR 68 A3-4
Airdrie Rd NW AIR 68 A1-2
Airport Rd MED 94 G1
Airport Rd NE CAL 22 T7
Airport Tr NE CAL 22 T6
Alandale Lk RCY 24 Y14-15
Alandale Pl 100 200 RCY 24 Y14-15
Alanwood St SE CAL 43 Q24
Albany Pl SE CAL 43 Q25
Alberni Rd SE CAL 43 Q25 49 Q26
Albert St NE AIR 68 B3
Albert St SE AIR 68 B-C3
Alberta Av OKO 76 C3
Alberta Av SE CAL 37 Q18
Alberta St BRO 90 B2
Alberta St CRS 62 A3
Alberts Cl RED 67 K7
Alcock Cl OKO 76 B2
Alcock St OKO 76 B2
Alcott Cr SE CAL 43 P25 49 P26
Alcott Rd SE CAL 43 P25 49 P26
Alder Cl OLD 62 C2
Alder Cr SE AIR 68 C4
Alder Way NW CAL 26 E12
Alderwood Cl SE CAL 43 Q24-25
Alderwood Pl SE CAL 43 Q25
Aldrich Cl RED 67 K7
Alexa Cl RCY 9 A2
Alexander Cr RED 67 J8
Alexander Cr NW CAL 28 O15
Alexander St SE CAL 37 Q18
Alexandra St MED 95 F5
Alfege St SW CAL 36 N19
Alford Av RED 67 J7
Algonquin Bay W LET 86 G-H4
Algonquin Pl W LET 86 G4
Algonquin Rd W LET 86 G4
Allan Cl RED 67 J7
Allan Cr SE CAL 43 P25
Allan St RED 67 J7 J8
Allandale Cl SE CAL 43 Q25
Allandale Rd SE CAL 43 Q25
Allard Cr RED 67 K7
Allden Pl SE CAL 43 Q25
Allen St NE AIR 68 B4
Allen St SE AIR 68 C3-4
Allison Cr RED 67 J-K7
Allison Dr SE CAL 43 Q25
Allowance Av MED 93 E5 95 F5
Allsop Av RED 67 J7
Allsop Cl RED 67 J7
Allsop Dr RED 67 J-K7
Allston Av SE CAL 43 Q24
Allwright Cl RED 67 K7
Almond Cr SE CAL 43 Q25
Alpine Cr SE AIR 68 C3
Alpine Mdws CAN 59 F7
Alpine Mdws RCY 32 Y20 33 Z20
Altadore Av SW CAL 36 M20
Altawana Av MED 92 D-E4
Altawana Dr MED 92 D4
Altena Cl RED 67 K8
Alton Cl RED 67 J7
Alton St RED 67 J7
Alyth Ct SE CAL 37 R18
Alyth Pl SE CAL 37 R-S18
Alyth Rd SE CAL 37 S18-19
Amber Av SE CAL 43 Q24
Amer Cl RED 67 J8
Amherst St SW CAL 36 O18
Amiens Cr SW CAL 36 L20
Amiens Rd SW CAL 36 L20
Amlee Cl RED 67 K8
Ammeter Cl RED 67 J-K8
Amos Pl MED 95 G-H6
Amy Cl RED 67 J-K7
Anaheim Bay NE CAL 31 Z12
Anaheim Cir NE CAL 31 Z12
Anaheim Cr NE CAL 31 Z12
Anaheim Ct NE CAL 31 Z12
Anaheim Gdns NE CAL 31 Z12
Anaheim Gn NE CAL 31 Z12
Anaheim Pl NE CAL 31 Z12
Anatapi La SW CAL 34 D18
Ancourt Rd SE CAL 43 Q24-25
Anders Cl RED 67 J7
Anders St RED 67 J7
Anderson Cl RED 67 J7
Anderson Cr TVY 74 C3
Anderson Gr SW CAL 47 K27
Anderson Rd SE CAL 49 P-Q27
Anderson Rd SW CAL 47 K27 48 L-O27
Andrews Cl RED 67 J7-8
Angus Rd W LET 86 F3
Anne Av SW CAL 36 O20
Anquetel St RED 67 J7-8
Ansett Cr RED 67 J8
Anson Av MED 94 F1
Antelope La BAN 57 C3
Antelope St BAN 57 C3
Aperture Dr W LET 87 H5
Apple Way NW CAL 26 D-E11
Applebrook Cir SE CAL 39 Z17
Appleburn Cl SE CAL 39 Z16
Applecrest Cr SE CAL 39 Y16
Applecrest Ct SE CAL 39 Y16
Applecrest Pl SE CAL 39 Y16
Applecroft Rd SE CAL 39 Z17
Applefield Cl SE CAL 39 Z17
Appleglen Pk SE CAL 39 Z16
Appleglen Pl 100 to 300 SE CAL 39 Z16
Applegrove Cr SE CAL 39 Y-Z16
Applegrove Pl SE CAL 39 Y-Z16
Applemead Cl SE CAL 39 Z17
Applemead Ct SE CAL 39 Z16-17
Applemont Cl SE CAL 39 Z17
Applemont Pl SE CAL 39 Z16-17
Appleridge Gn SE CAL 39 Z16
Appleside Cl SE CAL 39 Z16
Applestone Pk SE CAL 39 Z17
Applestone Pl 100 200 SE CAL 39 Z17
Appletree Cl SE CAL 39 Y17
Appletree Cr SE CAL 39 Y17
Appletree Rd SE CAL 39 Y17
Appletree Way SE CAL 39 Y17
Applewood Ct SE CAL 39 Z17
Applewood Dr SE CAL 39 Y16-17 Y-Z17
Applewood La SE CAL 39 Y-Z17
Applewood Pl 100 to 400 SE CAL 39 Y16-17 Y-Z17
Applewood Village NE CAL 30 V15
Applewood Way SE CAL 39 Z17
April Rd BRG 78 A-B2
Aquaduct Dr BRO 90 D-E3
Arb Cl RED 67 J7
Arbor Cr SE AIR 68 C3
Arbour Cr SE CAL 43 P-Q25
Arbour Butte Cr NW CAL 18 F6
Arbour Butte Pl NW CAL 18 F6
Arbour Butte Rd NW CAL 18 F6
Arbour Butte Way NW CAL 18 F6
Arbour Cliff Cl NW CAL 18 G7
Arbour Cliff Ct NW CAL 18 G7
Arbour Crest Cir NW CAL 18 F7
Arbour Crest Cl 100 200 NW CAL 18 F7
Arbour Crest Ct NW CAL 18 F6
Arbour Crest Dr NW CAL 18 F6-7
Arbour Crest Hts NW CAL 18 F6
Arbour Crest Mews NW CAL 18 E-F6
Arbour Crest Mt NW CAL 18 F6
Arbour Crest Rd NW CAL 18 F6
Arbour Crest Rise NW CAL 18 E6
Arbour Crest Ter NW CAL 18 F6
Arbour Crest Way NW CAL 18 F6
Arbour Estates Gn NW CAL 18 F7
Arbour Estates Ldg NW CAL 18 F7
Arbour Estates View NW CAL 18 F7
Arbour Estates Way NW CAL 18 F7
Arbour Glen Cl NW CAL 18 G6
Arbour Glen Gn NW CAL 18 G6
Arbour Grove Cl NW CAL 18 E-F7
Arbour Lake Dr NW CAL 18 E-F7 F-G6
Arbour Lake Gn NW CAL 18 G6-7
Arbour Lake Pl NW CAL 18 G6-7
Arbour Lake Rd NW CAL 18 E7 E-F7
Arbour Lake Way NW CAL 18 F-G7
Arbour Meadows Cl NW CAL 18 E7
Arbour Ridge Cir NW CAL 18 G6

Arbour Ridge / Berwick

Arbour Ridge Cl NW CAL 18 G6
Arbour Ridge Ct NW CAL 18 G6
Arbour Ridge Gn NW CAL 18 G6
Arbour Ridge Hts NW CAL 18 G6
Arbour Ridge Mews NW CAL 18 G6
Arbour Ridge Pk NW CAL 18 G6
Arbour Ridge Pl NW CAL 18 G6
Arbour Ridge Way NW CAL 18 G6
Arbour Stone Cl NW CAL 18 E7
Arbour Stone Cr NW CAL 18 E7
Arbour Stone Pl 100 200 NW CAL 18 E7
Arbour Stone Rise NW CAL 18 E6-7
Arbour Stone Way NW CAL 18 E7
Arbour Summit Cl NW CAL 18 G6-7
Arbour Summit Pl 100 to 300 NW CAL 18 G6-7
Arbour Vista Cl NW CAL 18 F6
Arbour Vista Gt NW CAL 18 G6-7
Arbour Vista Hill NW CAL 18 F6
Arbour Vista Hts NW CAL 18 F-G7
Arbour Vista Rd NW CAL 18 F6-7
Arbour Vista Ter NW CAL 18 F7
Arbour Vista Way NW CAL 18 F-G7
Arbour Wood Cl NW CAL 18 F7
Arbour Wood Cr NW CAL 18 F7
Arbour Wood Gt NW CAL 18 F7
Arbour Wood Mews NW CAL 18 E7
Arbour Wood Pl NW CAL 18 F7
Archer Dr RED 67 K7
Archer Rd SE CAL 37 R-S16
Archibald Cr RED 67 J8
Archibald Way TVY 74 C3
Archwood Rd SE CAL 43 Q-R25 49 Q26
Ardell Cl RED 67 J7
Ardiel Dr OKO 76 B2
Argent Cl RED 67 K7
Argyll Rd W LET 86 F3
Arlington Bay SE CAL 43 Q24
Arlington Dr SE CAL 43 P-Q24
Arlington Pl SE CAL 43 Q24
Armitage Cl RED 67 J7-8
Armstrong Cl RED 67 J7
Armstrong Cr SE CAL 43 P-Q25
Arnold Cl RED 67 K8
Arnot Av RED 67 K7
Arthur Cl RED 67 K8
Artists View Dr RCY 25 A-B13 B14
Artists View Gt RCY 25 B13
Artists View Pl RCY 25 A13
Artists View Way RCY 25 A13
Ash Av MED 93 D-E5 E5
Ash Cl RED 67 J8
Ash Cr SE CAL 38 U18
Ash St BRO 90 C1
Ash St OLD 62 C2
Ash Grove Rd S LET 88 H11
Ashley Av RED 67 J8
Ashley Cl CAN 58 F3
Ashley Cl RED 67 J8
Ashley Cr SE CAL 43 P24-25
Ashmore Cl RED 67 H-J8
Ashton Cl RED 67 K8
Ashwood Gn SE AIR 68 C3
Ashwood Rd SE AIR 68 C3
Ashworth Rd SE CAL 43 Q24
Askin Cl RED 67 J8
Asmundsen Av RED 67 J-K7
Asmundsen Cl RED 67 J7
Aspen Cir STM 71 C-D4
Aspen Cl OLD 62 C2
Aspen Cr SE AIR 68 C3-4
Aspen Cr SE CAL 38 U18
Aspen Dr RCY 9 C3
Aspen Dr NW CAL 26 E11-12
Aspen Glen CAN 59 C-D5
Aspen Gn RCY 32 Y20
Aspen Ldg STM 71 C4
Aspen Mews STM 71 D4
Aspen Pl S LET 88 H11
Aspen Pt STM 71 C-D4
Aspen Way NW CAL 26 E12
Aspen Creek Cr STM 71 C4
Aspen Creek Way STM 71 C-D4
Aspen Dale Ct SW CAL 34 F17
Aspen Dale Gt SW CAL 34 F17
Aspen Dale Way SW CAL 34 F17
Aspen Glen Cl SW CAL 34 F17
Aspen Glen Pl 100 to 400 SW CAL 34 F17
Aspen Meadows Ct 100 200 SW CAL 34 G17
Aspen Meadows Gn SW CAL 34 G17
Aspen Meadows Pl 100 200 SW CAL 34 G17
Aspen Meadows Way SW CAL 34 G17
Aspen Ridge Cr SW CAL 34 F-G17
Aspen Ridge La SW CAL 34 G16-17
Aspen Ridge Way SW CAL 34 F16-17
Aspen Summit Blvd SW CAL 34 E-F17
Aspen Summit Cl SW CAL 34 E-F17
Aspen Summit Dr SW CAL 34 F17
Aspen Summit Gt SW CAL 34 F17
Aspen Summit Hts SW CAL 34 F17
Aspen Summit Mews SW CAL 34 E-F17
Aspen Summit Pl 100 to 300 SW CAL 34 E-F17
Aspen Summit Way SW CAL 34 F17
Aspen Vista Pl 100 200 SW CAL 34 F16-17
Aspen Vista Rd SW CAL 34 F17
Aspen Vista Way SW CAL 34 F17
Assinger Av RED 67 K8
Assiniboia Pl W LET 86 G3
Assiniboia Rd W LET 86 G3
Assiniboine Rd SE CAL 43 Q25
Aster Pl SE AIR 68 B-C3
Astoria Cr SE CAL 43 P25 49 P26
Astra St S LET 88 F10
Athabasca Cr CRS 62 A2
Athabasca St CRS 62 A2
Athabasca St SE CAL 43 P24
Athabaska Rd W LET 86 G3
Athabaska Way W LET 86 G3
Athens Rd SE CAL 43 Q25 49 Q26
Athlone Rd SE CAL 43 P-Q25
Atkins Cl RED 67 J7
Atlanta Cr SE CAL 43 P-Q25
Atlas Dr SE CAL 43 P-Q24
Atlee Cl RED 67 J8
Atter Cl RED 67 J8
Attica Dr SE CAL 43 Q24
Atwell St RED 67 K7
Aubrey Cl RED 67 J7-8
Auburn Rd SE CAL 43 Q-R25
Aurora Dr NE HIG 77 B3
Aurora Pl SE CAL 43 Q25
Austin Dr RED 67 K7
Austin Rd SE CAL 43 Q25 49 Q26
Avalon Rd SE CAL 43 P25 49 P26
Averill St RED 67 K8
Avery Pl SE CAL 43 Q25
Avery St RED 67 J8
Aviation Blvd NE CAL 29 R11
Aviation Pk NE CAL 29 R-S11
Aviation Pl NE CAL 21 R10 29 R11
Aviation Rd NE CAL 29 R-S11
Aviation Way NE CAL 29 R-S11
Avonburn Rd SE CAL 43 P24
Avonlea Pl SE CAL 43 Q25
Ayers Av RED 67 J7
Ayers Cl RED 67 J7

B

Badger St BAN 57 C2
Bagot Av SW CAL 36 N18
Baile Cl RED 66 K5 67 K6
Bailey Ridge Cl TVY 74 E3
Bailey Ridge Pl TVY 74 E3
Baines Cr RED 66 K5
Baines Rd NW CAL 19 K10 27 K11
Baird Av COC 61 B5
Baird St RED 66 K-L5
Baker Av RED 66 K5
Baker Cr NW CAL 27 K11 28 L11
Baker Rd SW HIG 77 C1
Baker Creek Dr SW HIG 77 C1
Baker Creek Pl SW HIG 77 C1
Baker Creek Rise SW HIG 77 C1
Baldwin Cr SW CAL 42 N22
Balmoral St MED 93 E5-6
Balsam Av BRG 78 B3
Balsam Cr OLD 62 C2
Balsam Dr SW CAL 35 K17
Banded Peak Pl RCY 24 X14
Banff Av BAN 57 C3 D2
Banff Tr NW CAL 28 L14
Banister Dr OKO 76 B3
Banister Gt OKO 76 A2-3
Bankview Cl DRU 73 C-D6
Bankview Dr DRU 73 C-D6 D6
Bannerman Dr NW CAL 19 K10
Bannister Mnr SE CAL 53 P31
Bannister Rd SE CAL 48 O30 49 P30 53 P31
Bannon Av MED 94 G1
Bantry St NW CAL 29 R15
Barberry Walk SE CAL 35 K17
Barclay Parade SW CAL 6 C92 37 P16
Barclay Walk SW CAL 6 C91-92 37 P16
Barlow Tr RCY 14 T1
Barlow Tr NE CAL 14 T4-5 22 T10 T6 U7-8 30 T11-15 38 T16
Barlow Tr SE CAL 38 T17 U18-20 44 V23-25 50 V26-27
Barner Av RED 66 K5
Baroc Rd NW CAL 19 I9-10
Barr Rd NW CAL 27 K11-12
Barrett Dr RED 66 J-K5 K-L5 67 K6
Barrett Dr NW CAL 19 K10
Barrett Pl NW CAL 19 K10
Barron Cr NW CAL 27 K11
Barron Dr NW CAL 19 K10 27 K11
Barton Cr TAB 91 D3-4
Barton Dr TAB 91 D3-4
Bassett Cr MED 92 D3
Batchelor Cr NW CAL 27 K11
Battleford Av SW CAL 35 K20 36 L20
Bay Rd STM 71 B3
Bay Croft Rd SW CAL 42 M25
Bay Field Pl SW CAL 42 M25
Bay Ridge Dr SW CAL 42 L-M24 M25
Bay Shore Rd SW CAL 42 M25
Bay View Dr SW CAL 42 L24-25
Bay View Pl SW CAL 42 L25
Bay Wood Pl SW CAL 42 L25
Baycrest Ct SW CAL 42 L24
Baycrest Pl SW CAL 42 L24
Baylor Cr SW CAL 42 L-M25
Bayside Av SW AIR 68 E2
BAyside Dr SW AIR 68 D2
Bayside Ldg 100 200 SW AIR 68 D2
Bayside Pk SW AIR 68 D2
Bayside Pl STM 71 C3
Bayside Pl 100 to 400 SW AIR 68 E2
Bayside Pt SW AIR 68 D-E2
Bayside Rd SW AIR 68 D2
Bayside Rise SW AIR 68 D-E2
Bayview Cr STM 71 B3
Bayview Rd STM 71 B-C3
Beach Way SW HIG 77 C1
Beacham Cl NW CAL 20 N7
Beacham Rd NW CAL 20 M-N7
Beacham Rise NW CAL 20 N7
Beacham Way NW CAL 20 N7
Beacon Heights Rd BEI 69 A2
Beaconsfield Cl NW CAL 20 M7
Beaconsfield Cr NW CAL 20 M7-8
Beaconsfield Gt NW CAL 20 M7
Beaconsfield Pl NW CAL 20 M7
Beaconsfield Rd NW CAL 20 M7
Beaconsfield Rise NW CAL 20 M7
Beaconsfield Way NW CAL 20 M7
Beamish Park Dr BRO 90 C4
Bear St BAN 57 D2
Bearberry Bay NW CAL 20 M-N7
Bearberry Cl NW CAL 20 N7
Bearberry Cr NW CAL 20 N7
Bearberry Pl NW CAL 20 N7
Bearspaw Dr NW CAL 27 K11
Bearspaw Gn RCY 9 A3-4
Bearspaw Loop RCY 9 A3
Bearspaw Mdws RCY 17 A-B9
Bearspaw Rd RCY 9 Z1-3
Bearspaw Summit RCY 9 Z2
Bearspaw View RCY 9 B3
Bearspaw Way RCY 9 B3
Bearspaw Dam Rd RCY 17 Z10
Bearspaw Dam Rd NW CAL 17 B-C10 18 D-E10
Bearspaw Hills Pl RCY 9 Z2-3
Bearspaw Hills Rd RCY 9 Z2
Bearspaw Meadows Bay RCY 17 A8
Bearspaw Meadows Ct RCY 17 B8
Bearspaw Pointe Gn RCY 9 Z5
Bearspaw Pointe Pl RCY 9 Z5
Bearspaw Pointe Way RCY 9 Z4-5
Bearspaw Ridge Cr RCY 9 B4
Bearspaw Summit Pl RCY 9 Z2
Bearspaw Village Bay RCY 17 Z7
Bearspaw Village Cr RCY 17 Z7
Bearspaw Village Cv RCY 17 Z7
Bearspaw Village Dr RCY 17 Z6
Bearspaw Village Glen RCY 17 Z6-7
Bearspaw Village La RCY 17 Z6
Bearspaw Village Pl RCY 16 Y6 17 Z6 Z6
Bearspaw Village Rd RCY 17 Z6-7 Z8
Bearspaw Village Ridge RCY 17 Z6
Bearspaw Village View RCY 17 Z6-7
Bearspaw Vista Pl RCY 9 Z2-3
Beatty Cr RED 66 K5 67 K6
Beaufort Cr MED 94 F1
Beaupre Cr NW CAL 26 F12
Beauvais Pl S LET 88 H11
Beaver Pl BEI 69 A2
Beaver Rd NW CAL 19 J-K10
Beaver St BAN 57 D2
Beaver Dam Pl NE CAL 21 P10
Beaver Dam Rd NE CAL 21 P10 Q10 29 Q11
Beaver Dam Way NE CAL 21 P10
Beaverbrook Rd N LET 83 B8 84 B9
Beaverpond Ct N LET 84 B9
Beaverun Pl N LET 84 B9
Beddington Blvd NE CAL 20 N-O7 O8 21 P8
Beddington Cir NE CAL 21 P7
Beddington Cr NE CAL 21 P7
Beddington Dr NE CAL 20 O7 21 P7
Beddington Gdns NE CAL 21 P7
Beddington Gn NE CAL 21 P7
Beddington Pl NE CAL 21 P7
Beddington Rd NE CAL 20 O7 21 P7
Beddington Rise NE CAL 21 P7
Beddington Tr NE CAL 21 P-Q7
Beddington Tr NW CAL 12 M-N5 20 N-O6
Beddington Way NE CAL 21 P7
Bedfield Cl NE CAL 21 Q8
Bedfield Ct 100 200 NE CAL 21 Q8
Bedfield Gt NE CAL 21 Q8
Bedford Cir NE CAL 21 P-Q7
Bedford Dr NE CAL 21 P7-8
Bedford Mnr NE CAL 21 Q7-8
Bedford Pl 100 to 300 NE CAL 21 P7
Bedford Rd NE CAL 21 P-Q7
Bedridge Pl NE CAL 21 P7-8
Bedridge Rd NE CAL 21 P8
Bedridge Way NE CAL 21 P8
Bedwood Bay NE CAL 21 P8
Bedwood Cr NE CAL 21 P7-8
Bedwood Hill NE CAL 21 P8
Bedwood Pl NE CAL 21 P7-8
Bedwood Rd NE CAL 21 P7-8
Bedwood Rise NE CAL 21 P8
Beech Cr OLD 62 B-C1
Beech Rd S LET 88 H11
Beech St DRU 73 B-C6
Begonia Ct MED 94 H4 95 H5
Beil Av NW CAL 27 K11-12
Bel-Aire Dr SW CAL 42 N22
Bel-Aire Pl SW CAL 42 N22
Belanca Cr MED 94 F1
Belavista Cr SW CAL 42 N22
Belfast St MED 93 E5 94 F4
Bell St MED 94 G1
Bell St RED 66 K5
Bell St NW CAL 27 K12
Bell St SW CAL 41 J21
Belle North Rd NW CAL 19 J10 27 J11
Bellevue Av SE CAL 37 Q17
Belvedere Rd SW CAL 42 N22
Benchlands Dr COC 61 B-C6
Benchlands Pl COC 61 B6
Benchlands Ter 100 200 CAN 59 E6
Benchlands Trail CAN 59 E5-6 E6
Bencroft Pl COC 61 B-C6
Bennett Cr NW CAL 27 K11 28 L11
Bennett Ct MED 92 D3
Bennett St RED 66 K5
Benson Rd NW CAL 27 K11
Bent Tree Ct RCY 33 Z20
Bent Tree Pl RCY 33 Z20
Bentley Pl COC 61 B-C6
Benton Dr NW CAL 19 J-K10
Benton Dr W LET 86 H3 J-K4
Bergen Cr NW CAL 20 O7
Bergen Pl NW CAL 20 O7
Bergen Rd NW CAL 20 O7
Berkeley Pl W LET 87 H5
Berkley Cl NW CAL 20 O7-8
Berkley Cr NW CAL 20 N-O8
Berkley Ct NW CAL 20 O7
Berkley Dr NW CAL 20 M-N7
Berkley Gt NW CAL 20 M8
Berkley Pl NW CAL 20 O8
Berkley Rd NW CAL 20 O7-8
Berkley Rise NW CAL 20 O8
Berkley Way NW CAL 20 O7
Berkshire Blvd NW CAL 20 M-N7
Berkshire Cl NW CAL 20 N7
Berkshire Ct NW CAL 20 N7
Berkshire Mews NW CAL 20 N7
Berkshire Pl 100 to 300 NW CAL 20 O7
Berkshire Rd NW CAL 20 N-O7
Berkshire Village NW CAL 20 N7
Bermondsey Cr NW CAL 20 M-N8
Bermondsey Ct NW CAL 20 N7
Bermondsey Pl NW CAL 20 N8
Bermondsey Rd NW CAL 20 N7-8
Bermondsey Rise NW CAL 20 N7-8
Bermondsey Way NW CAL 20 N8
Bermuda Cl NW CAL 20 O7
Bermuda Ct NW CAL 20 O7
Bermuda Dr NW CAL 20 O7
Bermuda Gt NW CAL 20 O7
Bermuda La NW CAL 20 O7
Bermuda Pl NW CAL 20 O7
Bermuda Rd NW CAL 20 O7
Bermuda Way NW CAL 20 O7
Bernard Cl NW CAL 20 O7
Bernard Ct NW CAL 20 O7
Bernard Dr NW CAL 20 O7
Bernard Mews 100 to 500 NW CAL 20 O7
Bernard Pl NW CAL 20 O7
Bernard Rd NW CAL 20 O7
Bernard Way NW CAL 20 O6-7
Berry Av RED 66 K-L5
Berwick Cl NW CAL 20 N7
Berwick Cr NW CAL 20 N7

Berwick Ct NW *CAL* **20** N7
Berwick Dr NW *CAL* **20** N7
Berwick Hill NW *CAL* **20** N7
Berwick Pl NW *CAL* **20** N7
Berwick Rd NW *CAL* **20** N7
Berwick Rise NW *CAL* **20** N7
Berwick Way NW *CAL* **20** N7
Best Cr *RED* **66** L5
Bettenson St *RED* **66** K5
Beulah Vista Rd *RCY* **51** Z27
Beverley Blvd SW *CAL* **42** N22
Beverley Pl SW *CAL* **42** N22
Big Bell Cl *IRR* **69** B2
Big Four Ter SE *CAL* **37** P18
Big Hill Cir SE *AIR* **68** C4
Big Hill Gt SE *AIR* **68** C4
Big Hill Pl 100 200 SE *AIR* **68** C4
Big Hill Rd SE *AIR* **68** C-D4
Big Hill Way SE *AIR* **68** C-D4
Big Hill Springs Rd SW *AIR* . .**68** E1-2 E2-3
Big Horn St *BAN* **57** D1-2
Big Rock La *OKO* **76** D2
Big Rock Rd *OKO* **76** D2
Big Rock Tr *OKO* **75** D1 **76** D2
Big Springs Cr SE *AIR* **68** D4
Big Springs Ct 100 to 400 SE *AIR* . .
68 D4 **69** D5
Big Springs Dr SE *AIR* **68** D4 **69** D5
Big Springs Gn SE *AIR* **68** D4 **69** D5
Big Springs Hill SE *AIR* **68** D4 **69** D5
Big Springs Mews SE *AIR* **69** D5
Big Springs Rise SE *AIR* **69** D5
Big Springs Way SE *AIR* . .**68** D4 **69** D5
Billy Haynes Tr *OKO* **76** B5
Binder Cr *MED* **92** E2
Birch Av *BAN* **57** E2
Birch Av *CAN* **58** A2
Birch Av *MED* **93** E5
Birch Cl *OLD* **62** C1
Birch Cir SE *CAL* **38** U18
Birch Dr *BAN* **57** E1-2
Birch Pl S *LET* **88** H11
Birch Rd *OLD* **62** C1
Birch St *BRO* **90** C1
Birchwood Cl *DRU* **73** D6
Birchwood Pl *CAN* **58** E4
Bison Path St *CAL* **37** C17
Blacfoot Ter W *LET* **86** H3
Black Blvd *MED* **92** D3
Black & White Tr *MED* **95** K7
Black Rock Cr *CAN* **59** E6
Blackburn Rd SE *CAL* **37** P-Q19
Blackfoot Blvd W *LET* **86** G-H3
Blackfoot Cir W *LET* **86** G3
Blackfoot Cr W *LET* **86** G3
Blackfoot Ct W *LET* **86** H3
Blackfoot Rd W *LET* **86** G-H3
Blackfoot Tr SE *CAL*
. . . .**37** Q20 R-S18 **43** Q23 **49** R26
Blacklock Way *TVY* **74** D2
Blackthorn Bay NE *CAL* **21** P-Q9
Blackthorn Cr NE *CAL* **21** P-Q10
Blackthorn Gn NE *CAL* **21** P-Q10
Blackthorn Pl NE *CAL* **21** Q10
Blackthorn Rd NE *CAL* . .**20** O10 **21** P-Q10 Q9
Blackwell Bay *RCY* **9** Z4-5
Blair Av *BRO* **90** B1
Blakiston Dr NW *CAL* **27** K12
Blazer Estates Ridge *RCY* **17** Z9 A9
Blazier Park St *BRO* **90** C4
Blow St NW *CAL* **27** K12
Blue Grouse Ridge *CAN* **59** D5
Bluebell Ct *MED* **95** G-H5
Bluefox Bay N *LET* **83** B8 **84** B9
Bluefox Blvd N *LET* **84** B9
Bluefox Rd N *LET* **84** B9
Blueridge Bay *RCY* **17** B6
Blueridge Cl *RCY* **17** Z7
Blueridge Dr *RCY* **17** B6-7
Blueridge La *RCY* **17** B6
Blueridge Pl *RCY* **17** B7
Blueridge Rise *RCY* **17** A-B6
Blueridge View *RCY* **17** A-B7 B6
Bomford Cr *MED* **94** F2
Bonaventure Dr SE *CAL* . . . .
. . . .**43** P24-25 **49** P26-29
Bonita Cr NW *CAL* **26** F-G12
Bonnybrook Pl SE *CAL* **37** R18-19
Bonnybrook Rd SE *CAL* **37** R19 S19-20
Booth Cr *IRR* **69** B1
Botterill Cr *RED* **66** J5
Boulder Cr *CAN* **59** G6-7
Boulton Rd NW *CAL* **27** J-K11
Bow Av *BAN* **57** D1
Bow Cl *COC* **60** C2-3
Bow Cr *CAN* **58** A2
Bow Cr NW *CAL* . .**26** F-G11 G12 **27** H12 H13
Bow Ct *COC* **60** C3
Bow Ldg NW *CAL* **27** H13
Bow Pl *COC* **60** C3

Bow Pt *COC* **60** C3
Bow St *COC* **61** C5
Bow Tr SW *CAL* **35** H-J16 K17
Bow Way *COC* **60** C2
Bow Anne Rd NW *CAL* **26** G12
Bow Bottom Tr SE *CAL* . . . .
. . . .**49** R28-30 S30 **53** S31-32
Bow Falls Dr *BAN* **57** E2-3
Bow Green Cr NW *CAL* **26** F11
Bow Lake Pl NW *CAL* **26** F12
Bow Meadows Cr *CAN* **59** F-G7
Bow Meadows Dr *COC* **60** B-C2 C3
Bow Ridge Cl *COC* **60** C1
Bow Ridge Cr *COC* **60** B-C1 C2
Bow Ridge Ct 100 200 *COC* **60** C2
Bow Ridge Dr *COC* **60** C1-2
Bow Ridge Link *COC* **60** C1
Bow Ridge Rd *COC* **60** C1-2
Bow River Rd *CAN* **58** A2
Bow Valley Ct SE *CAL* **37** R16
Bow Valley Dr NE *CAL* **37** R16
Bow Valley La SE *CAL* **37** R16
Bow Valley Pkwy *LKL* **56** C-D5
Bow Valley Tr *RCY* **8** V-W2
Bow Valley Trail *CAN* . .**58** D4 E4 **59** E5 F5-6
Bow Village Ct NW *CAL* **26** F-G11
Bowbank Cr NW *CAL* **27** H-I12
Bowcliffe Cr NW *CAL* **26** F12
Bowcroft Pl *COC* **61** C6
Bowdale Cr NW *CAL* **26** G13
Bowers St NE *AIR* **68** B3
Bowfort Rd NW *CAL* **26** E-F12
Bowglen Rd NW *CAL* **26** F12
Bowglen Rd NW *CAL* **26** F11-12
Bowlen St NW *CAL* **28** L11-12
Bowmanten Pl NW *CAL* **26** F12
Bowmont Cr NW *CAL* **27** H13
Bowness Centre NW *CAL* **26** F11-12
Bowness Rd NW *CAL* . . . .
. . . .**26** E11 E-G12 **27** H12 H-I13 J15 **36** L-N16
Bowridge Cr NW *CAL* **26** E-F12
Bowridge Dr NW *CAL* **26** E-F12
Bowview Rd NW *CAL* **27** H13
Bowwater Cr NW *CAL* **27** H12
Bowwood Dr NW *CAL* . .**26** G12 **27** H12 H13
Box Springs Rd *MED* **92** B-C1
Boyce Cr NW *CAL* **28** N14-15
Boyce St *RED* **66** K5
Brabourne Mews SW *CAL* **48** M27
Brabourne Rd SW *CAL* **48** L27
Brabourne Rise SW *CAL* **48** L-M27
Bracebridge Cr SW *CAL* **48** M-N26
Bracewood Cr SW *CAL* **48** M27
Bracewood Dr SW *CAL* **48** L27
Bracewood Pl SW *CAL* **48** M27
Bracewood Rd SW *CAL* **48** M27
Bracewood Rise SW *CAL* **48** L27
Bracewood Way SW *CAL* **48** L-M27
Bracken Pt *BRG* **78** B3
Bracken Rd *BRG* **78** B-C2
Brackenridge Rd SW *CAL* **48** M26
Bradbury Dr SW *CAL* **48** M26-27
Braden Cr NW *CAL* **27** K11
Bradford St SW *CAL* **48** M-N27
Bradley Av SW *CAL* **48** M26
Brae Pl SW *CAL* **48** M26-27
Brae Rd SW *CAL* **48** M27
Braeburn Oaks SW *CAL* **48** L26
Braeburn Village SW *CAL* **48** L-M26
Braeglen Cl SW *CAL* **48** M26
Braeglen Cr SW *CAL* **48** M26
Braeglen Ct SW *CAL* **48** M26
Braeglen La SW *CAL* **48** M26
Braeglen Rd SW *CAL* **48** M26
Braemar St SW *CAL* **48** M26
Braemar St *MED* **93** E5-6
Braemar St *RCY* **32** Y20
Braeside Dr SW *CAL* . .**48** L-M27 M26-27
Braeside Pl SW *CAL* **48** M26
Bralorne Cr SW *CAL* **48** M-N26
Brampton Cr SW *CAL* **48** M-N26
Brandon St SE *CAL* **37** Q19-20
Brandy La SW *CAL* **48** M26
Braniff Cr SW *CAL* **48** M27
Braniff Pl 100 to 300 SW *CAL* . .**48** M-N27
Braniff Rd SW *CAL* **48** M27
Brantford Cr NW *CAL* **27** K12
Brantford Dr NW *CAL* **27** K12 **28** L12
Braton Pl SW *CAL* **48** M26-27
Braxton Brae SW *CAL* **48** M27
Braxton Pl 100 to 300 SW *CAL* . .**48** M27
Braxton Rd SW *CAL* **48** M27
Bray Cr *MED* **94** G3
Brazeau Cr *MED* **94** G3
Brecken Rd NW *CAL* **27** K12 **28** L12
Breen Cr NW *CAL* **27** K11
Breen Tr Rd NW *CAL* **27** K11
Bremner Av *RED* **66** J5

Brenner Cr NW *CAL* **19** K10
Brenner Dr NW *CAL* **19** J-K10
Brenner Pl NW *CAL* **19** K10
Brent Blvd *STM* **71** B3-4
Brentwood Blvd NW *CAL* . .**27** K12 **28** L12
Brentwood Cr *STM* **71** B3
Brentwood Dr E *STM* **71** B3
Brentwood Dr W *STM* **71** B-C3
Brentwood Gn NW *CAL* **27** J-K11
Brentwood Pl *STM* **71** C3
Brentwood Rd NW *CAL* **27** K12
Breskens Dr NW *CAL* **36** L20
Breton Bay NW *CAL* **19** K10
Breton Cl NW *CAL* **19** K10
Breton Pl NW *CAL* **19** K10
Briar Cr *STM* **71** B3
Briar Cr NW *CAL* **28** L-M15
Briar Pl *STM* **71** B3
Briarwood Cr *STM* **71** B3
Briarwood Dr *RCY* **9** B1
Briarwood Rd *STM* **71** B3
Brick Av *MED* **95** F7
Bridge Cr NE *CAL* **29** Q-R15
Bridge Dr W *LET* **82** E4
Bridge Rd *CAN* **58** F4
Bridge St *MED* **95** F6
Bridgefield Cir SW *AIR* **68** B1
Bridgefield Cl SW *AIR* **68** B1
Bridgefield Cr SW *AIR* **68** C1
Bridgefield Dr SW *AIR* **68** B-C1
Bridgefield La SW *AIR* **68** C1
Bridgefield Mews SW *AIR* **68** C1
Bridgefield Pl 100 200 SW *AIR* . .**68** C1
Bridlecreek Gn 100 to 500 SW *CAL* . . . .
. . . .**52** N33
Bridlecreek Gt SW *CAL* **52** N33
Bridlecreek Heath SW *CAL* **52** M-N33
Bridlecreek Pk SW *CAL* **52** N33
Bridlecreek Ter SW *CAL* **52** M-N33
Bridlecrest Blvd SW *CAL* **52** L32-33
Bridlecrest CR SW *CAL* **52** L32
Bridlecrest Dr SW *CAL* **52** L32
Bridlecrest Gdns SW *CAL* **52** L32
Bridlecrest Link SW *CAL* **52** L32
Bridlecrest Mnr SW *CAL* **52** L32
Bridlecrest Way SW *CAL* **52** L33
Bridleglen Mnr SW *CAL* **52** M32
Bridleglen Pk SW *CAL* **52** M32
Bridleglen Rd SW *CAL* **52** M32
Bridlemeadows Com SW *CAL* . .**52** L33
Bridlemeadows Mnr 1000 2000 SW *CAL* . .
. . . .**52** L33
Bridlepost Gn SW *CAL* **52** M33
Bridleridge Cir SW *CAL* **52** M33
Bridleridge Cr SW *CAL* **52** M33
Bridleridge Ct SW *CAL* **52** L-M33
Bridleridge Gdns SW *CAL* **52** M33
Bridleridge Hts SW *CAL* **52** L-M32
Bridleridge Link SW *CAL* **52** M33
Bridleridge Rd SW *CAL* **52** M33
Bridleridge View SW *CAL* **52** L-M33
Bridleridge Way SW *CAL* **52** M32-33
Bridlewood Av SW *CAL* **52** L-M33
Bridlewood Blvd SW *CAL* **52** M33
Bridlewood Cir SW *CAL* **52** M32
Bridlewood Cl SW *CAL* **52** M32
Bridlewood Com SW *CAL* **52** M32
Bridlewood Cr SW *CAL* **52** M32
Bridlewood Ct 100 to 400 SW *CAL* . . . .
. . . .**52** M33
Bridlewood Dr SW *CAL* **52** M33
Bridlewood Gdns SW *CAL* **52** J-K1
Bridlewood Gn SW *CAL* **52** M32
Bridlewood Gr SW *CAL* **52** M33
Bridlewood La 100 to 300 SW *CAL* . . . .
. . . .**52** M33
Bridlewood Link SW *CAL* . . .**52** M32-33
Bridlewood Link SW *CAL* . . .**52** M32-33
Bridlewood Mnr SW *CAL* **52** M33
Bridlewood Pk SW *CAL* **52** M33
Bridlewood Pl 100 to 400 SW *CAL* . . . . .
. . . .**52** M33
Bridlewood Rd SW *CAL* **52** M32-33
Bridlewood St SW *CAL* **52** M33
Bridlewood View SW *CAL* **52** M33
Bridlewood Way SW *CAL* **52** M33
Brier Estates Cr *MED* **92** C2
Brier Estates Way *MED* **92** C2
Brier Park Bay *MED* **92** C1
Brier Park Cr *MED* **92** C1
Brier Park Dr *MED* **92** C1
Brier Park Pl *MED* **92** C1
Brier Park Rd *MED* **92** C1-2 D2
Brier Park Way *MED* **92** C1
Brighton Dr NW *CAL* **28** L12
Brightondale Bay SE *CAL* **55** X31
Brightondale Cl SE *CAL* **55** X31
Brightondale Cr SE *CAL* **55** X31
Brightondale Gn SE *CAL* **55** X31

Brightondale Parade SE *CAL* . . .**55** X31
Brightondale Pk SE *CAL* **55** X31
Brightonstone Bay SE *CAL* **55** X31
Brisebois Dr NW *CAL* **27** K11-12
Britannia Dr SW *CAL* **36** N20 **42** N21
Britannia La SW *CAL* **36** O20
Broadview Rd NW *CAL* **36** L-M16
Brock Pl W *LET* **87** H5
Brockington Rd NW *CAL* **27** K11
Brookgreen Dr SW *CAL* **48** L26
Brooklyn Cr NW *CAL* **28** L12
Brookmere Bay 100 200 SW *CAL* . . . . .
. . . .**48** M26-27
Brookmere Cr SW *CAL* **48** M26-27
Brookmere Gdns SW *CAL* **48** L-M26
Brookmere Pl SW *CAL* **48** M26
Brookmere Rd SW *CAL* **48** M26
Brookpark Bay SW *CAL* **48** L-M26
Brookpark Blvd SW *CAL* **48** L-M26
Brookpark Cr SW *CAL* **48** L26
Brookpark Dr SW *CAL* . . .**48** L26-27 L-M26
Brookpark Gdns SW *CAL* **48** M26
Brookpark Mews SW *CAL* **48** L26
Brookpark Rise SW *CAL* **48** L26
Brooks Cr *RED* **66** K5
Broughton Cr *RED* **66** K5
Brown Cl *RED* **66** K5 **67** K6
Brown Cr NW *CAL* **27** K11
Brown Rd *LET* **89** J15
Brownsea Dr NW *CAL* **36** M16
Brunswick Av SW *CAL* **36** O20
Buckboard Rd NW *CAL* **19** H9-10
Buckthorn Cr NE *CAL* **21** P10
Buckthorn Rd NE *CAL* . . .**21** P10 **29** P11
Buffalo St *BAN* **57** D-E2
Builders Rd SE *CAL* . . .**37** P20 **43** P21-22
Bullhead Rd *CAL* **47** J27
Bullivant Cr *MED* **94** F-G3
Bulyea Cr NW *CAL* **27** K11
Bulyea Rd NW *CAL* **27** K11
Bunn Cr *RED* **66** L5
Burbank Cr SE *CAL* **48** N-O28
Burbank Rd SE *CAL* **43** Q21
Burgess Dr NW *CAL* **27** K12 **28** L12
Burleigh Cr SE *CAL* **43** Q21
Burma Rd NW *CAL* **10** F-G1 **11** I-K1
Burney Rd *BRG* **78** B-C3
Burns Av SE *CAL* **37** O18
Burns Cr *MED* **92** C3-4
Burnside Dr *BRG* **78** B-E4
Burnsland Rd SE *CAL* **37** P19-20
Burntall Dr *BRG* **78** B3
Burroughs Cir NE *CAL* **31** Z13
Burroughs Mnr NE *CAL* **31** Z13
Burroughs Pl NE *CAL* **31** Z13
Burton Pl *MED* **95** H6
Butler Cr NW *CAL* **27** K11-12
Butte Pl NW *CAL* **28** L12
Buttercup Ct *MED* **95** H5
Button Rd NW *CAL* **27** K11
Byer Cl *RED* **66** K5

C

C&E Tr *RED* **66** H1
Cabot St SW *CAL* **36** N19
Cactus Ridge SW *CAL* **35** I18
Cactus St *MED* **94** F2
Cactus Coulee Pl *MED* **94** J-K1
Cadogan Rd NW *CAL* **28** N12
Caen Av SW *CAL* **35** K20 **36** L20
Cairney Cr *MED* **95** H7
Cairns Way *MED* **95** H7
Calais Av SW *CAL* **36** L20
Calandar Rd NW *CAL* **28** M12
Calder Bay *MED* **95** H7
Calder Cir *MED* **95** H7
Calder Cr *MED* **95** H7
Calder Ct *MED* **95** H7
Calder Gn *MED* **95** H7
Calder Pl *MED* **95** H7
Calder Rd *MED* **95** H7
California Blvd NE *CAL* **31** Y14 Z13-14
California Pl 100 to 400 NE *CAL* **31** Z13-14
Calkins Pl SE *TVY* **74** D-E3
Calla Donna Pl SW *CAL* **42** N23
Calling Horse Dr *RCY* **16** Y10 **24** Y11
Calling Horse Estates Rd *RCY* . . .**16** X-Y10
Camara Ct *STM* **71** B4
Camas Ct *MED* **95** H5
Cambrai Av SW *CAL* **36** L-M20 M20
Cambria Pl *STM* **71** C4
Cambria Rd *STM* **71** C4
Cambrian Dr NW *CAL* **28** N12-13
Cambridge Pl *STM* **71** B4
Cambridge Pl NW *CAL* **28** N-O13

Cambridge Rd NW CAL 28 N-013
Cambridge Rd W LET 86 J4
Cambridge St MED 94 F4 95 F5
Cambridge Glen Dr STM 71 C4
Cambrille Cr STM 71 B-C4
Camden Ct STM 71 C4
Camden Pl STM 71 B4
Cameron Av SW CAL 36 N18
Cameron Cr RED 65 F7
Cameron Pl MED 95 J7-8
Cameron Pl S LET 88 G12
Cameron Rd MED 95 H7 H-J8
Cameron Rd S LET 88 G12
Cameron Way MED 95 J7-8
Camp Dr MED 94 F2
Campbell Av RED 65 F8
Campbell Cr MED 95 H7
Campbell Dr RCY 9 Z5
Campus Dr NW CAL 27 K13 28 L13
Campus Gt NW CAL 28 L13
Campus Pl 100 to 800 NW CAL 27 K13
Canada Olympic Dr SW CAL 26 E12-13
Canada Olympic Rd SW CAL 26 E12-13
Canada Olympic View SW CAL 26 E13
Canal Blvd STM 71 E2
Canal Gdn STM 71 E2
Canal St BRO 90 D3 D-E3
Canals Blvd SW AIR 68 B-C2
Canals Cir SW AIR 68 C2
Canals Dr SW AIR 68 C1-2
Canata Cl SW CAL 48 N28
Canaveral Cr SW CAL 48 028
Canaveral Rd SW CAL 48 028
Canberra Pl NW CAL 28 M12-13
Canberra Rd NW CAL 28 M12
Candiac Rd SW CAL 48 028
Candle Cr SW CAL 48 N29
Candle Ct SW CAL 48 N-029
Candle Pl 100 to 400 SW CAL 48 N28-29
Candle Ter SW CAL 48 N-029
Canfield Cr SW CAL 48 027
Canfield Gn SW CAL 48 028
Canfield Pl SW CAL 48 028
Canfield Rd SW CAL 48 027-28
Canfield Way SW CAL 48 027
Canford Cr SW CAL 48 027-28
Canford Pl SW CAL 48 028
Canmore Rd NW CAL 28 L-M13
Canna Bay SW CAL 48 028
Canna Cr SW CAL 48 028
Cannell Pl 100 200 SW CAL 48 028
Cannell Rd SW CAL 48 028
Cannes Rd SW CAL 48 028
Canniff Pl 100 to 300 SW CAL 48 029 49 P29
Cannington Cl SW CAL 48 029
Cannington Pl 100 to 300 SW CAL 48 028
Cannington Way SW CAL 48 028-29
Cannock Pl SW CAL 48 028
Cannock Rd SW CAL 48 N-028
Cannon Rd NW CAL 28 L11
Canoe Cir SW AIR 68 B-C1
Canoe Cl SW AIR 68 B2
Canoe Cr SW AIR 68 C2
Canoe Cv SW AIR 68 C2
Canoe Dr SW AIR 68 C2
Canoe Gt SW AIR 68 C2
Canoe Pl 100 200 AIR 68 B-C2
Canoe Rd SW AIR 68 B-C2
Canoe Sq 100 200 SW AIR 68 B-C2
Canoe Sq SW AIR 68 B2
Canova Cl 100 to 300 SW CAL 48 N28
Canova Pl 100 200 SW CAL 48 N27-28
Canova Rd SW CAL 48 N27-28
Canso Bay SW CAL 48 N28-29
Canso Cr SW CAL 48 N28-29
Canso Ct SW CAL 48 N28
Canso Gn SW CAL 48 N28
Canso Pl SW CAL 48 N28-29
Cantabrian Dr SW CAL 48 028
Canter Pl 100 to 300 SW CAL 48 N27-28
Canterbury Ct 100 200 SW CAL 48 N-028
Canterbury Dr SW CAL 48 N28 027-29
Canterbury Gdns SW CAL 48 029
Canterbury Pl 100 to 500 SW CAL 48 N27-28
Canterville Bay SW CAL 48 N28
Canterville Dr SW CAL 48 N28
Canterville Rd SW CAL 48 N28
Cantree Bay 100 200 SW CAL 48 028-29
Cantree Pl SW CAL 48 028
Cantree Rd SW CAL 48 028
Cantrell Bay SW CAL 48 029
Cantrell Dr SW CAL 48 028-29
Cantrell Pl 100 to 800 SW CAL 48 028
Canyon Blvd W LET 86 L7 L8
Canyon Cl CAN 59 F7
Canyon Cl W LET 87 K7
Canyon Ct W LET 86 L8 87 K7
Canyon Dr NW CAL 28 M12
Canyon Gdns W LET 86 L8
Canyon Gn W LET 86 L8
Canyon Pl CAN 59 E-F7
Canyon Rd CAN 59 E-F7
Canyon Ter 100 200 W LET 86 L7 87 K7
Canyon Meadows Dr SE CAL 49 P-S29 50 T29
Canyon Meadows Dr SW CAL 48 N28 029
Canyoncrest Pl LET 87 K7
Capilano Cr NW CAL 28 M11-12
Capitol Hill Cr NW CAL 28 L13-14
Capri Av NW CAL 28 L11 L-M12
Capri Cr NW CAL 28 L11
Card Cr RED 65 F7
Cardell St NE CAL 29 R15 37 R16
Cardiff Dr NW CAL 28 N-012
Cardiff Pl NW CAL 28 N12-13
Cardinal Av RED 65 F8
Cardston Cr NW CAL 28 M12-13
Caribou Dr NW CAL 28 M12-13
Caribou St BAN 57 D2
Carleton Pl W LET 87 H5
Carleton Rd W LET 87 H5
Carleton St NW CAL 36 N18-19
Carlyle Rd NW CAL 42 N24
Carmangay Cr NW CAL 28 M12
Carmel Cl NE CAL 31 Y12
Carmel Pl NE CAL 31 Y12
Carnarvon Way NW CAL 28 N12
Carney Rd NW CAL 27 K11 28 L11
Carol Dr NW CAL 28 M12-13
Carolina Cr COC 61 B-C5
Carolina Dr COC 61 B5-6
Carp Av BRO 90 E3
Carpenter Cir NW CAL 28 N15
Carpenter St RED 67 G8
Carr Cr MED 95 G7
Carr Cr OKO 76 A-B3
Carr Pl 100 200 OKO 76 B3
Carragana Cr NW CAL 28 L11
Carriage La RCY 24 Y13
Carroll Cr RED 65 F8 67 G8
Carry Cr MED 95 H7
Carry Ct MED 95 H-J7
Carry Dr MED 95 F6-7 G7 H7-8 J7
Carry Pl MED 95 H7
Carswell Rd MED 95 H7-8
Carter Cr MED 95 G8
Cartier St SW CAL 36 N18-19
Cartwright Av MED 93 E8 95 F8
Casale Pl CAN 59 H7
Casale St SW CAL 41 I22
Cascade Blvd W LET 86 K4 87 K5
Cascade Ct BAN 57 E2
Cascade Dr CAN 58 A2-3
Cascade Pl COC 60 C4
Cascade Rd NW CAL 28 L13
Cassils Rd BRO 90 B1-4
Cassino St S LET 84 E10 88 F10
Casson Gn NW CAL 27 J13
Castelani Cr MED 95 G7
Castle Cr RED 67 G7
Castle Pl COC 60 C4
Castle Rd NW CAL 28 L13
Castle Mountain Rd W LET 86 K4
Castlebrook Ct NE CAL 22 W10
Castlebrook Dr NE CAL 22 W10
Castlebrook Mews NE CAL 22 W10
Castlebrook Pl NE CAL 22 W10
Castlebrook Rd NE CAL 22 W10
Castlebrook Rise NE CAL 22 W10
Castlebrook Way NE CAL 22 W10
Castlebury Ct NE CAL 22 W10
Castlebury Rd NE CAL 22 W10
Castlebury Way NE CAL 22 W10
Castledale Cr NE CAL 22 W9-10
Castledale Gt NE CAL 22 W9-10
Castledale Pl NE CAL 22 W9
Castledale Way NE CAL 22 W9-10
Castlefall Cr NE CAL 22 W10 23 X10
Castlefall Gr NE CAL 22 W10
Castlefall Rd NE CAL 22 W10
Castlefall Way NE CAL 22 W10
Castleglen Cr NE CAL 23 X10
Castleglen Ct NE CAL 23 X10
Castleglen Pl NE CAL 23 X10
Castleglen Rd NE CAL 23 X10
Castleglen Way NE CAL 23 X10
Castlegreen Cl NE CAL 22 W10 23 X10
Castlegrove Pl NE CAL 22 W10
Castlegrove Rd NE CAL 22 W10
Castlegrove Way NE CAL 22 W10
Castlepark Bay NE CAL 23 X10
Castlepark Rd NE CAL 23 X10
Castlepark Way NE CAL 23 X10
Castleridge Blvd NE CAL 22 W9-10
Castleridge Cl NE CAL 23 X9-10
Castleridge Cr NE CAL 23 X9
Castleridge Dr NE CAL 22 W10 23 X10
Castleridge Rd NE CAL 23 X9-10
Castleridge Way NE CAL 23 X10
Caswell Cl RED 67 G8
Catalina Blvd NE CAL 31 Y13-14 Y-Z12
Catalina Cir NE CAL 31 Y12
Catalina Pl 100 200 NE CAL 31 Z13-14
Cataract Rd SW HIG 77 C1
Cathedral Mnr NW CAL 19 H10
Cathedral Rd NW CAL 28 L13
Cavan Pl MED 95 G-H7
Cavanaugh Pl NW CAL 28 M-N12
Cave Av BAN 57 E1
Cavendish Beach Bay CHE 70 E2
Cawder Dr NW CAL 28 M-N12
Cayuga Cr NW CAL 28 M12
Cayuga Cr W LET 86 G4
Cayuga Dr NW CAL 28 M-N12
Cayuga Pl W LET 86 G4
Cedar Av CAN 58 A2-3
Cedar Cr DRU 73 D8
Cedar Cr SW CAL 35 K16
Cedar Pl S LET 88 H-K11
Cedar Rd S LET 88 H11
Cedar Way NW CAL 26 E11-12
Cedar Ridge Cr SW CAL 47 K26
Cedar Ridge Dr SW CAL 47 K26
Cedar Ridge Pl SW CAL 47 K26 48 L26
Cedar Springs Gdns SW CAL 48 L27
Cedarbrae Cr SW CAL 47 K26 48 L26
Cedarbrae Dr SW CAL 47 K26
Cedarbrook Bay 100 200 SW CAL 47 K27 48 L27
Cedarbrook Cl SW CAL 47 K26 48 L26
Cedarbrook Pk SW CAL 48 L27
Cedarbrook Pl SW CAL 48 L26-27
Cedarbrook Way SW CAL 47 K27 48 L27
Cedardale Bay 100 200 SW CAL 47 K27
Cedardale Cr SW CAL 47 K27
Cedardale Hill SW CAL 47 K26-27
Cedardale Mews SW CAL 47 K27
Cedardale Pl 100 to 300 SW CAL 47 J-K26 J-K27
Cedardale Rd SW CAL 47 K26-27
Cedardale Rise SW CAL 47 K27
Cedargrove Ct 100 200 SW CAL 48 L27
Cedargrove La SW CAL 48 L27
Cedargrove Pl SW CAL 48 L27
Cedargrove Rd SW CAL 47 K27 48 L27
Cedargrove Way SW CAL 47 K27 48 L27
Cedarille Cr SW CAL 47 J-K26
Cedarille Dr SW CAL 47 K26-27
Cedarille Gn SW CAL 47 K26
Cedarille Pl SW CAL 47 K26
Cedarille Way SW CAL 47 K26
Cedarpark Dr SW CAL 48 L26
Cedarpark Gn SW CAL 48 L26
Cedarpark Gt SW CAL 48 L26
Cedarview Mews SW CAL 48 L26
Cedarwood Bay SW CAL 47 K27
Cedarwood Hill SW CAL 47 K27
Cedarwood Mews SW CAL 47 K27
Cedarwood Pk 100 200 SW CAL 47 K27
Cedarwood Pl SW CAL 47 K26-27
Cedarwood Rd SW CAL 47 K26
Cedarwood Rise SW CAL 47 K27
Ceduna La SW CAL 48 L27
Ceduna Pk SW CAL 48 L27
Celtic Rd NW CAL 28 N12
Cemetery Rd IRR 69 B1-2
Cemetery Rd SE CAL 37 Q19
Centre Av BLD 75 B6-7
Centre Av BRG 78 B2
Centre Av COC 61 B5
Centre Av HIG 77 B3
Centre Av OKO 76 B-C2
Centre Av E AIR 68 B3-4
Centre Av E CHE 70 C3-4
Centre Av NE AIR 69 B5
Centre Av NE CAL 37 Q-R16 S16 38 T-U16
Centre Av SW CAL 35 H16
Centre Av W AIR 68 B3
Centre Cr NE CAL 29 P11
Centre St BRO 90 A3 B-C3 C2-3
Centre St OKO 76 C2
Centre St STM 71 C3
Centre St N HIG 77 A-B2
Centre St N NW CAL 7 D91 12 02 20 08 21 P10 29 P11-15
Centre St S HIG 77 C2
Centre St S SW CAL 7 D92-94 37 P16-17 43 P21 P22
Centre A St NE CAL 29 P11 P12 P14
Centre A St NW CAL 29 P15
Centre B St NW CAL 29 P12-13 P14
Century Dr SE CAL 38 T16-17
Century Gt SE CAL 38 T16
Century Rise SE CAL 38 T16-17
Chalice Rd NW CAL 28 L11
Chalmers Cl RED 65 F8
Chamberlain Cl RCY 9 A2
Chamberlain Pl RCY 9 Z1
Champlain St SW CAL 36 N19
Chancellor Way NW CAL 28 N12
Chandler Rd NW CAL 27 K11 28 L11
Chapala Bay SE CAL 53 R35
Chapala Cl SE CAL 53 R35
Chapala Cr SE CAL 53 R34-35
Chapala Ct SE CAL 53 R35
Chapala Dr SE CAL 53 R34-35
Chapala Gr SE CAL 53 R35
Chapala Gt SE CAL 53 R35
Chapala Heath SE CAL 53 R35
Chapala Ldg SE CAL 53 R35
Chapala Rd SE CAL 53 R35
Chapala Sq SE CAL 53 R35
Chapala Ter SE CAL 53 R35
Chapala Way SE CAL 53 R-S35
Chapalina Cr SE CAL 53 Q34
Chapalina Cr SE CAL 53 Q35
Chapalina Mnr SE CAL 53 Q34
Chapalina Pl 100 200 SE CAL 53 Q34
Chapalina Way SE CAL 53 Q34
Chapalina Park Cr SE CAL 53 Q34
Chaparral Bay SE CAL 53 Q34
Chaparral Cir SE CAL 53 Q35
Chaparral Cl SE CAL 53 Q-R35
Chaparral Com SE CAL 53 R34
Chaparral Cr SE CAL 53 Q35 R34
Chaparral Ct 100 200 SE CAL 53 R34
Chaparral Cv SE CAL 53 R34-35
Chaparral Dr SE CAL 53 Q-R34 R35
Chaparral Gn SE CAL 53 S34
Chaparral Heath SE CAL 53 Q-R35
Chaparral Link SE CAL 53 R34
Chaparral Mews SE CAL 53 R-S34
Chaparral Mnr SE CAL 53 R34-35
Chaparral Pk SE CAL 53 R34
Chaparral Pl 100 to 300 SE CAL 53 R-S34
Chaparral Pt SE CAL 53 R34
Chaparral Rd SE CAL 53 R-S34
Chaparral St SE CAL 53 R34
Chaparral Ter SE CAL 53 Q35
Chaparral View SE CAL 53 Q34-35
Chaparral Way SE CAL 53 R-S34
Chaparral Ridge Bay SE CAL 53 S34
Chaparral Ridge Cir SE CAL 53 S34
Chaparral Ridge Dr SE CAL 53 S34
Chaparral Ridge Link SE CAL 53 S34
Chaparral Ridge Pt 100 to 300 SE CAL 53 S34-35
Chaparral Ridge Ter SE CAL 53 S34
Chaparral Ridge Way SE CAL 53 S34
Chapel Rd NW CAL 28 L11
Chapman Cir SE CAL 53 S35
Chapman Cl SE CAL 53 S35
Chapman Ct SE CAL 53 S35
Chapman Heath SE CAL 53 S35
Chapman Link SE CAL 53 S35
Chapman Mews SE CAL 53 S35
Chapman Pl SE CAL 53 S35
Chapman Rd SE CAL 53 S35
Chapman Ter SE CAL 53 S35
Chapman Way SE CAL 53 S35
Chappel Dr RED 65 F8 67 G8
Chardie Pl SW CAL 42 N23-24
Chardie Rd SW CAL 42 N23-24
Charlebois Dr NW CAL 28 L12
Charles Av SW CAL 36 N20 42 N22
Charles Carey CAN 58 G4
Charleswood Cr NW CAL 27 K12 28 L12
Charleswood Dr NW CAL 28 L12
Charlesworth Av COC 60 C4 61 C5
Charlesworth Cr BRO 90 C3
Chateau Estates 100 to 900 NE CAL 31 Z15
Chateau Pl NW CAL 28 L13
Chatham Dr NW CAL 28 L12
Chatham Pl NW CAL 28 L12
Chelsea St NW CAL 28 N13
Cheltenham Rd NW CAL 28 M-N12
Cherokee Dr NW CAL 28 L12
Cherokee Pl NW CAL 28 L-M12
Cherovan Dr SW CAL 42 N23
Cherry Way NW CAL 26 D-E11
Cherry Tree Walk SW CAL 35 K17
Chester Pl NW CAL 28 M-N13
Chestermere Station Way CHE 70 C-D2
Chestnut Walk SW CAL 35 K17
Cheyanne Meadows Gt N RCY 9 A1
Cheyanne Meadows Gt W RCY 9 Z2
Cheyanne Meadows Way RCY 9 Z2
Cheyenne Cr NW CAL 28 L12
Chicoutimi Dr NW CAL 28 L-M12
Chilcotin Cr W LET 86 G3
Chilcotin Rd NW CAL 28 L12
Chilcotin Rd W LET 86 G3
Child Av NE CAL 29 R15 37 R16

Childrens Gt NW CAL 27 J13
China Cl CAN 58 F3
Chiniki Dr COC 60 A-B4
Chinook Cl BEI 69 A2
Chinook Cr BRO 90 B-C1
Chinook Ct MED 92 E2
Chinook Dr COC 60 A-B4
Chinook Dr MED 92 E2-3
Chinook Dr SW CAL 42 N24
Chinook Hts S LET 88 H-J9
Chinook Pl MED 92 E3
Chinook Rd BEI 69 A2
Chinook Rd BRO 90 C1
Chinook St BRO 90 B-C1
Chinook Way BRO 90 B-C1
Chippendale Dr NW CAL 28 L12-13
Chippewa Cr W LET 86 G4
Chippewa Rd NW CAL 28 L11-12
Chisholm Av CRS 62 A2-3
Chisholm Cr NW CAL 28 L-M12
Chism Cl RED 67 G8
Chow Av MED 95 G-H8
Christie Pt SW CAL 35 H17
Christie Rd NW CAL 28 M12
Christie Briar Gn SW CAL 34 G17
Christie Briar Heath SW CAL 34 G17
Christie Briar La SW CAL 34 G17
Christie Briar Mnr SW CAL 34 G17
Christie Briar Row SW CAL 34 G17
Christie Cairn Heath SW CAL
. . . . .34 G17 35 H17
Christie Cairn Sq SW CAL 35 H17
Christie Estate Blvd SW CAL 34 G17
Christie Estate Gdns SW CAL 34 G17
Christie Estate Gr SW CAL 35 H17
Christie Estate Heath SW CAL 35 H17
Christie Estate Mnr SW CAL 34 G17
Christie Estate Ter SW CAL 34 G17
Christie Knoll Gn SW CAL . .34 G17 35 H17
Christie Knoll Hts SW CAL 34 G17
Christie Knoll Pt 100 to 400 SW CAL . . .
. . . . .34 G17
Christie Park Gdns SW CAL 35 H17
Christie Park Gn 100 200 SW CAL 35 H17
Christie Park Gt SW CAL 35 H17-18
Christie Park Hill SW CAL 35 H17
Christie Park Mews SW CAL 35 H17
Christie Park Mnr SW CAL 35 H17
Christie Park Ter SW CAL 35 H17
Christie Park View SW CAL 35 H17
Christman Av MED 93 E8 95 F8
Chula Blvd CAL 47 J27
Church Ct MED 95 G7
Church Ranches Blvd RCY . .9 Z2 A2 A-B3
Church Ranches Cl RCY 9 A2-3
Church Ranches Pl RCY 9 Z2
Church Ranches Rise RCY 9 A3
Church Ranches Way RCY 9 Z2-3
Churchill Dr SW CAL 42 N24
Cimarron Bay OKO 76 D3
Cimarron Blvd OKO 76 D3
Cimarron Cir OKO 76 D3
Cimarron Cl OKO 76 D-E3
Cimarron Com OKO 76 E3
Cimarron Cr OKO 76 D3
Cimarron Ct OKO 76 D3
Cimarron Dr OKO 76 D-E3
Cimarron Hill OKO 76 D3
Cimarron Pt OKO 76 D-E3
Cimarron Rise OKO 76 D3
Cimarron Tr OKO 76 D3
Cimarron Way OKO 76 D3
Cimarron Grove Bay OKO 76 E3
Cimarron Grove Cr OKO 76 E3
Cimarron Grove Dr OKO 76 E3
Cimarron Grove Way OKO 76 E3
Cimarron Meadows Bay OKO . .76 E2-3
Cimarron Meadows Cl OKO 76 E2-3
Cimarron Meadows Cr OKO 76 E2-3
Cimarron Meadows Link OKO 76 E3
Cimarron Meadows Way OKO 76 E3
Cimarron Park Bay OKO 76 E3
Cimarron Park Cl OKO 76 E3
Cimarron Park Pl OKO 76 E3
Citadel Bay NW CAL 19 H6
Citadel Blvd NW CAL 19 H6
Citadel Cir NW CAL 19 H6
Citadel Cl NW CAL 19 H6
Citadel Ct NW CAL 19 H6
Citadel Dr NW CAL 10 G5 18 G6 19 H6
Citadel Gdns NW CAL 19 H6
Citadel Gn NW CAL 11 I5
Citadel Gr NW CAL 19 I6
Citadel Gt NW CAL 18 G6 19 H6
Citadel Hts NW CAL 19 H6
Citadel La NW CAL 18 G6
Citadel Link NW CAL 19 H6
Citadel Mnr NW CAL 19 H6
Citadel Pass NW CAL 19 H6
Citadel Pk NW CAL 19 H6
Citadel Pt NW CAL 10 G5
Citadel Ter NW CAL 19 H6
Citadel Way NW CAL 10 G5
Citadel Acres Cl NW CAL 10 F-G5
Citadel Acres Pl NW CAL 10 F5
Citadel Bluff Cl NW CAL 10 G5
Citadel Crest Cir NW CAL . . .11 H5 19 H6
Citadel Crest Gn NW CAL 11 H5
Citadel Crest Heath NW CAL 11 H5
Citadel Crest Link NW CAL . . .10 G5 11 H5
Citadel Crest Pk NW CAL 11 H5
Citadel Crest Pl NW CAL 11 H5
Citadel Estates Hts NW CAL . .10 G5 18 G6
Citadel Estates Link NW CAL 18 G6
Citadel Estates Mnr NW CAL 10 G5
Citadel Estates Pl NW CAL 10 G5 18 G6
Citadel Estates Ter NW CAL 18 G6
Citadel Forest Cl NW CAL 10 F5 18 F6
Citadel Forest Link NW CAL 10 F5
Citadel Forest Pl NW CAL 10 F5
Citadel Hills Cir NW CAL 19 H-I6
Citadel Hills Gn NW CAL 19 H6
Citadel Hills Pl100 to 300 NW CAL19 H6
Citadel Meadow Bay 100 to 500 NW
CAL 10 G5 11 H5
Citadel Meadow Cl NW CAL 10 G5
Citadel Meadow Cr NW CAL 11 H5
Citadel Meadow Cv NW CAL 11 H5
Citadel Meadow Gr NW CAL 11 H5
Citadel Meadow Pt NW CAL 10 G5
Citadel Mesa Cl NW CAL 10 G5
Citadel Pass Cr NW CAL 19 H6
Citadel Pass Ct 100 200 NW CAL .19 H6
Citadel Peak Cir NW CAL 11 H5
Citadel Peak Mews NW CAL 11 H5
Citadel Ridge Cl NW CAL 10 G5
Citadel Ridge Gn NW CAL 18 G6
Citadel Ridge Pk NW CAL 10 G5
Citadel Ridge Pl NW CAL 18 G6
Citadel Vista Cl NW CAL 18 F6
Citadel Vista Gn NW CAL 10 F5 18 F6
Clarendon Rd NW CAL 28 M12
Claret St NW CAL 28 L11
Clark Av OKO 76 B-C3
Clark Cr MED 95 G-H7
Clark Cr RED 67 G7-8
Clarke Rd SW CAL 42 N24
Clatter St NW CAL 28 N12
Clay Av MED 95 F6
Clear Mountain Rise RCY 33 A16
Clelland Cr MED 95 H7
Clematis Ct MED 95 H5
Clennel Cr MED 95 H8
Cleveland Cr SE CAL 37 Q20
Cliff St SW CAL 36 O18
Cliffe Av SW CAL 36 O20
Clover Ct MED 95 H5
Clover La RCY 24 W11-15 32 W16-20
Coach Ct SW CAL 26 G15
Coach Bluff Cr SW CAL 26 G15
Coach Gate Ct SW CAL 35 H16
Coach Gate Pl SW CAL 35 H16
Coach Gate Way SW CAL 35 H16
Coach Grove Pl 100 to 300 SW CAL . . .
. . . . .35 H16
Coach Grove Rd SW CAL . . .27 H15 35 H16
Coach Hill Meadows SW CAL 26 G15
Coach Hill Mnr SW CAL 26 G15
Coach Hill Rd SW CAL 26 G15 27 H15
Coach Light Bay 100 to 500 SW CAL . . .
. . . . .35 H16
Coach Manor Rise SW CAL 27 H15 35 H16
Coach Manor Ter SW CAL 27 H15
Coach Ridge Bay SW CAL 26 G15
Coach Ridge Cl SW CAL 34 G16
Coach Ridge Pl SW CAL 34 G16
Coach Ridge Rd SW CAL 34 G16
Coach Ridge Rise SW CAL .26 G15 34 G16
Coach Side Cr SW CAL . . .26 G15 27 H15
Coach Side Pl SW CAL 26 G15
Coach Side Rd SW CAL . . .26 G15 27 H15
Coach Side Ter SW CAL 26 G15
Coachway Gdns SW CAL .26 G15 27 H15
Coachway Gn SW CAL 26 G15
Coachway La 100 to 300 SW CAL 26 G15
Coachway Rd SW CAL 26 G15
Coachwood Cr SW CAL . . .34 G16 35 H16
Coachwood Pl SW CAL . . .26 G15 27 H15
Coachwood Rd W LET 86 F4
Cobb Rd MED 95 G7
Coburg Av MED 93 E6 95 F6
Cochran Dr MED 92 C-D3
Cochrane Cr COC 60 B4
Cochrane Rd NW CAL 28 L-M13
Cockrill Ct MED 95 G7
Cocks Way MED 95 G-H7

Cody Range Cl RCY 9 B2
Cody Range Way RCY 9 B2 B2-3
Col James Walker CAN 58 G4
Colborne Cr SW CAL 36 N18
Cole St RED 67 G7-8
Coleman Rd NW CAL 19 K10 27 K11
Coleridge Cr NW CAL 28 N12
Coleridge Rd NW CAL 28 N12
Colgrove Av NE CAL 29 R15
Colleen Av SW CAL 42 N24
Colleen Cr SW CAL 42 N24
College Av NE CAL 94 G-H4
College Blvd RED 66 J4
College Cir RED 66 J3-4
College Ct RED 66 J4
College Dr MED 95 G5
College Dr S LET 88 J10
College La RED 66 J4
College La SW CAL 36 O17-18
College Rd MED 94 G4
College St RED 65 E-F8 F9
Collegiate Blvd NW CAL 27 K13
Collegiate Ct NW CAL 27 J-K13
Collegiate Pl 100 to 300 NW CAL . . . .
. . . . .27 J13 K13
Collegiate Rd NW CAL 27 J13
Collicut St NW CAL 42 N24
Collier Ct MED 95 H7
Collier Rd MED 95 H7
Collingwood Dr NW CAL . . .28 M12-13
Collingwood Pl NW CAL 28 M12
Collins Cr CRS 62 A2
Collins Cr MED 95 G7
Colonel Baker Pl SE CAL 37 R16
Colter Cr MED 92 D3
Columbia Bay W LET 86 J4
Columbia Blvd W LET .86 H3-4 H4 J4 87 H5
Columbia Pl NW CAL 28 M12
Columbia Pl W LET 86 J4
Comanche Rd NW CAL 28 M12
Comfort Cl RED 65 F8
Commerce St NW CAL 28 N12
Commercial Ct RCY 24 V12
Commercial Dr RCY 24 V12
Community Way OKO 76 D2
Concordia Pl W LET 87 H5
Conductor Blvd COD 85 A-B3
Confederation Village NW CAL . . .28 M12
Congo Cr SW CAL 42 L21
Congo Rd SW CAL 42 L21
Connaught Dr NW CAL 94 G3
Connaught Dr NW CAL 28 N12
Connell Cl RED 65 F8 67 G8
Conners Cr RED 65 F7
Conrad Cr NW CAL 19 K10 27 K11
Conrad Dr NW CAL . .19 K10 20 L10 28 L11
Conrad Pl RCY 33 Z16
Constable Pl NW CAL 28 M12-13
Constable Rd NW CAL 28 M12-13
Constance Av SE CAL 37 Q18
Cook Ct MED 95 G7
Cook Rd MED 95 H7
Cooney Rd MED 95 H7-8
Cooper Rd MED 95 H7
Coopers Bay SW CAL 68 E3
Coopers Cir SW AIR 68 E3
Coopers Cl SW AIR 68 E2-3
Coopers Crossing SW CAL 68 E3
Coopers Dr SW AIR 68 E2-3
Coopers Hts SW AIR 68 E3
Coopers Link SW AIR 68 E3
Coopers Mnr SW AIR 68 E3
Coote St RED 67 G8
Copithorne Rd NW CAL 28 M12-13
Copperfield Blvd SE CAL 55 X-Y32
Copperfield Cl SE CAL 55 Y32
Copperfield Com SE CAL 55 Y32
Copperfield Cr SE CAL 55 Y32
Copperfield Gdns 100 to 300 SE CAL . . .
. . . . .55 X32
Copperfield Gn 100 200 SE CAL . . . . .
. . . . .55 Y31-32
Copperfield Gr 100 to 300 SE CAL 55 Y32
Copperfield Gt SE CAL 55 X32
Copperfield Hts 100 to 400 SE CAL . . .
. . . . .55 X31-32
Copperfield Link SE CAL 55 Y31-32
Copperfield Mews 100 200 SE CAL . . .
. . . . .55 X-Y32
Copperfield Mnr 100 200 SE CAL . . . . .
. . . . .55 Y31-32
Copperfield Rise SE CAL 55 Y31
Copperfield Ter SE CAL 55 Y31
Copperfield View SE CAL 55 Y32
Copperfield Grand Blvd SE CAL .55 X-Z32
Copperstone Gr 100 to 300 SE CAL . . . .
. . . . .55 Y-Z32
Copperstone Gt SE CAL 55 Y31-32
Copperstone Pl SE CAL 55 Y31-32

Copperstone St SE CAL 55 Y32
Coral Cv NE CAL 31 Y11
Coral Pl S LET 88 G11
Coral Keys Ct 100 200 NE CAL . . .23 Y10
Coral Keys Dr NE CAL 23 Y-Z10
Coral Keys Pl 100 to 400 NE CAL .23 Y10
Coral Keys Villas 100 to 500 NE CAL . . .
. . . . .23 Y10
Coral Reef Bay NE CAL 23 Z9
Coral Reef Cl NE CAL 23 Z9-10
Coral Reef Cr NE CAL 23 Z9-10
Coral Reef Link NE CAL 23 Z10
Coral Reef Mnr 100 to 300 NE CAL . . .
. . . . .23 Z9-10
Coral Sands Ct NE CAL 31 Z11
Coral Sands Pl 100 200 NE CAL .31 Y-Z11
Coral Sands Ter 100 to 300 NE CAL . . . .
. . . . .31 Z11
Coral Shores Bay 100 200 NE CAL . . . .
. . . . .23 Y10 31 Y11
Coral Shores Cape 100 200 NE CAL . . .
. . . . .31 Y-Z11
Coral Shores Ct 100 200 NE CAL23 Y-Z10
Coral Shores Cv NE CAL 31 Z11
Coral Shores Dr NE CAL . . .23 Y10 31 Y11
Coral Shores Ldg 100 200 NE CAL . . . .
. . . . .23 Y-Z10
Coral Springs Bay NE CAL 23 Y9-10
Coral Springs Blvd NE CAL . . . .
. . . . .23 Y-Z10 31 Y-Z11
Coral Springs Cir NE CAL 23 Y9-10
Coral Springs Cl NE CAL 23 Z10
Coral Springs Ct NE CAL 23 Z9-10
Coral Springs Gdns NE CAL 23 Z10
Coral Springs Gn NE CAL 23 Z10
Coral Springs Gr NE CAL 23 Z10
Coral Springs Ldg 100 200 NE CAL . . . .
. . . . .23 Z10 31 Z11
Coral Springs Mews 100 200 NE CAL . . .
. . . . .23 Z9-10
Coral Springs Pk NE CAL 23 Z10
Coral Springs Pl 100 to 400 NE CAL . . .
. . . . .23 Z10 31 Z11
Corbitt Way MED 95 G7
Cornell Cr MED 94 F1
Cornell Pl NW CAL 28 N12
Cornell Rd NW CAL 28 N12
Cornett Dr RED 65 F8 F8 67 G8
Cornwallis Dr NW CAL 28 N12
Coronado Pl NW CAL 31 Y14
Coronation Dr SW CAL 36 N-O20
Corvette Cr S LET 88 F10
Cosgrove Cl RED 65 F8
Cosgrove Cr RED 65 F8
Cosgrove St NW CAL 28 L11
Costa Mesa Cl NE CAL 31 Y12
Costa Mesa Pl NE CAL 31 Y12
Costello Blvd SW CAL 35 H17
Cottage St NW CAL 28 N12
Cottonwood Bay MED 94 H2
Cottonwood Cl MED 94 H2
Cottonwood Cr SE CAL 38 U-V18
Cottonwood Ct MED 94 H2
Cottonwood Pl MED 94 H2
Cottonwood Rd MED 94 H2
Cottonwood St MED 26 D11-12
Cottonwood Way MED 94 H2-3
Cougar Bay N LET 83 B8 84 B9
Cougar Cr N LET 84 B9
Cougar Ct CAN 59 F6
Cougar Pl BAN 57 C2
Cougar Pl N LET 84 A-B9
Cougar Rd N LET 84 A-B9
Cougar St BAN 57 C2
Cougar Way N LET 84 A9
Cougar Creek Dr CAN 59 E-F6
Cougar Plateau Cir SW CAL . .26 F13-14
Cougar Plateau Gt SW CAL 26 E-F14
Cougar Plateau Mews 100 200 SW CAL
. . . . .26 F14
Cougar Plateau Pl SW CAL 26 F13
Cougar Plateau Way SW CAL 26 F14
Cougar Point Rd CAN 59 E5-6
Cougar Ridge Av SW CAL 26 F14
Cougar Ridge Bay SW CAL 26 F14
Cougar Ridge Cir SW CAL 26 F14
Cougar Ridge Cr SW CAL 26 F14
Cougar Ridge Ct SW CAL 26 F14
Cougar Ridge Dr SW CAL 26 E14 F14
Cougar Ridge Gr SW CAL 26 F14
Cougar Ridge Hts SW CAL 26 F14
Cougar Ridge La SW CAL 26 G14
Cougar Ridge Link SW CAL 26 F14
Cougar Ridge Pl SW CAL 26 F14
Cougar Ridge View SW CAL 26 F14
Cougarstone Bay SW CAL 26 E14
Cougarstone Cir SW CAL 26 E14

Cougarstone Cl SW *CAL* 26 E14
Cougarstone Com SW *CAL* 26 E14
Cougarstone Cr SW *CAL* 26 E14
Cougarstone Ct SW *CAL* 26 D-E14
Cougarstone Cv SW *CAL* 26 E14
Cougarstone Gdns 100 200 SW *CAL* . . .
. . . . .26 E14
Cougarstone Gr SW *CAL* 26 E14
Cougarstone Gt SW *CAL* 26 E14
Cougarstone Link SW *CAL* 26 E14
Cougarstone Mews SW *CAL* 26 E13
Cougarstone Mnr SW *CAL* 26 E13-14
Cougarstone Pk SW *CAL* 26 E14
Cougarstone Pl SW *CAL* 26 E14
Cougarstone Pt SW *CAL* 26 E13-14
Cougarstone Sq SW *CAL* 26 E14
Cougarstone Ter SW *CAL* 26 E13
Cougarstone Vill SW *CAL* 26 E14
Cougarstone Way SW *CAL* 26 E14
Coulee Pk SW *CAL* 26 G14
Coulee Ridge *RCY* 33 A20
Coulee View SW *CAL* 26 G14
Coultis Ct *BRO* 90 C4
Council Way SW *CAL* 36 N19
Country Club La *RCY* 9 A4
Country Club Pl *RCY* 9 B5
Country Hills Bay NW *CAL* 12 O5
Country Hills Blvd NE *CAL* . . . .
. . . . .13 Q-S4 14 T-W4 15 X-Z4
Country Hills Blvd NW *CAL* . . . .
. . . . .9 C4 10 E-F5 12 N-O5 19 H-K6 20 L-N6
Country Hills Cir 1000 2000 NW *CAL* . . .
. . . . .13 P5 21 P6
Country Hills Cl NW *CAL* 20 N-O6
Country Hills Cr NW *CAL* 12 O5 13 P5
Country Hills Ct 100 to 800 NW *CAL* . . .
. . . . .20 N-O6
Country Hills Cv NW *CAL* 12 O5 20 O6
Country Hills Dr NW *CAL* 13 P5
Country Hills Gdns NW *CAL* 12 O5
Country Hills Gn NW *CAL* 12 O5
Country Hills Gr NW *CAL* 13 P5
Country Hills Gt NW *CAL* 12 O5 20 O6
Country Hills Hts NW *CAL* 12 O5
Country Hills Ldg NW *CAL* 20 O6
Country Hills Link NW *CAL* 13 P5
Country Hills Mews NW *CAL* 13 P5
Country Hills Mnr NW *CAL* 12 O5
Country Hills Pk NW *CAL* 20 O6
Country Hills Pl 100 to 400 NW *CAL* . . .
. . . . .13 P5
Country Hills Rd NW *CAL* . . .12 O5 20 O6
Country Hills Rise NW *CAL* 13 P5
Country Hills Sq NW *CAL* 13 P5
Country Hills Ter NW *CAL* . . .12 O5 13 P5
Country Hills View NW *CAL* . .12 O5 20 O6
Country Hills Villas NW *CAL* 13 P5
Country Hills Way NW *CAL* 13 P-R3
Country Meadows Cl *TVY* 74 C2
Country Meadows St *TVY* 74 C2
Country Meadows Way *TVY* 74 C2-3
Country Village Bay NE *CAL* 13 Q4
Country Village Cape 100 to 400 NE
CAL .13 Q4
Country Village Cir NE *CAL* 13 P-Q4
Country Village Cv NE *CAL* 13 P4
Country Village Ldg NE *CAL* 13 Q4
Country Village Ln NE *CAL* 13 P4
Country Village Rd NE *CAL* . .12 O4 13 P4
Country Village Way NE *CAL* 13 P4
Cousins Ct *MED* 95 G7
Couture Cr SW *CAL* 41 K21-22
Cove Bay *CHE* 70 C2
Cove Cr *CHE* 70 C2
Cove Ct 100 200 *CHE* 70 B-C2
Cove Dr *CHE* 70 C2-3
Cove Hill *CHE* 70 C2-3
Cove Ldg *CHE* 70 C2
Cove Link *CHE* 70 C2
Cove Pl *CHE* 70 C2-3
Cove Point 100 200 *CHE* 70 C2
Cove Rd *CHE* 70 C2-3
Cove Rise *CHE* 70 C2
Covebrook Cl NE *CAL* 13 P2-3
Covebrook Gt NE *CAL* 13 P3
Covebrook Pl NE *CAL* 13 P2-3
Covecreek Cl NE *CAL* 13 Q2-3
Covecreek Gn NE *CAL* 13 Q2
Covecreek Gt NE *CAL* 13 Q2-3
Covecreek Pl NE *CAL* 13 Q2
Covehaven Cl NE *CAL* 13 P3
Covehaven Cr NE *CAL* 13 P3
Covehaven Ct NE *CAL* 13 P3
Covehaven Gdns NE *CAL* 13 P3
Covehaven Link NE *CAL* 13 P3
Covehaven Mews NE *CAL* . . . .
. . . . .12 O3 O4 13 P3 P4
Covehaven Rd NE *CAL* 13 P3-4
Covehaven Rise NE *CAL* 13 P3-4

Covehaven View NE *CAL* 13 P3
Covemeadow Cl NE *CAL* 13 P2
Covemeadow Cr NE *CAL* 13 P3
Covemeadow Rd NE *CAL* 13 P2
Coventry Blvd NE *CAL* 13 Q4
Coventry Cir NE *CAL* 13 Q4
Coventry Cl NE *CAL* 13 Q4
Coventry Cr NE *CAL* 13 Q4
Coventry Ct 100 200 NE *CAL* 13 Q4
Coventry Dr NE *CAL* 13 Q4
Coventry Gdns NE *CAL* 13 Q3
Coventry Gn NE *CAL* 13 Q4
Coventry Gt NE *CAL* 13 Q4
Coventry La NE *CAL* 13 Q-R4
Coventry Link NE *CAL* 13 Q3-4
Coventry Mews 100 200 NE *CAL* . . .13 Q4
Coventry Pl 100 200 NE *CAL* 13 Q4
Coventry Rd NE *CAL* 13 Q3-4
Coventry View NE *CAL* 13 Q3-4
Coventry Way NE *CAL* 13 Q4
Coventry Hills Blvd NE *CAL* 13 Q4
Coventry Hills Dr NE *CAL* 13 P3
Coventry Hills Way NE *CAL* 13 Q3
Covepark Cl NE *CAL* 13 P-Q3
Covepark Cr NE *CAL* 13 Q2
Covepark Dr NE *CAL* 13 Q2
Covepark Gn NE *CAL* 13 P3
Covepark Gt NE *CAL* 13 Q2
Covepark Mews NE *CAL* 13 P3
Covepark Pl NE *CAL* 13 P3
Covepark Rd NE *CAL* 13 Q3
Covepark Rise NE *CAL* 13 Q3
Covepark Sq NE *CAL* 13 P3
Covepark Ter NE *CAL* 13 Q3
Covepark Way NE *CAL* 13 Q3
Coverdale Ct 100 to 300 NE *CAL* .13 Q3-4
Coverdale Pl NE *CAL* 13 Q4
Coverdale Rd NE *CAL* 13 Q4
Coverdale Way NE *CAL* 13 Q4
Coverton Cir NE *CAL* 13 Q-R4
Coverton Cl NE *CAL* 13 R3-4
Coverton Ct NE *CAL* 13 R3-4
Coverton Gn NE *CAL* 13 Q3
Coverton Gt NE *CAL* 13 Q-R3
Coverton Hts NE *CAL* 13 R3
Coverton Mews NE *CAL* 13 R3
Covette Bay NE *CAL* 13 Q3
Covette Gn NE *CAL* 13 Q3-4
Covewood Cir NE *CAL* 13 Q3
Covewood Cl NE *CAL* 13 Q-R3
Covewood Gn NE *CAL* 13 Q-R3
Covewood Gt NE *CAL* 13 Q2-3
Covewood Link NE *CAL* 13 Q3
Covewood Mnr NE *CAL* 13 Q3
Covewood Pk NE *CAL* 13 Q3
Covewood Pl NE *CAL* 13 Q3
Coville Bay NE *CAL* 13 Q2
Coville Cir NE *CAL* 13 Q-R2
Coville Cl NE *CAL* 13 Q2
Coville Cr NE *CAL* 13 R3
Coville Gdns NE *CAL* 13 Q-R2
Coville Gt NE *CAL* 13 Q2
Coville Sq NE *CAL* 13 R3
Covington Bay 100 to 300 NE *CAL* . . . .
. . . . .13 Q-R4
Covington Cl NE *CAL* 13 R4
Covington Ct NE *CAL* 13 R4
Covington Mews NE *CAL* 13 R4
Covington Pl NE *CAL* 13 R4
Covington Rd NE *CAL* 13 Q-R4
Covington Rise NE *CAL* 13 R4
Cowan Cl NE *CAL* 65 F3
Cowan Cr *MED* 95 G7
Cowichan Ct W *LET* 86 G3
Coyote Dr *BAN* 57 C3
Coyote Way *CAN* 59 F6
Coyote Valley Rd *RCY* 8 W-X3
Crabapple Walk SW *CAL* 35 K16-17
Craig Rd *MED* 95 H7
Craig Rd SW *CAL* 42 N23
Cramond Cir SE *CAL* 54 V33-34
Cramond Cl SE *CAL* 54 V34
Cramond Cr SE *CAL* 54 V33-34
Cramond Dr SE *CAL* 54 V33-34
Cramond Pl 100 200 SE *CAL* . .54 V33-34
Cranberry Cl SE *CAL* 54 V34-35
Cranberry Gn SE *CAL* 54 V34
Cranberry Sq SE *CAL* 54 V34
Cranberry Way SE *CAL* 54 V34
Crane Rd *MED* 95 H7-8
Cranfield Cir SE *CAL* 54 V34
Cranfield Ct SE *CAL* 54 V34
Cranfield Gdns 100 to 400 SE *CAL* . . . .
. . . . .54 V33-34
Cranfield Gn 100 200 SE *CAL* . . .54 V34
Cranfield Gn SE *CAL* 54 V34
Cranfield Link SE *CAL* 54 V33
Cranfield Mnr SE *CAL* 54 V34

Cranfield Pk SE *CAL* 54 V34
Cranfield Pl SE *CAL* 54 V34
Cranleigh Bay 100 200 SE *CAL* 54 U33-34
Cranleigh Cl SE *CAL* 54 U-V34
Cranleigh Com SE *CAL* 54 U34
Cranleigh Dr SE *CAL* 54 U34
Cranleigh Gdns SE *CAL* 54 U34
Cranleigh Gn SE *CAL* 54 U33-34
Cranleigh Gt SE *CAL* 54 U34
Cranleigh Hts SE *CAL* 54 U34
Cranleigh Mews SE *CAL* 54 U34
Cranleigh Mnr SE *CAL* 54 U34
Cranleigh Pk SE *CAL* 54 U34
Cranleigh Pl SE *CAL* 54 U34
Cranleigh View 100 200 SE *CAL* . .54 U34
Cranleigh Way SE *CAL* 54 U34-35
Cranston Blvd SE *CAL* 54 U33-34 V34
Cranston Dr SE *CAL* 54 U34
Cranston Pl SE *CAL* 54 U34
Cranston Rd SE *CAL* 54 V35
Cranston Way SE *CAL* 54 U-V34
Cranwell Cl SE *CAL* 54 U-V34
Cranwell Cr SE *CAL* 54 U34
Cranwell Gn 100 200 SE *CAL* . .54 U-V35
Cranwell Link SE *CAL* 54 V34
Cranwell Mnr SE *CAL* 54 V34
Cranwell Pl SE *CAL* 54 U-V34
Craven Pl *MED* 95 G5
Crawford Cl *COC* 60 B-C2
Crawford Dr *COC* 60 C2
Crawford Pl *COC* 60 B-C2
Crawford Rd NW *CAL* 27 K11 28 L11
Crawford St *RED* 67 G7-8
Creek Gardens Cl NW *AIR* 68 A2
Creek Gardens Pl NW *AIR* 68 A2-3
Creek Springs Rd NW *AIR* 68 A2
Creek Springs Rise NW *AIR* 68 A2
Creekside Bay NW *AIR* 68 A2
Crescent Av SE *HIG* 77 C3
Crescent Blvd SW *CAL* 36 N-O20
Crescent Dr *BEI* 69 A-B2
Crescent Rd E *OKO* 76 C3
Crescent Rd NW *CAL* . . . .
. . . . . . .6 C91 28 N14-15 O15 29 P15
Crescent Rd W *OKO* 76 C2
Crescent St *DRU* 73 B6
Crestbrook Cr SW *CAL* 25 A12
Crestbrook Pl SW *CAL* 25 A12
Crestbrook Ter SW *CAL* 25 A12-13
Cresthaven Pl 100 to 500 SW *CAL* . . . .
. . . . .25 A-B12
Cresthaven Rise SW *CAL* 25 A12
Cresthaven View SW *CAL* 25 A12
Cresthaven Way SW *CAL* 25 A12
Crestmont Blvd SW *CAL* 25 A-B12
Crestmont Dr SW *CAL* 25 A-B12
Crestmont Way SW *CAL* 25 B12
Creston Cr NW *CAL* 28 L13
Crestridge Gt SW *CAL* 25 A-B12
Crestridge Hts SW *CAL* 25 B13
Crestridge Mews 100 200 SW *CAL* . . . .
. . . . .25 A12-13 B12-13
Crestridge Pl 100 200 SW *CAL* . .25 B12
Crestridge Way SW *CAL* 25 B12
Crestview Estates *RCY* 9 B1
Crestview Rd SW *CAL* 36 N19-20
Crestwood Dr *MED* 95 G6 G7
Crestwood Rd SE *CAL* 44 T22-23
Crimson Cl *CHE* 70 G1
Crimson La *CHE* 70 F1
Crockett Way *MED* 95 H7
Crockford Cr *MED* 92 C3
Crocus Cr *COC* 60 B4
Crocus Rd NW *CAL* 28 L-M11
Crocus St *MED* 94 F2
Crocus Ridge Cr *RCY* . .16 X10 24 X11
Crocus Ridge Dr *RCY* . . .16 W10 X10 24 X11
Cromwell Av NW *CAL* 28 M-N12
Cronquist Dr *RED* 66 H2-3 H3
Crooked Pond Gn *RCY* 33 B20
Crooked Pond Way *RCY* 33 B20
Crooker Ct *BRO* 90 C-D4
Cross Cr NW *CAL* 42 N24
Crowchild Tr NW *CAL* . . . .
. . . . . . .18 E7-8 G9 19 H-I10 27 J-K11
Crowchild Tr SW *CAL* . . .36 L18-20 42 L21
Crowfoot Cir NW *CAL* 18 F8
Crowfoot Cr NW *CAL* 18 F7-8
Crowfoot Gt 100 200 NW *CAL* . . .18 F7
Crowfoot Rd NW *CAL* 18 F7-8
Crowfoot Rise NW *CAL* 18 E-F8
Crowfoot Ter NW *CAL* 18 F7
Crowfoot Way NW *CAL* 18 F8
Crown Av SW *CAL* 36 N20
Croxford Pl NW *AIR* 68 B3
Croydon Rd NW *CAL* 28 N12
Crsytal Beach Bay *CHE* 70 F1-2
Crystal Green Bay *OKO* 76 B4

Crystal Green Cl *OKO* 76 B4
Crystal Green Ct *OKO* 76 B4
Crystal Green Dr *OKO* 76 B4-5
Crystal Green Gr *OKO* 76 B5
Crystal Green Mews *OKO* 76 B4
Crystal Green Mnr *OKO* 76 A-B5
Crystal Green Pl *OKO* 76 B4-5
Crystal Green Pt *OKO* 76 B4
Crystal Green Rise *OKO* 76 B4-5
Crystal Green Way *OKO* 76 B4
Crystal Ridge Bay *OKO* 76 C4
Crystal Ridge Cl *OKO* 76 B-C4
Crystal Ridge Cr *OKO* 76 B4
Crystal Ridge Ct *OKO* 76 B4
Crystal Ridge Dr *OKO* 76 C4
Crystal Ridge Gt *OKO* 76 C4
Crystal Ridge Link *OKO* 76 B4
Crystal Ridge Pl *OKO* 76 B4
Crystal Ridge Pt *OKO* 76 C4
Crystal Ridge Rise *OKO* 76 B-C4
Crystal Ridge Ter *OKO* 76 C4
Crystal Ridge View *OKO* 76 C4
Crystal Ridge Way *OKO* 76 B-C4
Crystal Shores Bay *OKO* 76 B4
Crystal Shores Cr *OKO* 76 A-B3 A-B4
Crystal Shores Ct *OKO* 76 B3-4
Crystal Shores Dr *OKO* 76 B3-4
Crystal Shores Gr *OKO* 76 A-B3
Crystal Shores Hill *OKO* 76 A-B4
Crystal Shores Hts *OKO* 76 A-B4
Crystal Shores La *OKO* 76 B3
Crystal Shores Ldg *OKO* 76 B4
Crystal Shores Mews *OKO* 76 B3
Crystal Shores Mnr *OKO* 76 B4
Crystal Shores Pl *OKO* 76 B4
Crystal Shores Pt *OKO* 76 B4
Crystal Shores Rd *OKO* 76 B3-4
Crystal Shores View *OKO* 76 B4
Cullen Creek Estates *RCY* . . .25 Z15 33 Z16
Culver Rd NW *CAL* 28 M-N12
Cumberland Rd NW *CAL* 28 N12-13
Cummer Pl *BRG* 78 B2-3
Cunliffe Cr *MED* 95 H7
Cunningham Cr *RED* 67 G8
Currie Ct *MED* 95 G-H7
Cuthbert Pl NW *CAL* 28 M12
Cuyler Rd *MED* 95 G7
Cymrie St NW *CAL* 28 N12
Cypress Cl *OLD* 62 C1
Cypress Way *MED* 95 H7
Cyprus Av SW *CAL* 42 L21
Cyprus Cr SW *CAL* 42 L21

D

Daines Av *RED* 67 H9
Dakota Rd W *LET* 86 G4
Dalarna Bay NW *CAL* 19 J10
Dalbeattie Gn NW *CAL* 19 J10
Dalbeattie Hill NW *CAL* 19 J9-10
Dalbrook Bay NW *CAL* 19 H-I9
Dalcastle Cl NW *CAL* 19 H9
Dalcastle Cr NW *CAL* 19 I8-9
Dalcastle Ct NW *CAL* 19 H9
Dalcastle Dr NW *CAL* 19 H9
Dalcastle Hill NW *CAL* 19 H9
Dalcastle Link NW *CAL* 19 H9
Dalcastle Mews 100 to 500 NW *CAL* . . .
. . . . .19 H9
Dalcastle Pl NW *CAL* 19 H-I9
Dalcastle Rise NW *CAL* 19 H9
Dalcastle Way NW *CAL* 19 H9 I8-9
Dalcroft Cr NW *CAL* 19 I-J9
Dalcroft Hill NW *CAL* 19 J9
Dale Cl *RED* 67 H9
Dalford Hill NW *CAL* 19 I9-10
Dalford Rd NW *CAL* 19 I10
Dalgetty Bay 100 200 NW *CAL* .19 I-J10
Dalgetty Dr NW *CAL* 19 J10
Dalgetty Hill NW *CAL* 19 I-J10
Dalgetty Pl NW *CAL* 19 J10
Dalgetty Village NW *CAL* 19 I10
Dalgleish Bay 100 to 300 NW *CAL* .19 I10
Dalgleish Rd NW *CAL* 19 I-J10
Dalham Cr NW *CAL* 19 I10
Dalhart Hill NW *CAL* 19 I9
Dalhart Rd NW *CAL* 19 I9 J10
Dalhousie Cr NW *CAL* 19 I10
Dalhousie Ct W *LET* 87 H-J5
Dalhousie Dr NW *CAL* . . .19 H-I9 I-J10
Dalhousie Rd NW *CAL* 19 I9-10
Dalhousie Rd W *LET* 87 H5
Dalhurst Cr NW *CAL* 19 I9
Dalhurst Gt NW *CAL* 19 I9
Dalhurst Pl NW *CAL* 19 J9
Dalhurst Way NW *CAL* 19 I-J9
Dalkeith Hill NW *CAL* 19 J10
Dallaire Av SW *CAL* 41 K21 42 L21

Dallyn St NW *CAL* 19 J10
Dalmarnock Cr NW *CAL* 19 J9-10
Dalmarnock Gn NW *CAL* 19 J9-10
Dalmead Cr NW *CAL* 19 J10
Dalmeny Bay 100 to 300 NW *CAL* . . .19 I9
Dalmeny Gt NW *CAL* 19 I9
Dalmeny Hill NW *CAL* 19 I8-9
Dalridge Hill NW *CAL* 19 I9-10
Dalroy Cr NW *CAL* 19 J10
Dalrymple Cr NW *CAL* 19 I9
Dalrymple Gn NW *CAL* 19 I9
Dalrymple Hill NW *CAL* 19 I9
Dalrymple Way NW *CAL* 19 I9
Dalsby Gn NW *CAL* 19 J9
Dalsby Rd NW *CAL* 19 J9-10
Dalton Bay NW *CAL* 19 J10
Dalton Cl *RED* 67 G9
Dalton Dr NW *CAL* 19 J9-10
Dalwood Way NW *CAL* 19 I9
Dalzell Pl NW *CAL* 19 I9
Dandell Cl *RED* 67 H9
Daniel Cl *RED* 67 H9
Daniel Cr *RED* 67 H9
Danielle Dr *RED* 67 G9-10
Danloe St NE *CAL* 29 R15
Dann Cl *RED* 67 H-J9
Daqing Av SW *CAL* 6 C92 7 D92 37 F16
Darling Cr *RED* 67 H9
Dartmouth Rd SE *CAL* 37 Q19 Q-R18
Davies St *INN* 63 D2
Davis Cl *RED* 67 H8-9
Davis Pl *OLD* 62 C1-2
Davison Dr *RED* 67 G-H9 H9
Dawe Cl *RED* 67 H9
Dawes Rd SE *CAL* 54 T35
Dawson St *RED* 67 G8-9
Day Cl *RED* 67 G8-9
Day St *MED* 95 F-G8
Daykin St *RED* 67 G9-10
De Foras Cl NW *HIG* 77 A1
De Havilland Blvd *MED* 94 F-G1
Decalta Rd *TVY* 74 D3 E3-4
Deer Bay SE *CAL* 50 T29
Deer Pl *CAN* 58 F3
Deer Pl SE *CAL* 50 T29
Deer St *BAN* 57 C-D2
Deer Lane Bay SE *CAL* 50 T30
Deer Lane Cl SE *CAL* 50 T30
Deer Lane Pl SE *CAL* 50 T30
Deer Lane Rd SE *CAL* 50 T30
Deer Park Pl 100 to 300 SE *CAL* . .54 T31
Deer Park Rd SE *CAL* 54 T31
Deer Park Way SE *CAL* 54 T31
Deer Ridge Cl SE *CAL* 49 S29-30
Deer Ridge Ct SE *CAL* 49 S30
Deer Ridge Dr SE *CAL* 49 S29-30
Deer Ridge La SE *CAL* 49 S30
Deer Ridge Mews SE *CAL* 49 S30
Deer Ridge Pl 100 200 SE *CAL* . .49 S30
Deer Ridge Way SE *CAL* 49 S28
Deer River Bay SE *CAL* 50 T29
Deer River Cir SE *CAL* 50 T29
Deer River Gn SE *CAL* 50 T29
Deer River Gt SE *CAL* 50 T29
Deer River Pl 100 200 SE *CAL* . .50 T29
Deer Run Bay SE *CAL* 54 T31
Deer Run Blvd SE *CAL* 50 T29-30
Deer Run Cl SE *CAL* 54 T31
Deer Run Cr SE *CAL* 54 T31
Deer Run Dr SE *CAL* 54 T31
Deer Run Pl SE *CAL* 54 T31
Deer Side Dr SE *CAL* 54 T-U31
Deer Side Pl 100 to 600 SE *CAL* . .54 T31
Deer Side Rd SE *CAL* 54 T31
Deerbow Cir SE *CAL* 53 S31
Deerbow Ct SE *CAL* 53 S31
Deerbow Gt SE *CAL* 53 S31
Deerbow Pl SE *CAL* 53 S31 54 T31
Deerbrook Bay SE *CAL* 54 U31
Deerbrook Cr SE *CAL* 54 U31
Deerbrook Ct SE *CAL* 50 U30 54 U31
Deerbrook Mews SE *CAL* 54 U31
Deerbrook Pl SE *CAL* 50 T30
Deerbrook Rd SE *CAL* 50 T-U30
Deercliff Rd SE *CAL* 50 T29
Deercrest Cl SE *CAL* 49 S30 50 T30
Deercrest Pl SE *CAL* 50 T30
Deercrest Way SE *CAL* 50 T30
Deercroft Pl 100 to 300 SE *CAL* . .54 T-U31
Deercroft Way SE *CAL* 54 T31
Deercross Pl SE *CAL* 50 T30
Deercross Rd SE *CAL* 50 T30
Deercross Way SE *CAL* 50 T30
Deerfield Bay SE *CAL* 49 S30
Deerfield Cir SE *CAL* 49 S30
Deerfield Ct SE *CAL* 49 S30
Deerfield Dr SE *CAL* 49 S30 50 T30
Deerfield Gdns 100 to 400 SE *CAL* . . . .
. . . . .49 S30 50 T30

Deerfield Gn SE *CAL* 49 S30 50 T30
Deerfield Mnr SE *CAL* 49 S30
Deerfield Pl SE *CAL* 49 S30
Deerfield Ter SE *CAL* 49 S30
Deerfield Village SE *CAL* 49 S30
Deerfoot Tr *RCY* 14 T1
Deerfoot Tr NE *CAL* . . . .
. . . . . . .14 T3-4 21 Q10 Q-R7 29 R13 S15
Deerfoot Tr SE *CAL* 38 T17 T19-20
. . . . .43 R21-25 49 R26 50 U28 54 V31
Deermeade Bay SE *CAL* 50 T30
Deermeade Pl SE *CAL* 50 T30
Deermeade Rd SE *CAL* 50 T30
Deermont Ct 100 to 500 SE *CAL* .49 S30
Deermont Pl SE *CAL* 49 S30
Deermont Rd SE *CAL* 49 S30
Deermont Way SE *CAL* 49 S30
Deermoss Bay SE *CAL* 50 T29
Deermoss Cr SE *CAL* 50 T29-30
Deermoss Pl SE *CAL* 50 T29-30
Deerpath Ct 100 500 600 SE *CAL* .49 S30
Deerpath Rd SE *CAL* 49 S30
Deerpoint Gdns SE *CAL* 49 S30
Deerpoint La SE *CAL* 49 S30
Deerpoint Rd SE *CAL* 49 R-S30
Deersaxon Cir SE *CAL* 49 S30 53 S31
Deersaxon Gt SE *CAL* 49 S30
Deersaxon Rd SE *CAL* 49 S30 53 S31
Deerview Ct 100 200 SE *CAL* .49 S29-30
Deerview Dr SE *CAL* 49 S29-30
Deerview Hts SE *CAL* 49 S29
Deerview Pl SE *CAL* 49 S30
Deerview Ter SE *CAL* 49 S29
Deerview Way SE *CAL* 49 S29-30
Deerwood Bay SE *CAL* 50 T30
Deerwood Rd SE *CAL* 50 T30
Del Monica Bay NE *CAL* 31 Z13
Del Monica Pl NE *CAL* 31 Z13
Del Monica Villas NE *CAL* 31 Y13
Del Ray Cl NE *CAL* 31 Z13
Del Ray Cr NE *CAL* 31 Z14
Del Ray Ct NE *CAL* 31 Z14
Del Ray Gt NE *CAL* 31 Z13-14
Del Ray Pl NE *CAL* 31 Z13
Del Ray Rd NE *CAL* 31 Z13-14
Del Rio Pl NE *CAL* 31 Y13
Delburne Rd *RED* 67 L7 L9
Deltor Cl *RED* 67 H9
Dempsey St *RED* 67 G9
Denise St *BRG* 78 B2
Denison Cr *RED* 67 H8-9
Denmark Cr *RED* 67 H9
Denovan Cr *RED* 67 G8-9
Densmore Cr *RED* 67 H9
Dentoom Cl *RED* 67 H9
Depalme St *RED* 67 H8
Deschner Cl *RED* 67 H10
Destination Pl *OLD* 62 D2
Dial St *INN* 63 C3
Diamond Bay 100 to 600 SE *CAL* .49 S28
Diamond Cr *BLD* 75 C7
Diamond Ct 100 to 800 SE *CAL* . .49 S28
Diamond Dr SE *CAL* 49 S28
Diamond Pt 100 200 SE *CAL* . .49 S27-28
Diamond St *RED* 67 G8
Diamond St Cl *RED* 67 G8-9
Diamond Ter SE *CAL* 49 S27-28
Diamond View SE *CAL* 49 S27-28
Diamond Willow Pt *RCY* 33 Z20
Dickenson Cl *RED* 67 G8
Dickenson Cr *RED* 67 G8
Dickson Stevenson Tr N *AIR* 68 A3
Diebert Cl SW *HIG* 77 C1
Dieppe Av N *CAL* 36 L19
Dieppe Blvd S *LET* 88 F10 F10-11
Dietz Cl *RED* 67 H9
Dillon Cl *RED* 67 H9
Dingman Cl *TVY* 74 D4
Discovery Dr SW *CAL* 34 F-G20
Discovery Hts SW *CAL* 34 F-G20
Discovery Pl 100 to 300 SW *CAL*34 F-G20
Discovery Rise SW *CAL* 34 F20
Discovery Ridge Bay 100 to 400 SW
CAL 34 D19-20
Discovery Ridge Blvd SW *CAL* 34 F20
Discovery Ridge Cir SW *CAL* 34 D20
Discovery Ridge Cr SW *CAL* 34 F20
Discovery Ridge Ct SW *CAL* 34 F20
Discovery Ridge Cv SW *CAL* 34 E-F20
Discovery Ridge Gdns SW *CAL* 34 E20
Discovery Ridge Gn SW *CAL* 34 E20
Discovery Ridge Gt SW *CAL* 34 E20
Discovery Ridge Heath SW *CAL* .34 E-F20
Discovery Ridge Hill SW *CAL* 34 E20
Discovery Ridge La SW *CAL* 34 E20
Discovery Ridge Ldg SW *CAL* 34 E20
Discovery Ridge Link SW *CAL* 34 F20
Discovery Ridge Mews SW *CAL* . . .34 E20
Discovery Ridge Mnr SW *CAL* 34 E20

Discovery Ridge Mt SW *CAL* 34 E20
Discovery Ridge Pk SW *CAL* 34 E20
Discovery Ridge Pl SW *CAL* 34 D19
Discovery Ridge Pt SW *CAL* 34 F20
Discovery Ridge Rd SW *CAL* 34 F20
Discovery Ridge Rise SW *CAL* 34 F20
Discovery Ridge Ter 100 200 SW *CAL* . . .
. . . . .34 D20
Discovery Ridge View SW *CAL* . . .34 F20
Discovery Ridge Way SW *CAL* .34 E19-20
Discovery Valley Cv SW *CAL* 34 F20
Discovery Woods Vill SW *CAL* 34 F20
Division Av N *MED* 92 A-D4
Division Av S *MED* 94 F4
Dixon Av *RED* 67 H8
Dixon Cl *RED* 67 H8-9
Dixon Cr *RED* 67 H8 H8-9
Doan Av *RED* 67 G9
Dobler Av *RED* 67 G8
Dobson Cl *RED* 67 H9
Dodds St *RED* 67 G-H8 G-H9
Dodoge Av *RED* 67 G9
Dogwood Av *CAN* 58 A2-3 B3
Dogwood Cr *CAL* 38 U18
Dogwood Way NW *CAL* 26 D11-12
Doherty Cl *RED* 67 H10
Doherty Pl NW *CAL* 10 F5
Dolan Cl *RED* 67 G9
Dominion St *MED* 93 E6
Don Ethell Blvd SW *CAL* 41 K21
Donald Cl *RED* 67 H9
Doncaster Av *RED* 67 G10
Donlevy Av *RED* 67 G9
Donnelly Cr *RED* 67 H9
Doran Cr *RED* 67 G9
Dorchester Av *RED* 67 G9-10
Dorchester Av SW *CAL* 36 N18
Douglas Av *RED* 67 H8-9
Douglas Ct *BRO* 90 C2
Douglas Ct *MED* 92 D3
Douglas Pl *OLD* 62 C1-2
Douglas Glen Bay 100 200 SE *CAL* . . . .
. . . . .50 T27
Douglas Glen Blvd SE *CAL* 50 T27
Douglas Glen Cir SE *CAL* 50 T26
Douglas Glen Cl 100 to 400 SE *CAL* . . .
. . . . .50 T27
Douglas Glen Com SE *CAL* 50 T27
Douglas Glen Cr SE *CAL* 50 T27
Douglas Glen Ct 100 200 SE *CAL* .50 T27
Douglas Glen Gdns 100 to 300 SE *CAL* .
. . . . .49 S26-27 50 T26-27
Douglas Glen Gn SE *CAL* 50 T27
Douglas Glen Gr SE *CAL* 50 T27
Douglas Glen Heath 100 to 300 SE *CAL*
. . . . .50 T27
Douglas Glen Hts SE *CAL* 50 T26-27
Douglas Glen Mews SE *CAL* 50 T27
Douglas Glen Mnr 100 200 SW *CAL* . . .
. . . . .50 T27
Douglas Glen Pk SE *CAL* 50 T-U27
Douglas Glen Pl SE *CAL* 50 T27
Douglas Glen Pt 100 to 600 SE *CAL* . . .
. . . . .49 S27 50 T27
Douglas Glen View SE *CAL* 50 T27
Douglas Park Blvd SE *CAL* 50 U28-29
Douglas Park Cl SE *CAL* 50 U28
Douglas Park Mews SE *CAL* 50 T-U28
Douglas Park Mnr SE *CAL* 50 U28-29
Douglas Park Pl SE *CAL* 50 U28-29
Douglas Park View 100 to 400 SE *CAL* .
. . . . .50 U29
Douglas Range Rd SE *CAL* .49 S28 50 T28
Douglas Ridge Blvd SE *CAL* 50 V28
Douglas Ridge Cir SE *CAL* 50 V29
Douglas Ridge Cl SE *CAL* 50 V28-29
Douglas Ridge Gn SE *CAL* 50 V29
Douglas Ridge Gr SE *CAL* 50 V29
Douglas Ridge Link SE *CAL* 50 U-V20
Douglas Ridge Mews 100 to 400 SE
CAL 50 V28
Douglas Ridge Pl 100 to 300 SE *CAL* . .
. . . . .50 V29
Douglas Ridge View SE *CAL* 50 V29
Douglas Ridge Way SE *CAL* 50 V29
Douglas Shore SE *CAL* 50 T28
Douglas Woods Bay SE *CAL* . . .50 V28-29
Douglas Woods Cl 100 200 SE *CAL* . . .
. . . . .50 U28
Douglas Woods Ct 100 to 300 SE *CAL* .
. . . . .50 U28
Douglas Woods Dr SE *CAL* 50 T-U28
Douglas Woods Gdns SE *CAL* 50 U28
Douglas Woods Gr SE *CAL* 50 U-V28
Douglas Woods Hill SE *CAL* 50 U-V28
Douglas Woods Hts SE *CAL* 50 U-V28
Douglas Woods Link SE *CAL* 50 T-U28
Douglas Woods Mews 100 to 500 SE
CAL 50 U-V28

Douglas Woods Mnr SE *CAL* 50 U28
Douglas Woods Pk SE *CAL* 50 U28
Douglas Woods Pl 100 to 800 SE *CAL* . .
. . . . .50 T-U28
Douglas Woods Pt 100 200 SE *CAL* . . . .
. . . . .50 U28
Douglas Woods Rd SE *CAL* 50 U28
Douglas Woods Rise SE *CAL* 50 U28
Douglas Woods Ter SE *CAL* 50 U28
Douglas Woods View SE *CAL* 50 U28
Douglas Woods Way SE *CAL* 50 U28
Douglasbank Bay 100 to 300 SE *CAL* . .
. . . . .50 T27-28
Douglasbank Cr SE *CAL* 50 T28
Douglasbank Ct 100 to 400 SE *CAL* . . .
. . . . .50 T27-28
Douglasbank Dr SE *CAL* 50 T27-28
Douglasbank Gdns SE *CAL* 50 T28
Douglasbank Gn 100 to 300 SE *CAL* . . .
. . . . .50 T27
Douglasbank Mews 100 200 SE *CAL* . . .
. . . . .50 T28
Douglasbank Pl 100 to 300 SE *CAL* . . .
. . . . .50 T28
Douglasbank Pt SE *CAL* 49 S27
Douglasbank Rise SE *CAL* 50 T27-28
Douglasdale Blvd SE *CAL* . . .50 T-U28 V28
Douglasdale Cr SE *CAL* 50 U-V29
Douglasdale Ct 100 to 400 SE *CAL* . . .
. . . . .50 U-V29
Douglasdale Pt SE *CAL* 50 U-V29
Douglasview Bay SE *CAL* 50 U28
Douglasview Blvd SE *CAL* 50 U28-29
Douglasview Cir SE *CAL* 50 U28-29
Douglasview Ct 100 200 SE *CAL* .50 V29
Douglasview Pk SE *CAL* 50 U28
Douglasview Rd SE *CAL* 50 U-V29
Douglasview Rise SE *CAL* 50 U28-29
Dovely Cr SE *CAL* 38 U19
Dovely Ct SE *CAL* 38 U19
Dovely Pk SE *CAL* 38 U19
Dovely Pl SE *CAL* 38 U19-20
Dovely Way SE *CAL* 38 U19
Dover Cr SE *CAL* 38 V-W19
Dover Pt SE *CAL* 38 U20
Dover Rd SE *CAL* 38 V19
Dover Meadow Cl SE *CAL* 38 V19
Dover Ridge Bay SE *CAL* 38 U19-20
Dover Ridge Cl SE *CAL* 38 V19
Dover Ridge Cr SE *CAL* 38 V19
Dover Ridge Dr SE *CAL* 38 U-V20 V19
Dover Ridge Pl SE *CAL* 38 U-V19
Doverbrook Rd SE *CAL* 38 U20
Dovercliffe Cl SE *CAL* 38 V19
Dovercliffe Rd SE *CAL* 38 V19
Dovercliffe Way SE *CAL* 38 V19
Dovercrest Dr SE *CAL* 38 U20
Dovercrest Pl 100 200 SE *CAL* .38 U-V20
Dovercrest Rd SE *CAL* 38 U20
Dovercrest Way SE *CAL* 38 U20
Dovercroft Pl SE *CAL* 38 V20
Dovercroft Rd SE *CAL* 38 U-V20
Doverdale Cr SE *CAL* 38 V18-19
Doverdale Mews SE *CAL* 38 V18-19
Doverglen Cr SE *CAL* 38 T-U20 U19-20
Doverglen Pl SE *CAL* 38 T-U20
Doverglen Pl 100 200 SE *CAL* . . . . . .
. . . . .38 T19-20 U20
Doverthorn Bay SE *CAL* 38 U19
Doverthorn Cl SE *CAL* 38 U19
Doverthorn Pl SE *CAL* 38 U19
Doverthorn Rd SE *CAL* 38 U19
Doverthorn Way SE *CAL* 38 U19
Dovertree Pl SE *CAL* 38 W18
Doverview Cr SE *CAL* 38 V20
Doverview Dr SE *CAL* 38 V19-20
Doverview Pl SE *CAL* 38 V19
Doverview Rd SE *CAL* 38 U-V20
Doverville Cr SE *CAL* 38 V-W18 V-W19
Doverville Way SE *CAL* 38 W18
Doverwood Pl SE *CAL* 38 V-W18
Dovista Ct SE *CAL* 38 U19
Dowd Cl *RED* 67 G10
Dowler St *RED* 67 H9
Downey Bay *OKO* 76 C3-4
Downey Gn *OKO* 76 C3
Downey Pl 100 to 300 500 600 800 *OKO*
. . . . .76 B3 C3-4
Downey Rd *OKO* 76 C3-4
Downing Cl *RED* 67 H10
Dr Anderson Park St *BRO* 90 C-D4
Dragoon St SW *CAL* 41 J21
Drake Cl *RED* 67 G8
Drever Cl *RED* 67 G9
Drummond Av *RED* 67 G-H10
Drummond Cl *RED* 67 G-H10
Drury Av NE *CAL* 29 R15

Dubois Cr *RED* **67** H10
Duckering Cl *RED* **67** H-J9
Dufferin Blvd SE *CAL* **51** X27
Dufferin Pl SE *CAL* **51** X26
Duffield Av *RED* **67** H9
Duffy Cl *RED* **67** G-H9
Dumas Cr *RED* **67** G-H9
Duncan Cr *RED* **67** G-H8
Duncan Pl *OLD* **62** C1
Dundee St *MED* **95** F5
Dunham Cl *RED* **67** H9
Dunham La *TVY* **74** C2-3
Dunham Pt *TVY* **74** C3
Dunkirk St S *LET* **88** F10-11
Dunlop St *RED* **67** H8
Dunmore Rd *MED* **95** G-H6 H-J7
Dunn Cl *RED* **67** G9
Dunning Cl *RED* **67** H8
Dunning Cr *RED* **67** H8
Durand Cr *RED* **67** G10
Durham Av SW *CAL* **36** N-O18
Durie Cl *RED* **67** H9
Duston Cr *RED* **67** H9-10
Duston St *RED* **67** H9
Duval Cl *RED* **67** G9
Duval Cr *RED* **67** G9
Dynes St *RED* **67** H10

E

Eagle Cr *BAN* **57** C2-3
Eagle Hts *CAN* **59** E6
Eagle Ldg *CAN* **59** E7
Eagle Pl N *LET* **84** B-C10
Eagle Pt *CAN* **59** E6
Eagle Rd N *LET* **84** B9-10
Eagle Birth Rd *MED* **94** H4
Eagle Butte Ranch Rd *RCY* **24** W-X11
Eagle Crest Pl SW *CAL* **42** M23
Eagle Ridge Dr SW *CAL* **42** M-N23
Eagle Ridge Pl SW *CAL* **42** M-N23
Eagle Terrace *CAN* **59** E6 E6-7
Eagle View Gt *COC* **61** B7
Eagle View Hts *COC* **61** B7
Eagle View Pl *COC* **61** B7
Eagleview Ct *MED* **94** H-J2
Eagleview Pl *MED* **94** J1-2
Eagleview Pl NW *HIG* **77** A2
Eakins Cr *RED* **67** G-H8
Eamon Rd NW *CAL* **17** C6 **18** D6
Earl Ct *BRO* **90** A3
Earl Grey Cr SW *CAL* **36** O18
East Cl *RED* **67** H8
East Chestermere Dr *CHE* **70** D-F3
East Glen Av *MED* **95** H8
East Glen Cr *MED* **95** H8
East Glen Ct *MED* **95** H8
East Glen Dr *MED* **95** H8
East Glen Pl *MED* **95** H8
East Glen St *MED* **95** H8
East Hangar Rd NE *CAL* . . .**22** T10 **30** T11
East Lake Av NE *AIR* **68** B4 **69** B5
East Lake Blvd NE *AIR* **68** B4 C4 **69** A-B5 B5
East Lake Blvd SE *AIR* **69** C-E5
East Lake Cir NE *AIR* **69** B-C5
East Lake Cr NE *AIR* . .**68** B4 B-C4 C4 **69** B5
East Lake Dr NE *AIR* **69** B5
East Lake Gn NE *AIR* **68** B4
East Lake Gt SE *AIR* **68** C4
East Lake Hill NE *AIR* **69** C5
East Lake Link NE *AIR* **68** B4
East Lake Ramp NE *AIR* **68** B4
East Lake Rd *STM* **71** C3-4
East Lake Rd NE *AIR* **68** C4 **69** B-C5 C5
East Lake Way NE *AIR* **68** B4
East Lakeview Pl 300 400 *CHE* . . .**70** E3
East Lakeview Rd *CHE* **70** E3 F2-3
East Park Pl *BRG* **78** C3
East Pine Rd *STM* **71** E3-4
East Ridge Blvd *CHE* **70** F5
East Ridge Rd *STM* **71** D3-4
Eastbrook Bay NW *CAL* **90** B-C3
Eastbrook Dr *BRO* **90** C3
Eastbrook Way *BRO* **90** B3
Easterbrook Pl SE *AIR* **68** C4
Eastman Cr *RED* **67** G8
Eastwood Cl *RED* **67** G-H7
Eastwood Cr *RED* **67** G7
Eau Claire Av SW *CAL* **6** B92 **36** O16
Eberglen Gr SW *CAL* **52** L32
Ebert Av *RED* **67** G7
Ebert Cl *RED* **67** G7
Echlin Ct *BRG* **78** B2
Echlin Dr *BRG* **78** B2
Edcath Bay NW *CAL* **19** J8
Edcath Ct NW *CAL* **19** J-K8
Edcath Mews NW *CAL* **19** J-K8
Edcath Pl 100 200 NW *CAL* **19** J8

Edcath Rd NW *CAL* **19** J8
Edcath Rise NW *CAL* **19** J8
Edelweiss Cr NW *CAL* **19** K8
Edelweiss Ct NW *CAL* **19** K8
Edelweiss Dr NW *CAL* **19** J8-9 K8-9
Edelweiss Pl 100 to 300 NW *CAL* **19** J-K8
Edelweiss Pt NW *CAL* **19** J-K9
Edelweiss Rd NW *CAL* **19** J-K8
Edendale Cr NW *CAL* **19** J8
Edendale Cr SE *AIR* **68** C3-4
Edendale Pl NW *CAL* **19** J8
Edendale Way NW *CAL* **19** J8
Edenstone Pl NW *CAL* **19** J8
Edenstone Rd NW *CAL* **19** J8
Edenstone View NW *CAL* **19** J8
Edenstone Way NW *CAL* **19** J8
Edenwold Cr NW *CAL* **19** K8
Edenwold Dr NW *CAL* **19** J-K8
Edenwold Gn NW *CAL* **19** K8
Edenwold Hts NW *CAL* **19** K7-8
Edenwold Pl NW *CAL* **19** K8
Edforth Cr NW *CAL* **19** J8
Edforth Pl 100 to 300 NW *CAL* . . .**19** J7-8
Edforth Rd NW *CAL* **19** J-K8
Edforth Way NW *CAL* **19** J8
Edgar Av *TVY* **74** D2-3
Edgar Industrial Av *RED* **64** A-B2
Edgar Industrial Bend *RED* **64** C2
Edgar Industrial Cl *RED* **64** A-B3
Edgar Industrial Cr *RED* **64** A-B2
Edgar Industrial Ct *RED* **64** B-C2
Edgar Industrial Dr *RED* **64** B2-3 C2 D2
Edgar Industrial Gn *RED* **64** B2
Edgar Industrial Link *RED* **64** B2
Edgar Industrial Pl *RED* **64** B3
Edgar Industrial Way *RED* **64** B-C2
Edge Cl *RED* **67** G8
Edgebank Cir NW *CAL* **19** J-K7
Edgebank Pl 100 to 700 NW *CAL* **19** J-K7
Edgebrook Blvd NW *CAL* **19** K6
Edgebrook Cir NW *CAL* **19** K7
Edgebrook Cl NW *CAL* **19** K7
Edgebrook Ct 100 200 NW *CAL* . . .**19** K7
Edgebrook Cv NW *CAL* **19** K6
Edgebrook Dr NW *CAL* **19** K6-7
Edgebrook Gdns 100 to 300 NW *CAL* . .
. . . .**19** K7
Edgebrook Gn NW *CAL* **19** K7
Edgebrook Gr 100 to 400 NW *CAL* .**20** L6
Edgebrook Hts NW *CAL* **19** K7
Edgebrook Ldg NW *CAL* **19** K6
Edgebrook Mews NW *CAL* **19** K7
Edgebrook Pk NW *CAL* **19** K6 **20** L6
Edgebrook Pl NW *CAL* **19** K7
Edgebrook Pt NW *CAL* **19** K7
Edgebrook Rd NW *CAL* **19** K7
Edgebrook Rise NW *CAL* **19** K7 **20** L7
Edgebrook Ter NW *CAL* **19** K7
Edgebrook View NW *CAL* . . .**19** K7 **20** L7
Edgebrook Way NW *CAL* **19** K7
Edgeburn Cr NW *CAL* **19** I7
Edgeburn Gdns NW *CAL* **19** I7
Edgeburn La NW *CAL* **19** I7
Edgeburn Pl NW *CAL* **19** I7
Edgebyne Cr NW *CAL* **19** I-J7
Edgedale Ct NW *CAL* **19** I8-9
Edgedale Dr NW *CAL* **19** I8
Edgedale Gdns 100 to 300 NW *CAL* . . .
. . . .**19** I-J8
Edgedale Pl NW *CAL* **19** I8-9
Edgedale Rd NW *CAL* **19** I8-9
Edgedale Way NW *CAL* **19** I8-9
Edgeford Pl NW *CAL* **19** I8
Edgeford Rd NW *CAL* **19** I8
Edgeford Way NW *CAL* **19** I8
Edgehill Bay NW *CAL* **19** I8
Edgehill Cl NW *CAL* **19** I8
Edgehill Cr NW *CAL* **19** I8
Edgehill Ct NW *CAL* **19** I8
Edgehill Dr NW *CAL* **19** I8
Edgehill Mews NW *CAL* **19** I8
Edgehill Pl 100 200 NW *CAL* **19** I8
Edgehill Rise NW *CAL* **19** I8
Edgeland Bay NW *CAL* **19** I8
Edgeland Cl NW *CAL* **19** I7-8
Edgeland Cr NW *CAL* **19** I7-8
Edgeland Ct NW *CAL* **19** I8
Edgeland Gt NW *CAL* **19** I7
Edgeland Mews NW *CAL* **19** I7
Edgeland Rd NW *CAL* **19** I7-8
Edgeland Rise NW *CAL* **19** I7
Edgemont Bay 100 to 600 NW *CAL* **19** J9
Edgemont Blvd NW *CAL* **19** I-J9 J-K7
Edgemont Ct NW *CAL* **19** J-K9
Edgemont Dr NW *CAL* **19** J9
Edgemont Hill NW *CAL* **19** J9
Edgemont Pl 100 to 300 NW *CAL* . .**19** J9
Edgemont Rd NW *CAL* **19** J9
Edgemont Rise NW *CAL* **19** J9

Edgemont Estate Dr NW *CAL* **19** J8-9
Edgemont Estate Rd NW *CAL* . . .**19** J8-9
Edgepark Blvd NW *CAL* **19** I7
Edgepark Cr NW *CAL* **19** I7
Edgepark Ct NW *CAL* **19** I7
Edgepark Dr NW *CAL* **19** I7
Edgepark Mews NW *CAL* **19** I-J7
Edgepark Pl NW *CAL* **19** I6-7
Edgepark Rd NW *CAL* **19** I-J6
Edgepark Rise NW *CAL* **19** I7
Edgepark Village NW *CAL* **19** I7
Edgepark Way NW *CAL* **19** I6 I-J7
Edgeridge Bay NW *CAL* **19** I6
Edgeridge Cir NW *CAL* **19** I6
Edgeridge Cl NW *CAL* **19** I6
Edgeridge Ct NW *CAL* **19** I7
Edgeridge Gdns 100 to 300 NW *CAL* . .
. . . .**19** K6
Edgeridge Gn NW *CAL* **19** J-K6
Edgeridge Gt NW *CAL* **19** J-K6
Edgeridge Mews NW *CAL* **19** K6
Edgeridge Pk NW *CAL* **19** J-K6
Edgeridge Pl 100 200 NW *CAL* . . .**19** J6-7
Edgeridge Ter NW *CAL* **19** K6
Edgeridge View NW *CAL* **19** K6
Edgeridge Way NW *CAL* **19** I7
Edgevalley Cir NW *CAL* **19** K7
Edgevalley Cl NW *CAL* **19** K7
Edgevalley Dr NW *CAL* **19** J7
Edgevalley Gdns NW *CAL* **19** J7
Edgevalley Gn 100 200 NW *CAL* . . .**19** J7
Edgevalley Ldg NW *CAL* **19** J7
Edgevalley Mews 100 to 300 NW *CAL* . .
. . . .**19** J7
Edgevalley Mnr NW *CAL* **19** J7
Edgevalley Pl NW *CAL* **19** J7
Edgevalley View NW *CAL* **19** J7
Edgevalley Way NW *CAL* **19** J-K7
Edgeview Dr NW *CAL* **19** J7
Edgeview Hts NW *CAL* **19** J7
Edgeview Pl 100 to 400 NW *CAL* .**19** I-J7
Edgeview Rd NW *CAL* **19** J7
Edgewood Blvd W *LET* **86** F4
Edgewood Cr W *LET* **86** F4
Edgewood Dr NW *CAL* **19** I8
Edgewood Pl NW *CAL* **19** I8
Edgewood Pl W *LET* **86** F4
Edgewood Rise NW *CAL* **19** I8
Edgington Av *RED* **67** G-H7
Edinburgh Rd SW *CAL* **36** N-O20
Edis Cl *RED* **67** G8
Edison Cr SW *CAL* **36** O19-20
Edmonton Tr NE *AIR* **68** B4
Edmonton Tr NE *CAL* . . . .
. . . .**7** E91-92 **29** P13-16 Q11-12 Q15 **37** Q16
Edmonton Tr SE *AIR* **68** C4
Edmund Way SE *AIR* **68** D3-4
Edward Av *TVY* **74** C3
Edward Cl *TVY* **74** C3
Edward St NE *CAL* **29** R-S15
Edwards Cr *RED* **67** G-H7 G-H8
Edwards Way NW *AIR* **68** B2-3
Edworthy St SW *CAL* **27** I15
Eggleton St *RED* **67** H7-8
Eide Park Dr *BRO* **90** C4
Elbow Dr SW *CAL* . . . .
. . . .**36** O18-20 **42** N25 O21-24 **48** N26-28 N-O29
Elbow Rise *BRG* **78** A3
Elbow Park La SW *CAL* **36** O19
Elbow River Cir *RCY* **32** X19
Elbow River Ct *RCY* **32** Y19
Elbow River Dr *RCY* **32** W-X19 Y19
Elbow River Pt *RCY* **32** W18-19
Elbow River Rd *RCY* **32** W-X19
Elder Av *MED* **95** H8
Elder St *RED* **67** G7-8
Elderwood Pl SE *AIR* **68** D4
Eldorado Cl NE *CAL* **31** Z14
Eldorado Pl 100 to 400 NE *CAL* .**31** Y-Z14
Eldorado Rd SE *AIR* **68** C3
Eldridge Cr *RED* **67** G8
Eldridge Rise SE *AIR* **68** D3
Elevator St *RED* **95** F6
Elgin Av SE *CAL* **54** W32
Elgin Bay SE *CAL* **54** V-W32
Elgin Cr SE *CAL* **54** W32
Elgin Ct SE *CAL* **54** W32-33
Elgin Dr SE *CAL* **54** W32
Elgin Gdns SE *CAL* **54** W32
Elgin Gn SE *CAL* **54** V32
Elgin Gt SE *CAL* **54** W32
Elgin Heath SE *CAL* **54** W32
Elgin Mews SE *CAL* **54** V32
Elgin Mnr SE *CAL* **54** W32
Elgin Pl SE *CAL* **54** W32-33
Elgin Rise SE *CAL* **54** W32-33
Elgin St SE *CAL* **54** W32
Elgin View SE *CAL* **54** W32-33

Elgin Way SE *CAL* **54** V-W32
Elgin Hill Rd *DRU* **73** C6
Elgin Park Com SE *CAL* **54** W32
Elgin Park Hill SE *CAL* **54** W32
Elgin Park Rd SE *CAL* **54** W32
Eline St *RED* **67** H8
Elizabeth Rd SW *CAL* **36** N20
Elizabeth St *OKO* **76** C2-3
Elizabeth St SE *CAL* **37** Q-R18
Elizabeth Way SE *AIR* **68** C4
Elk Cir *BAN* **57** D2
Elk St *BAN* **57** D2
Elk St *OKO* **76** C2
Elk Hill Hill SE *AIR* **68** C3
Elk Run Blvd *CAN* **59** F7
Elkin Cl *RED* **67** G8
Elkton Dr SW *CAL* **34** F-G19
Elkton Pl SW *CAL* **34** G19
Elkton Way SW *CAL* **34** G19
Ellenwood Dr *RED* **67** G-H8
Elliot Cl *RED* **67** H8
Elliot Rd S *LET* **88** G11-12
Elliott St *MED* **95** H8
Ellis Cl *RED* **67** G8
Ellis Cr SE *HIG* **77** C3
Ellis St *RED* **67** G7-8
Elm Av *OKO* **76** C3
Elm Cr S *LET* **88** H12
Elm Pl *OKO* **76** C3
Elm Pl S *LET* **88** H11-12
Elm Rd S *LET* **88** H11
Elm St *BRO* **90** C1
Elm St *MED* **95** F6
Elma St E *OKO* **76** C2-3
Elma St W *OKO* **76** C2
Elmont Bay 100 200 SW *CAL* . .**34** G18-19
Elmont Dr SW *CAL* **34** G19
Elmont Mews SW *CAL* **34** G18-19
Elmont Mnr SW *CAL* **34** G18
Elmont Rise SE *CAL* **34** G19
Elmwood Dr SE *CAL* **38** U18
Elsmore Pl SE *AIR* **68** C4
Elston Bay SE *AIR* **68** C3
Elston Pl SE *AIR* **68** C3
Elton Ct *BRG* **78** B2
Elveden Dr SW *CAL* **34** F-G19
Elwell Av *RED* **67** G-H8
Elwell Cl *RED* **67** G-H8
Ely Cl *RED* **67** G7-8
Emberdale Way SE *AIR* **68** C3
Emburry Cr *RED* **67** G7
Emerald Bay *RCY* **16** Y8-9
Emerald Ct SE *AIR* **68** C3
Emerald Rd SE *CAL* **49** Q27-28
Emerald Way *BLD* **75** C7
Emerald Bay Dr *RCY* **16** Y8-9
Emerson Rd SW *HIG* **77** C1
Empress Pl SE *AIR* **68** C3-4
England Cr *RED* **67** G8
Erickson Dr *RED* **67** G8
Erin Cir SE *CAL* **38** W20
Erin Cr SE *CAL* **38** W20
Erin Dr SE *AIR* **68** C4 D3-4
Erin Gr SE *CAL* **38** W20
Erin Link SE *CAL* **38** W20
Erin Pl SE *CAL* **38** W20
Erin Rd SE *CAL* **38** W20
Erin Croft Cr SE *CAL* **38** W19
Erin Croft Gn SE *CAL* **38** W19
Erin Croft Pl SE *CAL* **38** W19
Erin Dale Cr SE *CAL* **38** V19-20
Erin Dale Pl 100 200 SE *CAL* . .**38** V19-20
Erin Green Mews SE *CAL* **38** W20
Erin Green Pl SE *CAL* **38** V-W20
Erin Green Way SE *CAL* **38** V-W20
Erin Grove Bay SE *CAL* **38** W19
Erin Grove Cl SE *CAL* **38** W19
Erin Grove Ct SE *CAL* **38** W19
Erin Grove Gr SE *CAL* **38** W19
Erin Meadow Bay SE *CAL* **38** W19
Erin Meadow Cl SE *CAL* **38** W19
Erin Meadow Cr SE *CAL* **38** W19
Erin Meadow Gn SE *CAL* **38** W19
Erin Meadow Mnr SE *CAL* **38** W19
Erin Meadow Way SE *CAL* **38** W19
Erin Mount Cr SE *CAL* **38** V-W19
Erin Mount Pl 100 200 SE *CAL* .**38** V-W19
Erin Park Bay SE *CAL* **38** W19
Erin Park Cl SE *CAL* **38** W19
Erin Park Dr SE *CAL* **38** W19
Erin Ridge Ct SE *CAL* **38** V20
Erin Ridge Pl SE *CAL* **38** V20
Erin Ridge Rd SE *CAL* **38** V-W20
Erin Woods Blvd SE *CAL* **38** V20
Erin Woods Cir SE *CAL* **38** W20
Erin Woods Dr SE *CAL* **38** W19-20
Erin Woods Gn 100 300 SE *CAL* .**38** V20
Erin Woods La SE *CAL* **38** W19

Erin Woods Pl SE CAL 38 V20
Erin Woods Ter SE CAL 38 W19
Erlton Ct SE CAL 37 P19
Erlton Pl SE CAL 37 P18
Erlton Rd SE CAL 37 P18
Erlton St SE CAL 37 P18-19
Erlton Ter SW CAL 37 P19
Ermine Run Pl N LET 84 B9
Erminebend Pl N LET 84 B9
Erminedale Blvd N LET 84 B9
Ermineglen Rd N LET 84 B9
Ermineview Bay N LET 84 B9
Ermineview Rd N LET 84 B9
Ermineview Way N LET 84 B9
Escarpment Dr RCY 25 A14-15
Escarpment Pk RCY 33 A16
Escarpment Pl RCY 25 A14
Escott Cl RED 67 G7
Eton Rd W LET 86 J4
Evans Av RED 67 G8
Evansbrooke Hts NW CAL 12 L3
Evansbrooke Ldg NW CAL 12 L3-4
Evansbrooke Link NW CAL 12 L3
Evansbrooke Mnr NW CAL 12 L3
Evansbrooke Pk NW CAL 12 L4
Evansbrooke Pt NW CAL 11 K3 12 L3
Evansbrooke Rise NW CAL 12 L3-4
Evansbrooke Ter NW CAL 12 L3
Evansbrooke Way NW CAL 11 K3 12 L3
Evanscove Cir NW CAL 12 L3
Evanscove Hts NW CAL 12 L3
Evanscove Pl NW CAL 12 L3
Evanscreek Ct 100 200 NW CAL 12 L3
Evansford Gr NW CAL 12 L-M3
Evansford Rd NW CAL 12 L-M3
Evansmeade Cir NW CAL 12 L3-4
Evansmeade Cl NW CAL 12 L-M3
Evansmeade Com NW CAL 12 L-M3
Evansmeade Cr NW CAL 12 L4
Evansmeade Mnr NW CAL 12 L3-4
Evansmeade Pt 100 200 NW CAL 12 L-M4
Evansmeade Way NW CAL 12 L3-4
Evanston View NW CAL 12 L3
Everbrook Cr SW CAL 52 L31
Everbrook Dr SW CAL 52 L-M31
Evercreek Bluffs Cr SW CAL 48 L30
Evercreek Bluffs Gt SW CAL 48 L30
Evercreek Bluffs Mews 100 200 SW CAL 47 K30 48 L30
Evercreek Bluffs Pt SW CAL 48 L30
Evercreek Bluffs Rd SW CAL 48 L30
Evercreek Bluffs View SW CAL 48 L30
Evercreek Bluffs Way SW CAL 48 L30
Everglade Bay SE AIR 68 D4
Everglade Cir SW CAL 47 K30
Everglade Dr SE AIR 68 D4
Everglade Gt SW CAL 47 K30
Everglade Link SW CAL 47 K30
Everglade Pl SW CAL 47 K30 48 L30
Everglade Way SW CAL 47 K30
Everglen Cl SW CAL 52 L31
Everglen Com 100 to 400 SW CAL 52 L-M33
Everglen Pl SW CAL 52 L32
Everglen Rise SW CAL 52 L31-32
Everglen Rise SW CAL 52 L32
Everglen Way SW CAL 52 L31-32
Evergreen Av SW CAL 52 M31
Evergreen Bay SW CAL 48 M30
Evergreen Blvd SW CAL 52 M31
Evergreen Cir CAN 58 F3
Evergreen Cir SW CAL 52 M31
Evergreen Cl SW CAL 48 M-N30
Evergreen Com SW CAL 52 M31
Evergreen Cr SW CAL 48 M30
Evergreen Ct SW CAL 48 M-N30
Evergreen Cv SW CAL 48 M30
Evergreen Dr SW CAL 48 M-N30 52 M31
Evergreen Gdns SW CAL 48 M-N30
Evergreen Gr SW CAL 48 M30
Evergreen Heath 100 200 SW CAL 48 M30 M-N29
Evergreen Hill SW CAL 48 M29-30
Evergreen Hts SW CAL 48 N30
Evergreen La SW CAL 48 M30
Evergreen Ldg SW CAL 48 M30
Evergreen Link SW CAL 48 N30
Evergreen Mews 100 200 SW CAL 48 M30
Evergreen Mnr SW CAL 48 M30
Evergreen Pl 100 200 SW CAL 48 N30
Evergreen Plz 100 200 SW CAL 48 M30 52 M31
Evergreen Pt SW CAL 48 N30
Evergreen Rise SW CAL 48 M30
Evergreen Sq SW CAL 52 M31
Evergreen St SW CAL 48 N30
Evergreen Ter SW CAL 48 N29
Evergreen View SW CAL 48 N30
Evergreen Village SW CAL 21 P9
Evergreen Way SW CAL 48 N30
Evergreen Park Cl BRO 90 C2
Everhollow Gn 100 200 SW CAL 52 L31
Everhollow Heath SW CAL 52 L31
Everhollow Mews SW CAL 52 L31
Everhollow Mnr SW CAL 52 L31
Everhollow Pk SW CAL 48 L30 52 L31
Everhollow Pl SW CAL 52 L31
Everhollow Rise SW CAL 52 L31
Everhollow Way SW CAL 52 L31
Everitt Cr RED 67 G8
Evermeadow Dr SW CAL 52 L31
Evermeadow Gt SW CAL 52 L31-32
Evermeadow Heath SW CAL 52 L31
Evermeadow Mnr SW CAL 52 L31
Evermeadow Pl SW CAL 52 L31
Evermeadow Rd SW CAL 52 L31-32
Everoak Cl SW CAL 52 L-M31
Everoak Dr SW CAL 52 L31
Everoak Gdns SW CAL 52 L31
Everoak Gn SW CAL 52 L31
Everoak Pk SW CAL 52 L-M31
Everoak Pl SW CAL 52 L31
Everridge Cl SW CAL 52 L31
Everridge Com SW CAL 52 L32
Everridge Ct SW CAL 52 L31-32
Everridge Dr SW CAL 52 L-M32
Everridge Mews SW CAL 52 L31
Everridge Mnr SW CAL 52 L32
Everridge Pk SW CAL 52 L31
Everridge Pl SW CAL 52 L31
Everridge Rd SW CAL 52 L32
Everridge Way SW CAL 52 L-M32
Eversole Cr RED 67 G7-8
Everstone Av SW CAL 52 M32
Everstone Blvd SW CAL 52 M32
Everstone Ct SW CAL 52 M32
Everstone Dr SW CAL 52 M31-32
Everstone Gt SW CAL 52 M32
Everstone Link SW CAL 52 M32
Everstone Pl SW CAL 52 M31-32
Everstone Rd SW CAL 52 M32
Everstone Rise SW CAL 52 M32
Everstone Way SW CAL 52 M32
Eversyde Av SW CAL 52 L-M32
Eversyde Bay SW CAL 52 M31
Eversyde Blvd SW CAL 52 M32
Eversyde Cl SW CAL 52 M32
Eversyde Ct SW CAL 52 L-M32
Eversyde Gdns SW CAL 52 M32
Eversyde Heath SW CAL 52 M32
Eversyde Mnr SW CAL 52 M31
Eversyde Rd SW CAL 52 M31
Eversyde St SW CAL 52 M31-32
Eversyde Way SW CAL 52 M31
Everwillow Blvd SW CAL 52 M31
Everwillow Cir SW CAL 52 M31
Everwillow Cl SW CAL 52 M31
Everwillow Gn SW CAL 52 M31
Everwillow Pl SW CAL 52 M31
Everwoods Cl SW CAL 52 L31
Everwoods Rd SW CAL 52 L31
Ewart Cr MED 95 H8
Excell St RED 67 G-H7
Exeter Cr RED 67 H7
Exshaw Rd NW CAL 28 L-M13

F

Factory St MED 95 F6
Fairbank Rd RED 64 F4
Fairchild St MED 94 F1
Fairholm Dr CAN 58 D-E4
Fairholme Pl BAN 57 E1
Fairmont Bay S LET 88 J11
Fairmont Blvd S LET 88 J11-12
Fairmont Cr S LET 88 J11
Fairmont Ct S LET 88 J12
Fairmont Cv S LET 88 J10-11
Fairmont Gt S LET 88 J11
Fairmont Link S LET 88 J11
Fairmont Pl S LET 88 J11
Fairmont Pt S LET 88 J11
Fairmont Rd S LET 88 J11
Fairmont Ter LET 88 J11
Fairmont Garden Rd S LET 88 J11-12
Fairmont Park La S LET 88 J11
Fairmont Park Ldg S LET 88 J11
Fairmount Dr SE CAL 43 P23-25 49 P26-27
Fairview Av BRO 90 B3
Fairview Cl BRO 90 B3
Fairview Cr BRO 90 B3
Fairview Cr SE CAL 43 P23
Fairview Dr LKL 56 C-D4
Fairview Dr SE CAL 43 P23-24
Fairview Estates BRO 90 B3
Fairview Rd BRO 90 B3
Fairview Way BRO 90 B3
Fairway Av RED 64 F4 66 G3
Fairway Dr COD 85 C1
Fairway Dr NW HIG 77 B1-2
Fairway La NW HIG 77 B2
Fairway Rd S LET 88 J11
Fairway St S LET 88 J11
Fairway View NW HIG 77 B1
Fairway Plaza Rd S LET 88 J11
Fairways Bay NW AIR 68 B1
Fairways Cir NW AIR 68 B1
Fairways Cl NW AIR 68 B1-2
Fairways Cr NW AIR 68 B1
Fairways Dr NW AIR 68 B1
Fairways Gr NW AIR 68 A1
Fairways Ldg NW AIR 68 B1
Fairways Mews NW AIR 68 B1
Fairways Pl NW AIR 68 B1
Falaise Av SW CAL 35 K20 36 L20
Falaise St S LET 88 F10
Falbury Bay NE CAL 31 Y11
Falbury Cr NE CAL 31 Y11
Falchurch Cr NE CAL 23 X10
Falchurch Pl NE CAL 23 X10
Falchurch Rd NE CAL 23 X10
Falcon St BAN 57 C2-3
Falconcrest Village NE CAL 23 Y9-10
Falconer Ter NE CAL 23 Y10
Falconridge Blvd NE CAL 23 X9-10 31 X11
Falconridge Cl NE CAL 31 X11
Falconridge Cr NE CAL 31 X11
Falconridge Dr NE CAL 31 X-Y11
Falconridge Gdns NE CAL 23 Y10
Falconridge Pl NE CAL 31 X11
Faldale Cl NE CAL 23 Y10
Fallingworth Bay NE CAL 23 X10
Fallingworth Ct NE CAL 23 X10
Fallingworth Pl NE CAL 23 X10
Fallswater Cr NE CAL 31 Y11
Fallswater Gt NE CAL 31 Y11
Fallswater Rd NE CAL 31 Y11
Falmead Bay NE CAL 23 X10
Falmead Cl NE CAL 23 X10
Falmead Pl NE CAL 23 X10
Falmead Rd NE CAL 23 X10
Falmere Ct NE CAL 23 X9-10
Falmere Rd NE CAL 23 X9-10
Falmere Way NE CAL 23 X-Y9
Falsbridge Dr NE CAL 31 X11
Falsbridge Gt NE CAL 31 X11
Falsby Ct NE CAL 23 X10 31 X11
Falsby Pl NE CAL 23 X10 31 X11
Falsby Rd NE CAL 31 X11
Falsby Way NE CAL 23 X10
Falshire Cl NE CAL 23 X10
Falshire Dr NE CAL 23 X-Y10
Falshire Pl NE CAL 23 Y10
Falshire Ter NE CAL 23 X10
Falshire Way NE CAL 23 Y9
Falton Cl NE CAL 23 Y10
Falton Ct NE CAL 23 Y10
Falton Dr NE CAL 23 Y9-10
Falton Mews NE CAL 23 Y10
Falton Rd NE CAL 23 Y10 31 Y11
Falton Rise NE CAL 23 Y10
Falton Way NE CAL 23 Y10
Falwood Cr NE CAL 31 X-Y11
Falwood Pl NE CAL 31 X-Y11
Falwood Way NE CAL 31 Y11
Falworth Bay NE CAL 23 X10
Falworth Ct NE CAL 23 X10
Falworth Pl NE CAL 23 X10 31 X11
Falworth Rd NE CAL 23 X10 31 X11
Falworth Way NE CAL 23 X10
Farnham Dr SE CAL 43 Q24
Farr Cr NE AIR 68 B3
Farrell Av RED 66 G3
Farrell Rd SE CAL 43 P-Q23
Farrin Av NW CAL 26 G12
Fawn Cr SE CAL 43 P23
Fay Rd SE CAL 43 P24
Fenton Rd SE CAL 43 P24
Fern Cr S LET 88 G10
Fern Rd RED 64 F3
Ferncliff Cr SE CAL 43 P23
Fernie Pl SE CAL 43 P23
Festubert Av SW CAL 41 J21-22
Fielding Dr SE CAL 43 P24
Finlay Ct MED 92 E2
Fir Dr SE CAL 38 U18
Fir St RED 64 F3-4
Fisher Av COC 61 C5
Fisher Cr OKO 76 C4
Fisher Rd SE CAL 43 P22-23
Fisher St OKO 76 C4
Fisher St SE CAL 43 P22-23
Fishermans Bend RCY 33 A20
Fishermans Ldg RCY 33 A20
Fishermans Pt RCY 33 A20
Fitzgerald Rise CAN 59 H7
Flagstaff Cl RED 66 G3
Flanders Av SW CAL 36 L20
Flavelle Rd SE CAL 43 P24
Fleet St MED 94 F1
Fleetwood Dr SE CAL 43 P-Q23
Fletcher Rd NW AIR 68 B3
Flett Cr NE AIR 68 B3-4
Flett Dr NE AIR 68 B3 B3-4
Flett Pl 100 200 NE AIR 68 A-B3
Flint Pl SE CAL 43 P23
Flint Rd SE CAL 43 P23-24
Flower Dew Av SW CAL 41 J21
Foley Rd SE CAL 43 P23
Fonda Cl SE CAL 38 V16
Fonda Cr SE CAL 38 V16
Fonda Ct 100, 400 to 700, 1000 to 1200 SE CAL 38 V16-17
Fonda Dr SE CAL 38 V-W16
Fonda Gn SE CAL 38 V16-17
Fonda Hill SE CAL 38 V16
Fonda Mews SE CAL 38 V16
Fonda Pl SE CAL 38 V16-17
Fonda Rise SE CAL 38 V16
Fonda Way SE CAL 38 V16-17
Foothills Village NW CAL 27 K14
Ford St BLD 75 B6
Fordham Cr SE CAL 38 V16
Forego Av SE CAL 38 W16 39 X16
Forest Cl RED 66 G3
Forest Cr SE CAL 38 W16 39 X16
Forest Ct SE CAL 38 V16
Forest Gn SE CAL 39 X16
Forest Gr SE CAL 38 V16
Forest Mews SE CAL 38 V16
Forest Pl SE CAL 38 W16 39 X16
Forest Rd SE CAL 38 W16 39 X16
Forest Way SE CAL 39 X16
Forest Grove Pl SE CAL 38 W16-17
Forestry Av S LET 88 H11-12
Forge Rd SE CAL 43 P22
Foritana Rd SE CAL 38 W16-17
Forlee Dr SE CAL 38 W16-17
Forman Cr SE CAL 38 W16
Fortalice Cr SE CAL 38 W16-17
Fortress Dr SW CAL 34 F19
Fortress Mnr 100 200 SW CAL 34 F19
Fortress Rise SW CAL 34 F19
Fortune Rd SE CAL 38 W16
Foster Rd SE CAL 43 P23
Foundry St MED 95 F5-6
Fountain Dr RED 66 G3
Fountain Rd SE CAL 43 Q23
Fountain Walk SW CAL 6 A94 36 N17
Fourier Dr SE CAL 38 W16
Fowler Dr NW CAL 28 N14
Fox Cr RED 64 F3-4
Fox St BAN 57 C2
Foxbend Cr N LET 84 B9
Foxwell Rd SE CAL 43 P23
Franklin Dr SE CAL 43 P23
Fraser Rd SE CAL 43 Q24
Frazer Av BRO 90 B1-2 C2
Fredson Dr SE CAL 43 P-Q24
Freeman Way NW HIG 77 A1
Freemont Cl RED 64 F3-4
Freeport Blvd NE CAL 14 T5
Freeport Dr NE CAL 14 T5
Freeport Ldg NE CAL 14 T5
Freeport Pl NE CAL 14 T5
Freeport Way NE CAL 14 T5
Fresno Pl100 200 NE CAL 31 Z12
Frobisher Blvd SE CAL 43 Q23
Frontage Rd CAN 59 D-E5
Frontenac Av TVY 74 C3
Frontenac Av SW CAL 36 N-018
Fulham St SE CAL 43 P23-24
Fullerton Rd SE CAL 43 P-Q24
Fyffe Rd SE CAL 43 P-Q23

G

Gaetz Av RED 64 B-F5 66 G-K5
Gainsborough Cr SW CAL 35 J20
Gainsborough Gt SW CAL 35 I-J20
Galbraith Dr SW CAL 35 J20 41 J21-22
Galbraith St RED 64 D3
Galway Cr SW CAL 35 J20
Garden Cr SW CAL 36 018
Garden La SW CAL 36 018
Garden Pl MED 92 D-E2
Garden Way DRU 73 D-E8
Gardner Pl MED 95 G-H7
Garland St SW CAL 35 J18
Garnet Cl BLD 75 C7
Garrick Dr SW CAL 35 J20 41 J21
Garrison Blvd SW CAL 36 L19-20
Garrison Gt SW CAL 36 L19

Garrison / Hawkcliff

Garrison Sq SW *CAL* 36 L19
Garrow Av *BRO* 90 B3
Garrow Cr *BRO* 90 B3
Garry Cr NE *CAL* 29 P-Q11
Garry Dr W *LET* 86 F3
Gascony La SW *HIG* 77 C1
Gatefield Av SW *CAL* 35 J18
Gateway Dr SW *CAL* 35 I18
Gateway Pl SW *CAL* 35 I18
Gaza Cr SW *CAL* 42 L21
Gee St *RED* 64 C3-4
Gehring Rd *MED* 94 H4
Gehrke Cl *RED* 64 D3-4
George Cr *RED* 64 D4
George St *TVY* 74 C-D3
George Craig Blvd NE *CAL* 29 S11 30 T11
George Fox Tr *COC* 60 C1-3
Georgia St SW *CAL* 35 I17-18
Georgian Villas 200 to 400 NE *CAL* 31 X15 Y15
Gershaw Dr *MED* 94 F3 G2 H1
Gibson Cl *RED* 64 C4
Gilbert Cr *RED* 64 C4
Gilchrist Cr *RED* 64 C4
Gillespie Cr *RED* 64 C3
Gilmer Pl SW *CAL* 41 J21
Gilmore Av *RED* 64 C4
Gish St *RED* 64 C3
Gissing Dr SW *CAL* 35 J20
Glacier Av S *LET* 88 G11-12
Glacier Dr *BAN* 57 E1
Glacier Dr *CAN* 59 F6-7
Glacier Dr S *LET* 88 G11
Glacier Dr SW *CAL* 35 J20 41 J21
Glacier Pl SW *CAL* 35 J20
Gladeview Cr SW *CAL* 35 J20
Gladstone Gdns SW *CAL* 35 I20
Gladstone Pk SW *CAL* 35 I20
Gladstone Rd NW *CAL* 28 N15 36 N16
Gladys Ridge Rd SW *CAL* 35 I18
Glamis Dr SW *CAL* 35 I20 41 I21-22
Glamis Gdns SW *CAL* 35 I20 41 I21-22
Glamis Gn SW *CAL* 35 I20
Glamis Ter SW *CAL* 35 I20
Glamorgan Cr SW *CAL* 35 I20
Glamorgan Dr SW *CAL* 35 J20
Glamorgan Pl 200 to 400 SW *CAL* 35 I20
Glamorgan Way SW *CAL* 35 I20
Glasgow Dr SW *CAL* 35 I17-18
Glass Cl *RED* 64 C4
Glen Av *BAN* 57 E2
Glen Cr *BAN* 57 E2
Glen Dr *MED* 95 K8
Glenbow Dr *COC* 60 B3-4
Glenbrook Bay *COC* 60 B4
Glenbrook Cr *COC* 60 B4
Glenbrook Dr SW *CAL* 35 I19
Glenbrook Gn SW *CAL* 35 I19
Glenbrook Mews *COC* 60 B4
Glenbrook Mnr SW *CAL* 35 I19
Glenbrook Pl *COC* 60 B4
Glenbrook Pl SW *CAL* 35 I19
Glenbrook Rd *COC* 60 B4
Glenbrook Village SW *CAL* 35 I19
Glenbrook Villas SW *CAL* 35 I18
Glencastle St SW *CAL* 35 J18
Glencoe Rd SW *CAL* 36 O19
Glendale Blvd *RED* 64 C3-4
Glendale Pl *COC* 60 B3
Glendale St *STM* 71 D-E3
Glendale Way *COC* 60 A-B3
Glendeer Cir SE *CAL* 43 R23
Gleneagle Pl SW *CAL* 35 I19
Gleneagles Blvd *COC* 61 B-C7
Gleneagles Cl *COC* 61 B6-7
Gleneagles Dr *COC* 61 B6-7
Gleneagles Gn *COC* 61 C8
Gleneagles Gt *COC* 61 B6
Gleneagles Ldg *COC* 61 C7
Gleneagles Pt *COC* 61 B-C7
Gleneagles Ter *COC* 61 B-C8
Gleneagles View *COC* 61 B-C7
Glenfield Rd SW *CAL* 35 I18
Glengrove Cl SW *CAL* 35 I19
Glenhill Cr *COC* 60 B3-4
Glenhill Ct *COC* 60 C3
Glenhill Dr *COC* 60 B-C3
Glenhill Pl *COC* 60 C3
Glenmere Rd SW *CAL* 35 J18
Glenmore Gn SW *CAL* 42 N22
Glenmore Tr *RCY* 33 C20
Glenmore Tr SE *CAL* 43 Q-R22 S24 44 T-W24 45 X24
Glenmore Tr SW *CAL* 34 F20 41 J-K21 42 M22
Glenmore Bridge Rd SW *CAL* 42 M21-22
Glenmore Hill Rd SW *CAL* 42 M-N21
Glenmount Cr SW *CAL* 35 J17-18
Glenmount Dr SW *CAL* 35 J18
Glenpark Cr SW *CAL* 35 J18
Glenpatrick Cr *COC* 60 B-C4
Glenpatrick Ct *COC* 60 B3
Glenpatrick Dr *COC* 60 B-C4
Glenpatrick Dr SW *CAL* 35 I19
Glenpatrick Pl *COC* 60 B3
Glenpatrick Rd *COC* 60 B3
Glenport Rd *COC* 60 B-C3
Glenridge Av *STM* 71 E2-3
Glenside Dr SW *CAL* 35 I18
Glenview Cr SW *CAL* 35 I18
Glenview Dr SW *CAL* 35 I18
Glenway Dr SW *CAL* 35 J19-20
Glenway Pl SW *CAL* 35 J19
Glenwood Av SW *CAL* 35 J18
Glenwood Bay *COC* 60 B3-4
Glenwood Cr *COC* 60 B3-4
Glenwood Cr SW *CAL* 35 J18
Glenwood Ct *COC* 60 B3
Glenwood Dr SW *CAL* 35 J18
Glenwood Pl *COC* 60 B3-4
Glenwood St *STM* 71 D-E3
Gloucester Cr SW *CAL* 35 J19-20
Gloucester Dr SW *CAL* 35 J20
Goard Cl *RED* 64 C3-4
Goddard Av NE *CAL* 29 P-Q11
Golan Av SW *CAL* 41 K21 42 L21
Golan St SW *CAL* 42 L21
Golden West Av *RED* 64 D2-3 E2
Goldenrod Ct *MED* 94 H4 95 H5
Golf Course Rd *BAN* 57 E4
Good Cr *RED* 64 C-D3
Goodacre Cl *RED* 64 C3
Goodall Av *RED* 64 C3
Gooding La *TVY* 74 D3
Gopher St *BAN* 57 D1
Gordon Dr SW *CAL* 35 J20 41 J21
Gordon St *RED* 64 C3-4
Gosling Way SE *CAL* 38 U18-19
Government Rd N *BLD* 75 B6
Government Rd S *BLD* 75 B-C6
Governor Dr SW *CAL* 35 J20
Grafton Cr SW *CAL* 35 J20
Grafton Dr SW *CAL* 35 J20
Graham Dr SW *CAL* 35 I18-19
Graham's Pl NE *CAL* 31 Z11
Granada Dr SW *CAL* 35 I18
Grand Beach Bay *CHE* 70 E-F2
Grand Oaks Dr SW *CAL* 35 J17-18
Grand River Blvd W *LET* 87 K5-6
Grande Blvd *COC* 60 B-C4
Grande Point Ests *STM* 71 C4
Grandstand Ter SE *CAL* 37 Q18
Grandview Blvd *RED* 67 G6
Granite Ridge *RCY* 33 Z19
Granlea Pl SW *CAL* 35 I18
Grant Cr SW *CAL* 35 J18-19
Grant St *RED* 64 D3-4
Granville Cr SW *CAL* 35 J18
Granville St SW *CAL* 35 J18
Grassi Pl 100 to 300 *CAN* 58 F3
Grassi Pl *CAN* 58 F3
Gray Cr *MED* 92 C3
Gray Dr *RED* 64 D3
Great Lakes Pl S *LET* 88 G-H11
Great Lakes Rd S *LET* 88 G11
Green Meadow Cr *STM* 71 C3
Green Meadow Dr *STM* 71 C4
Green Meadow Pl *STM* 71 C3
Green View Cr *STM* 71 C3-4
Green View Way *STM* 71 C3-4
Greenbriar Blvd NW *CAL* 26 E12
Greenbriar Cr NW *CAL* 26 D-E12
Greenbriar Ct NW *CAL* 26 D-E12
Greenbriar Pl NW *CAL* 26 E12
Greenbriar Rd NW *CAL* 26 D-E12
Greenbriar Way NW *CAL* 26 D-E12
Greenbrook Cr *BRO* 90 C4
Greenbrook Dr *BRO* 90 C4
Greenbrook Rd *BRO* 90 B3-4 C4
Greenbrook Way *BRO* 90 C4
Greene Cl *RED* 64 D4
Greenfield Rd NE *CAL* 29 P-Q11
Greenham Cr *RED* 64 C4
Greenhill Cr NE *CAL* 29 P-Q11
Greenridge Rd SW *CAL* 35 J18
Greenview Cl N *LET* 84 C10
Greenview Dr NE *CAL* 29 P-Q11
Greenview Pl NE *CAL* 29 P-Q11
Greenwood Cr SW *CAL* 35 J20
Greenwood Ct *MED* 92 E2
Gregson Cr *RED* 64 C4
Greig Cl *RED* 64 C4
Greig Dr *RED* 64 C3
Grey Av *CRS* 62 B2
Greyhound Way SW *CAL* 36 M16-17
Greystone Cl *BRO* 90 D4
Grier Av NE *CAL* 29 P-Q11
Grier Pl NE *CAL* 21 Q10
Grier Ter 100 200 NE *CAL* 21 P-Q10
Griffin Rd *COC* 60 C3
Griffin Rd E *COC* 61 C5-6
Griffin Rd W *COC* 60 C4
Griffin Industrial Pt *COC* 61 C6
Griffiths Av *RED* 64 C-D4
Grimson St *RED* 64 C3
Grizzly Cr *CAN* 59 F6
Grizzly St *BAN* 57 D2
Grosvenor Pl SW *CAL* 35 J18
Grote Cr *RED* 64 C4
Grotto Cl *CAN* 59 F6
Grotto Pl *CAN* 59 F6
Grotto Rd *CAN* 58 A2 59 F6
Grotto Ter *CAN* 59 F7
Grotto Way *CAN* 59 F6
Grove Av *DRU* 73 B6
Grove Pl *DRU* 73 B6-7
Grove Hill Pl SW *CAL* 35 J18
Grove Hill Rd SW *CAL* 35 I-J18
Gummow Cl *RED* 64 C-D3
Gunn St *RED* 64 C3

H

Hackamore Tr *RCY* 16 X9
Hackney Dr *TAB* 91 E2
Haddock Rd SW *CAL* 42 N25
Haddon Rd SW *CAL* 42 O24-25
Hager Pl SW *CAL* 42 N25 48 N26
Haliburton Cr *RED* 64 E-F3
Halifax Cr NW *CAL* 28 L-M14
Hall Cr *RED* 64 E4
Halladay Av *RED* 64 E4
Hallbrook Dr SW *CAL* 42 N25
Hallbrook Pl SW *CAL* 42 N25
Hallgren Av *RED* 64 E4-5
Hallmark Pl SW *CAL* 42 N25
Halman Cr *RED* 64 E3
Hamilton Cl *RCY* 9 A4
Hamilton Ct *MED* 93 C5
Hamilton Dr *RCY* 9 A4 B4
Hamilton Dr *RCY* 9 Z4
Hamilton Dr *RED* 64 E3-4
Hamilton St NW *CAL* 28 L15
Hamlet Rd SW *CAL* 42 N24
Hammond Av *CRS* 62 A-B2
Hammond Cr *RED* 64 E3
Hampshire Cir NW *CAL* 19 I6
Hampshire Cl NW *CAL* 19 I6
Hampshire Ct 100 to 500 NW *CAL* 19 I6
Hampshire Gr NW *CAL* 19 I6
Hampshire Pl 100 to 300 NW *CAL* 19 I6
Hampstead Cir NW *CAL* 19 J6
Hampstead Cl NW *CAL* 19 I-J6
Hampstead Gdns 100 200 NW *CAL* 19 K6
Hampstead Gn NW *CAL* 19 K6
Hampstead Gr NW *CAL* 19 K6
Hampstead Heath 100 200 NW *CAL* 19 J6
Hampstead Hill NW *CAL* 19 J6
Hampstead Mnr NW *CAL* 19 K6
Hampstead Pl 100 200 NW *CAL* 19 I-J6
Hampstead Pt NW *CAL* 19 K6
Hampstead Rd NW *CAL* 19 K6
Hampstead Rise NW *CAL* 11 K5
Hampstead Ter NW *CAL* 11 K5 19 K6
Hampstead View NW *CAL* 19 K6
Hampstead Way NW *CAL* 19 J6
Hampton Cr SW *CAL* 35 K19
Hamptons Bay NW *CAL* 11 J5
Hamptons Blvd NW *CAL* 19 I-J6
Hamptons Cir NW *CAL* 11 I-J5
Hamptons Cl NW *CAL* 11 I-J5
Hamptons Cv NW *CAL* 11 I5
Hamptons Dr NW *CAL* 11 J5 19 K6
Hamptons Gdns 100 to 300 NW *CAL* 11 J5 19 J6
Hamptons Gn NW *CAL* 11 I5 19 I6
Hamptons Gr NW *CAL* 19 I6
Hamptons Heath NW *CAL* 19 I-J6
Hamptons Hts NW *CAL* 11 J-K5
Hamptons Ldg 100 200 NW *CAL* 11 J5 19 J6
Hamptons Link NW *CAL* 11 J5
Hamptons Mews 100 to 500 NW *CAL* 19 I-J6
Hamptons Mnr NW *CAL* 11 I5
Hamptons Pk NW *CAL* 19 I6
Hamptons Pl NW *CAL* 11 J5
Hamptons Rise NW *CAL* 11 J5
Hamptons Sq 100 200 NW *CAL* 11 I5
Hamptons Ter NW *CAL* 11 J5 19 J6
Hamptons Way NW *CAL* 11 I-J5
Hanna St *RED* 64 E4
Hanover Rd SW *CAL* 42 N25
Harcourt Rd SW *CAL* 42 N24
Hardisty Pl SW *CAL* 42 O25
Hargrave Way *MED* 92 D3
Harley Rd SW *CAL* 42 N25
Harlow Av NW *CAL* 28 O11-12
Harmon Pl SW *CAL* 42 O24
Harmony Pl *TAB* 91 E2
Harper St NW *CAL* 28 O11
Harris Pl NW *CAL* 27 J13
Harris St *MED* 92 E2
Harrison 100 to 400 *CRS* 62 A2
Harrison Pl *CRS* 62 A2
Harrison St *CRS* 62 A2
Harrow Cr SW *CAL* 42 O25
Harrow Pl SW *CAL* 42 O25
Hart Cr *RED* 64 E4
Hartford Pl NW *CAL* 28 O11
Hartford Rd NW *CAL* 28 O11-12
Harvard Av *MED* 94 G1
Harvard Cr W *LET* 86 H3-4
Harvard St NW *CAL* 28 O12
Harvest Gn *TAB* 91 E2
Harvest Creek Cl NE *CAL* 13 Q5 21 Q6
Harvest Creek Ct 100 200 NE *CAL* 13 Q5 21 Q6
Harvest Glen Ct NE *CAL* 13 Q5 21 Q6
Harvest Glen Hts NE *CAL* 21 Q6
Harvest Glen Link NE *CAL* 13 Q5 21 Q6
Harvest Glen Mews NE *CAL* 21 Q6
Harvest Glen Pl 100 200 NE *CAL* 21 Q6
Harvest Glen Rise NE *CAL* 13 Q5 21 Q6
Harvest Glen Way NE *CAL* 21 Q6
Harvest Gold Cir NE *CAL* 21 P6
Harvest Gold Hts NE *CAL* 13 P5
Harvest Gold Mnr NE *CAL* 21 P6
Harvest Gold Pl NE *CAL* 21 P6
Harvest Grove Cl NE *CAL* 13 Q5
Harvest Grove Gn NE *CAL* 13 Q5
Harvest Grove Pl 100 to 300 NE *CAL* 13 Q5
Harvest Grove Pl NE *CAL* 13 Q5
Harvest Hills Bay NE *CAL* 21 P6
Harvest Hills Blvd NE *CAL* 12 O4 13 P4 P5 21 P6
Harvest Hills Blvd NE *CAL* 13 P3
Harvest Hills Dr NE *CAL* 13 P-Q5 21 P-Q6
Harvest Hills Gt NE *CAL* 13 Q4-5
Harvest Hills Link NE *CAL* 21 Q6
Harvest Lake Cr NE *CAL* 13 Q5
Harvest Lake Dr NE *CAL* 13 Q5 21 Q6
Harvest Lake Gn 100 to 300 NE *CAL* 13 Q5
Harvest Lake Link NE *CAL* 13 Q5
Harvest Lake Village NE *CAL* 13 Q5
Harvest Lake Way NE *CAL* 13 Q5
Harvest Oak Cir NE *CAL* 13 P5
Harvest Oak Cr NE *CAL* 13 P5
Harvest Oak Dr NE *CAL* 13 P5
Harvest Oak Gn NE *CAL* 13 P5
Harvest Oak Gt NE *CAL* 13 P5
Harvest Oak Pl NE *CAL* 13 P5
Harvest Oak Rise 100 200 NE *CAL* 13 P5
Harvest Oak View NE *CAL* 13 P5
Harvest Oak Way NE *CAL* 13 P-Q5
Harvest Park Cir NE *CAL* 13 P5 21 P6
Harvest Park Ct NE *CAL* 13 P-Q5
Harvest Park Gt NE *CAL* 13 P5 21 P6
Harvest Park Mews NE *CAL* 13 P-Q5
Harvest Park Pl NE *CAL* 13 P-Q5
Harvest Park Rd NE *CAL* 13 P5
Harvest Park Ter NE *CAL* 13 P5 21 P6
Harvest Park Way NE *CAL* 13 P5
Harvest Rose Cir NE *CAL* 21 P6
Harvest Rose Gdns NE *CAL* 21 P6
Harvest Rose Pk NE *CAL* 21 P6
Harvest Rose Pl NE *CAL* 21 P6
Harvest Wood Gt NE *CAL* 13 Q5
Harvest Wood Link NE *CAL* 13 Q5
Harvest Wood Pl NE *CAL* 13 Q5
Harvest Wood Rd NE *CAL* 13 Q5
Harvest Wood Way NE *CAL* 13 Q5
Harvetta Rd SE *CAL* 44 T21
Harvey Cl *RED* 64 E4
Harvey Hills *RCY* 9 A-B1
Harvey Pl SW *CAL* 42 O24
Harvie Heights Rd *CAN* 58 A2 B2-3
Harwood St *BRG* 78 B3
Haste St *RED* 64 E-F3
Hastings Cr SE *CAL* 37 R20
Hatcher Ct *MED* 92 C4
Hatcher Dr *MED* 92 B4 93 B5 B5
Haultain Pl SW *CAL* 42 O24-25
Haven Pl *TAB* 91 E2
Havenhurst Cr SW *CAL* 42 O25
Haverhill Rd SW *CAL* 42 N24
Hawk Av *BAN* 57 C2
Hawkbury Cl NW *CAL* 18 G7
Hawkbury Pl NW *CAL* 18 G7 19 H7
Hawkcliff Ct NW *CAL* 19 I7
Hawkcliff Gt NW *CAL* 19 H-I7
Hawkcliff Mews NW *CAL* 19 I8
Hawkcliff Pl NW *CAL* 19 H-I8

Hawkcliff Way NW *CAL* **19** H-I8 I7
Hawkdale Bay 100 to 300 NW *CAL* **18** G7
Hawkdale Cir NW *CAL* **18** G7
Hawkdale Cl NW *CAL* **18** G7 **19** H7
Hawkdale Gt NW *CAL* **18** G7
Hawkdale Pl NW *CAL* **18** G7-8
Hawke Cr *MED* **93** B-C5
Hawkey Cr NE *AIR* **68** B3
Hawkfield Cr NW *CAL* **18** G7
Hawkfield Pl NW *CAL* **18** G7
Hawkfield Rise NW *CAL* **18** G7
Hawkfield Way NW *CAL* **18** G7
Hawkford Cr NW *CAL* **19** H-I7
Hawkford Ct NW *CAL* **19** H7
Hawkford Gt NW *CAL* **19** H7
Hawkford Pl NW *CAL* **19** H7
Hawkford Way NW *CAL* **19** H7
Hawkhill Ct 100 200 NW *CAL* **19** I7
Hawkhill Mews NW *CAL* **19** I7-8
Hawkhill Pl 100 to 600 NW *CAL* **19** I7
Hawkhill Rd NW *CAL* **19** I7
Hawkhill Way NW *CAL* **19** I7
Hawkland Cir NW *CAL* **18** G6 **19** H6
Hawkland Cr NW *CAL* **18** G6 **19** H6
Hawkland Pl 100 to 400 NW *CAL* **18** G6 **19** H6
Hawkley Valley Pl NW *CAL* **19** H8
Hawkley Valley Rd NW *CAL* **19** H8
Hawkmount Cl NW *CAL* **19** H6
Hawkmount Gn NW *CAL* **19** H6-7
Hawkmount Hts NW *CAL* **19** H7
Hawkridge Ct NW *CAL* **19** H7-8
Hawkridge Pl NW *CAL* **19** H8
Hawks Ct NW *CAL* **19** H8
Hawks Pl NW *CAL* **19** H8
Hawksbrow Dr NW *CAL* **19** H7-8
Hawksbrow Mews 100 to 300 NW *CAL* **19** H7-8
Hawksbrow Pl NW *CAL* **19** H8
Hawksbrow Pt NW *CAL* **19** H7
Hawksbrow Rd NW *CAL* **19** H-I8
Hawkside Cl NW *CAL* **18** G7 **19** H7
Hawkside Mews 100 to 700 NW *CAL* **18** G7 **19** H7
Hawkside Pk NW *CAL* **19** H7
Hawkside Rd NW *CAL* **18** G7-8
Hawksley Bay NW *CAL* **19** H8
Hawksley Cr NW *CAL* **19** H8
Hawkslow Bay NW *CAL* **19** H8
Hawkslow Ct NW *CAL* **19** H8
Hawkslow Pl NW *CAL* **19** H8
Hawkstone Cl NW *CAL* **19** H7
Hawkstone Ct 100 200 NW *CAL* **19** H7
Hawkstone Dr NW *CAL* **18** G6 **19** H6 H-I7
Hawkstone Gt NW *CAL* **19** H6-7
Hawkstone Mnr 100 to 600 NW *CAL* **19** H6-7
Hawkstone Pl NW *CAL* **19** H-I7
Hawktree Bay 100 200 NW *CAL* **19** H-I7
Hawktree Cir NW *CAL* **19** I6-7
Hawktree Cl NW *CAL* **19** H6-7
Hawktree Gn NW *CAL* **19** H-I6
Hawkview Manor Bay NW *CAL* **19** H7-8
Hawkview Manor Cir NW *CAL* **19** H7
Hawkview Manor Ct 100 to 300 NW *CAL* **19** H7
Hawkview Manor Link NW *CAL* **19** H7-8
Hawkview Manor Pl 100 200 NW *CAL* **19** H7
Hawkview Manor Rd NW *CAL* **19** H7
Hawkville Cl NW *CAL* **18** G7
Hawkville Mews NW *CAL* **18** G7
Hawkville Pl NW *CAL* **18** G7
Hawkwood Blvd NW *CAL* **19** H7
Hawkwood Cr NW *CAL* **18** G7
Hawkwood Dr NW *CAL* **18** G7-8
Hawkwood Hill NW *CAL* **19** H7-8
Hawkwood Pl NW *CAL* **18** G7-8
Hawkwood Rd NW *CAL* **18** G7
Hawkwood Way NW *CAL* **18** G7-8
Hawthorn Cr *OLD* **62** C1
Hawthorn Dr NE *CAL* **20** O10 **21** P10
Hawthorn Way *OLD* **62** C1
Hawthorne Av *MED* **92** C4 **93** B5 C5
Hawthorne Cr NW *CAL* **28** L15
Hawthorne Pl N *LET* **84** C10
Hawthorne Rd N *LET* **84** C10
Hay Pl *IRR* **69** B2
Hays Ct *MED* **92** D3
Hays Dr SW *CAL* **42** O25
Haysboro Cr SW *CAL* **42** N24
Hayward Cl *MED* **92** C4
Hazelwood Cr SW *CAL* **42** O25 **48** O26
Hazlett Cl *RED* **64** E3
Headlands Cl *COC* **61** B5-6
Healy Dr SW *CAL* **42** O24
Hearne Ct *MED* **92** B4
Heath Cl *RED* **64** E4
Heather Cr *BRO* **90** B2
Heather Pl N *LET* **84** C9-10
Heather Pl SW *CAL* **42** N25 **48** N26
Heather Rd N *LET* **84** C10
Heckbert Ct *MED* **92** C4
Heirloom Cr *TAB* **91** E2
Hemingway Cr *MED* **93** B-C5
Hemlock Cr SW *CAL* **35** K16
Henderson Cr *MED* **93** B-C5
Henderson Lake Blvd S *LET* **88** G10-11 H10
Hendon Dr NW *CAL* **28** O11-12
Hendon Pl NW *CAL* **28** O12
Hendricks Dr *IRR* **69** B1-2
Henefer Rd SW *CAL* **42** O25
Henwood St SW *CAL* **41** K21
Hepworth Cl *RED* **64** E3-4
Herald Dr *MED* **92** D3
Heritage Av *MED* **93** B5
Heritage Bay SW *CAL* **41** K24
Heritage Blvd W *LET* **82** E3 **86** F3-4 F4
Heritage Cir W *LET* **86** F4
Heritage Cl W *LET* **86** F4
Heritage Cr *OKO* **76** C4
Heritage Cr W *LET* **86** F3-4
Heritage Ct *MED* **92** B4 **93** B5
Heritage Ct W *LET* **86** F3-4
Heritage Dr *OKO* **76** C3-4
Heritage Dr *TAB* **91** D-E2
Heritage Dr SE *CAL* **43** P24 Q-R23
Heritage Dr SW *CAL* **42** N-O24
Heritage Gn W *LET* **86** F4
Heritage Gt *OKO* **76** C4
Heritage Gt SE *CAL* **43** Q23
Heritage La *OKO* **76** C3-4
Heritage La W *LET* **82** E4 **86** F4
Heritage Pl *MED* **92** B4 **93** B5
Heritage Pl 100 to 300 *RCY* **25** C15 **33** C-D16
Heritage Pl *TAB* **91** E2
Heritage Pl W *LET* **86** F4
Heritage Pt W *LET* **86** F4 **87** F5
Heritage Rd SW *CAL* **42** O24
Heritage Rd W *LET* **86** F4
Heritage Meadows Rd SE *CAL* **43** R23-24
Heritage Meadows Way SE *CAL* **43** Q-R23
Heritage Woods Dr *RCY* **25** C15
Hermary St *RED* **64** E4
Heston St NW *CAL* **28** N11-12 O11
Hewitt Ct *MED* **93** C5
Hewson Av *RED* **64** E3
Hidden Cir NW *CAL* **12** L5 **20** L6
Hidden Cl NW *CAL* **20** L6
Hidden Cr NW *CAL* **12** L5 **20** L6
Hidden Ct NW *CAL* **12** L5
Hidden Cv 100 to 300 NW *CAL* **12** L-M5
Hidden Gn NW *CAL* **12** L5 **20** L6
Hidden Mews NW *CAL* **11** K5
Hidden Pk NW *CAL* **12** L5
Hidden Pt NW *CAL* **20** L6
Hidden Way NW *CAL* **11** K5
Hidden Creek Bay NW *CAL* **12** M4
Hidden Creek Blvd NW *CAL* **12** M4
Hidden Creek Cir NW *CAL* **12** M-N4
Hidden Creek Cr NW *CAL* **12** M4
Hidden Creek Cv NW *CAL* **12** M4
Hidden Creek Dr NW *CAL* **12** M4
Hidden Creek Gdns NW *CAL* **12** M4
Hidden Creek Gn NW *CAL* **12** M4
Hidden Creek Hts NW *CAL* **12** M4
Hidden Creek Mews NW *CAL* **12** M4
Hidden Creek Mnr NW *CAL* **12** M4
Hidden Creek Pk NW *CAL* **12** M4
Hidden Creek Pl NW *CAL* **12** M4
Hidden Creek Pt NW *CAL* **12** N4
Hidden Creek Rd NW *CAL* **12** M4
Hidden Creek Rise NW *CAL* **12** M4
Hidden Creek Ter NW *CAL* **12** M-N4
Hidden Creek View NW *CAL* **12** M4
Hidden Creek Way NW *CAL* **12** M-N4
Hidden Hills Pl100 to 300 NW *CAL* **11** K5
Hidden Hills Rd NW *CAL* **11** K5
Hidden Hills Ter NW *CAL* **11** K5
Hidden Hills Way NW *CAL* **11** K5
Hidden Ranch Blvd NW *CAL* **12** L5
Hidden Ranch Cir NW *CAL* **12** L5
Hidden Ranch Cl NW *CAL* **11** K5
Hidden Ranch Cr NW *CAL* **12** L5
Hidden Ranch Ct NW *CAL* **12** L5
Hidden Ranch Hill NW *CAL* **11** K5
Hidden Ranch Mews NW *CAL* **11** K5 **12** L5
Hidden Ranch Pl 100 to 300 NW *CAL* **12** L5
Hidden Ranch Rd NW *CAL* **11** K5 **12** L5
Hidden Ranch Ter NW *CAL* **11** K5 **12** L5
Hidden Ranch Way NW *CAL* **11** K5 **12** L5
Hidden Ridge Bay NW *CAL* **12** L-M5
Hidden Ridge Cl NW *CAL* **12** L5
Hidden Ridge Ct NW *CAL* **12** L5
Hidden Ridge Pl NW *CAL* **12** L5
Hidden Ridge View NW *CAL* **12** L5
Hidden Spring Cir NW *CAL* **12** M5
Hidden Spring Cl NW *CAL* **12** M5
Hidden Spring Ct NW *CAL* **12** M5
Hidden Spring Gn NW *CAL* **12** L5
Hidden Spring Mews 100 200 NW *CAL* **12** L5
Hidden Spring Pl NW *CAL* **12** M5
Hidden Vale Cl NW *CAL* **12** M5 **20** M6
Hidden Vale Cr NW *CAL* **20** M6
Hidden Vale Ct NW *CAL* **20** M6
Hidden Vale Pl 100 to 600 NW *CAL* **12** M5
Hidden Valley Cr NW *CAL* **12** M5
Hidden Valley Dr NW *CAL* **11** K5 **12** L-M5 **19** K6
Hidden Valley Gdns NW *CAL* **12** M5
Hidden Valley Gn NW *CAL* **12** M-N5
Hidden Valley Gr 100 to 400 NW *CAL* **12** M5
Hidden Valley Gt NW *CAL* **12** M-N5
Hidden Valley Hts NW *CAL* **12** M5 **20** M6
Hidden Valley Ldg 100 to 300 NW *CAL* **12** M5
Hidden Valley Link NW *CAL* **12** M5
Hidden Valley Mnr 100 to 300 NW *CAL* **12** M5
Hidden Valley Pk NW *CAL* **12** M5
Hidden Valley Pl 100 to 300 NW *CAL* **12** M5 **20** M6
Hidden Valley Villas NW *CAL* **12** M5
Higdon Av *MED* **95** H6
High St SE *CAL* **54** W31
High Country Bay NW *HIG* **77** A-B1
High Country Dr NW *HIG* **77** A1
High Country Pl NW *HIG* **77** A-B1
High Glen Bay NW *HIG* **77** A1
High Glen Pl NW *HIG* **77** A1
High Park Way NW *HIG* **77** A1
High Point Estates 100 200 *CHE* **70** E-F5
High Ridge Cl NW *HIG* **77** A1
High Ridge Cr NW *HIG* **77** A1
High Ridge Ct NW *HIG* **77** A1
High Ridge Pl NW *HIG* **77** A1
High View Gt NW *HIG* **77** A-B1
High View Pk 100 200 NW *HIG* **77** B1
High View Pt NW *HIG* **77** B1
Highfield Av SE *CAL* **37** Q20
Highfield Blvd SE *CAL* **37** R19-20
Highfield Cir SE *CAL* **37** Q20
Highfield Cr SE *CAL* **37** R20 **43** R21
Highfield Pl SE *CAL* **37** Q20
Highfield Rd SE *CAL* **37** Q19
Highland Cir *STM* **71** A2
Highland Cl *STM* **71** A2
Highland Pl NE *CAL* **28** O11 **29** P11
Highland Green Dr NW *HIG* **77** A1
Highland Green View NW *HIG* **77** A1
Highlands Blvd W *LET* **86** F3
Highlands Pl W *LET* **82** E3 **86** F3
Highlands Rd W *LET* **86** F3
Highwood Pl NW *CAL* **28** O11
Highwood Tr SW *HIG* **77** C1
Highwood Village Gt NW *HIG* **77** A1
Highwood Village Pl 100 to 400 NW *HIG* **77** A1
Hill Cr *RED* **64** E4
Hill Rd *MED* **95** F5
Hill Rd NE *CAL* **37** R-S16
Hill St SW *DRU* **73** C5
Hillary Cr SW *CAL* **42** N25
Hillcrest Av SW *CAL* **36** O18
Hillcrest Blvd *STM* **71** A-B2
Hillgreen Pl SW *CAL* **42** N25 **48** N26
Hillgrove Cr SW *CAL* **42** N25
Hillgrove Dr SW *CAL* **42** N25 **48** N26
Hillvale Cr *STM* **71** B2
Hillvoew La *STM* **71** B2
Hilton Av SW *CAL* **28** O11
Hilton Cr *MED* **92** C4 **93** C5
Hobart Rd SW *CAL* **42** N25
Hobart W McNeill *CAN* **58** G4
Hobbs Way *MED* **92** B-C4
Hochwald Av SW *CAL* **35** K19 **36** L19
Hochwald Ct SW *CAL* **35** K19 **36** L19
Hodson Cr *OKO* **76** B3
Hodson Pl *OKO* **76** B3
Hodson Way *OKO* **76** B3
Hogarth Cr SW *CAL* **42** O25
Holden Pl SW *CAL* **42** N24
Holden Rd SW *CAL* **42** N24
Holland St NW *CAL* **28** N11
Holly Dr SE *CAL* **38** U18
Holly St NW *CAL* **28** N11-12 O11
Hollyburn Rd SW *CAL* **42** N25
Holmes St *RED* **64** E4
Holmwood Av NW *CAL* **28** O11
Holsom Rd *MED* **94** G1
Holt Cr *MED* **93** C5
Holt St *RED* **64** E4
Holy Cross La SE *CAL* **37** P18
Home Bay 100 SE *HIG* **77** B3
Home Pl 500 SE *HIG* **77** B3-4
Home Rd NW *CAL* **27** I13-14
Homestead Bay 300 NE *HIG* **77** B3
Homestead Cl 200 NE *HIG* **77** B3-4
Homestead Pl *TAB* **91** E2
Homestead Pl 600 SE *HIG* **77** B4
Homestead Tr 400 SE *HIG* **77** B4
Homestead Way NE *HIG* **77** B3
Honeysuckle Rd N *LET* **84** C10
Hoodoo Cr *CAN* **59** F6
Hooke Rd SW *CAL* **42** N25
Hoover Pl SW *CAL* **42** N24-25
Hope St SW *CAL* **36** O18
Hopewell Pl NE *CAL* **30** U11
Hopewell Way NE *CAL* **30** U11
Hoppe Mews SW *CAL* **41** K21
Horizon View Ct *RCY* **25** Z14
Horizon View La *RCY* **25** Z15
Horizon View Pl *RCY* **25** A15
Horizon View Rd *RCY* **25** Z14 **33** Z17
Horn Cr *RED* **64** E3
Horn St *RED* **64** E3-4
Horne Blvd *MED* **92** C4
Horner Ct *MED* **93** C5
Horton Rd SW *CAL* **42** O24-25
Hospital Dr NW *CAL* **27** K14-15
Hospital Pl *CAN* **59** E5
Hounslow Dr NW *CAL* **28** N11-12
Howarth St *RED* **64** E3
Howarth St Cl *RED* **64** E4
Howe Rd *LET* **89** G-H15
Howlett Av *RED* **64** E3
Hub Av SW *CAL* **42** N25
Hubalta Rd SE *CAL* **38** W18 **39** X18
Hubert St *TVY* **74** C-D3
Huckvale Cr *MED* **94** G3
Hudson Cr *MED* **93** B5
Hudson Rd NW *CAL* **28** O12
Hudson Way *MED* **93** B5
Huget Cr *RED* **64** E4
Huggard Rd *RCY* **24** V13 V14
Hughes Cr *MED* **93** C5
Hull Av SW *CAL* **42** O24
Hull Cr *MED* **92** C4
Hull Way *MED* **92** C4
Humber Cl *RED* **64** E3
Hunt Cr *MED* **93** B5
Huntbourne Gn NE *CAL* **21** P9
Huntbourne Gt NE *CAL* **21** P9
Huntbourne Hill NE *CAL* **21** P9
Huntbourne Pl NE *CAL* **21** P-Q9
Huntbourne Rd NE *CAL* **21** P9
Huntbourne Way NE *CAL* **21** P9
Huntchester Cr NE *CAL* **21** P-Q9
Huntchester Rd NE *CAL* **21** P9
Huntcroft Pl NE *CAL* **21** P8
Huntcroft Rd NE *CAL* **21** P8
Huntcroft Way NE *CAL* **21** P8
Hunter Cl *RED* **64** E4
Hunter Ct *MED* **92** B4
Hunter Dr *DRU* **72** B1 C2
Hunter St NW *CAL* **28** O12
Hunter's Cr *OKO* **76** C-D2
Hunter's Gt *OKO* **75** C1 **76** C2
Hunter's Mews *OKO* **75** C1 **76** C2
Hunter's Pl *OKO* **76** C-D2
Hunterbow Cr NW *CAL* **20** O9
Hunterbrook Pl 100 to 300 NW *CAL* **20** N8
Hunterbrook Rd NW *CAL* **20** N8
Hunterburn Cr NW *CAL* **20** N8
Hunterburn Hill NW *CAL* **20** N8-9
Hunterburn Pl NW *CAL* **20** N8
Huntercove Pl NW *CAL* **20** O9
Huntercrest Rd NW *CAL* **20** O9
Hunterdale Pl NW *CAL* **20** O9
Hunterdale Rd NW *CAL* **20** O9
Hunterfield Pl NW *CAL* **20** O8
Hunterfield Rd NW *CAL* **20** O8
Hunterhaven Pl NW *CAL* **20** O8-9
Hunterhaven Rd NW *CAL* **20** O8
Hunterhorn Cr NE *CAL* **21** Q9
Hunterhorn Dr NE *CAL* **21** Q9
Hunterhorn Gdns NE *CAL* **21** P8
Hunterhorn Gt NE *CAL* **21** Q9
Hunterhorn La NE *CAL* **21** Q9
Hunterhorn Mnr NE *CAL* **21** P-Q9
Hunterhorn Pl NE *CAL* **21** Q9
Hunterhorn Rd NE *CAL* **21** Q9
Hunterhorn Ter NE *CAL* **21** Q9
Hunterplain Hill NW *CAL* **20** O8
Hunterquay Hill NW *CAL* **20** N8
Hunterquay Pl NW *CAL* **20** N8
Hunterquay Rd NW *CAL* **20** N8
Hunterquay Way NW *CAL* **20** N8
Huntерslea Cr NW *CAL* **20** O8
Hunterston Bay NW *CAL* **20** O8
Hunterston Cr NW *CAL* **20** O8
Hunterston Hill NW *CAL* **20** N-O8

Hunterston Pl NW *CAL* **20** 08
Hunterston Rd NW *CAL* **20** 08
Huntertown Cr NW *CAL* **20** 08
Huntervalley Rd NW *CAL* **20** 08
Hunterview Dr NW *CAL* **20** N-08
Hunterville Rd NW *CAL* **20** 09
Hunterwood Rd NW *CAL* **20** 09
Huntford Cl NE *CAL* **21** P9
Huntford Gn NE *CAL* **21** P9
Huntford Hill NE *CAL* **21** P9
Huntford Rd NE *CAL* **21** P9
Huntford Way NE *CAL* **21** P9
Huntham Gt NE *CAL* **21** P8
Huntham Pl 100 to 300 NE *CAL* . . .**21** P8
Huntham Rd NE *CAL* **20** 08 **21** P8
Huntington Cl NE *CAL* **21** P-08
Huntington Gn NE *CAL* **21** P8
Huntington Park *DRU* **73** D7
Huntington Rd NE *CAL* **21** P8
Huntington Ridge NE *CAL* **20** 09
Huntington St NE *CAL* **21** Q8
Huntington Way NE *CAL* **21** P8
Huntington Park Bay NW *CAL* . . .**20** N-08
Huntington Park Gn NW *CAL* **20** N-08
Huntington Park Pl NW *CAL* **20** 08-9
Huntley Cl NE *CAL* **21** P8-9
Huntley Ct *MED* **92** B-C4
Huntley Rd NE *CAL* **21** P-08
Huntley Way NE *CAL* **21** P-08
Huntmeadow Rd NE *CAL* **21** P-Q9
Huntridge Cr NE *CAL* **20** 08 **21** P8
Huntridge Gt NE *CAL* **21** P8-9
Huntridge Hill NE *CAL* **21** P8-9
Huntridge Pl NE *CAL* **21** P8
Huntridge Rd NE *CAL* **21** P8
Huntridge Way NE *CAL* **21** P8
Hunts Cr NW *CAL* **20** 09
Hunts Dr *DRU* **73** D7
Hunts Pl *DRU* **73** D7
Hunts Pl NW *CAL* **20** 09
Huntsbay Rd NW *CAL* **20** 09
Huntstrom Bay 100 200 NE *CAL* . .**21** Q8
Huntstrom Dr NE *CAL* **21** Q8
Huntstrom Pl NE *CAL* **21** Q8
Huntstrom Rd NE *CAL* **21** Q8
Huntsville Cr NW *CAL* **21** P9
Huntwell Ct 100 200 NE *CAL* **21** Q8
Huntwell Pl 100 200 NE *CAL* **21** Q8
Huntwell Rd NE *CAL* **21** Q8
Huntwell Way NE *CAL* **21** Q8
Huntwick Cr NE *CAL* **21** P8
Huntwick Hill NE *CAL* **21** P8
Huntwick Way NE *CAL* **21** P8
Huron Av NW *CAL* **28** N11
Huron Pl S *LET* **88** G-H11
Hurst Rd SE *CAL* **37** R18
Husky Oil Gdns SW *CAL* **26** E12-13
Hussar St SW *CAL* **41** J21
Hussar Tr SW *CAL* **41** I21
Hutchings Ct *MED* **92** C4
Hutchinson Av *MED* **94** G4
Hutton Cr SW *CAL* **42** O25
Hutton Pl SW *CAL* **42** O25
Huxley Gn *MED* **92** C4
Huxley Pl SW *CAL* **42** N24-25
Hy-Grade Cr *DRU* **73** C6 D6
Hyler Pl SW *CAL* **42** N24
Hyslop Dr SW *CAL* **42** O24

I

Icefields Pkwy *LKL* **56** A2
Ijsselmeer St SW *CAL* **41** J21
Imperial Cl *OLD* **62** B1
Imperial Dr *OLD* **62** B1-2
Imperial Dr SE *TVY* **74** D-E4
Imperial Rd *OLD* **62** B1
Imperial Way SW *CAL* **36** O20
Indian Flats Rd *CAN* **59** F-G7
Industrial Av *MED* **95** F6-7
Industrial Pl *CAN* **58** D4
Industrial Rd *BRO* **90** D2-3
Ingle Cl *RED* **67** K7
Inglewood Cl *RED* **67** K-L7
Inglewood Cv SE *CAL* **37** S17
Inglewood Dr *RED* **67** K-L7
Inglewood Gr SE *CAL* **37** S17
Inglewood Ldg SE *CAL* **37** S17
Inglewood Pt SE *CAL* **37** S17
Inglis Cr *RED* **67** K7
Ingram Park Dr *BRO* **90** C4
Inverlake Rd *CHE* **70** B1-2
Invermere Dr *CHE* **70** D1
Inverness Blvd SE *CAL* **54** W31
Inverness Cl SE *CAL* **54** W31
Inverness Ct SE *CAL* **54** W31
Inverness Cv SE *CAL* **54** W31-32
Inverness Dr SE *CAL* **54** V-W32

Inverness Gdns SE *CAL* **54** V-W31
Inverness Gn SE *CAL* **54** W31
Inverness Gr SE *CAL* **54** V31-32
Inverness Gt SE *CAL* **54** W31
Inverness La SE *CAL* **54** W31
Inverness Pk SE *CAL* **54** W31-32
Inverness Pl SE *CAL* **54** V32
Inverness Rd SE *CAL* **54** W31
Inverness Rise SE *CAL* **54** V-W31
Inverness Sq SE *CAL* **54** W31
Inverness View SE *CAL* **54** W31-32
Inverness Way SE *CAL* **54** V-W31
Ireland Cr *RED* **67** L7
Ireland Ct *MED* **92** C3
Iris Ct *MED* **95** H5
Irish St *RED* **67** K7
Iron Av *MED* **95** F7
Ironside St *RED* **67** K7
Iroquois Cr W *LET* **86** G4
Irricana Rd NE *AIR* **69** A5-6
Irving Cr *RED* **67** K7
Iverson Cl *RED* **67** L7
Ives Cr *RED* **67** L7
Ivey Cl *RED* **67** K7

J

Jackson Cl *RED* **64** C3
Jackson Pl *MED* **95** H6
Jackson Pl NW *CAL* **27** J13
Jacobs Cl *RED* **64** C-D2
Jacques Lodges SW *CAL* **36** L17
Jail Rd *LET* **85** E14-15
James St *RED* **64** C2-3
James McKevitt Rd SW *CAL* . . . .
. . . .**48** N-O30 **52** M31 N33
Jamieson Av NE *CAL* **29** R15
Janko Cl *RED* **64** C3
Jarvis Av *RED* **64** C3
Jasper Way *BAN* **57** E1
Jay St *BAN* **57** C2
Jenkins Dr *RED* **64** C3
Jensen Dr NE *AIR* **68** B3
Jensen Ldg NE *AIR* **68** B3
Jensen Pl NE *AIR* **68** B3
Jensen Hts Ct NE *AIR* **68** B3
Jensen Hts Pl NE *AIR* **68** B3
Jerry Potts Blvd W *LET* **86** G3-4
Jerusalem Way SW *CAL* **42** M-N25
Jessup Av *RED* **64** C3
Jewell St *RED* **64** C2-3
Jo-Ann Trucking Rd *BRO* **90** A2
John St *TVY* **74** D2
John Gardam Av SW *CAL* **41** K21
John Laurie Blvd NW *CAL* . . . .
. . . .**18** F7 G7-8 **19** I-J9 **28** L11 N11-12
Johns St *RED* **64** C3
Johnson Pl SW *CAL* **41** K21 **42** L21
Johnstone Dr *RED* **64** C2-3 D2
Joice Cl *RED* **64** C3
Joliet Av SW *CAL* **36** N19
Jones Cr *RED* **64** C3
Juniper Dr NW *CAL* **26** D-E12
Juniper Rd *DRU* **73** D-E8
Juniper Rd NW *CAL* **28** L15
Juniper Ridge *CAN* **59** D5

K

Kamenka Gn *CAN* **58** G-H3
Kananaskis Dr SW *CAL* **42** N23
Kananaskis Rd *CRO* **79** A4-5
Kananaskis Way *CAN* **59** E5 F5-6
Kane Cl *RED* **64** B4
Kanell Dr NE *HIG* **77** B3
Kara Cr *BRO* **90** B2
Keats Way *RED* **64** B-C3
Kee St *RED* **64** B-C4
Keen Cr *RED* **64** B4
Keewatin St SW *CAL* **42** N-O23
Keho Pl S *LET* **88** H11
Keith Cl *RED* **64** B3
Kellington Cl *BRO* **90** B3
Kelloway Cr *RED* **64** B4
Kelly St *RED* **64** B4
Kelowna Cr SW *CAL* **42** N22-23
Kelsey Pl SW *CAL* **42** N23
Kelvin Pl SW *CAL* **42** O24
Kelwood Cr SW *CAL* **35** J18
Kelwood Dr SW *CAL* **35** J18
Kelwood Pl SW *CAL* **35** J18
Kemp Av *RED* **64** B4
Kendall Cr *RED* **64** B4
Kendall Rd SW *CAL* **42** O23
Kendrew Dr *RED* **64** B3-4
Kenmare Cr SW *CAL* **35** K19
Kennedy Dr *RED* **64** B-C4

Kennedy Dr *TVY* **74** D3
Kennedy Dr SW *CAL* **42** N22-23
Kennings Cr *RED* **64** B4
Kenny Cl *RED* **64** B3
Kenosee Pl SW *CAL* **42** N23
Kensington Av *MED* **94** G3
Kensington Cr NW *CAL* **36** N16
Kensington Rd NW *CAL* **36** L-N16
Kent Pl SW *CAL* **42** N23
Kent St *RED* **64** B3
Kentish Dr SW *CAL* **42** O23
Kentwood Dr *RED* **64** B4
Kerfoot Cr SW *CAL* **42** N23
Kerr Cl *RED* **64** B4
Kerry Park Rd SW *CAL* **35** J19
Kerry Wood Dr *RED* **64** F2 F4 **66** G3-4
Kerry Wood Mews *RED* **64** F4
Kerrydale Rd SW *CAL* **35** K19
Kershaw Cl *RED* **64** B4-5
Kerwood Cr SW *CAL* **42** N23
Ketchen Av SW *CAL* **41** J21
Kew St SW *CAL* **42** N23
Kidd Cl *RED* **64** B3
Kilburn Cr *RED* **64** B4
Kildare Cr SW *CAL* **35** J-K19
Kildonan Cr SW *CAL* **42** N23
Kildonan Pl 1000 1100 SW *CAL* **42** N22-23
Kilkenny Rd SW *CAL* **35** J-K19
Killarney Glen Ct 100 to 600 SW *CAL* . .
. . . .**35** K19
Killearn Av SW *CAL* **42** N23
Kincaid Castle SW *CAL* **35** I17
Kincora Bay 100 to 700 NW *CAL* . . . . .
. . . .**11** J-K4 **12** L4
Kincora Blvd NW *CAL* **11** K4
Kincora Cv 100 200 NW *CAL* .**11** K4 **12** L4
Kincora Dr NW *CAL* **11** K4
Kincora Gdns NW *CAL* **11** K4
Kincora Gr NW *CAL* **11** K4
Kincora Hill NW *CAL* **11** J-K4
Kincora Hts NW *CAL* **11** K4
Kincora Ldg NW *CAL* **11** K4 **12** L4
Kincora Mnr NW *CAL* **11** K4
Kincora Pk NW *CAL* **11** K4
Kincora Pl 100 200 NW *CAL* **11** K4
Kincora Pt NW *CAL* **11** K4
Kincora Rise NW *CAL* **11** K3-4
Kincora Ter NW *CAL* **11** K4
Kincora View NW *CAL* **11** K4
Kincora Glen Bay NW *CAL* **11** K3
Kincora Glen Cr NW *CAL* **11** K3-4
Kincora Glen Gn NW *CAL* **11** K3-4
Kincora Glen La NW *CAL* **11** J-K3 K3-4
Kincora Glen Mews NW *CAL* **11** K3
Kincora Glen Rd NW *CAL* **11** K3
Kincora Glen Rise NW *CAL* **11** K3-4
King Cl *RED* **64** B4
Kingfisher La *CHE* **70** G2
Kings Alley SW *CAL* **48** L27
Kings Bay 100 to 300 S *LET* **88** J9
Kings Cr S *LET* **88** J9
Kings Gt S *LET* **88** J9
Kings Mews S *LET* **88** J9
Kings Pl S *LET* **88** J9
Kings Rd S *LET* **88** J9
Kingsland Ct SW *CAL* **42** O23
Kingsland Pl SW *CAL* **42** O23
Kingsland Village SW *CAL* **42** O23
Kingsmere Cr SW *CAL* **42** O23
Kingston Dr *RED* **64** B4
Kingston St SW *CAL* **27** K15 **28** L15
Kingsway Av *MED* **95** F5
Kinsale Rd SW *CAL* **35** K19
Kipling St *MED* **94** G4 **95** G5
Kirby Pl SW *CAL* **42** O23-24
Kirby St *RED* **64** B4
Kirk Cl *RED* **64** B4
Kirkland Cl *RED* **64** B-C3
Kirkland Dr *RED* **64** B3-4
Kirkwood Cr *RED* **64** C3-4
Kirsch Cl *RED* **64** B-C4
Kirton Cr *RED* **64** B4-5
Kitson Cl *RED* **64** B3
Klamath Pl SW *CAL* **42** O23
Klondike Av SW *CAL* **42** N23
Kluane Dr *BAN* **57** E2
Knight Av *CRS* **62** A2
Knight Pl *CRS* **62** A2
Knight St *OKO* **76** C3
Knowles Av *OKO* **76** B-C2
Knowles Pl *OKO* **76** B2
Kodiak Blvd N *LET* **84** B9-10
Kootenay Av *BAN* **57** E2
Kootenay Pl W *LET* **86** G3-4
Korea Av SW *CAL* **41** J22
Korea Pl SW *CAL* **41** J22
Kovac St *RED* **64** B4

Krause Cr *RED* **64** B3-4
Kyte Cr *RED* **64** B4-5

L

Lachine Ct SW *CAL* **42** L22
Lacombe Way SW *CAL* **42** L22
Ladbrooke Dr SW *CAL* **41** K21
Ladbrooke Pl SW *CAL* **41** K21
Ladwig Cl *RED* **67** J9
Lady MacDonald Cr *CAN* **59** F6-7
Lady MacDonald Dr *CAN* **59** F7
Lafayette Blvd W *LET* **86** H4 **87** H5
Lafayette Cr W *LET* **86** H4 **87** H5
Lafayette Pl W *LET* **86** H4 **87** H5
Lagrange Cr *RED* **67** K8-9
Laguna Cir NE *CAL* **31** Y12-13
Laguna Cl NE *CAL* **31** Y-Z12
Laguna Way NE *CAL* **31** Y11 Y-Z12
Laird Cl *RED* **67** K8
Laird Ct SW *CAL* **42** L22
Lake Ct SW *CAL* **41** K23
Lake Ridge *OLD* **62** D1
Lake Acadia Gn SE *CAL* **49** Q29
Lake Acadia Pl SE *CAL* **49** Q29
Lake Acadia Rd SE *CAL* **49** Q29
Lake Adams Cr SE *CAL* **49** P28
Lake Adams Pl SE *CAL* **49** P28
Lake Arrow Gn SE *CAL* **49** Q29
Lake Arrow Rd SE *CAL* **49** Q-R29
Lake Arrow Way SE *CAL* **49** Q29
Lake Aspen Rd SE *CAL* **48** O28 **49** P28
Lake Bevan Dr *BRO* **90** B3
Lake Bevan Pl *BRO* **90** B3
Lake Bonaventure Pl SE *CAL* **49** P29
Lake Bonavista Dr SE *CAL* **49** P-R28 Q-R29
Lake Bonavista Gn SE *CAL* **49** Q28
Lake Christina Cl SE *CAL* **49** R28
Lake Christina Pl SE *CAL* **49** Q-R28
Lake Christina Rd SE *CAL* **49** R28
Lake Christina Way SE *CAL* **49** R28
Lake Crimson Cl SE *CAL* **49** Q29
Lake Crimson Dr SE *CAL* **49** Q29
Lake Emerald Cr SE *CAL* **49** Q27-28
Lake Emerald Pl SE *CAL* **49** Q28
Lake Emerald Rd SE *CAL* **49** Q27-28
Lake Erie Gn SE *CAL* **49** P-Q28
Lake Erie Pl 100 200 SE *CAL* **49** P28
Lake Erie Rd SE *CAL* **49** P28
Lake Erie Way SE *CAL* **49** Q28
Lake Fraser Ct SE *CAL* **49** P28
Lake Fraser Dr SE *CAL* **49** P27-29
Lake Fraser Gn SE *CAL* **49** P28
Lake Fraser Gt SE *CAL* **49** P28
Lake Fraser Pl 100 200 SE *CAL* . . .**49** P28
Lake Fraser Way SE *CAL* **49** P28
Lake Geneva Pl SE *CAL* **49** R28-29
Lake Geneva Rd SE *CAL* **49** R28-29
Lake Huron Bay SE *CAL* **49** R28
Lake Huron Cr SE *CAL* **49** R28
Lake Huron Pl SE *CAL* **49** R27-28
Lake Linnet Cl SE *CAL* **49** Q27-28
Lake Linnet Gn SE *CAL* **49** Q27-28
Lake Louise Dr *LKL* **56** C4 D2-3
Lake Louise Way SE *CAL* **49** Q28
Lake Lucerne Cl SE *CAL* **49** R29
Lake Lucerne Cr SE *CAL* **49** Q29
Lake Lucerne Dr SE *CAL* **49** Q-R29
Lake Lucerne Rd SE *CAL* **49** Q29-30
Lake Lucerne Way SE *CAL* **49** Q-R29
Lake Mead Cr SE *CAL* **49** P28-29
Lake Mead Dr SE *CAL* **49** P-Q29
Lake Mead Gn SE *CAL* **49** P28-29
Lake Mead Pl SE *CAL* **49** P28-29
Lake Mead Rd SE *CAL* **49** P29
Lake Michigan Cr SE *CAL* **49** R-S28
Lake Michigan Dr SE *CAL* **49** R28
Lake Michigan Rd SE *CAL* **49** R28
Lake Moraine Gn SE *CAL* **49** Q28
Lake Moraine Pl 100 200 SE *CAL* **49** P28
Lake Moraine Rd SE *CAL* **49** P28
Lake Moraine Rise SE *CAL* **49** P28
Lake Moraine Way SE *CAL* **49** P-Q28
Lake Newell Bay *BRO* **90** B4
Lake Newell Cr *BRO* **90** B4
Lake Newell Cr SE *CAL* **49** P27-28
Lake Newell Ct *BRO* **90** B3-4
Lake Newell Gn SE *CAL* **49** P27-28
Lake Newell Mews *BRO* **90** B4
Lake Ontario Cl SE *CAL* **49** Q-R29 R28
Lake Ontario Pl 100 to 400 SE *CAL* . .
. . . .**49** R28-29
Lake Ontario Rd SE *CAL* **49** R28
Lake Patricia Pl SE *CAL* **49** Q-R28
Lake Placid Bay SE *CAL* **49** Q29
Lake Placid Cl SE *CAL* **49** Q29

Lake Placid Dr SE CAL 49 P-Q29
Lake Placid Gn 100 to 400 SE CAL 49 P-Q29
Lake Placid Hill SE CAL 49 Q29
Lake Placid Pl SE CAL 49 P29
Lake Placid Rd SE CAL 49 Q29
Lake Placid Rise SE CAL 49 Q29
Lake Rosen Cr SE CAL 49 P27-28
Lake Rosen Rise SE CAL 49 P27-28
Lake Simcoe Cl SE CAL 49 P29
Lake Simcoe Cr SE CAL 49 P29
Lake Simcoe Ct SE CAL 49 P29
Lake Simcoe Gn SE CAL 49 P29
Lake Simcoe Rise SE CAL 49 P29
Lake Stafford Cr BRO 90 A3
Lake Stafford Dr BRO 90 A-B3 B3-4
Lake Stafford Way BRO 90 A3
Lake Sundance Cr SE CAL 49 R28-29
Lake Sundance Pl SE CAL 49 R28-29
Lake Sylvan Cl SE CAL 49 R28
Lake Sylvan Dr SE CAL 49 R28
Lake Sylvan Pl SE CAL 49 R28
Lake Tahoe Gn SE CAL 49 Q29
Lake Tahoe Pl SE CAL 49 Q29
Lake Topaz Cr SE CAL 49 P27-28
Lake Twintree Bay SE CAL 49 Q28-29
Lake Twintree Cr SE CAL 49 Q28-29
Lake Twintree Dr SE CAL 49 Q-R29
Lake Twintree Pl SE CAL 49 R29
Lake Twintree Rd SE CAL 49 R29
Lake Twintree Way SE CAL 49 R29
Lake Wapta Pl SE CAL 49 R28
Lake Wapta Rd SE CAL 49 R28
Lake Wapta Rise SE CAL 49 R27-28
Lake Wapta Way SE CAL 49 R28
Lake Wasa Gn SE CAL 49 P28
Lake Wasa Pl SE CAL 49 P28
Lake Waterton Cr SE CAL 49 Q28
Lake Waterton Way SE CAL 49 Q28
Lake Willow Rd SE CAL 49 P28
Lake Wood Pl 100 200 SE CAL 49 P28-29
Lakehill Cr S LET 88 H11
Lakeland Cr S LET 88 G11
Lakeland Ct BRO 90 B3
Lakemount Blvd S LET 88 G11-12 H11
Lakemount Pl S LET 88 G-H11
Lakepoint Rd S LET 88 H10-11
Lakeridge Blvd S LET 88 H10-11
Lakeshore Rd S LET 88 H10-11
Lakeside Blvd STM 71 D3
Lakeside Cr SW CAL 41 K22
Lakeside Rd S LET 88 H10-11
Lakeside Greens Cl CHE 70 D1-2
Lakeside Greens Cr CHE 70 D1
Lakeside Greens Ct 100 to 300 CHE 70 E1
Lakeside Greens Dr CHE 70 D2 D-E1
Lakeside Greens Gt CHE 70 E1
Lakeside Greens Pl 100 to 500 CHE 70 D1-2 E1
Lakeview Bay CHE 70 E1
Lakeview Cr BRO 90 B4
Lakeview Cv CHE 70 E2
Lakeview Dr S LET 88 G11 H10
Lakeview Dr SW CAL 41 J-K21 K22
Lakeview Gt CHE 70 F1
Lakeview Inlet CHE 70 E1-2
Lakeview Rise CHE 70 F3
Lakeview Shores CHE 70 E1-2
Lakeview Shores Ct CHE 70 E1-2
Lakeway Blvd S LET 88 G11
Lakewood Gn BRO 90 B4
Lakewood Rd BRO 90 B3
Lakewood Rd S LET 88 G11
Lakhota Cr W LET 86 G3
Lakhota Rd W LET 86 G3
Lamar Cl RED 67 J10
Lamb Cl RED 67 J9
Lamb Ct MED 95 H6
Lambert Av NE CAL 37 R-S16
Lamone Av SW CAL 36 L20
Lamont Cl RED 67 J9
Lamont Ct SW CAL 42 L22-23
Lampard Cr RED 67 J-K8 J-K9
Lampson Av BEI 69 A3
Lancaster Dr RED 67 J-K8 J-K9
Lancaster St MED 94 G1
Lancaster Way SW CAL 41 K22
Lancing Av SW CAL 42 L22
Landmark Estates NW CAL 27 J12
Landsdown Estates CHE 70 F4-5
Landsdown Estates 100 to 300 CHE 70 F4-5
Lane Cr SW CAL 41 K22
Laneham Pl SW CAL 42 L-M21
Lang Cl RED 67 J10
Lang Cr MED 94 F3
Lang Pl OKO 76 B5
Langford Cr RED 67 K8-9
Langriville Dr SW CAL 42 L-M22
Langton Dr SW CAL 42 L21
Lansdowne Av SW CAL 36 N-O20
Lanterman Cl RED 67 J9-10
Larch Av CAN 58 D3
Larch Av CRO 81 J14
Larch Av DRU 73 B6
Larch Cl CAN 58 D3
Larch Cr CAN 58 D3
Larch Ct SW CAL 42 L22
Larch Pl 100 to 1100 CAN 58 D3 D3-4 D4
Larch Way NW CAL 26 D-E11
Lariat Loop RCY 16 W10 W-X9
Larkspur Ct MED 95 H5
Larkspur Rd N LET 84 C10
Larkspur Way SW CAL 42 L22
Las Americas Villas NE CAL 31 Z12
LaSalle Cr SW CAL 41 J-K21
Lassiter Ct SW CAL 41 K22-23
Lathom Cr SW CAL 41 K22
Lauden Av OKO 76 C2
Laurel Cr BRO 90 B-C2
Laurel Cr SW CAL 42 L22
Laurentian Pl W LET 87 J5
Laurentian Way SW CAL 42 M22
Laurier Ct SW CAL 42 L23
Laut Av CRS 62 B2
Laut Cr CRS 62 B2
Laval Av SW CAL 36 N19
Laval Blvd W LET 87 H-J5 J5
Laval Ct W LET 86 J4 87 J5
Laval Pl W LET 87 J5
Laval Rd W LET 87 J5
LaValencia Gdns NE CAL 31 Y13
LaValencia Gn NE CAL 31 Y13
Law Cl RED 67 K8
Law Dr SW CAL 41 J-K22
Lawford Av RED 67 J9
Lawrence Cr RED 67 J8-9
Lawrence Ct SW CAL 42 L22-23
Lawrence Grassi Ridge CAN 58 G3-4 H4
Lawson Pl SW CAL 41 K21
Laxton Pl SW CAL 42 L-M21
Laycock Dr NE CAL 29 P11
Laycock Dr NW CAL 29 P11
Layzell Rd SW CAL 42 L21
Leaside Av S LET 84 E10 88 F10-11
Leaside Dr SW CAL 41 K22-23
Leduc Cr SW CAL 41 K22
Lees St RED 67 J8-9
Leeson Ct SW CAL 42 L22
Lefroy Ct SW CAL 42 L22-23
Legare Dr SW CAL 41 K22-23
Legsby Rd SW CAL 42 L22
Lemoyne Cr W LET 86 H4
Lenton Pl SW CAL 42 M21
Leonard Cr RED 67 J9
Lepine Ct SW CAL 41 K22 42 L22
Lethbridge Cr SW CAL 41 J-K22
Leung Cl RED 67 J-K8
Levis Av SW CAL 36 N19
Lewis Cl RED 67 K8
Lewis Dr SW CAL 41 K22
Lewis Mackenzie Pl SW CAL 41 K21 42 L21
Liddell Ct SW CAL 41 K23
Lilac Way NW CAL 26 E12
Lily Ct MED 94 H4 95 H5
Limit Av CRS 62 A2-3
Lincoln Dr SW CAL 42 L-M22
Lincoln Gn SW CAL 35 J-K20
Lincoln Mnr SW CAL 41 J-K21
Lincoln Pl SW CAL 35 J-K20
Lincoln Way SW CAL 41 J-K21
Linden Dr SW CAL 41 K23 42 L23
Lindsay Av RED 67 K9
Lindsay Dr SW CAL 41 K22
Lindstrom Dr SW CAL 42 L22-23
Lineham Av OKO 76 C3
Lineham Acres Cl NW HIG 77 A-B2
Lineham Acres Dr NW HIG 77 B2
Lineham Acres Gr 100 400 NW HIG 77 A-B2
Lineham Acres Pl NW HIG 77 B2
Link Ct MED 92 E2-3
Link St CRS 62 A2
Linn Cl RED 67 J9
Lionel Cr SW CAL 42 L22
Liri Av SW CAL 41 J22
Liri Mews SW CAL 41 J22
Lismer Gn NW CAL 27 J13
Lissington Dr SW CAL 42 L-M21
Lister Cr RED 67 J9
Little Ravine Rd CAN 59 D5
Littlewood Bay RCY 16 W10
Livingstone Dr SW CAL 41 K22-23
Livingstone Estates Rd RCY 16 W7-8
Lloyd Cr SW CAL 42 L22
Lochend Dr RCY 8 W-X2
Lock Cr OKO 76 B3
Lock Pl OKO 76 B3
Locke Ct SW CAL 41 K22-23
Lockinvar Rd SW CAL 41 K21-22
Lockwood Av RED 67 J9
Lodge Cr SW CAL 41 J-K21
Logan Cl RED 67 J9
Logan Cr SW CAL 41 J-K22
Lokier Av MED 92 D3
Lombardy Cr SW CAL 42 L22
London Av MED 95 F6
London St SW CAL 27 K14-15
Londonderry Cr SW CAL 41 K21-22
Lone Pine Cr RCY 9 B2
Long Beach Ldg CHE 70 F1-2
Longeway Pl RCY 24 V-W13
Longmoor Way SW CAL 41 J-K22
Longridge Dr SW CAL 42 L22
Longview Coal Tr NW HIG 77 A1
Longwood Ct SW CAL 42 L22-23
Loohend Rd RCY 8 W2
Lord Cl RED 67 J9
Lorne Pl SW CAL 42 L22
Los Alamos Cr NE CAL 31 Z11-12
Los Alamos Pl 100 to 300 NE CAL 31 Z11-12
Lott Creek Blvd RCY 33 B20
Lott Creek Dr RCY 33 A20
Lott Creek Dr RCY 33 Z20
Lott Creek Hollow RCY 33 A20
Lougheed Cir BAN 57 E2
Lougheed Cl RED 67 J-K9
Lougheed Dr SW CAL 42 L22
Louise Rd SW CAL 42 L22
Lount Cr BEI 69 B2
Lowe Ct SW CAL 42 L23
Lowell Ct SW CAL 41 K23
Lower Springbank Rd RCY 33 B17 C-D18 D19
Lower Springbank Rd SW CAL 34 F19-20
Loyola Pl W LET 87 H5
Ludor Cl BRO 90 B3
Lund Cl RED 67 J9
Lupine Ct MED 95 H5
Luxstone Blvd SW AIR 68 D2-3
Luxstone Cr SW AIR 68 D3
Luxstone Gr 100 200 SW AIR 68 D2-3
Luxstone Pk SW AIR 68 D3
Luxstone Pl 100 200 SW AIR 68 D3
Lyle Av SW CAL 42 L-M22
Lynch Cr SW CAL 42 L22
Lynn Rd SE CAL 44 T23
Lynnbrook Bay SE CAL 43 S23
Lynnbrook Cl SE CAL 43 S22
Lynnbrook Gt SE CAL 43 S22
Lynnbrook Pl SE CAL 43 S22-23
Lynnbrook Rd SE CAL 43 S22-23
Lynndale Cr SE CAL 44 T23
Lynndale Rd SE CAL 44 T23
Lynnover Cr SE CAL 43 S23 44 T23
Lynnover Pl 100 to 300 SE CAL 43 S23
Lynnover Rd SE CAL 43 S23
Lynnover Way SE CAL 43 S23
Lynnridge Bay SE CAL 43 S22
Lynnridge Ct SE CAL 43 S22
Lynnridge Mews SE CAL 43 S22
Lynnridge Pl SE CAL 43 S22
Lynnridge Village SE CAL 43 S22
Lynnview Cr SE CAL 43 S22
Lynnview Ct SE CAL 43 S22
Lynnview Pl SE CAL 43 S21-22
Lynnview Rd SE CAL 43 S22 S22 44 T22
Lynnview Rise SE CAL 43 S22
Lynnview Ter SE CAL 43 S21
Lynnview Way SE CAL 43 S22
Lynnwood Dr SE CAL 44 T22-23
Lynx La RCY 16 X9
Lynx Pl N LET 84 A10
Lynx Rd N LET 84 A-B10
Lynx St BAN 57 D1-2
Lynx Meadows Ct RCY 17 B8
Lynx Meadows Dr RCY 17 B8-9
Lynx Ridge Blvd RCY 17 B9
Lynx Ridge Rd RCY 17 A-B9
Lyons Cl RED 67 K8
Lyons Creek Rd CRO 80 F-G8
Lysander Cr SE CAL 43 S23
Lysander Dr SE CAL 43 S22-23
Lysander Pl 100 to 300 SE CAL 43 S23
Lytton Cr SE CAL 43 S23 44 T23

M

MacDonald Av SE CAL 37 Q17
MacDonald Pl CAN 58 E-F3
MacDonnell Av SW CAL 41 J21
MacEwan Dr NW CAL 20 L-M6 L-M7
MacEwan Ter NW CAL 20 L6
MacEwan Glen Cl NW CAL 20 M7
MacEwan Glen Dr NW CAL 20 L-M7
MacEwan Glen Mews NW CAL 20 L7
MacEwan Glen Pl 100 200 NW CAL 20 L-M7
MacEwan Glen Rd NW CAL 20 L7
MacEwan Glen Way NW CAL 20 L-M7
MacEwan Meadow Cr NW CAL 20 M6
MacEwan Meadow Gt NW CAL 20 M6
MacEwan Meadow Link NW CAL 20 M6
MacEwan Meadow Rise NW CAL 20 L-M6
MacEwan Meadow Way NW CAL 20 L6
MacEwan Park Cir NW CAL 20 L7
MacEwan Park Cl NW CAL 20 L6-7
MacEwan Park Gn NW CAL 20 L7
MacEwan Park Gt NW CAL 20 M7
MacEwan Park Hts NW CAL 20 L6
MacEwan Park Link NW CAL 20 M6-7
MacEwan Park Mnr NW CAL 20 L7
MacEwan Park Pl NW CAL 20 L6-7
MacEwan Park Rd NW CAL 20 L-M6
MacEwan Park Rise NW CAL 20 L6-7
MacEwan Park View NW CAL 20 L7
MacEwan Park Way NW CAL 20 L-M7
MacEwan Ridge Cir NW CAL 20 L6
MacEwan Ridge Cl NW CAL 20 L6
MacEwan Ridge Gt NW CAL 20 L6
MacEwan Ridge Pl NW CAL 20 L6
MacEwan Ridge View NW CAL 20 L6
MacEwan Ridge Village 100 200 NW CAL 20 L6
MacEwan Valley Gt NW CAL 20 L6
MacEwan Valley Mews 100 to 300 NW CAL 20 L-M6
MacEwan Valley Rd NW CAL 20 L-M6
MacFarlane Av RED 67 H7
MacKay Dr SW CAL 42 O22
Mackay Rd NW CAL 27 J13-14
MacKenzie Cr RED 67 H7-8
MacKenzie Way SW AIR 68 C2
MacKid Cr NE CAL 30 T15
MacKid Rd NE CAL 30 T14-15
MacLeay Rd NE CAL 30 T15
MacLeod Cl RED 67 H7
Macleod Dr W LET 87 J5
MacLeod Tr MED 92 E4
Macleod Tr SE CAL 7 D92-94 37 P16-17 42 O23-25 48 O26-28 53 P31-32
Macleod Tr SW CAL 37 P18-20 42 O21 43 P21 P21
Macleod Tr SW HIG 77 C1-2
Maddock Cr NE CAL 31 X15 39 X16
Maddock Dr NE CAL 39 X-Y16
Maddock La NE CAL 39 X16
Maddock Way NE CAL 31 X15 39 X16
Madeira Cl NE CAL 31 X15
Madeira Cr NE CAL 31 X15
Madeira Dr NE CAL 31 X15
Madeira Gt NE CAL 31 X15
Madeira Pl 100 200 NE CAL 31 X15
Madeira Rd NE CAL 31 X15
Madeira Way NE CAL 31 X15
Madigan Ct NE CAL 31 Y15
Madigan Dr NE CAL 31 X15 Y15 39 Y16
Madigan Village NE CAL 31 Y15
Madison Av SW CAL 36 O20
Madison Ct STM 71 C3
Madison Dr IRR 69 B2
Madison St TVY 74 D3-4
Maggie St SE CAL 37 Q17
Mah Cr RED 67 H7
Maidstone Bay NE CAL 31 X15
Maidstone Cr NE CAL 31 X15
Maidstone Dr NE CAL 31 X15
Maidstone Gn 100 200 NE CAL 31 X15
Maidstone Pl NE CAL 31 X15
Maidstone Rd NE CAL 31 X15
Maidstone Way NE CAL 31 X15
Main St CAN 58 E4
Main St DRU 73 C7
Main St IRR 69 B2
Main St TVY 74 C-D3
Main St N AIR 68 B3
Main St S AIR 68 C-E3
Maitland Cr NE CAL 31 Y14
Maitland Dr NE CAL 31 Y14-15
Maitland Gn NE CAL 31 Y14
Maitland Gt NE CAL 31 Y14
Maitland Hill NE CAL 31 Y15
Maitland Pl 100 200 NE CAL 31 Y15
Maitland Rd NE CAL 31 Y14-15
Maitland Rise NE CAL 31 Y14
Maitland Way NE CAL 31 Y15
Majestic Gt RCY 33 A20
Majestic Pl TAB 91 B-C2
Majestic Pt RCY 33 A20
Majestic View RCY 33 A20
Major Stewart La SE CAL 37 R-S17
Malcolm Cr RED 67 H7
Malibou Rd SW CAL 42 N-O22 43 P-Q22
Mallard Alley CAN 58 E4

Malvern Cl NE *CAL* **39** Y16
Malvern Cr NE *CAL* **31** Y15
Malvern Ct NE *CAL* **39** Y16
Malvern Dr NE *CAL* **31** Y15 **39** Y16
Malvern Gn NE *CAL* **31** Y15
Malvern Gt NE *CAL* **31** Y15
Malvern Pl NE *CAL* **31** Y15
Malvern Rd NE *CAL* **31** Y15 **39** Y16
Malvern Way NE *CAL* **31** Y15 **39** Y16
Manchester Rd SE *CAL* **37** P-Q19
Manhattan Rd SE *CAL* **37** Q20
Manilla Rd SE *CAL* **37** Q20
Manitoba Rd SE *CAL* **37** P-Q20
Manitou Rd SE *CAL* **37** P-Q20
Manning Cl NE *CAL* **29** S15
Manning Rd NE *CAL* **29** S15 **37** S16
Manning St *RED* **67** H7-8
Manor Rd *IRR* **69** B1
Manor Rd SW *CAL* **42** O22
Manor Park Cr *BRO* **90** A3
Manora Cr NE *CAL* **31** Y14
Manora Dr NE *CAL* . . .**31** X14-15 X-Y14 Y15
Manora Hill NE *CAL* **31** X14-15
Manora Pl NE *CAL* **31** X14-15
Manora Rd NE *CAL* **31** X14-15
Manora Rise NE *CAL* **31** X14-15
Manora Way NE *CAL* **31** X14-15
Many Horses Bay *RDW* **61** A3
Many Horses Cir *RDW* **61** A3
Many Horses Cl *RDW* **61** A3
Many Horses Cr *RDW* **61** A3
Many Horses Ct *RDW* **61** A-B3
Many Horses Dr *RDW* **61** A3
Many Horses Gdn *RDW* **61** A3
Many Horses Gn *RDW* **61** A-B3
Many Horses Gt *RDW* **61** B3
Many Horses Pk *RDW* **61** B3
Many Horses Pl *RDW* **61** A3-4
Many Horses Rd *CAL* **41** H23-24
Many Horses Rise *RDW* **61** A3-4
Maple Av *CRS* **62** A2
Maple Av *MED* **93** E5
Maple Dr *BRO* **90** C-D1
Maple Dr NW *CAL* **26** E12
Maple Gdns *STM* **71** B3
Maple Pl *CRS* **62** A2
Maple Pl *STM* **71** C3
Maple Pl SW *CAL* **42** O22
Maple St *OKO* **76** C3
Maple Walk *CRS* **62** A2
Maple Way SE *AIR* **69** D5
Maple Court Cr SE *CAL* **49** R26
Maple Green Way *STM* **71** B-C3
Maple Grove Cr *STM* **71** B-E3
Maple Leaf Rd *STM* **71** C3-4
Maple Tree Way *STM* **71** B3
Maplebend Dr SE *CAL* **49** R26-27
Maplebrook Pl SE *CAL* **49** Q26
Mapleburn Dr SE *CAL* **49** R27
Maplecreek Dr SE *CAL* **49** R26
Maplecrest Rd SE *CAL* **49** R26-27
Maplecroft Rd SE *CAL* **49** R26
Mapledale Pl SE *CAL* **49** Q-R26
Mapleford Rd SE *CAL* **49** R26-27
Mapleglade Cl SE *CAL* **49** R27
Mapleglade Cr SE *CAL* **49** R27
Mapleglade Dr SE *CAL* **49** R27
Mapleglade Pl SE *CAL* **49** R27
Mapleglen Cr SE *CAL* **49** R26
Maplegrove Pl SE *CAL* **49** Q26
Maplemont Rd SE *CAL* **49** R26
Mapleridge Cr SE *CAL* **49** R26
Mapleridge Ests *STM* **71** C3
Mapleshire Cr SE *CAL* **49** R26-27
Mapleton Dr SE *CAL* **49** Q-R26
Maplewood Cr SE *CAL* **49** Q26
Maplewood Dr *BLD* **75** C7
Maplewood Dr *STM* **71** B-C3
Maplewood Ests *STM* **71** B-C3
Maplewood Gn *STM* **71** C3-4
Maplewood Pl *BLD* **75** C7
Maplewood Way *BLD* **75** C7
Maranda Cl NE *CAL* **30** V-W15
Marbank Dr NE *CAL* **30** V-W15
Marbank Pl NE *CAL* **30** W15
Marbank Way NE *CAL* **30** V14-15
Marbrooke Cir NE *CAL* . . . .
. . . .**30** W15 **38** W16 **39** X16
Marbury Pl NE *CAL* **38** W16
Marchand Cr NE *CAL* **38** W16
Marcombe Cr NE *CAL* **30** W15
Marcombe Dr NE *CAL* **30** W15
Marcombe Pl NE *CAL* **30** W15
Marcombe Rd NE *CAL* **30** W15
Marcombe Way NE *CAL* **30** W15
Marda Link SW *CAL* **36** L19
Mardale Cr NE *CAL* **30** W14
Mardale Dr NE *CAL* **30** W14-15
Mardale Rd NE *CAL* **30** W14-15
Mardale Way NE *CAL* **30** W14
Margaret Av SE *CAL* **37** Q18
Margate Cl NE *CAL* **30** V-W15
Margate Pl NE *CAL* **30** V15
Margodt Cl *INN* **63** D1-2
Marian Cr NE *CAL* **30** W15
Marian Rd NE *CAL* **30** W15
Marian Way NE *CAL* **30** W15
Marina Dr *CHE* **70** C1-2
Marina Rd *CHE* **70** C2
Marion Cr *RED* **67** H7-8
Mariposa Dr NE *CAL* **29** S15 **30** T15
Mariposa Pl NE *CAL* **29** S15
Markerville Rd NE *CAL* **30** T15 **38** T16
Markle Cr *RED* **67** H8
Markwick Dr *MED* **94** G4 **95** G5
Marlborough Dr NE *CAL* **30** V-W15
Marlborough Pl NE *CAL* .**30** W15 **31** X14-15
Marlborough Way NE *CAL* . .**30** V15 **38** V16
Marlowe Pl NE *CAL* **29** Q14
Marlyn Ct NE *CAL* **30** V14
Marlyn Pl 100 200 NE *CAL* **30** V14
Marlyn Way NE *CAL* **30** V14-15 W14-15
Marmot Cr *BAN* **57** C2-3
Marmot Pl *BAN* **57** C3
Marmot Rd N *LET* **84** A9
Marmot St *BAN* **57** C3
Marpole Bay NE *CAL* **30** V15
Marpole Pl NE *CAL* **30** V15
Marpole Rd NE *CAL* **30** V15
Marquette St SW *CAL* **36** N18-19
Marquis Pl SE *AIR* **69** E5
Marquis Way SE *AIR* **69** D-E5
Marquis of Lorne Tr SE *CAL* . . . .
. . . .**53** R-S34 **54** U-V33 **55** X-Z32
Marsden Rd NE *CAL* **29** Q14
Marsella Ct SE *AIR* **69** D5
Marsh Rd NE *CAL* **7** E92 **37** Q16
Marshall Av *MED* **95** G5
Marshall Dr *BRO* **90** C1
Marshall Rd NE *CAL* **30** W15
Marshall Rise NW *HIG* **77** A1
Marsham Rd NE *CAL* **30** W15
Martell Rd NE *CAL* **30** W15 **38** W16
Martelo Ct NE *CAL* **30** V15
Marten St *BAN* **57** C-D2
Martha's Cl NE *CAL* **22** W8
Martha's Gn NE *CAL* **22** W8
Martha's Mnr 100 to 300 NE *CAL* . . . . . .
. . . .**22** W8 **23** X8
Martha's Pl NE *CAL* **22** W8
Martha's Way NE *CAL* **22** W8
Martha's Haven Gdns NE *CAL* **22** W8
Martha's Haven Gn NE *CAL* **22** W8
Martha's Haven Gt NE *CAL* **22** W8
Martha's Haven Heath NE *CAL* **22** W8
Martha's Haven Mnr NE *CAL* **22** W8
Martha's Haven Parade NE *CAL* .**22** W8-9
Martha's Haven Pk NE *CAL* **22** W8
Martha's Haven Pl NE *CAL* **22** W8
Martha's Haven Way NE *CAL* **22** W8
Martha's Meadow Cl NE *CAL* **22** W8
Martha's Meadow Cl NE *CAL* **22** W8
Martha's Meadow Dr NE *CAL* **22** W8
Martha's Meadow Gn NE *CAL* **22** W8
Martha's Meadow Gt NE *CAL* **22** W8
Martha's Meadow Link NE *CAL* . . .**22** W8
Martha's Meadow Pl NE *CAL* **22** W8
Martin Av *MED* **92** C-D3
Martin Av *OKO* **76** B-C2
Martin Cl *RED* **67** H7-8
Martin Pl *IRR* **69** B2
Martin Crossing Cl NE *CAL* **22** W8
Martin Crossing Cr NE *CAL* **23** X9
Martin Crossing Ct NE *CAL* **22** W9
Martin Crossing Cv NE *CAL* **22** W8-9
Martin Crossing Dr NE *CAL* **22** W9
Martin Crossing Gn NE *CAL* **22** W9
Martin Crossing Gr NE *CAL* **23** X9
Martin Crossing Link NE *CAL* **23** X8
Martin Crossing Mnr NE *CAL* **22** W8-9
Martin Crossing Pk NE *CAL* **22** W9
Martin Crossing Rise NE *CAL* **22** W9
Martin Crossing Way NE *CAL* **23** X8
Martinbrook Link NE *CAL* **22** W9
Martinbrook Pl 100 to 300 NE *CAL* .**23** X9
Martinbrook Rd NE *CAL* **22** W9
Martindale Bay NE *CAL* **23** X8
Martindale Blvd NE *CAL* **22** W8 W9 **23** X8 X9
Martindale Cl NE *CAL* **23** X9
Martindale Cr NE *CAL* **22** W9 **23** X9
Martindale Ct NE *CAL* **23** X9
Martindale Dr NE *CAL* **23** X8-9
Martindale Gt NE *CAL* **22** W9
Martindale Mews NE *CAL* **23** X9
Martinglen Cl NE *CAL* **22** W9
Martinglen Link NE *CAL* **22** W9
Martinglen Mews NE *CAL* **22** V-W9
Martinglen Pl NE *CAL* **22** W9
Martinglen Way NE *CAL* **22** W9
Martingrove Ct NE *CAL* **23** X9
Martingrove Dr NE *CAL* **23** X9
Martingrove Mews NE *CAL* **23** X9
Martingrove Pl NE *CAL* **23** X9
Martingrove Rd NE *CAL* **23** X9
Martingrove Way NE *CAL* **23** X9
Martinpark Way NE *CAL* **22** W9
Martinridge Cr NE *CAL* **22** W9
Martinridge Gr NE *CAL* **22** W9
Martinridge Pl NE *CAL* **22** W9
Martinridge Rd NE *CAL* **22** W9
Martinridge Way NE *CAL* **22** W9
Martinvalley Cr NE *CAL* **23** X8
Martinvalley Ct NE *CAL* **23** X8
Martinvalley Pl NE *CAL* **23** X8
Martinvalley Rd NE *CAL* **23** X8
Martinvalley Way NE *CAL* **23** X8
Martinview Cl NE *CAL* **22** W9
Martinview Cr NE *CAL* **22** W9
Martinview Rd NE *CAL* **22** W9 **23** X9
Martinwood Ct NE *CAL* **23** X9
Martinwood Mews NE *CAL* **23** X9
Martinwood Pl 100 to 300 NE *CAL* .**23** X9
Martinwood Rd NE *CAL* **23** X9
Martinwood Way NE *CAL* **23** X9
Marwood Cir NE *CAL* **38** V-W16
Marwood Pl NE *CAL* **38** W16
Marwood Rd NE *CAL* **38** V-W16
Marwood Way NE *CAL* **38** W16
Maryland Pl SW *CAL* **42** N22
Maryvale Cr NE *CAL* **30** W15
Maryvale Dr NE *CAL* **30** V-W15
Maryvale Pl NE *CAL* **30** V15
Maryvale Rd NE *CAL* **30** V-W15
Maryvale Way NE *CAL* **30** W15
Massey Pl SW *CAL* **42** N22
Matador Cr NE *CAL* **30** T15
Matheson Dr NE *CAL* **29** S15 **30** T15
Maunsell Cl NE *CAL* **30** T15
Maunsell Dr NE *CAL* **30** T15
Maxwell Av *RED* **67** H7
Mayberry Cl *RED* **67** H-J8
Mayday Walk SW *CAL* **35** K17
Mayfair Cl SE *AIR* **69** D5
Mayfair Rd SW *CAL* **42** O22
Mayland Dr NE *CAL* **30** T15
Maynard Rd SE *CAL* **38** T16
Mayor Magrath Dr N *LET* **84** E9-10
Mayor Magrath Dr S *LET* . . . .
. . . .**88** F9-10 G10 J10-11 K11
McBlane Cl *RED* **67** H8
McBride Cr *RED* **67** H7
McCaig Cr *MED* **95** H6
McCall Gdns NE *CAL* **21** Q9-10
McCall Way NE *CAL* **22** T7-10 **30** T11
McCaskill Dr *CRS* **62** A2-3
McConnel Cl *RED* **67** H-J6 H-J7
McCool Cr *CRS* **62** C2
McCool St *CRS* **62** C3
McCracken Cr NE *AIR* **68** B3
McCulloch Cr *IRR* **69** B1-2
McCullough Cr *RED* **67** H8
McCune Av *RED* **67** H7
McCutcheon Dr *MED* **92** D2 D3
McCutcheon Pl *MED* **92** C2-3
McDougall Cr *RED* **67** H8
McDougall Ct NE *CAL* **37** Q16
McDougall Rd NE *CAL* **7** E92 **37** Q-R16
McGill Blvd W *LET* **86** J4 **87** H5 J5
McGill St *RED* **67** H7-8
McGonigal Dr NE *CAL* **29** S15 **30** T15
McHugh Ct NE *CAL* **30** T14
McHugh Pl NE *CAL* **30** T14-15
McHugh Rd NE *CAL* **30** T14-15
McIntosh Av *MED* **92** D4
McIntosh Av *RED* **67** H7
McIntosh Rd NE *CAL* **30** T15 **38** T16
McIvor Blvd SE *CAL* **55** X-Y31
McKee Cl *RED* **67** H7
McKenna Cr SE *CAL* **54** U-V33
McKenna La SE *CAL* **54** U-V33
McKenna Mews SE *CAL* **54** U33
McKenna Mnr SE *CAL* **54** V33
McKenna Pl SE *CAL* **54** U-V33
McKenna Rd SE *CAL* **54** U33
McKenna Way SE *CAL* **54** U33
McKenzie Cr *MED* **92** C3
McKenzie Dr SE *CAL* **54** V32-33
McKenzie Pl SE *CAL* **54** V32
McKenzie Lake Bay 100 to 1000 SE *CAL* **54** V31
McKenzie Lake Blvd SE *CAL* **54** U32-33 V31
McKenzie Lake Cr SE *CAL* **54** V31-32
McKenzie Lake Cv 100 to 300 SE *CAL* **54** V32
McKenzie Lake Gdns SE *CAL* **54** U-V31
McKenzie Lake Gn SE *CAL* **54** V32
McKenzie Lake Gt SE *CAL* **54** V31-32
McKenzie Lake Is SE *CAL* **54** V31-32
McKenzie Lake Ldg SE *CAL* **54** V32
McKenzie Lake Mnr SE *CAL* **54** V32
McKenzie Lake Pl SE *CAL* **54** V31
McKenzie Lake Pt SE *CAL* **54** V32
McKenzie Lake View SE *CAL* **54** V32
McKenzie Lake Way SE *CAL* . . .**54** V31-32
McKenzie Towne Av SE *CAL* **54** W31 **55** X31
McKenzie Towne Blvd SE *CAL* **54** V-W31 **55** X31
McKenzie Towne Dr SE *CAL* **54** W32
McKenzie Towne Gt SE *CAL* **54** W31 **55** X31
McKenzie Towne Link SE *CAL* **55** X31
McKernan Ct SE *CAL* **54** V32-33
McKernan Pl SE *CAL* **54** V32-33
McKernan Rd SE *CAL* **54** V32
McKerrell Cl SE *CAL* **54** V33
McKerrell Cr SE *CAL* **54** V32-33
McKerrell Ct SE *CAL* **54** V32-33
McKerrell Gdns 100 200 SE *CAL* .**54** V32
McKerrell Pl 100 to 500 SE *CAL* . .**54** V32
McKerrell Way SE *CAL* **54** V32
McKillop Pl N *LET* **84** D-E10
McKinley Bay SE *CAL* **54** U32-33
McKinley Ct SE *CAL* **54** U-V32
McKinley Pl SE *CAL* **54** U32-33
McKinley Rd SE *CAL* **54** U32-33
McKinley Rise SE *CAL* **54** U32
McKinley Way SE *CAL* **54** U-V32
McKinnon Cr *RED* **67** H7
McKinnon Cr NE *CAL* **30** T15 **38** T16
McKinnon Dr NE *CAL* . . .**30** T14-15 **38** T16
McKinnon Pl 100 200 NE *CAL* **30** T15 **38** T16
McKinnon Rd NE *CAL* **30** T14
McKinnon Ter NE *CAL* **30** T14
McKittrick Pl *BRO* **90** C3
McKnight Blvd NE *CAL* **29** Q-S11 **30** T-W11 **31** X-Y11
McKnight Blvd NW *CAL* **28** O11
McLaren Village NW *CAL* **27** J-K12
McLean St *RED* **67** H8
Mcleod Cr *OLD* **62** C3
McLevin Cr *RED* **67** H8
McMaster Blvd W *LET* **86** H-J4
McMillan Av *RED* **67** H7
McNab Cl *DRU* **72** B2
McNab Park St *BRO* **90** C-D4
McNeely Ct *MED* **95** G5
McNeill Rd NE *CAL* **29** S15
McPhee St *RED* **67** H7
McPherson Rd NE *CAL* **37** Q-R16
McRae St *OKO* **76** C3
McTavish Pl NE *CAL* **29** S11 **30** T11
McTavish Rd NE *CAL* **29** S11
McVicar St *RED* **67** H6-7
Meadow Bay *RCY* **9** C2
Meadow Cl *COC* **60** C2
Meadow Ct *COC* **60** C2-3
Meadow Dr *RCY* **9** B2 C2
Meadow Pl *COC* **60** B-C2
Meadow Pl SE *AIR* **69** D5
Meadow Way *COC* **60** B-C2
Meadow Brook Bay 100 to 600 SE *AIR* **69** D5-6
Meadow Brook Dr SE *AIR* **69** D5
Meadow Brook Gt SE *AIR* **69** D5-6
Meadow Lake Cl *BRO* **90** C4
Meadow Lake Gt *BRO* **90** C4
Meadowbrook Dr *BRO* **90** C4
Meadowlark Blvd N *LET* **84** B9-10 C10
Meadowlark Cr SW *CAL* **42** O22
Meadowlark Pl N *LET* **84** C10
Meadowlark Rd SE *AIR* **69** D5
Meadows La *MED* **95** J6
Meadowview Cr *BRO* **90** B1
Meadowview Pl SW *CAL* **42** O22
Meadowview Rd SW *CAL* **42** O22
Medalta Av *MED* **95** F6
Medford Pl SW *CAL* **42** N22
Meeres Cl *RED* **67** H7
Melville Pl SW *CAL* **42** N-O22
Memorial Dr NE *CAL* . . . .
. . . . . .**7** D-E92 **37** Q-R16 **38** V-W16 **39** X-Y16
Memorial Dr NW *CAL* . . . .
. . . .**6** A-B91 **28** O15 **36** M16 O16
Memorial Dr SE *CAL* **38** T16-17 U16
Meota Rd NE *CAL* **29** S15 **30** T15
Meredith Rd NE *CAL* **7** E92 **37** Q16
Merganser Dr E *CHE* **70** E3-4
Merganser Dr W *CHE* **70** E1-2
Meridian Rd NE *CAL* . . .**30** T15 U14 **38** T16
Merrill Dr NE *CAL* **29** Q13
Metcalf Av *RED* **67** H8
Michener Cl *RED* **67** G7
Michener Cr *RED* **67** G7
Michener Dr *RED* **67** G6
Michener Gn *RED* **67** G7
Michichi Dr *DRU* **73** B6

Michiels St *RED* 67 H7
Michigan Pl S *LET* 88 G11
Micmac Blvd W *LET* 86 G4
Micmac Pl W *LET* 86 G4
Midbend Cr SE *CAL* 53 P32
Midbend Pl 100 to 300 SE *CAL* 53 P31-32
Midcrest Cr SE *CAL* 53 P31
Midcrest Rise SE *CAL* 53 P31
Middle Springs Dr *BAN* 57 E1
Middleton Dr SE *CAL* 30 T15
Midglen Dr SE *CAL* 53 Q31
Midglen Gdns SE *CAL* 53 Q31
Midglen La SE *CAL* 53 Q31
Midglen Pl 100 to 300 SE *CAL* 53 Q31
Midglen Rd SE *CAL* 53 Q31
Midglen Ter 100 to 300 SE *CAL* 53 Q31
Midglen Way SE *CAL* 53 Q31
Midlake Blvd SE *CAL* 53 P31 Q31
Midlake Gn SE *CAL* 53 Q31
Midlake Pl SE *CAL* 53 Q31
Midland Cr SE *CAL* 53 Q32
Midland Pl 100 200 SE *CAL* 53 Q32
Midlawn Cl SE *CAL* 53 P31
Midlawn Gn SE *CAL* 53 P31
Midlawn Pl SE *CAL* 53 P31
Midnapore Pl SE *CAL* 53 P31
Midpark Blvd SE *CAL* 53 P32
Midpark Cl SE *CAL* 53 Q32
Midpark Cr SE *CAL* 53 P31-32
Midpark Dr SE *CAL* 53 P31-32
Midpark Gdns SE *CAL* 53 P31
Midpark Gt SE *CAL* 53 P32
Midpark Hill SE *CAL* 53 P31
Midpark Pl SE *CAL* 53 P-Q31
Midpark Rise SE *CAL* 53 P-Q31
Midpark Way SE *CAL* 53 P32
Midridge Bay SE *CAL* 49 Q30
Midridge Cl SE *CAL* 53 P-Q31
Midridge Cr SE *CAL* 53 P-Q31
Midridge Dr SE *CAL* 53 P-Q31
Midridge Gdns SE *CAL* 53 P31
Midridge Gn SE *CAL* 53 P31
Midridge Pl 100 200 SE *CAL* 49 P30 53 P31
Midridge Rd SE *CAL* 53 P-Q31
Midridge Rise SE *CAL* 53 Q31
Midvalley Cr SE *CAL* 53 Q-R32
Midvalley Dr SE *CAL* 53 Q-R31
Midvalley Pl 100 to 300 SE *CAL* 53 Q31-32 R31-32
Midvalley Rd SE *CAL* 53 Q31-32
Midvalley Rise SE *CAL* 53 Q31
Midvalley Way SE *CAL* 53 Q31-32
Mill St *MED* 95 F5-6
Millar Rd NE *CAL* 30 T15
Millbank Bay SW *CAL* 52 O31
Millbank Cl SW *CAL* 52 O31
Millbank Cr SW *CAL* 52 O31
Millbank Ct SW *CAL* 52 O31
Millbank Dr SW *CAL* 52 O31
Millbank Hill SW *CAL* 52 O31
Millbank Rd SW *CAL* 52 O31
Millcrest Ct SW *CAL* 52 N31
Millcrest Gn SW *CAL* 52 N31
Millcrest Pl SW *CAL* 52 N31
Millcrest Rd SW *CAL* 52 N31
Millcrest Rise SW *CAL* 52 N31
Millcrest Way SW *CAL* 52 N31
Miller Av NW *CAL* 28 N14
Millican Rd SW *CAL* 44 T22
Milligan Dr *OKO* 76 B3
Millpark Pl SW *CAL* 48 O30 52 O31
Millpark Rd SW *CAL* 52 N31
Millpark Rise SW *CAL* 52 N-O31
Millpark Way SW *CAL* 52 N-O31
Millrise Blvd SW *CAL* 52 O31
Millrise Cl SW *CAL* 52 N-O31
Millrise Cr SW *CAL* 52 N31
Millrise Dr SW *CAL* 52 N-O31
Millrise Gn SW *CAL* 52 N31
Millrise Hill SW *CAL* 48 N30 52 N31
Millrise La SW *CAL* 52 O31
Millrise Mews SW *CAL* 52 O31
Millrise Mnr SW *CAL* 52 N31
Millrise Pt SW *CAL* 48 O30 52 O31
Millrise Sq 100 to 400 SW *CAL* 52 M-N31
Millrise Way SW *CAL* 48 O30 52 O31
Millside Cr SW *CAL* 48 O30 52 O31
Millside Ct SW *CAL* 52 O31
Millside Dr SW *CAL* 52 O31
Millside Pl SW *CAL* 52 O31
Millside Rd SW *CAL* 52 O31
Millside Way SW *CAL* 52 O31
Millview Bay 100 to 500 SW *CAL* 48 M30 N30 52 M31 N31
Millview Com SW *CAL* 52 N31
Millview Ct 100 200 SW *CAL* 52 N31
Millview Dr SW *CAL* 52 N31
Millview Gdns 100 200 SW *CAL* .. 52 N31
Millview Gn SW *CAL* 52 M31
Millview Gt SW *CAL* 52 M31
Millview Mnr SW *CAL* 52 N31
Millview Pk SW *CAL* 52 M-N31
Millview Pl 100 to 300 SW *CAL* 48 N30 52 N31
Millview Rd SW *CAL* 52 N31
Millview Rise SW *CAL* 52 N31
Millview Sq SW *CAL* 52 N31
Millview Way SW *CAL* 52 N31
Millward Pl NE *CAL* 30 T15
Millward Rd NE *CAL* 30 T15
Milne Dr NE *CAL* 30 T15
Milne Pl *MED* 95 G5
Minto Av *MED* 93 E6
Misano Av SW *CAL* 41 J22
Misano Ct 100 to 600 SW *CAL* .. 41 J22
Mission Rd SW *CAL* 36 O19 37 P19
Mist Rd SW *HIG* 77 C1
Misty Morning Dr *RCY* 33 Z20
Mitchell Av *RED* 67 H7
Mitchell Cr *MED* 92 D3
Modesto Rd W *LET* 86 H4
Mohawk Rd W *LET* 86 F-G4 G4
Molly Bannister Dr *RED* 66 J5
Monarch Gt SE *AIR* 69 D5
Moncton Rd NE *CAL* 29 Q14
Mons Av SW *CAL* 36 L20
Montalban Av NW *CAL* 27 I13
Montalban Cr NW *CAL* 27 I13
Montalban Dr NW *CAL* 27 I13
Montana Cr NW *CAL* 27 I13
Montana Dr NW *CAL* 27 I13
Montane Rd *CAN* 59 F5
Montcalm Cr SW *CAL* 36 N18-19
Monterey Av NW *CAL* 27 I14
Monterrey Sq NE *CAL* 31 Y14
Montgomery Av NW *CAL* 27 I14
Montgomery Blvd NW *CAL* 27 I14
Montgomery Rd NW *CAL* 27 I14
Montgomery View NW *CAL* 27 I-J14
Montreal Av SW *CAL* 36 N18
Montrose Cr NE *CAL* 29 Q14
Montserrat Dr NW *CAL* 27 H13
Monument Pl SE *CAL* 38 U16
Moodie Rd NE *CAL* 30 T15
Moon Cr *RED* 67 H7
Moor St SW *CAL* 42 O22
Moorcroft Rd SW *CAL* 42 N22
Moore Cr *RED* 65 F6
Moorgate Pl SW *CAL* 42 N22
Moose St *BAN* 57 C-D2
Moraine Rd *CAN* 59 F6
Moraine Rd NE *CAL* 30 U15 38 U16
Moraine Lake Rd *LKL* 56 D3
Moreuil Ct SW *CAL* 36 L-M20
Morley Cr NW *CAL* 28 L12-13
Morley Tr NW (Banff Trail) *CAL* 28 L12 L-M13
Morley Tr NW (Dalhousie) *CAL* 19 H10
Moro Dr SW *CAL* 36 L19
Morris *CAN* 58 G4
Morris Av *RED* 67 H8
Morris Cr SE *AIR* 69 D-E5
Morris Ct *MED* 95 G5
Morris Pl SE *AIR* 69 D-E5
Morris Rd SE *AIR* 69 D5
Morrison St *TVY* 74 C3
Morrison St SW *CAL* 36 N18
Morrow Ct *MED* 92 D3
Morton Av NE *CAL* 29 Q-R14
Moseley Cl *RED* 67 H7
Mossip Av *CRS* 62 A2
Motherwell Rd NE *CAL* 30 T14-15
Mount Peechee Pl *CAN* 58 E4
Mount Rundle Pl *CAN* 58 E4
Mount Aberdeen Cir SE *CAL* 50 V30
Mount Aberdeen Cl SE *CAL* 50 V29
Mount Aberdeen Gr SE *CAL* 50 V29-30
Mount Aberdeen Link SE *CAL* .. 50 V29-30
Mount Aberdeen Mnr SE *CAL* 50 V29
Mount Alberta Bay SE *CAL* 54 V31
Mount Alberta Ct SE *CAL* 54 U-V31
Mount Alberta Gn SE *CAL* 54 U31
Mount Alberta Mnr SE *CAL* 54 U31
Mount Alberta Pl 100 200 SE *CAL* 54 U31
Mount Alberta View SE *CAL* 54 U-V31
Mount Alderson Cr W *LET* 87 J-K5
Mount Alderson Pl W *LET* 87 J5
Mount Allan Cir SE *CAL* 50 V30
Mount Apex Cr SE *CAL* 50 V30
Mount Apex Gn SE *CAL* 50 V30
Mount Assiniboine Cir SE *CAL* .. 54 U32
Mount Assiniboine Gt SE *CAL* .. 54 U32-33
Mount Assiniboine Pl 100 200 SE *CAL* 54 U32
Mount Backus Cr W *LET* 87 J-K5
Mount Backus Pl W *LET* 87 J-K5
Mount Belcher Pl SE *CAL* 54 U32
Mount Blakiston Bay W *LET* .. 86 K4 87 K5
Mount Blakiston Pl W *LET* 86 K4 87 K5
Mount Blakiston Rd W *LET* .86 K4 87 J-K5
Mount Brazeau Rd W *LET* 86 J-K4
Mount Brewster Cir SE *CAL* .50 V30 54 V31
Mount Brewster Pl SE *CAL* 54 V31
Mount Burke Blvd W *LET* .. 86 J4 87 J5 K5
Mount Cascade Cl SE *CAL* 54 U32
Mount Cascade Pl 100 to 400 SE *CAL* 54 T-U32
Mount Copper Gn SE *CAL* 54 U32
Mount Copper Pk 100 200 SE *CAL* 54 U32
Mount Cornwall Cir SE *CAL* 54 V31
Mount Cornwall Mews 100 200 SE *CAL* 54 V31
Mount Crandell Bay W *LET* 86 K4
Mount Crandell Cr W *LET* 86 K4
Mount Douglas Cir SE *CAL* 50 V30
Mount Douglas Cl SE *CAL* 50 V30
Mount Douglas Ct 100 to 400 SE *CAL* 50 V29-30
Mount Douglas Gn 100 to 400 SE *CAL* 50 V30
Mount Douglas Mnr 100 to 300 SE *CAL* 50 V30
Mount Douglas Pl 100 to 400 SE *CAL* 50 V30
Mount Douglas Pt SE *CAL* 50 U29 V30
Mount Douglas Villas SE *CAL* 50 V30
Mount Gibraltar Hts SE *CAL* 54 U33
Mount Gibraltar Pl SE *CAL* 54 U33
Mount Kidd Gdns SE *CAL* 54 U32-33
Mount Kidd Pt SE *CAL* 54 U33
Mount Kidd Rd SE *CAL* 54 U33
Mount Lorette Cl SE *CAL* .. 50 V30 54 V31
Mount Lorette Pl 100 to 400 SE *CAL* 50 V30 54 V31
Mount McKenzie Bay SE *CAL* .. 50 V29-30
Mount McKenzie Dr SE *CAL* 50 V29-30 54 V31
Mount McKenzie Gdns 100 to 300 SE *CAL* 54 V31
Mount McKenzie Vill SE *CAL* .. 54 U-V31
Mount McKenzie Way SE *CAL* .. 54 U-V31
Mount Norquay Gt SE *CAL* 54 T-U32
Mount Norquay Pk 100 200 SE *CAL* 54 U32
Mount Norquay Rd *BAN* 57 C-D1
Mount Reliant Pl SE *CAL* 54 U32
Mount Robson Cir SE *CAL* 54 U32
Mount Robson Cl SE *CAL* 54 U32
Mount Robson Gt SE *CAL* 54 U32
Mount Royal Ct SW *CAL* .. 35 K20 36 L20
Mount Royal Pl W *LET* 86 J4
Mount Rundle Bay W *LET* 87 K5
Mount Rundle Blvd W *LET* 87 K5
Mount Rundle Pl W *LET* 87 K5
Mount Rundle Rd W *LET* 87 K5
Mount Rundle Way W *LET* 87 K5
Mount Selkirk Cl SE *CAL* 54 V31
Mount Selkirk Pl SE *CAL* 54 V31
Mount Sparrowhawk Ldg SE *CAL* .54 U32
Mount Sparrowhawk Pl 100 to 400 SE *CAL* 54 U32
Mount Victoria Pl 100 to 300 SE *CAL* 54 U31-32
Mount Yamnuska Ct SE *CAL* 54 U33
Mount Yamnuska Pl SE *CAL* 54 U33
Mountain Av *BAN* 57 E1-2
Mountain Av *CAN* 58 D4 D4 59 D5 E5
Mountain Av *CRS* 62 A2-3
Mountain Cir SE *AIR* 69 D5
Mountain La *BAN* 57 E2
Mountain Pl *OKO* 76 B-C2
Mountain St *CAN* 59 E5
Mountain St *COC* 61 B5
Mountain St *OKO* 76 B2-3 C2-3
Mountain Goat La *BAN* 57 D1-2
Mountain Park Cir SE *CAL* 54 U31
Mountain Park Dr SE *CAL* 54 U31-33
Mountain River Estates Rd *RCY* .. 32 V17
Mountain View Cl *OLD* 62 B2-3
Mountview Cr NE *CAL* 29 Q14
Muir Av *RED* 67 H8
Muir Cr *MED* 92 C3
Muldrew Cr *RED* 67 H7-8
Munro Cr *RED* 67 H7
Munro Dr NE *CAL* 30 T15
Munson St *CRS* 62 B2
Murdoch Cl *CRS* 62 B2
Murdoch St *CRS* 62 A-B2
Murdock Pl *IRR* 69 B2
Murphy Av *RED* 67 H8
Murphy Pl NE *CAL* 30 T15 38 T16
Murphy Rd NE *CAL* 30 T15
Murray Pl *MED* 92 D4
Murray Pl NE *CAL* 30 T15 38 T16
Murray Hill Rd *DRU* 72 A1
Muskoka Dr NE *CAL* 29 S15 37 S16
Muskrat St *BAN* 57 D2

N

Nagel Av *RED* 64 D4
Nagway Ct *RCY* 9 A5
Nagway Rd *RCY* 9 A5 B5
Nahanni Dr *BAN* 57 E2
Namaka Cr NW *CAL* 28 N11-12
Nance Av *RED* 64 C-D4
Nanton Av *CRS* 62 A-B2
Nanton Rd NW *CAL* 28 N11
Nash St *RED* 64 D4
Natalie St *MED* 95 F8
Neal Cl *RED* 64 D4
Nebraska Rd W *LET* 86 H4
Neilly Av *RED* 64 D4
Neilson Cl *RED* 64 C-D4
Nellis Av *RED* 64 C4
Nelson Rd NW *CAL* 28 N11
Nelson St *RED* 64 D4
Nemiskam Rd NW *CAL* 20 N10 28 N11
Nesbitt Rd NW *CAL* 20 N-O10 28 N-O11
Nevada Pl W *LET* 86 G-H4
Nevada Rd W *LET* 86 H4
Neville Cl *RED* 64 D4
New Pl SE *CAL* 37 R-S17
New St SE *CAL* 37 R-S17
New Bow La SE *CAL* 37 R-S17
New Brighton Cir SE *CAL* 55 X31
New Brighton Cl SE *CAL* 51 X30
New Brighton Dr SE *CAL* .51 X30 55 X-Y31
New Brighton Gt SE *CAL* 55 X31
New Brighton Link SE *CAL* 55 X31
New Brighton Mews 100 200 SE *CAL* 55 X31
New Brighton Mnr SE *CAL* 55 X31
New Brighton Pl 100 to 400 SE *CAL* 51 X30 55 X31
New Brighton Way SE *CAL* 55 Y31
Newcastle Gn *DRU* 73 C5
Newcastle Rd *DRU* 73 C5
Newcastle Tr *DRU* 72 C4 73 C5-6
Newcombe Cr *RED* 64 D4
Newcombe Pl NW *CAL* 20 N10 28 N11
Newell Cr *BRO* 90 B3-4
Newlands Av *RED* 64 C-D4
Newton Cr *RED* 64 D4
Nichols Cr *RED* 64 D4
Nickle Rd NW *CAL* 28 N11
Nicola Pl NW *CAL* 28 N11
Nina Gdns NE *CAL* 37 R16
Ninga Rd NW *CAL* 20 N10
Nipawin Cr NW *CAL* 28 N11
Nipigon Rd S *LET* 88 G11-12
Niska Pl W *LET* 86 G3
Niven Pl NW *CAL* 20 N10 28 N11
Niven Rd NW *CAL* 28 N11
Niven St *RED* 64 D3-4
Noble Av *RED* 64 C4
Noble Ct *MED* 92 E2
Noble Rd NW *CAL* 28 N11
Nokomis Pl NW *CAL* 20 N10 28 N11
Nolan Rd NW *CAL* 28 N-O11
Nolan St *RED* 64 C4-5
Norby Cr *RED* 64 C4
Nordegg Cr *RED* 64 C4-5
Nordegg Cr NW *CAL* 28 N11
Norfolk Dr NW *CAL* 20 O10
Norfolk Rd NW *CAL* 20 O10
Norfolk Way NW *CAL* 20 O10
Normandy Dr SW *CAL* 36 L19-20
Normandy Rd S *LET* 88 F10
Norquay Ct NW *CAL* 28 N11
Norquay Dr NW *CAL* 28 N11
Norquay Hts NW *CAL* 28 N11
Norquay St *RED* 64 C4-5
Norris Cl *RED* 64 D4
Norris Rd NW *CAL* 20 N10 28 N11
Norseman Pl NW *CAL* 20 N10
Norseman Rd NW *CAL* 20 N10
North Rd *BEI* 69 A2-3
North Dinosaur Tr *DRU* 72 B2-3 73 B5-6
North Haven Dr NW *CAL* 20 N10 28 N11
North Railway Av *DRU* 73 C7
North Railway St *OKO* 76 C3-4 D4-5
North River Dr *DRU* 72 C3-4
North Royalite Way *TVY* 74 D4
Northcote Rd NW *CAL* 28 N11
Northey Av *RED* 64 C-D4
Northland Dr *RED* 65 B6
Northland Dr NW *CAL* 19 J10 27 J11
Northlands Cr *MED* 92 B4
Northlands Way *MED* 92 B4
Northmount Cr NW *CAL* 20 O10 28 O11
Northmount Dr NW *CAL* 27 K11 28 L-N12 O11
Northmount Pl NW *CAL* 20 O10 21 P10

Northridge / Patterson

Northridge Dr *OKO* **76** C2
Northway St *BEI* **69** B3
Norton Av *RED* **64** C4
Norwest Cl *RED* **64** D4
Nose Hill Dr NW *CAL* **17** C10 **18** E9-10 F8-9 G6-7
Notre Dame Pl W *LET* **86** H4
Notre Dame Rd W *LET* **86** H4
Nottingham Gt NW *CAL* **20** N10
Nottingham Rd NW *CAL* **20** N10
Nurse St *RED* **64** C4
Nutana Pl NW *CAL* **28** N11-12
Nyberg Av *RED* **64** D4
Nyman Cr *RED* **64** C-D4 C-D5

O

O'Brien Cr *RED* **64** E2
Oak Av *BRO* **90** C-D2
Oak Av *OKO* **76** C3
Oak Dr *RED* **64** E2
Oak Dr S *LET* **88** H11
Oak St *RED* **64** E3
Oakbriar Cl SW *CAL* **48** L-M26
Oakbury Pl SW *CAL* **47** K26 **48** L26
Oakchurch Bay SW *CAL* **41** K25
Oakchurch Cr SW *CAL* **41** K25
Oakchurch Pl SW *CAL* **41** K25
Oakcliffe Dr SW *CAL* **41** K25
Oakcliffe Pl SW *CAL* **41** K25
Oakdale Pl SW *CAL* **42** L25
Oakfern Cr SW *CAL* **41** K25
Oakfern Rd SW *CAL* **41** K25
Oakfern Way SW *CAL* **41** K24
Oakfield Dr SW *CAL* **41** K25 **47** K26-27 **48** L27
Oakfield Mnr SW *CAL* **48** L27
Oakfield Pl SW *CAL* **41** K25
Oakhampton Pl 100 200 SW *CAL* **41** K25 **42** L25
Oakhill Dr SW *CAL* **42** L25
Oakhill Pl 100 to 700 SW *CAL* **41** K25 **42** L25 **47** K26 **48** L26
Oakland Gt SW *CAL* **41** K25
Oakland Pl 100 200 SW *CAL* **41** K25
Oakland Rd SW *CAL* **41** K25
Oakland Way SW *CAL* **41** K25
Oaklawn Pl SW *CAL* **47** K26 **48** L26
Oakmere Cl *CHE* **70** D1
Oakmere Gn *CHE* **70** D1
Oakmere Pl 100 200 *CHE* **70** D1
Oakmere Pt *CHE* **70** D1
Oakmere Way *CHE* **70** D1
Oakmoor Cr SW *CAL* **47** K26
Oakmoor Dr SW *CAL* **47** K26 **48** L26
Oakmoor Pl 100 200 SW *CAL* **47** K26
Oakmoor Village SW *CAL* **48** L26
Oakmoor Way SW *CAL* **48** L26
Oakmount Ct SW *CAL* **41** J-K24
Oakmount Dr SW *CAL* **41** J25 J-K24
Oakmount Pl SW *CAL* **41** K25
Oakmount Rd SW *CAL* **41** K24-25
Oakmount Way SW *CAL* **41** J-K25
Oakridge Gdns SW *CAL* **42** L25 **48** L26
Oakridge Gt SW *CAL* **47** K26
Oakridge Pl 100 to 300 SW *CAL* **47** J-K26
Oakridge Rd SW *CAL* **47** K26
Oakridge Way SW *CAL* **47** K26
Oakside Bay 100 200 SW *CAL* **41** K25 **42** L25
Oakside Cir SW *CAL* **41** K25 **42** L25
Oakside Cl SW *CAL* **41** K25
Oakside Gt SW *CAL* **41** K25 **42** L25
Oakside Pl SW *CAL* **41** K25 **42** L25
Oakside Rd SW *CAL* **42** L25
Oaktree Cl SW *CAL* **48** L26
Oaktree La SW *CAL* **48** L26
Oakvale Pl SW *CAL* **48** L26
Oakview Pl SW *CAL* **47** K26
Oakville Cr *RED* **64** E-F3
Oakwood Dr SW *CAL* **41** K25
Oakwood La SW *CAL* **48** L26
Oakwood Pl 100 to 600 SW *CAL* **41** J25 K25 **47** J26 K26
Oates Gn *RED* **64** E3
Oberlin Av *RED* **64** F3
Ockley Cl *RED* **64** F3
Odell Gn *RED* **64** E3
Odstone Gn *RED* **64** F2-3
Ogden Av *RED* **64** F3
Ogden Cr SE *CAL* **43** S23
Ogden Dr SE *CAL* **43** S23-24
Ogden Rd SE *CAL* **37** R19-20 S20 **44** T22-23 U23
Ogden Rise SE *CAL* **43** S23
Ogden Way SE *CAL* **43** S23
Ogden Dale Pl SE *CAL* **44** U23
Ogden Dale Rd SE *CAL* **44** U22-23
Ogilvie Cl *RED* **64** E2
Ogmoor Cr SE *CAL* **43** S23 **44** T23
Ogmoor Pl SE *CAL* **43** S23 **44** T23
Ohio Cl *RED* **64** F3
Ojibwa Pl 100 to 300 W *LET* **86** H4
Ojibwa Rd W *LET* **86** G3-4 H3-4
Okalta Dr *TVY* **74** E3
Okotoks Dr *OKO* **76** B3
Old Banff Coach Rd *RCY* **25** B-C14
Old Banff Coach Rd SW *CAL* **26** D-G14 G15
Old Canmore Rd *CAN* **59** E-F5
Old Cemetery Rd *MED* **94** F-G4
Oldbury St *RED* **64** F3
Oldford Cl *RED* **64** E2
Oldring Cr *RED* **64** E2
Oleander Dr *RED* **64** F3
Oliver Av *MED* **95** F5-6
Oliver St *RED* **64** E3
Olsen St *RED* **64** F3
Olympia Bay SE *CAL* **44** T24
Olympia Cr SE *CAL* **44** T24
Olympia Dr SE *CAL* **44** T24
Olympia Pl SE *CAL* **44** T24
Olympic Dr *CAN* **58** F3
Olympic Gn *RED* **64** E-F3
Olympic Way SE *CAL* **37** Q17
Onaway Av *RED* **64** E3
ONeil Cl *RED* **64** E2
Onslow Sq *RED* **64** F3
Opal Av *RED* **64** E-F3
Openview Cl *RED* **64** F3
Orchard Gn *RED* **64** F3
Orchard Way *STM* **71** E3
Orchard Park Rd *STM* **71** E2-3
Oreston Cl *RED* **64** F3
Orient Gn *RED* **64** E3
Orillia Park Rd *RED* **64** F3
Oriole Rd N *LET* **84** B10
Orr Dr *RED* **64** E2
Ortona St S *LET* **88** F11
Orwell Cl *RED* **64** F2-3
Osborne Cr SW *CAL* **36** L18
Osborne St *RED* **64** F2-3
Osler Av *CRS* **62** A2-3
Osler Cr *RED* **64** E2
Oslo Cl *RED* **64** F3
Osmond Cl *RED* **64** E-F2
Ottawa St *RED* **64** E3
Otter La *BAN* **57** C3
Otter St *BAN* **57** D2
Otterbury Av *RED* **64** F3
Overdown Dr *RED* **64** E3 F2
Ovington Cl *RED* **64** F2-3
Owens Cl *RED* **64** F2
Owl Haven *RCY* **33** B20
Owl St *BAN* **57** C2
Oxbow St *RED* **64** F3
Oxford Av *MED* **94** F1
Oxford Av *RED* **64** E3
Oxford Pl W *LET* **86** J4
Oxford Rd W *LET* **86** J3-4 J4
Oyen Cr *RED* **64** E-F3

P

Pacific Av *OKO* **76** C3
Pacific Rd NE *CAL* **29** Q11
Pacific St *MED* **93** C6
Padmore *CAN* **58** G4
Page Av *RED* **64** C-D5
Palermo Way SW *CAL* **42** M25
Palis Way SW *CAL* **42** L-M25
Palisade Dr SW *CAL* **42** L25
Palisan Pl SW *CAL* **42** M25
Palisbriar Pk 100 200 SW *CAL* **48** L-M26
Paliscliffe Rd SW *CAL* **42** L25 **48** L26
Palisdale Rd SW *CAL* **42** M25 **48** M26
Palisfield Pl SW *CAL* **42** M25 **48** M26
Palishall Rd SW *CAL* **42** M25 **48** M26
Palismount Pl SW *CAL* **42** L25
Palisprior Rd SW *CAL* **42** M25
Palistone Rd SW *CAL* **42** L25 **48** L26
Palisview Pl SW *CAL* **42** L25
Paliswood Bay SW *CAL* **42** M25
Paliswood Gt SW *CAL* **42** L25
Paliswood Pk 100 200 SW *CAL* **42** M25
Paliswood Pl SW *CAL* **42** L-M25
Paliswood Rd SW *CAL* **42** L-M25
Paliswood Way SW *CAL* **42** L-M25
Palliser Dr SW *CAL* **41** K25 **42** L25 M25
Palliser Pl *MED* **93** C6
Palliser Pl SW *CAL* **42** L25
Palliser Tr *CAN* **58** C-D4 **59** D-E5
Palliser Way *MED* **93** C6
Pallo Cl *RED* **64** D5
Palm Rd S *LET* **88** H11
Palm Way NW *CAL* **26** D-E11
Palmer Rd NE *CAL* **30** T11
Palomino Blvd *RCY* **16** X9
Pamely Av *RED* **64** D5
Panamount Blvd NW *CAL* **12** 04
Panamount Cl 100 200 NW *CAL* **12** 04
Panamount Cr NW *CAL* **12** 04
Panamount Ct 100 200 NW *CAL* **12** 04
Panamount Dr NW *CAL* **12** 04
Panamount Gdns NW *CAL* **12** N-04
Panamount Gn NW *CAL* **12** 03-4
Panamount Gr 100 200 NW *CAL* **12** N4 04
Panamount Gt NW *CAL* **12** 04
Panamount Hill NW *CAL* **12** 04
Panamount Hts NW *CAL* **12** 04
Panamount La NW *CAL* **12** N-04
Panamount Link NW *CAL* **12** 04
Panamount Mews NW *CAL* **12** 04 **13** P4
Panamount Pk NW *CAL* **12** 04
Panamount Pl 100 200 NW *CAL* **12** N-04
Panamount Rise NE *CAL* **12** 03-4
Panamount Sq NW *CAL* **12** 04
Panatella Bay NW *CAL* **12** 03
Panatella Blvd NW *CAL* **12** N-03
Panatella Cir NW *CAL* **12** 03-4
Panatella Cl NE *CAL* **12** 03
Panatella Ct 100 to 500 NW *CAL* **12** 03-4
Panatella Dr NW *CAL* **12** 03
Panatella Gt NW *CAL* **12** 03 **13** P3
Panatella Pl 100 200 NW *CAL* **12** 03
Panatella Tr NE *CAL* **12** 03
Panatella View NW *CAL* **12** 03
Panatella Way NW *CAL* **12** 03
Panorama Bay *RCY* **24** W-X13
Panorama Hts NW *CAL* **12** L3
Panorama Rd *RCY* **24** X14-15 **32** X16-20
Panorama Rd NW *CAL* **12** L3-4
Panorama Hills Bay 100 200 NW *CAL* **12** N5
Panorama Hills Blvd NW *CAL* **12** 04-5
Panorama Hills Cir NW *CAL* **12** N5
Panorama Hills Cl NW *CAL* **12** N-05
Panorama Hills Com NW *CAL* **12** 05
Panorama Hills Cr NW *CAL* **12** 05
Panorama Hills Ct NW *CAL* **12** 05
Panorama Hills Cv NW *CAL* **12** 04-5
Panorama Hills Dr NW *CAL* **12** N4-5 05
Panorama Hills Gdns NW *CAL* **12** N5
Panorama Hills Gn NW *CAL* **12** 05
Panorama Hills Gr NW *CAL* **12** 05
Panorama Hills Heath NW *CAL* **12** 04-5
Panorama Hills Hts NW *CAL* **12** 04-5
Panorama Hills La 100 200 NW *CAL* **12** 05 **13** P5
Panorama Hills Ldg NW *CAL* **12** N5
Panorama Hills Link NW *CAL* **12** N4-5
Panorama Hills Mews NW *CAL* **12** N-05
Panorama Hills Mnr NW *CAL* **12** 05
Panorama Hills Pk NW *CAL* **12** 05
Panorama Hills Pl NW *CAL* **12** 05
Panorama Hills Pt NW *CAL* **12** N5
Panorama Hills Rd NW *CAL* **12** 05
Panorama Hills Rise NW *CAL* **12** N-05
Panorama Hills Sq NW *CAL* **12** 05
Panorama Hills Ter 100 to 300 NW *CAL* **12** N4-5
Panorama Hills View NW *CAL* **12** N5
Panorama Hills Way NW *CAL* **12** 05
Paradise Rd *CHE* **70** B-C1
Pardue Cl *RED* **64** C-D5
Parish Way *MED* **93** C6
Park Av *BAN* **57** E1-2
Park Av SW *CAL* **36** 020
Park Cr *MED* **92** D4
Park Cr NE *CAL* **29** R15
Park Dr *BRO* **90** C4
Park Dr *RED* **66** H3
Park La *OLD* **62** D1
Park La SW *CAL* **36** 018
Park Pl *BRG* **78** C3
Park Pl *BRO* **90** A2
Park Pl *DRU* **72** B4
Park Pl *TAB* **91** B-C2
Park Pt *BRG* **78** C3
Park Rd *STM* **71** C-D3
Park Rd SE *CAL* **37** P18
Park St *TAB* **91** A1-2
Park Estates Dr SE *CAL* **49** Q-R30
Park Estates Pl 100 200 SE *CAL* **49** Q-R30
Park Lane Dr *STM* **71** D3-4
Park Meadows Blvd N *LET* **84** C9-10
Park Meadows Cr *OLD* **62** C-D2
Park Meadows Ct *MED* **95** H-J6
Park Meadows Dr *MED* **95** J6
Park Meadows La *MED* **95** H-J6
Park Meadows Pl *MED* **95** J6
Park Meadows Pl *OLD* **62** C1-2
Parkdale Blvd NW *CAL* **27** J-K15 **35** K16
Parkdale Cr NW *CAL* **27** K15
Parke Av *RED* **64** C-D5
Parker Av *MED* **92** D3
Parkglen Cr SE *CAL* **49** R-S30
Parkglen Pl 100 200 SE *CAL* **49** R-S30 **53** S31
Parkglen Rd SE *CAL* **53** R-S31
Parkhill Pl SW *CAL* **37** P19
Parkhill St SW *CAL* **37** P19
Parkland Blvd SE *CAL* **49** R-S30 **53** S31
Parkland Cl *BRO* **90** B4
Parkland Cr SE *CAL* **49** R30
Parkland Dr *BRO* **90** B4
Parkland Gn SE *CAL* **49** R29-30
Parkland Hill SE *CAL* **49** R30
Parkland Pl *BRO* **90** B4
Parkland Pl SE *CAL* **49** R30
Parkland Rise SE *CAL* **49** R30
Parkland Way *BRO* **90** B4
Parkland Way SE *CAL* **49** R30
Parklane Pl *STM* **71** C-D3
Parklane Way *STM* **71** D3
Parkmere Gn *CHE* **70** C1-2
Parkridge Cr SE *CAL* **53** S31
Parkridge Dr SE *CAL* **53** S31-32
Parkridge Gn SE *CAL* **53** S31
Parkridge Hill SE *CAL* **53** S31
Parkridge Pl 100 200 SE *CAL* **53** S31
Parkridge Rd SE *CAL* **53** S31
Parkridge Rise SE *CAL* **53** S31
Parkridge View SE *CAL* **53** S31
Parkridge Way SE *CAL* **53** S31
Parkside Blvd *COD* **85** B4
Parkside Cr SE *CAL* **49** R30
Parkside Dr *COD* **85** B4
Parkside Dr *RED* **64** D4
Parkside Dr S *LET* **88** F10-11 F-G11
Parkside Dr SE *CAL* **49** R30
Parkside Gn SE *CAL* **49** R30
Parkside Pl SE (Parkland) *CAL* **49** R30
Parkside Pl SE (Ranchlands) *CAL* **19** H9
Parkside Pt *COD* **85** B4
Parkside Way SE *CAL* **49** R30
Parkvalley Dr SE *CAL* **53** R-S31
Parkvalley Gt SE *CAL* **53** R31
Parkvalley Pl SE *CAL* **53** R-S31
Parkvalley Rd SE *CAL* **53** R-S31
Parkvalley Way SE *CAL* **53** S31
Parkview Close *MED* **93** D5
Parkview Cr *BLD* **75** B-C7
Parkview Cr SE *CAL* **53** R31
Parkview Dr *MED* **93** C-D5 D6
Parkview Ests *STM* **71** C3
Parkview Gn SE *CAL* **49** R30 **53** R31
Parkview Pl *BLD* **75** B-C7
Parkview Pl 100 200 SE *CAL* **53** S31
Parkview Way SE *CAL* **49** R30 **53** R31
Parkvista Cr SE *CAL* **53** R-S31
Parkvista Pl SE *CAL* **53** R-S31
Parkway Av *RED* **64** D4
Parkwood Cl SE *CAL* **49** Q-R30
Parkwood Cr *STM* **71** C-D3
Parkwood Dr SE *CAL* **49** Q-R30
Parkwood Pl *STM* **71** C-D3
Parkwood Pl 100 200 SE *CAL* **49** R30
Parkwood Rise SE *CAL* **49** R30
Parkwood Way SE *CAL* **49** R29-30
Parlby Cr *RED* **66** H2
Parsons Cl *RED* **65** D6
Partridge Bay *RCY* **24** Y14 **25** Z14 Z14
Partridge Ct *RCY* **25** Z14
Partridge Pl *RCY* **25** Z14
Partridge St *MED* **93** C-D6
Pasadena Gdns NE *CAL* **31** Y13
Pasadena Gn NE *CAL* **31** Y13
Passchendale Av SW *CAL* **36** L-M20
Passchendale Rd SW *CAL* **36** L-M20
Paterson Cr *RED* **64** D5
Patina Ct SW *CAL* **27** H15
Patina Dr SW *CAL* **27** H-I15
Patina Gn 100 200 SW *CAL* **27** H15
Patina Hill SW *CAL* **27** H15
Patina La SW *CAL* **27** H15
Patina Pk SW *CAL* **27** H15
Patina Pl 400 500 SW *CAL* **27** H15
Patina Pt SW *CAL* **27** H15
Patina Rise SW *CAL* **27** H15
Patina Ter SW *CAL* **27** H15
Patina View SW *CAL* **27** H15
Patrician St *CAN* **58** F3
Patrician Village NW *CAL* **27** K14 **28** L14
Patrick Av SW *CAL* **26** G14
Patrick St SW *CAL* **26** G14
Patrick View SW *CAL* **27** H14
Patrol Av *MED* **93** D6
Patterson Bay SW *CAL* **27** H14-15
Patterson Blvd SW *CAL* **26** G14 **27** H14-15
Patterson Cl SW *CAL* **26** G14
Patterson Cr SW *CAL* **27** H14-15
Patterson Dr SW *CAL* **27** H14
Patterson Gn SW *CAL* **26** G14 **27** H14
Patterson Gr SW *CAL* **26** G13-14

Patterson / Ranchlands

Patterson Gt SW *CAL* 26 G15 27 H15
Patterson Hill SW *CAL* 26 G14 G15 27 H15
Patterson Mews SW *CAL* 27 H14-15
Patterson Mt 100 200 SW *CAL* 27 H15
Patterson Pk SW *CAL* 27 H14
Patterson Pl SW *CAL* 27 H14
Patterson Pt SW *CAL* 26 G14
Patterson Rd *OKO* 76 C2-3
Patterson Rise SW *CAL* 26 G15 27 H15
Patterson View SW *CAL* 26 G14-15
Patton Ct 100 200 SW *CAL* 42 M-N25
Patton Pl SW *CAL* 42 M-N25
Patton Rd SW *CAL* 42 N25 48 N26
Payne Cl *RED* 64 D5
Peacekeepers Way SW *CAL* 41 K21
Peaks Dr *CAN* 58 G4
Pearson Cr *RED* 64 D5
Pebble Pl S *LET* 88 G11
Pederson Dr *RCY* 9 Z5
Pegasus Rd NE *CAL* 30 T11
Pegasus Way NE *CAL* 30 T11
Peigan Ct W *LET* 86 G3
Peigan Tr SE *CAL* 38 U-W20 39 X20
Pekisko Rd SW *HIG* 77 C1
Penbrooke Cl SE *CAL* 39 Y17
Penbrooke Cr SE *CAL* 39 Y16
Penbrooke Dr SE *CAL* 39 X-Y17
Penbrooke Pl SE *CAL* 39 Y16
Penbrooke Rd SE *CAL* 39 Y16
Penbrooke Way SE *CAL* 39 Y16
Penedo Cr SE *CAL* 39 X17
Penedo Pl SE *CAL* 39 X-Y17
Penedo Way SE *CAL* 39 X-Y17
Penland Way *MED* 93 C6
Penmeadows Cl SE *CAL* 39 X16-17
Penmeadows Pl SE *CAL* 39 X16-17
Penmeadows Rd SE *CAL* 39 X16
Pennington Cr *RED* 64 D5
Pennsburg Dr SE *CAL* 39 X17
Pennsburg Pl SE *CAL* 39 X17
Pennsburg Rd SE *CAL* 39 X17
Pennsburg Way SE *CAL* 39 X17
Pennsylvania Rd SE *CAL* 39 X16
Penrith Cr SE *CAL* 39 X17
Penrith Pl SE *CAL* 39 X17
Pensacola Cl SE *CAL* 39 X17
Pensacola Cr SE *CAL* 39 X17
Pensacola Ct W *LET* 86 H4
Pensacola Walk SE *CAL* 38 W17 39 X17
Pensacola Way SE *CAL* 39 X17
Pensdale Cr SE *CAL* 39 X17
Pensdale Rd SE *CAL* 39 X17
Pensville Cl SE *CAL* 39 X-Y16
Pensville Rd SE *CAL* 39 X-Y16
Penswood Pl SE *CAL* 39 Y16
Penswood Rd SE *CAL* 39 Y16
Penswood Way SE *CAL* 39 Y16
Penworth Cl SE *CAL* 39 X16
Penworth Cr SE *CAL* 39 X16
Penworth Ct SE *CAL* 39 X16
Penworth Dr SE *CAL* 39 X16
Penworth Gn SE *CAL* 39 X16
Penworth Pl SE *CAL* 39 X16
Penworth Rd SE *CAL* 39 X16
Penworth Rise SE *CAL* 39 X16
Penworth Way SE *CAL* 39 X16
Perry Cr *MED* 93 C6
Phair Av NE *CAL* 29 R15
Pheasant Bay *BRO* 90 A-B2
Pheasant Rd *BRO* 90 A2
Pheasant Rd N *LET* 84 B10
Phelan Cl *RED* 64 D5
Phelan Cr *RED* 64 C-D5
Phelan St *RED* 64 D5
Philpott Ct *BRO* 90 B3
Pigeon St *MED* 93 D5-6
Pika Pl *BAN* 57 C2-3
Pine Av *BRG* 78 B3-4
Pine Av *BRO* 90 C2
Pine Cr S *LET* 88 H11
Pine Ct *MED* 93 D6
Pine Pl *CRS* 62 A2
Pine Pl *DRU* 73 D-E7
Pine Pl SW *CAL* 35 K17
Pine Rd *STM* 71 E3
Pine St NW *CAL* 26 D11-12
Pinebrook Cl NE *CAL* 31 Y13
Pinebrook Pl NE *CAL* 31 Y13
Pinebrook Way *RCY* 33 C19
Pinecliff Cl NE *CAL* 31 Y13
Pinecliff Dr NE *CAL* 31 Y13
Pinecliff Gr NE *CAL* 31 Y13
Pinecliff Rd NE *CAL* 31 Y13
Pinecliff Way NE *CAL* 31 Y13
Pinecone La *RCY* 33 C-D19
Pinecrest Cr NE *CAL* 31 X14
Pinecrest Way NE *CAL* 31 X14
Pinegreen Bay NE *CAL* 31 X14
Pinegreen Cl NE *CAL* 31 X14
Pinegrove Cl NE *CAL* 31 Y14
Pinehill Pl NE *CAL* 31 X-Y14
Pinehill Rd NE *CAL* 31 X-Y14 Y13-14
Pineland Bay NE *CAL* 31 X-Y13
Pineland Cl NE *CAL* 31 X13
Pineland Pl 100 to 300 NE *CAL* 31 X-Y13
Pineland Rd NE *CAL* 31 X-Y13
Pinelore Pl NE *CAL* 31 Y13
Pinemeadow Pl NE *CAL* 31 Y13
Pinemeadow Rd NE *CAL* 31 Y13
Pinemill Mews 100 200 NE *CAL* 31 X13-14
Pinemill Rd NE *CAL* 31 X13
Pinemill Way NE *CAL* 31 X13
Pinemont Bay NE *CAL* 31 X14
Pinemont Gt NE *CAL* 31 X14
Pinemont Pl NE *CAL* 31 X14
Pinemont Rd NE *CAL* 31 X14
Pinepoint Dr NE *CAL* 31 X14
Pinepoint Pl 100 200 NE *CAL* 31 X14
Pinepoint Rd NE *CAL* 31 X14
Pineridge Gn NE *CAL* 30 W14 31 X14
Pineridge Rd NE *CAL* 31 Y14
Pineridge Way *RCY* 33 C19
Pineset Pl 100 to 300 NE *CAL* 31 X14
Pineside Pl NE *CAL* 31 X14
Pineson Pl NE *CAL* 31 X-Y13
Pinestream Pl 100 to 300 NE *CAL* 31 X13
Pinetown Pl 100 200 NE *CAL* 31 X13
Pinetree Bay 100 200 NE *CAL* 31 Y14
Pinetree Cr NE *CAL* 31 Y14
Pinetree Dr *RCY* 33 C18 C19
Pinetree Pl NE *CAL* 31 Y14
Pinetree Rd NE *CAL* 31 Y14
Pinewind Cl NE *CAL* 31 X13
Pinewind Rd NE *CAL* 31 X13
Pinewood Cl *RED* 64 D4
Pinewood Cr *CAN* 58 D-E4
Pinewood Dr NE *CAL* 38 V18
Pinnacle Dr *LKL* 56 C4
Pinnacle Ridge Dr *RCY* 25 A14-15 B15
Pinnacle Ridge Pl 100 to 400 *RCY* 25 B15
Pinta Gdns NE *CAL* 37 R16
Pioneer Cr *MED* 93 D6
Pioneer Dr *IRR* 69 B2
Pioneer Rd *CAN* 59 F6
Piper Cl *RED* 64 C5
Piper Dr *RED* 64 D5
Pipestone Rd *LKL* 56 B-C4
Pitt Av SW *CAL* 36 N19
Plainsview Rd *STM* 71 C3
Pleasant Park Cl *BRO* 90 C1
Pleasant Park Ct *BRO* 90 C1-2
Pleasant Park Gn *BRO* 90 C1-2
Pleasant Park Rd *BRO* 90 C1
Plum Tree Pl SW *CAL* 35 K17
Point Dr *MED* 93 C-D6
Point Dr NW *CAL* 27 J15
Point McKay Cr NW *CAL* 27 J15
Point McKay Ct NW *CAL* 27 J15
Point McKay Gdns NW *CAL* 27 J15
Point McKay Gr NW *CAL* 27 J15
Point McKay Rd NW *CAL* 27 J15
Point McKay Ter NW *CAL* 27 J15
Police Point Dr *MED* 93 C6
Pope Av *COC* 61 B5
Poplar Av *OKO* 76 C3
Poplar Av NE *HIG* 77 B3
Poplar Ct *MED* 93 D6
Poplar Rd SW *CAL* 35 K16
Poplar St *BRO* 90 C1
Poplar St *DRU* 73 B6
Poplar St NW *CAL* 26 D11-12
Porcelain Av *MED* 95 F7
Porcupine Av *MED* 93 C-D6
Porcupine Pl *BAN* 57 C3
Porter Pl *MED* 95 G-H7
Porter St *COD* 85 A-B2
Porters Hill *MED* 95 F8
Portland St SE *CAL* 37 R18
Pottery St *MED* 95 F6
Powell St *COC* 61 B5
Power House Rd *MED* 92 E1-2
Prairie Ct *MED* 93 C6
Prairie Dr *MED* 93 D6
Prairie Meadows Cl *BRO* 90 B1
Prairie Meadows Rd *BRO* 90 B1
Premier Cl *DRU* 73 C5
Premier Cr *DRU* 73 C5
Premier Rd *DRU* 73 C-D5
Premier Way NW *CAL* 36 N19
Prendergast Pl *CAN* 58 F3
Prestick Pond Ter SE *CAL* 54 W31
Preston Av *MED* 93 C6
Prestwick Av SE *CAL* 50 W30
Prestwick Bay SE *CAL* 50 W30
Prestwick Blvd SE *CAL* 50 W30 54 W31
Prestwick Cir SE *CAL* 50 W30 54 W31
Prestwick Cl 100 to 300 SE *CAL* 50 W30
Prestwick Cr SE *CAL* 50 W30 54 W31
Prestwick Ct 100 SE *CAL* 50 W30
Prestwick Cv SE *CAL* 54 V-W31
Prestwick Dr SE *CAL* 50 W30
Prestwick Gdns SE *CAL* 54 W31
Prestwick Gn SE *CAL* 54 W31
Prestwick Gr SE *CAL* 54 W31
Prestwick Gt SE *CAL* 50 W30 51 X30
Prestwick Heath SE *CAL* 50 V30
Prestwick Hts SE *CAL* 50 W30
Prestwick La SE *CAL* 50 W30
Prestwick Ldg SE *CAL* 54 V-W31
Prestwick Mews 100 200 SE *CAL* 50 V30 54 V31
Prestwick Mnr SE *CAL* 50 W30
Prestwick Parade SE *CAL* 50 W30
Prestwick Pk SE *CAL* 54 W31
Prestwick Pl SE *CAL* 50 W30 51 X30
Prestwick Pt 100 200 SE *CAL* 50 V-W30
Prestwick Rd SE *CAL* 54 W31
Prestwick Rise SE *CAL* 50 W30
Prestwick Row SE *CAL* 54 W31
Prestwick St SE *CAL* 50 W30
Prestwick Ter 100 to 300 SE *CAL* 50 V-W30
Prestwick View SE *CAL* 50 W30
Prestwick Way SE *CAL* 50 W30 54 W31
Prestwick Acres La SE *CAL* 50 W30 51 X30
Prestwick Estate Gt SE *CAL* 50 W30
Prestwick Estate Link SE *CAL* 50 W30
Prestwick Estate Way SE *CAL* 50 W30 54 W31
Primrose Dr *MED* 94 G4 95 G5 H5
Primrose Pl N *LET* 84 C9
Prince St *MED* 93 E5
Princess Av *MED* 93 E5
Princess Pl *BRO* 90 A3
Princeton Cr W *LET* 86 H3
Princeton Rd W *LET* 86 H3
Princeton Way SW *CAL* 6 B92 36 O16
Pringle St *MED* 93 E5
Promenade Pk SE *CAL* 54 W31
Promenade Way SE *CAL* 54 W31
Prominence Hill SW *CAL* 27 H15
Prominence Hts SW *CAL* 27 H15
Prominence Path SW *CAL* 27 H14-15
Prominence Pk SW *CAL* 27 H15
Prominence Pl *TAB* 91 C1-2
Prominence Pl SW *CAL* 26 G15
Prominence Pt SW *CAL* 27 H15
Prominence Rise SW *CAL* 27 H15
Prominence View SW *CAL* 27 H15
Prominence Way SW *CAL* 27 H15
Pronghorn St *MED* 93 C-D6
Prospect Av SW *CAL* 36 N18
Prospect Cl *CAN* 58 G4
Prospect Ct *CAN* 58 G4
Prospect Dr *MED* 92 E3
Prospect Hts *CAN* 58 G4
Prospect Pt *CAN* 58 F4
Prospect Rise *CAN* 58 G4
Pump Hill Bay SW *CAL* 48 M-N26
Pump Hill Cl SW *CAL* 42 M25 48 M26
Pump Hill Cr SW *CAL* 48 M26
Pump Hill Dr SW *CAL* 42 M25
Pump Hill Gdns 100 to 300 SW *CAL* 42 M25
Pump Hill Gn SW *CAL* 48 M26
Pump Hill Gt SW *CAL* 48 M26
Pump Hill Ldg SW *CAL* 42 M25
Pump Hill Mews SW *CAL* 48 M26
Pump Hill Pl SW *CAL* 42 M25 48 M26
Pump Hill Rd SW *CAL* 48 M26
Pump Hill Rise SW *CAL* 42 M25
Pump Hill View SW *CAL* 48 M26
Pump Hill Way SW *CAL* 42 M25
Pump Valley Ct SW *CAL* 42 M-N25
Pumphouse Av SW *CAL* 36 L-M17
Pumphouse Rd SW *CAL* 36 M16-17
Pumpmeadow Cr SW *CAL* 42 M25
Pumpmeadow Pl SW *CAL* 42 M25
Pumpridge Pl 100 300 SW *CAL* 42 M25
Purcell Pl *BRO* 90 C3
Purdue Ct W *LET* 86 H3-4

Q

Quail Pl N *LET* 84 B10
Qualicum Beach Bay *CHE* 70 F1-2
Quebec Av SW *CAL* 36 N18
Queen St *MED* 93 E5 E6
Queen Alexandra Cl SE *CAL* 49 R29
Queen Alexandra Rd SE *CAL* 49 R29
Queen Alexandra Way SE *CAL* 49 R-S28
Queen Anne Cl SE *CAL* 49 S29 50 T29
Queen Anne Pl 100 200 SE *CAL* 49 S28
Queen Anne Rd SE *CAL* 49 S28-29
Queen Anne Way SE *CAL* 49 S28-29
Queen Charlotte Dr SE *CAL* 49 S29
Queen Charlotte Gt SE *CAL* 49 S29
Queen Charlotte Pl SE *CAL* 49 S29
Queen Charlotte Rd SE *CAL* 49 S29
Queen Charlotte Way SE *CAL* 49 S29
Queen Isabella Cl SE *CAL* 49 R29
Queen Tamara Pl SE *CAL* 49 S28
Queen Tamara Rd SE *CAL* 49 S28
Queen Tamara Way SE *CAL* 49 S28
Queens Rd W *LET* 87 H-J5
Queens Way *BRO* 90 A3
Queensland Cir SE *CAL* 49 S28
Queensland Dr SE *CAL* 49 R-S29
Queensland Estates SE *CAL* 49 R29
Queensland Gt SE *CAL* 49 S29
Queensland Hill SE *CAL* 49 S29
Queensland Pl 100 to 600 SE *CAL* 49 S28-29
Queensland Rd SE *CAL* 49 S29
Queensland Rise SE *CAL* 49 S29
Queenston Gdns SE *CAL* 49 S29
Queenston Hts SE *CAL* 49 S29 50 T29
Queenston Ter SE *CAL* 49 S29 50 T29
Quentin Av SW *CAL* 36 M20
Quentin Ct SW *CAL* 36 M20
Quentin Pl SW *CAL* 36 L-M20
Quentin St SW *CAL* 36 M20
Quesnay Wood Dr SW *CAL* 36 L19-20
Quigley Cl 100 200 *COC* 60 B2
Quigley Dr *COC* 60 B1-3

R

Raabis St *RED* 65 F9 67 G9
Rabbit St *BAN* 57 C-D2
Radcliffe Bay SE *CAL* 38 V16-17
Radcliffe Cl SE *CAL* 38 U-V16
Radcliffe Cr SE *CAL* 38 U-V16
Radcliffe Ct SE *CAL* 38 U16
Radcliffe Dr SE *CAL* 38 U16-17
Radcliffe Pl 100 200 SE *CAL* 38 U16
Radcliffe Rd SE *CAL* 38 U-V16
Radford Rd NE *CAL* 29 Q-R15
Radisson Ct *MED* 95 J7
Radisson Dr SE *CAL* 38 U17
Radisson Pl *MED* 95 J7
Radisson Pl SE *CAL* 38 V17
Radisson Village SE *CAL* 38 U-V16
Radley Pl 100 200 SE *CAL* 38 V16
Radley Way SE *CAL* 38 V16
Radnor Av NE *CAL* 29 R15
Rae Cr *MED* 95 J8
Rae Cr SE *CAL* 38 U17
Rae Ct *MED* 95 J8
Rae Pl *MED* 95 J8
Rae St *MED* 95 J8
Railway Av *BAN* 57 D1
Railway Av *BRO* 90 D3-4 E4
Railway Av *CAN* 58 E4 59 E5
Railway Av *COD* 85 B2-3
Railway Gt SW *AIR* 68 C2
Railway St *CRS* 62 B2-3
Railway St *MED* 93 E5
Railway St E *COC* 61 C5-6
Railway St SE *CAL* 43 Q-R23
Railway St SW *AIR* 68 C2-3
Railway St SW *HIG* 77 D2
Railway St W *COC* 60 B4 61 B5
Rainbow Av *BAN* 57 E2
Rainbow Falls Dr *CHE* 70 G1
Rainbow Falls Way *CHE* 70 G1
Raintree Village NW *CAL* 19 H9
Ramage Cl 100 to 800 *RED* 65 F10 67 G10
Ramage Cr *RED* 65 F10 67 G9
Ramsay St SE *CAL* 37 Q18
Ramsey Av *RED* 65 F9 67 G9
Ramsey Cl *RED* 65 F9
Ranch Rd *OKO* 76 B5
Ranch Estates Bay 100 to 600 NW *CAL* 19 H8
Ranch Estates Dr NW *CAL* 19 H8
Ranch Estates Pl 100 to 1000 NW *CAL* 19 H8
Ranch Estates Rd NW *CAL* 19 H8
Ranch Glen Dr NW *CAL* 18 G8-9
Ranch Glen Pl 100 to 400 NW *CAL* 18 G8-9
Ranchero Bay NW *CAL* 18 G8
Ranchero Dr NW *CAL* 18 G8
Ranchero Gn NW *CAL* 18 G8
Ranchero Pl 100 200 NW *CAL* 18 G8
Ranchero Rd NW *CAL* 18 G8
Ranchero Rise NW *CAL* 18 G8
Ranchlands Bay NW *CAL* 18 F-G8
Ranchlands Blvd *MED* 93 C6
Ranchlands Blvd NW *CAL* 18 G9 19 H9
Ranchlands Cr NW *CAL* 18 F8
Ranchlands Ct 100 to 300 NW *CAL* 18 F8
Ranchlands Gr NW *CAL* 18 F8-9

Ranchlands Meadows NW *CAL* ..19 H8-9
Ranchlands Pl NW *CAL* 18 F-G8
Ranchlands Rd NW *CAL* 18 F-G8
Ranchlands Ridge NW *CAL* ..18 G9 19 H9
Ranchlands Sq NW *CAL* 19 H9
Ranchlands Way NW *CAL* 18 F8
Ranchridge Bay 100 to 400 NW *CAL* ...
..................18 G8 19 H9
Ranchridge Cr NW *CAL* 18 G8 19 H8
Ranchridge Ct 100 to 600 NW *CAL* 18 G8
Ranchridge Dr NW *CAL* 18 G8
Ranchridge Pl NW *CAL* 18 G8
Ranchridge Rd NW *CAL* 18 G8
Ranchridge Way NW *CAL* 18 G8
Ranchview Cir NW *CAL* 18 G9
Ranchview Cr NW *CAL* 18 G9 19 H9
Ranchview Ct 100 to 500 NW *CAL* .19 H9
Ranchview Dr NW *CAL* ..18 G8 19 H8 H9
Ranchview Link NW *CAL* 19 H9
Ranchview Mews 100 to 300 NW *CAL* ..
..................19 H9
Ranchview Pl 100 to 500 NW *CAL* .18 G9
Ranchview Rd NW *CAL* 18 G8-9
Ranchview Ter NW *CAL* 18 G8-9
Randall Ct *MED* 92 D3
Randall St *RED* 67 G8-9
Randolph St *RED* 65 F9
Range Cr NW *CAL* 18 G8
Range Dr NW *CAL* 18 F-G8
Range Gdns NW *CAL* 18 G8
Range Gn NW *CAL* 18 G8
Range Pl NW *CAL* 18 G8
Range Way NW *CAL* 18 F-G8
Ratcliffe St *RED* 65 F10 67 G10
Ravenna Av SW *CAL* 41 J21
Ravine Dr *MED* 95 G5
Ray Av *RED* 65 F8
Ray McBride St *CAN* 58 C4
Raymond Cl *TVY* 74 D2
Raynard Ct SE *CAL* 38 U-V17
Reader Cr NE *CAL* 29 Q15
Red Crow Blvd W *LET* ...86 F3 G3 G3-4
Red Deer Av *DRU* 72 B1
Red Deer Dr *MED* 92 E2 E2 94 F2
Red Oak Blvd *MED* 95 J7
Red Oak Ct *MED* 95 J7
Red Oak Pl *MED* 95 J7
Redcliff Dr *MED* 94 F2
Redwood Bay *MED* 95 J7
Redwood Cr *MED* 95 J7
Redwood Cr SE *CAL* 38 U-V18
Redwood Ct *MED* 95 J7
Redwood Gn *MED* 95 K7
Redwood Pl *MED* 95 J7
Redwood Rd S *LET* 88 H11
Redwood St *MED* 95 J-K7 K8
Redwood Way *MED* 95 J-K7
Redwood Meadows Cl *RDW* 61 B2
Redwood Meadows Ct *RDW* ...61 B2-3
Redwood Meadows Dr *RDW* ...61 B-C2
Reeves Cr *RED* 67 G8
Reflection Cv *RCY* 33 A20
Regal Cr NE *CAL* 29 R15
Regal Pk 100 to 600 NE *CAL* ..29 R15
Regent Cr NE *CAL* 29 Q15
Reichley St *RED* 65 F10 67 G9-10
Reighley Cl *RED* 65 F9
Reinholt Av *RED* 65 F9 67 G9
Remington Rd NE *CAL* 29 Q-R15
Renfrew Dr NE *CAL* 29 Q-R14 R15
Research Pl NW *CAL* 27 K12
Research Rd NW *CAL* 27 K12
Research Way NW *CAL* 27 K12
Research Centre Rd *LET* 89 G-H13
Retreat Rd *COC* 61 A5
Revie Cl *RED* 65 F9
Rice Av *MED* 95 J-K8
Rice Bay *MED* 95 K8
Rice Ct *MED* 95 J8
Rice Dr *MED* 95 K8
Rice Gn *MED* 95 K8
Rice Pl *MED* 95 J-K8
Rich Cl *RED* 65 F9
Richard Ct SW *CAL* 41 K21
Richard Pl SW *CAL* 41 K21
Richard Rd SW *CAL* ....
........35 K20 36 L20 41 K21-22
Richard Way SW *CAL* 41 K21
Richards Cl *RED* 65 F8
Richards Cr *OLD* 62 C3
Richards Cr *RED* 65 F8
Richardson Link SW *CAL* 35 K20
Richardson Rd SW (CFB Calgary) *CAL* ..
..................41 J21
Richardson Rd SW (Mt. Royal College)
CAL 35 K20
Richardson Way SW *CAL* 35 K20
Richelieu Ct SW *CAL* 35 K20
Richland Rd SW *CAL* 29 R14-15

Richmond Meadows SW *CAL* 35 I19
Richmond Rd SW *CAL* ....
..........35 H-I20 J-K19 36 L19 L-M18 M17
Riddell Pl SW *CAL* 38 U-V17
Rideau Cl *MED* 95 H-J7
Rideau Cl SW *AIR* 68 C3
Rideau Cr *MED* 95 J7
Rideau Ct *MED* 95 J7
Rideau Gn *MED* 95 J7
Rideau Pl *MED* 95 J7
Rideau Pl SW *CAL* 36 O19
Rideau Rd SW *CAL* 36 O19
Rideout Av *RED* 67 G9
Ridge Rd *CAN* 59 F7
Ridge Rd *STM* 71 D2-3
Ridge Rd SW *CAL* 36 N19
Ridgebrook Dr SW *AIR* 68 C3
Ridgegate Way SW *AIR* 68 C3
Ridgewood Blvd W *LET* 86 G4
Ridgewood Cr W *LET* 86 G4
Riel Pl SE *CAL* 38 U17
Riley Ct *MED* 92 D2
Riley Pl NE *HIG* 77 B3
Riley St NE *HIG* 77 B3
Ritson Cl *RED* 67 G9
River Av *COC* 61 B-D5
River Dr N *BRG* 78 B3
River Dr S *BRG* 78 B3
River Pl 100 200 *COC* 61 D5
River Rd *CAN* 58 E4
River Rd *MED* 92 E4 93 E5
River Way *COC* 61 D5-6
River Bend Dr *RED* 65 B7-8
River Ridge Cl *MED* 92 D1-2
River Ridge Cl *RCY* 32 Y17
River Ridge Dr *MED* 92 D1-2
River Ridge Dr *RCY* 32 Y17
River Rock Cir SE *CAL* 44 T25
River Rock Cr SE *CAL* 44 T25 50 T26
River Rock Ct SE *CAL* 44 T25
River Rock Gn SE *CAL* 44 T25
River Rock Mnr SE *CAL* 44 T25 50 T26
River Rock Pl SE *CAL* 44 T25 50 T26
River Rock Rd SE *CAL* 44 T25
River Rock Way SE *CAL* 44 T25
River Way Gt *COC* 61 D5
Riverbend Dr SE *CAL* 43 S24-25
Riverbend Gt SE *CAL* 43 S24
Riverbirch Bay SE *CAL* 43 S24
Riverbirch Cr SE *CAL* 43 S24
Riverbirch Ct SE *CAL* 43 S24
Riverbirch Pl SE *CAL* 43 S24
Riverbirch Rd SE *CAL* 43 S24
Riverbrook Cl W *LET* 87 J-K5
Riverbrook Ct SE *CAL* 43 S24
Riverbrook Pl SE *CAL* 43 S24
Riverbrook Rd SE *CAL* 43 S24
Riverbrook Way SE *CAL* 43 S24
Rivercrest Cir SE *CAL* 44 T24
Rivercrest Cl SE *CAL* 44 T24
Rivercrest Cr SE *CAL* 44 T24
Rivercrest Ct W *LET* 87 K5
Rivercrest Dr SE *CAL* 44 T24
Rivercrest Pl SE *CAL* 44 T24
Rivercrest Vill SE *CAL* 44 T24
Rivercrest Way SE *CAL* 44 T24
Rivercroft Cl SE *CAL* 44 T24
Riverdale Av SE *CAL* 36 N-O20
Riverdale Ter W *LET* 87 K5
Riverfront Av SE *CAL* 7 D-E92 37 P-Q16
Riverfront Av SW *CAL* 6 C92 37 P16
Riverglen Cl SE *CAL* 44 T24
Riverglen Cr SE *CAL* 43 S24-25
Riverglen Dr SE *CAL* 44 T24-25
Riverglen Pk SE *CAL* 44 T25
Riverglen Pl 100 200 SE *CAL* .44 T24-25
Riverglen Rd SE *CAL* 44 T25
Riverglen Way SE *CAL* 44 T24-25
Rivergreen Cr SE *CAL* 43 S24
Rivergreen Pl 100 200 SE *CAL* .43 S24
Rivergreen Rd W *LET* 87 J5
Riverpark Blvd W *LET* 87 K5
Riverside Bay NW *HIG* 77 B1
Riverside Bay 100 200 SE *CAL* .43 R-S24
Riverside Cir SE *CAL* 43 R-S24
Riverside Cl SE *CAL* 43 R-S24
Riverside Cr NW *HIG* 77 B1
Riverside Cr SE *CAL* 43 S24
Riverside Ct NW *HIG* 77 B1
Riverside Dr *DRU* 73 D8
Riverside Dr *RED* 64 E5 65 C-D6 E6
Riverside Dr E *DRU* 73 C7
Riverside Dr N *HIG* 77 A-B1
Riverside Dr W *DRU* 72 C4 73 C5 C6
Riverside Dr W *OKO* 76 C2
Riverside Gdns NW *HIG* 77 B1
Riverside Gt *OKO* 76 C2
Riverside Mews 100 200 SE *CAL* 43 R-S24
Riverside Pl *COC* 60 C3-4

Riverside Pl NW *HIG* 77 B1
Riverside Pl SE *CAL* 43 S23-24
Riverside Rd NW *HIG* 77 B1
Riverside Rd SE *CAL* 43 S24
Riverside Way *OKO* 76 C2
Riverside Way SE *CAL* 43 S24
Riverstone Blvd W *LET* 87 J5-6
Riverstone Cl SE *CAL* 44 T24-25
Riverstone Cr SE *CAL* 44 T25
Riverstone Ct SE *CAL* 44 T25
Riverstone Cv 100 200 SE *CAL* 44 T24-25
Riverstone Pl SE *CAL* 44 T24-25
Riverstone Rd *CAN* 59 F6
Riverstone Rd SE *CAL* 44 T24
Rivervalley Cr SE *CAL* 43 S24-25
Rivervalley Dr SE *CAL* 43 S25
Rivervalley Pl SE *CAL* 43 S24-25
Riverview Av *RED* 64 E4 66 H3
Riverview Bay SE *CAL* 43 S25
Riverview Cir *COC* 60 C-D4
Riverview Cir SE *CAL* 43 S25 49 S26
Riverview Cl *COC* 60 C-D4
Riverview Cl SE *CAL* 43 S25
Riverview Ct *BAN* 57 E2
Riverview Ct *COC* 60 D4
Riverview Ct SE *CAL* 43 S24-25
Riverview Dr *COC* 60 C-D4
Riverview Dr SE *CAL* 43 S24-25
Riverview Gdns SE *CAL* 43 S25
Riverview Gn 100 to 400 *COC* 60 D4
Riverview Mews SE *CAL* 43 S25
Riverview Pk SE *CAL* 43 S25
Riverview Pkwy W *LET* 87 K6-7
Riverview Pl *CAN* 58 E4
Riverview Pl 100 to 900 SE *CAL* .49 S26
Riverview Pt SE *CAL* 43 S25
Riverview Ter SE *CAL* 43 S25
Riverwood Cir SE *CAL* 43 S25 44 T25
Riverwood Cl SE *CAL* 44 T25
Riverwood Cr SE *CAL* 44 T25
Riverwood Ct SE *CAL* 44 T25
Riverwood Mnr *LET* 87 J5
Riverwood Mnr SE *CAL* 44 T25
Robert Rd NE *CAL* 29 N15
Robert St *TVY* 74 D-E2
Roberts Cr *RED* 67 G9
Robertson Way *MED* 94 F-G3
Robin Rd N *LET* 84 B10
Robinson Cr *MED* 95 J8
Robinson Cr *RED* 65 F9
Robinson Dr *MED* 95 J8
Robinson Dr *OKO* 76 B3
Robinson Pl *MED* 95 J8
Robinson Rd *MED* 95 F8 J8
Robinson Rd *RCY* 33 A16-17
Robson Cr SE *CAL* 38 U17
Roche St *RED* 67 G9
Rochon Av *RCY* 51 Z27
Rockaway Bay NW *CAL* 9 C5
Rockaway Dr NW *CAL* 9 C5
Rockaway View NW *CAL* 9 C5
Rockbluff Cl NW *CAL* 9 B-C5
Rockbluff Pl NW *CAL* 9 B-C5
Rockborough Gn 100 200 NW *CAL* .
..................9 C5 10 D5
Rockborough Pk NW *CAL* 10 D5
Rockcliffe Bay NW *CAL* 9 C5
Rockmont Ct NW *CAL* 9 C5
Rockvalley Dr NW *CAL* 9 B-C5
Rocky Bear Pl *RCY* 9 Z2-3
Rocky Mountain Blvd W *LET* 87 K5
Rocky Ridge Bay 100 to 500 NW *CAL* ..
..............17 C6 18 D6
Rocky Ridge Blvd NW *CAL* 9 C5 17 C6
Rocky Ridge Cir NW *CAL* 9 C5 17 C6
Rocky Ridge Cl 100 200 NW *CAL* .9 B-C5
Rocky Ridge Cr NW *CAL* ...9 C5 10 D5
Rocky Ridge Ct 100 200 NW *CAL* .17 C6
Rocky Ridge Cv 100 to 400 NW *CAL* ...
..................9 C5 17 C6
Rocky Ridge Dr NW *CAL* ..9 B5 17 B6 C6
Rocky Ridge Gdns NW *CAL* 17 C6
Rocky Ridge Gn NW *CAL* 9 C5
Rocky Ridge Gt NW *CAL* 9 C5
Rocky Ridge Heath NW *CAL* 9 C5
Rocky Ridge Hts NW *CAL* 9 C5
Rocky Ridge Ldg NW *CAL* ...9 C5 10 D5
Rocky Ridge Mews 100 to 300 NW *CAL* .
..................17 C6
Rocky Ridge Pl NW *CAL* 9 C5
Rocky Ridge Pt NW *CAL* 9 C5
Rocky Ridge Rd NW *CAL* ..10 D2 18 D6-7
Rocky Ridge Sq NW *CAL* 18 D6
Rocky Ridge View 100 to 600 NW *CAL* .
..............9 B-C5 17 B-C6
Rocky Spring Cir NW *CAL* 9 B-C5
Rocky Spring Gn NW *CAL* 9 B5
Rocky Spring Gt NW *CAL* 9 B4-5
Rocky Spring Heath NW *CAL* 9 B5

Rocky Spring Pl NW *CAL* 9 B5
Rocky Spring Rise NW *CAL* 9 B5
Rocky Spring Ter 100 200 NW *CAL* .9 B5
Rocky Spring Way NW *CAL* 9 B5
Rocky Vista Cir NW *CAL* 17 C6 18 D6
Rocky Vista Cir NW *CAL* 9 C5
Rocky Vista Dr NW *CAL* ...17 C6 18 D6
Rocky Vista Gdns NW *CAL* 17 C6
Rocky Vista Pk NW *CAL* 17 C6
Rocky Vista Ter NW *CAL* 18 D6
Rockyledge Cr NW *CAL* 9 C5
Rockyledge Rise NW *CAL* 17 B6
Rockyledge St NW *CAL* ...9 B5 17 B6
Rockyledge Ter NW *CAL* 9 B5
Rockyledge View NW *CAL* ...17 B-C6
Rockypoint Cv NW *CAL* 9 C5
Rockyvale Dr NW *CAL* 9 C5
Rockywood Pk NW *CAL* 9 B-C5
Rodeo Ridge *RCY* 16 Y8-9
Rogers Cr *RED* 65 F9 67 G9
Roland St *RED* 67 G9
Rolling Acres Dr *RCY* 9 Z1 A1
Rolling Acres Pl *RCY* 9 A1
Rollis St *RED* 65 F8 67 G8
Ronan Pl *MED* 95 G7 H6-7
Root Cl *RED* 67 G9
Rose Cr *RED* 65 F9
Rose St *MED* 94 F2
Rose Way NW *CAL* 26 D-E11
Rosehill Dr NW *CAL* 28 N13
Roselake St NW *CAL* 28 N13
Roselawn Cr NW *CAL* 28 N13
Roselawn Pl NW *CAL* 28 N13
Rosery Dr NW *CAL* 28 N13
Rosery Pl NW *CAL* 28 N13
Rosetree Cr NW *CAL* 28 N13
Rosetree Rd NW *CAL* 28 N13
Rosevale Dr NW *CAL* 28 N13
Roseview Dr NW *CAL* 28 N13
Rosewood Dr *RCY* 25 Z15
Rosewood Rd NW *CAL* 28 N13
Ross Av *COC* 61 B5
Ross Pl *CRS* 62 B2
Ross Rd NW *CAL* 28 N14
Ross St *CRS* 62 A-B2
Ross St *MED* 93 E6
Ross St *RED* 67 G6-9
Ross Glen Cr *MED* 95 H8
Ross Glen Ct *MED* 95 H8
Ross Glen Dr *MED* 95 J7 J-K8 K8
Ross Glen Gn *MED* 95 H8 H-J8
Ross Glen Pl *MED* 95 H7-8
Ross Glen Rd *MED* 95 J7-8
Ross Glen Way *MED* 95 H8
Ross Haven Av *MED* 95 J7
Ross Haven Cr *MED* 95 J7
Ross Haven Ct *MED* 95 J7
Ross Haven Pl *MED* 95 J7
Ross Haven Way *MED* 95 J7
Ross Heights Ct *MED* 95 H-J8
Ross Heights Gn *MED* 95 H8
Ross Heights Pl *MED* 95 H8
Ross View Bay *MED* 95 J8
Ross View Cl *MED* 95 J8
Ross View Ct *MED* 95 J8
Ross View Pl *MED* 95 J8
Rossburn Cr SW *CAL* 35 I-J16
Rosscarrock Gt SW *CAL* 35 J16-17
Rossdale Av *MED* 95 J8
Rossdale Cr *MED* 95 H8
Rossdale Ct *MED* 95 J8
Rossdale Dr *MED* 95 J8
Rossdale Rd *MED* 95 H8
Rossdale Rd SW *CAL* 35 J17
Rossdale St *MED* 95 H8
Rossdale Way *MED* 95 H8
Rossland Av *MED* 95 J8
Rossland Bay *MED* 95 J8
Rossland Blvd *MED* 95 J8
Rossland Cr *MED* 95 J8
Rossland Ct *MED* 95 J8
Rossland Dr *MED* 95 J8
Rossland Gn *MED* 95 J8
Rossland Pl *MED* 95 J8
Rossland Rd *MED* 95 J8
Rossland St *MED* 95 J8
Rossland Way *MED* 95 J8
Rossmere Av *MED* 95 J7-8
Rossmere Bay *MED* 95 J8
Rossmere Cl *MED* 95 J8
Rossmere Cr *MED* 35 J16-17
Rossmere Ct *MED* 95 J7-8
Rossmere Gn *MED* 95 J8
Rossmere Pl *MED* 95 J8
Rossmere Rd SW *CAL* 35 J16-17
Rossmere Way *MED* 95 J8
Rossmount Rd SW *CAL* 35 J17

Roth Cr *RED* **67** G8
Rouleau Cr SE *CAL* **38** U17
Roundup Way SE *CAL* **37** Q17-18
Rovers Av *RED* **65** F9 **67** G9
Rowell Cl *RED* **65** F9 **67** G9
Rowland La *OKO* **76** B5
Rowley Cl *TVY* **74** D2
Rowntree Cr *RED* **65** F9 **67** G9
Roxboro Rd SW *CAL* **36** 019 **37** P19
Roxboro Glen Rd SW *CAL* **37** P19
Royal Av *TVY* **74** C2-3
Royal Av SW *CAL* **36** N-018
Royal Bay 100 to 500 NW *CAL* **18** D6
Royal Ct 100 to 800 NW *CAL* **18** D6
Royal Mnr NW *CAL* **18** D6
Royal Rd *BRO* **90** A3
Royal Rd NW *CAL* **18** D6
Royal Ter NW *CAL* **18** D6
Royal Abbey Ct 100 200 NW *CAL* **10** D5
Royal Abbey Rise NW *CAL* **10** D5 **18** D6
Royal Birch Bay 100 200 NW *CAL* **10** E5
Royal Birch Blvd NW *CAL* **10** E5
Royal Birch Cir NW *CAL* **18** E6
Royal Birch Cl NW *CAL* **10** E5 **18** E6
Royal Birch Cr NW *CAL* **10** E5
Royal Birch Gdns NW *CAL* **10** E5 **18** E6
Royal Birch Gn NW *CAL* **18** E6
Royal Birch Gr NW *CAL* **18** E6
Royal Birch Gt NW *CAL* **18** E6
Royal Birch Heath 100 200 NW *CAL* **10** E5
Royal Birch Hill NW *CAL* **10** E5
Royal Birch Hts NW *CAL* **10** E5 **18** E6
Royal Birch Mews 100 200 NW *CAL* **10** E5
Royal Birch Mnr NW *CAL* **10** E5 **18** E6
Royal Birch Pl 100 200 NW *CAL* **18** E6
Royal Birch Pt NW *CAL* **18** D6
Royal Birch Rd NW *CAL* **18** E6
Royal Birch Rise NW *CAL* **10** E5 **18** E6
Royal Birch St NW *CAL* **10** E5 **18** E6
Royal Birch Ter NW *CAL* **10** E5
Royal Birch View 100 to 300 NW *CAL* **10** E5 **18** E6 E-F6
Royal Birch Way NW *CAL* **10** E5
Royal Birkdale Cr NW *CAL* **10** D5 **18** D6
Royal Birkdale Ct NW *CAL* **10** D5 **18** D6
Royal Birkdale Dr NW *CAL* **10** D5
Royal Crest Bay 100 to 500 NW *CAL* **18** E6
Royal Crest Ct NW *CAL* **18** E6
Royal Crest Pl 100 200 NW *CAL* **18** E6
Royal Crest Pt NW *CAL* **18** E6
Royal Crest Ter NW *CAL* **18** E6
Royal Crest Way NW *CAL* **18** E6
Royal Elm Bay NW *CAL* **18** D6
Royal Elm Dr NW *CAL* **18** D6
Royal Elm Mews NW *CAL* **18** D6
Royal Elm Rd NW *CAL* **18** D6
Royal Elm Way NW *CAL* **18** D6
Royal Highland Ct NW *CAL* **10** D5 **18** D6
Royal Highland Rd NW *CAL* **10** D5
Royal Oak Bay 100 200 NW *CAL* **10** D4-5 D-E5
Royal Oak Cape NW *CAL* **10** E5
Royal Oak Cir NW *CAL* **10** D5
Royal Oak Com NW *CAL* **10** D5
Royal Oak Cr NW *CAL* **10** D5
Royal Oak Ct 100 200 NW *CAL* **10** D5
Royal Oak Cv NW *CAL* **10** D5
Royal Oak Dr NW *CAL* **18** D-E6
Royal Oak Gdns NW *CAL* **10** D5
Royal Oak Gdns 100 to 300 NW *CAL* **10** E5
Royal Oak Gn NW *CAL* **10** D5
Royal Oak Gr NW *CAL* **10** D5
Royal Oak Gt NW *CAL* **10** D5
Royal Oak Hts NW *CAL* **10** D5
Royal Oak Link NW *CAL* **10** D5
Royal Oak Mews 100 to 300 NW *CAL* **10** D5
Royal Oak Mnr NW *CAL* **10** E5
Royal Oak Pl 100 200 NW *CAL* **10** D5
Royal Oak Pt NW *CAL* **10** D5
Royal Oak Ter NW *CAL* **10** E5
Royal Oak View NW *CAL* **10** D5
Royal Oak View NW *CAL* **10** E5
Royal Oak Way NW *CAL* **10** D-E5
Royal Ridge Bay NW *CAL* **18** D6
Royal Ridge Hill NW *CAL* **18** E6
Royal Ridge Mews NW *CAL* **18** D-E6
Royal Ridge Mnr NW *CAL* **18** D6
Royal Ridge Mt NW *CAL* **18** D6
Royal Ridge Rise NW *CAL* **18** E6
Royal Ridge Tr NW *CAL* **18** D6
Royal Troon Ct NW *CAL* **10** D5
Royal View Cr NW *CAL* **18** D6
Royalite Way *TVY* **74** D4
Rummel Pl *CAN* **58** F4
Rundle Av *BAN* **57** E2
Rundle Av *MED* **95** J-K8
Rundle Cr *MED* **95** K8
Rundle Cr NE *CAL* **29** R15
Rundle Dr *CAN* **58** A2 F4
Rundle Mnr NE *CAL* **30** V-W13
Rundle Pl SW *AIR* **68** C-D3
Rundle Rd *MED* **95** K8
Rundle Way *MED* **95** J-K8
Rundle Plant La *CAN* **58** F3-4
Rundlecairn Gt NE *CAL* **30** W14
Rundlecairn Pl NE *CAL* **30** W14
Rundlecairn Rd NE *CAL* **30** W14
Rundlecairn Rise NE *CAL* **30** W14
Rundlecairn Way NE *CAL* **30** W14
Rundlefield Cl NE *CAL* **30** W14
Rundlefield Cr NE *CAL* **30** W14
Rundlefield Rd NE *CAL* **30** W14
Rundlehill Dr NE *CAL* **30** W13
Rundlehill Pl NE *CAL* **30** W13
Rundlehill Rd NE *CAL* **30** W13
Rundlehill Way NE *CAL* **30** W13
Rundlehorn Cir NE *CAL* **30** V14
Rundlehorn Cr NE *CAL* **30** W13-14
Rundlehorn Dr NE *CAL* **30** V-W14 **31** X-Y14
Rundlehorn La NE *CAL* **30** W13
Rundlehorn Ter NE *CAL* **30** V14
Rundlelawn Cl NE *CAL* **30** V13
Rundlelawn Ct NE *CAL* **30** V13
Rundlelawn Gn NE *CAL* **30** V-W13
Rundlelawn Pk NE *CAL* **30** V-W13
Rundlelawn Pl NE *CAL* **30** V13
Rundlelawn Rd NE *CAL* **30** V13
Rundlelawn Way NE *CAL* **30** V13
Rundlemere Bay NE *CAL* **30** V13
Rundlemere Ct NE *CAL* **30** V13
Rundlemere Gn NE *CAL* **30** V13
Rundlemere Pl NE *CAL* **30** V13-14
Rundlemere Rd NE *CAL* **30** V13-14
Rundleridge Cl NE *CAL* **30** V14
Rundleridge Dr NE *CAL* **30** V-W14
Rundleridge Pl NE *CAL* **30** V14
Rundleridge Rd NE *CAL* **30** V14
Rundleridge Way NE *CAL* **30** V14
Rundleside Cr NE *CAL* **30** W13
Rundleside Dr NE *CAL* **30** W13
Rundleson Pl 100 to 400 NE *CAL* **30** V-W13
Rundleson Rd NE *CAL* **30** V13
Rundleson Village NE *CAL* **30** V13
Rundleson Way NE *CAL* **30** V-W13
Rundleview Cl NE *CAL* **30** W13
Rundleview Dr *CAN* **58** F3
Rundleview Dr NE *CAL* **30** W13
Rundleview Rd NE *CAL* **30** W13
Rundleville Dr NE *CAL* **30** W13-14
Rundleville Pl 100 to 400 NE *CAL* **30** W13-14
Rundlewood Bay NE *CAL* **30** W13-14
Rundlewood Cl NE *CAL* **30** W14
Rundlewood Dr NE *CAL* **30** W13-14
Rundlewood La NE *CAL* **30** W13
Rundlewood Pl NE *CAL* **30** W14
Rundlewood Rd NE *CAL* **30** W14
Runnell Pl NE *CAL* **30** V13
Rupert Cr *RED* **67** G8 G8-9
Rupert Rd NE *CAL* **29** R15
Russell Cr *RED* **65** F8-9
Russell Rd NE *CAL* **29** R14-15
Russett Ct NE *CAL* **30** V13
Russett Rd NE *CAL* **29** Q14-15
Rutgers Cr *LET* **86** H-J3
Rutgers Rd W *LET* **86** H3-4
Rutherford Cl *RED* **67** G9
Rutherford Dr *RED* **65** F8 **67** G8 G9
Rutherford Pl *RED* **67** G9
Rutherford St *MED* **92** C3
Rutland Rd SW *CAL* **35** K19
Rutledge Cr *RED* **65** F9
Ruttan Cl *RED* **67** G9
Ryan Cl *RED* **65** F9
Ryerson Bay W *LET* **86** J4
Ryerson Pl W *LET* **86** J-K4
Ryerson Rd W *LET* **86** J-K4

S

Saamis Cl *MED* **94** J4
Saamis Dr *MED* **92** D1
Saamis Rotary Way *MED* **94** J3-4
Sable Dr SE *CAL* **38** U-V18
Sabrina Bay 100 to 300 SW *CAL* **48** 027
Sabrina Rd SW *CAL* **48** 026-27
Sabrina Way SW *CAL* **48** 027
Sackville Dr SW *CAL* **48** N26-27
Sacramento Dr SW *CAL* **48** 026-27
Sacramento Pl SW *CAL* **48** 027
Saddleback *LKL* **56** B4
Saddleback Rd NE *CAL* **23** X7
Saddleback Way NE *CAL* **23** X7
Saddlecreek Cr NE *CAL* **22** W7 **23** X7
Saddlecreek Ct 100 200 NE *CAL* **22** W7 W8 **23** X7 X8
Saddlecreek Cv NE *CAL* **23** X8
Saddlecreek Gt NE *CAL* **23** X8
Saddlecreek Pl NE *CAL* **23** X7
Saddlecreek Pt 100 to 300 NE *CAL* **22** W7 **23** X7
Saddlecreek Pt NE *CAL* **23** X7-8
Saddlecreek Ter NE *CAL* **23** X8
Saddlecreek Way NE *CAL* **23** X7-8
Saddlecrest Blvd NE *CAL* **23** Y6-7
Saddlecrest Cl NE *CAL* **23** X-Y7
Saddlecrest Pk NE *CAL* **23** Y6-7
Saddlecrest Pl NE *CAL* **23** Y6-7
Saddlefield Cr NE *CAL* **23** Y7
Saddlefield Dr NE *CAL* **23** Y7-8
Saddlefield Gr NE *CAL* **23** Y7-8
Saddlefield Mnr NE *CAL* **23** Y8
Saddlefield Pl 100 200 NE *CAL* **23** Y8
Saddlefield Rd NE *CAL* **23** Y7
Saddlehorn Cl NE *CAL* **23** X7
Saddlehorn Cr NE *CAL* **23** X7
Saddlehorn Dr NE *CAL* **23** X-Y7
Saddleland Cl NE *CAL* **23** Y7
Saddleland Ct NE *CAL* **23** Y7
Saddleland Dr NE *CAL* **23** Y7
Saddleland Way NE *CAL* **23** Y7
Saddlemead Cl NE *CAL* **23** X7
Saddlemead Gn NE *CAL* **23** Y7
Saddlemead Rd NE *CAL* **23** X8 Y7
Saddlemead Way NE *CAL* **23** X-Y7
Saddlemont Blvd NE *CAL* **23** X8 Y7
Saddlemont Cl NE *CAL* **23** Y7-8
Saddlemont Cr NE *CAL* **23** Y7
Saddlemont Rd NE *CAL* **23** Y7
Saddlemont Way NE *CAL* **23** Y7-8
Saddleridge Cl NE *CAL* **23** X7
Saddleridge Dr NE *CAL* **23** X7-8
Saddleridge Rd NE *CAL* **23** X7-8
Saddletowne Cir NE *CAL* **23** X-Y8
Saddletree Cl NE *CAL* **23** X7
Saddletree Dr NE *CAL* **23** X7
Saddletree Way NE *CAL* **23** X7
Sage Cl *MED* **94** J4
Sage Gate *MED* **94** J4
Sage Pl *MED* **94** J4
Sage Rd *MED* **94** J4
Sage Way NW *CAL* **26** D-E11
Sage Hill Dr NW *CAL* **11** J2 K3
Sage Hill Gdns NW *CAL* **11** J-K3
St. Andrew Rd N *LET* **83** C8
St. Andrews Pl NW *CAL* **27** K14 **28** L14
St. Anne Pl N *LET* **83** C8
St. Arthur Rd N *LET* **83** C8
St. Barbara's Ter *CAN* **58** F3
St. Basil Rd N *LET* **83** C8
St. Catherine Rd N *LET* **83** C8
St. Charles Rd N *LET* **83** C8
St. Christopher Pl N *LET* **83** C8
St. David Rd N *LET* **83** C8
St. Edward Blvd N *LET* **83** C8
St. Francis Rd N *LET* **83** C8
St. George Rd N *LET* **83** C8
St. George's Dr NE *CAL* **37** R-S16
St. James Blvd N *LET* **83** C8
St. James Cr N *LET* **83** C8
St. Julien Dr SW *CAL* **36** L20
St. Julien Rd *BAN* **57** D2
St. Julien Way *BAN* **57** D2-3
St. Mary's Cr *BRO* **90** B-C2
St. Monica Av SE *CAL* **37** R-S17
SAIT St NW *CAL* **28** N14-15
SAIT Way NW *CAL* **28** N15
Salem Av SW *CAL* **36** M17
Salina St SW *CAL* **48** N26
Salisbury Av *RED* **67** J6
Salisbury Av SE *CAL* **37** Q17
Salisbury St SE *CAL* **37** Q18
Salish Bay *LET* **86** F-G3
Salish Pl W *LET* **86** G3
Samis Rd NE *CAL* **7** D91 **29** P15 **37** P16
San Diego Cr NE *CAL* **31** Y11
San Diego Gn NE *CAL* **31** Y11
San Diego Mnr NE *CAL* **31** Z11
San Diego Pl NE *CAL* **31** Y-Z11
San Diego Way NE *CAL* **31** Y-Z11
San Fernando Cr NE *CAL* **31** Z12
San Fernando Pl 100 200 NE *CAL* **31** Z12
Sanctuary Rd SE *CAL* **38** T18-19
Sandalwood Cl NW *CAL* **20** M6
Sandalwood Ct NW *CAL* **20** M6
Sandalwood Gt NW *CAL* **20** M6
Sandalwood Hts NW *CAL* **20** M6
Sandalwood Pl 100 200 NW *CAL* **20** M6
Sandarac Cir NW *CAL* **20** M7
Sandarac Dr NW *CAL* **20** M6-7
Sandarac Pl 100 200 NW *CAL* **20** M-N7
Sandarac Rd NW *CAL* **20** M-N7
Sandarac Vill NW *CAL* **20** M7
Sandarac Way NW *CAL* **20** M-N7
Sanderling Cl NW *CAL* **20** M-N6
Sanderling Ct NW *CAL* **20** N6
Sanderling Dr NW *CAL* **20** N6
Sanderling Hill NW *CAL* **20** N6
Sanderling Pl 100 to 300 NW *CAL* **20** N6
Sanderling Rd NW *CAL* **20** N6
Sanderling Rise NW *CAL* **20** N6
Sanderling Way NW *CAL* **20** N6
Sanderson Av *MED* **92** C-D4
Sandford Cr *MED* **94** J4
Sandhurst Av NW *CAL* **36** L17
Sandpiper Cir NW *CAL* **20** M-N6 N7
Sandpiper Ct NW *CAL* **20** M6
Sandpiper Dr NW *CAL* **20** N6
Sandpiper Gt NW *CAL* **20** M6
Sandpiper La *CHE* **70** G2
Sandpiper La NW *CAL* **20** N6
Sandpiper Link NW *CAL* **20** N6
Sandpiper Mews NW *CAL* **20** N6
Sandpiper Pl 100 200 NW *CAL* **20** M-N7
Sandpiper Rd NW *CAL* **20** M-N6
Sandpiper Rise NW *CAL* **20** N6
Sandpiper Way NW *CAL* **20** M-N6
Sandpoint Pk NW *CAL* **20** M6
Sandringham Cl NW *CAL* **20** M6
Sandringham Ct 100 to 300 NW *CAL* **20** M6
Sandringham Pl 100 to 700 NW *CAL* **20** M6
Sandringham Rd NW *CAL* **20** M6-7
Sandringham Way NW *CAL* **20** M7
Sandstone Cr SE *AIR* **68** D4
Sandstone Ct *OKO* **76** B2
Sandstone Ct NW *CAL* **20** N7
Sandstone Dr *OKO* **76** B2
Sandstone Dr NW *CAL* **20** M-N6
Sandstone Gt *OKO* **76** B2
Sandstone Hill NW *CAL* **20** N7
Sandstone Mews *OKO* **76** B2
Sandstone Pl *MED* **95** J6
Sandstone Pl *OKO* **76** B2
Sandstone Pl100 200 NW *CAL* **20** N7
Sandstone Pt *OKO* **76** B-C2
Sandstone Rd NW *CAL* **20** N7
Sandstone Rd W *LET* **88** L10
Sandstone Rise NW *CAL* **20** N7
Sandstone Ter *CAN* **59** F7
Sandstone Way NW *CAL* **20** N7
Sandstone Way S *LET* **88** K-L10
Sandstone Ridge Cr *OKO* **76** B2
Sandy Beach Cv *CHE* **70** E2
Santa Maria Gdns NE *CAL* **37** R16
Santana Bay 100 to 300 NW *CAL* **20** N6
Santana Cr NW *CAL* **20** N6
Santana Ct NW *CAL* **20** N6
Santana Hill NW *CAL* **20** N6-7
Santana Mews 100 to 300 NW *CAL* **20** N6
Santana Mnr NW *CAL* **20** N6-7
Santana Pl 100 300 NW *CAL* **20** N6-7
Santana Rd NW *CAL* **20** N6-7
Sarah King Ct *BRO* **90** C4
Saratoga Cl NE *CAL* **31** Z11-12
Saratoga Pl 100 200 NE *CAL* **31** Y-Z11
Sarcee Pl W *LET* **86** F-G3
Sarcee Rd NW *CAL* **35** K19-20
Sarcee Rd W *LET* **86** F-G3
Sarcee Tr NW *CAL* **11** I1 **19** H9 H-I6 I7-8
Sarcee Tr SW *CAL* **26** G13-14 **35** I16-19
Sarson St *BRO* **90** C2
Saskatchewan St *CRS* **62** A2
Saunders Cr *MED* **94** J4 **95** J5
Savoy Cr *RED* **67** M6
Saxon Pl NW *CAL* **48** N26
Saxony La SW *HIG* **77** C1
Scandia Bay 100 to 400 NW *CAL* **18** E9
Scandia Hill NW *CAL* **18** E9
Scandia Pt NW *CAL* **18** E9
Scandia Rise NW *CAL* **18** D-E9
Scanlon Bay NW *CAL* **18** E8
Scanlon Gn NW *CAL* **18** D-E8
Scanlon Gt NW *CAL* **18** D-E8
Scanlon Hill NW *CAL* **18** E8
Scanlon Pl NW *CAL* **18** E8
Scarboro Av SW *CAL* **36** M17
Scarpe Dr NW *CAL* **36** L-M20
Scenic Dr N *LET* **83** B8 D7
Scenic Dr S *LET* **83** E7 **87** F7 G7-8 **88** J9-10
Scenic Gdns NW *CAL* **18** E8
Scenic Gn NW *CAL* **18** E-F9
Scenic Hts S *LET* **87** H8
Scenic Pl NW *CAL* **18** E9
Scenic Rd NW *CAL* **18** E9
Scenic Rise NW *CAL* **18** E-F9
Scenic Way NW *CAL* **18** E-F8 E-F9
Scenic Acres Blvd NW *CAL* **18** E8-9

Scenic Acres Dr NW *CAL* 18 E9
Scenic Acres Gt NW *CAL* 18 E9
Scenic Acres Link NW *CAL* 18 D8
Scenic Acres Ter NW *CAL* 18 E9
Scenic Bow Pl 100 200 NW *CAL* 18 E10 26 E11
Scenic Bow Rd NW *CAL* 18 D-E10
Scenic Cove Bay NW *CAL* 18 E8
Scenic Cove Cir NW *CAL* 18 F8
Scenic Cove Ct NW *CAL* 18 E-F8
Scenic Cove Dr NW *CAL* 18 E-F8
Scenic Cove Pl NW *CAL* 18 F8
Scenic Glen Bay 100 to 300 NW *CAL* 18 E8-9
Scenic Glen Cl NW *CAL* 18 E8-9
Scenic Glen Cr NW *CAL* 18 E9
Scenic Glen Gt NW *CAL* 18 E9
Scenic Glen Mews NW *CAL* 18 E9
Scenic Glen Pl 100 to 300 NW *CAL* 18 E9
Scenic Hill Cl NW *CAL* 18 E8-9
Scenic Park Cr NW *CAL* 18 E9
Scenic Park Gt NW *CAL* 18 E9
Scenic Park Pl 100 200 NW *CAL* . .18 E9
Scenic Ridge Cr NW *CAL* 18 E9-10
Scenic Ridge Ct NW *CAL* 18 E9
Scenic Ridge Gn NW *CAL* 18 E9-10
Scenic Ridge Link NW *CAL* 18 E9
Scenic Ridge Pl NW *CAL* 18 E9-10
Scenic Ridge Way NW *CAL* 18 E9
Scenic View Bay 100 to 400 NW *CAL* 18 E8
Scenic View Cl NW *CAL* 18 E7-8
Scenic View Gt NW *CAL* 18 E8
Sceptre Cl NW *CAL* 18 D8-9
Sceptre Ct 100 to 300 NW *CAL* . .18 D8-9
Schiller Bay NW *CAL* 18 D-E9
Schiller Cr NW *CAL* 18 D9
Schiller Pl 100 200 NW *CAL* 18 D-E9
Schneider Cr *MED* 95 J5
Schooner Cl NW *CAL* 18 D8
Schooner Cv 100 to 700 NW *CAL* .18 D8
Schooner Ldg 100 to 500 NW *CAL* 18 D8
Schubert Gt NW *CAL* 18 D8
Schubert Hill NW *CAL* 18 D7-8
Schubert Pl 100 to 800 NW *CAL* . .18 D8
Schuler Pl *MED* 95 J5
Scimitar Bay 100 to 800 NW *CAL* .18 E9
Scimitar Cir NW *CAL* 18 E10
Scimitar Ct NW *CAL* 18 E10
Scimitar Heath 100 200 NW *CAL* .18 E10
Scimitar Ldg NW *CAL* 18 E10
Scimitar Pt NW *CAL* 18 E9-10
Scimitar Rise NW *CAL* 18 E10
Scimitar View NW *CAL* 18 E10
Scotia Bay NW *CAL* 18 E8
Scotia Ldg NW *CAL* 18 E8
Scotia Pt 100 to 300 NW *CAL* 18 E8
Scotland St SW *CAL* 36 M17
Scott Bay *MED* 95 K5
Scott Cr *MED* 95 J5
Scott Ct *MED* 95 K5
Scott Gn *MED* 95 J-K5
Scott St *RED* 67 J6
Scripps Ldg NW *CAL* 18 E8
Scurfield Dr NW *CAL* 18 D8-9 E8
Scurfield Pl 100 200 NW *CAL* 18 E8
Scurfield Way NW *CAL* 18 E8
Seattle Dr SW *CAL* 48 O26
Selkirk Blvd *RED* 67 J6
Selkirk Dr SW *CAL* 48 N26
Selkirk Rd W *LET* 86 J4
Semrau Dr *MED* 92 C1
Seneca Pl W *LET* 86 J4
Senlac St SW *CAL* 36 M17
Sentinel Rd *LKL* 56 B-C4
Service Rd *BLD* 75 C6
Service Rd *COD* 85 B1
Service Rd *TAB* 91 B-C4 D2
Settler Way *CAN* 59 E-F6
Seven Chiefs Rd SW *CAL* 47 J27
Seven Persons Cr *MED* 94 H-J4
Seven Persons Dr *MED* 94 J4
Seymour Av SW *CAL* 48 O26
Shaganappi Tr NW *CAL* 11 J3 K5 19 K6-9 20 L6-7 27 J11-14
Shale St *MED* 95 F7
Shalom Way SE *CAL* 53 P32
Shamrock Av SW *CAL* 48 O27
Shamrock Cl *RED* 67 J6
Shamrock Pl SW *CAL* 48 O26-27
Shannon Av SW *CAL* 52 N32
Shannon Cir SW *CAL* 52 N31
Shannon Cl *OLD* 62 B2
Shannon Cl SW *CAL* 52 O32
Shannon Com SW *CAL* 52 N32
Shannon Cr *MED* 95 J5
Shannon Cr SW *CAL* 52 N32
Shannon Ct SW *CAL* 52 O31-32
Shannon Dr *MED* 95 J5

Shannon Dr *OLD* 62 B2 B2-3 B3
Shannon Dr SW *CAL* 52 N-O32
Shannon Gdns SW *CAL* 52 M-N32
Shannon Gn SW *CAL* 52 N31
Shannon Hill *CAL* 52 N31
Shannon Link SW *CAL* 52 N31-32
Shannon Mews 100 200 SW *CAL* .52 N32
Shannon Mnr SW *CAL* 52 N31-32
Shannon Pl SW *CAL* 52 N-O31
Shannon Rd SW *CAL* 52 N31-32
Shannon Sq 100 to 400 SW *CAL* 52 M-N31
Shannon Ter SW *CAL* 52 N31
Shannon Way SW *CAL* 52 N-O31
Shannon Estate Ter SW *CAL* .52 M-N31 M-N32
Shantara Gr *RCY* 25 A14
Shantz Cr *CRS* 62 B2
Sharon Av SW *CAL* 36 M17
Sharpe Cr *MED* 95 J5
Shaw Cr *MED* 95 J5
Shaw Rd SW *CAL* . . .48 O30 52 O31 53 P31
Shawbrooke Bay SW *CAL* 52 N32
Shawbrooke Cir SW *CAL* 52 N32
Shawbrooke Cl SW *CAL* 52 N32
Shawbrooke Cr SW *CAL* 52 N32
Shawbrooke Ct SW *CAL* 52 N32
Shawbrooke Dr SW *CAL* 52 N32
Shawbrooke Gn SW *CAL* 52 M-N32
Shawbrooke Mnr SW *CAL* 52 N32
Shawbrooke Pk SW *CAL* 52 M-N32
Shawbrooke Pl SW *CAL* 52 N32
Shawbrooke Rd SW *CAL* 52 N32
Shawbrooke Rise SW *CAL* 52 N32
Shawcliffe Bay SW *CAL* 52 O31-32
Shawcliffe Cir SW *CAL* 52 O32
Shawcliffe Ct SW *CAL* 52 O31-32
Shawcliffe Gn SW *CAL* 52 O31-32
Shawcliffe Gt SW *CAL* 52 O32
Shawcliffe Pl SW *CAL* 52 O32
Shawcliffe Rd SW *CAL* 52 O31-32
Shawfield Bay SW *CAL* 52 O32
Shawfield Ct SW *CAL* 52 N32
Shawfield Dr SW *CAL* 52 O32
Shawfield Gt SW *CAL* 52 O32
Shawfield Pl SW *CAL* 52 O32-33
Shawfield Rd SW *CAL* 52 N-O32
Shawfield Way SW *CAL* 52 N32
Shawglen Ct SW *CAL* 52 O32
Shawglen Pl SW *CAL* 52 O32
Shawglen Rd SW *CAL* 52 O32
Shawglen Rise SW *CAL* 52 O32
Shawglen Way SW *CAL* 52 O32
Shawinigan Ct 100 200 SW *CAL* 52 N-O32
Shawinigan Dr SW *CAL* 52 N-O32
Shawinigan La SW *CAL* 52 N-O32
Shawinigan Pl 100 to 300 SW *CAL* 52 N-O32
Shawinigan Rd SW *CAL* 52 O32
Shawinigan Rise SW *CAL* 52 O32
Shawinigan Way SW *CAL* 52 N-O32
Shawmeadows Bay SW *CAL* 52 O32
Shawmeadows Cl SW *CAL* 52 O31-32
Shawmeadows Cr SW *CAL* 52 O32
Shawmeadows Gt SW *CAL* .52 O32 53 P32
Shawmeadows Pl SW *CAL* 52 O32
Shawmeadows Rd SW *CAL* 52 O32
Shawmeadows Rise SW *CAL* 52 O32
Shawnee Bay SW *CAL* 48 N30
Shawnee Cr SW *CAL* 48 N-O30
Shawnee Ct SW *CAL* 48 O30
Shawnee Dr SW *CAL* 48 N-O30
Shawnee Gdns 100 to 300 SW *CAL* 48 N29
Shawnee Gr SW *CAL* 48 N30
Shawnee Gt SW *CAL* 48 O30
Shawnee Link SW *CAL* 48 O30
Shawnee Mews SW *CAL* 48 N-O30
Shawnee Mnr 100 to 300 SW *CAL* 48 N-O30
Shawnee Pl SW *CAL* 48 O30
Shawnee Rd SW *CAL* 48 N30
Shawnee Rise SW *CAL* 48 N30
Shawnee View SW *CAL* 48 N30
Shawnee Way SW *CAL* 48 N30
Shawnessy Alley SE *CAL* 53 P31-32
Shawnessy Blvd SW *CAL* 52 N-O31
Shawnessy Ct SW *CAL* 52 O32
Shawnessy Dr SW *CAL* 52 O31-32
Shawnessy Ter SW *CAL* 52 O32
Shawville Blvd SE *CAL* 53 P32-33
Shawville Gt SE *CAL* 53 P33
Shawville Link SE *CAL* 53 P33
Shawville Pl SE *CAL* 53 P32
Shawville Rd SE *CAL* 53 P33
Shawville Rise SE *CAL* 53 P32
Shawville Way SE *CAL* 53 P33
Sheep River Bay *OKO* 75 C-D1
Sheep River Blvd *OKO* 75 D1

Sheep River Cl *OKO* 75 D1
Sheep River Cr *OKO* 75 C-D1
Sheep River Crest *OKO* 75 D1
Sheep River Ct *OKO* 75 D1
Sheep River Dr *OKO* 75 C-D1
Sheep River Gn *OKO* 75 D1
Sheep River Heath *OKO* 75 C-D1
Sheep River Hill *OKO* 75 D1
Sheep River Hts *OKO* 75 D1
Sheep River La *OKO* 75 C-D1
Sheep River Link *OKO* 75 C-D1
Sheep River Mews *OKO* 75 D1
Sheep River Pl *OKO* 75 C-D1
Sheep River Pt *OKO* 75 D1
Sheep River Ter *OKO* 75 D1
Shelbourne St SW *CAL* 36 M17
Sheldon Pl NW *CAL* 27 I13
Shellian La *CAN* 58 H4
Sheol Rd *LKL* 56 B3
Shepard Pl SE *CAL* 44 U25
Shepard Rd SE *CAL* 31 Z15 39 Z16-20 44 U25 45 Z21-25 51 Z26-30
Shepherd Dr *MED* 94 H4 H5
Sheppard Rd SW *HIG* 77 C1
Sheridan Pl W *LET* 86 J4
Sheridan Rd W *LET* 86 J4
Sheriff King Pl SE *CAL* 53 P-Q34
Sheriff King Rd SE *CAL* 53 P-Q34
Sherman Av SW *CAL* 48 O26
Sherriff King St SW *CAL* 52 O34-35
Sherwood Blvd NW *CAL* 11 J4
Sherwood Com NW *CAL* 11 J4
Sherwood Cr *OLD* 62 B2
Sherwood Cr *RED* 67 J6
Sherwood Cr W *LET* 86 F-G4
Sherwood Ct NW *CAL* 11 J4
Sherwood Cv NW *CAL* 11 J4
Sherwood Gdns NW *CAL* 11 J4
Sherwood Gn NW *CAL* 11 I-J4
Sherwood Heath NW *CAL* 11 J4
Sherwood Hill NW *CAL* 11 J4
Sherwood Ldg NW *CAL* 11 J4
Sherwood Pl 100 to 400 W *LET* . . .86 F4
Sherwood Prom NW *CAL* 11 J4
Sherwood Pt NW *CAL* 11 J4
Sherwood Rise NW *CAL* 11 J4
Sherwood Ter NW *CAL* 11 J4
Sherwood View NW *CAL* 11 J4
Sherwood Way NW *CAL* 11 J4
Shields Cr *MED* 94 H4
Shillington Cr SW *CAL* 48 O26
Shirley St *MED* 93 E8 95 F8
Short Rd NW *CAL* 26 G13 27 H14
Short Rd SW *CAL* 36 M17
Sibbald St SW *COC* 61 B5
Sidney St *CAN* 59 E5
Sidon Cr SW *CAL* 35 I19
Sienna Bay SW *CAL* 35 H19
Sienna Heights Hill 100 to 400 SW *CAL* 34 G18 35 H18 H19
Sienna Heights Way SW *CAL* 34 G18 35 H19
Sienna Hills Ct SW *CAL* 35 H19
Sienna Hills Dr SW *CAL* 35 H19
Sienna Hills Gt SW *CAL* 35 H19
Sienna Hills Link SW *CAL* 35 H19
Sienna Hills Pl SW *CAL* 35 H19
Sienna Hills Ter 100 200 SW *CAL* .35 H19
Sienna Hills View SW *CAL* 35 H19
Sienna Park Bay 100 to 300 SW *CAL* .34 G18-19
Sienna Park Cr SW *CAL* 34 G18
Sienna Park Ct SW *CAL* 34 G18
Sienna Park Dr SW *CAL* 34 G18 G19 35 H19
Sienna Park Gdns 100 200 SW *CAL* 34 G19
Sienna Park Gn SW *CAL* 34 G19
Sienna Park Gr SW *CAL* 34 G19
Sienna Park Heath 100 200 SW *CAL* 34 G18
Sienna Park Link SW *CAL* 34 G18
Sienna Park Pl SW *CAL* 34 G19 35 H19
Sienna Park Ter SW *CAL* 34 G18-19
Sienna Park View SW *CAL* .34 G19 35 H19
Sienna Ridge Bay SW *CAL* 35 H19
Sienna Ridge Ldg SW *CAL* 35 H19
Sierra Av *MED* 94 J3
Sierra Bay *MED* 94 J3
Sierra Blvd *MED* 94 J3-4
Sierra Cl *OLD* 62 A3
Sierra Cr SW *CAL* 48 O26
Sierra Dr *MED* 94 J3
Sierra Dr *OLD* 62 B3
Sierra Pl *OLD* 62 A3
Sierra Rd *OLD* 62 B3
Sierra Madre Cr SW *CAL* 35 H20
Sierra Madre Ct 100 to 800 SW *CAL* 35 H20

Sierra Morena Blvd SW *CAL* 34 G19 G20 35 H19 H20
Sierra Morena Cir SW *CAL* .34 G20 35 H20
Sierra Morena Cl SW *CAL* 35 H20
Sierra Morena Ct 100 to 1100 SW *CAL* 34 G20 35 H20
Sierra Morena Gdns SW *CAL* 34 G20
Sierra Morena Gn 100 to 300 SW *CAL* 34 G19
Sierra Morena Gr SW *CAL* 34 G20
Sierra Morena Ldg SW *CAL* 34 G20
Sierra Morena Mews SW *CAL* 35 H20
Sierra Morena Pk SW *CAL* 34 G20
Sierra Morena Pl 100 to 900 SW *CAL* 34 G20 35 H20
Sierra Morena Rd SW *CAL* 34 G19
Sierra Morena Ter 100 to 300 SW *CAL* 35 H19-20
Sierra Morena Vill SW *CAL* 35 H20
Sierra Morena Way SW *CAL* 34 G19
Sierra Nevada Cl SW *CAL* .34 G20 35 H20
Sierra Nevada Gn SW *CAL* 34 G20
Sierra Nevada Pl 100 to 300 SW *CAL* 34 G20
Sierra Nevada Rise SW *CAL* 34 G20 35 H20
Sierra Nevada Way SW *CAL* 34 G20
Sierra Vista Bay 100 200 SW *CAL* 35 H19
Sierra Vista Cir SW *CAL* 34 G19 35 H19
Sierra Vista Cl SW *CAL* 35 H19
Sierra Vista Ter 100 200 SW *CAL* .34 G20
Sifton Av *RED* 67 J6
Sifton Blvd SW *CAL* 36 N-O20
Signal Hill Bay SW *CAL* 35 H18
Signal Hill Cir SW *CAL* 35 H-I18 I19
Signal Hill Ct 100 to 300 SW *CAL* 35 H18 I19
Signal Hill Ctr SW *CAL* 35 H20
Signal Hill Dr SW *CAL* . .34 G18 35 H18-19
Signal Hill Gn SW *CAL* 35 I18
Signal Hill Hts SW *CAL* 35 I18-19
Signal Hill La SW *CAL* 35 I18
Signal Hill Mews SW *CAL* 35 H-I19
Signal Hill Pl 100 to 400 SW *CAL* 35 H-I19
Signal Hill Pt 100 to 300 SW *CAL* 35 H-I19
Signal Hill Ter SW *CAL* 35 H19
Signal Hill View SW *CAL* 35 H-I19
Signal Hill Way SW *CAL* 35 H19
Signal Ridge Ct SW *CAL* 35 H18
Signal Ridge Hts SW *CAL* 35 H18-19
Signal Ridge Link SW *CAL* 35 H18-19
Signal Ridge Pl SW *CAL* 35 H18-19
Signal Ridge View SW *CAL* 35 H18-19
Signature Cl SW *CAL* 35 H18
Signature Ct *TAB* 91 D2
Signature Ct 100 to 300 SW *CAL* .35 H18
Signature Hts SW *CAL* 35 H18
Signature Link SW *CAL* 35 H18
Signature Mews SW *CAL* 35 H18
Signature Mnr SW *CAL* 35 H18
Signature Pk SW *CAL* 35 H-I18
Signature Pl SW *CAL* 35 H18
Signature Pt 100 200 SW *CAL* 34 G18 35 H18
Signature Rise SW *CAL* 35 H18
Signature Ter 100 200 SW *CAL* . .35 H18
Signature Vill SW *CAL* 35 H18
Signature Way SW *CAL* 35 H18
Sikome Cir SE *CAL* 53 S33
Sikome Rd SE *CAL* 53 S33
Silcher St *MED* 95 J5
Sillak Cr *MED* 94 H4 95 H5
Silver Birch Way NW *CAL* 26 E12
Silver Brook Dr NW *CAL* 18 G9-10
Silver Brook Rd NW *CAL* 18 G9-10
Silver Brook Way NW *CAL* 18 G9
Silver Creek Blvd NW *AIR* 68 A2
Silver Creek Cl NW *CAL* 18 F9
Silver Creek Cr NW *CAL* 18 E-F9
Silver Creek Dr NW *AIR* 68 A2
Silver Creek Dr NW *CAL* 18 F9
Silver Creek Gn NW *CAL* 18 F9
Silver Creek Mews 200 300 NW *CAL* 18 F9
Silver Creek Mnr NW *CAL* 18 F9
Silver Creek Pl NW *CAL* 18 E9
Silver Creek Way NW *CAL* 18 F9
Silver Crest Cr NW *CAL* 18 F10
Silver Crest Dr NW *CAL* 18 F-G10
Silver Crest Gn NW *CAL* 18 F10
Silver Crest Rd NW *CAL* 18 F-G10
Silver Hill Cr NW *CAL* 18 F9-10
Silver Hill Pl NW *CAL* 18 F10
Silver Hill Rd NW *CAL* 18 F10
Silver Hill Way NW *CAL* . .18 F9-10 G9-10
Silver Mead Bay NW *CAL* 18 F-G10
Silver Mead Cl NW *CAL* 18 G10
Silver Mead Cr NW *CAL* 18 F-G10
Silver Mead Rd NW *CAL* 18 F-G10
Silver Ridge Cl NW *CAL* 18 G10

Silver Ridge Cr NW CAL ... 18 F10
Silver Ridge Ct NW CAL ... 18 G9
Silver Ridge Dr NW CAL ... 18 F9-10 F-G10
Silver Ridge Gn NW CAL ... 18 F9
Silver Ridge Pl NW CAL ... 18 F10
Silver Ridge Rd NW CAL ... 18 G9
Silver Ridge Rise NW CAL ... 18 F-G9
Silver Ridge Way NW CAL ... 18 F9
Silver Springs Blvd NW CAL ... 18 F9 F-G10
Silver Springs Cr NW CAL ... 18 G9
Silver Springs Dr NW CAL ... 18 G10
Silver Springs Gn NW CAL ... 18 G9
Silver Springs Gt NW CAL ... 18 G9-10
Silver Springs Hill NW CAL ... 18 G10
Silver Springs Mews NW CAL ... 18 G9
Silver Springs Pl NW CAL ... 18 G9
Silver Springs Rd NW CAL ... 18 E-G9
Silver Springs Rise NW CAL ... 18 G9
Silver Springs Way NW AIR ... 68 A2
Silver Springs Way NW CAL ... 18 G9-10
Silver Valley Bay NW CAL ... 18 F10
Silver Valley Blvd NW CAL ... 18 E-F10
Silver Valley Dr NW CAL ... 18 F-G10
Silver Valley Pl NW CAL ... 18 F10
Silver Valley Rd NW CAL ... 18 E-F10
Silver Valley Rise NW CAL ... 18 F10
Silverdale Cr NW CAL ... 18 G10
Silverdale Dr NW CAL ... 18 G10 26 G11
Silverdale Pl NW CAL ... 18 G10
Silverdale Rd NW CAL ... 18 G10 26 G11
Silvergrove Bay NW CAL ... 18 F8-9
Silvergrove Cl NW CAL ... 18 F9
Silvergrove Cr NW CAL ... 18 F8
Silvergrove Ct NW CAL ... 18 F8-9
Silvergrove Dr NW CAL ... 18 F-G9
Silvergrove Gdns NW CAL ... 18 F9
Silvergrove Gn NW CAL ... 18 F9
Silvergrove Hill NW CAL ... 18 F9
Silvergrove Mews NW CAL ... 18 F9
Silvergrove Mnr NW CAL ... 18 F9
Silvergrove Pl 100 to 300 NW CAL ... 18 F-G9
Silvergrove Pl NW CAL ... 18 F8
Silvergrove Rd NW CAL ... 18 F9
Silvergrove Rise NW CAL ... 18 F-G9
Silvergrove Way NW CAL ... 18 F9
Silverpark Cl OLD ... 62 B2-3
Silverpark Estate Cl OLD ... 62 B2
Silverstone Bay NW CAL ... 18 G9
Silverstone Mews NW CAL ... 18 G9
Silverstone Mnr NW CAL ... 18 G9
Silverstone Pl NW CAL ... 18 G9
Silverstone Rd NW CAL ... 18 G9
Silverthorn Cl 100 to 400 OLD ... 62 A2-3
Silverthorn Dr NW CAL ... 18 F9
Silverthorn Rd OLD ... 62 B2-3
Silverthorn Rd NW CAL ... 18 F9
Silverthorn Way NW CAL ... 18 F9
Silvertip Cl CAN ... 59 F6
Silvertip Pt CAN ... 59 D6
Silvertip Rd CAN ... 59 D6
Silvertip Ridge CAN ... 59 D6
Silvertip Tr CAN ... 59 D5-6 E5-6
Silverview Dr NW CAL ... 26 G11
Silverview Pl NW CAL ... 26 G11
Silverview Pt NW CAL ... 18 F9
Silverview Rd NW CAL ... 18 G10 26 G11
Silverview Way NW CAL ... 18 G10 26 G11 27 H11
Silverwoods Dr RCY ... 9 B2
Simcoe Bay SW CAL ... 34 G18
Simcoe Blvd SW CAL ... 34 G18 35 H18
Simcoe Cir SW CAL ... 34 G18 35 H18
Simcoe Cl SW CAL ... 34 G18
Simcoe Cr SW CAL ... 34 G18 35 H18
Simcoe Gt SW CAL ... 34 G18 35 H18
Simcoe Link SW CAL ... 34 G18
Simcoe Mews SW CAL ... 34 G18
Simcoe Pl SW CAL ... 34 G18
Simcoe Rd SW CAL ... 34 G18 35 H18
Simcoe Rise SW CAL ... 34 G18
Simcoe Ter SW CAL ... 34 G18 35 H18
Simcoe View 100 200 SW CAL ... 34 G18
Simcrest Gr SW CAL ... 34 G18
Simcrest Hts 100 to 300 SW CAL ... 35 H18
Simcrest Mnr SW CAL ... 35 H18
Simcrest Pt SW CAL ... 34 G18 35 H18
Simmons Ct MED ... 95 J5
Simon Fraser Blvd W LET ... 86 J4
Simons Cr NW CAL ... 20 010
Simons Rd NW CAL ... 28 011 29 P11
Simpson Cr MED ... 94 J4
Sinai St SW CAL ... 42 L21
Sinclair Cr SW CAL ... 48 N26
Sirocco Dr SW CAL ... 35 H-I18
Sirocco Pl SW CAL ... 35 H-I18
Sissons Cr MED ... 94 J4
Skyline Cr NE CAL ... 29 Q11
Skyline Way NE CAL ... 29 Q11
Slack St MED ... 95 J5
Slate Rd LKL ... 56 B3-4
Slater Rd STM ... 71 E3
Slater Way STM ... 71 E3
Sleigh Dr RDW ... 61 A3
Slocan Rd SW CAL ... 48 N26
Slopes Gdns SW CAL ... 34 D19
Slopes Gr SW CAL ... 34 D18
Slopes Pt SW CAL ... 34 D18
Slopes Rd SW CAL ... 34 D18-19
Slopeview Dr SW CAL ... 34 D18-19
Smeaton Av MED ... 95 J5
Smed Ln SE CAL ... 45 X22
Smelter Av MED ... 95 F6
Smith Av CRS ... 62 B1-2
Smith Cl MED ... 95 J5
Smith St NE AIR ... 68 B3
Smith St SE AIR ... 68 B-C3
Smith Dorrien Spray Trail CAN ... 58 E2-3 F2
Smithson St MED ... 94 J4 95 J5
Smythe Av MED ... 92 D3
Snowberry Cir RCY ... 33 Z20
Snowberry Gt RCY ... 33 Z20
Snowberry Pl RCY ... 33 Z20
Snowberry Pt RCY ... 33 Z20
Snowberry View RCY ... 33 Z20
Snowdon Cr SW CAL ... 48 N26
Solace Ridge Pl RCY ... 25 A13-14
Somercrest Cir SW CAL ... 52 033
Somercrest Cl SW CAL ... 52 N-033
Somercrest Gdns SW CAL ... 52 N32-33
Somercrest Gr SW CAL ... 52 N32-33
Somercrest Mnr SW CAL ... 52 033
Somercrest St SW CAL ... 52 N32-33
Somerglen Cl SW CAL ... 52 033
Somerglen Com SW CAL ... 52 N-033
Somerglen Cr SW CAL ... 52 033
Somerglen Ct SW CAL ... 52 033
Somerglen Cv SW CAL ... 52 033
Somerglen Heath SW CAL ... 52 033
Somerglen Pk SW CAL ... 52 033
Somerglen Pl SW CAL ... 52 033
Somerglen Rd SW CAL ... 52 033
Somerglen Way SW CAL ... 52 N33
Somerset Cir SW CAL ... 52 033
Somerset Cl RED ... 67 J6
Somerset Cl SW CAL ... 52 033
Somerset Cr SW CAL ... 52 N33
Somerset Ct SW CAL ... 52 033
Somerset Dr SW CAL ... 52 N-033
Somerset Gt SW CAL ... 52 033
Somerset Mnr SW CAL ... 52 N33
Somerset Pk SW CAL ... 52 N-033
Somerset Sq SW CAL ... 52 033
Somerset Way SW CAL ... 52 N33
Somerside Bay SW CAL ... 52 N33
Somerside Cl SW CAL ... 52 N33
Somerside Com SW CAL ... 52 N32
Somerside Cr SW CAL ... 52 N33
Somerside Dr SW CAL ... 52 N32
Somerside Gn 100 200 SW CAL 52 M-N32
Somerside Gr SW CAL ... 52 N32-33
Somerside Mnr SW CAL ... 52 N32-33
Somerside Pk SW CAL ... 52 N32-33
Somerside Pl SW CAL ... 52 N33
Somervale Cl SW CAL ... 52 033
Somervale Ct SE CAL ... 53 P33
Somervale Dr SW CAL ... 52 033
Somervale Gn SW CAL ... 52 033
Somervale La SW CAL ... 52 033 53 P33
Somervale Link SW CAL ... 52 033
Somervale Path SW CAL ... 52 033
Somervale Pk SW CAL ... 52 033 53 P33
Somervale Pl SW CAL ... 52 033
Somervale View SW CAL ... 52 033
Somme Av SW CAL ... 36 L20 L-M19
Somme Blvd SW CAL ... 36 M19-20
Somme La SW CAL ... 36 L19-20
Somme Mews SW CAL ... 36 L19
Somme Mnr SW CAL ... 36 L19-20
Somme Way SW CAL ... 36 L19-20
Sonora Av SW CAL ... 36 M17
Sorrel Mews SW CAL ... 36 L19
Sorrel Pl SW CAL ... 48 027
Souch Bay MED ... 95 J5
South Boundary Rd MED ... 94 K2-4 95 K5-6
South Dale Ct MED ... 95 H6
South Dinosaur Tr DRU ... 72 B1 C1-2
South Parkside Dr LET ... 88 G10-11
South Railway Av DRU ... 73 C5-6 C-D7
South Railway St MED ... 93 E5 95 F6
South Railway St OKO ... 76 C3
South Ridge Cl COC ... 61 D-E5
South Ridge Cr MED ... 94 H-J4
South Ridge Dr COC ... 61 D5
South Ridge Dr MED ... 94 H-K4
South Shore Dr BRO ... 90 B3
South West Dr MED ... 94 G2-3
Southampton Dr SW CAL ... 48 N26-27
Southbank Rd OKO ... 76 E4
Southbow Pl SW CAL ... 48 N26
Southcreek Pl SE AIR ... 68 D3
Southdale Bay SW CAL ... 48 N27
Southdale Cl SW CAL ... 48 N27
Southdale Cr SW CAL ... 48 N27
Southdale Pl SW CAL ... 48 N27
Southdale Rd SW CAL ... 48 N27
Southglen Dr SW CAL ... 48 N27
Southglen Pl SW CAL ... 48 N27
Southland Cir SW CAL ... 42 025
Southland Cr SW CAL ... 48 N-026
Southland Dr SE CAL ... 49 Q26
Southland Dr SW CAL ... 47 K26 48 L-026
Southland Gn SW CAL ... 48 026
Southmount Pl SW CAL ... 48 N-027
Southport La SW CAL ... 48 026
Southport Rd SW CAL ... 48 026
Southport Way SW CAL ... 48 026-27
Southridge Blvd LET ... 88 L10
Southridge Dr OKO ... 76 C-E2
Southridge Rd S LET ... 88 L10
Southview Ct MED ... 95 H6
Southview Dr MED ... 95 H5-6 H7
Southview Pl MED ... 95 H6
Southwood Dr SE CAL ... 38 V18
Southwood Rd TVY ... 74 E3
Sovereign Cr SW CAL ... 36 L17
Spadina Dr SW CAL ... 48 N26
Sparrow Pl RCY ... 8 X-Y2
Spence Av BRO ... 90 B1
Spencer St MED ... 95 G5
Spencer St RED ... 67 J6
Spiller Rd SE CAL ... 37 P-Q19 Q18
Spokane St SW CAL ... 48 N26
Sprague Way MED ... 94 H4 95 J5
Spray Av BAN ... 57 E2
Spray Dr CAN ... 58 A2
Spray Lakes Rd CAN ... 58 F3 G4
Spring Cr SW CAL ... 34 F20
Spring Mews SW CAL ... 34 F20
Spring View SW CAL ... 34 F20
Spring Bok Av SW CAL ... 41 J21
Spring Creek Cr CAN ... 58 E4
Spring Dale Cir SE AIR ... 68 C4 69 C5
Spring Dale Ct SE AIR ... 68 C-D4
Spring Dale Gt SE AIR ... 68 D4 69 D5
Spring Gate Estates RCY ... 32 Y17
Spring Grove Cr SE AIR ... 68 D-E4 69 D-E5
Spring Haven Cl SE AIR ... 68 D4
Spring Haven Cr SE AIR ... 68 D-E4
Spring Haven Ct 500 to 900 SE AIR ... 68 D-E4
Spring Haven Mew 100 SE AIR ... 68 D-E4
Spring Haven Rd SE AIR ... 68 D4
Spring Meadows La RCY ... 24 X-Y15
Spring Shire Estates RCY ... 32 Y17
Spring Valley Cl SW CAL ... 34 F19
Spring Valley La SW CAL ... 34 F19
Spring Valley Mews SW CAL ... 34 F19
Spring Valley Pt 100 200 SW CAL ... 34 F18-19
Spring Valley Ter SW CAL ... 34 F18-19
Spring Valley View SW CAL ... 34 F18-19
Spring Valley Way SW CAL ... 34 F19
Spring Village La SW CAL ... 34 G19
Springbank Bay SW CAL ... 34 G19
Springbank Blvd SW CAL ... 34 F-G20
Springbank Cr SW CAL ... 34 F19
Springbank Ct SW CAL ... 34 F19-20
Springbank Dr SW CAL ... 34 F19
Springbank Mews SW CAL ... 34 G19
Springbank Mt SW CAL ... 34 G19
Springbank Pl 100 to 400 SW CAL ... 34 F19-20
Springbank Rd RCY ... 24 V-W14 25 Z14
Springbank Rd RCY ... 25 B-C14
Springbank Rd (Township Rd 244) RCY ... 24 W-X14
Springbank Rise SW CAL ... 34 F19
Springbank Ter SW CAL ... 34 G19-20
Springbank View SW CAL ... 34 F19
Springbank Way SW CAL ... 34 F20
Springbank Community School Rd RCY ... 16 V7-8
Springbank Heights Dr RCY ... 16 W6-7
Springbank Heights Loop RCY ... 16 V6-7 W6 W7
Springbank Heights Rd RCY ... 8 V5 16 V6 W7
Springbett Dr RED ... 67 H6
Springbluff Bay SW CAL ... 34 F19
Springbluff Blvd SW CAL ... 34 G19
Springbluff Gt SW CAL ... 34 G19
Springbluff Hts SW CAL ... 34 F-G19
Springbluff Link SW CAL ... 34 F19
Springborough Blvd SW CAL ... 34 G18
Springborough Cr SW CAL ... 34 F18
Springborough Gn SW CAL ... 34 F-G18
Springborough Gt SW CAL ... 34 G18
Springborough Pt SW CAL ... 34 G1
Springborough Way SW CAL ... 34 G1
Springfield Av RED ... 67 J
Springfield Pl SW CAL ... 48 N2
Springhill Cr SW CAL ... 34 F1
Springland Cr RCY ... 25 C1
Springland Way RCY ... 25 B14-1
Springland Manor Dr RCY ... 25 B-C1
Springmere Cl CHE ... 70 D
Springmere Dr CHE ... 70 D
Springmere Key CHE ... 70 E
Springmere Link CHE ... 70 D
Springmere Pl 100 200 CHE ... 70 D
Springmere Rd CHE ... 70 D-E
Springmere Way CHE ... 70 D
Springridge Estates RCY ... 25 A1
Springs Cr BAN ... 57 E2-4
Springs Cr SE AIR ... 68 D4
Springs Ct 100 SE AIR ... 69 D5
Springs Pl 100 to 300 SE AIR ... 68 D4
Springside St RCY ... 24 Y14-15
Springwood Cr SE AIR ... 68 D3-4
Springwood Dr SW CAL ... 48 N26
Springwood Pl SW CAL ... 42 N25 48 N26
Spruce Av BRG ... 78 B3-4
Spruce Av BRO ... 90 C1-2
Spruce Centre SW CAL ... 35 K16
Spruce Cl MED ... 94 K4
Spruce Dr DRU ... 73 D8
Spruce Dr RED ... 66 H5 67 H6
Spruce Dr S LET ... 88 H11
Spruce Dr SW CAL ... 35 I-J16 K16-17
Spruce La STM ... 71 E3
Spruce St BAN ... 57 C2
Spruce Way MED ... 94 K4 95 J-K5 K5
Spruce Way NW CAL ... 26 E11-12
Spruce Bank Cr SW CAL ... 35 J-K16
Spruce Grove La SW CAL ... 42 M25
Spruce Meadows Ct MED ... 95 K5
Spruce Meadows Dr SW CAL ... 52 M-N34
Spruce Meadows Tr SW CAL 52 L-034 M33
Spruce Meadows Way SW CAL 52 N34-35
Spruce Park Dr STM ... 71 E3
Sprucegrove Cr SE AIR ... 68 D4
Sprucegrove Gt SE AIR ... 68 D4
Sprucegrove Way SE AIR ... 68 D4
Spyhill Cr NW CAL ... 20 010 21 P10
Spyhill Rd NW CAL ... 20 010 21 P10
Squamish Blvd W LET ... 86 F3
Squamish Cr W LET ... 86 F3
Squamish Ct W LET ... 86 F3
Squamish La W LET ... 86 G3
Squamish Rd W LET ... 86 F-G3
Squirrel Cr CAN ... 58 F3
Squirrel St BAN ... 57 C-D2
Stafford Av N LET ... 83 C7-8
Stafford Bay 100 to 400 N LET ... 83 C8
Stafford Blvd N LET ... 83 C7-8
Stafford Dr N LET ... 83 C-D8 D-E8
Stafford Dr S LET ... 83 E8 87 F8
Stafford Pl CRS ... 62 A2
Stafford Rd N LET ... 83 C8
Stafford St CRS ... 62 A2
Stafford St MED ... 95 J5
Staffordville Cr N LET ... 83 C8
Stampede Ter SE CAL ... 37 Q17-18
Standish Cl RED ... 67 J6
Stanfield Ct MED ... 94 K4
Stanfield Pl MED ... 94 K4
Stanfield Way MED ... 94 J4 95 J5 J5
Stanhope Av RED ... 67 J6
Stanley Av OKO ... 76 C3
Stanley Cl RED ... 67 J6
Stanley Cr SW CAL ... 36 020 42 021 43 P21
Stanley Dr SW CAL ... 36 020 37 P20
Stanley Pl SW CAL ... 37 P20
Stanley Rd SW CAL ... 37 P20 43 P21-22
Stanton St RED ... 67 J6
Stapeford Cr MED ... 95 J5
Stark Av MED ... 94 K4
Stark Bay MED ... 95 K5
Stark Ct MED ... 94 K4
Stark Mews MED ... 94 K4
Stark Way MED ... 94 K4 95 K5
State Rd SW CAL ... 36 L17
Station Blvd COD ... 85 B2-3
Station St COD ... 85 A-B3
Steel St MED ... 95 F6
Steele Av SW CAL ... 41 J21
Stein Cr MED ... 95 J5
Stevens St CRS ... 62 A-B2
Stevenson St MED ... 94 J4
Stewart Dr MED ... 92 D3
Stewart Gn SW CAL ... 35 H20
Stewart St RED ... 67 J6
Stimson Rd SW HIG ... 77 C1
Stirling Cl RED ... 67 J6
Stock St MED ... 95 J5
Stockton Av OKO ... 76 C4

Stockton Pl *OKO* 76 C4
Stone Cr *MED* 94 J4
Stonecreek Pl *CAN* 59 D6
Stonecreek Rd *CAN* 59 D6
Stonegate Cl NW *AIR* 68 A3
Stonegate Cr *MED* 95 J5
Stonegate Cr NW *AIR* 68 A3
Stonegate Dr NW *AIR* 68 A3
Stonegate Pl 100 200 NW *AIR* . .68 A3
Stonegate Rd NW *AIR* 68 A3
Stonegate Way NW *AIR* 68 A2-3
Stonehaven Rd SW *CAL* 48 N-O27
Stonehill Dr SE *CAL* 14 T4
Stonehill Gt SE *CAL* 14 T4
Stonemere Pt *CHE* 70 C2
Stonepine Cv *RCY* 33 Z19
Stonepine Dr *RCY* 33 Z19
Stonepine Gt *RCY* 33 Z19
Stoney Cr W *LET* 86 F3
Stoney Pl W *LET* 86 F3
Stoney Tr NE *CAL* . .13 P-Q2 14 T2 15 X2
Stoney Tr NW *CAL*
. . . . .11 H5 K5 12 N2 18 D9-10 D-E7 D11-12
Stoney Tr SW 26 D13-14 34 D17
Storrs Cr *MED* 95 J5
Storrs Pl *MED* 94 K4 95 K5
Storybook Gdns NW *CAL* 18 F-G8
Storybook Ter 100 200 NW *CAL* .18 F-G8
Strabane Cl SW *CAL* 35 H16
Strachan Ct *MED* 95 J6
Strachan Rd *MED* 94 J-K4 95 J5 J6
Stradbrooke Pl SW *CAL* 35 H17
Stradbrooke Rise SW *CAL* 35 H17
Stradbrooke Way SW *CAL* 35 H17
Straddock Cr SW *CAL* 34 G16
Straddock Ter SW *CAL* 34 G16
Stradwick Pl SW *CAL* 35 H16
Stradwick Pt SW *CAL* 35 H16
Stradwick Rise SW *CAL* 35 H16
Stradwick Way SW *CAL* 35 H16
Strandell Cr SW *CAL* 35 H-I16
Stranraer Pl SW *CAL* 35 H16
Strasbourg Bay SW *CAL* . .34 G17 35 H17
Strasbourg Gn SW *CAL* 35 H17
Stratford Pl SW *CAL* 35 H16
Stratham Bay SW *CAL* 35 H17
Strathaven Bay 100 to 300 *STM* . .71 A-B4
Strathaven Cir SW *CAL* 34 G16
Strathaven Cr *STM* 71 A-B4
Strathaven Dr *STM* 71 B4
Strathaven Gt SW *CAL* . .34 G16 35 H16
Strathaven Mews SW *CAL* 34 G16
Strathaven Pl 100 *STM* 71 A4
Strathbury Bay 100 200 SW *CAL* . . . . .
. . . . .34 G16 35 H16
Strathbury Cir SW *CAL* 35 H16
Strathbury Gt SW *CAL* 35 H16
Strathbury Pl SW *CAL* 35 H16
Strathbury Rise SW *CAL* 35 H16
Strathcairn Pl SW *CAL* 35 H16
Strathcanna Ct SW *CAL* 35 H17
Strathclair Pl SW *CAL* 35 H16
Strathclair Rise SW *CAL* 35 H16
Strathcona Bay *STM* 71 A3
Strathcona Bay SW *CAL* 35 H17
Strathcona Blvd *STM* 71 A3
Strathcona Blvd SW *CAL* 34 G16-17
Strathcona Cl SW *CAL* 35 H-I16
Strathcona Cr *STM* 71 A3
Strathcona Cr SW *CAL* 35 H-I16
Strathcona Dr SW *CAL*
. . . . .34 F-G16 G16-17 35 H16-17
Strathcona Hill SW *CAL* 35 H16
Strathcona Mews 100 to 500 SW *CAL* . .
. . . . .35 H16-17
Strathcona Pl SW *CAL* 35 H16-17
Strathcona Rd *STM* 71 A3
Strathcona Rd SW *CAL* 35 H16
Strathcona St *CRS* 62 A2
Strathcona St SW *CAL* 41 I21-22
Strathdale Cl SW *CAL* 34 G17
Strathearn Cr SW *CAL* 35 H-I17
Strathearn Gdns SW *CAL* 35 I17
Strathearn Pl SW *CAL* 35 H17
Strathearn Rise SW *CAL* 35 H-I17
Strathford Bay 100 to 400 *STM* . .71 A4
Strathford Blvd *STM* 71 A-B3
Strathford Cl *STM* 71 B4
Strathford Cr *STM* 71 B4
Strathford Glen *STM* 71 A4
Strathford Pl *STM* 71 B3-4
Strathlea Av SW *CAL* 34 E-F16
Strathlea Cl SW *CAL* 34 E16
Strathlea Cm SW *CAL* 34 E16
Strathlea Cr SW *CAL* 34 F16
Strathlea Ct SW *CAL* 34 F16
Strathlea Gn SW *CAL* 34 F16
Strathlea Gr SW *CAL* 34 F16
Strathlea Gt SW *CAL* 34 F16

Strathlea Mnr SW *CAL* 34 F16
Strathlea Pl SW *CAL* 34 F16
Strathlorne Bay SW *CAL* 35 H17
Strathlorne Cr SW *CAL* 35 H17
Strathlorne Mews SW *CAL* 35 H17
Strathmore Lakes Bay *STM* 71 D2
Strathmore Lakes Cr *STM* 71 D2
Strathmore Lakes Way *STM* 71 D2
Strathridge Bay SW *CAL* 34 G16
Strathridge Cl SW *CAL* 34 G16
Strathridge Cr SW *CAL* 34 G16
Strathridge Ct SW *CAL* 34 F16
Strathridge Gdns SW *CAL* 34 G16
Strathridge Gt SW *CAL* 34 G16
Strathridge Hts SW *CAL* 34 F16
Strathridge Pk SW *CAL* 34 G16
Strathridge Pl 100 200 SW *CAL* . .34 G16
Strathridge Way SW *CAL* 34 G16
Strathroy Bay SW *CAL* 35 H16
Strathwood Bay SW *CAL* . .34 G16 35 H16
Stratton Cl *MED* 94 K4 95 K5
Stratton Cr SW *CAL* 35 H16
Stratton Ct SW *CAL* 35 H16
Stratton Pk SW *CAL* 35 H16-17
Stratton Pl SW *CAL* 35 H16
Stratton Ter SW *CAL* 35 H16
Stratton Way *MED* 94 J-K4
Stratton Hill Bay SW *CAL* 35 H16
Stratton Hill Rise SW *CAL* 35 H16-17
Stravanan Bay 100 to 300 SW *CAL* . . . .
. . . . .35 H16
Strickland Bay 100 200 SW *CAL* .35 H17
Strong Av *MED* 94 J4
Sudbury Av SW *CAL* 36 M17
Suffolk St SW *CAL* 36 L17
Sugnature La *TAB* 91 D2
Sullivan Rd SW *HIG* 77 C1
Sulpher Ct *BAN* 57 E1
Sulpher Mountain Cr *BAN* 57 E2
Sumac Rd NW *CAL* 28 L15
Summer St SW *CAL* 36 M17
Summerfield Blvd SE *AIR* 68 D3-4
Summerfield Cl SW *AIR* 68 E3
Summerfield Rd SE *AIR* 68 D3
Summerwood Pl 100 to 500 SE *AIR* 68 D3
Summerwood Rd SE *AIR* 68 D3
Summit Pl *RCY* 9 Z2
Summit St SW *CAL* 36 M17
Sun Ridge Cl NW *AIR* 68 B3
Sun Canyon Cr SE *CAL* 53 R-S32
Sun Canyon Link SE *CAL* 53 R32
Sun Canyon Pk SE *CAL* 53 S32
Sun Canyon Way SE *CAL* 53 R32
Sun Harbour Cl SE *CAL* 53 S33
Sun Harbour Cr SE *CAL* 53 S33
Sun Harbour Gn SE *CAL* 53 R33
Sun Harbour Pl SE *CAL* 53 S33
Sun Harbour Rd SE *CAL* 68 D3
Sun Harbour Way SE *CAL* 53 R-S33
Sun Ridge Cr NW *AIR* 68 B3
Sun Ridge Pl NW *AIR* 68 B2-3
Sun Valley Blvd SE *CAL* . .53 P-Q32 R32
Sun Valley Dr SE *CAL* 53 Q-S32
Sunbank Ct SE *CAL* 53 Q32
Sunbank La SE *CAL* 53 Q32
Sunbank Pl SE *CAL* 53 Q32
Sunbank Rd SE *CAL* 53 Q32
Sunbank Way SE *CAL* 53 Q32-33
Suncastle Bay SE *CAL* 53 R32-33
Suncastle Cr SE *CAL* 53 R33
Suncastle Dr SE *CAL* 53 R32-33
Suncastle Gt SE *CAL* 53 R32-33
Suncastle Pl SE *CAL* 53 Q-R32
Suncastle Rd SE *CAL* 53 R32
Suncrest Way SW *CAL* 53 Q-R32
Sundance Bay *MED* 94 J3
Sundance Ct *MED* 94 J3
Sundance Pl SE *AIR* 68 D3
Sundance Rd *BAN* 57 D-E1
Sundance Rd *MED* 94 J3
Sunderland Av SW *CAL* 36 M17
Sundown Bay *MED* 94 J3
Sundown Cl SE *CAL* 53 P-Q33
Sundown Ct *MED* 94 J-K3
Sundown Gn SE *CAL* 53 Q33
Sundown Link SE *CAL* 53 Q33
Sundown Mnr SE *CAL* 36 L18
Sundown Pl SE *CAL* 53 Q33
Sundown Rd *MED* 94 J-K3
Sundown Rd SE *CAL* 53 Q33
Sundown Way SE *CAL* 53 Q33
Sunflower Ct *MED* 95 H5
Sunhaven Bay 100 200 SE *CAL* 53 R32-33
Sunhaven Ct SE *CAL* 53 R32
Sunhaven Cl SE *CAL* 53 R32
Sunhaven Link SE *CAL* 53 R32
Sunhaven Pl SE *CAL* 53 R32-33
Sunhaven Rd SE *CAL* 53 R32

Sunhaven Way SE *CAL* 53 R32
Sunhurst Cr SE *CAL* 53 Q32
Sunhurst Ct SE *CAL* 53 Q32
Sunhurst Pl SE *CAL* 53 Q32
Sunhurst Rd SE *CAL* 53 Q32
Sunhurst Rise SE *CAL* 53 Q-R32
Sunlake Cir SE *CAL* 53 Q-R33
Sunlake Cl SE *CAL* 53 Q33
Sunlake Gdns SE *CAL* 53 R33
Sunlake Link SE *CAL* 53 R33
Sunlake Mnr SE *CAL* 53 Q33
Sunlake Rd SE *CAL* 53 Q-R33
Sunlake St SE *CAL* 53 Q-R33
Sunlake Way SE *CAL* 53 Q33
Sunmeadows Cr SE *CAL* 53 Q-R32
Sunmeadows Ct SE *CAL* 53 Q33-34
Sunmeadows Pl SE *CAL* 53 Q33-34
Sunmeadows Rd SE *CAL* 53 Q33
Sunmills Ct SE *CAL* 53 Q32
Sunmills Dr SE *CAL* 53 Q32-33 R33
Sunmills Gn SE *CAL* 53 Q32
Sunmills Pl 100 200 SE *CAL* 53 Q33
Sunmount Bay 100 200 SE *CAL* .53 R32
Sunmount Cl SE *CAL* 53 Q-R32
Sunmount Cr SE *CAL* 53 R32
Sunmount Ct SE *CAL* 53 Q32
Sunmount Gdns SE *CAL* 53 Q32
Sunmount Pl 100 200 SE *CAL* . . .53 R32
Sunmount Rd SE *CAL* 53 R32
Sunmount Rise SE *CAL* 53 R32
Sunnyhill La NW *CAL* 28 O15
Sunnyside Cr *RED* 67 J6
Sunnyside Pl SE *AIR* 68 D3-4
Sunnyside Rd *LET* 85 C-D13
Sunpark Dr SE *CAL* 53 Q32-33
Sunpark Gt SE *CAL* 53 P32
Sunpark Plaza SE *CAL* 53 P32-33
Sunridge Blvd NE *CAL* 30 U13
Sunridge Way NE *CAL* 30 U-V14
Sunrise Bay *MED* 94 J4
Sunrise Cir *MED* 94 J4
Sunrise Cir SE *CAL* 53 S32-33
Sunrise Cr *OLD* 62 B2
Sunrise Cr *TAB* 91 D-E3
Sunrise Cr SE *CAL* 53 S32-33
Sunrise Ct *MED* 94 J4
Sunrise Gt *MED* 94 J4
Sunrise Link SE *CAL* 53 S33
Sunrise St *MED* 94 J4
Sunrise Way *MED* 94 J4
Sunset Av *MED* 94 J3
Sunset Av SW *CAL* 36 L17
Sunset Blvd *TVY* 74 D2-4
Sunset Cl SE *CAL* 53 R33
Sunset Cr *MED* 94 J3
Sunset Cr *OKO* 76 B3
Sunset Cr SE *CAL* 53 Q33
Sunset Cv SE *CAL* 53 Q33
Sunset Dr *MED* 94 J3
Sunset Dr *TVY* 74 D2
Sunset Gn *CRS* 62 B2
Sunset Hts *CRS* 62 A-B2
Sunset Pl 100 to 300 *OKO* 76 B3
Sunset Pl 100 200 SE *CAL* 53 R33
Sunset Rd *MED* 94 J3
Sunset Way *CRS* 62 A1-2 B1-2
Sunset Way NE *HIG* 77 B3
Sunset Way SE *CAL* 53 R33
Sunshine Cl SE *HIG* 77 C4-5
Sunshine Ct SE *HIG* 77 C4
Sunshine Pl SE *HIG* 77 C4
Sunshine Tr SE *HIG* 77 C5
Sunshine Way SE *HIG* 77 C4-5
Suntree La *OKO* 76 B2-3
Suntree Pl 100 to 500 *OKO* 76 B3
Sunvale Cr SE *CAL* 53 Q33
Sunvale Ct SE *CAL* 53 Q33
Sunvale Dr SE *CAL* 53 Q33
Sunvale Mews SE *CAL* 53 Q33
Sunvale Pl SE *CAL* 53 Q33
Sunvale Rd SE *CAL* 53 Q33
Sunvista Cl SE *CAL* 53 R33
Sunvista Cr SE *CAL* 53 R33-34
Sunvista Ct 100 200 SE *CAL* .53 R33-34
Sunvista Pl SE *CAL* 53 R33
Sunvista Rd SE *CAL* 53 R33
Sunvista Way SE *CAL* 53 R33
Sunwood Gt SE *CAL* 53 R33
Sunwood Pk SE *CAL* 53 R33
Sunwood Pl SE *CAL* 53 R33
Sunwood Rd SE *CAL* 53 R33
Sunwood Way SE *CAL* 53 R33
Superior Av SW *CAL* 36 M17
Surrey St SW *CAL* 36 L17
Sussex Cr SW *CAL* 48 N26
Sutherland Dr *BRO* 90 B-C4 C3-4
Sutton Cl *RED* 67 J6

Swan Way *MED* 95 J5
Sweetwater Pl *RCY* 33 Z20
Sydenham Rd SW *CAL* 36 N18
Sydney Cl *RED* 67 J6
Sydney Dr SW *CAL* 48 N26
Sylvan Pl SE *AIR* 68 D4
Sylvan Rd S *LET* 88 G-H11
Sylvester Cr SW *CAL* 48 O26
Symons Valley Pkwy NW *CAL*
. . . . .11 J-K3 12 L3
Symons Valley Rd NW *CAL* 11 K3-4

T

Tache Av NW *CAL* 21 P10
Talon Av SW *CAL* 36 N18
Tamarac Cr SW *CAL* 35 K16
Tanner Cl SE *CAL* 69 C5
Tanner Dr SE *AIR* 69 C-D5
Taracove Cr NE *CAL* 23 X-Y8
Taracove Gt NE *CAL* 23 Y8
Taracove Ldg 100 200 NE *CAL* . .23 Y8
Taracove Pl 100 200 NE *CAL* . . .23 Y8
Taracove Rd NE *CAL* 23 Y8-9
Taracove Way NE *CAL* 23 Y8
Taracove Estate Dr NE *CAL* . . .23 X-Y8
Taradale Cl NE *CAL* 23 X-Y9
Taradale Dr NE *CAL* 23 X-Z9
Taraglen Ct NE *CAL* 23 Y9
Taraglen Pl NE *CAL* 23 Y9
Taraglen Rd NE *CAL* 23 Y9
Taralea Bay NE *CAL* 23 Y9
Taralea Cir NE *CAL* 23 Y9
Taralea Cr NE *CAL* 23 Y9
Taralea Gdns NE *CAL* 23 X-Y9
Taralea Gn NE *CAL* 23 Y9
Taralea Mnr NE *CAL* 23 Y9
Taralea Pk NE *CAL* 23 Y9
Taralea Pl NE *CAL* 23 X-Y9
Tararidge Cl NE *CAL* 23 Y9
Tararidge Ct NE *CAL* 23 Y9
Tararidge Dr NE *CAL* 23 Y9
Tararidge Pl NE *CAL* 23 Y9
Taravista Cr NE *CAL* 23 Z9
Taravista Ct NE *CAL* 23 Y8
Taravista Dr NE *CAL* 23 Y8
Taravista Gdns NE *CAL* 23 Z9
Taravista Mews NE *CAL* 23 Z9
Taravista St NE *CAL* 23 Y9
Taravista St NE *CAL* 23 Y9
Taravista Way NE *CAL* 23 Z9
Tarawood Cl NE *CAL* 23 Y8
Tarawood Gr NE *CAL* 23 Y8
Tarawood La NE *CAL* 23 Y8
Tarawood Pl 100 200 NE *CAL* . . .23 Y8
Tarington Cl NE *CAL* 23 Y9
Tarington Ct NE *CAL* 23 Z9
Tarington Gdns NE *CAL* 23 Z9
Tarington Gn NE *CAL* 23 Y-Z9
Tarington Ldg NE *CAL* 23 Z9
Tarington Link NE *CAL* 23 Y9
Tarington Mnr NE *CAL* 23 Z9
Tarington Pk NE *CAL* 23 Y-Z9
Tarington Pl NE *CAL* 23 Z9
Tarington Rd NE *CAL* 23 Y9
Tarington Way NE *CAL* 23 Z9
Tartan Blvd W *LET* 86 F3
Tartan Cir W *LET* 86 F2-3
Taunton Rd NW *CAL* 29 P11
Tavender Rd NW *CAL* . .20 O10 21 P10
Taylor Av *MED* 95 K8
Taylor Bay *MED* 95 K8
Taylor Bay *RCY* 9 Z4
Taylor Blvd *MED* 95 K8
Taylor Cir *MED* 95 K8
Taylor Cl *MED* 95 K8
Taylor Cr *MED* 95 K8
Taylor Cr NE *CAL* 21 P10 29 P11
Taylor Ct *MED* 95 K8
Taylor Dr *RED* 64 A-F3 F4 66 H-K4
Taylor Mews *MED* 95 K8
Taylor Pl *MED* 95 K8
Taylor Rd *MED* 95 K8
Taylor Way SE *AIR* 69 C5
Teakwood Av SE *CAL* 38 V18
Tecumseh Rd SW *CAL* 36 L18
Temple Blvd W *LET* 86 H4 J3-4
Temple Cl NE *CAL* 31 X12
Temple Cr W *LET* 86 H4
Temple Dr NE *CAL* . .31 X-Y11 X-Y12
Temple Gdns NE *CAL* 31 X12
Temple Gn NE *CAL* 31 X12
Temple Mews NE *CAL* 39 Y16
Temple Pl NE *CAL* 31 X12
Temple Rd NE *CAL* 31 X12
Temple Way NE *CAL* 31 X12-13
Templebow Pl 100 to 300 NE *CAL* 31 X11

Templebow Rd NE *CAL* 31 X11
Templebow Way NE *CAL* 31 X11
Templeby Cl NE *CAL* 31 Y11
Templeby Cr NE *CAL* 31 X-Y11
Templeby Dr NE *CAL* 31 X-Y11
Templeby Gt NE *CAL* 31 Y11
Templeby Pl 100 to 500 NE *CAL* 31 X-Y11
Templeby Rd NE *CAL* 31 Y11
Templeby Way NE *CAL* 31 Y11
Templegreen Bay NE *CAL* 31 X-Y12
Templegreen Dr NE *CAL* 31 X11-12
Templegreen Pl NE *CAL* 31 Y12
Templegreen Rd NE *CAL* 31 Y12
Templehill Bay NE *CAL* 31 X12
Templehill Cr NE *CAL* 31 X12
Templehill Dr NE *CAL* 31 X12
Templehill Pl NE *CAL* 31 X12
Templehill Rd NE *CAL* 31 X12
Templemont Cir NE *CAL* 31 X11
Templemont Dr NE *CAL* 31 X11
Templemont La NE *CAL* 31 X11
Templemont Pl 100 to 300 NE *CAL* 31 X11
Templemont Rd NE *CAL* 31 X11
Templemont Way NE *CAL* 31 X11
Templeridge Bay NE *CAL* 31 X12
Templeridge Cl NE *CAL* 31 X11-12
Templeridge Cr NE *CAL* 31 X12
Templeridge Pl NE *CAL* 31 X12
Templeridge Way NE *CAL* 31 X12
Templeside Bay NE *CAL* 31 X12
Templeside Cir NE *CAL* 31 X12
Templeside Gt NE *CAL* 31 X12
Templeside Pl NE *CAL* 31 X12
Templeside Rd NE *CAL* 31 X12
Templeson Cr NE *CAL* 31 Y12
Templeson Gt NE *CAL* 31 Y12
Templeson Pl NE *CAL* 31 Y11-12
Templeson Rd NE *CAL* 31 Y12
Templeson Way NE *CAL* 31 Y12
Templeton Bay NE *CAL* 31 Y12
Templeton Cir NE *CAL* 31 Y12-13
Templeton Gt NE *CAL* 31 Y12-13
Templeton Pl NE *CAL* 31 Y12
Templeton Rd NE *CAL* 31 Y12
Templevale Dr NE *CAL* 31 X-Y12
Templevale Gt NE *CAL* 31 Y12
Templevale Pl 100 to 300 NE *CAL* .31 Y12
Templevale Rd NE *CAL* 31 Y11-12
Templevale Way NE *CAL* 31 Y12
Templeview Dr NE *CAL* 31 X-Y12
Templeview Gt NE *CAL* 31 Y12
Templeview Pl 100 200 NE *CAL* .31 X-Y12
Templeview Way NE *CAL* 31 X-Y12
Templewood Dr NE *CAL* 31 X12
Templewood Mews NE *CAL* 31 X12
Templewood Pl 100 to 400 NE *CAL* . . . .
. . . . .31 X12
Templewood Rd NE *CAL* 31 X12
Terrace Bay *MED* 93 C5-6
Terrace Cr *MED* 93 C6
Terrace Dr *MED* 93 C5-6
Terrace Pl *CAN* 59 E6
Terrace Pl *MED* 93 C6
Terrill Rd *MED* 92 D3
Terry Rd NW *CAL* 28 O11
Thacker St SW *CAL* 41 J21
Thames Cl NW *CAL* 20 O10
Thames Pl NW *CAL* 20 O10
Thelma St *TAB* 91 A1
Theodore Pl NW *CAL* 20 O10
Thistle Bay *STM* 71 C3
Thistle Pl NW *CAL* 21 P10
Thistle Way *STM* 71 C3
Thomas Dr *STM* 71 B-C3
Thomas Pl *STM* 71 C3
Thomas St NE *CAL* 29 P11
Thompson Cr *MED* 95 H6-7
Thomson Av NE *CAL* 37 R16
Thorburn Dr SE *AIR* 69 D5
Thornaby Cr NW *CAL* 20 O10
Thornaby Rd NW *CAL* 20 O10
Thornaby Way NW *CAL* 20 09-10
Thornbank Dr NW *CAL* 21 P10
Thornbird Rd SE *AIR* 69 D5
Thornbird Rise SE *AIR* 69 D5
Thornbird Way SE *AIR* 69 D5
Thornbriar Gn *STM* 71 C3
Thornbriar Rd NW *CAL* 29 P11
Thornburn Dr NW *CAL* . .20 O10 21 P10
Thornburn Pl *STM* 71 C3
Thornburn Rd *STM* 71 C3
Thorncliffe Cr NW *CAL* 21 P10
Thorncliffe Pl NW *CAL* . . .21 P10 29 P11
Thorncrest Rd NE *CAL* 29 P11
Thorncrest Rd NW *CAL* 29 P11
Thorndale Cl SE *AIR* 69 C-D5
Thorndale Pl *STM* 71 C3
Thorndale Pl NW *CAL* . . .20 O10 21 P10
Thorndale Rd NW *CAL* . . .28 O11 29 P11

Thorneycroft Dr NW *CAL* 20 O10
Thornfield Cl SE *AIR* 69 C5
Thornfield Pl SE *AIR* 69 C5
Thornhill Dr NW *CAL* 20 O10 28 O11
Thornhill Pl NW *CAL* 28 O11 29 P11
Thornlee Cr NW *CAL* 20 O10 28 O11
Thornleigh Cl SE *AIR* 69 C5-6
Thornleigh Way SE *AIR* 69 C5
Thornton Rd NW *CAL* 21 P10 29 P11
Thornwood Cl NW *CAL* 20 O10
Thornwood Pl NW *CAL* 20 09-10
Thorson Cr *OKO* 76 B3
Thorson Pl *OKO* 76 B3
Three Sisters Dr *CAN* 58 F3 F-G4
Three Sisters Pkwy *CAN* 59 H5-6
Tiller Pl SE *AIR* 69 C-D5
Timber Ridge Way *RCY* 9 A-B1
Tipping Cl SE *AIR* 69 D5
Tipton Pl NW *CAL* 20 O10
Tipton Rd NW *CAL* 20 O10
Tongue Rd SW *HIG* 77 C1
Toronto Cr NW *CAL* 27 K15 28 L15
Torrice Av SW *CAL* 41 J21
Touchwood Dr NW *CAL* 20 O10
Tournament La SW *CAL* 52 M-N34
Tournament St SW *CAL* 52 M34
Tower Lane Dr SW *AIR* 68 C3
Townsend St NE *CAL* 37 R16
Tractor Av *MED* 95 F5-6
Trafford Cr NW *CAL* 28 O11
Trafford Dr NW *CAL* . .20 O10 28 O11 29 P11
Trafford Pl NW *CAL* 28 O11
Trailer Ct Rd *CRO* 79 B4
Trans-Canada Hwy *BAN* 57 B2-3
Trans-Canada Hwy *CAL*
. . . . . . .25 A-B12 26 E12 30 U-W14 31 X-Y14
Trans-Canada Hwy *CHE* 70 B1 D3 E5
Trans-Canada Hwy *RCY*
. . . . .24 V-W12 25 Z12 A12
Trans Canada Way *MED* 95 J5-6
Trap Rd SW *HIG* 77 C1
Trapper Rise *CAN* 59 E-F6
Trasimene Cr SW *CAL* 35 K20 36 L20
Travis Cr NE *CAL* 21 P10
Travis Pl NE *CAL* 21 P10
Travis St NE *CAL* 21 P10
Travois Cr NW *CAL* 21 P9-10
Travois Pl NW *CAL* 21 P9-10
Tregillus St NW *CAL* 21 P9-10
Trelle Dr NE *CAL* 21 P10 29 P11
Trent Rd W *LET* 86 J4
Trinity Pl W *LET* 87 H5
Trollinger St NE *CAL* 21 P10
Tsuu T'ina Dr *RDW* 61 C1-2
Tucker Rd SE *AIR* 69 C5
Tudor Bay S *LET* 88 J9
Tudor Blvd S *LET* 88 J9
Tudor Cr S *LET* 88 J9
Tudor Pl S *LET* 88 J9
Tuffy's Haven *STM* 71 C3
Tunnel Mountain Dr *BAN* 57 D-E3
Tunnel Mountain Rd *BAN* 57 C-D3
Turner Av *MED* 95 K8
Turner Bay *MED* 95 K8
Turner Blvd *MED* 95 K8
Turner Cir *MED* 95 K8
Turner Cl *MED* 95 K8
Turner Cr *MED* 95 K8
Turner Ct *MED* 95 K8
Turner Dr *MED* 95 K8
Turner Dr *TVY* 74 E3
Turner Gn *MED* 95 K8
Turner Gt *TVY* 74 E2-3
Turner Pl *MED* 95 K8
Tuscany Blvd NW *CAL* 17 C8 18 D8
Tuscany Cl NW *CAL* 17 C8
Tuscany Dr NW *CAL* 17 B-C8 C7
Tuscany Hill NW *CAL* 17 C9
Tuscany Way NW *CAL* 17 B7 C8
Tuscany Estates Cl NW *CAL* 17 C9
Tuscany Estates Cr NW *CAL* . . .17 B-C9
Tuscany Estates Dr NW *CAL* . . .17 B-C9
Tuscany Estates Pt NW *CAL* 17 C9
Tuscany Estates Rise NW *CAL* . .17 B-C9
Tuscany Estates Ter NW *CAL* . . .17 B-C9
Tuscany Glen Gn NW *CAL* 17 C9
Tuscany Glen Gt NW *CAL* 17 C9
Tuscany Glen Pk NW *CAL* 17 B-C9
Tuscany Glen Pl NW *CAL* 17 B8-9 C9
Tuscany Glen Rd NW *CAL* 17 C8-9
Tuscany Glen Way NW *CAL* 17 C8-9
Tuscany Hills Bay NW *CAL* . .17 C8 18 D8
Tuscany Hills Cir NW *CAL* 17 C8
Tuscany Hills Cl NW *CAL* 17 C8
Tuscany Hills Cr NW *CAL* 17 C8
Tuscany Hills Mews NW *CAL* 17 C8
Tuscany Hills Pk NW *CAL* 17 C8
Tuscany Hills Pt NW *CAL* 17 C8
Tuscany Hills Rd NW *CAL* 17 C8

Tuscany Hills Ter NW *CAL* 17 C8
Tuscany Hills Way NW *CAL* 17 C8
Tuscany Meadows Bay NW *CAL* 17 C9
Tuscany Meadows Cl NW *CAL* 17 C9
Tuscany Meadows Cm NW *CAL* 17 C9
Tuscany Meadows Cr NW *CAL* 17 C9
Tuscany Meadows Ct NW *CAL* 17 C8-9
Tuscany Meadows Dr NW *CAL* 17 C9
Tuscany Meadows Heath NW *CAL* .17 C9
Tuscany Meadows Hts NW *CAL* . .17 C8-9
Tuscany Meadows Mews 100 200 NW
CAL 17 C9
Tuscany Meadows Pl NW *CAL* 17 C9
Tuscany Ravine Bay NW *CAL* 17 C9
Tuscany Ravine Cr NW *CAL* 17 C9
Tuscany Ravine Ct NW *CAL* . .17 C9 18 D9
Tuscany Ravine Ldg NW *CAL* .17 C9 18 D9
Tuscany Ravine Mews NW *CAL* 17 C9
Tuscany Ravine Mnr NW *CAL* .17 C9 18 D9
Tuscany Ravine Pt NW *CAL* 18 D9-10
Tuscany Ravine Rd NW *CAL*
. . . . .17 C8-9 18 D9-10
Tuscany Ravine Ter NW *CAL* .17 C9 18 D9
Tuscany Ravine View NW *CAL* 17 C9
Tuscany Ridge Cl NW *CAL* 17 B-C8
Tuscany Ridge Com NW *CAL* 17 B7-8
Tuscany Ridge Cr NW *CAL* 17 B7-8
Tuscany Ridge Gn NW *CAL* 17 B8
Tuscany Ridge Heath NW *CAL* . . .17 B7-8
Tuscany Ridge Hts NW *CAL* 17 B7
Tuscany Ridge Mews NW *CAL* 17 B7
Tuscany Ridge Pk NW *CAL* 17 B-C8
Tuscany Ridge Pl NW *CAL* 17 C8
Tuscany Ridge Ter NW *CAL* 17 B8
Tuscany Ridge View NW *CAL* 17 B-C8
Tuscany Springs Bay NW *CAL* 17 C6
Tuscany Springs Blvd NW *CAL*
. . . . .17 B-C6 C7-8
Tuscany Springs Cir NW *CAL* 17 C7
Tuscany Springs Gdns NW *CAL* . . .17 C7
Tuscany Springs Gn NW *CAL* 17 C6-7
Tuscany Springs Gr NW *CAL* 17 B-C8
Tuscany Springs Hill NW *CAL* . . .17 B-C7
Tuscany Springs Hts NW *CAL* 17 C6-7
Tuscany Springs Pk NW *CAL* 17 C7
Tuscany Springs Pl NW *CAL* 17 C6-7
Tuscany Springs Rd NW *CAL* 17 C7
Tuscany Springs Rise NW *CAL* 17 C7
Tuscany Springs Ter NW *CAL* . . .17 B-C7
Tuscany Springs Way NW *CAL* . . .17 C6-7
Tuscany Valley Dr NW *CAL* 17 B-C7
Tuscany Valley Gn NW *CAL* 17 B-C7
Tuscany Valley Gt NW *CAL* 17 C7-8
Tuscany Valley Hill NW *CAL* 17 C7
Tuscany Valley Hts NW *CAL* 17 C7
Tuscany Valley La NW *CAL* 17 C7
Tuscany Valley Pk NW *CAL* 17 B-C8
Tuscany Valley Rd NW *CAL* 17 C7
Tuscany Valley Rise NW *CAL* . . .17 B-C7
Tuscany Valley View NW *CAL* 17 C7
Tuscany Valley Way NW *CAL* 17 C7-8
Tuscany Village Ct NW *CAL* 17 C8
Tuscany Vista Cr NW *CAL* 17 B8
Tuscany Vista Ct NW *CAL* 17 B8-9
Tuscany Vista Pt NW *CAL* 17 B8
Tuscany Vista Rd NW *CAL* 17 B8-9
Tuscarora Cir NW *CAL* 17 C7
Tuscarora Cl NW *CAL* 17 C8 18 D8
Tuscarora Cr NW *CAL* 17 C7
Tuscarora Hts NW *CAL* 17 C7
Tuscarora Mews NW *CAL* 18 D7
Tuscarora Mnr NW *CAL* 18 D7
Tuscarora Pl NW *CAL* 17 C7 18 D7
Tuscarora Pt NW *CAL* 17 C8
Tuscarora View NW *CAL* . . .17 C8 18 D8
Tuscarora Way NW *CAL* 18 D7
Tusslewood Bay NW *CAL* 17 C6
Tusslewood Dr NW *CAL* 17 B6 C7
Tusslewood Gr NW *CAL* 17 C6
Tusslewood Hts NW *CAL* 17 B6-7
Tusslewood Ter 100 to 300 NW *CAL*
. . . . .17 B-C6
Tusslewood View NW *CAL* 17 C6-7
Tweed Av *MED* 92 D3-4
Tweed St NE *CAL* 21 P10
Twin Hill Cl *DRU* 73 D7
Two Pine Dr *BRG* 78 A-B2
Tye St NW *CAL* 28 L-M14

U

Udell Rd NW *CAL* 27 K13-14
Ulrich Rd NW *CAL* 27 K13-14
Ulster Rd NW *CAL* 27 K14
Ulysses St NW *CAL* 27 K14
Umber Pl NW *CAL* 27 J-K14
Underhill Dr NW *CAL* 27 J13 J-K14
Underhill Pl NW *CAL* 27 J13-14

Underwood Pl NW *CAL* 27 K13-14
Ungava Rd NW *CAL* 27 J-K14
Unity Pl NW *CAL* 27 J11
University Ct 100 to 400 NW *CAL* .27 K13
University Dr NW *CAL* 27 K14 28 L14
University Dr W *LET*
. . . . .82 D3 86 F3-4 G4 87 H-J5
University Gt NW *CAL* 27 K13
University Pl NW *CAL* 27 K13-14
University Way NW *CAL* 27 K13
Unwin Rd NW *CAL* 27 K14
Upland Av *BRO* 90 A2
Upland Blvd *BRO* 90 A-C2
Upland Cr *BRO* 90 A2
Upland Ct *BRO* 90 A2
Upland Ct *MED* 95 G5
Upland Dr *MED* 95 G5
Upland Gn *BRO* 90 A2
Upland Link *BRO* 90 A2
Upland Mnr *BRO* 90 A2
Upland Pl *BRO* 90 A2
Upland Rd *BRO* 90 A2
Upland St *BRO* 90 A2
Upland Tr *BRO* 90 A2
Uplands Blvd N *LET* 84 A-B9
Uplands Pl *RCY* 25 A-B14
Uplands Rd NW *CAL* 27 K13-14
Uplands Way *RCY* 25 B14
Upper Pl NW *CAL* 27 K13-14
Upton Pl NW *CAL* 27 K13-14
Uralta Rd NW *CAL* 27 K14
Urbana Rd NW *CAL* 27 K14
Urquhart Rd NW *CAL* 27 K14
Ursenbach Rd NW *CAL* 27 K14
Usher Rd NW *CAL* 27 K13-14
Utah Cr NW *CAL* 27 K14
Utah Dr NW *CAL* 27 J-K14
Utah Pl NW *CAL* 27 K14
Uxbridge Dr NW *CAL* 27 K14

V

Valdes Pl NW *CAL* 27 J12
Valencia Pl NW *CAL* 19 I10
Valencia Rd NW *CAL* 19 I10 27 I11
Valentine Cr SE *CAL* 39 X17
Valhalla Dr NW *CAL* 27 I11
Valiant Dr NW *CAL* 27 I-J12
Valiant Pl NW *CAL* 27 I12
Vallance Cr NW *CAL* 27 I11
Valley Rd *TVY* 74 C-D4
Valley Rd W *LET* 87 G-H5
Valley Tr *TVY* 74 C4 D3
Valley Brook Cir NW *CAL* 25 C11-12
Valley Brook Ct 100 200 NW *CAL* . . . . . .
. . . . .25 C11-12
Valley Creek Cr NW *CAL* 25 B11
Valley Creek Pl NW *CAL* 25 B11
Valley Creek Rd NW *CAL* 25 B11
Valley Crest Cl NW *CAL* 25 A11-12
Valley Crest Ct 100 to 300 NW *CAL*
. . . . .25 A-B11
Valley Crest Gdn NW *CAL* 25 A11
Valley Crest Rise NW *CAL* 25 A11
Valley Glen Bay 100 200 NW *CAL* .25 C11
Valley Glen Hts NW *CAL* 25 C11
Valley Meadow Cl NW *CAL* 25 C11-12
Valley Meadow Cr NW *CAL* 25 C11
Valley Meadow Gdns NW *CAL* 25 C11
Valley Ponds Cr NW *CAL* 25 B12
Valley Ponds Pl NW *CAL* 25 B11
Valley Ponds Way NW *CAL* 25 B11-12
Valley Ridge Av *BLD* 75 B6-7
Valley Ridge Blvd NW *CAL* .25 B11 C11-12
Valley Ridge Ct 100 200 NW *CAL* .25 B11
Valley Ridge Dr NW *CAL* 25 A-B11 C11
Valley Ridge Gn NW *CAL* 25 B11
Valley Ridge Hts NW *CAL* 25 B11 C12
Valley Ridge Pk NW *CAL* 25 B11
Valley Ridge Pt NW *CAL* 25 B-C11
Valley Springs Rd NW *CAL* 25 C11
Valley Springs Ter 100 to 300 NW *CAL*
. . . . .25 C11
Valley Stream Cir NW *CAL* 25 A11-12
Valley Stream Cr NW *CAL* 25 A-B12
Valley Stream Mnr NW *CAL* 25 A11-12
Valley Stream Pl NW *CAL* 25 A11-12
Valley Woods Ldg NW *CAL* 17 A-B10
Valley Woods Pl 100 to 300 NW *CAL* . . .
. . . . .17 B10 25 A-B11
Valley Woods Way NW *CAL* 25 A-B11
Valleyview Av *MED* 92 E2 94 F2
Valleyview Dr *MED* 92 E2
Valleyview Pk SE *CAL* 38 U19
Valleyview Rd NE *CAL* . . .29 S14 30 T14
Valois Av SW *CAL* 36 N19
Valparaiso Pl NW *CAL* 19 II-I10
Van Horne *CAN* 58 G4 59 G5

Van Horne Cr NE *CAL* 29 S14
Vance Pl NW *CAL* 27 J11
Vancouver Cr NW *CAL* 27 J11-12
Vandale Pl NW *CAL* 27 I12
Vandergrift Cr NW *CAL* 27 J12
Vandoos Gdns NW *CAL* 27 I-J11
Vandoos Pl NW *CAL* 27 I11
Vandoos Rd NW *CAL* 27 I-J11
Vandoos Vill NW *CAL* 27 J11
Vandyke Pl NW *CAL* 27 I12
Vandyke Rd NW *CAL* 27 I12
Vanguard Pl NW *CAL* 27 I11
Vanguard Rd NW *CAL* 27 I11
Vanstone Cr NW *CAL* 27 I11
Vanstone Rd NW *CAL* 27 I11
Vantage Bay NW *CAL* 27 I11-12
Vantage Cr NW *CAL* 27 I11
Vantage Pl NW *CAL* 27 I11
Varal Pl NW *CAL* 27 J12
Varal Rd NW *CAL* 27 J12
Varanger Pl NW *CAL* 27 I12
Varbay Pl NW *CAL* 27 J12
Varbow Pl NW *CAL* 27 J12
Varbrook Pl NW *CAL* 27 J12
Varcourt Pl NW *CAL* 27 J12
Varcove Pl NW *CAL* 27 J12
Varcrest Pl NW *CAL* 27 J12
Vardana Pl NW *CAL* 27 J12
Vardana Rd NW *CAL* 27 J12
Vardell Pl NW *CAL* 27 J12
Vardell Rd NW *CAL* 27 J12
Varley Dr NW *CAL* 27 J13
Varmoor Pl NW *CAL* 27 J12-13
Varmoor Rd NW *CAL* 27 J12-13
Varna Cr NW *CAL* 27 I12-13
Varna Pl NW *CAL* 27 I12
Varscliff Pl NW *CAL* 27 I12
Varscliff Rd NW *CAL* 27 I12
Varsconna Pl NW *CAL* 27 J12
Varsdale Pl NW *CAL* 27 I12
Varsfield Pl NW *CAL* 27 I12
Varshaven Pl NW *CAL* 27 J12
Varsity Cl NW *CAL* 27 H11-12
Varsity Cr 100 200 NW *CAL* 27 I12
Varsity Dr NW *CAL* 27 H-J11 J-K12
Varsity Gn NW *CAL* 27 H-I11
Varsity La NW *CAL* 27 J11-12
Varsity Pl NW *CAL* 27 H11
Varsity Rd NW *CAL* 27 H-I11
Varsity Estates Bay 100 to 500 NW *CAL* 19 H10 27 H11
Varsity Estates Cl NW *CAL* 19 H10
Varsity Estates Cr NW *CAL* 19 H10
Varsity Estates Ct NW *CAL* 19 H-I10
Varsity Estates Dr NW *CAL* 19 H10 27 H11
Varsity Estates Gdns NW *CAL* 19 I10
Varsity Estates Gn NW *CAL* 19 H10 27 H11
Varsity Estates Gr NW *CAL* 19 I10 27 I11
Varsity Estates Link NW *CAL* 19 I10 27 I11
Varsity Estates Mews 100 to 300 NW *CAL* 19 H10
Varsity Estates Pk NW *CAL* 19 I10
Varsity Estates Pl 100 to 1000 NW *CAL* 19 H10
Varsity Estates Rd NW *CAL* 19 H-I10
Varsity Estates Rise NW *CAL* 19 H10 27 H11
Varsity Estates Ter 100 to 300 NW *CAL* 19 H10
Varsity Estates View NW *CAL* 19 H10
Varsity Estates Village NW *CAL* 19 I10
Varsity Green Bay 100 200 NW *CAL* 27 H-I11
Varsity Ridge Gt NW *CAL* 27 I11
Varsity Ridge Ter NW *CAL* 27 I11
Varslea Pl NW *CAL* 27 J12
Varsplain Pl NW *CAL* 27 J12
Varston Pl NW *CAL* 27 J12
Varsville Pl NW *CAL* 27 J12
Vartown Pl NW *CAL* 27 J12
Varview Pl NW *CAL* 27 I12
Varwood Pl NW *CAL* 27 J12
Vaughan St NE *CAL* 29 S14
Vauxhall Cr NW *CAL* 27 J12
Vegas Rd NW *CAL* 27 J11
Vegas Way NW *CAL* 27 J11
Veiner Rd *BRO* 90 D2-3
Veiner St NE *CAL* 29 S14
Ventura Cr N *LET* 83 C-D7
Ventura La NE *CAL* 29 S13 30 T13
Ventura Pl N *LET* 83 C7
Ventura Pl NE *CAL* 30 T14
Ventura Rd N *LET* 83 D7
Ventura Rd NE *CAL* 30 T14
Ventura Ter NE *CAL* 30 T14
Ventura Way NE *CAL* 30 T13-14
Vercheres St SW *CAL* 36 N19
Verdun Pl NW *CAL* 27 J11
Vermillion St NE *CAL* 29 S13-14
Vermillion Lakes Dr *BAN* 57 C1
Vernon Pl NW *CAL* 27 K12
Verona Dr NW *CAL* 27 J11
Veronica Pl NW *CAL* 27 I11
Veronica Rd NW *CAL* 27 I11
Verulum Pl NW *CAL* 27 I12
Veteran's Way *CAN* 58 E4
Veterans Way NW *CAL* 27 J15
Vicary Pl NW *CAL* 27 I12
Viceroy Dr NW *CAL* 19 I10 27 I11
Viceroy Pl NW *CAL* 27 I11
Victoria Av *MED* 95 F5
Victoria Cr NW *CAL* 28 M14
Victoria Beach Bay *CHE* 70 E-F2
Vienna Dr NW *CAL* 19 I10 27 I11
Villa Cr NW *CAL* 27 J12
Villa St *DRU* 73 B6
Village Av *OKO* 76 D2
Village Gdns SW *CAL* 27 I15
Village Hts SW *CAL* 27 H15
Village La *OKO* 76 D2
Village Mews SW *CAL* 27 H-I15
Village Rd *LKL* 56 B-C4
Village Ter SW *CAL* 27 H-I15
Village Way *STM* 71 D2-3
Villosa Ridge Dr *RCY* 16 X9 X-Y10
Villosa Ridge Pt *RCY* 16 X9
Villosa Ridge Way *RCY* 16 X9-10
Vimy Way SW *CAL* 36 L-M20
Vincent Dr NW *CAL* 27 J12
Vincent Pl NW *CAL* 27 J12
Vintage Meadows Ct *MED* 95 H-J6
Vintage Meadows Pl *MED* 95 H-J6
Violet Ct *MED* 95 H5
Virginia Dr NW *CAL* 27 I-J11
Virginia St NE *AIR* 68 B3-4
Virginia St SE *AIR* 68 B3-4
Viscount Av *MED* 94 G1
Viscount Dr NW *CAL* 27 J11
Vissar Cr NW *CAL* 27 J11
Visser Pl *OKO* 76 B3
Visser Way *OKO* 76 B3
Vista Cr NE *CAL* 29 S13-14
Vista Dr *MED* 94 K4 95 K5
Vista Pl *MED* 94 K4 95 K5
Vista Rd *MED* 94 K4 95 K5
Vista Rd NE *CAL* 29 S14
Vista St NE *CAL* 29 S13-14
Voyageur Dr NW *CAL* 27 I11-12 J11

W

W T Hill Blvd S *LET* 84 E11 88 F11
Waddy La *STM* 71 D2-3
Wade Cl *RED* 66 H3
Waghorn Cl *RED* 66 J4
Wainright Pl SE *CAL* 49 P26
Wainright Rd SE *CAL* 49 P26
Wakefield Dr SW *CAL* 35 I17
Waldron Av *OKO* 76 B3
Waldron Pl *OKO* 76 B3
Wales Gn *STM* 71 D2
Walker Blvd *RED* 66 H3
Wallace Cl *RED* 66 H-J4
Wallin Cr *RED* 66 H-J3
Walnut Dr NW *CAL* 35 J16
Walrond Rd SE *CAL* 49 Q26
Walsh Rd W *LET* 82 E2-3
Walters Way *MED* 92 C1
Waneta Cr SE *CAL* 49 P26
Wapiti Cl *CAN* 59 E6
Wapiti Dr SE *CAL* 49 P26
Ward Cr *RED* 66 H-J4
Warren Rd SE *CAL* 49 P26
Warwick Dr *RED* 66 G-H3
Warwick Dr SW *CAL* 35 I16
Wascana Cr SE *CAL* 49 P26
Wascana Rd SE *CAL* 49 P26
Washington Av *MED* 93 E6
Washington Way *MED* 93 E6
Waskasoo Cr *RED* 65 F6
Waskatenau Cr SW *CAL* 35 I17
Waterloo Dr SW *CAL* 35 J16
Waterstone Cr SE *AIR* 68 D4
Waterstone Gt SE *AIR* 68 D3-4
Waterstone Pl 100 to 300 SE *AIR* 68 D4 E3-4
Waterton Rd S *LET* 88 H11-12
Watson Rd SE *CAL* 49 P26
Watson St *RED* 66 H4
Watt St *BRG* 78 B-C3
Waverley Dr SW *CAL* 35 I16
Weaselhead Rd *CAL* 41 H23-24
Webb Cl *RED* 66 H3
Webster Dr *RED* 66 H2-3
Weddell Cr *RED* 66 H3
Weddenburn Rd SE *CAL* 49 P26
Wedgewood Dr *RED* 66 L-M3
Wedgewood Dr SW *CAL* 35 J16
Wedgewood La *RED* 66 L3-4
Welch Cr *OKO* 76 B3
Welch Pl 100 200 *OKO* 76 B3-4
Well St *BRO* 90 D3
Wellington Cv *STM* 71 D2
Wellington Pl SW *CAL* 35 J16
Welliver St *RED* 66 H3
Wells St *RED* 66 H4
Welton Cr *RED* 66 G4
Wentworth Av SW *CAL* 26 E15
Wentworth Cir SW *CAL* 26 E-F15
Wentworth Cl SW *CAL* 34 E-F16
Wentworth Cr *OKO* 76 B3
Wentworth Cr SW *CAL* 26 D-E15
Wentworth Cv SW *CAL* 26 E-F15
Wentworth Dr SW *CAL* 26 E15 F15 34 F16
Wentworth Gdns SW *CAL* 26 F15 34 F16
Wentworth Gn SW *CAL* 26 F15
Wentworth Gr SW *CAL* 26 E15 34 E16
Wentworth Gt SW *CAL* 26 F15 34 F16
Wentworth Heath SW *CAL* 26 E15
Wentworth Hts SW *CAL* 26 E15
Wentworth Link SW *CAL* 26 F15 34 F16
Wentworth Mews SW *CAL* 34 E16
Wentworth Mnr SW *CAL* 26 E15 34 E16
Wentworth Pk 100 200 SW *CAL* 26 F15
Wentworth Pl 100 to 700 SW *CAL* 26 F15 34 F16
Wentworth Pt 100 200 SW *CAL* 26 E15
Wentworth Rd SW *CAL* 26 F15
Wentworth Rise SW *CAL* 26 E15
Wentworth View SW *CAL* 26 E15 34 E16
Wentworth Way SW *CAL* 26 F15
West Aarsby Rd *COC* 60 A-B3
West Andison Cl *COC* 60 B3
West Barrett Pl *COC* 60 B3
West Beynon Rise *COC* 60 A-B3
West Boothby Cr *COC* 60 B2
West Broatch Pl *COC* 60 B2
West Callaway Pl *COC* 60 B3
West Campus Blvd NW *CAL* 27 J14
West Campus Dr NW *CAL* 27 J13
West Campus Pl NW *CAL* 27 J13-14
West Campus Rd NW *CAL* 27 J13
West Campus Wat NW *CAL* 27 J13
West Cedars Pt SW *CAL* 26 F15
West Cedars Rise SW *CAL* 26 F-G15
West Chapman Pl *COC* 60 B3
West Chestermere Dr *CHE* 70 D-F2
West Copithorne Pl *COC* 60 B2-3
West Creek Bay 100 to 300 *CHE* 70 E1
West Creek Blvd *CHE* 70 E1
West Creek Cir *CHE* 70 E-F1
West Creek Cl *CHE* 70 E1
West Creek Cr *CHE* 70 E1
West Creek Ct 100 200 *CHE* 70 E1
West Creek Dr *CHE* 70 E1
West Creek Glen *CHE* 70 E1
West Creek Ldg *CHE* 70 E1
West Creek Mews 100 200 *CHE* 70 F1
West Creek Pond *CHE* 70 E1
West Creek Springs 200 300 *CHE* 70 E1
West Edge Rd *COC* 60 B2-3
West Gissing Rd *COC* 60 B2-3
West Glen Cr SW *CAL* 35 I17
West Hall Pl *COC* 60 B2
West Howes Pl *COC* 60 B3
West Kerfoot Pl *COC* 60 B2-3
West Lakeview Cir *CHE* 70 E-F1
West Lakeview Cl *CHE* 70 F1
West Lakeview Cr *CHE* 70 E1
West Lakeview Dr *CHE* 70 F1-2
West Lakeview Passage *CHE* 70 E1-2
West Lakeview Pl *CHE* 70 F1
West Lakeview Pt *CHE* 70 F1
West MacKay Cr *COC* 60 B3
West McDonald Pl *COC* 60 B3
West McDougal Rd *COC* 60 A3 A-B2
West McGonigle Pl *COC* 60 A-B3
West McManus Rd *COC* 60 B3
West Meadows Ct *RCY* 32 X20
West Meadows Estates *RCY* 32 W-X20 X20
West Meadows Pl *RCY* 32 W20
West Meadows Pl SW *CAL* 26 F-G15
West Mitford Cr *COC* 60 B2
West Moore Pl *COC* 60 B2
West Murphy Pl *COC* 60 A-B3
West Park Cl *RED* 66 H3
West Park Cr *RED* 66 H3 H3-4
West Park Dr *CHE* 70 B-C2
West Park Pl *COC* 60 B3
West Pine Rd *STM* 71 E2
West Ranch Pl 100 to 300 SW *CAL* 26 F15
West Ranch Rd SW *CAL* 26 F-G15
West Ridge Rd *STM* 71 D2
West Spicer Pl *COC* 60 A-B2
West Springs Cl SW *CAL* 26 G14
West Springs Ct SW *CAL* 26 G14-15
West Springs Gt SW *CAL* 26 G14
West Springs Pl SW *CAL* 26 G15
West Springs Rd SW *CAL* 26 G14-15
West Springs Way SW *CAL* 26 G14-15
West Terrace Bay 100 200 *COC* 60 B2
West Terrace Cl *COC* 60 B2
West Terrace Cr *COC* 60 B2
West Terrace Dr *COC* 60 B1
West Terrace Pl 100 to 300 *COC* 60 B1-2
West Terrace Pt 100 200 *COC* 60 B2
West Terrace Pt *COC* 60 B2
West Terrace Rd *COC* 60 B1-2
West Terrace Rise *COC* 60 B1
West Tower Pl *COC* 60 B2
West Valley Rd SW *CAL* 25 C12
Westbluff Bay *RCY* 33 B16
Westbluff Ct *RCY* 25 C15 33 C16
Westbluff Dr *RCY* 25 B-C15
Westbluff Pl *RCY* 25 C15 33 C16
Westbluff Rd *RCY* 25 B15
Westbluff Ridge *RCY* 33 B16
Westbrook Cr *BRO* 90 B-C1
Westchester Bay *CHE* 70 G1-2
Westchester Blvd *CHE* 70 F-G1
Westchester Cv *CHE* 70 F-G1
Westchester Gn *CHE* 70 F1
Westchester Key *CHE* 70 F1-2
Westchester Rd *STM* 71 D2
Westchester Way *CHE* 70 F-G1
Westdale St *STM* 71 D2
Western Dr *CRS* 62 C2-3
Western Headworks Pathway SE *CAL* 45 X-Y25
Westerner Dr *RED* 66 M5 67 M6
Westfall Cr *OKO* 76 E2
Westfall Dr *OKO* 76 D2
Westfall Gn *OKO* 76 E2
Westgate Av *RED* 66 G4
Westlake Bay *STM* 71 D1-2
Westlake Cir *STM* 71 D2
Westlake Rd *STM* 71 D2
Westland Gt *OKO* 76 D2
Westland Rd *OKO* 76 D2
Westland St *OKO* 76 D2
Westmeadows Rd *RCY* 33 B-C17
Westminster Dr SW *CAL* 35 I17
Westminster Pl SW *CAL* 35 I16-17
Westmount Blvd *OKO* 76 A2
Westmount Blvd NW *CAL* 36 M-N16
Westmount Cir 100 to 400 *OKO* 76 A2
Westmount Cr *OKO* 76 A2
Westmount Ct 100 200 *OKO* 76 A2
Westmount Dr *STM* 71 D2
Westmount Pl *OKO* 76 A2
Westmount Rd *OKO* 76 A2
Westmount Rd NW *CAL* 36 L-M16
Westmount Way *OKO* 76 A2
Weston Ct SW *CAL* 26 F14
Weston Dr SW *CAL* 26 F15
Weston Gn SW *CAL* 26 F14-15 G14
Weston Mnr SW *CAL* 26 F14
Weston Pk SW *CAL* 26 F-G14
Weston Pl SW *CAL* 26 F14
Weston Rise SW *CAL* 26 F14-15
Weston Way SW *CAL* 26 F14-15
Westover Dr SW *CAL* 35 I16-17
Westpark Village *STM* 71 C-D2
Westpoint Bay SW *CAL* 26 G15
Westpoint Ct SW *CAL* 26 G15
Westpoint Gdns SW *CAL* 26 G15
Westridge Cl *OKO* 76 D2
Westridge Cr *OKO* 76 D2
Westridge Cr SW *CAL* 26 F15
Westridge Dr *OKO* 76 D2
Westridge Gn *OKO* 76 E2
Westridge Rd *OKO* 76 D2
Westridge Rise *OKO* 76 E2
Westridge Park Dr *RCY* 33 B16-17
Westrock Rd *COC* 60 B3
Westside Dr *COC* 60 B3
Westside Dr W *LET* 82 C2 D2-3
Westview Dr SW *CAL* 35 I16
Westview Pl *STM* 71 D2
Westview St *STM* 71 D2
Westwinds Cr NE *CAL* 22 W10
Westwinds Dr NE *CAL* 22 V-W10 30 V-W11
Westwinds Village SW *CAL* 35 I18
Westwood Cr SW *CAL* 35 I17
Westwood Dr SW *CAL* 35 I16-17
Westwood Rd *RCY* 33 B-C16
Westwood St *STM* 71 D2
Westwood Ter SW *CAL* 35 I-J17
Wheatland Av SW *CAL* 35 I17
Wheatland Gn *STM* 71 D2
Wheatland Pl *STM* 71 D2
Wheatland Tr (Highway 817) *STM* 71 C2 E2
Wheeler Pl *STM* 71 D2
Wheeler St *STM* 71 D2

Whiskey Jack Cr BAN 57 C2
Whispering Woods Ter RCY 33 Z20
Whitaker Bay NE CAL 30 V12
Whitaker Cl NE CAL 30 V12
Whitaker Ct NE CAL 30 V12
White Av BRG 78 B-C3
White Cr BRG 78 B-C3
White Pl BRG 78 C3
White Oak Cr SW CAL 35 I16
White Pine Way NW CAL 26 E11-12
Whitebow Pl NE CAL 30 W11
Whitefield Cl NE CAL 30 V12
Whitefield Cr NE CAL 30 W11-12
Whitefield Dr NE CAL 30 V12
Whitefield Pl NE CAL 30 V12
Whiteglen Cr NE CAL 30 W12
Whitehaven Cr NE CAL 30 V11
Whitehaven Rd NE CAL 30 V11
Whitehill Gt NE CAL 30 W11
Whitehill Pl 100 to 500 NE CAL . .30 W11
Whitehill Way NE CAL 30 W11
Whitehorn Cr NE CAL 30 V12
Whitehorn Dr NE CAL 30 V-W12
Whitehorn Pl 100 to 400 NE CAL .30 W12
Whitehorn Rd LKL 56 B5
Whitehorn Rd NE CAL 30 W12
Whitehorn Way NE CAL 30 V12
Whiteland Bay NE CAL 30 W11 31 X11
Whiteland Dr NE CAL 30 W11
Whiteland Gt NE CAL 30 W11
Whitemont Dr NE CAL 30 W11
Whitemont Pl NE CAL 30 W11
Whiteram Cl NE CAL 30 V12
Whiteram Ct NE CAL 30 V12
Whiteram Gt NE CAL 30 V12
Whiteram Hill NE CAL 30 V12
Whiteram Mews NE CAL 30 V-W11
Whiteram Pl NE CAL 30 V12
Whiteram Way NE CAL 30 V11-12
Whiteridge Cr NE CAL 30 W11-12
Whiteridge Pl 100 200 NE CAL . . .30 W12
Whiteridge Rd NE CAL 30 W12
Whiteridge Way NE CAL 30 W11-12
Whiteside Av RED 66 H3
Whiteside Cr RED 66 H4
Whiteside Cr NE CAL 30 W12
Whiteside Rd NE CAL 30 W12
Whitestone Cr NE CAL 30 W12
Whitestone Rd NE CAL 30 W12
Whitestone Way NE CAL 30 W12
Whiteview Bay NE CAL 30 W12
Whiteview Cl NE CAL 30 W12
Whiteview Pl NE CAL 30 W12-13
Whiteview Rd NE CAL 30 W12-13
Whitewood Bay NE CAL 30 W11
Whitewood Pl 100 200 NE CAL . .30 W11
Whitewood Rd NE CAL 30 W11
Whitfield Av CRS 62 A2
Whitlock Cl NE CAL 30 V-W12
Whitlock Pl 100 200 NE CAL . . .30 V12
Whitlock Way NE CAL 30 V-W12
Whitlow Cr NE CAL 30 V-W11
Whitlow Pl NE CAL 30 V-W11
Whitman Cl NE CAL 30 V12
Whitman Cr NE CAL 30 V12
Whitman Pl 100 to 300 NE CAL 30 V12-13
Whitmire Bay NE CAL 30 V12
Whitmire Rd NE CAL 30 V12
Whitmire Vill NE CAL 30 V12
Whitnel Cl NE CAL 30 V12-13
Whitnel Ct NE CAL 30 V-W12
Whitnel Pl NE CAL 30 V12
Whitney Cr SE CAL 49 P26
Whitworth Pl NE CAL 30 V11
Whitworth Rd NE CAL 30 V11
Whitworth Way NE CAL 30 V11
Whoop-Up Dr W LET 86 H3-4 87 G5
Wigmore Cl RED 66 H4
Wilcox St SE CAL 49 Q27
Wild Rose Dr RCY 33 C16
Wild Rose Dr TAB 91 B4
Wild Rose Gt TAB 91 B4
Wild Rose Way TAB 91 B4
Wilde Rd SE CAL 49 P26
Wilderness Dr SE CAL 49 Q27
Wilderness Pl SE CAL 49 P27
Wildflower Cr STM 71 D1
Wildflower Cv STM 71 D1
Wildflower Hill RCY 16 X-Y9
Wildflower Rd STM 71 D1
Wildrose Av BRO 90 D1
Wildrose Cr BRO 90 C1-2
Wildrose Ct BRO 90 C-D1
Wildwood Cr W LET 86 G4
Wildwood Dr SW CAL . . .27 I15 J15 35 J16
Wildwood Rd W LET 86 G4
Wilkes Rd SE CAL 49 Q27
Wilkins Gn RED 66 H-J3
Wilkinson Pl SE CAL 49 P-Q27

Willacy Dr SE CAL 49 Q27
Willamette Dr SE CAL 49 Q27
Willamina Cr SE CAL 49 P-Q27
Willard Rd SE CAL 49 Q27
Willesden Dr SE CAL 49 Q27
William St COC 61 B5
William St SE CAL 37 Q17-18
Williams Pl BRG 78 B2
Williams St CAN 59 E5
Willingdon Blvd SE CAL 49 Q27
Willoughby Cr SE CAL 49 Q27
Willow Av BRO 90 C1
Willow Av DRU 73 B-C6
Willow Cr SE CAL 35 K16
Willow Dr STM 71 D2
Willow Gn OLD 62 C1
Willow La OLD 62 C1
Willow Pt CAN 59 F5
Willow Pt DRU 73 D-E8
Willow Way OLD 62 C1
Willow Way NW CAL 26 E11
Willow Bend Pl SE CAL 49 Q26
Willow Brook Bay NW AIR 68 B2
Willow Brook Cl 100 to 400 NW AIR .68 B2
Willow Brook Cr NW AIR 68 B2
Willow Brook Dr NW AIR 68 B2
Willow Brook Dr SE CAL 49 Q26
Willow Brook Gt NW AIR 68 B2
Willow Brook Rd NW AIR 68 B2
Willow Grove Cr SE CAL 49 P-Q26
Willow Park Dr SE CAL 49 P-Q26
Willow Park Gn SE CAL 49 Q27
Willow Park Pl SE CAL 49 Q26
Willow Ridge Pl BLD 75 C6
Willow Ridge Pl SE CAL 49 P26-27
Willow Ridge Rd SE CAL 49 P26
Willowburn Cr SE CAL 49 Q26
Willowcrest Rd SE CAL 49 Q26
Willowdale Cr SE CAL 49 Q26
Willowfern Dr SE CAL 49 Q26-27
Willowglen Pl SE CAL 49 Q-R27
Willowgreen Dr SE CAL 49 Q26
Willowind Pl SE CAL 49 Q26
Willowisp Rd SE CAL 49 Q27
Willowmere Cl CHE 70 D1
Willowview Rd SE CAL 49 Q26
Wilmer Rd SE CAL 49 Q27
Wilshire Pl SW CAL 35 J16
Wilson Cr RED 66 H-J3 J4
Wilson Pl CAN 58 F3
Wilson Rd SE CAL 49 Q27
Wilson St OKO 76 B3
Wilson Way CAN 58 H4
Wilton Pl SE CAL 49 Q27
Wiltshire Blvd RED 66 G-H3
Wiltshire Pl RED 66 G3
Wilverside Way SE CAL 49 P-Q27
Wimbledon Cr SW CAL 35 I16
Wimbledon Dr SW CAL . . .27 I15 35 I16
Winchester Cr SW CAL 35 I17
Windermere Blvd CHE 70 C-D2
Windermere Rd SW CAL 35 I-J16
Windmill Way RCY 16 X-Y10 24 X11
Windsor Av TVY 74 D2-3
Windsor Cr SW CAL 42 N-O21
Windsor Pl STM 71 D2
Windsor St NW CAL . . .27 K14 28 L14 L15
Winslow Cr SW CAL 35 I16
Winston Dr SW CAL 35 I16-17
Winter Dr OLD 62 D1
Winter Hts SW CAL 26 F13
Winterbourne Cr SE CAL 49 P-Q26
Wintergreen Rd BRG 78 A-B3
Winters Way OKO 76 B5
Wishart St RED 66 H3
Wolf Cl RDW 61 B2
Wolf Cr RDW 61 B2
Wolf Ct RDW 61 B2-3
Wolf Dr RDW 61 B2
Wolf St BAN 57 D1-2
Wolfe St SW CAL 36 N18-19
Wolfwillow Pt RCY 33 A20
Wolfwillow Ridge RCY 33 Z20
Wolverine St BAN 57 D2
Wong Av RED 66 H3
Wood Cr SW CAL 48 M28
Wood St MED 95 F6
Wood Crest Cl SW CAL 48 L29
Wood Crest Pl 100 200 SW CAL 48 L-M29
Wood Oak Pl SW CAL 48 M29
Wood Oak Way SW CAL 48 M29
Wood Valley Bay 100 to 300 SW CAL . .
. . . . .47 J-K28
Wood Valley Ct 100 200 SW CAL .47 K29
Wood Valley Dr SW CAL 47 K28-29
Wood Valley Gt SW CAL 47 K29
Wood Valley Mews SW CAL 47 K28
Wood Valley Pl 100 to 300 SW CAL . . . .
. . . . .47 K28-29

Wood Valley Rd SW CAL 47 K28-29
Wood Valley Rise SW CAL 47 K29
Wood Willow Bay SW CAL 48 M29
Wood Willow Cl SW CAL 48 M29
Wood Willow Pl SW CAL 48 M29
Woodacres Cr SW CAL 48 L29
Woodacres Ct SW CAL 48 L29
Woodacres Dr SW CAL 48 L29
Woodacres Pl SW CAL 48 L29
Woodacres Rd SW CAL 48 L29
Woodacres Way SW CAL 48 L29
Woodbend Rd SW CAL 49 P-Q26
Woodbend Way OKO 76 C-D3 D2-3
Woodbine Blvd SW CAL 47 K28-29
Woodborough Cr SW CAL 47 K28
Woodborough Pl SW CAL 47 K28
Woodborough Rd SW CAL 47 K28
Woodborough Ter SW CAL 47 K28
Woodbriar Cir SW CAL 47 K28
Woodbriar Gt SW CAL 47 K28
Woodbriar Pl 100 to 700 SW CAL .47 K28
Woodbrook Cl SW CAL 47 K27
Woodbrook Ct SW CAL 47 K27-28
Woodbrook Gn SW CAL 47 K27-28
Woodbrook Mews 100 to 300 SW CAL .
. . . . .47 K27-28
Woodbrook Pl SW CAL 47 K27
Woodbrook Rd SW CAL 47 K27-28
Woodbrook Way SW CAL 47 K27-28
Woodburn Cr OKO 76 C-D2
Woodcroft Pl SW CAL 48 M28
Woodfern Ct SW CAL 47 K27
Woodfern Dr SW CAL 47 K27
Woodfern Pl 100 200 SW CAL . .47 K27
Woodfern Rd SW CAL 47 K28
Woodfern Rise SW CAL 47 K28
Woodfern Way SW CAL 47 K28
Woodfield Cl SW CAL 48 L28
Woodfield Cr SW CAL 47 K29
Woodfield Ct SW CAL 47 K29
Woodfield Dr SW CAL 48 L28-29
Woodfield Gn SW CAL 48 L28-29
Woodfield Pl 100 to 300 SW CAL . . . .
. . . . .48 L28-29
Woodfield Rd SW CAL 47 K29 48 L29
Woodfield Way SW CAL 47 K29
Woodford Cl SW CAL 48 L27-28
Woodford Ct SW CAL 48 L27
Woodford Ct SW CAL 48 L27-28
Woodford Dr SW CAL 48 L27
Woodford Pl SW CAL 48 L27
Woodgate Bay SW CAL 48 M29
Woodgate Cl SW CAL 48 M29
Woodgate Rd OKO 76 C-D2
Woodglen Cir SW CAL 48 L28
Woodglen Cl SW CAL 48 L28
Woodglen Cr SW CAL 48 L28
Woodglen Ct SW CAL 48 L28
Woodglen Gr SW CAL 48 L28
Woodglen Gt SW CAL 48 L28
Woodglen Mews SW CAL 48 L28
Woodglen Pl OKO 76 C2
Woodglen Pl 100 to 400 SW CAL .48 L28
Woodglen Rd SW CAL 48 L28
Woodglen Rise SW CAL 48 L28
Woodglen Way SW CAL 47 K27
Woodgreen Cr SW CAL 48 M28
Woodgreen Dr SW CAL 48 M29
Woodgreen Pl SW CAL 48 M28
Woodgrove Bay OKO 76 D3
Woodgrove Cr SW CAL 48 M28-29
Woodhaven Bay 100 to 500 SW CAL . . .
. . . . .47 K29
Woodhaven Cr SW CAL 47 K29
Woodhaven Dr OKO 76 C2-3 D2-3
Woodhaven Mnr SW CAL 48 L29
Woodhaven Pl 100 to 400 SW CAL . . . .
. . . . .47 K29
Woodhaven Rd SW CAL 47 K29
Woodhaven View SW CAL 48 L29
Woodhill Ct SW CAL 48 L-M28
Woodhill Pl SW CAL 48 L28
Woodhill Rd SW CAL 48 L28
Woodland Cl RCY 8 X1
Woodland Cl RED 66 L3-4
Woodland Cr SE CAL 49 P-Q26
Woodland Dr RED 66 L3-4 L4 L-M3
Woodland Gn RCY 8 X1-2
Woodland La RCY 8 Y2
Woodland Pl RCY 8 Y2
Woodland Rd INN 63 D2
Woodland Rd RCY 8 Y1
Woodland Way RCY 8 X1
Woodlark Dr SW CAL 27 I15
Woodman Av MED 93 E6
Woodmark Cr SW CAL 48 L28
Woodmark Pl SW CAL 48 L27-28
Woodmeadow Cl SW CAL 48 M28
Woodmont Cr SW CAL 47 K28

Woodmont Ct 100 200 SW CAL ..47 K28
Woodmont Dr SW CAL 47 K28
Woodmont Gn SW CAL 47 K28
Woodmont Gt SW CAL 47 K28
Woodmont Pl SW CAL 47 K28
Woodmont Rd SW CAL 47 K28
Woodmont Rise SW CAL 47 K28
Woodmont Ter SW CAL 47 K28
Woodmont Way SW CAL 47 K28
Woodpark Av SW CAL 48 L-M28
Woodpark Bay 100 200 SW CAL ..48 L27
Woodpark Blvd SW CAL 48 L29 M28
Woodpark Cir SW CAL 48 L28
Woodpark Cl SW CAL 48 L27-28
Woodpark Cr SW CAL. 48 M27
Woodpark Ct 100 to 300 SW CAL 48 M28
Woodpark Gn 100 to 300 SW CAL 48 L28
Woodpark Link SW CAL 48 M27-28
Woodpark Pl 100 to 400 SW CAL 48 M28
Woodpark Rd SW CAL 48 M28
Woodpark Ter 100 200 SW CAL ..48 L28
Woodpark Way SW CAL 48 M28
Woodpath Rd SW CAL 47 K29
Woodpath Ter SW CAL 47 K29
Woodridge Cl SW CAL 48 M29
Woodridge Dr SW CAL 48 L-M29
Woodridge Pl 100 to 300 SW CAL 48 M29
Woodridge Ter SW CAL 48 L-M29
Woodrow Cl RED 66 H3
Woodrow Pl OKO 76 C-D2
Woodside Bay NW AIR 68 A-B1
Woodside Bay 100 to 300 SW CAL . .
. . . . .48 L28-29
Woodside Blvd NW AIR 68 A-B1
Woodside Cir NW AIR 68 B1
Woodside Cir SW CAL 48 L-M29
Woodside Cl NW AIR 68 B1
Woodside Cr NW AIR 68 B2
Woodside Ct NW AIR 68 B1
Woodside Dr NW AIR 68 B1-2
Woodside Gt NW AIR 68 B1
Woodside Gt SW CAL 48 M29
Woodside La CAN 58 D3
Woodside La NW AIR 68 B2
Woodside Link NW AIR 68 B2
Woodside Mews NW AIR 68 A-B2
Woodside Pk NW AIR 68 B1
Woodside Pl OKO 76 C-D3
Woodside Pl 100 200 NW AIR . . .68 B2
Woodside Pl SW CAL 48 L28-29
Woodside Rd NW AIR 68 B2
Woodside Rd SW CAL 48 L28-29
Woodside Rise NW AIR 68 B1-2
Woodside Way NW AIR 68 B2
Woodsman La SW CAL 47 K28
Woodstock Pl 100 200 SW CAL 48 L-M28
Woodstock Rd SW CAL 48 L-M28
Woodstock Way SW CAL 48 L-M28
Woodsworth Cl RED 66 H4
Woodsworth Rd SE CAL 49 Q26
Woodvale Bay 100 200 SW CAL ..48 L28
Woodvale Cr SW CAL 48 L28-29
Woodvale Rd SW CAL 48 L28-29
Woodview Bay OKO 76 C-D3
Woodview Bay SW CAL 48 M28
Woodview Cr SW CAL 48 L28
Woodview Ct SW CAL 48 L28
Woodview Dr SW CAL 48 L-M28
Woodview Pl SW CAL 48 L28
Woodview Rd SW CAL 48 L28
Woodview Ter SW CAL 48 L28
Woolley Pl MED 95 G-H7
Worcester Dr SW CAL 35 I-J16
Wright Av RED 66 H-J3

Y

Yankee Valley Rd SE AIR 68 E4 69 E5
Yardmaster Av COD 85 B2-3
Yoho Tinda Rd BRG 78 A3
York Pl W LET 86 J4 87 J5
Young Rd BRO 90 C-E2
Ypres Gn SW CAL 36 L20
Ypres La SW CAL 36 L20
Ypres Mews SW CAL 36 L20
Ypres Way SW CAL 36 L20
Yuill St MED 93 E6

Z

Zoo Rd NE CAL 37 R16-17